Preface

This book is the result of the Fourth European Conference of Psychology and Law, held in Barcelona in April, 1994. We would like to thank people who collaborated in the scientific and organising committees of the conference. Of special importance for the success of the meeting was the fine work of Jordi Bajet, Rosa Maria Martínez, Domènec Pérez, Maria Reales, Gemma Domingo, Begoña Orozco and Isabel Clemente.

Two institutions played a key role in supporting this event: The Catalan Board of Psychologists and the Center of Legal Studies of the Justice Department of Catalonia. The former provided financial support for the conference as well as valuable logistic and administrative assistance. The latter provided the facilities for the conference.

The preparation of this book has meant hard work for contributors and editors. The original papers were screened, completed and updated during the time that has elapsed since the Conference. We appreciate very much the patience shown by the authors, who committed themselves to a series of tasks that were necessary to produce the book in its final state. *Advances in Psychology and Law: International Contributions* would have not been possible without the altruistic and continuous collaboration of the colleagues of the first editor of this book at the Center of Legal Studies: Carlos Ferrer, Maribel Baños, Luis de Santiago, Orestes Martínez, Núria Rius-Pastor and Eulalia Luque. The editors would like to give special thanks to Antonio Marchal whose painstaking work over the past year in preparing the final copy has been indispensable. And last but not least, we want to express our gratitude to Elisabeth Abu Homos, Bianka Ralle and Christoph Schirmer from De Gruyter for their constant support and suggestions throughout all the editorial process.

The Editors

Contents

Part III: Witnesses and Expert Testimony

Part IV: Juries and Tribunals

Part V: Child Development and Delinquency

Part VI: Psychological Factors Related to Crime

Part IX: Correctional Evaluation

Epilogue

Introduction

Santiago Redondo, Vicente Garrido, Jorge Pérez and
Rosemary Barberet

The IV conference on Psychology and Law, held in Barcelona, was a success in terms of participation. More delegates than ever before met at the Centre d'Estudis Jurídics, a section of the Catalonian Justice Department devoted to the study of legal issues. This book continues the tradition of the "Psychology and Law" series in publishing the most outstanding contributions of that conference. Since the very nature of this book is an edited collection of conference proceedings, it is unavoidable that to a certain degree, the reader gets the "melting pot" sensation, but the editors do not necessarily consider this a mistake: the European expansion in the area of Psychology and Law is great and varied, and this volume must reflect this fact.

Perhaps this book, more than its predecessors, expands on the characteristics of legal and criminological psychology in Southern Europe, and particularly in Spain. In this respect it is fortunate that psychology can build a legacy of empirical research. In the first part of the book ("Law and Psychology in Different Countries"), Helmut Kury focuses on the difference between two research traditions: "At least in western industrial nations as the USA and Great Britain for example, criminology is conceived as a discipline of empirical social science, whereas in many parts of Europe (...) it is considered a discipline of the science of law". However, as Kury's article shows, many areas are being researched with notable energy, and so it is possible to envision a future which includes a truly empirical science of criminology in Europe.

The situation in South America is more fragmentary, a logical fact if we consider the different cultures and political structures that coincide there. Dr. Popolo underlines the advances taking place in the areas of expert appraisals and advice in judicial decision-making, but stresses the important objectives which have not yet been achieved, in particular the prevention of antisocial behaviour and the co-ordination among disciplines and institutions involved in the development of legal and criminological sciences, in which psychology plays a leading role. Unfortunately, Dr. Popolo passed away during the edition of this book. As a co-founder of the Ibero-American Society of Psychology and Law, Dr. Popolo's work on psychology in the courtroom will remain as a testament to his interest in Psychology and Law, and on a personal level, he will be sadly missed by his academic colleagues and, in particular, by the editors of this book.

Portugal is also in a emergent situation. As R. Abrunhosa points out, "this kind of specialisation is giving now its first steps". But as also has occurred in Spain (Garrido & Redondo, 1992), Portugal now has a penal code that supports the role of psychology as a important tool in the rehabilitation of offenders. This offers hope: "So, we have an official framework to lean on and start to do something. And from I have said above, it seems that we are doing it".

The other two chapters focus on specific matters in two countries: euthanasia in the Netherlands and family law in Germany after reunification. Altogether Part I adds to the chapters of the previous books of the series in the intent to clarify the evolution of legal and criminological psychology in Europe.

Part II, Victimology, reflects the very broad expansion that this field has witnessed. Matters are as diverse as the cognitive processes employed by offenders before committing a crime, and the importance of the victim's role in confronting the crime; the buffering effects of personality traits in post-victimisation; the victimological aspects of computer-crimes; victimisation in intimate relationships and victims experience and fear of crime; all of them indicate that we have truly advanced since the beginning of the seventies. Now we approach the study of the victim as an active agent, seeing him or her as someone who suffers and also as someone who can contribute to prevent criminal behaviour.

Psychology has many things to say in a field that by its nature is very psychological: Witnesses and Expert Testimony (Part III). Children continue to attract much of the interest of researchers in this subject, but the "art of interrogation" receives attention, as well as the examination of the role of the expert. It is interesting to note that the police can take advantage of the work developed by psychologists in interrogation and credibility, overcoming the "experience from the police detectives" as the only valid argument in deciding how to conduct this kind of fact-finding. And we welcome papers such as the "The Effects of Distraction on Police Officer Shooting Behavior", where the authors explain that psychology can help police practice in near-fatal events.

"Juries and Tribunals" is the other main topic in the Legal Psychology arena. The psychology of juries has been a focus of great interest in the last few years in Spain because its employment in the criminal justice system is now (1996) a reality. The papers presented by Sobral ("Enquiry on Judicial Decisions"), Garrido Martín and Herrero ("Influence of the Prosecutor's Plea on the Judge's Sentencing in Sexual Crimes"), De la Fuente et al. ("Formal Pattern in Jury Decision Making"), De Paúl ("Models in Jury Decision Making") and Arce et al. ("Inquisitorial Jury Selection through Scientific Support") are good examples of current research undertaken by Spanish legal psychologists. This part is complemented by a reflection on the judge's role from the socio-psychological perspective, by R. Jakob. He concludes with an audacious challenge: "For all persons involved it makes more sense to cope with the personality of the judge. To reach this aim, possibilities of self-experience should be offered obligatorily to trainees, individually or in groups".

Part V, Child Development and Delinquency, is represented in this book by classical as well as non-conventional papers. By classical, we are referring to the paramount importance of the longitudinal study continued by David Farrington since the seventies. Of the many derivations of the Cambridge Study are studies regarding prevention, which demonstrate without doubt preventive measures applied in the first few years of life are the most important. Self-report research is also a classic theme of study and there is no research in Spain more complete than that undertaken by Montañés, Rechea and Barberet. For first time we have a rigorous study which can be compared with international research. The Spanish contribution ends with the paper by Jarne et al. about the long term effects of divorce in the psychological adjustment of children, another very new theme of research in our country.

This part ends with two additional papers. The first is a very suggestive one ("Adoption and Murder", by P.D. Jaffé), structured around the discussion of a case, while engaging in a review of this phenomenon; the author argues that adoption homicide is "a rare event too often ignored", and we think that perhaps it is time for more thorough research. The other paper, "Custodian's Gender and Gender Disorders in the Child Development", by Czerederecka and Jaskiewicz, ends with a hopeful conclusion that, we think, reflects much of the effort of psychologists in family courts all over the world: "(...) in cases of family break-up, fathers can potentially be the main custodian as well as mothers. However, they should incorporate a striving for the establishment of better mutual contacts between mother and child into their child-raising activities to a much greater extent and not concentrate on conflict with their former spouse, seeking social support for such forms of behaviour".

Five studies carried out in a variety of European countries have been grouped together under the title "Psychological Factors Related to Crime" (Part VI). Luberto et al. tell of the low crime rate among psychiatric patients, and stress the importance of family and social integration in preventing anti-social conduct among that population.

McMurran presents two studies which emphasise the connections between outcome expectations and the consumption of alcoholic beverages and crime. In a third study carried out in Spain, Martín and Rodríguez theorise the role that socio-cognitive skills may play in the genesis of female crime.

Jackson et al. describe an offender profiling technique which is based on in-depth interviews with a limited number of convicted murderers plus the extensive experience of detectives in the homicide field. Finally, Garrido reflects on the fields of application of criminal psychology and on the work of psychologists in these areas.

Part VII deals with intervention with drug dependent offenders. In their first two studies carried out in Québec, Brochu and Guyon analyse the link between drug consumption and crime. In the first such study, the authors acknowledge the high rate of drug addiction among prison inmates, and reflect on their need for treatment.

In the second, carried out on drug addicts attending a rehabilitation centre, the sociodemographic characteristics of drug abuse among subjects both with and without criminal records are compared.

Marco expounds on the problems which arise from the rate of heroin abuse in Spanish prisons and acknowledges the good results achieved in prisons in Catalonia on programmes based on the administration of agonistic opiates. Lastly, Sanchis et al. narrate the stimulating experience of a therapeutic community inside a prison designed for the treatment of drug-dependent inmates from Catalonian prisons.

"Correctional Treatment and Prison Initiatives" is the generic title of part VIII. Jaffa et al. tackle the complex subject of children who live in prison with their mothers, and propose changes with a view to avoiding negative psychological consequences and promoting mental hygiene in both mothers and children.

In a second work, Clemente recounts the construction of an Organisational Assessment Instrument for prisons based on research carried out in Spanish prisons. Behar et al. present differences in feelings and emotions about prison, comparing inmates both with and without a history of self-inflicted injuries or attempted suicide, with preventative aims in mind. Dahle's study focuses on the construct of Therapy-Motivation in the application of psychotherapy to prison inmates.

Queral et al. discuss a programme of treatment by means of the organisation of progressive phases in a Catalonian penitentiary, and show positive results with aggressive prisoners. Those who took part in the programme reduced both the length of time they spent in prison and the amount of disciplinary problems when in prison to a greater degree than those who did not. The last study in this section deals with the same subject matter. Montero et al. present the good results achieved in personal hygiene, disputes, social climate and participation in educational programmes after the application of three treatment programmes in the Barcelona women's prison.

The last section of the book (Part IX) focuses on correctional evaluation. As Anguera shows in her first paper on methodological advances, correctional evaluation is a most relevant matter as it contributes information as to how effective programmes are with a view to optimising the results, the effectiveness and the quality of programmes in correctional centres. On the same subject, Sánchez-Meca's paper is a good referent with regard to the technique of meta-analysis in evaluating the results of treatment in correctional centres.

In his contribution, Holling reflects on the advantages and disadvantages of the treatment of young offenders who are also consumers of alcohol in institutions and in the community. The author champions the establishment of ties between both areas.

The section and the volume itself end with an interesting work on correctional rehabilitation in Europe. Redondo, Garrido and Sánchez-Meca present the results of a meta-analysis of 57 studies in six European countries. The fact that this was the first meta-analysis carried out in Europe on studies from different countries renders it of special interest (Lösel, 1995). The study reveals optimistic results on rehabilitation and concludes that programmes based on cognitive-behavioural techniques obtain the best results.

The meeting at Barcelona was a very exciting one. Many people from Spain joined people from all over Europe to share knowledge, and to continue giving support to the European Association of Psychology and Law. We hope this book is a good example of that vitality. Similar to what happened at the meeting held in Pamplona, Spain in 1991, where Spanish and British legal psychologists met, as well as the three previous conferences, the Barcelona conference showed that "Pyschology and Law" is a marriage that promises longevity.

References

Garrido, V. & Redondo, S. (1992). Psychology and Law in Spain. In F. Lösel, D. Bender and T. Bliesener (Eds.), *Psychology and Law. International Perspectives.* (pp. 526-534). Berlin: De Gruyter.

Lösel, F. (1995). Management of Psychopaths. Paper presented at NATO ASI; Psychopathy. Alvor, Portugal.

Contributors

Trenti Alessia, Dipartamento di Scienze Morfologiche e Medico-Legali dell'Università di Modena Policlinico, Via del Pozzo 71, 41100 Modena, Italy

Ana Alonso, Centre Penitenciari d'Homes de Barcelona, Entença 155, 08029 Barcelona, Spain

Marisa Alonso-Quecuty, Department of Cognitive Psychology, University of La Laguna (Campus de Guajara), 38205 La Laguna, Tenerife, Spain

M. Teresa Anguera, Faculty of Psychology, University of Barcelona, Passeig de la Vall d'Hebron 171, 08035 Barcelona, Spain

Ramón Arce, Department of Social Psychology, University of Santiago de Compostela, 15706 Santiago de Compostela, La Coruña, Spain

Jordi Bajet, Gerència de Suport Judicial de Barcelona ciutat, Ronda de Sant Pere 35, 08010 Barcelona, Spain

Anna Costanza Baldry, University of Rome 'La Sapienza', Via dei Marsi 78, 00185 Roma, Italy

Rosemary Barberet, Instituto Andaluz Interuniversitario de Criminología, Facultad de Derecho, Universidad de Sevilla, Avenida del Cid s/n, 41004 Sevilla, Spain

Júlia Behar, Departament de Metodologia i Ciències del Comportament, Facultat de Psicologia, Universitat de Barcelona, Passeig de la Vall d'Hebron 171, 08035 Barcelona, Spain

Wolfgang Bilsky, Psychologisches Institut IV, Westfälische Wilhelms-Universität Münster, Fliednerstrasse 21, D-48149 Münster, Germany

John R. Blad, Faculteit der Rechtsgeleerdheid, Erasmus Universiteit Rotterdam, P.O. Box 1738, 3000 DR Rotterdam, The Netherlands

Serge Brochu, International Center for Comparative Criminology, University of Montréal (Qc), P.O. Box 6128, Station A, Montréal H3C 3J7, Canada

Judith Caballero, Centre Penitenciari Brians, 08781 Sant Esteve de Sesrorives, Barcelona, Spain

Laura Campos, Department of Cognitive Psychology, University of La Laguna (Campus de Guajara), 38205 La Laguna, Tenerife, Spain

Alícia Casals, Centre Penitenciari Brians, 08781 Sant Esteve de Sesrorives, Barcelona, Spain

Miguel Clemente, Department of Social Psychology, Universidad Complutense de Madrid (Campus de Somosaguas), 28223 Madrid , Spain

Anna Cordomí, Departament de Justícia de la Generalitat de Catalunya, Pau Claris 81, 08010 Barcelona, Spain

Alicja Czerederecka, Department of Forensic Psychology, Institute of Forensic Research, ul. Westerplatte 9, 31-033 Kraków, Poland

Klaus-Peter Dahle, Institut für Forensische Psychiatrie, Freie Universität Berlin, Limonenstrasse 27, D-12203 Berlin, Germany

Juan Horacio Del Popolo, Chile, 925 4P Dpto 10, Mendoza, Argentina

E. Inmaculada De la Fuente Solana, Departamento de Psicología Social y Metodología de las Ciencias del Comportamiento, Facultad de Psicología, Universidad de Granada (Campus Universitario de Cartuja), 18071 Granada, Spain

Adriaan Denkers, Dept. of Social Psychology / VU Centre for Police Sciences, Vrije Universiteit Amsterdam, Van der Boechorststraat 1, 1081 BT Amsterdam, The Netherlands

Deirdre Suzette Enthoven, Dept. of Social Psychology / VU Centre for Police Sciences, Vrije Universiteit Amsterdam, Van der Boechorststraat 1, 1081 BT Amsterdam, The Netherlands

Miguel Angel Esteban, Centre Penitenciari de Dones de Barcelona, Wad Ras 98, 08005 Barcelona, Spain

Thomas Fabian, Hochschule für Technik, Wirtschaft und Kultur Leipzig (FH), Fachbereich Sozialwesen, Postfach 66, D-04251 Leipzig, Germany

Francisca Fariña, Area of Basic Psychology, Faculty of Social Sciences, University of Vigo, Rua Sierra, 40, 36002 Pontevedra, Spain

David P. Farrington, Institute of Criminology, University of Cambridge, 7 West Road, CB3 9DT Cambridge, UK

Vicente Garrido Genovés, University of Valencia, Faculty of Psychology and Education, 46010 Valencia, Spain

Eugenio Garrido Martín, Departamento de Psicología, Facultad de Psicología, Avenida de la Merced, 109-131, 37005 Salamanca, Spain

Rui Abrunhosa Gonçalves, Department of Psychology, Instituto de Educação, University of Minho (Campus de Gualtar), 4700 Braga, Portugal

Giorgio Gualandri, Istituto di Medicina Legale e delle Assicu Azioni dell'Università di Modena Policlinico, Via del Pozzo 71, 41100 Modena, Italy

Louise Guyon, Quebec Research and Intervention Group on Psychoactive Substances, 101401 Lajeunesse, Montréal (Qc), H3L 2E2, Canada

J. C. M. Herbrink, Netherlands Institute for the Study of Criminality and Law Enforcement, Witte Singel 103, 2313AA Leiden, The Netherlands

Estefanía Hernández-Fernaud, Department of Cognitive Psychology, University of La Laguna (Campus de Guajara), 38205 La Laguna, Tenerife, Spain

Carmen Herrero Alonso, Departamento de Psicología, Facultad de Psicología, Avenida de la Merced, 109-131, 37005 Salamanca, Spain

Dick J. Hessing, Faculteit der Rechtsgeleerdheid, Erasmus Universiteit Rotterdam, P.O. Box 1738, 3000 DR Rotterdam, The Netherlands

Clive R. Hollin, Department of Psychology, University of Leicester, Leicester LEI 7RH, UK

Immaculada Ibern Regàs, Departament d'Atenció Especialitzada, Centre Penitenciari Quatre Camins, Apartat Oficial 335, 08400 Granollers, Barcelona, Spain

Janet L. Jackson, Netherlands Institute for the Study of Criminality and Law Enforcement, Witte Singel 103, 2313AA Leiden, The Netherlands

Philip D. Jaffé, Faculty of Psychology and Education Sciences, and Institute of Legal Medicine, University of Geneva, 9 route de Drize, 1227 Carouge, Switzerland

Raimund Jakob, Arbeitgruppe für Rechtspsychologie und Politische Psychologie, Universität Salzburg, Churfürststrasse 1, A-5020 Salzburg, Austria

Adolfo Jarne, Departament de Personalitat, Avaluació i Tractament Psicològics, Facultat de Psicologia, Universitat de Barcelona, Passeig de la Vall d'Hebron, 171, 08035 Barcelona, Spain

Teresa Jaskiewicz-Obydzinska, Department of Forensic Psychology, Institute of Forensic Research, ul. Westerplatte 9, 31-033 Kraków, Poland

Leendert Koppelaar, CIRCON, Oosteinde 15-17, 1017 WT Amsterdam, The Netherlands

P. van Koppen, Netherlands Institute for the Study of Criminality and Law Enforcement, Witte Singel 103, 2313AA Leiden, The Netherlands

Adelheid Kühne, Universität Hannover, FB Erziehungswissenschaften I, Bismarckstrasse 2, D-30173 Hannover, Germany

Helmut Kury, Max-Planck-Institut für Ausländisches und Internationales Strafrecht, Günterstalstrasse 73, D-79100 Freiburg im Breisgau, Germany

Friedrich Lösel, Institute of Psychology, University of Erlangen-Nürnberg, Bismarckstrasse, 1, D-91054 Erlangen, Germany

Salvatore Luberto, Institute of Forensic Medicine of Modena, Via del Pozzo 71, 41100 Modena, Italy

Andrés Marco, Centre Penitenciari d'Homes de Barcelona, Entença 155, 08029 Barcelona, Spain

Ana M. Martín-Rodríguez, Departamento de Psicología Social, Facultad de Psicología, Universidad de La Laguna (Campus de Guajara), 38205 La Laguna, Tenerife, Spain

Ignacio Martín Tamayo, Departamento de Psicología Social y Metodología de las Ciencias del Comportamiento, Facultad de Psicología, Universidad de Granada (Campus Universitario de Cartuja), 18071 Granada, Spain

Jesús Martínez, Centre Penitenciari de Dones de Barcelona, Wad Ras 98, 08005 Barcelona, Spain

Mary McMurran, East Midlands Centre for Forensic Mental Health, Arnold Lodge, Cordelia Close, Leicester LE5 0LE, UK

Juan Montañés-Rodríguez, Unidad de Criminología, Facultad de Derecho, Universidad de Castilla-La Mancha, Plaza de la Universidad 1, 02071 Albacete, Spain

José M. Montero, Centre Penitenciari d'Homes de Barcelona, Entença 155, 08029 Barcelona, Spain

Paula Montero Brasero, Departament d'Atenció Especialitzada, Centre Penitenciari Quatre Camins, Apartat Oficial 335, 08400 Granollers, Barcelona, Spain

Josep Moya, CAPIP, Providència 60, 08901 L'Hospitalet de Llobregat, Barcelona, Spain

Joan C. Navarro, Centre Penitenciari Brians, 08781 Sant Esteve de Sesrorives, Barcelona, Spain

J.F. Nijboer, Professor of Law and Judge, Department of Criminal Law, University of Leiden, P.O. Box 9520, 2300 RA Leiden, The Netherlands

Ana Ortega Martínez, Departamento de Psicología, Universidad de Jaen, 23071 Jaén, Spain

Pilar de Paúl, Social Psychology Department, Universidad Complutense de Madrid (Campus de Somosaguas), 28223 Madrid, Spain

Roel Pieterman, Faculteit der Rechtsgeleerdheid, Erasmus Universiteit Rotterdam, P.O. Box 1738, 3000 DR Rotterdam, The Netherlands

Volker Pieters, Klinik und Poliklinik für Psychiatrie und Psychotherapie der Ernst-Moritz-Arnd-Universität Greifswald, Ellernholzstrasse 1-2, 17487 Greifswald, Germany

Francisco Pons, Faculty of Psychology and Education Sciences, and Institute of Legal Medicine, University of Geneva, 9 route de Drize, 1227 Carouge, Switzerland

Joan Pere Queralt, Centre Penitenciari Brians, 08781 Sant Esteve de Sesrorives, Barcelona, Spain

Santiago Real, Department of Social Psychology, University of Santiago de Compostela, 15706 Santiago de Compostela, La Coruña, Spain

Cristina Rechea-Alberola, Unidad de Criminología, Facultad de Derecho, Universidad de Castilla-La Mancha, Plaza de la Universidad 1, 02071   Albacete, Spain

Santiago Redondo, Centre of Legal Studies, Roger de Flor 196, 08013 Barcelona, Spain

Elena Requena, Departament de Personalitat, Avaluació i Tractament Psicològics, Facultat de Psicologia, Universitat de Barcelona, Passeig de la Vall d'Hebron, 171, 08035 Barcelona, Spain

Hélène Rey Wicky, Faculty of Psychology and Education Sciences, and Institute of Legal Medicine, University of Geneva, 9 route de Drize, 1227 Carouge, Switzerland

Ana M. Rodríguez-Rodríguez, Departamento de Psicología Social, Facultad de Psicología, Universidad de La Laguna (Campus de Guajara), 38205 La Laguna, Tenerife, Spain

Julio Sánchez Meca, Departamento de Psicología Básica y Metodología, Facultad de Psicología, Universidad de Murcia (Campus Universitario de Espinardo), Apartado 4021, 30080 Murcia, Spain

J. Ricardo Sanchis Mir, Departament d'Atenció Especialitzada, Centre Penitenciari Quatre Camins, Apartat Oficial 335, 08400 Granollers, Barcelona, Spain

Sílvia Serra, Centre Penitenciari Brians, 08781 Sant Esteve de Sesrorives, Barcelona, Spain

Jorge Sobral Fernández, Departamento de Psicología Social y Básica, Facultad de Filosofía y Ciencias de la Educación, Universidad de Santiago de Compostela (Campus Sur), 15706 Santiago de Compostela, La Coruña, Spain

Carles Soler Departament de Justícia de la Generalitat de Catalunya, Pau Claris 81, 08010 Barcelona, Spain

Montserrat Soto Fernández, Departament d'Atenció Especialitzada, Centre Penitenciari Quatre Camins, Apartat Oficial 335, 08400 Granollers, Barcelona, Spain

Michael Stadler, Institute of Psychology and Cognition Research, University of Bremen, P.O. Box 330440, D-28334 Bremen, Germany

Jaap van der Steen, CIRCON, Oosteinde 15-17, 1017 WT Amsterdam, The Netherlands

Mónica Timón, Departament de Personalitat, Avaluació i Tractament Psicològics, Facultat de Psicologia, Universitat de Barcelona, Passeig de la Vall d'Hebron, 171, 08035 Barcelona, Spain

Humberto Trujillo Mendoza, Departamento de Psicología Social y Metodología de las Ciencias del Comportamiento, Facultad de Psicología, Universidad de Granada (Campus Universitario de Cartuja), 18071 Granada, Spain

Carlos Vila, Department of Social Psychology, University of Santiago de Compostela, 15706 Santiago de Compostela, La Coruña, Spain

Renate Volbert, Institut für Forensische Psychiatrie, Freie Universität Berlin, Limonenstrasse 27, D-12203 Berlin, Germany

Aldert Vrij, Department of Psychology, University of Portsmouth, King Charles Street, PO1 2ER Portsmouth, UK

Peter Wetzels, Kriminologisches Forschungsinstitut Niedersachsen (KFN), Lützerodestrasse 9, D-30161 Hannover, Germany

Frans Willem Winkel, Dept. of Social Psychology / VU Centre for Police Sciences, Vrije Universiteit Amsterdam, Van der Boechorststraat 1, 1081 BT Amsterdam, The Netherlands

Patrizia Zavatti, Istituto di Medicina Legale e delle Assicu Azioni dell'Università di Modena Policlinico, Via del Pozzo 71, 41100 Modena, Italy

Part I
Law and Psychology in Different Countries

Law and Psychology in Europe: Current Status and Future Perspectives[1]

Helmut Kury

Introduction

Legal psychology is one of the oldest disciplines of applied psychology; its origin can be traced back to the end of the 19th and the beginning of the 20th century. For example, at the end of last century, *Münsterberg* had been working in the field of applied psychology including legal psychology. He emigrated to the USA where he became one of the founders of legal psychology; there, he continued his research in legal psychology (see *Münsterberg* 1908). Already at the end of the 18th century there existed publications dealing with the psychological aspects of delinquency - at a time indeed, which did not know any academic psychology in our modern sense (see e.g., *v. Eckartshausen* 1791; *Schaumann* 1792; *Muench* 1799; see also *Gross* 1898).

The importance of legal psychology has experienced ups and downs during its more than 100-year-old history, but it has definitely increased over the last years, at least in several Western countries. The upswing of legal psychology has been taking place especially over the past 20 years. *Diamond* (1992, p.5) emphasizes that although *Münsterberg* had written his studies on legal psychology already at the beginning of this century, "it is only 15 years since the first review of psychology and law appeared in the *Annual Review of Psychology*". In the year 1977 the first issue of *Law and Human Behaviour* was published which is the official journal of the American Psychology and Law Society, and nowadays it is also the journal of the American Psychological Association's Division of Psychology and Law. *Tapp* (1976) wrote one of the first readers on forensic psychology in the USA nearly 20 years ago. One of the first modern volumes on legal and criminal psychology was edited by *Toch* (1961). Before 1973, only a few psychological institutes in the USA offered training courses in legal psychology; often, they even did not offer one single course at all. However, nine years later, in 1982, one fourth of the graduate programs in psychology offered at least one training course and numerous others started to offer more detailed and elaborated programs. "Yet this short period of less than 20 years has been a dramatic level of activity" (*Diamond* 1992, p.V; see also

---

[1]   I am especially indebted to Daniela Kirstein for helping me to produce the results.

Bartol & Bartol 1987, p.16; *Ogloff* 1992, p.2). According to *Weiner* and *Hess* (1987, p.XI), "Forensic psychology has become a rapidly emerging professional speciality". With respect to the situation in Canada, *Ogloff* (1989) reports on a survey at Canadian psychological institutes. Here, it could be observed that only 3 out of 26 of the institutes offered graduate courses, despite the fact that 62% simultaneously stated that their faculty was engaged in legal psychological research and/or in practice within the fields of legal psychology. Research, however, is obviously still restricted to few fields of legal psychology. *Roesch* (1990, p.1) emphasizes that during the past 12 years of appearance of the journal *Law and Human Behaviour* which is, as already mentioned, the official journal of the American Psychology Law Society, almost one third of all articles published dealt with the topics expert witness, jury decision making and eye-witness testimony. The author regrets that this way the large field of legal psychology had been strongly limited. *Kagehiro* and *Laufer* stress in the preface of their *Handbook of Psychology and Law* (1992, p.XI): "The narrow focus of psycholegal research continues to be the despair of writers in the field". *Lösel* (1989), too, who repeatedly points out the upswing of legal psychology during the past years, is right in highlighting the large gaps in research in this field.

As already mentioned, the Western industrial nations have experienced a clear increase in discussions on legal psychological matters and especially in empirical research during the past 15-20 years. Authors generally refer to the situation in Great Britain, the Netherlands or Germany, but mostly in the USA. *Bartol* and *Bartol* (1987, p.17) emphasize that "the 1970's saw a literature and research explosion in all areas of forensic psychology, which had, as *Loh* (1981) observes, 'come of age'". *Melton* (1987, p.681), too, emphasizes the strong increase in legal psychology in the USA, but he regrets at the same time that the scope of topics is still restricted: "psycholegal studies may be fairly termed as psychology's new growth industry. Besides the development of new professional organizations (e.g., the American Psychology-Law Society of the American Psychological Association), there has been a mushrooming of scholarship on psychology and law, albeit still predominantly in relatively narrow areas of criminal and family law". According to *Lösel et al.* (1992, p.VII), psychology in the field of law does not only have a long-standing tradition, "but is also characterized by a recent upswing. Research in this area has significantly intensified during the past 15 years". One reason why psychologists are increasingly summoned before the court since the 50s can be seen, according to *Loh* (1981, p.323), in the "increased professionalization (...) the rapid growth of mental health professions during this period, and the formulation of legal doctrines of insanity consistent with modern psychiatry". During the past decades, psychology has developed considerable knowledge that can be used especially by criminology and legal psychology: "Psychologists have made many contributions to the explanation, prevention, and treatment of offending (...)." (*Farrington* 1992, p.35).

Germany, too (at least the former Federal Republic of Germany) has experienced a clear increase in legal psychology during the past years in research as well as in practical application. For example, for some years there have been groups of psychologists who are engaged in forensic expert reports in court, especially when matters of criminal and family law are concerned (see e.g., *Arntzen* 1994; *Fabian & Wetzels* 1991). The scope of research topics is slowly expanding (see e.g., *Egg* 1991). According to *Kaiser* (1992, p.31), "(...) - after a period of eventual development - one can now speak of a newly established criminological psychology that is in keeping with a great and long tradition and lives up especially to modern expectations (...)."

A survey of the literature on the number of journals, congresses, meetings and research projects indeed proves the rising importance of legal psychology during the past 15-20 years (see *Lösel* 1989). Despite this positive development, we must not forget that legal psychology is attributed a rather marginal position within psychological research; but, after all, this position has been strengthened. The following point should also be taken into account: When we speak of an increase in the importance of legal psychology, to which countries does this rise apply? If we analyze the pertinent literature in the Federal Republic of Germany, then our lack of knowledge in foreign languages, except for English and perhaps French, inevitably forces us to limit ourselves to German or Anglo-American, i.e. English, maybe Dutch, and North-American literature. There, reports on the situation of legal psychology in non-English-speaking countries are very scarce. We even know little about the situation in France or Spain, and I think we know very little about the situation in Russia or Poland.

Two important English readers published by *Garrido* and *Redondo* (1992) and *Garrido Martín* (1994) give an overview of the current situation of legal psychology in Spain, which reveals an old and rich tradition in this field. As it is also the case with the majority of the other countries, legal psychology has systematically developed only within the past years (*Garrido Martín* 1994, p.304). The handbook of *Mira y López* (1932) meant a landmark in Spanish legal psychology. There, besides legal-psychological topics such as credibility and the relative importance of objective test methods, criminological topics such as prevention, causes and treatment of delinquency are discussed. The increasing number of publications in legal psychology gives proof of its positive development in Spain, especially from the mid-80s on. The volume of *Jiménez Burillo* and *Clemente Díaz* (1986) is frequently considered to mark the turning point in Spanish legal psychology; there, scientists as well as practicians discuss important themes (see also *Morales et al.* 1986). *Ávila Espada* (1987) describes the relevance of forensic psychology to law. During the past years, several research groups have been engaged in forensic expert reports on credibility. *Mira* and *Diges*, for example, published results on the issue of recognition, especially of faces (1984; 1986; see also *Garrido Martín* 1986). *Prieto et al.* (1990) examined the influence of results of expert reports about credibility in court, depending on their presentation and precision. *Clemente* (1987) comprehensively examines female delinquency, *Sobral* and *Arce* (1990) summarize the results of research on sentencing (see also *Arce et al.* 1990; *Garrido & DeElena* 1990). *Garzon* and *Seoane* (1988) examined the court as a social institution, considering its relationship to attitudes and norms of society.

A relatively broad research area in Spain, covers criminal psychology, especially the incarceration of offenders, their rehabilitation and the development of alternatives to imprisonment. In particular, *Garrido Genovés* (1982; 1987) from the University of Valencia has been empirically engaged for several years in problems of prison psychology and treatment research and has published numerous volumes. No doubt, he is "one of the driving forces regarding the empirical studies on penitentiary treatment" (*Garrido Martín* 1994, p.308; see in this respect also e.g., *Sancha Mata et al.* 1987; *Valverde* 1991a; 1991b). *Portero Carbo et al.* (1987) provided an interesting study on treatment experiences in the Penitentiary Center for Young People in Barcelona. In Spain, from the 70s on, only the prison psychologists drew the attention to the role of psychology in law (*Garrido & Redondo* 1992, p.526). In the 80s, the interest in psychology generally grew stronger, also on the part of the law. More and more, psychologists had been granted positions with administrative and political influence. Unfortunately, the universities have expressed only little interest in legal psychology (*Garrido & Redondo* 1992, p.526). Despite all the difficulties that legal psychology still has to cope with in Spain, *Garrido* and *Redondo* (1992, p.533) came to the following conclusion in their very informative overview: "On the other hand, we must not forget the important progress made by legal psychology in the last 10 years, both in terms of social recognition and the number of jobs occupied. This is the reason why legal psychology is one of the most promising fields in current Spanish psychology".

Lösel et al. (1992) published a reader on the occasion of the Second European Conference on Law and Psychology 1990 in Nuremberg which also contains two relevant review articles on the situation of legal psychology in Italy and Poland (see also *Kury* 1987). *Traverso* and *Manna* (1992) report on the situation in Italy, where although legal psychology has a long tradition, as is generally known, it is strongly bound to clinical psychology and to the exploration of the causes of delinquency (see also *Gulotta* 1987). *Stanik* (1992) states in his article on Poland, that there the term legal psychology (and not only in Poland, see above) is defined very vaguely. This is also true for other countries of the Eastern bloc, as our study reveals (see below).

Due to the aforementioned language problems, the analyses of literature about legal psychology usually need to confine themselves to English-language publications and therefore inevitably concentrate on few countries. Even the situation in the home country, for example in Germany, is scarcely known especially with respect to legal psychological practice, at least if we consider the partly inconsistent information found in the pertinent literature (see *Kury* 1983). A few years ago, a first survey of the situation of legal psychology in training and research was conducted by us in the German-speaking countries of Austria,

Switzerland and Germany (*Kury* 1994; see also on the situation of forensic psychiatry e.g., *Foerster* 1983; 1988; 1989; 1992). A few results will be reported below.

If we know little yet about legal psychology in Western countries, then we know still less about its situation in Eastern Europe. Thus, we decided to conduct a first survey in European countries in 1994, focusing on Eastern Europe. The following countries participated in the survey - Western Europe: Austria, Belgium, Cyprus, Denmark, Finland, France, Germany, Greece, Iceland, Ireland, Italy, Luxembourg, The Netherlands, Norway, Portugal, Spain, and Sweden - Eastern Europe: Bulgaria, Croatia, Czech Republic, Estonia, Hungary, Lithuania, Poland, Russia, Slovakian Republic, Slovenia, and Turkey. Furthermore, China participated from outside Europe. In planning this survey, we were fully aware of the considerable difficulties such a survey could involve. First, it was extraordinarily difficult to find adequate interviewees. We worked out a questionnaire and had it translated into English. Due to the very restricted knowledge of the English language in some countries, misunderstandings occurred now and then. Some interviewees, such as from Poland, sent us material or answered our questions in their own language. Only the fact that the Max Planck Institute for Foreign and International Criminal Law employs internationally oriented foreign-language referees and permanently takes in guests, particularly from Eastern Europe, enabled us to include this material in our analysis at all. Once again, misunderstandings caused by problems with translations could not always be avoided. Sometimes, our questionnaires were not answered completely. We must also bear in mind that the individual countries often have very different legal systems, a fact which also affects issues in legal psychology, particularly in forensic psychology. Thus, it is quite understandable that our survey, which was conducted in a short period of time, cannot give but first impressions of the situation of legal psychology in Europe which need to be complemented by further studies. As far as we know, an extensive long-term survey within member organizations was carried through by the "European Federation of Professional Psychologists Associations". The results of this survey are not available to us.

I shall now present some results of our survey of the situation of legal psychology in Western and Northern Europe, followed by results for Eastern Europe. All information I present here is given by at least two independent local experts. I only present a piece of information when both experts questioned had given similar and not contradictory information.

Legal Psychology in Western and Northern Europe

Overview of essential results of the survey

There are considerable differences in training in legal psychology within the surveyed countries (see Table 1): In Denmark, for example, the universities offer training in forensic psychology for jurists at the Law School, but not within psychological studies, while in France, training is offered for psychologists by several universities, such as in Rouen, Lille or Rennes; the forensic courses, however, are mostly held by and for physicians. In France, the demand for training in legal psychology has been expressed increasingly, particularly by psychologists and jurists, and also by social workers. Austria merely provides training in forensic or legal psychology on a rather low level for psychologists. In Portugal, training in legal psychology has been provided since 1991, at least on paper; some universities have obviously announced training courses, but have not yet realized them. Sweden offers no official training at universities; in Lund, however, postgraduates have the opportunity of attending periodical training courses. The same is true for Finland where courses are offered only irregularly, except for continuation courses (in criminal psychology) held for the 21 prison psychologists. As expected, in the Netherlands the training programs in legal psychology are extensive. Although legal psychology is not an independent subject, it is however taught at numerous universities. Furthermore, institutions offer quite an extensive in-service training as well as courses for postgraduates. From Denmark, Finland, Austria and Sweden, we received rather skeptical estimations regarding the future perspective of training in legal psychology: it is assumed that the prevailing low level of training in legal psychology shall at best be maintained. Experts in France, the Netherlands, Portugal, Norway and Spain predict a more or less high increase for their countries. Estimations as to the general situation of research in legal psychology are similarly skeptical. The central topics of research are partly different. In Denmark, research is done on witness examination, sexual abuse of children and similar topics. In Finland, research focuses on family aggression, imprisonment and victimology; in Sweden, there is research on children as witnesses, drug career offenders, but there are also opinion polls on penal law. In France, the emphasis is - as expected - on clinical, legal psychological topics. Research in the Netherlands is quite differentiated, it concerns the following topics: juveniles in the criminal procedure, prognosis, violence in the family, police behavior etc. In Portugal, studies are being conducted above all in the form of case studies and offender profiles.

On an average, the percentage of research with respect to all psychological research is estimated to be 2-3% (maximum 5%). The percentage of legal psychologists with respect to all psychologists is also estimated to be very small, namely, less than 10%. For Denmark, the absolute number of legal psychologists equals about 5-10, for Finland 23, for Sweden 30-40, for the Netherlands 150, for Austria 170, for Portugal even 200-250 and for France 380. It goes without saying that these figures are mostly based on estimations and ought thus not to be overinterpreted. It can only give a first impression. Of course, these absolute figures must be considered in relation to the size of the country, and especially the population figure.

Table 1: Legal Psychology / Western Europe

	Education				Research			Activity fields		
	DEG	DEV	% FORE	% PSY RE	DEV	% FOPS	N FORE	PERMI	CRIM RE	ASSO
Austria	no	(↑)	7%	< 5%	(↑)	about 5%	170	yes	(yes)	yes
Belgium		←			↑			--	yes	no
Cyprus	no	↑	0%	0%	↑	0%	0		no	no
Denmark		↑	very small	5%	↑	5%	5-10	yes	yes	no
Finland	no	←	very small	0.5-2%	←	< 1%	23	no	no	no
France	no	(↑)			↑		380	yes	yes	yes
Germany	no		5%	3%		5-10%	1500 (incl. part time)	no	yes	yes
Greece	no	↑	0%		↑					
Iceland	no full	education in	psychology	very small	↑	very small	1 (20 part time)	no	no	no
Ireland	no	↑		very small	↑	1-2%	6-10	no	no	no
Italy								yes	yes	
Luxembourg	no	education in	psychology	0%	↑	very small	very small	no	no	no
The Netherlands	no	←	< 1%	< 1%	←	7%	150	no	yes	yes
Norway	no	←	very small	small	(↑)		25-30	no	no	no
Portugal	yes	(↑)	0.5%	small	←	very small	200-250	no	no	no
Spain	no	←	< 1%	small	←	very small	40	no	yes	yes
Sweden	no	↑	0.1%	0.5%	←	1%	30-40	no	yes	yes

DEG : Degree
DEV : Development
% FORE : % of forensic psychology in psychology
% PSY RE : % of psychological research
N FORE : N forensic psychologists
% FOPS : % of forensic psychologists of all psychologists

PREMI : For court: Special permission necessary
CRIM RE : Criminological research
ASSO : Associations of forensic psychologists
↑ : Increasing
→ : Constant

→ : Decreasing
(↑) : Moderate increasing
(yes) : Tends to yes
(no) : Tends to no

In principle, as to their fields of activity, legal psychologists are allowed - with the exception of Denmark - to act as forensic experts in court. As mentioned before, in Denmark they are generally not accepted in court. In criminal cases, however, and in cases involving child sexual abuse, they are summoned before the court sporadically. In this country, psychologists need an official admission to the court which is hardly ever given. In France, they are admitted to both penal and family courts, but they compete strongly with psychiatrists. The situation in Portugal is similar. The conditions in the Netherlands seem to be rather favorable. In Finland and Portugal, legal psychologists are not engaged in criminological research; in other countries such as for example Denmark and Austria, the situation is similar. In Denmark as well as in Finland and Portugal there have been no more professional federations of forensic psychology for 30 years. In Austria, a section of forensic psychology has existed since January 1994 within the Professional Federation of Austrian Psychologists.

This cursory overview unveils the considerable differences in the situation of legal psychology as to training and research as well as to its practical fields of activity. In sum we can say that, as expected, legal psychology is generally not at all well-developed in Europe nor in all countries either.

Before presenting some results on the situation in Eastern Europe, I will give a short overview of the situation in Germany as another Western country based on a survey we conducted of all German psychological institutes some years ago (see *Kury* 1994).

The situation in Germany

In Germany, research and training in the field of legal psychology have a long tradition. Already at the end of the last century, *Münsterberg* taught legal psychology in Germany; he later emigrated to the USA where he was one of the initiators of legal psychology (see above). At the beginning of this century, psychologists appeared in court sessions as forensic experts for the first time. Despite this long-standing tradition, legal psychologists play only a minor role in Germany, in the training of psychologists in universities as well as in research. The "Berufsverband Deutscher Psychologen" (BDP, Professional Federation of German Psychologists) has a special section "legal psychology". The "Deutsche Gesellschaft für Psychologie" (DGfPs, German Society of Psychology) which is an association of psychologists scientifically engaged in research and training also founded a special section for legal psychology at the biannual meeting in Vienna in 1984. This section regularly holds workshops and conferences. In 1989, *Lösel* published the results of a systematic analysis of German-language journals edited between 1950-1989. Among other findings, he discovered that the frequency of publications in the field of legal psychology had clearly increased.

Some years ago, the special section for legal psychology of the German Society of Psychology (DGfPs) carried out its own study on the current situation of legal psychology at the university institutes of psychology in the former Federal Republic of Germany. The response rate of this study was not very high and the results can only be generalized with restrictions. This survey found out that the situation of legal psychology in teaching and research at Western German psychological university institutes is not a good one. The persons responsible for legal psychology at the Departments of Psychology mostly have a lower degree and there are no special chairs for this subject. The possibilities to reach a good professional position in an institute are unfavorable for legal psychologists, and therefore young scientists feel the pressure to change to another specialization.

In addition to this study, we decided to conduct another questionnaire-based survey by means of a fully standardized instrument of data collection on the current situation of legal psychology in research and training at Austrian, Swiss and German Psychological University Institutes. The section for legal psychology of the German Society of Psychology supported our study.

We developed two versions of the questionnaire: version A containing 39 items for institutes which offer training and research on legal psychology and version B containing 13 items for institutes which offer neither training nor research in legal psychology. The data collection covered the period between the winter term 1988/1989 and the beginning of the winter term 1990/1991, thus comprising a period of nearly 4 terms. The questionnaire contains items referring to the following fields: 1. general presentation of legal psychology at those institutes where a diploma can be achieved for studies in psychology, 2. training in legal psychology, 3. research in legal psychology, 4. how do students make use of offers of training in legal psychology, 5. aspects independent from training and research, 6. coordination and cooperation, 7. chronological/historical development of legal psychology in training and research at the institute, 8. assessment of and attitudes towards legal psychology.

The study was conducted at all psychological university institutes in the German-speaking countries Austria, Switzerland and Germany where a diploma can be obtained in psychology. In addition, we sent our questionnaire to some university institutes offering psychology as a subsidiary subject. The study was conducted between early August 1990 and early March 1991. The response rate of the mail survey was 100% (after sometimes several reminders) for the institutes offering a diploma in psychology studies. As to the situation in East Germany, in the mean time the reunification of both German countries took place. Our results described the situation in the former German Democratic Republic. However, current information of 1993 reveals that the situation of legal psychology in East Germany until now is not better than before the reunification.

A diploma for studies in psychology is offered at 41 German university institutes (37 in Western Germany, 4 in Eastern Germany), in Austria at 4 institutes and in Switzerland at 3 institutes. In Western Germany, 37 institutes offer a diploma in psychology, 27 (73%) of which offer legal psychology in training or research. All these 27 institutes which have legal psychology offer training but only 17 (63%) offer research (see Table 2). The proportion of training is, however, rather low: The average proportion of training in legal psychology compared to psychological training on the whole amounts to 3% in Germany, in Austria also 3%, in Switzerland 2%. At the universities, these figures range from 1% to 6%. Referring to the 4 terms mentioned above, the average figure of training courses per term which deal exclusively with legal psychology equals 2 in Western Germany, 3.0 in Eastern Germany, 3.0 in Austria and 0.5 in Switzerland. The average figure of training courses per week equals 3.5 in Western Germany, 3.0 in Eastern Germany, 6 in Austria and 0.5 in Switzerland. In Western Germany, only 6 institutes offered legal psychology as a required optional subject from the winter term 1988/1989 to the beginning of the winter term 1990/1991. 16 institutes, i.e. 60% of all institutes in Western Germany which offer legal psychology, also offer their students the opportunity to participate in training courses in legal psychology at neighboring faculties, especially at faculties of law, to a lesser degree at the faculty of medicine and in one single case at faculties of other subjects of social science. In Western Germany, only 7 institutes have a fixed training curriculum for legal psychology, which is almost one third of the total number of institutions offering legal psychology.

Table 2: Legal Psychology in Education and Research in German Speaking Countries (1991)

	Psychological institutes with course of study for diploma	Institute with legal psychology		Institute with teachings in legal psychology		Institute with research in legal psychology	
Germany/West	37	27	(73%)	27	(100%)	17	(63%) [1]
Germany/East	4	4	(100%)	4	(100%)	1	(25%) [2]
Austria	4	4	(100%)	3	(75%)	2	(50%)
Switzerland	3	2	(66%)	2	(100%)	2	(100%)

[1] Missing 3; [2] Missing 1

Nevertheless, 18 institutes in Western Germany, i.e., after all two thirds of all institutes offering courses in legal psychology, also prepare forensic expert reports, in particular for the courts. Only 10 of these institutes also partially engage students for forensic expert reports within the training in legal psychology, while five institutes engage students regularly. This means that approximately every second institute with courses in legal psychology offers its students the possibility to experience directly the process of drawing up forensic expert reports; this seems to be of rather great importance for their training. Four institutes regularly offer colloquia.

As to the situation of *research* in legal psychology, seventeen (63%) Western German institutes are engaged in research. Interviews with university staff members reveal that the average percentage of research in legal psychology is seven in proportion to research on the whole. The estimations of the staff members lie between 1% and 20%. At nine institutes research is financed by universities, and at another nine institutes obtain financing from other sources. Sixteen institutes made statements regarding the contents of their fields of research (see Table 3). Table 3 clearly shows that in Western Germany forensic-psychological research focuses upon the field of forensic psychology (in this connection, particularly on penal law) as well as on criminal psychology. Incarceration and resocialisation also constitute a focal point of forensic-psychological research. The results found earlier e.g., by *Lösel* (1989) can herewith be confirmed.

Table 3: Research Fields in Legal Psychology in German Speaking Countries (1991)

		Germany/West	Germany/East	Austria	Switzerland
I. Diagnostic and intervention	Forensic psychology:				
	- Penal law	8	1		
	- Civil law	2			1
	- Public law	2		1	
II. Action in justice administration	1. Psychology and law:				
	- Psychology of legal proceedings	1			
	- Psychology of criminal investigations	3			
	2. Psychology of law	2		1	
III. Prison / resocialisation		4			
IV. Criminal psychology		8			1

Regarding the acceptance of training courses in legal psychology by students in Western Germany, an average of 26% of psychology students attend courses in legal psychology, the figures ranging from 3% to 100%. A maximum of three institutes offer a compulsory course in a compulsory subject within legal psychology. In Western German Institutes, 3.5% of all diploma and doctoral theses on the average deal with subjects of legal psychology. The proportion of legal-psychological practical training courses also equals 3.5% compared to the overall number of practical studies. The persons interviewed judge the interest of psychology students in legal-psychological training courses to be average.

We found a clear positive trend in the general development of legal psychology at Western German universities. Only one institute stated that training courses in legal psychology had already been offered regularly before 1949. Another eleven institutes took up legal psychology between 1950 and 1979, and another twelve institutes joined in between 1980 and 1989. We can recognize a strong increase in legal-psychological training courses and research during the 80s at Western German university institutes; in the meantime, two institutes have canceled their offers. Nine institutes estimate that their offers in legal-psychological training courses and research have clearly increased within the last five years. Eleven Western German institutes believe that research possibilities in legal psychology will increase, ten Western German institutes estimate that there will not be any changes and four institutes expect a decrease. Estimations of trends for training in legal psychology reveal similar results.

The institutes brought forward the following points that could support the desired development of training in legal psychology:

- Expansion of the teaching staff's capacity by increasing the personnel and the financial means; because of the current period of financial shortage there will hardly be any chance to achieve this expansion;
- Curricular institutionalization; equal status for legal psychology compared to other subjects, e.g., as a required optional subject or as a priority topic in another partial subject;
- An increase in the number of training courses;
- Structural institutionalization: creation of legal-psychological departments, and professorial chairs;
- Expansion of intradisciplinary coordination and cooperation.

With respect to research in legal psychology, the following points were mentioned:

- Improvements in both the number of staff and the financial situation;
- Expansion of coordination and cooperation;
- Curricular institutionalization.

On the whole, psychological institutes that offer legal psychology emphasize that students are undoubtedly interested in legal psychology or that their interest might easily be roused. Students seem to be highly interested if there exists a compact program in legal psychology, instead of scattered single courses that are offered at irregular intervals every now and then.

It is quite interesting that those institutes that do not provide legal psychology in training or research strongly favor the development and support of legal psychology at their own institute. Only one institute states that there will probably be no offer in legal psychology in the future; whereas the remaining institutes state that they might possibly provide legal psychology in future. According to the institutes, the main reasons for not offering legal psychology are: 1. other priorities, 2. lacking interest of staff or lacking lecturers.

Fifteen institutes in Western Germany favor the introduction of a specialized type of psychologist, namely the "Forensic Psychologist", similar to the "Clinical

Psychologist/Psychotherapist" because of the social relevance of this discipline and the mostly insufficient professional training of forensic practitioners. However eight institutes object to the introduction of a forensic psychologist, putting forward that they fear a devaluation of the diploma in psychology and favor postgraduate training and examination in legal psychology for diploma psychologists. Eighteen institutes favor the development of legal psychology into an independent partial subject, however, in order to prevent legal psychology, a discipline of practical relevance, from losing importance. Furthermore, legal psychology is an independent subject in its contents and methods within applied psychology. Eight institutes reject this development, arguing that legal psychology is connected too closely to the other subjects or that the examination rules for psychology do not guarantee the quality of a completed training in legal psychology.

Legal Psychology in Eastern Europe and the Eastern Bloc

In the following section, we give some information on a survey concerning the situation of forensic psychology in Eastern Europe. Due to scarce relevant information in the literature available, this task could be accomplished - if at all - only by an expert survey conducted in the individual countries. Even if taking into account the close contacts between the Max Planck Institute for Foreign and International Criminal Law and most of the countries, a survey of the situation of legal psychology could be realized only partially in the short period of time available, especially if we take into account the problems regarding Eastern Europe caused by long distance and language barriers. Apart from these technical problems, such a survey also entails considerable difficulties as to its contents; these countries partially have different legal systems, a circumstance which naturally has an impact on the issues of legal psychology, particularly of forensic psychology. Furthermore, there often exists little experience in legal psychology, and its definition varies. This already being the case with the Federal Republic of Germany, it cannot be expected that countries which differ as much as e.g. Russia and China define (and translate into and from their own language) legal psychology similarly. We have tried to reduce this problem by providing wide definitions for psychological/legal terms. However, we were merely able to alleviate this problem. Moreover, it was very difficult, especially in Eastern Europe, to find experts in the field of legal psychology with sufficient knowledge of the situation of legal psychology in their own country.

Considering this background, I can give but first impressions of the results of our survey; these impressions need to be completed by results obtained later on. We did not cover Eastern European countries exclusively, but almost all European countries - focusing, however, on Eastern Europe. Many countries provided useful information, though some information was not complete. In addition, we included some large countries from the Eastern Bloc outside Europe, such as China. A total of eleven countries from the Eastern Bloc - not included Turkey - provided information, at least partially. We asked (as in the survey conducted in Western European countries) especially for information on three topics: training, research and fields of activity in legal psychology and of the legal psychologists. Table 4 shows the essential results.

Training in legal psychology

Six out of eleven Eastern Bloc countries, i.e. only about one half of those included in the analysis provide mostly more or less partial training courses in legal psychology or related fields within the discipline of psychology. In some countries, such as China and Estonia, legal psychology is also taught at universities, albeit at the faculty of law. Some other countries, such as Turkey and Hungary, provide training in legal psychology only as continuation courses for postgraduates. Only Bulgaria, Croatia, Russia, the Czech and the Slovakian Republic offer university training in legal psychology within psychology studies exceeding more than a few hours. In most cases, this training is concentrated in and restricted to a few universities of the respective country. Eight out of eleven Eastern Bloc countries offer training in legal psychology outside the university, in general for postgraduates. It is striking that training institutions are usually state organizations: the Ministry of the Interior (Bulgaria, Russia), police academies (China and Lithuania), national defense institutions (Estonia), state departments of forensic medicine (Turkey) or judicial authorities (Slovakian Republic). It must be assumed that training in legal psychology is not independent in the aforementioned countries, whereas the independence of teaching is natural for university training in Western countries. Obviously, state institutions provide training according to their own ideas for the majority of - if not for all - legal psychologists who, in turn, are engaged for state tasks within the legal system, a fact which surely influences the contents of the training. Western countries, too, partly offer training in legal psychology outside the universities; however, this occurs in mostly independent institutions such as professional federations of psychology, etc., which provide training courses. Partly, prison authorities provide training in legal psychology as far as incarceration and resocialisation are concerned.

None of the surveyed countries - except for the Slovakian Republic - offer a special degree for studies in legal psychology. In general, the curriculum is not standardized; some training institutions provide only single and often irregular courses in legal psychology. The following countries offer relatively comprehensive training in legal psychology: Bulgaria, Croatia with two terms at the university, in Russia at few universities, e.g. in St. Petersburg, the Czech and the Slovakian Republic. In general, the contents of the training are restricted to traditional topics - especially topics belonging to forensic and criminal psychology, such as expert reports for the courts, criminal prevention and psychology of the offender.

Table 4: Legal Psychology / Eastern Europe

	Education				Research			Activity fields		
	DEG	DEV	% FORE	% PSY RE	DEV	% FOPS	N FORE	PERMI	CRIM RE	ASSO
Bulgaria	no	↑	very small	3%	→	35% of applied psychologists	80	yes	yes	yes
Croatia	no	→		< 5%	→	15%	165	no		no
Czech Republic	no	↑	very small	very small	penology → crimology ↑		120	yes	yes	yes
Estonia		→	2-3%	5%	→	1%	7-8	yes	little	no
Hungary				small	↑		40-60	no	yes	yes
Lithuania	no	↑	very small	small	↑		10	no	no	yes
Poland	no	→	very small	very small	↑	8-10% (20-25% part time)	200	no	yes	no
Russia	no	→(↑)	2-3%	1-2%	↑	2-3%	500	no	yes	yes
Slovakian Republic	yes	↑	5-10%		(↑)	14%	160	no (except registered)	yes	yes
Slovenia	no	→↑	0%	0%	→	very small	very small	no	no	no
Turkey	no	→↑	very small	very small	(↑)		20	no	yes	no
China	no	↑		very small	↑		1500, members of section		(yes)	yes

DEG	: Degree	PREMI	: For court: Special permission necessary
DEV	: Development	CRIM RE	: Criminological research
% FORE	: % of forensic psychology in psychology	ASSO	: Associations of forensic psychologists
% PSY RE	: % of psychological research	↑	: Increasing
N FORE	: N forensic psychologists	→	: Constant
% FOPS	: % of forensic psychologists of all psychologists		

→	:	Decreasing
(↑)	:	Moderate increasing
(yes)	:	Tends to yes
(no)	:	Tends to no

As expected, the Eastern countries did not show as strong an increase in legal psychology as could be observed in some of the Western countries during the past years. Of course, the economic and financial reality of the Eastern countries is responsible for this situation, but also current wars, such as in Croatia. The problems caused by the process of reorientation after the opening of the Eastern Bloc understandably push questions related to training in legal psychology into the background. Thus, it is not astonishing that one third of the countries in our survey have diminished their offers of legal psychology. However, in China, a strong increase can be observed. Experts from Lithuania, Russia, Turkey and the Slovakian Republic mention a moderate increase. The data are relativized by the fact that for all countries the percentage of training in legal psychology - if training is offered at all - amounts to a very low figure, namely to approximately 5%. However, it must be taken into consideration that the percentage for Western Europe (the Federal Republic of Germany) also amounts to about 5%. But in general, psychology in the Eastern Bloc is not so well developed, due to various economic and political problems and also because of the Iron Curtain which had rendered nearly all contacts to Western colleagues impossible during a long period of time. In East and West, however, training in legal psychology plays only a marginal role within psychology studies.

Research

As expected, the situation of research in the field of legal psychology is similar to the situation of training - yet slightly more positive. All countries covered in our survey report that there exists research in this field. Closer examination of the data reveals, however, that research is mostly restricted to a few empirical studies on more or less classic legal psychological/criminological themes. The following research themes were mentioned most frequently: incarceration, personality of the offender, treatment of offenders, criminality and mental illness, crime prognosis and juvenile delinquency. Research themes mentioned less frequently are: the fear to punishment, psychology of punishing (Croatia), the population's consciousness of law, public opinion on criminality (Russia), justice research (Czech Republic), victimological themes (Slovakian Republic).

The future development of research is generally judged with skepticism. The majority of countries in our survey suppose that the development will stagnate or, at least, increase slightly. The percentage of research in the field of legal psychology in relation to psychological research on the whole is estimated as being very low, i.e. less than 5% almost without exception. The experts interviewed who are not only psychologists, but also partly sociologists and jurists unanimously state that training as well as research in legal psychology should be developed further.

The total number of legal psychologists naturally differs strongly according to the population figure of the country. In general, the number of legal psychologists is relatively small. Estimates as to the total number of legal psychologists are for example: 300 (out of 1,500 members of section) in China, 500 in Russia, 80 in Bulgaria, 160 for the Slovakian Republic and 120 for the Czech Republic, 165 for Croatia, 200 for Poland. Clearly lower figures were established for the remaining countries. Mostly less than 5% of all psychologists are legal psychologists, for Russia the figure equals 2-3%.

Fields of activity

As expected, in almost all Eastern Bloc countries, legal psychologists draw up expert reports for the courts and are employed in prisons. These are nearly always their main fields of activity. The situation in the West is similar (see above). Only in China, legal psychologists are not allowed to act in prisons or courts. There, the 300 legal psychologists are exclusively engaged in training, particularly in the training of jurists. In the other countries, legal psychologists may act as forensic psychologists, as experts in court when penal and family matters are involved; in general, they can act alone, but often they are not admitted unless they cooperate with psychiatrists. In Estonia, they are only accepted by penal courts. The data for Russia reveal a very small number of public psychologists who may act as experts in court. In Turkey, the courts accept psychologists only if they cooperate with psychiatrists or physicians to whom they are subordinate. Here, the final decision as to expert reports rests with the physician. In Hungary, legal psychologists may act independently in family courts as well as in juvenile courts. In matters of criminal responsibility (criminal cases) or legal capacity (civil cases) they can only act in cooperation with psychiatrists.

Forensic psychologists are offered many opportunities in the Slovakian Republic. They are accepted in family, civil as well as in penal cases. In Bulgaria, the Czech Republic and Estonia, forensic psychologists need special permission in order to be accepted by courts. In Estonia, supplementary training courses have to be attended for this purpose. In the other countries, basically every psychologist can be appointed by the court. Also with regard to prisons, psychologists are relatively independent in the Slovakian Republic. They are employed in particular in medical and treatment services within prisons and may even be appointed director of a prison. In the other countries, forensic psychologists are employed in adult and youth prisons and in treatment-oriented centers, if there are any such centers at all.

In general, very few or no psychologists at all are engaged in criminological research; here we have to take into account that criminological research is rather underdeveloped as compared to Western countries. If they are engaged in criminological research at all, then it is mostly under the supervision of jurists. In the Eastern Bloc, too, criminological research, if done at all, is dominated by jurists. Independent professional fields for legal psychologists exist in China, Croatia (only for psychologists working in prison), Lithuania (since 1988 there exists a subgroup "deviant behavior") and in the Slovakian Republic. Here, there exist even two subsections: the forensic section of the Slovakian Society of Psychology and furthermore, since 1992, the independent subsection "psychology" of permanently registered psychological experts in court.

It can be noted that legal psychologists in Eastern countries mostly act in prisons and prepare expert reports for the courts. They are seldom engaged in criminological research. As we know, this is also true for Western countries, such as the Federal Republic of Germany, however, mostly on a higher level. It is striking that legal psychology is relatively well-developed in the Slovakian Republic and that the fields of work for legal psychologists are quite broad there.

Discussion

Our analysis gives a first, still rather cursory overview of the situation of legal psychology in European countries. As expected, the positive development of legal psychology frequently observed did not show in all the surveyed countries. The development has been stagnating or even decreasing, particularly in a number of Eastern Bloc countries, but also in some Western European states. As far as the Eastern Bloc countries are concerned, this situation results from difficulties in the political and economic reality. As already mentioned above, legal psychology, especially forensic psychology, depends on the development and humanization of law. In the German Penal Code, alterations of rules concerning criminal responsibility ensure a more frequent consultation and presence of psychologists when decisions of the court are concerned (§§20, 21 German Penal Code). This is also the case with family law where alterations in divorce legislation have occurred such as the term "well-being of the child" ("Kindeswohl") being introduced when decisions on tutelage and parental responsibility/contact are involved (*Böttger et al.* 1988; *Kury* 1991). More and more, these alterations had required to make use of psychological expert knowledge with court decisions, resulting in a trend towards an increasing humanization of these decisions. In the Eastern bloc countries, a comparable development in legislation mostly cannot be observed and/or has not been fully completed yet. The vital development of legislation and as well the development of jurisdiction will surely bring about the need for more psychological expert knowledge in the future.

Legal psychology is one of the minor disciplines even within psychology. The further development of legal psychology will essentially depend on the development of both justice administration and the legal consciousness. Unlike in western industrial systems, legal psychology has obviously been less successful in emphasizing its rank and significance in traditional social systems, where it often plays only a minor role, such as forensic medicine in questions regarding expert reports, in criminal and civil law. While both law and medicine are old sciences with a long-standing cooperation, psychology did not fully appear until this century.

Psychology may no doubt contribute essentially to issues of forensic reports, a fact it still must prove; for this purpose experts need to be trained. Forensic medicine needs to surrender fields of activity, a change which will not occur without opposition. For this reason it is not surprising that psychology is still restricted to few fields of legal psychology in some countries.

Psychology itself ought to be more concerned with the unexplored fields within the broad realm of legal psychology by increasing the number of research projects. Research in legal psychology is still mostly devoted to few current issues, as e.g. imprisonment or questions concerning forensic psychology, expert opinions on credibility or problems in the field of family law. For legal psychology to become an essential part of applied psychology, we need a problem-oriented integration of results and experiences of all disciplines of basic research in psychology (*Lösel* 1987). This is a considerable challenge for psychologists who are engaged in this field, since they would be required to have a very comprehensive psychological knowledge. During the past years, forensic expert reports in cases involving family law which have been increasingly ordered by family courts in Germany due to legal alterations can be drawn up only if the forensic psychologist does not have knowledge exclusively in law but also in development psychology, psychodiagnostics, social psychology, personal psychology and psychopathology to state only the most important ones. Without a well-founded training in these fields and without linking up these areas of research with forensic questions, the drawing up of qualified expert reports can hardly be achieved. The often poor or even bad quality of expert reports is caused by a lack of training of forensic psychologists and also by their working alone without supervision and support by the colleagues, and without being monitored.

In many countries the number of psychologists occupied with legal psychology is on the rise and rightly so. Psychology is capable of making more fruitful contributions to a great deal more issues in the fields of law and law application as well as criminology as is currently the case. During the past decades, practitioners in various professional fields have recognized the potential advantage psychological knowledge may bring about - this recognition resulted in an increasing number of psychologists who were offered important positions. In Germany, according to *Lösel* (1992, p.102), approximately 300 psychologists are working in prisons, about 250 at safety standards authorities ("Technische Überwachungsvereine"). There, they are testing drivers with problems in road traffic, and approximately another 100 psychologists have full-time jobs as forensic experts in courts. Just in this field, the work in court means a job on the side for many psychologists. Approximately 1,600 members of the Professional Federation of German Psychologists belong to the section of forensic and criminal psychology, i.e. about 10% of all members of the Professional Federation of German Psychologists are in any way occupied with issues of forensic and criminal psychology.

This represents a challenge to psychology. At least in western industrial nations such as the USA and Great Britain, criminology is conceived as a discipline of empirical social science, whereas in large parts of Europe, particularly in the Eastern Bloc, but also in Germany, it is considered a discipline of the science of law; but the science of law, however, is by no means an empirical social science. In this connection, too, we ought to doubt old traditional regulations and think them over. The advantage of US-American and partly also of English criminology over criminological research in Germany and in many other European countries is that psychologists and sociologists, i.e. social scientists, act independently and are in a leading manner engaged in criminological research. In Germany, despite all progress in social sciences, the dominance of jurists over psychologists in criminology poses great problems for the further development of this discipline. The international competitiveness of European criminological research shall in the future depend on how far we will succeed in engaging predominantly social scientists in the discipline of social science, i.e. criminology. Here, as in other fields of legal psychology, too, the importance of empirical social sciences, among which psychology is one of the most essential, has to be emphasized time and again, not only for reasons of professional politics, but also in order to promote science itself. In Germany, over the past years, a clear increase in the importance of psychology for criminology can be observed. The rising number of criminological publications written by psychologists is proof of this trend (see e.g. *Kaiser, Kury & Albrecht* 1988). In this connection, psychology should branch out more strongly in forensic psychology but also in criminology. Psychologists should more often bring in their expert knowledge in order to help to solve crime problems; they also should intensify their participation in research.

If the law is intended to guide human behavior, then the science of law is a science of human behavior, and hence above all a science of psychology. Law created and elaborated by jurists and politicians serves as a means to influence and guide human behavior. The assessment of the influence of law on human behavior is an empirical issue which cannot be explained by jurists and, because of reasons of independence, also should not be explained by them. Evaluation research has always attached great importance to the principle that the person who is carrying out treatment programs should not test their functioning at the same time, and rightly so. The risk to create conflicting interests would simply be too high and the vital independence of research would be endangered. Also, the functioning of law should not be tested by those who create law, even if they were able to. In this connection, too, the principle applies: "Essentially, a person can function as a psychologist or a lawyer but not both" (*Hess* 1987, p.44). Already at the beginning of this century, *Pound* (1912) stressed the importance of social sciences for the understanding of the effects of law. "It is not enough to compare the laws themselves. It is much more important to study their social operation and the effects which they produce, if any, when into action". This demand appears to be so timely because it was only fulfilled partially up to now, if at all.

The practice demonstrates the importance of permanent testing of legal rules and their efficiency. After the alteration of certain legal rules, one often wonders why a rule could have been in force for such a long time. "The probability is always given that any portion of law needs reexamination to determine how far it fits the society it purports to serve" (*Llewellen* 1931, p.1222). In this connection, *Saks* (1989, p.1110) points out that "the law and its practitioners are careful, thoughtful, and rigorous about many things. But those things do not include the nature of social and behavioral phenomena, cause and effect relationships, or the effects of the interventions made by the law". These aspects have to be introduced by the social sciences (see also *Monahan & Walker* 1990). *Rasch* (1994, p.252), a forensic psychiatrist, put the critical question with respect to the participation of psychologists in law, how much psychology in the contact with delinquents or in penal procedure was possible or necessary. "How much psychology does law 'endure', since psychologists are surely the strongest rivals of jurists".

It will also depend on the psychologists themselves how far they "become more involved in the law and have greater influence on legal policy" (...) "we may need to be more creative in our approaches to the uses of social science in law" *(Freeman & Roesch* 1992, p.571). Here, psychology must not shirk its responsibility.

References

Arce, R., Sobral, J., & Fariña, F. (1990). The influence of the individual juror's psychosocial profile on his verdict. *Social Action and the Law, 12,* 73-94.

Arntzen, F. (1994). *Das Bochumer Institut für Gerichtspsychologie.* Unpubl. Manuscr. Bochum.

Ávila Espada, A. (1987). Evaluación de la competencia legal. *Papeles del Psicólogo, 30,* 14-25.

Bartol, C.R. (1983). *Psychology and American law.* Belmont/Ca.: Wadsworth.

Bartol, C.R., & Bartol, A.M. (1987). History of forensic psychology. In: Weiner, J.B., & Hess, A.K. (Eds.), *Handbook of forensic psychology* (pp. 3-21). New York: Wiley.

Böttger, A., Kury, H., Kuznik, R., & Mertens, R. (1988). Kriterien der gutachterlichen Schuldfähigkeitsbeurteilung und ihr Einfluß auf die richterliche Entscheidung. In: Kaiser, G., Kury, H., & Albrecht, H.-J. (Eds.), *Kriminologische Forschung in den 80er Jahren* (pp. 323-373). Freiburg, 2 vols.

Clemente, M. (1987). *Delincuencia femenina. Un enfoque psicosocial.* Madrid: UNED.

Diamond, S.S. (1992). Foreword. In: Kagehiro, D.K., & Laufer, W.S. (Eds.), *Handbook of psychology and law* (pp. V-IX). New York: Springer.

v. Eckartshausen, K. (1791). *Über die Notwendigkeit psychologischer Kenntnisse bey Beurtheilung der Verbrechen.* München.

Egg, R. (Ed.) (1991). *Brennpunkte der Rechtspsychologie. Polizei - Justiz - Drogen.* Bonn: Forum.

Fabian, Th., & Wetzels, P. (1991). Zur gegenwärtigen Praxis von forensischen Psychologen und Psychologinnen: Ergebnisse einer Befragung. *Praxis der Forensischen Psychologie, 1,* 10-17.

Farrington, D.P. (1992). Psychological contributions to the explanation, prevention, and treatment of offending. In: Lösel, F., Bender, D., & Bliesener, T. (Eds.), *Psychology and law* (pp. 35-51). Berlin: De Gruyter.

Foerster, K. (1983). Die forensische Psychiatrie an den Universitäten der Bundesrepublik Deutschland, in Österreich und in der Schweiz. *Forensia, 4,* 73-79.

Foerster, K. (1988). Die Weiterbildung in forensischer Psychiatrie im internationalen Vergleich. *Forensia, 9,* 257-261.

Foerster, K. (1989). Zur Situation der Weiterbildung in forensischer Psychiatrie in der Bundesrepublik Deutschland. Ergebnisse einer Umfrage. *Nervenarzt, 60,* 243-245.

Foerster, K. (1992). Forensische Psychiatrie in der psychiatrischen/nervenärztlichen Weiterbildung. In: Jehle, J.-M. (Ed.), *Kriminologie als Lehrgebiet* (pp. 87-96). Wiesbaden.

Freeman, R.J., & Roesch, R. (1992). Psycholegal education: Training for forum and function. In: Kagehiro, D.K., & Laufer, W.S. (Eds.), *Handbook of psychology and law* (pp. 567-576). New York: Springer.

Garrido, E., & DeElena, J. (1990). Peritaje judicial y decisión judicial. En actas del II Congreso Nacional de Psicología Social VI (pp. 181-192). Barcelona.

Garrido Genovés, V. (1982). *Psicología y tratamiento penitenciario: Una aproximación.* Madrid: EDERSA.

Garrido Genovés, V. (1987). Tratamiento de los delincuentes en la comunidad. In: Pérez Sánchez, J. (Ed.), *Bases psicológicas de la delincuencia y de la conducta antisocial* (pp. 102-118). Barcelona.

Garrido, V., & Redondo, S. (1992). Psychology and law in Spain. In: Lösel, F., Bender, D., & Bliesener, T. (Eds.), *Psychology and law* (pp. 526-534). Berlin: De Gruyter.

Garrido Martín, E. (1986). El testigo visual en los juicios. In: Morales, J.F., Blanco, A., Huici, C., & Fernandez, J.M. (Eds.), *Psicología social aplicada* (pp. 93-112). Bilbao.

Garrido Martín, E. (1994). Psychology and law. *Applied Psychology: An International Review, 43,* 303-311.

Garzón, A., & Seoane, J. (1988). Dimensiones políticas en psicologia judicial. In: Seoane, J., & Rodriguez, A. (Eds.), *Psicología política.* Madrid: Pirámide.

Gross, H. (1898). *Criminalpsychologie.* Graz: Leuschner & Lubensky's.

Gulotta, G. (Ed.) (1987). *Trattato di psicologia giudiziaria nel sistema penale.* Milano: Giuffrè.

Haney, C. (1980). Psychology and legal change: On the limits of a factual jurisprudence. *Law and Human Behaviour, 4,* 147-200.

Hess, A.K. (1987). Dimensions of forensic psychology. In: Weiner, J.B., & Hess, A.K. (Eds.), *Handbook of forensic psychology* (pp. 22-49). New York: Wiley.

Hommers, W. (1993). Zum Begriff der Rechtspsychologie unter professioneller Perspektive. *Praxis der Rechtspsychologie, 3,* 11-21.

Jiménez Burillo, F., & Clemente Díaz, M. (Eds.) (1986). *Psicología social y sistema penal.* Madrid: Alianza Universidad.

Kagehiro, D.K., & Laufer, W.S. (Eds.) (1992). *Handbook of psychology and law.* New York: Springer.

Kaiser, G. (1992). Psychological contributions to criminology: Perspectives of a law scientist. In: Lösel, F., Bender, D., & Bliesener, T. (Eds.), *Psychology and law* (pp. 22-34). Berlin. New York: de Gruyter.

Kaiser, G., Kury, H., & Albrecht, H.-J. (Eds.) (1988). *Kriminologische Forschung in den 80er Jahren.* Freiburg, 3 vols.

Kury, H. (1983). Psychologie im Bereich der Kriminologie: Chancen und Probleme. *Psychologische Rundschau, 34,* 72-85.

Kury, H. (Ed.) (1987). Ausgewählte Fragen und Probleme forensischer Begutachtung. Köln et al.

Kury, H. (1991). Zur Begutachtung der Schuldfähigkeit: Ausgewählte Ergebnisse eines empirischen Forschungsprojektes. In: Egg, R. (Ed.), *Brennpunkte der Rechtspsychologie. Polizei - Justiz - Drogen* (pp. 331-350). Bonn: Forum.

Kury, H. (1994). *Zur Situation der Rechtspsychologie in den deutschsprachigen Ländern.* Unpubl. Manuscr. Freiburg 1994.

Llewellen, K.N. (1931). Some realism about realism: Responding to Dean Pound. *Harvard Law Review, 44,* 1222-1264.

Lösel, F. (1987). Konzeptuelle Probleme und Heuristiken der Angewandten Sozialpsychologie. In: Schultz-Gambard, J. (Ed.), *Angewandte Sozialpsychologie* (pp. 29-42). München: Psychologie VerlagsUnion.

Lösel, F. (1989). Zur neueren Enwicklung der Rechtspsychologie: Versuch einer Standortbestimmung. In: Schönpflug, W. (Ed.), *Bericht über den 36. Kongreß der Deutschen Gesellschaft für Psychologie in Berlin.* Vol.2 (pp. 291-306). Göttingen.

Lösel, F. (1992). Psychology and law: Overtures, crescendos, and reprises. In: Lösel, F., Bender, D., & Bliesener, T. (Eds.), *Psychology and law* (pp. 3-21). Berlin.

Lösel, F. (1992a). Aus- und Weiterbildung in forensischer, Kriminal- und Rechtspsychologie. In: Jehle, J.-M. (Ed.), *Kriminologie als Lehrgebiet* (pp. 97-122). Wiesbaden.

Lösel, F., Bender, D., & Bliesener, T. (1992). International perspectives on psychology and law: An introduction. In: Lösel, F., Bender, D., & Bliesener, T. (Eds.), *Psychology and law* (pp. VII-XVII). Berlin: De Gruyter.

Loh, W.D. (1981). Perspectives on psychology and law. *Journal of Applied Social Psychology, 11*, 314-355.

Melton, G.B. (1987). Training in psychology and law. In: Weiner, J.B., & Hess, A.K. (Eds.), *Handbook of forensic psychology* (pp. 681-697). New York: Wiley.

Mira, J.J., & Diges, M. (1984). Psicología del testimonio: Un problema metodológico. *Revista de Psicología General y Applicada, 39*, 1059-1074.

Mira, J.J., & Diges, M. (1986). Procesos intervinierendes en la evidencia de testigos. In: Jiménez Burillo, J., & Clemente Díaz, M. (Eds.), *Psicología social y sistema penal* (pp. 301-326). Madrid: Alianza.

Mira y López, E. (1932). *Manual de psicología jurídica*. Barcelona: Salvat.

Monahan, J., & Walker, L. (1990). *Social science in law: Cases and materials*. New York: Foundation Press, 2nd ed.

Morales, J.F., Blanco, A., Huici, C., & Fernández, J.M. (Eds.) (1986). *Psicología social aplicada*. Bilbao: Dexlée de Breowver.

Muench, J.G. (1799). *Über den Einfluß der Criminalpsychologie auf ein System des Criminal-Rechts, auf menschliche Gesetze und Cultur der Verbrecher*. Nürnberg: Steinische Buchhandlung.

Münsterberg, H. (1908). *On the witness stand: Essays on psychology and crime*. New York: Doubleday.

Ogloff, J.R.P. (1989). Law and psychology in Canada. *Canadian Psychology, 31*, 61-73.

Ogloff, J.R.P. (1992). Introduction. In: Ogloff, J.R.P. (Ed.), *Law and psychology: The broadening of the discipline* (pp. 1-7). Durham/NCarol.

Portero, P., Redondo, S., & Roca, M. (1987). El tratamiento penitenciario. Una aproximación conductual. In: Pérez, J. (Ed.), *Bases psicológicas de la delincuencia y de la conducta antisocial* (pp. 143-184). Barcelona: PPU.

Pound, R. (1912). The scope and purpose of sociological jurisprudence. *Harvard Law Review, 25*, 489.

Prieto, A., Diges, M., & Bernal, M. (1990). El impacto del testigo prescencial sobre el jurado. In: Sobral, J., & Arce, R. (Eds.), *La psicología social en la sala de justicia. El jurado y el testimonio* (pp. 12-31). Barcelona: Paidós.

Rasch, W. (1994). Mit differenzierender Optik sich dem Gegenstand Kriminaltherapie nähern. In: Steller, M., Dahle, K.-P., & Basqué, M. (Eds.), *Straftäterbehandlung* (pp. 251-254). Pfaffenweiler.

Roesch, R. (1990). From the editor. *Law and Human Behaviour, 14*, 1-3.

Saks, M.J. (1989). Legal policy analysis and evaluation. *American Psychologist, 44*, 1110-1117.

Sancha Mata, V., Clemente Díaz, M., & Miguel Toval, J.J. (Eds.) (1987). *Delincuencia. Teoría e investigación*. Madrid: Alpe Editores.

Schaumann, J.G. (1792). *Ideen einer Kriminalpsychologie*. Halle.

Sobral, J., & Arce, R. (Eds.) (1990). *La psicología social en la sala de justicia*. Barcelona: Paidós.

Stanik, J.M. (1992). Psychology and law in Poland. In: Lösel, F., Bender, D., & Bliesener, T. (Eds.), *Psychology and law* (pp. 546-553). Berlin: De Gruyter.

Tapp, J.L. (1976). Psychology and the law: An overture. In: Rosenzweig, M.L., & Porter, L.W. (Eds.), *Annual Review of psychology*. Vol.27, Palo Alto/Cal.

Toch, H. (Ed.) (1961). *Legal and criminal psychology*. New York: Holt, Rinehart & Winston.

Traverso, G.B., & Manna, P. (1992). Law and psychology in Italy. In: Lösel, F., Bender, D., & Bliesener, T. (Eds.), *Psychology and law* (pp. 535-545). Berlin: De Gruyter.

Valverde, J. (1991a). Juvenile delinquency: The behavioural patterns of maladapted adolescents. In: Seva, A. (Ed.), *The European handbook of psychiatry and mental health* (pp. 1575-1585). Zaragoza.

Valverde, J. (1991b). Prison and mental health. In: Seva, A. (Ed.), *The European handbook of psychiatry and mental health* (pp. 1312-1319). Zaragoza.

Weiner, J.B., & Hess, A.K. (Eds.) (1987). *Handbook of forensic psychology*. New York: Wiley.

Psychology and Law in Latin America: State of the Art

Juan Horacio Del Popolo

In this paper, I propose, first, to outline briefly the state of the art of Psychology and Law in Latin America. Then, I shall comment some issues I consider of the utmost importance for the progress of this discipline as it faces the far-reaching transformations that have affected daily life in Latin America as well as in the rest of the world. Finally, I shall endeavor to formulate some proposals aimed at adding dynamism to the role of Psychology and Law in its multiple interactions with Law.

Before undertaking a description of the state of the art in Latin America, I think it is necessary to remark that, as regards the interaction between Psychology and Law, a series of queries arise which I have taken into account upon devising the instruments that will allow an evaluation of the situation in the region:

1. Considering the irreversible processes of change that have altered traditional functions in daily life, are Psychology and Law performing a mitigating role or an innovative and creative one? Are we serving an obsolete system?
2. What is and what can be the scope of Psychology and Law in the new and ever-changing environment which surrounds us?
3. Is the relationship between Psychology and Law interactive or does it involve friction? Does it show a mutual ignorance in many areas?
4. Is the body of knowledge of the behavioral sciences adequately enhanced by the interaction between Psychology and Law?
5. Is it necessary to re-define "Psychology and Law" operationally, starting from global visualizations of the problem of social dysfunction?

State of the Art

Methodology and instruments used for the exploration

With the purpose of evaluating the state of the art of the disciplines of Psychology and Law in Latin America, the following steps were taken:

1. A questionnaire was developed (see below).
2. The material presented at the last two scientific meetings of specialists researching the interaction between Psychology and Law was analyzed.

The following questionnaire was sent to different institutions in Latin America:

Questionnaire

1. In your country, are there university professorships of Psychology and Law, Forensic Psychology, Criminal Psychology or any others related to the specialization "Psychology and Law"? (Please mark your answer).
Yes   No   I do not know.
A. Designation of the course.
B. How many courses are there?
C. Faculty or institution where you know that the course is taught.
D. In which stage of the course of study is the academic activity carried on?
E. If possible, please provide the name of the full professor in charge of the subject.
F. When was the professorship created?
G. If possible, please enclose pertinent syllabi.

2. Are there in your country post-graduate degrees or seminars for those majoring in the above-mentioned disciplines?
A. Please, provide a list and mention in which cities they are offered
B. Please, provide the name of the lecturer in charge and, if possible, the respective syllabi.

3. In your country, are there research programs or projects at the university, governmental, foundation or specialized institutions level, that deal with the above-mentioned subjects?
A. Name of the project or program.
B. When did the project or program start?
C. What areas are they researching?
D. Do you know who the director of the project is? Please, provide his/her name and address.
E. Where are these activities carried out?

4. Please, indicate the existence of:
A. Applications of Psychology and Law in your country (or of sciences related to the interaction between Psychology and Law) in the following areas:
   - Administration of justice.
   - Penal and correctional institutions.
   - Security centers.
   - Areas of law-making, as logistic support for decisions.
   - Executive and administrative powers.
   - Centers that offer treatment to victim.
   - Child abuse.
   - Family violence.
   - Battered women.
   - Others.

B. Institutions that aim to resolve conflicts, or any other entity where these disciplines are applied.

5. Are there laws or proposed laws, in your country, related to the profession of forensic or juridical psychologists, or that refer to the interaction between Psychology and Law?
A. Please provide relevant documentation.

6. Are there international institutions in your country that give support to these disciplines or that are entrusted to make them known?
7. Books published, specialized journals, research carried out in your country related to the specialization.

8. Are there multidisciplinary teams working on the subject?
A. If so, please, provide a list.
B. What are the opinions about it?

9. Is the specialization well-known among psychologists?
A. Is it known by other professionals?
B. What are the opinions about it?

10. What do you propose in order to develop the specialization in your country?
11. Please, add any data that you deem relevant.

This questionnaire was sent in December 1993 to 67 educational, governmental and university centers related to the subject matter or that might have been connected to it in Latin America.

Results

What follows is a summarized description of the results obtained from the answers to the questionnaire.

Considering that it is very probable that the data gathered are incomplete, I would appreciate very much receiving extra information so as to perfect the work. An extended version of the results is forthcoming.

I shall examine the state of the art of the interaction by countries.

The psychological disciplines that devote themselves to the mentioned interaction receive different designations that do not always involve different contents.

In Chile, there are professorships of "Psychology and Law" at the faculty of law of the Diego Portales University, and of "Criminal Psychology", also at the faculty of law but at the University of Chile. There are also systemic therapy centers and institutions that provide support to victims and to women, where the above-mentioned disciplines are put into practice. Additionally, teams of psychologists work for the Police and for the Gendarmery.

In Guatemala, it seems that there does not exist, nor has there ever existed, a program or specialization dealing with Psychology and Law. However, there is great interest in the development of these studies at the Department of Psychology of the Francisco Marroquin University, according to what was stated by its director, Dr. Luis Recinos.

In Peru the discipline of Psychology and Law as such is not known; notwithstanding, general and clinical psychologists work in the fields of justice (providing expert testimony), in the penal area (rehabilitation) and in cases of child abuse (providing support).

The professorships in Peru, are: "The Psychology of Delinquents", at the Federico Villarreal National University and "Criminal Psychology" at the San Marcos Major University ("UNMSM"). The pertinent syllabi stress the clinical characteristics of psychopaths. At the San Marcos Major University, aspects of prison policies are examined.

No post-graduate courses are taught; there is no record of any seminar on Psychology and Law having been offered in the past.

No law backs up the discipline.

In Brazil, according to the information received and particularly at the University of the State of Río de Janeiro, there is important activity related to Psychology and Law. A course in Psychology and Law has been taught since 1986. This is a two year post-graduate course that offers psychologists a specialization, enabling them to theorize, to do research and to provide psychological assistance in areas of the legal institutions.

The University of the State of Río de Janeiro is the only one in Brazil that teaches this specialization systematically.

As part of this course, seminars on subjects related to the interaction are organized periodically, such as the seminar on "Psychology and Legal Institutions".

However, in the State of Río de Janeiro there is no position of psychologist within the Judiciary, though there is some professional work in prisons, at juvenile courts and in schools for juvenile deviants.

As part of the specialized course in Psychology and Law, the following subjects are taught: "Semiology of Personality Dysfunctions" I and II; "Basic Law Concepts"; "Forensic Psychopathology"; "Social Pathology"; "Psychology and Law" I, II and III; "Institutional Psychology"; "Methodology for Higher Education" (optional). Candidates attend multidisciplinary lectures and must submit a research paper. The complete course comprises 630 hours of teaching.

In the area of interaction between Psychology and Law, in Río de Janeiro, the following subjects are taught at the Faculty of Humanities "Peter II", at the University of the State of Río de Janeiro and at Gama Filho University: "Psychology and Law", "Criminal Psychology" and "Psychology and Legal Institutions".

Psychologists work at penitentiaries, other correctional institutions, private foundations and associations, centers that provide support to victims and that deal with child abuse and family violence, as well as at juvenile courts.

In Mexico, according to the data provided by the head of the Department of Psychology of the Ibero American University, Dr. José Antonio Visseda Heras, the specialization dealing with the interaction between Psychology and Law has not been sufficiently developed, though students receive training at different penitentiaries, with good results.

The Autonomous National University of Mexico informs that at its faculty of Law, "Criminology" is taught, and that at the faculty of Psychology, "Behavioral Rehabilitation" is one of the subjects, since 1969 and 1971, respectively.

Furthermore, in Mexico City private seminars in the specialization exist, and a number of research programs are in progress. Psychology and Law is applied in the areas of the administration of justice, in penal and correctional institutions, in private foundations and associations, in centers that provide support to victims and that deal with child abuse, family violence and battered women.

In Uruguay, psychologists act, predominantly, in the juvenile courts.

In Argentina, different and multiple professorships deal with the interaction between Psychology and Law. The subject is taught in Buenos Aires, Mar del Plata, Córdoba, San Luis Mendoza and Rosario.

The first professorship of this discipline in Argentina was created in Rosario in 1960. The lecturer was Dr. Antonia Ramos de Nemeth and it was a four-month course. Special reference must be made to the work of Professor Horas, in San Luis, Argentina, and of the Spanish psychologist Mira y López.

In Mendoza, Argentina, "Psychology and Law" is taught at the undergraduate level during the last year of course of study, lasting the whole academic year. Students are trained in juvenile correctional institutions, civil, juvenile and criminal courts, the Criminal Bureau, the Provincial penitentiary and other centers that provide different services to the community. At the post-graduate level, as a part of the specialization in Criminology, Psychology and Law is taught in the first year.

By the end of the 80s, the Association of Forensic Psychologists of the Argentine Republic was founded. It publishes a journal periodically, entitled: "Forensic Psychology".

In 1993, the Ibero American Association of Psychology and Law was created, with representatives from Spain, the USA, Colombia, Argentina, Mexico, Chile, Uruguay and Brazil. The institution is very active in the promotion of the discipline.

Both associations offer post graduate courses and seminars.

Generally speaking, and considering the data emerging from the questionnaire, it appears that in Latin America specialized publications are few; applied research, post-graduate training, seminars on the specialization and teams working multidisciplinarily are scarce. Psychology and Law is seldom taken into account when drawing up new laws or as grounds for the decisions of the Executive and Administrative powers.

Congresses

So as to complete our evaluation of the present state of affairs of the interaction between Psychology and Law in Latin America, I shall analyze the papers presented at two of the most important congresses held on the subject:

1. The Congress held in Madrid, Spain, from the 5th to the 10th July 1992.
2. The XXIth Ibero American Congress held in Santiago, Chile, from the 4th to the 9th of July 1993.

As regards the first Congress, seven works were submitted to the Symposium Committee, three of which were by Latin American authors (one from Brazil and two from Argentina).

As regards "Free Theme Papers", thirty one were submitted by Argentina, twenty by Spain, six by Brazil, three by Chile, one by Venezuela and one by Portugal.

In addition to the number of works submitted, it is important to point out that multiple interactions between Psychology and Law were dealt with, namely: The Psychology of the Victim, Offenders, Minors and Adolescents, Expert Appraisals, The Role of the Psychologist, Psychology and the Administration of Justice, The Family, Mediation, The Psychology of Witnesses, Penitentiary, Psychology, Specific Difficulties in the Interaction with Civil Law, Training, Engineering of Knowledge, Imputability, AIDS, Female Delinquency, and others.

In the second congress considered, organized by the Ibero American Society of Psychology, no works on the specialization were submitted either to the workshops or to the round tables, although in the area of Symposiums there were five papers (two from Chile, one from Brazil, one from Bolivia and one from Argentina).

Three works from Latin America formed part of the poster session, all of them from Argentina and related to the behavior of criminals; as "Free Reports", Argentina submitted four works, Venezuela three, Brazil one and Chile one, the majority of which dealt with adoption and aspects of childhood and youth.

Analysis of the Results

The countries that seem to have reached a greater development in the structuring of the discipline in academic and professional arenas are: Argentina, Brazil, Mexico, Venezuela and Chile.

In the rest of Latin America, the discipline has not been adequately elaborated, according to the answers to the questionnaire and from the participation of specialists of different countries in the above-mentioned Congresses.

As for the subjects that deal with the interaction between Psychology and Law, their designations vary greatly, overlapping in some areas. In this respect, greater consensus and clarification of contents would be very convenient.

To summarize, in Latin America, there is a significant lack of:

1. Applied research.
2. Post-graduate training.
3. Participation of psychology in the following areas:

A. The drafting of new laws.

B. The implementation of policies of the executive and administrative powers.

4. In only a few countries of Latin America are there laws that back up the work of psychologists in fields related to law.

5. There is a lack of specialized publications.

6. Only a small number of multidisciplinary teams are engaged in the specialization.

7. Among psychologists, there is no real knowledge about the possible applications of the interaction between psychology and law.

A Proposal

From the results obtained and the material examined, it appears that most professional applications and scientific contributions of psychology to the legal field are centered upon:

A. The area of expert appraisals and advice in judicial decision-making.

B. The provision of assistance.

C. To a much lesser degree, the area of prevention.

Although all these activities are fruitful and relevant, I believe there is an aspect on which we must insist. The areas referred to above (expert appraisals, assistance and prevention) may be - and in fact, in my opinion, are - serving obsolete models of the law, no longer useful in coping with the new problems involved in social dysfunctions.

The vast majority of patterns and constructs that operate at present in the juridical arena belong, at least as regards their underlying principles, to the scientific concepts generally accepted at the beginning of this century.

During the last hundred years, psychology has made relevant contributions that require the design of new juridical model able to meet the innovations necessary to redress social dysfunctions.

Technological and scientific developments have reached such a degree that the traditional juridical infrastructure is no longer able to respond to them. This is a point of friction and not of interaction, where the knowledge provided by the behavioral sciences is in danger of being used only in a very small proportion of instances.

Consequently, and due to the complexity and density of the sciences devoted to the study of behavior at different levels, we are being challenged to implement adequate technological juridical structures as well as satellite services, in order to carry out a real process of effective transformations in holistic interaction.

The lack of strategies that would allow the modification of many obsolete constructs of law, that have to be updated to conform to the present knowledge on behavior, results in the unavoidable mistake of resorting to voluntarisms that waste the new data, decrease the efficiency of the results and produce changes that, at most, are merely palliative to aged structures.

If we do not acknowledge the seriousness of the present situation, we may be contributing - on a large scale - to an increase in the dysfunctions of an obsolete system.

Thus, it is imperative that the psychologist, from his or her own field of work and co-operating with integral engineering with other scientists, be in a position to:

1. Attract attention to the implicit and explicit assumptions of those constructs of the law that have become obsolete in the light of the behavioral sciences.
2. Propose new patterns and engineering, together with redressings, in the juridical system, after the due diagnosis based on the pertinent circumstances, so as to meet the present demands of society. It is mandatory that we make use of the recently acquired knowledge while avoiding investing in depleted institutions.
3. Co-operate in the implementation of the pertinent new patterns.

Unfortunately, in our research, we have found that all these essential tasks are being overlooked.

Universities, scientific or academic societies and institutions may quite well assume these responsibilities, creating working groups that will presently offer, to the government and the corresponding institutions, adequate and thorough proposals for the integral redressing of the legal system that will support the transformation and recycling of its operators, in the light of the present knowledge on behavior.

In this way, we would accomplish the formulation of alternative proposals to positivism (where the psychologist merely satisfies the demands generated by the obsolete legal system in force) to transcend to a position from which behavioral scientists propose new outlooks, in accordance with the specific environment in which the system being studied is immersed, so that learning is not confined only to academic premises and research teams.

The transformation will be worthwhile and will probably allow exponential growth of the interaction between psychology and law that, for the time being, is obstructed in the many bottle-necks of an inert and aged system.

Some new ground has already been broken towards this end but there is still much to be done.

Obviously, this effort to articulate the interaction between both disciplines will only be successful if we pursue it armed with an extensive knowledge of the specific subsystems involved - the legal and psychological ones, among others. Only this way will be able to reach our proposed goal.

Criminological and Legal Psychology in Portugal: Past, Present and Future

Rui Abrunhosa Gonçalves

Introduction

Portugal is a small European country with a rich cultural past. Due to its geographical situation and most assuredly its recent past, which includes a dictatorial regime of almost fifty years (1926-1974), the support and interest given to the social sciences and psychology in particular has been, until the late seventies, almost non-existent.

In this paper our purpose is to present the state of affairs of criminological and legal psychology in Portugal, bearing in mind that if psychology, in general, is a recent scientific field in our country, this kind of specialization is now taking its first steps. To help in understanding this point, it is important to provide some historical and retrospective data that will lead us to three major points that we think are the best landmarks for describing the present situation. The first one deals with professional careers, the second with the scientific production and the third with academic instruction. Based on these aspects we will finally outline some prospective ideas for this area of research and professionalization for Portuguese psychologists.

Historical Data

The existence of official and regular courses of psychology in Portuguese universities was made possible only after the April 25th, 1974, revolution. In 1976, the Universities of Lisbon, Coimbra and Oporto created the first five year degree in psychology. More recently (1991), another psychology degree was created at the University of Minho in Braga. Until then and only since 1963, one could get a degree in psychology only at a private institution in Lisbon, the Superior Institute of Applied Psychology, but the existence of the profession was far from being socially recognized or accepted. It was only in the last decade that this became a reality.

With great influence from the French and Belgian traditions and with a general psychoanalytical tendency, the first courses were basically composed of a three year "block" of "general disciplines" (developmental psychology, social psychology, statistics, psychopathology, etc.), and in the two remaining years, students would choose between the three main and traditional areas of psychology (clinical, educational or organizational), and do some supervised training (3-4 months). This simplistic and somewhat narrow view of professional preparation soon became obsolete, and several efforts at various universities emerged, not only to improve the curricula but also to provide more realistic and applied training of psychologists, regarding either their scientific value or their professional demands. In the mid eighties all courses introduced new disciplines and provided a broader spectrum of scientific interests for psychology students. Concerning our main subject, it must be pointed that a significant turn of events occurred in 1986 at the University of Oporto. The first step towards the creation of Criminological and Legal Psychology in Portugal was made there by Professor Candido da Agra.

From our previous exposition it may seem that because that the institutionalization of psychology is very recent among us, there were no people interested in this science in Portugal. Those who did want to be psychologists were obliged to go abroad to study; France, Belgium and Switzerland were the main countries of demand. Related to this were the backgrounds of university professors: psychoanalytical orientation in clinical psychology, the importance of tests and testing, projective techniques, the I.Q. discussion, etc. Subjects such as crime, delinquency, prisons or justice in general, were not relevant then and were clearly the "property" of law courses and forensic medicine. Actually, a century ago, the first publications that could be found regarding these matters were Ph.D. dissertations in Medicine greatly influenced by the works of Lombroso (cf., Gonçalves, 1992; Pina, 1939, 1960). Furthermore, it was at the beginning of the century that crime and delinquency research was made possible with the creation in 1901 of the Anthropometric Bureau (Postos Anthropométricos) of Lisbon, Oporto and Coimbra, whose mission was to examine delinquents, proceed to their anthrophometric identification and psychological profile in order to recommend them for suitable treatment or incarceration in adequate prisons. A specialized periodical (The Criminal Anthropology Review/Revista de Anthropologia Criminal) appeared then; however, only two issues were produced.

In 1918, Luiz Viegas transformed the Anthropometric Bureau of Oporto into the "Department of Criminal Anthropology, Experimental Psychology and Civil Identification of Oporto". It was the first time in Portugal that psychology was officially linked to research in this area. Some years later, the three Bureaus were converted into Institutes of Criminology (of Lisbon, Oporto and Coimbra) and for several decades they were the main producers of research in topics such as crime and delinquency, prisons and correctional treatment or justice related issues. From 1937 to 1980 they were the principal editors of the *Bulletin of the Penitentiary Administration and the Institutes of Criminology*, which contained the most important research produced in Portugal in this area during this period (cf., Gonçalves, 1992). Only in 1979 we can find there an article written by a psychologist (Alves, 1979), which in a way pre-announced that, finally, we were entering the field.

Present Situation

The eighties were undoubtedly the decade when psychologists began to enter and to play an important role in the Portuguese "justice world". Several facts were central to this process. First, as we have already said, it was then possible to obtain an officially recognized degree in psychology in our country which dissolved the marginal stereotype that was attached sometimes to the profession. Although the curriculum had no emphasis in disciplines concerning justice issues, one could say that the initial and fundamental step had been taken. Second, a new Penal Code was approved by the government in 1982, which strongly emphasized the importance of resocialisation and social and psychological interventions in justice decisions. Third, as a result of all of this, new institutions, such as the Social Reinsertion Institute (SRI), were created and the existing ones were forced to encompass the new penal philosophy clearly oriented towards alternatives measures to imprisonment and resocialisation. This last aspect generated new and numerous opportunities for psychologists to obtain employment either at penal institutions or in a profession somewhat similar to probation officers. The Department of Juvenile Justice also improved their acquisition of psychologists. Given this general picture, we will now be more precise by focusing our attention on three points that best describe the present situation for criminological and legal psychology in Portugal: professional careers, scientific production and academic instruction.

Professional careers

Figure 1 is an adapted version of Blumstein and Larson's (1972) juridical and penal scheme to the Portuguese situation. It will help us to see where an adult individual who commits a felony may meet psychologists through his or her passage through our penal system and at the same time provide us information about the different functions or jobs that they perform.

The first "meeting" may occur when the offender, after being arrested by the police, is presented to the court and the judge determines that there is evidence to support that he or she should proceed to trial. At this point the judge also decides whether the individual remains under custody or whether he or she may go home and wait there for the trial. In both cases and taking into account the circumstances of the case, the judge may find it useful to obtain a full and circumstantiated report of the offender, of his or her family or social background and certainly a detailed description of his or her personality in order to pronounce an appropriate sentence. At this point the psychologist working in SRI court teams is asked to conduct an

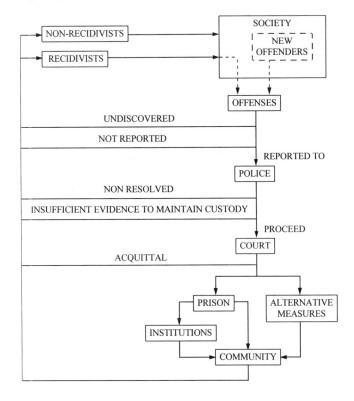

Figure 1: Juridical and Penal Flowchart (Adapted from Blumstein and Larson, 1972, to the Portuguese Situation)

inquiry and present a report afterwards - called "psychological expertise" - which contains the information gathered, by means of interviewing, psychological testing and observation, in order to help the judge to make a decision. This decision can range from alternative measures to prison to prison itself. If an alternative measure such as probation or work on the behalf of the community should be ordered, again the custody of the offender is given to the SRI services and a probation officer - it might be a psychologist or another social worker (sociologist, legal professional or social service worker) - will be designated to the accompanying role. This kind of function, that is mostly characterized as supervisional, is, as you may see, unspecific, because in fact no special training is needed to accomplish it, while the previously mentioned one clearly involves the presence of the psychologist and his or her specific knowledge.

If the person is sentenced to prison, another kind of psychologist will intervene there. In this professional group, psychologists are employed along with other social science professionals (as in the case of probation officers) as Superior Reeducational Officers (SRO), and as such to work directly with the inmates, providing them support during their imprisonment. The SROs are employed by the

General Prisons Administration Office and therefore respond directly to the prison warden. Their main task consists of helping the offender through his or her process of adaptation to prison and assuring him or her conditions such as access to work, work training, education, leisure, outside contacts, etc. that can contribute to preventing recidivism. However, one should not see this professional as a prison psychologist, but more as a "crisis counselor", because after all he or she is a prison administration officer and his or her opinion is relevant in internal matters related to the inmate's sentence, such as placement in a more open regime or the possibility of visiting his or her spouse or relatives for a few days or finally in being granted parole. This aspect is quite important because it is difficult for inmates to see them as impartial in the system and surely they try hard to do this. Another point I want to emphasize regarding these professionals is their great workload (bureaucracy, reports, inmate's demands) and their insufficient number (the ratio is generally 1 officer to 100 inmates).

Also in prisons, offenders may make contact with psychologists placed there by the SRI. Their main task is to provide and encourage the prisoner's liaison to the outside world, mostly with his or her family and when they are near to parole release, to assure that they will have work and social support that prevents them from reoffending. Like the SROs, these professionals also participate in regular meetings of the prison staff to provide information about the offenders and their outside environment and to help decide whether or not they should be placed in more flexible conditions of custody or if they deserve parole.

Again, this function is performed by psychologists as well as other social workers, which means that one need not be a psychologist to do these jobs, and of course that not all these officers are psychologists. However, we estimate that 30% of the professional personnel in SRI or performing SRO functions are psychologists.

In addition, we can say that this procedure is very similar to the one that involves juveniles who commit crimes, and we can find psychologists in functions that correspond to those in the adult penal system. In short, we can say that psychologists who work in the Portuguese juridical and penal system are much more oriented to dealing with delinquency and crime, either as a support to juridical decisions or in a remedial and rehabilitative way. It seems that a more important effort should be made in the field of primary prevention and also in terms of specific contributions that may show the value of our approaches.

Scientific production

In this section, we are going to present some data concerning the progressive growth of information and research produced by Portuguese psychologists in the last few years.

If it is true that before 1980, articles, books or papers by Portuguese psychologists about juvenile or adult delinquency, prisons or other related subjects were practically non-existent and that the few exceptions included only theoretical approaches (cf. Gonçalves, 1992), after 1980 a growing percentage of works related to these issues began to appear in a more consistent and less theoretical way. This "boom" can be explained naturally by the increasing number of psychologists working in this area but much more work is expected if we take into account the number of professionals. On the other hand, much of the research produced stems from academic sources. Some examples are given in the next paragraphs.

In 1981, under the general title "Portuguese Prisons File" the periodical "Raiz & Utopia" published 12 articles, in which two of them were authored by psychologists. Four years later another periodical, "Infância e Juventude" (num. 2, 1985), which is edited by the General Juvenile Administration Office, presented a thematic issue about delinquency and aggression where more than half of the articles were authored by psychologists as well. Finally, in 1986 an issue of "Análise Psicológica" (Série IV, num. 3/4), under the significant title "Psychology and Law", joined various articles of psychologists and law professionals with the particularity that one of these was the late Secretary of Justice, Mr. Laborinho Lúcio. This can be considered a landmark because it was the first time that psychologists, judges and other law professionals and academics emphasized the importance of the relationship between the two areas of psychology and law.

Since 1988 and throughout the last five years a considerable amount of scientific production in this field can be listed, not only regarding theoretical aspects but also showing empirical concerns. The "scientific menu" of these articles/books is vast and it surely reveals a wide list of themes under research: The relationships between psychology and justice (e.g., Agra, 1992; Barroso & Gonçalves, 1992); delinquency and psychology (e.g., Carvalho, 1991; Fleming, Maia & Sousa, 1992); Fonseca, 1993; murder (e.g., Fatela, 1988); juvenile delinquency (e.g., Matos, Oliveira, Rosa & Aguiar, 1990); prisons, suicide in prisons and correctional treatment (e.g., Gonçalves, 1989, 1993; Gonçalves & Vieira, 1989); psychological expertise in courts (e.g., Silva, 1993); drugs and prisons (e.g., Pereira & Costa, 1989; Soares, 1989); psychosocial aspects of police (e.g., Ventura, 1991).

Another positive aspect of this growing interest is that the number of publications has increased, with the edition of new periodicals clearly devoted to these issues: Penal Themes (Temas Penitenciários), Police and Justice (Polícia e Justiça) and the Portuguese Review of Criminal Science (Revista Portuguesa de Ciência Criminal). Finally, several important meetings took place in Portugal in the last years, such as the congress on "Rethinking Delinquency" (in Braga, in 1992) and the 25th International Congress of the Academy of Law and Mental Health that was held in 1993 in Lisbon. On both occasions the participation of Portuguese psychologists was very strong, which reveals again their increasing interest in this area.

Academic instruction

As we have already mentioned, the early curricula of university psychology undergraduate courses in Portugal did not include any disciplines that could be directly related to this area of research and profession (e.g., forensic psychology, criminal psychology, psychology of delinquency, etc.), nor did the new psychology graduates have any form of participation in post-graduate courses related to these topics. Law and medical schools were the traditional monopolizers of this knowledge. In the mid-eighties, C. Agra (1986), at the University of Oporto, modified the curricula of the last two years of psychology studies, introducing a new area called "Psychology of Deviant Behavior" which was intended to fill the gap between Psychology, Law and Justice. However, the excessive scope of this denomination soon introduced some confusion, since mental illness, delinquency, drug or alcohol addiction can all be labeled as deviant behaviors and, consequently, one could be simply doing clinical psychology under a different name, even if a transdisciplinary approach was clearly assumed by Agra and his colleagues (cf., Agra, 1986). Nevertheless, it surely was an important start and gave the opportunity to open new places for training (in juveniles, prisons, centers for drug dependents, etc.) and, above all, it started to alert psychologists to the importance that the field of justice could hold for them.

But what was to be done with the psychologists that had been working for some time in the justice system and have to perform their jobs without any theoretical or technical knowledge? In 1991, two answers were given in Lisbon and Oporto. At Lisbon, the Superior Institute of Applied Psychology started a post-graduate course under the title of "Legal Psychology" and in Oporto, again under the orientation of Cândido da Agra, a post-graduate course in "Criminology" and another one in "Drug Dependence" were created. Although the practical results of these efforts are yet to be seen, mostly by studying if the people involved modified their processes of work, it appears that the courses have successfully responded to the demands of the professionals, whose rush to apply to the courses clearly demonstrated their eagerness to learn more and consequently to improve their performance.

In the newly created Psychology course which started in 1991 at the University of Minho (Braga), we are trying to learn from the difficulties of the past and to ensure adequate instruction for those psychologists who wish to work in the juridical system in the future. In this sense we have created a two-year training period named "Psychology of Justice and Social Reinsertion", where we provide the students with theoretical and practical skills that can be useful to face specific professional problems, either when working with juveniles, in courts, prisons or in social reinsertion. Other more specific subjects of study are victimology, psychology of testimony, police work, correctional treatment, crime prevention, delinquency and urban planing. To grasp this multitude of topics we think that an integration of various areas of knowledge is necessary, such as a social-clinical psychology, environmental psychology, psychopathology, penal law and sociology.

The main and overall concern is prevention and great emphasis is put on the necessity of doing research to know more about this topic. In 1980, David Farrington argued that research should be the primary concern of prison psychologists in England. As we are fresh newcomers to the field of justice in Portugal, I would propose that this concern should be spread out to every juridical context we are entering. Clearly, it is the most effective way of avoiding errors.

Last but not least, we give much importance to ethical questions and each aspect of the program is confronted in terms of its applicability to current situations and the ethical procedures involved. Although no specific legislation is available in Portugal concerning these issues, we think that future "justice psychologists" must have a clear picture of the professional contexts where they will work and the ethical implications of their attitudes and behaviors, either on individuals and institutions or on themselves and their professional standards. One of our concerns now is to establish in our Association of Portuguese Psychologists (APPORT) an ethical code of conduct for those psychologists who intend to work in the justice field. In doing so, we will be following other examples, namely the U.S.A., where specific recommendations were developed concerning the particular case of being a "justice psychologist" (cf., American Psychological Association, 1978).

Final Remarks

The three points that we have outlined give a fairly close picture of the state of the "psychology of justice", at the moment, in Portugal. Obviously, we have much to learn and we intend to do it. Globally, our problems are in no way different from other European societies. However, it is true that our economical development has not yet overcome the historical delay of nearly fifty years of dictatorship and another twenty of trying to put ourselves together. Nevertheless, our Penal Code is clearly recognized as particularly advanced, since it focuses on alternative measures to imprisonment, the reduction of the length of prison sentences and gives credit to rehabilitation and psychological and social intervention. So, we have an official frame to lean on and to start to do something. And from what I have said above, it seems that we are doing it. I hope that at a future meeting, along with other Portuguese colleagues, we may tell you more about our work, our results and our future.

References

Agra, C. (1986). Projecto da psicologia transdisciplinar do comportamento desviante e auto-organizado (A project of a self-organized and deviant behaviour psychology). *Análise Psicológica, 3/4,* 311-318.

Agra, C. (1992). Justiça sábia, ciência justa (Wise justice, just science). *Boletim da Universidade do Porto, 3-4 (II),* 47-49.

American Psychological Association (1978). Report of the task force on the role of psychology in the criminal justice system. *American Psychologist, 133*, 1099-1133.

Alves, A. M. (1979). Teoria/terapia comportamental e instituição prisional (Behaviour theory and therapy and prison institution). *Boletim da Administração Penitenciária e dos Institutos de Criminologia, 34*, 88-116.

Barroso, J. & Gonçalves, R. A. (1992). *Psicologia e intervenção social de justiça (Psychology and social intervention justice)*. Oporto: APPORT.

Blumstein, A. & Larson, R. (1972). Models of a total criminal justice system. In M. D. Mesarovic and A. Reisman (Eds.), *Systems approach and the city* (pp. 253-313). Amsterdam: Amsterdam Publ. Co.

Carvalho, H. A. (1991). Ser delinquente: Sintoma de patologia da personalidade (Being delinquent: A symptom of personality's pathology). *Temas Penitenciários, 5-6*, 25-29.

Dossier Prisões Portuguesas (Portuguese prisons file) (1981). *Raiz and Utopia, 17/18/19*, 15-75.

Farrington, D. P. (1980). The professionalization of English prison psychologists. *Professional Psychology, 11*, 855-862.

Fatela, J. (1988). *O sangue e a rua (The blood and the street)*. Lisboa: Publicações D. Quixote.

Fonseca, A. C. (1993). Nível de desenvolvimento moral, empatia e delinquência (Level of moral development, empathy and delinquency). *Revista Portuguesa de Pedagogia, 2*, 175-194.

Fleming, M., Maia, A. C. & Sousa, A. (1992). Adolescência e perturbações do comportamento: A passagem ao acto sob a forma de "roubo" e "destruição" (Adolescence and behaviour problems: Theft and destruction acting-outs). *Revista de Psicologia e de Ciências da Educação, 3/4*, 67-82.

Gonçalves, R. A. (1989). Educar e punir: A prática da psicologia em ambiente prisional (Educating and punishing: The practice of psychology in prison environments). In J. F. Cruz, Rui A. Gonçalves and Paulo P. P. Machado (Eds.), *Psicologia e educação. Investigação e intervenção* (pp. 569-579). Oporto: APPORT.

Gonçalves, R. A. (1992). A investigação no domínio das prisões e da delinquência em Portugal: Papel e contributo da psicologia (Research in prisons and delinquency in Portugal: Role and contributions of psychology). *Jornal de Psicologia, 10 (1)*, 3-12.

Gonçalves, R. A. (1993). *A adaptação à prisão: Um processo vivido e observado (Adaptation to prison: A lived and observed process)*. Lisboa: Direcção Geral dos Serviços Prisionais.

Gonçalves, R. A. & Vieira, H.(1989). Um modelo multidimensional para a prevenção do suicídio na prisão (A multidimensional model for preventing suicides in prisons). *Temas Penitenciários, 2*, 7-17.

Matos, M. G., Oliveira, L., Rosa, J. & Aguiar, J. (1990). Uma ilha na Lua? A propósito de um trabalho desenvolvido no Instituto Padre António Oliveira (An island in the moon? Notes regarding the work developed in a Juvenile institution). *Infância e Juventude, 3*, 51-58.

Pereira, A. P. & Costa, L. (1989). Nos limites do social - Droga no meio prisional (In the limits of society - Drugs in the prison). *Temas Penitenciários, 2*, 19-25.

Pina, L. (1939). L'anthropologie criminelle et l'Institut de Criminologie de Oporto (aperçu historique). *Boletim dos Institutos de Criminologia, IV*.

Pina, L. (1960). Instituto de Criminologia do Porto. Resenha historico-bibliográfica (Institut of Criminology of Oporto. Historical and bibliographical survey). *Trabalhos do Instituto de Criminologia do Porto*.

Silva, J. P. (1993). A propósito do exame psicológico no âmbito penal (About the psychological assessement in the penal field). *Análise Psicológica, 1(XI)*, 29-36.

Soares, M. C. B. (1989). Consulta de psicologia a toxicodependentes em meio prisional (Psychological counseling with imprisoned drug addicts). *Temas Penitenciários, 1*, 55-60.

Ventura, J. P. (1991). Diferencia Avaliação psicológica no interior do aparelho policial português (Differentiation in the Portuguese police). *Polícia e Justiça, II Série (1)*, 53-66.

Euthanasia in the Netherlands: Policies, Practices and Public Opinion

Dick J. Hessing, Roel Pieterman and John R. Blad

Introduction

Matters of life and death are vital to all living things. As long as organisms live in a primarily *natural* environment, survival is the key question. But humans have succeeded in creating an environment, which is primarily *cultural*. Human societies are decreasingly influenced by natural evolution and increasingly by conscious development. Improvements in the conditions of living are among the most striking differences between industrial societies and those that depend on other means of providing food, shelter and clothing.

The classical self-conception of the medical profession centred around the quality of life. When death came near, for the doctors it was time to leave. Dying was a matter for religious professionals and for family and friends. But over the last hundred years there has been a dramatic change in this key attitude in the medical paradigm. As medicine became ever more successful in postponing death, it inevitably became more and more involved with dying at the same time. By now it is virtually impossible for doctors to avoid questions about the quality of dying.

Because matters of life and death are so important, it is little wonder that many values, norms and taboos centre around these issues. All societies strongly condemn the killing of fellow humans and many of them also condemn suicide. The criminal codes of states invariably threaten those who do kill others or assist them in killing themselves with severe penalties. Such provisions underline the importance of living. The increasing importance of dying, however, presents us with a dilemma. How can we do justice to the importance of living and to the importance of dying in the same culture?

It is this dilemma that concerns the debate about euthanasia. One thing seems clear from the previous argument: as long as modern developments continue, it will be impossible to avoid the dilemma or to solve it by neglecting the importance of dying. The many values, norms and taboos that have to do with the importance of living will eventually have to be adjusted to the importance of dying.

We feel that in this situation two cultural tools are needed. One is universal: pragmatism. "If we know the problem doesn't go away, let's face it." The other is originally a product of Western culture, but it has spread around the globe: scientific analysis. "If we have to face the problem, let's do it as objectively and impartially as possible." This second cultural tool is an expression of what Gellner calls "the rational spirit". Fundamental to this spirit are "a universal conceptual currency" and an *"esprit d'analyse"*. What this means is that "all facts are located within a single continuous logical space". One important implication of this is that "there are no special, privileged, insulated facts or realms (...) living in insulated independent logical spaces of their own" (1983: 21). Adhering to Western values related to this rational spirit means, in this context, that there is no valid argument to exclude the topic of euthanasia from scientific analysis.

We are fortunate that recent developments in the Netherlands allow us to present a first but already rather detailed picture of Dutch policies, practices and public opinion related to euthanasia. From approximately 1970 onward there has been a public debate in which doctors, politicians, private organisations, personnel from the criminal justice system and "the public" have participated. Criminal prosecutors and courts have produced case decisions on the subject and more recently the legislature has produced new rules. Also, since 1989 three books have been published about research on euthanasia. First, one of us has investigated the existence and content of (in)formal "policies" concerning euthanasia in hospitals and nursing homes for the elderly (Blad, 1991). Second, the State Committee Research on Medical Practice Concerning Euthanasia has published its report, including research by Van der Maas, Van Delden and Pijnenborg under the title *Medical Decisions involving the End of Life* (1991). Third, Van der Wal published his dissertation on *Euthanasia and help with suicide by family doctors* (1992).

In this paper we will first discuss the policies of the Dutch criminal justice system concerning euthanasia. Second, we focus on medical policies and practices. Third, we will analyse the results of public opinion studies and draw conclusions regarding the relationship between the legal, political and actual euthanasia situation in the Netherlands.

Before we go on, it is important to define euthanasia and to clarify what, in the Dutch context, is not euthanasia. *Euthanasia* is defined as an act (or omission) intended to shorten life carried out by a person other than the person concerned upon the request of the latter. This is sometimes also called "voluntary euthanasia". *Not euthanasia* are the following forms of medical action:

a. withholding or withdrawing medical treatment upon the express and serious request of the patient; medical treatment negating this request means maltreatment;

b. withholding or withdrawing medical treatment in cases where such a treatment would be useless according to current medical insights; there is no medical obligation to treat the patient any longer;

c. pain-relief with medication that has the side-effect of shortening life, provided that the relief is necessary and proportionate to the suffering of the patient.

Policies and Practices of the Dutch Criminal Justice System

Towards the end of the sixties it was the doctors themselves who began to address the criminal justice system and legal experts in general with questions about the implications of criminal paragraphs related to euthanasia and physician assisted suicide (PAS) for their medical discretion (Van den Berg, 1969). Were doctors obliged to do all they can, and if they did less, were they criminally liable? And, if a patient suffers severely from a painful and/or consuming disease, asks and later begs his doctor to put an end to his life, should the doctor then be obliged to refrain from this act or could he be allowed to help his patient to die? In other words, the question of the quality of dying was raised.

Dutch criminal law, like such laws everywhere, sets clear limits. However, physicians began to claim that in their professional capacity these normative limits were no longer valid. Both "ending life at express and serious request" and "assisting at suicide" were frequently happening, and with complete impunity. Moreover, they claimed, patients had emancipated and wanted the right to decide about their own life and death. Should the right to voluntary euthanasia not be acknowledged in a liberal and pluralistic society? The discussion remained one between medical and legal professionals until the both tragic and dramatic case against Mrs. Postma from Leeuwarden in 1973. This criminal trial had two consequences. First, it triggered widespread attention and support for voluntary euthanasia and from then on the professional problem became a truly public and social one. Second, from that moment on the substantial norm to be protected by law began to change in the direction proposed by the medical profession.

Mrs. Postma (a general practitioner but not acting in this capacity) put an end to the life of her mother on her repeated request, with a morphine injection. She was prosecuted and convicted; the court rejected the legal defence of "necessity", reasoning that the daughter should first have tried to alleviate her mother's suffering with other means. But more importantly, the court explicitly agreed with the statement delivered at trial by the Inspector-General of the Health Department, that medical doctors cannot be obliged anymore to prolong life at any price and that under certain conditions it can be legitimate to intentionally use pain-relieving medication with a life-shortening effect. The court expressed its permissive attitude towards euthanasia in its sentence: one week suspended imprisonment.

In a number of cases that followed, the courts developed a set of criteria for euthanasia by doctors. If and when doctors commit euthanasia or PAS in accordance with these criteria they will not be convicted by the courts. Given the fact that Dutch criminal procedure entitles public prosecutors not to prosecute if this is not in the public interest, this situation amounts to a de facto decriminalisation. In fact these criteria have been inserted by the Ministry of Justice in a policy-directive for the public prosecutors. As a result, all cases that are reported to the public prosecutor and that meet these criteria are, as a rule, not prosecuted. In 1989 two cases out of the 338 reported cases were prosecuted, while in 1990 none of the 451 reported cases was prosecuted.

In December 1993 the Dutch Senate approved the Government Bill to change the *Law regarding the disposal of the dead* to provide for a legal basis for the reporting procedure (Ministerie van Justitie, 1993). This procedure asks the doctor to voluntarily report a case of euthanasia to the coroner, who then investigates the situation, and reports to the public prosecutor. The latter will decide to waive the case when it seems that it is in conformity with the case-law criteria for "careful euthanasia". These are the following:

1. The patient has requested euthanasia after being fully informed about his medical condition and prognosis;
2. The doctor has assured himself that the patient has a long-lasting desire to die and has voluntarily requested this after careful consideration of all the options available;
3. The doctor has consulted one or more independent colleague(s);
4. The doctor has consulted with the family, unless the patient denied approval to do so;
5. When the patient is no longer capable of expressing himself, euthanasia may be committed on the basis of an earlier written request - not older than five years - by the patient, provided the doctor is convinced that this written request was voluntarily made after due consideration;
6. The doctor has kept a diary describing the course of the disease and the deliberations and decisions in the medical treatment.

It must, however, be noticed that these criteria should only act as a check-list and not as a guarantee that a physician who meets all these criteria will not be prosecuted. In concluding this paper we will return to this fact.

Medical Policies and Practices

Blad's study indicates that in 1989 32.6% of all hospitals and 22.7% of all nursing homes had a formal policy that permitted euthanasia. In 11.6% of the hospitals and 32.1% of the nursing homes there was a non-permissive policy. On the basis of the documents collected from the institutions the investigator could draw the following conclusions: in the determination of the policy the confessional denomination of the institutions seems to be of no significant importance. Much more determinant appeared to be the size of the institutions, measured according to the number of beds.

Van der Wal conducted a broad empirical research into the involvement of family doctors in euthanasia and PAS, using 263 cases that were reported by doctors to the public prosecutor and material that was collected by sending an anonymous questionnaire to 1,042 randomly chosen doctors.

On average the doctors reported 74 cases of euthanasia per year and 25 cases of assisted suicide. By extrapolation of these findings for all family doctors Van der

Wal concludes that they are involved in 2,007 cases of euthanasia or assistance with suicide each year. It is interesting to note that 53% of the doctors did not report any such case for the period of investigation. The average percentage per year of doctors who were not involved is even higher, 76%. About one third of the doctors (30%) reports one or two cases in which they were involved over the four years under investigation. A small number of them (5%) reports more than six cases in those four years.

Earlier we summed up the criteria that courts and prosecutors use to decide about the appropriateness of euthanasia or suicide. Van der Wal concludes that a "large majority of the family doctors adequately honour" these criteria. At the same time, however, he concludes that a "substantial number of family doctors do not work according the standing procedural criteria".

Two of the elements in these criteria are "unbearable suffering" and "absence of prospective". In court a doctor may be excused for committing euthanasia or assisting with suicide if the patient's suffering was intolerable and if there was no hope of recovering. The following table (Van der Wal, 1992: 33) shows that these conditions were met in most cases, but more so in the eyes of the patient than in the doctor's opinion.

Table 1: Unbearable Suffering and Absence of Prospective According to Patients and Doctors (From Van der Wal, 1992: Table 4.6)

Strength of conviction	Unbearable suffering according to:		Absence of prospective according to:	
	Patient	Doctor	Patient	Doctor
Very strong	85%	60%	98%	91%
Strong	13%	34%	2%	8%
Moderate	2%	6%	-	-

Further information is presented concerning the patients' life expectancies as estimated by the doctors. In 42% of the cases the doctors expected their patient to die within one week, when they committed euthanasia or assisted with suicide. In a further 21% their estimate was two weeks. In 16% of the cases they expected their patient to die within two to four weeks. For 11% their estimate was a maximum of three months and for the remaining 10% it was longer than three months. This means that in almost 80% of all cases the patient would probably have died within four weeks.

Van der Wal also describes the circumstances under which doctors commit euthanasia or assist with suicide. These data were relevant to the question of whether or not doctors generally act carefully enough. The following table shows that several persons are normally present either near the bed of the patient or in the house at the time the doctor commits euthanasia or assists with suicide.

Van der Wal indicates that in only three percent of the cases the doctor was the only one present. In one percent the patient was completely alone. He states, "In almost half the cases the partners and one or more children were present; in twelve percent of the cases other relatives were also present". He concludes that euthanasia and assistance with suicide are not only medical-technical acts with legal and moral implications but also social events for the patients and the ones they leave behind (see Table 2).

Table 2: Persons Present at the Bedside or in the House of the Patient (n=370) (From Van der Wal, 1992: Table 10.1)

Persons present	At the bedside	In the house
District nurse	13%	4%
Another professional	16%	7%
The patient's partner	78%	17%
The patient's child(ren)	62%	24%
Other relatives	25%	22%
Friend(s)	23%	7%
Other person(s)	10%	4%

In 1991 *Medical Decisions involving the End of Life* was published by the Ministry of Justice and the Ministry of Welfare, Health and Culture. The empirical part of this study was carried out by Van der Maas, Van Delden and Peijnenborg (1991). The questions Van der Maas et al. tried to answer express the wish for a complete picture of those aspects of medical practice that have to do with the death of patients. In a broad sense, therefore, the research was aimed at information regarding "medical decisions involving the end of life". These decisions were defined as "all decisions made by doctors about how to act or not act which serve the purpose of hastening the patient's end of life or those decisions where doctors take into account the probability that by acting or not acting in a certain way they will hasten the patient's end of life".

One of the most important findings of Van der Maas et al. is "that requests for euthanasia or PAS are for the majority of Dutch physicians part of their practice". They stress that these requests indicate that the euthanasia situation is not "a marginal situation involving only a limited number of physicians". The same can be said about the active involvement of physicians with euthanasia and PAS; they are part and parcel of "normal medical practice". The following table shows clearly that these statements are not exaggerated.

The fact that only a small percentage of nursing home doctors is involved must be explained by the fact that they treat a specific kind of patient. All their patients are old and many of them are very ill. Most patients under their care die because the treatment is stopped or not started (again).

Each year approximately 130,000 people die in the Netherlands. In the year 1990 the exact number was 128,786. The following percentages refer to this total number of deaths. The numbers are all estimates based upon research. In sum, in almost 40% of all deaths a medical decision is taken involving the end of life is involved.

Table 3: Self-reported Experience and Attitudes of Physicians in Relation to Euthanasia and PAS (From Van der Maas et al., 1991: Tables 5.1 and 5.3)

Experience/Attitude	Family doctors (n=152)	Nursing home doctors (n=50)	All physicians (n=405)
Never discussed the subject	2%	15%	5%
Received at least one request to act in the "near future"	92%	53%	84%
Received at least one request to act "when the time comes"	80%	57%	76%
Was at least once actively involved	62%	12%	54%
Was never actively involved although involvement is conceivable	28%	60%	34%
Would not do it but would refer to other physician	6%	26%	8%
Is opposed in principle and would not refer to other physician	3%	2%	4%

In 17.5% (1990: 22,500) of all cases people died because treatment was stopped or not started or resumed. In a further 17.5% people died as a result of the treatment where the shortening of life was either a secondary aim or a recognised side effect. In the majority of these cases people died as a result of increasing pain relief. Three categories remain. Euthanasia is committed in 1.8% (1990: 2,300) of all deaths. PAS is involved in 0.3% (1990: almost 400) of all deaths. And in a further 0.8% (1990: 1,000), physicians are actively involved in the death of a patient in cases where there is no explicit request.

Van der Maas et al.'s research is extremely rich in detail and depth. The general representation of the findings above does not do justice to this richness at all. However, the following opinions of physicians about the subject matter are specifically relevant for our purposes, because we also present public opinion data.

As Table 3 shows, only a small fraction of the physicians (4%) is absolutely opposed to euthanasia and PAS. All others are either willing to be actively involved in these matters themselves (90%) or, at least, are prepared to refer patients who make requests to colleagues who are willing (6%). This is accepted, normal medical practice among physicians and it is little wonder that the State Committee therefore advised, among other things, that this subject be incorporated in the medical training curriculum.

The majority of physicians feels that every case of euthanasia should be reviewed in some way (61%). Most others feel that review may be needed in some cases (31%), preferably by a committee of peers in each hospital or nursing home (47%), or by independent medical-ethical committees (35%), or by one colleague especially appointed as confidential doctor (31%).

Public Opinion and Political Dominance

Already in 1950 respondents in a survey were asked, "*If a person suffers from a painful, incurable disease, and both the patient and the family request a doctor to perform euthanasia, do you feel that the doctor should be allowed to hasten the death painlessly?*". A majority of fifty-four percent of the respondents felt that doctors were not allowed to do that. Especially the religious respondents (71% of the Roman Catholics, 60% of the Reformed and 50% of the Protestants) rejected euthanasia. However, the majority (55%) of the non-religious respondents were in favour. Since then there have been massive changes in the religious affiliations; at present the majority of the Dutch do not have any such affiliation.

Between 1966 and 1991 the Dutch Cultural Planning Bureau (SCP) asked the question "*Do you feel that euthanasia should be possible?*" ten times to a national representative sample of more than 1,500 respondents. While in 1966 the majority (49%) still thought this should not be possible, since 1975 the majority is in favour of that possibility. In the last survey (1991) 58% were in favour. A large section of over 30% of the respondents answers that "it depends". In the period between 1966 and 1991 the percentage of respondents that are opposed has decreased from 24% to 9%.

These surveys show that since the mid-seventies the majority of the Dutch population is in favour of the (legal) possibility of euthanasia. This tolerant attitude coincides with the fact that criminal prosecution has followed the lead of the courts decisions on this matter. Virtually no case of euthanasia is prosecuted, even though several hundred such cases are reported the last three or four years. The question then arises as to how it is possible that euthanasia is still forbidden by formal law. For an answer to this question we have to turn to the central characteristic of the political landscape of the Netherlands.

Ever since World War II the Christian-Democrats have held a central position in governmental power in the Netherlands. Given the number of seats in Parliament for the three main parties and the fact that the left wing (Social-Democrats) and the right wing (Liberals) are too far apart on most political issues, it has been impossible to form a governmental coalition without a contribution from the Christian-Democrats. In each coalition, therefore, they were the dominant party.

Especially with regard to topics regarding life and death such as abortion and euthanasia the Christian-Democrats were in a unique position to determine the political point of view. Notwithstanding the fact that both the Social-Democrats, the

Liberals and other parties - together forming a clear political majority - were in favour of officially decriminalising euthanasia and PAS, the Christian-Democrats were able to effectively block any proposal not in accordance with their views.

The most recent survey about euthanasia was held by NIPO in January 1993, on request of the Dutch Society for Voluntary Euthanasia, using a representative sample of 1,145 respondents. An overwhelming majority answered that someone who is in a hopeless situation should be allowed to request euthanasia. The respondents voting for the Christian-Democratic party are clearly the least tolerant. However, a majority of them is also in favour. How then is it possible that the Christian-Democrats in parliament are so reluctant?

To understand the complicated relationship between the opinions of voters on the one hand and political decisions of the parties in power on the other, we use the data collected by the National Voters Study from 1986 (reported in Hillebrand, 1992). In this study political candidates and voters were asked the same question. The scale that was presented to the respondents went from 1 (= Government should forbid euthanasia under all circumstances) to 7 (= a doctor is always allowed to perform euthanasia if a patient requests him to do so). The results are presented in the next table.

Table 4: Attitudes Toward Euthanasia: Political Candidates and Voters (From Hillebrand, 1992: Table 10.7)

	Social-Democrats			Christian-Democrats			Liberals		
	mean	s.d.	N	mean	s.d.	N	mean	s.d.	N
Political candidates	5.5	1.0	64	2.7	1.2	43	5.4	1.1	19
Voters	5.2	1.8	440	3.8	2.1	403	5.1	1.6	211
	$t = 1.29$, n.s.			$t = 3.33$, $p < 0.05$			$t = 1.34$, n.s.		

Question: Is euthanasia on request of the patient allowed?
Scale: 1 = always forbidden; 7 = always allowed

The results show an interesting pattern. In the case of Social-Democrats and Liberals we can see that the political candidates show a slightly more tolerant attitude towards euthanasia than their voters, while in the case of the Christian-Democrats this is the other way around (and statistically significant): the voters are much more tolerant than the political candidates they are voting for. This can be explained by the fact that to become a political candidate for the Christian-Democrats, one has to have very strict attitudes towards topics that are part of a central belief of that party and their counterpart religions. So, in fact a relatively small fraction of the religious groups in the Netherlands controls the official policy of their religious groups regarding euthanasia, and consequently, of the political parties with which they are affiliated. Future changes in the political landscape of Dutch politics may change this situation and bring policies, practices and public opinion more in line with each other.

References

Blad, J.R. (1991). *Tussen lots-en zelfbeschikking* (Between fate and self-determination). Arnhem: Gouda Quint.

Commissie Onderzoek Medische Praktijk inzake Euthanasie (Commission on the Study of Medical Practice concerning Euthanasia) (1991). *Medische beslissingen rond het levenseinde* (Medical decisions concerning the end of life). The Hague: Government Printinghouse.

Gellner, E. (1983). *Nations and nationalism*. Oxford: Blackwell.

Hillebrand, R. (1992). *De antichambre van het parlement* (The antichambre of parliament). Leiden: DSWO press.

Ministerie van Justitie (Department of Justice) (1993). *Euthanasia reporting procedure is given legal foudation*. Den Haag: MVJ/Directie Voorlichting.

Nederlandse Vereniging voor Vrijwillige Euthanasie (Dutch Voluntary Euthanasia Society) (1993). *Resultaten NIPO-enquête januari 1993* (Results of the opinion survey of the Dutch Institute for Public Opinion Research).

Van den Berg, J.H. (1969). *Medische macht en medische ethiek*. Nijkerk: Callenbach (Also published under the title Medical Power and Medical Ethics. New York: Norton, 1978).

Van der Maas, P.J., Van Delden, J.J.M., & Pijnenborg, L. (1991). *Medische beslissingen rond het levenseinde: Het onderzoek voor de Commissie Onderzoek Medische Praktijk inzake Euthanasie* (Medical decisions concerning the end of life: The study for the Commission on the Study of Medical Practice concerning Euthanasia). The Hague: Government Printinghouse. (See also Van der Maas, P.J., J.J.M. van Delden, L. Pijnenborg in C.W.N. Looman (1993). Euthanasia and other medical decisions concerning the end of life, *The Lancet*, 338, Sept. 14, 669-674).

Van der Wal, G. (1992). *Euthanasie en hulp bij zelfdoding door huisartsen* (Euthanasia and assistance with suicide by family doctors). Rotterdam: W.Y.T.

Psychological Aspects of the Family Law Reform and the Influences in Legislation after the German Unification

Adelheid Kühne

Introduction

This report will point out some topics of social legal studies important for legislation and legal practice in the view of legal psychology. Unfortunately there is not enough psychological research in Germany concerning family and guardianship law.

First, briefly, I would like to review the current studies concerning the situation of the child in families after separation and divorce, in foster - or in mother or father - only families respectively. I begin with a description of the legal position of the child in Germany, and an analysis of the child and family circumstances and the conditions of socialization follow. The conclusions will point out psychological aspects in legislation to improve the situation of children after separation and divorce or illegitimate children living in one-parent families.

The Legal Position of the Child Today

During the last few decades opinion grew steadily that the legal position of the child should be assimilated towards the reality of the family and the society. Children should no longer be the objects of "parental authority". After World War II, discussions started concerning the illegitimate child and the situation of divorce orphans in the former Federal Republic of Germany.

The main statement of the dogmatism of family law was the idea of "the best interest of the child". But it still lacks a precise legal definition. The definition of Goldstein, Freud and Solnit (1973, 43) that for "the best interest of the child" as the "less damaging alternative for the child" is generally accepted. There are different opinions among different professions as to what the "best interest of the child" means.

Since the marriage reform law (1977), the principle of broken marriage is the only reason for divorce. Since January 1, 1980, there is an act to regulate "parental custody" instead of "parental authority". Welfare institutions and the Federal Constitution Court pushed the reform law. The law court had to allocate personal custody from the viewpoint of the best interest of the child. The parent who is not entitled to custody has the right of access to the child, if there are no serious reasons for withholding such a right. A report from a social worker in a welfare institution is compulsory. In contested cases, the law court can order a psychological expert opinion. This holds for 5 to 10 % of all cases. Children over the age of 14 have to be heard; but the judge can also hear younger children.

Awarding custody to a third person or institution is possible, if both parents are not able to educate the child. Since the decision of the Federal Constitution Court on November, 5, 1982, joint custody is possible if both parents agree (Luthin, 1984).

In the Federal Republic of Germany there is no right of access for an illegitimate's father, but the guardianship court can deliberate upon it after a petition (Zenz, 1981).

After unification, the family law of the former Federal Republic of Germany was brought into effect in both parts of the country.

The Analysis of the Child's and Family's Circumstances

In the last few decades the custody of children is the main task of the family. Nauck (1989) describes a reducing rate of foster children from 121,000 in the year 1950 to 65,000 in the year 1980 and a reducing rate of children in welfare institutions in the same time from 48,000 to 1,200. This shows that there is in most cases a so-called normal family biography (design). This leads at the same time to a prognosis of normal family life for children and adolescents.

On the bases of a statistical longitudinal analysis, Nauck (1989) conducted a study to describe the family circumstances concerning the normative expectations in the so-called old Löndern of the Federal Republic of Germany in the middle of the eighties.

Nauck (1991) added beyond that individual data of 6,380 interviews of natural, foster, step and adoptive children. He collected information on 12,687 children between the age below 2 to 26 years in a cross sectional study.

Nauck's aim was to describe the different types of biological, legal and social parent-child-relationships. The so-called normal design of child relationship is the life in one household community with the natural married parents. Nauck (1991) asks for the number of children living in their family of origin, or as an illegitimate child, step or adoptive child and whether they have suffered during their life from the death of one parent, separation or divorce.

The results of the study point out that more than 85 % of children under age in the old Federal Republic of Germany live in families of the type (1), the "normal family design", which means that more than 90 % of the children are living together with their natural and married parents. On coming of age this rate reduces to 80 %.

Children living in stepfamilies (type 2) form the second majority, meaning that they are living together in the same household with a remarried parent and the new partner. In more than 80 % of all cases the children are living together with the natural mother and the stepfather. The probability of becoming a stepchild is increasing in early childhood; that means that 0.6 % of all children under the age of 2, nearly 3 % (2.7 %) under the age of 4 and more than 4 % at the age of 18 are living as a stepchild.

1.5 % of all stepchildren accompany their mothers (85 %) into the new family, the so-called type 3. Type 4 means that the children (1.6 %) are living in a mother-headed family while their fathers remarried in the majority (85 %) of all cases.

The smallest rate of 0.8 % of the children are half orphans living together with one natural parent and the unmarried new partner.

In summary, nearly 1 % of all children under the age of 2 years are stepchildren, the rate increase to 3.3 % till the age of 4, till the age of 12 the rate reaches 8.6 % and till coming of age, 10 %.

The rate of illegitimate children (type 6) is 4.5 % between 2 years and below 10 years. There are no more illegitimate children in the recent Federal Republic of Germany because of marriage of the mother with a stepfather.

In comparison to these results, in Great Britain and France more than 60 % of the mothers of illegitimate children marry the natural father on account of a decreasing marriage rate. In Great Britain the reason is found in the overwhelming majority of lower middle class parents. But there is no convincing interpretation of this fact for France (Willenbacher, 1992).

Illegitimate children are living in most cases together with their mother and only in a small percentage with their natural fathers. In Germany the custody for illegitimate children belongs to the mother; compared with this the illegitimate father is not awarded custody and he has no right of access to the child after separation.

In summary more than 80 % of all children are living in the original family through their whole childhood and adolescence (Nauck, 1991, 403). The rest of the children do not remain in a mother or father only family but live with a so called multiple parentship.

Only in a few cases do children live for a long time together with their unmarried natural parent. There is no actual decision for a marriage ceremony or a planned parentship (Nauck ,1991); that means that the birth of an illegitimate child is in most cases unplanned.

Following the results of the analysis of Nauck (1991) most of all children live together with their natural mother. Usually that means in the separation process the natural father will leave and the stepfather will enter the family.

Family Establishing and Family Separation Processes

Family establishing processes are the appearance of a new partner, beginning a new partnership, living together with the new partner and then the marriage with him.

Children experience these processes predominantly as illegitimate children of their mothers or after divorce becoming stepchildren.

Following the analysis of Nauck (1991, 412) more than 80 % of all children do not see a family establishing or family separation process. There are more family establishing processes with nearly 14 % (13.8 %) of all cases than those concerning separation (8.3 %) or divorce (7.7 %). The correlation between family separation and family establishing processes is r=.62; that means, the more family separation processes, the more family establishing processes and vice versa the child will live to see. With regard to children under age there are series of events.

A quicker series of events to observe in the former German Democratic Republic and still today in Great Britain is this: an early marriage follows an early birth of the child or the children, and then after the divorce a soon second remarriage. The statistical data give no answer to the question of the second divorce rate.

Hofer et al. (1992) suppose subjective specific and different causes for separation. He presumes for husbands job specific stress factors, discrepancy of sexual desires and the efforts of emancipation of the wife. On the other side wives give hints of overwhelming financial and living condition problems, violent struggles, psychological problems of the partner, less support and authoritarian behavior. Wives estimate in retrospect more negative marriages than the husbands and declare to have seen family problems earlier (Rottleuthner-Lutter, 1989).

Empirical family research asks for the correlation between the gender of the child and the risk of divorce. Following the results of American divorce research (Morgan, Lye & Condran, 1988) the risk of families with daughters is 9 % higher than in marriages with a son. A socio-economic study of Diekmann and Klein (1991) points out a 19 % higher risk with a daughter than with a son. A low correlation exists between family separation and family establishing processes, which means that the probability of a remarriage is a little bit less for a woman with a son. In Germany the lowest risk of divorces was in the years between 1959 and 1963. The risk for experiencing a divorce is higher for children born about 1950 and after 1974.

The Situation of Mother - or Father - Only Families

Good socialization conditions are needed of all children for a good emotional, cognitive and social development, independent from birth within or outside matrimony. Socialization conditions depend on family atmosphere, economic situation, lifestyle and cultural expectations. But they are estimated differently in different parts of Europe, i.e. the economic situation in Spain is very important versus the promotion of sports in Great Britain (Kühne, 1992).

The overwhelming majority of illegitimate children live in mother-only families; only a few in father-only families. The higher economic level of the father obtains the development for the child in contrast to mother-only families with lower financial resources (Gutschmidt,1986).

It has been pointed out the bad economic situation of divorced women but the economic level of the mother with an illegitimate child is much worse because of her being younger, with a low level of employment training and insufficient housing conditions. But on the other side, the mothers have few problems with their children. The interpretation is possible that the fact of illegitimate status is not as important as the reaction of the mother to it.

There is not enough research in Germany describing the effects and consequences of separation and divorce for the children's behavior and biography. Therefore I will describe some results of American research, but being cognizant of the problems of transferability to European conditions.

Richards (1991) provides a description of the kinds of reaction expected from children after parental divorce. Typically, children show signs of upset - anger, depression, anxiety - during the time of a separation and these overt signs are likely to persist for one year or so. School work may deteriorate, at least for a time. Richard (1991) points out that the nature of a child's response to separation is variable and will depend on age, gender and the relationships with their parents before, during and after the separation.

Parents, children and divorces are variable, depending in the way in which such family events are dealt with by the law and other social institutions in different societies and by social groups within them.

Seltzer (1991) points out that children living in mother-only families suffer from a lack of contact to their fathers. The reduction of social contact between father and child corresponds to the reduction of the maintenance to the child. Elliott and Richards (1991) searched for correlations between the "destructive behavior" and "feeling unhappy and worried" and school work in mathematics and reading. High scores in the behavior scales and low scores in school achievement were observed in the whole sample of children in the age of 7 to 16. After the remarriage of one parent the scores of behavior variables increase once more, but school achievement is not influenced.

McLanahan and Booth (1991) pointed out a high marriage rate of children after parental divorce. The most frequent consequence of the divorce for the child is an early divorce after his or her own marriage, an increase in alcohol or drug misuse or - for the daughters - an illegitimate maternity. These effects are equal for all ethnic and cultural minorities.

The remarriage of the mother does not reduce the consequences of divorce for the daughter; on the contrary the untimely school leaving and early maternity for daughters increase. These consequences are not to seen in one parent families that have been widowed.

The socio-economic situation of the one parent family is very important in the view of socio-legal research. The income of a (white) one parent family in the USA is only 50 % of the income of a married family. The result is a decrease to near poverty, which means economic instability, bad housing conditions, reduction of social status and social support. In the USA and in Great Britain social status decreases, another decrease follows later on with the reduction of school education and employment training. This kind of reduction of the social status is only observed since World War II.

Cherlin, Furstenberg et al. (1992) present the results of two longitudinal studies from Great Britain and the USA to investigate the effects of divorce on children in comparison with children living in two-parent families. Parents and teachers rated behavior problems and achievements in reading and mathematics of the children at age 11 and ages 11 to 16. Children whose parents divorced or separated between the two time points were compared to children whose families remained intact. For boys, the apparent effect of separation and divorce on behavior problems and achievement at the later point of time was sharply reduced by considering behavior problems, achievement levels, and family difficulties that were present at the earlier time point, before any of the families had broken up. For girls the reductions in the apparent effect of divorce occurred to a lesser but still noticeable extent once preexisting conditions were considered.

McLanahan and Booth (1988) summarize the results of their research in three theories of integrational consequences to describe the effects of single motherhood on their children. These effects are lower academic achievement, or premature parenthood, as compared to children from two parent families:

a. the   economic deprivation argument: which attributes the disadvantages associated with the mother-only family to the lack of parental investment; consequences are also fewer extracurricular activities, including summer travels and camps; all these activities are positively related to school achievement. Children need to leave school earlier in order to earn money for their families or to take care of younger siblings. McLanahan and Booth remark that the studies supporting this theory do not distinguish between low income as a cause or as a consequence of divorce.

b. the socialization argument: which claims that negative outcomes are due to dysfunctional parental values and parent-child relationships. Socialization theorists argue variously that single mothers are more accepting of divorce and out-of-wedlock birth and therefore their children are more likely to become single parents themselves. They claim that single mothers have less influence over their children's behavior because of a lack of parental attachment, parental involvement and supervision. McLanahan and Booth point out that children from mother-only families do not differ from children in unhappy or high conflict families. This finding suggests that it is family conflict rather than divorce that is the determining factor in children's behavior.

c. the neighborhood argument which point out that outcomes are due to structural or neighborhood characteristics such as social isolation, a lack of community resources, social network and peer-group activities. On the other hand many mother-only families are isolated in "underclass" neighborhoods with high levels of poverty and disorganization, circumstances supporting an increase in antisocial activities.

Mother-only families are mostly living in economically and socially isolated neighborhoods which, in turn, lower the opportunity for economic mobility and raise the likelihood that children will leave school and/or become teen parents. This argument incorporates elements of the economic-deprivation and the socialization perspectives.

The problems of all studies founding these theories are the small, non-representative samples and the lack of replication with larger databases.

Farrington (1996) describes a correlation between low parental control, low income, and social status and the development of an antisocial personality in the biography of boys and adolescents in London. In general there are few chances for social mobility, the children leave school earlier and become teen-parents.

The Situation in the Federal Republic of Germany

The question is how can we improve the situation of the children today.

The rate of divorces increases slowly but continuously in the former FRG; there was only a high increase before the law reform in 1975 in the FRG.

The increase in the former GDR was also continuos but with a break in 1992 after the unification. The development is shown in the following table:

Table 1: Divorces and the Rate of Affected Children

	Number of divorces		Number of affected children	
	former FRG	former GDR	former FRG	former GDR
1960	48,878	24,540	45,067	22,214
1970	76,520	27,407	86,057	32,647
1975	106,829	41,632	107,216	47,100
1980	96,222	44,794	78,972	46,075
1989	126,628	50,063	89,552	50,194
1992	124,698	10,312	91,747	9,630

One way to improve the situation was the Child and Youth Welfare Act which came into effect in 1991, that means in all cases of divorce the welfare institute is to ask and offer counseling in problematic and litigious cases and to propose solutions. If there is no possibility to mediate between the parties, a psychological expert opinion is requested for help and decision making.

The situation in the FRG today shows that most of the children live together with their mother (more than 85 %) and the father has only the right of access. The joint custody is one custody model but only 5-10 % of the parents prefer this model. The joint custody does not work to decrease the consequences of the separation because the child believes in most cases in the reconstruction of the family.

Consequences

The following proposed consequences result from the psychological and socio-legal research and the political discussion of lawyers, psychologists and solicitors to improve the situation of the children.

Consequences for the legislation

1. Improvement of the psychological, social, and economic situation, corresponding to the international standards, such as a guarantee of family income, child care, counseling in case of conflicts.
2. No more differences between children being born within or outside a marriage in all aspects of life and rights.
3. Joint custody for unmarried parents.
4. Improvement of the economic and social situation of the mother-only family.
5. Right of access as a right of the child and not only of the parent.
6. Possibility of personal custody for social parents (stepparents).
7. Improvement of counseling to reduce the conflicts between the parents and to improve the psychological energy of the parent for parental care.
8. Drawing up an educational plan concerning the development of the child in the future
    * school education, extracurricular activities, etc.,
    * residence of the child,
    * right of access with the other parent without parental custody,
    * distribution of the maintenance,
9. Possibility for the "child solicitor" to represent the child at the law court.

Consequences for the psychological expert

1. Better cooperation between all interacting parties such as psychological experts, lawyers, social workers at the welfare institutions to guarantee the best interest of the child.
2. Psychological counseling and mediation to solve family problems.
3. Better education and advanced studies for psychological experts.

References

Cherlin, A.J., Furstenberg, F.F. et al. (1992). Longitudinal effects of Divorce on Children in Great Britain and the United States. *Science, Vol. 2*, 1386-1389.

Diekmann, A., Klein, T. (1991). *Geschlecht von Kindern und Ehescheidungsrisiko*. Berne - Karlsruhe: o.V.

Elliott, B.J., Richards, M.P.M. (1991). Children and divorce: educational performance and behaviour, before and after parental separation. *International Journal of Law and the Family*.

Farrington, D. (1996). Psychological influences on the development of antisocial personality. In: Davies, G., Lloyd-Bostock, S., McMurran, M. & Wilson, C. (Eds.): *Psychology, Law and Criminal Justice*. Berlin - New York: de Gruyter.

Goldstein, J., Freud, A., Solnit, J. (1973). *Beyond the best interest of the child*. New York: Free Press.

Gutschmidt, G. (1986). *Kind und Beruf. Alltag alleinerziehender Mitter*. Weinheim: Juventa.

Hofer, M., Klein-Allermann, E., Noack, P. (1992). Familienbeziehungen - Eltern und Kinder in der Entwicklung. Goettingen: Verlag für Psychologie - Dr. C.J. Hogrefe.

Kühne, A. (1992). The child in the European legal system. In: Lösel, F., T. Bliesener, D. Bender (Eds.): *Psychology and law - International Perspectives*, Berlin - New York: Walter de Gruyter.

Luthin, H. (1984). Gemeinsames Sorgerecht nach der Scheidung. Bielefeld: Ernst u. Werner Gieseking.

McLanahan, S., K. Booth (1988). Mother only families: Problems, Reproduction, and Politics. Institute on research on Poverty. *Discussion Paper no.* 855-857.

Morgan, S.P., Lye, D., & Condran, G. (1988). Sons, daughters, and the risk of marital disruption. *American Journal of Sociology, 94*, 110-129.

Nauck, B. (1989). Individualistische Erklaerungsansätze in der Familienforschung: die rational-choice-Basis von Familienoekonomie, Ressourcen- und Austauschtheorien. In: Nave-Herz, R., Markefka, M. (Eds.): Handbuch der Familien- und Jugendforschung, Bd. 1, *Familienforschung, 45-61*. Neuwied: Luchterhand.

Nauck, B. (1991). Familien- und Betreuungssituation im Lebenslauf von Kindern. In: Bertram, H. (1991): *Die Familie in Westdeutschland. DJI: Familiensurvey 1*. Opladen: Leske und Buderich, 389-428.

Richards, M. (1991). Children and Parence after Divorce. Paper presented at the 7th World Conference of the International Society on Family Law, Opatija.

Rottleuthner-Lutter, M. (1989). Ehescheidungen. In: Nave-Herz, R., Markefka, M. (Eds.): *Handbuch der Familien- und Jugendforschung, Bd. 1, Familienforschung*. Neuwied: Luchterhand, 607- 624.

Seltzer, J.A. (1991). Relationship between fathers and children who live apart. The father's role after separation. *Journal of Marriage and the Family, 53*, 79-102.

Willenbacher, B. (1992). Die Illusion der Gleichheit von Familienstrukturen am Beispiel der Alleinerziehenden in England, Frankreich und der BRD. Unpublished manuscript: Deutscher Soziologentag 1992.

Zenz, G. (1981). *Kindesmißhandlung und Kindesrechte*. Frankfurt: Suhrkamp.

Part II
Victimology

Criminal Behavior and the Pre-Victimization Process: Three Studies on Neutralization, Redefinition, and Desensitization[1]

Frans Willem Winkel

Introduction

Moral restraint theory suggests that persons will commit crimes in the absence of moral restraints to do so, or if they have learned to overcome these inhibitors. An excess of definitions favorable to violating the law would thus typify persons committing crimes (Sutherland & Cressey, 1960). Parallel to this theoretical position Fattah (1991) contends that pcc's (persons committing crimes) go through a particular set of mental operations, prior to committing a crime, which he refers to as the pre-victimization process. After clarifying this process, drawing heavily on Fattah's analysis, we will report on three empirical studies exploring aspects of this process in more detail. Study 1 will focus on the constituting processes of neutralization, redefinition/autolegitimation and desensitization. Studies 2 and 3 will focus on strategies to change these processes. Study 2 considers the effectiveness of a specific alternative sanction, called the "focusing on victims-program", while study 3 compares the effectiveness of a victim-focused versus a perpetrator-focused strategy.

The Pre-Victimization Process

The process consists of a chain of cognitive operations - taking place before the act is committed - which are, for the victimizer neither "separable nor distinguishable" (Fattah, 1991: 136). It can be split into three processes, namely neutralization, redefinition / autolegitimation, and desensitization. The focus of neutralization is the victimizer and its aim is to neutralize the mechanisms of formal and informal social control. It makes it possible to overcome moral inhibitions and inner restraints that have been built up through socialization. Parallel to Sykes and Matza (1957) five techniques are distinguished: (1) denial of responsibility, (2) denial of injury, (3) denial of the victim, (4) condemnation of the condemners, and (5) appeal to higher loyalties (see also: Winkel, 1993).

---

[1] Further work on the victimological aspects of this chapter facilitated by a grant from the ACHMEA-Foundation (Stichting *Achmea* Slachtoffer en Samenleving).

The focus of the second process is the behavior or victimization act. Its main aim is to strip this behavior of its delinquent, immoral or illegal character. The desensitization process has the prospective victim as its focus. Its aim is to desensitize the victimizer to the pain and suffering inflicted upon the victim, thus making it possible to perform the behavior without feeling guilty about it. Table 1, taken from Fattah (1991:140) provides an overview of the various desensitization techniques.

Table 1: The Desensitization Process (Fattah, 1991)

Techniques of desensitization	Victimizer's attitude to the victim	Redefinition of the Act
Denial of the victim	The victim does not exist	The act is victimless. It is simply a norm violation
Reification, Deindividuation, Depersonalization of the victim	The victim is only an object, a nonperson, and a tool	The act is victimless. It is a simply a norm violation
Denial of Injury to the victim	The victim will not be hurt. The victim will enjoy the act (sexual victimization)	The act is harmless The act is enjoyable
Blaming the victim	The victim is guilty The victim is the true aggressor	The act is an act of justice, of retaliation, of self defense, and a means of getting even
Devaluing, Denigrating, Derogating the victim	The victim is deserving. The victim is worthless. The victim is blameworthy	The act is necessary and warranted (moral obligation). The act is blameless (morally right)

The notion of a pre-victimization process implies that there is an association with self-report measures of criminal behavior. For example, persons committing a lot of crime - who are highly "crime oriented" - should more strongly deny the presence of a victim as a result of their behavior than persons who are less crime oriented. Study 1 was set up to examine this relation empirically.

Study 1

Method

Sample The sample consisted of 152 subjects: 125 boys and 27 girls. Their age varied from 13 to 19 years: the majority was 15 or 16 years of age (73%). A substantial portion (72%) had had previous police contacts. Most subjects (115) came from a school offering primary vocational training. Questionnaires were administered there during regular class-sessions. The remaining 37 subjects were gathered via various Alternative Sanctions Agencies (ASA). These subjects were handled individually via the agency-coordinators. In other words, these subjects were officially registered delinquents, referred to the ASA by a juvenile judge or public prosecutor.

Measures The two central constructs - crime orientation and aspects of the pre-victimization process - were measured through a questionnaire. To measure crime orientation we used a scale for self-reported delinquency (Junger-Tas & Kruissink, 1990) composed of 22 crimes of (1) low (graffiti, vandalism, joy riding), (2) intermediate (burglary, bicycle theft, unlawful entry in homes) and (3) high seriousness (assaults, threats of violence, actual violence, arson). Subjects were asked to indicate if, and how often they had committed these crimes, at what age, and if they had acted alone or with others. Per subject a weighted average per seriousness-category was computed on the basis of frequency * weight (1, 2, or 3). Then, scores were summed over seriousness-categories. In this way, crime orientation scores varied between 0 and 38.

To measure the pre-victimization process nine subscales were developed on the basis of a thorough review of the relevant literature (Jesness, 1962; Tyler, 1990; Wells, 1980; Sykes & Matza, 1957; Fattah, 1991). These scales relate to:

- Moral Justifications ($n = 11$ items; $\alpha = .83$),
- Appeal to Higher Loyalties ($n = 2$ items, $\alpha = .46$),
- Diffusion of Responsibility ($n = 7$ items, $\alpha = .67$),
- Condemning the Condemners ($n = 5$ items, $\alpha = .61$),
- External Attribution ($n = 6$ items, $\alpha = .54$),
- Victim Blaming ($n = 5$ items, $\alpha = .57$), and
- Perceived Psychological Damage to
  Assault Victims ($n = 11$ items, $\alpha = .75$),
  Robbery Victims ($n = 11$ items, $\alpha = .72$),
  Burglary Victims ($n = 11$ items, $\alpha = .75$).

Responses were in terms of 5 point scales with the anchors "strongly (un)justified" and "strongly (dis)agree".

Results

Data were analyzed multivariately on the basis of a 2 (Crime Orientation; median split low versus high) x 2 (Subject Status; ASA-registered or not) design. This analysis revealed a main effect for "Crime Orientation" (F 9, 128 = 3.91, $p < .01$) and an interaction approaching significance (F 9, 128 = 1.88, $p = .06$). In Table 2 the relevant means are summarized.

Table 2: Pre-Victimization Processes by Low and High Crime Orientedness: Means and (standard deviations)

Neutralization/ Redefinition/ Desensitization	Crime orientedness		
	Low	High	F
Moral justification/ Palliative comparison	4.28 (0.49)	3.73 (.76)	26.29***
Appeal to higher loyalties	3.28 (.99)	2.49 (1.13)	19.43***
Diffusion of responsibility	3.96 (.69)	3.59 (.79)	8.94***
Condemning the condemners	3.11 (.76)	2.61 (.87)	13.05***
External attribution	3.17 (.72)	3.14 (.80)	< 1
Victim blaming	3.09 (.77)	3.26 (.88)	1.46
Perceived damage to victims of assault	3.89 (.53)	3.67 (.50)	6.37**
Perceived damage to robbery victims	3.67 (.55)	3.55 (.55)	1.46
Perceived damage to victims of burglary	3.62 (.57)	3.42 (.57)	4.51*

Scale Range: (1)-(5); ***p < .0001; **p < .01; *p < .05

Table 2 suggests that a stronger orientation for crime is associated with a stronger justification of various criminal behaviors and utilizing palliative comparisons more frequently. High crime oriented subjects recognized a series of conditions under which such behavior was perceived as a justified response. Furthermore, these subjects tended to diffuse the responsibility for the consequences of such behavior, to appeal to higher loyalties and to condemn the condemners. Finally, these subjects tended to ignore or minimize the adverse consequences of criminal behavior for victims. Given the interaction our results suggest that ASA-registered subjects with high crime orientedness also more strongly engage in external attributions for criminal behavior.

Study 2

The model of the pre-victimization process provides us with clear guidelines on how to counter criminal behavior, or to reduce the likelihood of future criminal responses. Making persons aware of the seriousness of their behavior, for example by stressing their personal responsibility, their *personal* involvement even in "gang" crimes, or by elucidating the "transparency" of their excuses, exemplifies an intervention relating to the first two processes described. Making persons aware that real and "ordinary" people might get victimized through their behavior illustrates the third process. The focus on victims program - a recently introduced alternative sanction for juvenile offenders in the Netherlands - currently utilizes interventions aimed at all three processes. For a detailed description of the contents of this program we refer to Winkel (1993).

To assess the impact of the program on delinquents an evaluation study was conducted. Two hypotheses were tested, namely: (1) program exposure will result in more favorable scores on (a) the perceived seriousness of criminal behavior, (b) the recognition of victimizing consequences resulting from such behavior and (c) on the awareness of victimization, the idea that the behavior "creates" a victim; and (2) relative to non-recidivists, recidivists will report less favorable scores; thus offenses will be considered (a) less serious, (b) awareness of adverse consequences will be lower, as well as (c) victimization-awareness. To examine potential differences in learning effects or differential response to the program, relevant interactions were explored, between recidivists and non-recidivists. It would be valuable to know for example, if recidivists learn relatively less.

Method

Sample The total sample participating in the study comprises 87 juvenile offenders. A clear majority are male (n = 77); 10 subjects are female. Their mean age is 16.5 years (sd = 1.30), varying from 13 to 19 years. Most subjects committed property crimes (burglary), followed by acts of aggression against property (vandalism, arson) or against persons (physical abuse; attempted manslaughter). All subjects were referred to the program through the criminal justice system (juvenile judge and public prosecutor) after consulting the coordinator "alternative sanctions". After exposure to the program 23 subjects re-appeared in the criminal documentation register (at least, at the level of the prosecuting attorney) within a period of at least three up to 15 months (yielding a recidivism rate of 26%). These subjects will be considered recidivists. Preliminary analyses reveal no significant differences between recidivists and non-recidivists as to age (t <1), educational level (F <1), self-reported crimes prior to the program (Mann-Whitney $U(80) = 522.5, p = .11$; a nonparametric test was conducted because of skewed distributions), prior police contacts ($X^2 = 3.58, p = .06$) and prior conviction record (Mann-Whitney $U = 464.0$, n.s.). Correlations between these variables and the dependent measures were moreover generally insignificant.[2]

---

[2]   The total set of correlations consists of 2 (pre-post test) x 3 (dependent measures) x 5 (background characteristics, age, educational level , prior record, etc) = 30 correlations. Five

Measures Dependent measures were assessed through a questionnaire, developed by the RDC (Research and Documentation Center), which was distributed both at the beginning and at the end of the program. The total questionnaire consists of five portions. Some of these will not be considered here because of unsatisfactory reliabilities (*alpha* < .60) or conceptual ambiguities, in light of the theoretical model presented above.

Three scales were constructed on the basis of a reliability-analysis (Cronbach's alpha-criterion). Reliabilities were satisfactory, ranging from .77 for the Perceived Seriousness Scale (PSS), to .80 for the Perceived Adverse Consequences (PACS), to .73 for the Awareness of Victimization-scale (AVS). PSS consists of a set of nine crimes, such as pickpocketing from an old lady and destroying a telephone booth. Perceived seriousness responses were in terms of five point rating scales. The average over nine items yields the total PSS-score per subject: these scores thus run from zero (minimum) to five (maximum). Total (rescaled) PACS and AVS-scores had an identical range. To measure PAC subjects were presented three crimes and were requested to consider which of 20 adverse consequences were related to these crimes. For each crime a higher number of marked consequences yields a higher score. To measure AV subjects were presented with nine crimes, the same ones as used for PS. Subjects were requested to consider who could be a victim of these crimes. Per crime a subject's score consists of the number of correct minus the number of incorrect marks; the average over nine crimes yields a total score per subject, which was rescaled afterwards to a 0-5 range.

Results

On all three dependent measures 2x2 analyses of variance[3] were conducted, including "time" (pre test-post test) and "offender status" (recidivist-non-recidivist) as factors. The first factor, depicting a potential learning effect due to program exposure, constitutes a "within subjects" factor, offender status being a "between subjects" factor.

On *Perceived Seriousness* the analysis revealed significant main effects for offender status ($F(1, 85) = 7.76$, $p < .01$), and for the time factor ($F(1, 85) = 22.80$, $p < .00$). In line with hypothesis 2(a) recidivists ($M = 3.35$) considered the criminal behavior presented to be less serious (M non-recidivists = 3.72). Moreover subjects' pretest-scores ($M = 3.52$) were significantly lower that their post-test scores ($M = 3.72$). Parallel to hypothesis 1(a) the program thus had a beneficial impact on perceived seriousness. However, this latter effect was qualified by a significant time x offender status interaction ($F(1, 85) = 10.48$, $p < .00$). Non-recidivists' post-test

---

were significant, but should be discarded in view of the multivariate *p*-level. Moreover the pattern is in no way interpretable.

[3] Analyses of covariance, controlling for "background characteristics" do not diverge from the ANOVA's reported here.

scores were more favorable than their pre-test-scores, but at a borderline level of significance ($T(63) = 1.51$, $p = .06$); for recidivists perceived seriousness on the post-test was significantly higher ($T(22) = 4.56$, $p = .00$). This interaction is graphically represented in Figure 1. The figure suggests that the desired increase in perceived seriousness is much more salient for recidivists (cp. "ceiling effect" in the non-recidivist group).

The analysis of perceived adverse consequences revealed a significant main effect for "time" ($F(1, 50) = 11.81$, $p <.00$). Neither the offender status main effect ($F < 1$), nor the interaction effect ($F < 1$) were significant. Only hypothesis 2(b) is thus confirmed: results suggest that subjects were more aware of adverse consequences, resulting from offending, after exposure to the program. The program had a favorable impact on subjects' awareness of victimizing consequences. Figure 1 provides a graphical illustration of these outcomes.

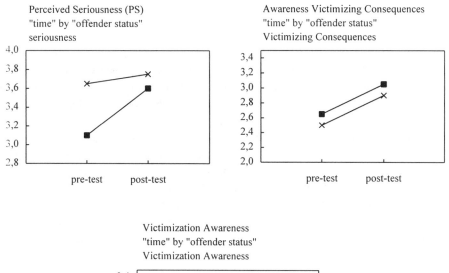

Figure 1: Focus on Victims (Alternative Sanction) Program: Impact on the Pre-Victimization Process

The analysis on "victimization awareness" revealed a similar picture. A significant main effect was observed for "time" ($F(1, 85) = 22.80, p < .00$). The offender status main effect ($F(1, 80) < 1$) and interaction ($F(1, 85) = 2.27, p < .10$) were insignificant. According to Figure 1 subjects' awareness of victimization increased during exposure to the program. This result confirms hypothesis 1(c).

In summarizing the major outcomes we would like to note that hypothesis 1 is consistently confirmed. The program had a clear beneficial impact on the perceived seriousness of criminal behavior, on the awareness of victimizing consequences, and on victimization-awareness. If the theoretical model presented here is correct, this conclusion suggests that the program actually stimulates internal inhibition, and might thus contribute to reducing or preventing future offending. In view of the recidivism-rate relating to the program, which contrasts favorably with rates obtained in other "alternative sanction" programs, there is sufficient ground to continue and expand the program.

Study 3

A mass media campaign aimed at discouraging various forms of sexual intimidation was recently initiated by the Dutch government. Its emphasis is on all sorts of undesirable (and sometimes criminal) male-female interactions. The aim is to change males' stereotypical conceptions of dating behavior. Inter alia the idea that macho behavior is basically preferred by females is challenged. Study 3 examines the impact of a video - especially created for the purpose of the campaign - in which two types of persuasive strategies - a perpetrator and a victim-focused message - were used. The perpetrator-focused message specifically considers negative consequences the actor may encounter, such as getting arrested by the police, encountering the criminal justice system, and meeting negative reactions from the social environment. A victim-focused message explicitly considers the fact that the behavior may have detrimental consequences for women, and that the behavior may cause psychological distress for victims.

Method

Sample Participants (n = 198) came from various types of secondary education: 53 were involved in technical/administrative education; 80 in general and 65 in "preparatory scientific" training. Sixty-two subjects were male; 136 subjects were female. Their average age was 16 years. Sixty-nine subjects were exposed to a victim-focused message; 63 to a perpetrator-focused message, while 66 subjects served as controls (no communication). A slight age-difference emerged between groups ($F_{(2, 194)} = 3.86; p < .05$). Control subjects were on average 16.2 years, victim-exposed 16, and perpetrator-exposed subjects 15.8 years. No differences emerged in gender compositions. All subsequent analyses were controlled for age.

Independent variable Two videos were constructed out of an already existing documentary[4], encompassing three central scenarios: (1) a group of boys are spying on a group of girls who are dressing at a sports center. Fragments of conversations among the boys are heard, including statements "I would like to tie her up, and screw her" and bets, such as "if you grab her cunt, I'll pay you 'X'", and "if you grab her tits, I'll pay you Dfl 2.50". The boys are hanging around, obviously waiting for the girls to come out. When a girl is leaving the center one of the boys (Hans) grabs her, touches her breasts and kisses her. When a motorcyclist passes by, noticing the incident, the girl is able to get loose and escape the scene. While fleeing, Hans is still yelling threats at her. At night, the boys are taken in by the police; (2) *Linda*, who works at a supermarket, is regularly bothered by her boss. While refilling the shelves he stands too close behind her, telling her that she is special, etc. For a total period of six years she doesn't dare to tell anyone about what is going on. After her boss sexually assaulted her in the backroom, she becomes very afraid of males and boys; she feels filthy and ashamed. Eventually her boyfriend finds out about it, after observing her strange responses to mass media sexual violence. They decide to report the incident to the police. Her boss gets convicted, but she loses her job in the meantime; (3) In a disco *Peter* is acquainted with a girl and asks her if she wants to go out with him. Outside, while fondling, he starts talking about sexual intercourse, and the need to use a condom so as not to contract AIDS. As he tries to undo her pants, she tells him that she does not want this. He then gets furious, and forces her to the ground, saying "if you say A, you have to say B also". She tries everything possible to resist him, holds her legs tight together, and begs him to let her go. He threatens her with a sharp object, and if people are passing by he shuts her mouth with his hands. While other people are passing by she is able to get loose and runs away. Later on, Peter is arrested by the police. Interspersed with these three scenarios are youngsters - both boys and girls - commenting on sexual violence, on dating and (motives underlying) macho behavior in male-female interactions.The victim-focused message specifically considered the Linda-scenario, and left out scenario (3). This video thus more strongly focuses on the negative psychological consequences of sexual victimization for the victim. Discussed are post traumatic responses such as fear of males, feelings of fear of being touched, even by intimates, the reluctance to openly talk about the incident, and feelings of self-blame, guilt and shame. The perpetrator-focused video especially considered the Peter-scenario. Moreover, a police officer throws light on the issue of sexual intimidation, while images of a jail are shown. This video thus more heavily concentrates on the negative consequences for the perpetrator, including formal responses from the criminal justice system, and negative reactions from the social environment.

---

[4]   *Boys and Sexual Violence*, developed by RIAGG Groningen (M. Bonink, E. Damen; Prevention Department) and Rutgershuis Groningen (R. Croon, T. Teuben; Prevention Department).

Measures In total five measures were taken from a questionnaire: (1) evaluation of macho behavior (e.g. "girls love groups of boys showing off"), (2) Sexual Intimidation Myth Acceptance (e.g. "Girls want to be taken violently"), (3) Conditional Acceptance of Forced Sex (e.g. "A boy may force a girl into sex, if she has had sex with him previously"), and (4) the perceived likelihood of negative consequences for the perpetrator and of victims' suffering psychological harm (5). Reliabilities of these multi-item measures ranged from .67 to .86.

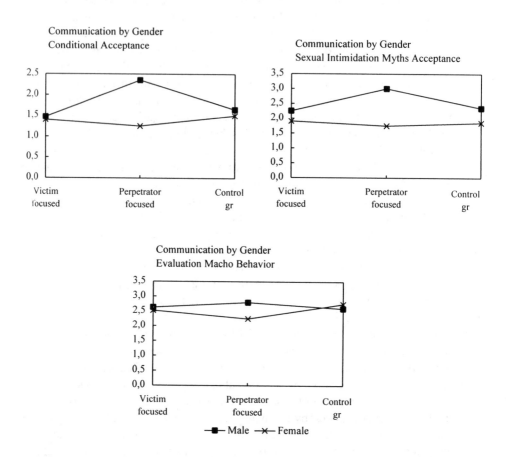

Figure 2: Victim-Focused and Perpetrator-Focused Strategy: Impact on the Pre-Victimization Process

Results

Substantial numbers of subjects reported experiences with various forms of sexual intimidation. Unwanted touching, either as a victim or as a perpetrator, was reported by 50% (often: 5%; very often: 2%); some experience with unwanted kissing by 24% (often: 2%); hearing or making unwanted sexual remarks by 51% (often: 6%; very often 3%). Unwanted sex in bed was uncommon: only 3% reported such experiences. No gender differences emerged in reported experiences.

Data were first analyzed multivariately on the basis of a 3 (type of communication) by 2 (gender) design. This analysis revealed significant main effects for type of communication ($F_{m(10, 366)} = 3.38; p < .01$), for gender ($F_{m(5, 183)} = 7.98; p < .01$), and a significant communication by gender-interaction ($F_{m(10, 368)} = 2.27; p < .01$). This interaction merits further attention here.

Communication by gender effects emerged on the evaluation of macho behavior ($F_{(2, 187)} = 3.75; p < .05$), on myths acceptance ($F_{(2, 187)} = 5.07; p < .01$), and on conditional acceptance ($F_{(2, 187)} = 8.60; p < .01$). On all three variables a similar pattern emerged (see: Figure 2).

For male subjects - the central target of the communication - the perpetrator-focused message appeared to backfire. Males exposed to this message evaluated macho behavior in interacting with girls more positively. Instead of weakening myths about sexual intimidation, this message seems to strengthen them. Moreover, the message appeared to enhance males' conditional acceptance of coerced sex. In males, the perpetrator-focused message resulted in various unwanted outcomes, which did not emanate from a victim-focused strategy. Thus, in order to change the pre-victimization process a victim-focused strategy appears to be more effective.

Conclusion

The theoretical model outlined here suggests that pcc's go through a particular (victim-related) set of cognitive operations before actually committing a crime. Interventions aimed at changing delinquent/criminal behavior should then incorporate a "victim-focused" component, making persons aware of the adverse psychological impact of their behaviors for crime victims. Study 1 offered some empirical support for this model through documenting a positive association between crime orientation - a self-report measure of criminal behavior - and various aspects of the previctimization process. Results inter alia revealed that crime orienteation is positively related to denying, ignoring, or minimizing the adverse consequences of criminal behavior for victims. Studies 2 and 3 suggested that the pre-victimization process is changeable. Study 2 revealed that juvenile delinquents can be made more aware of these adverse consequences through an alternative sanction program. Moreover, study 3 offered some experimental support that a victim-focused strategy will be more effective than the "traditional" perpetrator-focused strategy. Again, the "nothing works" paradigm (Andrews & Bonta, 1994) is thus refuted: victim-focused measures appear to make a difference.

References

Andrews, D.A., & Bonta, J. (1994). *The psychology of criminal conduct.* Cincinnati, Ohio: Anderson.

Fattah, Ezzat A. (1991). *Understanding criminal victimization. An introduction to theoretical victimology.* Scarborough, Ontario: Prentice Hall.

Jessness, C. (1962). *Manual for the jessness inventory.* Palo Alto, CA: Consulting Psychologists Press.

Junger-Tas, J. & Kruissink, M. (1990). *Ontwikkeling van de jeugdcriminaliteit: periode 1980-1988.* Arnhem: Gouda Quint.

Sutherland, E.H. & Cressey, D.R. (1960). *Principles of criminology* (6th Edition). Chicago: Lippincott.

Sykes, G., & Matza, D. (1957). Techniques of neutralization: a theory of delinquency. *American Sociological Review*, 22, 664-670.

Tyler, T. (1990). *Why people obey the law.* Appendix A: Questionnaire used in the first wave of the Chicago Study. New Haven: Yale University Press.

Wells, K. (1980). Adolescents' attributions for delinquent behavior. *Personality and Social Psychology Bulletin*, 6, 63-67.

Winkel, F.W. (1993). Opvattingen van jeugdige delinquenten over crimineel gedrag: 2 studies naar gunstige definities en gerichtheid op criminaliteit. *Tijdschrift voor Ontwikkelingspsychologie*, 20, 2, 151-171.

Criminal Victimization and Well-Being:
A Prospective Study on the Direct and Buffering Effects of Personality Traits[1]

Adriaan Denkers and Frans Willem Winkel

Two studies were conducted to investigate the direct and buffering effects of personality traits on the well-being of victims of crime. The personality traits Hardiness, Locus of Control, Evaluation Style, Relative Vulnerability and Style of Information Processing were examined. In study 1 the expected direct effects of personality traits on well-being emerged. Factor analyses showed a distinct protective factor, Self-confidence, and a sensitizing factor, Dependence. Study 2 was conducted among victims of crime and a control group of non-victims. The expected relations between the trait-factors and well-being were reconfirmed. However, the trait-factors had no bearing on the magnitude of the consequences of victimization on well-being. Moreover, victimization does not seem to influence well-being.

Introduction

Among victim assistance workers, mass media reports and theorists, there seems to be broad consensus about the notion that criminal victimization can cause dramatic psychological distress (Agnew, 1985; Frieze, Hymer & Greenberg, 1987). The research literature however suggests that the effects of stressful life events, including criminal victimization, on well-being are hardly as dramatic as expected (Agnew, 1985; Kessler, Price & Wortman, 1985). Correlations between life event-scores and well-being seldom exceed .30, which indicates that such events at best explain 9% of well-being (Cohen & Edwards, 1987). A possible explanation for this weak relationship is that personality traits and/or social factors might mitigate the detrimental consequences of victimization (Zika & Chamberlain, 1987).

This study focuses on the influence of personality traits on well-being. Two models depicting the nature of the influence of personality traits have dominated research in the past few decades: the stress buffer model and the main effects model. The buffering model suggests that personality traits influence the extent to which

---

[1] This study was carried out as part of a C.D.W.O. grant from the Dutch Department of Justice. Authors would also like to acknowledge the continued support from the ACHMEA-Foundation (Stichting *Achmea* Slachtoffer en Samenleving) to the VUA Program "Kwaliteit Slachtofferhulp".

individuals are affected by stressful events, either by tempering or amplifying the negative consequences. This implies that after a stressful event the influence of personality traits is, at least, more powerful than in the absence of stress. Alternatively, the main effects model suggests that personality traits have effects on well-being that are independent of the presence or absence of a stressor (Taylor & Brown, 1988).

Many studies are designed to investigate buffer effects of personality traits. This has generated a lot of information about the effects of personality traits. Nevertheless, conclusions about the direct or buffering nature of these effects still remains debatable, mainly because of methodological obstacles. For instance, many studies lack a control condition consisting of non-victims (e.g. Kobassa, Maddi, Pucetti & Zola, 1985). An effect of personality traits among a group of victims doesn't necessarily support the buffer model, but could also be due to a direct effect. For instance, Kushner, Riggs, Foa and Miller (1993) reported a negative relationship between perceptions of control and post-traumatic stress among 140 female sex-crime victims. Further analysis revealed that the severeness of the crime had no influence on this relationship. This seems to suggest that the influence of perceptions of control on post traumatic stress is not a function of the "degree to which one is victimized". Although this does not rule out the possibility of a buffering effect, this study rather seems to indicate a direct effect of perceptions of control.

To our knowledge, in all research on the influence of personality traits on the social-psychological aftermath of criminal victimization, as well as stressful life events in general, these traits were assessed after the incident took place. The main reason for post-event-assessment is that it is considered impossible to measure personality traits before the incident occurred (Gibbs, 1989). Moreover, theoretically there are no serious objections to this practical solution, because personality traits are by definition supposed to be relatively stable over time and situations. However, empirical evidence seems to dramatically undermine this assumption. For instance, criminal victimization can have a negative effect on both fear of crime and perceptions of control (Gibbs, 1989; Janoff-Bulman & Frieze, 1983). A more serious crime will evoke a more serious deterioration of both variables. A thus found interaction between victimization and perceptions of control on fear of crime might not be caused by the buffering qualities of control, but be due to the heterogeneous nature of the impact of the crimes in the survey.

Examining the nature (direct or buffering) of the influence of personality traits on well-being and attempting to avoid methodological pitfalls seems thus to demand A) a pre-victimization measurement of personality traits and well-being; and B) that both victims and non-victims be included in the study.

Psychologists have dedicated much of their attention unraveling which personality traits enable people to cope effectively with stressful life-events. This search has produced an impressive list of possibly relevant traits. Most of these are supposed to have (direct or buffering) beneficial effects on well-being, such as hardiness (Kobassa, 1979), locus of control (Rotter, 1966), and positive evaluation style (Lazarus, 1981). Considerably less attention has been devoted to traits that have (direct or buffering) negative effects on well-being, such as an emotional style of information processing (Kreitler & Kreitler, 1988), feelings of relative vulnerability (Perlof, 1983), and need for affiliation (Hill, 1987). Personality traits that have a positive influence on well-being or mitigate the detrimental effects of the stressful event will subsequently be labelled *protective traits*. Likewise, the term *sensitizing traits* will refer to traits that have a negative influence on well-being or cause people to be susceptible for the negative consequences of stressful events.

This paper will discuss two studies. The first study will examine personality traits and well-being in a representative sample of the Dutch population. The second will focus on the well-being of a group of respondents out of this sample who have subsequently been victimized, and a matched control group of non-victims. From the perspective of the direct effects model, we expect protective traits (hardiness, locus of control and evaluation style), both in study 1 and in study 2, to be positively related to well-being (Hypothesis 1). Similarly, sensitizing traits (emotional style of information processing, relative vulnerability an need for affiliation) are in both studies expected to be negatively related to well-being (Hypothesis 2). From the buffering model perspective, particularly victims that are characterized by low scores on protective and high scores on sensitizing traits are expected to suffer negative consequences of the event, while others will not, or hardly be influenced (Hypothesis 3; Colins, Taylor & Skogan, 1990; Lazarus, 1993).

During the past decades personality psychologists have, with mixed results, tried to reduce the structure of human personality to a couple of central dimensions (Eysenk, 1987). The literature hardly refers to any attempts to find central dimensions underlying the personality traits under examination in this study. This will exploratively be investigated in Study 1 of this paper.

Study 1

Method

Subjects A computerized questionnaire was presented to 3,411 subjects connected to the panel of Stichting Telepanel. This sample is reasonably representative of the Dutch population.

Procedure The Stichting Telepanel operates with a computerized method of data-gathering. Participating households get the use of a personal computer and modem. With the aid of these devices the central computer of the Stichting Telepanel on a weekly basis sends questionnaires to the connected households. Participants may respond at any time during the weekend that suits them. When the respondents have filled out the questionnaire, their answers are automatically returned to the central computer.

Measures The questionnaire consists of personality and well-being scales. To assess personality six scales were used: Internal/External Locus of Control (den Hertog, 1992; Rotter, 1966), consisting of 18 items (e.g. "I determine what happens to me") that form a reliable scale ($\alpha = .74$); Hardiness (Denkers, 1992) consisting of five items (e.g. "I'm well able to work under strain") that form a reliable scale ($\alpha = .77$); Evaluation style, operationalized by 4 items (e.g. "To what degree did you enjoy the past year") evaluating the past year ($\alpha = .65$; Winkel, 1989); Need for Affiliation (Hill, 1987), consisting of 3 items (e.g. "If I feel unhappy or depressed, I turn to others"), that form a reliable scale ($\alpha = .78$); Relative vulnerability (Perlof, 1983), consisting of three items (e.g. "Compared to others in your street, do you expect to have a greater, equal or smaller chance of becoming a victim of crime?") that form a reliable scale ($\alpha = .78$); and Style of Information Processing (Kreitler & Kreitler, 1988), consisting of eight items (e.g. "I often react emotionally") that form a reliable scale ($\alpha = .64$).

The questionnaire also entailed two well-being scales. The first can be considered a general measure of well-being: a Dutch translation (Heesink, 1989) of the five item "Satisfaction With Life" Scale of Diener, Emmons, Larsen and Griffon (1985; e.g. "In most ways my life is ideal"). The second well-being scale is more crime specific: Fear of Crime (Winkel, 1989), consisting of three items about the degree to which respondents feel tense, afraid and aggravated while thinking of the possibility of becoming a crime victim ($\alpha = .82$).

Results

To examine the direct effect of personality traits on Fear of Crime and Satisfaction With Life, regression analyses were conducted. First, socio-demographical characteristics, age, gender, and having/lacking a partner, were entered, followed by the personality traits. The results of these analyses are presented in Table 1.

Table 1 reveals that the personality traits are associated to the well-being measures, Satisfaction With Life and Fear of Crime, in the expected manner (Hypotheses 1 and 2). Exceptions to this are the relationships between the sensitizing personality traits (Information Processing Style, Need for Affiliation and Relative Vulnerability) and Satisfaction With Life. These personality traits seem to have no, or even a positive influence on Satisfaction With Life. Furthermore Evaluation Style seems to be unrelated to Fear of Crime.

A factor analysis was conducted to explore which dimensions underlie the personality traits. This factor analysis resulted in a solution with two factors (eigenvalue > 1), explaining 48% of the variance. The Varimax rotated solution is presented in Table 2.

Table 1: Correlations and Multiple Regression-Analysis Predicting Satisfaction with Life and Fear of Crime with Socio-Demographic Variables and Personality Traits (n = 3401)

	Satisfaction with life				Fear of crime			
	r	β	t	r^2	r	β	t	r^2
step 1: Socio-demographic variables								
partner	.12	.09	6.04**		.02	.02	.92	
age	-.04	-.09	-6.42**		-.11	-.08	-5.16**	
gender	.04	.06	3.72**		.21	.14	8.18**	
				2%				6%
step 2: Personality traits								
Hardiness	.16	.05	3.13**		-.25	-.10	-5.20**	
Locus of control	.27	.17	10.40**		-.22	-.14	-7.84**	
Evaluation style	.50	.46	30.21**		-.09	-.01	-.30	
Style of inf.proc.	-.02	.08	5.39**		.19	.10	6.11**	
Relative vulner.	-.05	-.03	-1.82		.12	.07	4.45**	
Need for affiliation	.05	.04	2.85**		.12	.06	3.82**	
				30%				13%

* $p < 0.05$; ** $p < 0.01$

The results presented in Table 2 show that the first factor contains Locus of Control, Evaluation Style and Hardiness, while the second factor embraces Need for Affiliation and Style of Information Processing. The factor analysis also displays a modest loading of Relative Vulnerability and a considerable loading of Hardiness on Factor 2. Nevertheless, from a logical point of view, we decided to consider the first three traits as one and the last three as the other factor. The first factor consisting of protective traits can be described by the term Self-confidence as introduced by Holahan and Moos (1987). Individuals with a high score on the factor Self-confidence consider themselves hardy, have the idea that they are in control, and are inclined to evaluate matters positively. The second factor includes sensitizing traits and can be typified by the term Dependence (Bornstein, 1992).

Table 2: Varimax Rotated Solution of the Factor Analysis on Personality Traits

	Factor 1	Factor 2
Factor 1		
Locus of control	.75	-.10
Evaluation Style	.69	.02
Hardiness	.61	-.46
Factor 2		
Need for affiliation	.25	.81
Style of information processing	-.28	.60
Relative vulnerability	-.09	.31

Dependent individuals are characterized by an emotional style of information processing, have a strong need for Affiliation, and feel more vulnerable than others.

Discussion

In general, the considered personality traits seem to have the expected direct effects on well-being. Individuals with a high Fear of Crime level are characterized by low scores on protective traits and high scores on sensitizing traits. The Satisfaction With Life of individuals is strongly related to the protective traits. However, no consistent association is found between Satisfaction With Life and the sensitizing traits. The significant correlations underline the direct effects of personality traits on well-being; protective traits have a positive and sensitizing traits a negative influence on well-being.

The factor analysis suggests a partition into protective and sensitizing traits too. These two factors can respectively be labeled Self-confidence and Dependence. In study 2 we will try to economize by using these two factor-scores instead of the measures of the separate personality traits.

Study 2

Method

Subjects Out of the sample of Study 1, 108 respondents reported to be victimized between September 1992 and March 1993: 33 reported household burglary, 25 contact-robbery, 36 threat, 10 assault and 6 sex-related crime. Physical injury was reported by 19% and financial loss by 51% of the victims. After the crime, 46% of the victims reported the offense to the police, in 18% of the cases others reported the crime, and 37% of the crimes were not reported. Besides the victims a matched control group consisting of 116 respondents was selected. This group was matched by the variables gender, age, degree of urbanization and living-situation. These variables are often noted to influence well-being and coping with stressful events. The control respondents do not differ from the victimized respondents on the above-mentioned matching variables. However, a difference was found on the presence of a partner in the household; 59.4% of the victims reported living with a partner, whereas among non-victims 79.5% mentioned a partner in the household.

Procedure On a weekly basis, members of the panel were asked if they had been victimized during the past week. An affirmative answer was followed by a list of crimes. If the respondents had been victims of one of the relevant crimes (household burglary, contact-robbery, threat, assault or sex-related crime) a questionnaire automatically appeared on the screen of their personal computer. An almost identical questionnaire was presented to respondents in the control condition.

Measures In study 2 the dependent measures were identical to those in study 1. Both scales appeared to be reliable (Satisfaction With Life: $\alpha = .89$; and Fear of Crime: $\alpha = .81$). Using a median-split of the factor-scores constructed in study 1, the respondents were divided into those who scored high and those who scored low on the factors, Self-confidence and Dependence.

Results The design of this study offers the opportunity to examine to which extent Satisfaction With Life and Fear of Crime after the crime differ from their equivalent before the crime took place. With Satisfaction With Life as the dependent variable we first conducted a mixed 2 (victimization: no/yes) x 2 (Self-confidence: low/high) x 2 (Dependence: low/high) x 2 (measurement: pre-/post-) MANOVA, of which the latter is a within-subjects factor.

The results of this analysis indicate that neither the pre-nor post-victimization measurement of Satisfaction With Life among victims differs from the measurements among non-victims, $F(1, 198) < 1$. This suggests that victimization has no influence on Satisfaction With Life.

However, the post-measurement ($M = 4.84$) of both groups showed a decline of Satisfaction With Life compared to the pre-measurement ($M = 4.98$), $F(1, 198) = 4.28$; $p < .05$. This decline could have been caused by a seasonal influence: The pre-measurement (among most respondents) was conducted in the summer, while the post-measurement was conducted throughout the year (e.g. Howarth & Hoffman, 1984).

With regard to the factor Self-confidence, only a significant direct effect was found, $F(1, 198) = 36.79$; $p < .001$. Respondents with higher scores on the factor Self-confidence reported, both in the pre- and post- victimization measurement, being more satisfied with life. This result confirms Hypothesis 1.

The results concerning the factor dependence are less clear cut. A victimization x dependence interaction was observed, $F(1, 198) = 4.56$; $p < .05$. This interaction seems to be mainly caused by the pre-victimization measurement, $F_{pre-measurement}(1.202) = 4.89$; $p < .05$; $F_{post-measurement}(1.202) < 1$. Among non-victims the factor dependence appears to be negatively related to Satisfaction With Life. Unexpectedly, among victims-to-be the reversed relation was observed. This result indicates that future non-victims and future victims differ.

Next, a marginally significant victimization x dependence x pre-/post-measurement interaction was observed, $F(1, 198) = 3.59$; $p = .06$. This interaction appears to be caused by victims with low scores on the factor dependence. This group of victims shows no decline of Satisfaction With Life after their victimization. Dependent victims as well as respondents out of the control condition do report a deteriorated Satisfaction With Life. The results involving the factor dependence are summarized in Figure 1.

With Fear of crime as dependent variable we first conducted a mixed 2 (victimization: no/yes) x 2 (Self-confidence: low/high) x 2 (Dependence: low/high) x 2 (measurement: pre-/post-)MANOVA, of which the latter is a within-subjects factor. The results of this analysis suggest no Fear of Crime differences between victims and non-victims, nor differences between the pre- and post- measurement. However, significant direct effects in the expected direction of both personality factors were observed. Respondents who scored above the median on the factor Self-confidence report less Fear of Crime than those who scored below the median, $F(1, 198) = 8.64$; $p < .01$. Similarly, - as expected - low Dependence-scores are associated with less Fear of Crime, $F(1, 198) = 8.24$; $p < .01$.

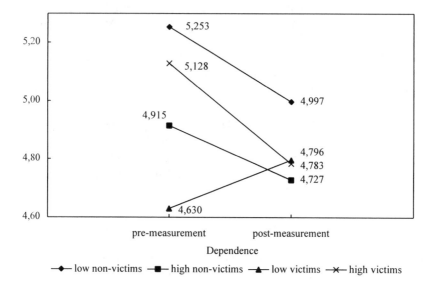

Figure 1: The Influence of the Factor Dependence on Pre- and Post- Satisfaction with Life among Victims and Non-Victims

Discussion

The results reported appear to suggest that crime victims' well-being was not substantially reduced. Both Satisfaction With Life and Fear of Crime seem not to be affected by the event. This outcome contrasts sharply with mass media reports, with the ideas of many theorists, and with the experiences of victim assistance workers, as well as with our own implicit expectations. As was mentioned in the introduction, life event scores generally explain 9% of well-being (Cohen & Edwards, 1987). Besides criminal victimization, such scores are build up out of many events, such as divorce, death of a partner and job loss. Undergoing only one of these events is likely to explain less than the full 9% of well-being. However, the proportion of variance of well-being that is explained by "criminal victimization" in this study seems to be almost trivial.

The personality traits in this study can be divided into two factors: Self-confidence and Dependence. Individuals with high Self-confidence scores are hardy, think that they are in control and tend to evaluate positively. Those with high Dependence-scores are characterized by an emotional style of information processing, a high need for affiliation, and feelings of relative vulnerability. These factors appeared to be consistently related to well-being in the expected direction, supporting the direct effects model. An exception to this is the relation between the factor Dependence and Satisfaction With Life. The absence of this relation might be due to the finding that future non-victims report a negative and future victims unexpectedly report a positive relation between Dependence and Satisfaction With Life in the pre-victimization measurement. These outcomes suggest that people differ in their objective risk of future victimization. A greater "objective victimization risk" might be caused by many different factors, e.g., life-style, presentation-style or the appearance of an individual. It seems reasonable to assume that people with a greater objective victimization risk also experienced more criminal victimizations in the past. The finding that Dependence and Satisfaction With Life are positively related within the group with a greater victimization risk, might indicate that in the long term victims benefit more from high than low Dependence.

Shortly after the victimization, the buffering effect of Dependence seems to be in the expected direction. Low Dependent victims show an increase and high Dependent victims a decrease of their Satisfaction With Life. Dependent personality traits, in the short term, seem to have a negative influence on coping with victimization. This suggests that individuals who are more emotional information processors, more in need of affiliation and who feel relatively more vulnerable, first "overreact", but in the long run are better coopers than their less Dependent fellow-victims. The Short term interaction effect between Dependence and victimization appeared as the only (weak) support for the buffer model. The absence of more support for the buffer model could be due to the lack of a direct influence of victimization. Hence, if victimization has no impact on well-being, how are its consequences for well-being to be buffered?

The short time period between the victimization and the post-victimization questionnaire (two weeks) could be one of the reasons for the lack of effect of victimization on well-being. The victims might not yet be fully aware of "what hit them"; their emotions might still be frozen. The dominance of personality over situation influence on well-being might be a second explanation of the absence of a victimization effect. These two explanations have contradicting practical implications. The first explanation suggests that it is probably impossible to make a proper diagnosis of the impact of the event so shortly after it took place. Therefore, contact between the victim and a victim assistance agency could, following this explanation, be established more effectively at a later point in time, when assessment of the consequences of the victimization is possible. Counter to this, the second explanation suggests that victim assistance agencies could be more effective if instead of focusing on victims and their struggle with the event, their aim would be on clients that are afraid or depressive, and how these clients can overcome this relatively "stable" state of mind. Following this second explanation, the recent victimization functions as a "justification" to acquire help; those who had been unhappy for a long time are finally recognized as such through the event. The cause of their misfortune however lies elsewhere. Because of its important practical implications it seems important to shed some light on the plausibility of these two explanations. Therefore, more research using a comparable method but following victims for a longer period of time could be worthwhile.

References

Agnew, R.S. (1985). Neutralizing the impact of crime. *Criminal Justice and Behavior, 12*, 221-239.

Bornstein, R.F. (1992). The dependent personality: developmental, social and clinical perspectives. *Psychological bulletin, 112*, 3-23.

Cohen, S., Edwards, J.R. (1987). Personality characteristics as moderators of the relationship between stress and disorder. In R.W.J. Neufeld (ed). *Advances in the investigation of psychological stress*, New York, Wiley.

Collins, R.L., Taylor, S.E., & Skogan, L.A. (1990). A better world or a shattered vision? Changes in life perspectives following victimization. *Social Cognition, 8*, 263-285.

Denkers, A.J.M. (1992). Pretest van de Vragenlijst. Amsterdam: Vrije Universiteit.

Diener, E., Emmons, R.A., Larsen, R.J., & Griffin, S. (1985). The satisfaction with life scale. *Journal of Personality Assessment, 49*, 71-75.

Eysenk, M.W. (1987). Personality, stress arousal, and cognitive processes in stress transactions. In R.W.J. Neufeld (ed). *Advances in the investigation of psychological stress*. New York: Wiley.

Frieze, I.H., Hymer, S., & Greenberg, M.S. (1987). Describing the crime victim: Psychological reactions to victimization. *Professional Psychology: Research and Practice, 18*, 299-315.

Gibbs, M. (1989). Factors in the victim that mediate between disaster and psychopathology: A review. *Journal of Traumatic stress, 2*, 489-514.

den Hertog, P.C. (1992). De "ie-18 locus of control"-vragenlijst: betrouwbaarheid en validiteit van een gewijzigde versie. *Nederlands Tijdschrift voor de Psychologie, 47*, 82-87.

Hill, C. A. (1987). Affiliation motivation: People who need people... but in different ways. *Journal of Personality and Social Psychology, 52*, 1008-1018.

Heesink J. (1989). *Schaalanalyses voor het project 'Het proces van sociale integratie van jong-volwassenen' II: werk, opleiding en welzijn*. Amsterdam: Vrije Universiteit.

Holahan, C.J., & Moos, R.H. (1987). Personal and contextual determinants of coping strategies. *Journal of Personality and Social Psychology, 52*, 946-955.

Howarth E., & Hoffman, M.S. (1984) A multidimensional approach to the relationship between mood and weather. *British Journal of Psychology, 75*, 15-23.

Janoff-Bulman, R., & Frieze, I.H. (1983). A Theoretical perspective for understanding reactions to victimization. *Journal of Social issues 39*, 1-17.

Kessler, R.C., Price, R.H., & Wortman, C.B. (1985). Social factors in Psychopathology: Stress, Social Support, and Coping Processes. *Annual Review of Psychology, 36*, 531-572.

Kobassa, S.C. (1979). Stressful life events, personality, and health: An inquiry into hardiness. *Journal of Personality and Social Psychology, 42*, 707-717.

Kobassa, S.C., Maddi, S.R., Puccetti, M.C., & Zola, M.A. (1985). Effectiveness of hardiness, exercise and social support as resources against illness. *Journal of Psychosomatic Research, 29*, 525-533.

Kreitler, S., & Kreitler, H. (1988). Trauma and anxiety: The cognitive approach. *Journal of Traumatic Stress, 1*, 35-56.

Kushner, M.G., Riggs, D.S., Foa, E.B., & Miller, S.M. (1993). Perceived controllability and the development of post-traumatic stress disorder in crime victims. *Behaviour-Research-and-Therapy, 31*, 105-110

Lazarus, R.S. (1981). The stress and coping paradigm. In C. Eisdorfer, D. Cohen, A. Kleinman, & P. Maxim (Eds.), *Theoretical Bases for Psychopathology*. New York: Spectrum.

Lazarus, R.S. (1993). From psychological stress to the emotions: A history of changing outlooks. *Annual Review of Psychology, 44*, 1-21.

Perlof, L.S. (1983). Perceptions of vulnerability to victimization. *Journal of Social Issues, 39*, 41-61.

Rotter, J.B. (1966). Generalized expectancies for internal versus external control of reinforcement. *Psychological Monographs, 80*, heel nummer 609.

Taylor, S.E., & Brown, J.D. (1988). Illusion and well-being: A social psychological perspective on mental health. *Psychological Bulletin, 103*, 193-210.

Winkel, F.W. (1989). Responses to criminal victimization: Evaluating the impact of a police assistance program and some social psychological characteristics. *Police Studies: The International Review of Police Development, 12*, 59-72.

Zika, S., & Chamberlain, K. (1987). Relation of hassles and personality to subjective well-being. *Journal of Personality and Social Psychology, 53*, 155-162.

Victimological Aspects of Computer Crimes

Trenti Alessia

The problem of "computer science victimization", that is, victimization related to illicit or indirect use of computer techniques, has been discussed only recently.

In fact, only in 1984 was the problem of computer science victimization examined for the first time, on the occasion of preparatory works for the VIIth Congress held by the United Nations for the prevention of crime and treatment of offenders (Sarzana, 1986).

During this Congress, the Resolution concerning "The declaration relative to fundamental principles of justice" was approved. This declaration, subdivided into two subsections, one concerning the victims of criminality and the other the victims of abuses of power, pointed out that the classical concept of victim necessarily must be dynamic and, in any case, adaptable to the possible changes in national legislations meant to prevent and fight abuses of computer techniques and the consequent violation of individual "privacy".

Recent victimological studies (Tranchina, 1975; Paradiso, 1983) that go beyond the stereotype of the victim as merely a passive object of the crime, have pointed out the importance of the "computer science victim" as a cause of the far-reaching, social dangerousness of "computer crimes". In fact, the victim represents such a substantial and decisive opportunity for the unpunished perpetration of crime that many authors have claimed (Correra & Martucci, 1986), that the victim is the best accomplice of the computer criminal. That is particularly true if we consider that most episodes of this kind are characterized by a constant attitude of the victim towards covering up the crime (Szabo, 1977).

This kind of attitude, on the other hand, is not rooted in an irrational illogical behavior in any way, but, rather comes from precise motivations:

1. The unawareness of being a victim or, in any case, of the ways to protect one from victimization. Edelhertz (1970) has underlined the importance of the fact that the criminal relies on the ignorance and negligence of the victim for this kind of crime.

2. The complexity and high cost of trials: the victim, although aware of the legal means available, generally prefers not to take legal action fearing that financial losses due to trial are greater than those caused by the crime. On this subject, Bequai (1976) asserts that many times, in cases of computer crime, reporting the case might be neither useful, nor exact, nor advantageous, as "a

simple case of computer crime could cause the collapse of a small investigating agency";

3. The personal profit obtained by the victims from the entire transaction induces them to consider it more advantageous to come directly to an arrangement with the criminal through an extrajudicial compromise than to initiate a penal procedure;

4. The fear that police investigation and also the divulgation of the crime can lead to a negative reputation with discredit of the image and commercial prestige of the firm and consequent decrease in turnover;

5. The sensation that the investigating and judging authorities are not completely prepared to prepare a case for trial, with consequent losses of time;

6. The victims' preferences to manage reservedly the consequences of crimes suffered, induce them to entrust the investigations to private detectives rather than to report all infractions discovered. The managers in charge who have been cheated or defrauded, having received confirmation of the crime, close the case with discretion, sharing the committed offense and restricting its gravity.

Besides, these motivations account for the fact that more and more frequently, within computer science victimology the concepts of "crime-couple" or "shared responsibility" are discussed in that the victim is at the same time responsible for the crime suffered (Ingrassia & Paterna, 1989).

The consequences of this behavior are varied: first, the collaboration of the victim is a very important factor in the prevention and suppression of computer crime. Non-reporting, in fact, prevents police and detective agencies from learning the mechanisms of the crime and then being able to intervene both preventively and repressively. In addition, the knowledge of computer crimes, not only on the part of the detective authorities but also of the public, can bring enormous advantages to computer organizations, at least on a preventive level, not only through a better estimation of imperfections or risks to which the enterprise is exposed, but also through the arrangement of more and specific precautionary measures.

Another decisive consequence of non-reporting is the attitude of superiority and self-assurance of the criminal him or herself, who, besides being in a situation of total impunity, perceives that his or her prestige is increased. This awareness of the high probability that the crimes will neither be discovered nor be reported, induces him or her not only to become a recidivist, but also to blackmail the victim. We know of cases in which, paradoxically, the victim merely transferred the offenders to another sector of the organization and also often increased their salaries so that they would not reveal their crimes (Spreutels, 1985; Sarzana, 1986).

These behaviors reflect the general characteristics of the victims of white-collar-crime; in fact, this kind of criminality is undoubtedly less evident than traditional criminality, thus provoking less social alarm; besides, the "dark figure" is also in this case inevitably elevated because of the "victim's silence" (Paradiso, 1983; Sieber, 1986).

Such a situation is also due to the fact that there is no law obliging the victims to file a report and inform the police of every case of computer crime in which they have been involved, and this fact is true not only for Italy.

Numerous attempts have been made to obtain the collaboration of the victim of computer science criminality and various solutions have been suggested (see Recommendation N(89)9 of the Council of Europe, adopted by the Committee of Ministers on September 13, 1989).

The first, and the most radical, implied the legal obligation for the victim to report to the police every crime committed in computer system, and considered non-reporting as a crime whose seriousness depends on the nature of the activities of the institutions involved.

Such a recommendation had already been called for many authors (Kling, 1980; Walsh & Schram, 1980; Levi, 1987), in consideration of the fact that the ignorance of the real extent of the problem of computer crime affected victims, criminals and shareholders negatively. In fact, while the victims were unaware of the risks they ran, the perpetrators were encouraged to become recidivists, and the shareholders, unaware of the real situation, were incapable of accomplishing a management strategy.

Some American states (e.g. Georgia) have already adopted specific laws on computer crimes, which explicitly call for the obligation of reporting by the victim, exactly is the case of financial crimes. Such a provision, however, has proved to be significantly foreign to the legal traditions of many States which have reaffirmed that it is up to the victim to decide whether to appeal to justice, treat the case extrajudicially, or, if it is an employee's crime, request the dismissal of the person involved (Couch, 1981).

Furthermore, numerous doubts have been expressed with regard to the difficulties of controlling such an obligation by regulations: in particular, whether it is correct to extend it to all computer crimes; whether it is correct to assess the obligation of reporting to the seriousness of the damage; to which competent authority the crime should be reported, etc.

On this subject, The Criminal Law Act of 1967 (UK), reasoning that the obligation of reporting for computer crimes can raise questions of inequality with reference to those crimes for which such obligation is not juridically implied, abolished, in fact, the general crime of omission of reporting to the police (for every crime) on the basis that in the United Kingdom there was not a general duty for the public to report every crime committed, such that creating a specific obligation of reporting for computer crimes, was considered inopportune (Wasik, 1991).

The second solution proposed, less rigid than the previous one, was to introduce the obligation of reporting, not to the police, but, at least in some particular cases, to a specific supervisory body changed with the task of examining the circumstances in which the crime occurred and acting as an intermediary with judicial authorities.

This kind of organization already exists in some countries: The American Bank Protection Act, for example, requires that banks report all frauds and losses over 1,000 dollars to a supervisory body in the bank sector, and delay or non-reporting is heavily punished.

The objections to this system were based, on the one hand, on the impossibility of applying it to any kind of computer crime and victim; and on the other, on the fact that the possibility of adopting such a solution depended not only on the structure of control systems in similar sectors of a member state, but also on the general policy concerning the implication and obligation of the victim-firm.

Another proposal suggested establishing fictitious "courts" made up of real and potential victims, together with representatives of judicial bodies, in order to prepare the case for a fictitious trial where computer crimes can be discussed anonymously. These trials would have made it possible to report crimes, thus helping the companies, institutions and public understand how these crimes work and consequently the risks and the weak points of the systems.

Finally, among the other solutions proposed, there was a suggestion that all computer systems of medium-large complexity should exhibit a special security certificate issued by a special body of experts responsible for the maintenance of security measures. Such experts would have the obligation to report any kind of violation discovered during their inspections.

The principle victims of this type of criminality are (e.g. Delord-Raynal, 1983; Correra and Martucci, 1986):

1. The State, probably the most vulnerable, because the capillary distribution over the territory of peripheral administration gives the computer-criminal greater access to the data banks used in public services. The situation is paradoxal: the State shares the responsibility for the crime both because of the lack of an adequate law and because of the impossibility of controlling all the computer services over the national territory.

2. Businesses, particularly banks, which nowadays have reached practically complete automation on an organizational level. Concerning businesses, the crime does not aim at the simple theft of money, but at the extraction of information kept by the technologically advanced firm, such as: theft of patents, financial data, marketing methodologies and fiscal information. Moreover, in this sector the discovery of the crime occurs, in most cases, accidentally, because the information stolen does not disappear from the computer and there is no trace of the intrusion; so businesses can be an unaware victim, a victim unable to discover the offender, or, on the contrary, an aware and conniving victim.

3. Citizens, who are harmed from two points of view: first of all, the economic damage caused by the crimes committed against businesses, are indirectly reflected on consumers. For example, enterprises raise the prices of goods and/or services to recover investments in the security of computers and protection of electronic files. Secondly, citizens are directly victimized through the violation of their right to privacy (Ingrassia & Paterna, 1989).

In the United States all the large multinational holdings use the information given by special "agencies" that can be telephonically contacted by anybody; this information concerns the character, lifestyle, financial situation, previous offenses and any other characteristics of the subjects with whom the companies have a business relationship (Baldassare, 1974).

The "victimization" of citizens will be progressively increased by the development of telematics with particular regard to interactive home media. These interactive home media, already widespread in the USA and northern Europe, allow the request or use of particular services via a keyboard connected to the television set. In this way, the citizen becomes at the same time criminal-victim of the computer, spontaneously providing exact details about his or her private life and financial situation, details that can be used by other people not only to violate privacy but also to commit computer crimes (Criner, 1980).

On this subject, various authors (Di Gennaro & Breda, 1972) talk of a real "electronic prejudice" that could exist against individual citizens - entered in a great data-bank as information available to thousands of managers - by the use of objective but rigid data, deprived of any relation with human experience.

Technological progress and the new computer reality have not only potentiated the so-called "generical predisposition to being a victim", but they have also favored a "specific predisposition" to victimization of computer crimes, thanks also to the attitudes shown at the different computer, financial, and telematic levels.

A particular aspect that affects not only the process of victimization, but also and especially the elevated social dangerousness of these crimes is the peculiar psychological bond between the computer criminal and his or her victim.

The classification into "irreplaceable" victims and "replaceable" victims is validly recognized by most of the criminological literature: the former are those who become victims for a precise intersubjective relationship with the criminal-agent, and the latter are those who assume this role independently from that relation (Gulotta & Vagaggini, 1976).

Most computer science victims fall into the second category because in this kind of criminality the criminal generally does not have a personal relationship with his or her victim, who is often anonymous or quite absent: consider, for example, the frauds or thefts committed against bank users, where the meeting between the criminal and his or her victim is completely fortuitous (Delord-Raynal, 1983).

In fact, the relation between the subjects of computer crimes is characterized in a different way from what is normally established among the subjects in different criminal schemes. While the latter include physical and personal contact, computer crimes come about through a psychic activity that does not involve any kind of physical aggression, and frequently the victim is not a real, defined person but an abstraction or legal fiction (Ferracuti & Newman, 1972).

This absence of human contact between criminal and victim not only delays inhibiting mechanisms but facilitates acting-out, which in this case is the perpetration of the crime. Furthermore, this will occur without the perpetrator's regret for his or her victim, since the latter is not personified, or without any kind of remorse, even as far as to feeling less guilty.

On a psychological level, the victims sometimes turn out to be imprudent or negligent, or sometimes they are greedy social climbers who, by aiming to gain from computer access, show themselves to be ingenuous and unfortunate cheats, by becoming victims themselves (Ingrassia & Paterna, 1989).

Therefore, these real victims can be victimized either by chance or because they have unconsciously favored possible damage from a computer thus encouraging and reinforcing other people's criminal purposes or facilitating the perpetration of the crime.

From a criminodynamic point of view it is already accepted that in crimes characterized by an impersonal victim, such as computer crimes, the dangerousness is greater because the target is the acquisition of personal utility, and the passive subject is part of the motivation of the crime only for what he or she represents or owns, as an "instrument" in achieving such utilitaristic purposes (Mantovani, 1984).

Besides, the ascertained impossibility of controlling criminal behavior with deterrence techniques or with therapies, has led victimologists to be convinced that it is more useful to change the victim's behavior rather than the criminal's.

As a result, the victim has lately acquired great criminological importance both for the prevention and the repression of computer crimes (Tranchina, 1975; Viano, 1976).

In fact, the victim represents the first trace in the reconstruction of computer crime; moreover, the individual's knowledge of the behavior of being a victim and occasions that favor crime, preventively leads to making individuals responsible by preventing their negligence favoring the criminal conduct and reducing victim-like predispositions.

References

Baldassare, A. (1974). *Privacy e Costituzione. L'esperienza statunitense*. Roma: Bulzoni.

Bequai, A. (1976). Computer crime: a growing and serious problem. *Police Law Quarterly., 6/1*,22.

Correra, M., & Martucci, P. (1986). *I reati commessi con l'uso del computer*. Padova: Cedam.

Couch, R. (1981). A suggested legislative approach to the problem of computer crime. *Washington and Lee Law Review, 38*, 4, 1173-1194.

Criner, K. (1980). US videotex activities and policy concerns in 4 telecomunications policy.

Delord-Raynal, Y. (1983). Les victimes de la delinquance d'affaires. *Victimology: an International Journal, 8, 1/2*, 68-79.

Di Gennaro,G., & Breda, R.(1972). I calcolatori nel settore della difesa sociale. Efficienza di servizio e garanzia individuale. *Indice Penale, 3*, 399.

Edelhertz, H.(1970). *The nature, impact and prosecution of white-collar crime*. Washington, DC: US Government Printing Office.

Ferracuti, F., & Newman, J. (1972). Perceptions cliniques et psychologiques de la déviance. *Conseil de l'Europe. Etudes Relatives à la Recherche Criminologique, IX*, 23. Strasbourg.

Gulotta, G., & Vagaggini, M. (1976). The offender-victim system. In C.A. Viano (Ed). *Victim and Society*, pp. 50-59.Washington.

Ingrassia,G., & Paterna, G. (1989). *Comunicazione sociale. Crimini e Devianze nel Post-Moderno Informatico.* Torino: Giappichelli.

Kling, R. (1980). Computer abuse and computer crime as organisational activities. *Computer and Law Journal, 2*, 403.

Levi, M. (1987). *Regulating fraud: white collar crime and the criminal process.* London: Tavistock.

Mantovani, F. (1984). *Il Problema della Criminalità.* Padova: Cedam.

Paradiso, P. (1983). *La Criminalità negli Affari. Un Approccio Criminologico.* Padova: Cedam.

Recommandation n°R(89)9. (1990). *La Criminalité Informatique.* Conseil de l'Europe. Strasbourg.

Sarzana, C. (1986). Giustizia e assistenza per le vittime. *Criminologia, 5/6*, 3.

Sieber, U. (1986). *The International Handbook on Computer Crime.* Chichester: John Wiley & Sons.

Spreutels, S.P. (1985). La responsabilità penale connessa ad abusi nell'applicazione informatica. *Il Diritto dell'Informazione e dell'Informatica, 1*, 123.

Szabo, D. (1977). *La criminalité d'affaires: aspects criminologiques.* Paper presented at the First European Congress of social defence on economic criminality. Roma, pp.9-11.

Tranchina, G. (1975). Premesse per uno studio sulla rilevanza della vittima nella dinamica dei fatti criminosi. *Il Tommaso Natale, 1*, 39.

Viano, E.C. (1976). *Victim and society*, p. XII. Washington, DC. Visage Press.

Walsh, M.E., & Schram, D.D. (1980). The victim of white-collar crime:accuser or accused?. In G. Geis, E. Stotland (Eds.), *White-collar Crime: Theory and Research*, p.5. Beverly Hills, Calif.: Sage Publications.

Wasik, M. (1991). *Crime and the Computer.* Oxford: Clarendon Press.

Victimization in Close Relationships:
On the Darkness of "Dark Figures"

Peter Wetzels and Wolfgang Bilsky

Introduction

Detailed knowledge of the amount and the structure of crime is of central interest to politicians and administrators in almost every society. Information of this kind is highly relevant with respect to political and social planning and legal decision making. Aside from this criminal and social policy, access to sound empirical data on the prevalence and incidence of different forms of crime is important within other domains as well. Research into fear of crime and public attitudes towards crime and punishment, for instance, needs valid information about previous criminal victimizations of the persons under study. In every explanatory model of fear of crime, for example, persons' experiences with criminal acts serve as one of the central independent variables (see Fattah, 1993; Kury & Würger, 1993). If information about victimization is not reliable and valid, however, the conclusions drawn will be misleading.

One standard source of information are victims' reports to the police on the criminal incidents which happened to them. Victims' reporting behavior as well as the recording behavior of police officers are crucial to official *police crime statistics.* Consequently, comprehensive and reliable reporting behavior is a necessary but not sufficient condition for a politically and scientifically useful data base. It is well known, however, that many criminal events never come to the knowledge of the authorities. This is why victims are frequently called the gate-keepers of the criminal justice system. The reliability of police statistics is further affected by the fact that the proportion of crime which is not reported to the police is neither constant over time nor across different kinds of offenses (see for example the results of the British Crime Survey; cf. Mayhew & Maung, 1992). Thus, different crime rates calculated on the basis of police statistics may better reflect changes of reporting and recording behavior than actual changes in the incidence of criminal acts. Because of these shortcomings, police statistics are only a rather poor indicator of the actual amount of crime experienced and an unreliable guide to changes in crime rates (Mayhew, 1993).

Representative *victim surveys* are seen as one means to overcome (at least partly) the double bias of underreporting and underrecording which is inherent to police crime statistics. One of the major purposes of victim surveys is to capture all criminal victimizations experienced by the interviewees as either reported or unreported to the police in order to calculate so-called *dark figures* (i.e., the ratio of reported and not reported criminal incidents). These dark figures can then be used to estimate the "true" amount of crime within a given society with respect to the offenses and the population under study by taking into account the rate of unreported incidents.

While this procedure seems quite promising at first glance, the range of criminal incidents which can be detected by victim surveys is restricted by sampling procedures and methods of data collection. First, representative surveys are mostly based on household samples, thus focusing on incidents which can happen to private persons and their household. They normally disregard several other forms of crime, for instance victimless crime and crime against business. In addition, they usually are unable to reach certain subpopulations which are at special risk of victimization, as for example homeless people or prostitutes. Second, interview methods are based on retrospective questioning. This means that data are restricted to those victimizing incidents which are experienced consciously and which furthermore are accessible to recall and retrieval processes. Within these limits, victim surveys strive to paint a picture as complete as possible of the crime burden of the population under study.

However, there are some additional shortcomings of victim surveys, which have been mentioned by numerous researchers for many years but without showing any impact on victim survey research until today. This regards the problem that violent crimes committed by non-strangers are not identified reliably by victim surveys. Consequently, the amount of violent crime is seriously underestimated.

Twenty years ago Biderman already wrote, for example, that assaults "(...) in a high proportion involve as victim and offender family members, lovers, and others who have an ongoing social relationship to each other. (...) 'crime' may not be the category of the mental card file under which that event is stored by the respondent and hence is not an event to which his memory associates when in the context of an interview about crimes, he is asked whether an event of a certain type happened to him" (Biderman, 1975, p.162). Sparks (1981, p.23) argued similarly, when stating that "many crimes by spouses, family members, etc., are not mentioned to survey interviewers". More recently Heidensohn (1991) supposed that the British Crime Survey might underestimate the rate of domestic assault in particular because of the interview setting. This setting did not exclude the possibility that the interviewees were in the same room with their assailants during the interview, thus possibly inhibiting respondents to mention violent acts experienced within that particular relationship. Lynch (1993, p.173) commented on the same topic: "Many events that clearly satisfy the conceptual definition of crime are not regarded as such, because they are committed by intimates or acquaintances or because retribution is exacted instantaneously. These do not enter into the frame of reference when the respondent's mind is on crime".

Gottfredson (1986, p.261) has noted, that an underestimation of non-stranger assaults in victim surveys would in turn lead to an overestimation of the proportion of violent acts experienced outside the home. Consequently, the picture of the spatial correlates of violent victimization as painted by victim surveys might be seriously distorted.

Evidence from Past Research on Family Violence

Interestingly enough, the problem of the underestimation of violent victimization has obviously been recognized since the early beginning of victim survey research. Furthermore, coincidental with the development of victim survey research, the importance of intrafamily violence has more and more been recognized within the social sciences. Today family violence researchers constitute an established interdisciplinary scientific community with its own specialized journals and conferences. Unfortunately however, family violence research has developed quite separately from criminology in general and from victim survey research in particular until today (cf. Smith, 1994). This is surprising, taking into account that most forms of behavior labeled as family violence clearly meet legal definitions of crime in most societies. Although the problem of underreporting of physical and sexual victimization experiences in victim surveys has thus been known for more than twenty years, and despite the fact that during that period family violence researchers have developed both theoretical concepts and empirical methods (including survey measures) to analyze just this problem of violence between closely related persons, this know-how has not been incorporated into criminological victim survey research.

In accordance with the above cited statements of criminologists, survey research on family violence provides empirical evidence that criminological victim surveys seriously underestimate the amount of physical violence occurring within families or family-like settings. This finding holds for both face-to-face-interviews as carried out in the first national survey on family violence in the USA in 1975 (Straus, Gelles & Steinmetz, 1980), and telephone interviews, a method used in the second national survey in the USA in 1985 (Straus & Gelles, 1990). The National Family Violence Resurvey (NFVR), for example, yielded a much higher incidence rate of physical violence between marital partners than the US National Crime Survey (NCS). Straus and Gelles (1990) reported the incidence rate revealed by the NFVR to be 73 times higher than the comparable NCS rate.

This comparison, however, has to be treated cautiously because different measures were employed in the respective surveys. Nevertheless, because of positive results of validational studies of the NFVR-measure (the Conflict Tactics Scale; Straus, 1990), it seems unreasonable to attribute these discrepancies entirely to measurement error (i.e. overreporting in the NFVR). Instead, as Straus and Gelles (1990, p.99) stated, "The most likely reason for this tremendous discrepancy lies in differences between the context of the NCS and the other studies. The NCS is presented to respondents as a study of crime, whereas the others are presented as studies on family problems. The difficulty with a 'crime survey' as the context of determining incidence rates of intrafamily violence is that most people think of being kicked by their spouse as wrong, but not a 'crime' in legal sense".

Hypotheses

The statements cited above and the results of previous family violence research point to the central role of the victim-offender-relationship in studying violent victimization: Similar events are likely to be interpreted quite differently depending on the social context of their occurrence (e.g., family Vs non-family). From a cognitive psychological point of view it seems quite clear that schemes of social roles and scripts of social events will affect the encoding and the subsequent retrieval of experiences. With respect to violent encounters between victims and offenders, these cognitive schemes and scripts are particularly dependent on the relationship between the actors involved.

Research on family violence up to now has used several categories of victim-offender relations. As Weis (1989) pointed out, there are at least three different kinds of relation which are treated under the more general heading of family violence: (1) Kin relationship, i.e. victim and offender are related through birth or marriage; (2) intimate relationship, i.e. victim and offender know each other in a close and personal way; (3) domestic relationship, i.e. victim and offender share the same household. While different legal criteria may apply to these forms of interpersonal relations, all of them share one central psychological feature: they differ from relationships to acquaintances and strangers with respect to shared biographical experiences and a higher degree of mutual personal involvement. To emphasize this common feature, interpersonal relations which are characterized by such a high degree of mutual personal involvement and shared biographical experiences are labeled *close relationships* therefore. Used in this sense, the concept of close relationship is very similar to the psychological definition of family given by Schneewind (1991).

As regards the interacting person's own perspective, social relations can be distinguished according to the intensity of normative, socially attributed and/or subjectively experienced closeness. Thus, *close relationship* is a *fuzzy concept*, which is at least partly specified by subjective and interindividually varying criteria. There are differences in the degree of closeness, i.e. closeness is not a dichotomous but a continuous variable. Marital partnership or blood relationship, for example, may or may not be experienced as close, depending on the subjectively perceived quality of the respective interpersonal relation.

It is of special importance for victimological research that there are explicit rules that guide and control social interactions in such close relationships. These rules guarantee the protection of these relations against meddling from outside, thus being a necessary prerequisite of privacy and intimacy. They are part of *role schemes*, i.e.

of cognitive structures that organize one's knowledge about appropriate behavior in certain social situations. Furthermore, there exist *event schemes* or *scripts* which describe (and prescribe) appropriate behavioral sequences in frequently reoccurring situations. Such schemes facilitate the application of special categories to individual instances and events in order to identify them as members of a larger, more familiar group. Following these lines of reasoning, it is plausible to assume that the processes of perception, evaluation, classification, memorizing, and recall of events within close relationships are very different from those outside. The psychological characteristics outlined before have some crucial consequences for the choice of adequate methods in surveying victimization experiences in close relationships (Wetzels, 1993). First, special *instructions* are necessary to direct the interviewees' attention towards the focal interest of the study, i.e. experiences with closely related persons. Otherwise, cognitive schemes relevant for recall and retrieval of the interesting events will not be activated. Second, the *interview setting* must guarantee the interviewees that they can give information about victimization experiences, particularly violent acts committed by a closely related offender, without risking a violation of the rules of privacy.

Considering the aforementioned results of previous research and our theoretical reasoning, we hypothesized that conventional methods of victim survey research lead to a serious underestimation of the prevalence of violent victimization experiences. More specifically we put forward the following three hypotheses:

1. Research strategies and interview techniques employed in most victim surveys until today lead to a systematic *underestimation* of *violent* crimes, especially of physical violence. This is caused by the fact that victim surveys are less likely to identify victimizations within *family settings* and other *close social relationships* - despite the victimizing events meeting legal criteria of criminal law.

2. Underestimation of *violent* victimization is disproportionally high in certain *subpopulations*. Especially prevalence rates of violence against women and elderly people will be more heavily underestimated by conventional victim surveys.

3. By far the *most violent* victimizations in close relationships which are not reported to interviewers during face-to-face-interviews in victim surveys have not been reported to the police either. Consequently, dark figures calculated on the basis of data derived from such conventional victim survey research are supposed to underestimate the actual amount of violent crime not reported to the police. There is a considerable number of criminal incidents which, while experienced by the respondents and meeting legal criteria of crime, are neither reported in survey interviews nor to the police. These incidents form what is called the *double dark figure* of police crime statistics and victim survey research (Schneider, 1993, p.47).

Furthermore, we contend that this remaining part of the "dark field" of crime can be considerably reduced by some methodological improvements as outlined below. Particularly by integrating measures from family violence research into criminological victim surveys the identification of victims of violence, especially victims of closely related offenders, is supposed to be clearly enhanced.

Method

In the KFN-victim survey conducted in Spring, 1992 we tried to improve the usual interviewing in victim surveys by using an additional research kit for investigating victimization in close relationships. Following a face-to-face-interview similar to those employed by other victim surveys, the interviewees received a *drop-off questionnaire* together with an unmarked envelope and a seal. This written questionnaire was introduced as a set of questions on family conflicts and problems with closely related persons. Having filled in this questionnaire in the absence of the interviewer, the respondents put it into the envelope, sealed the envelope and handed them over to the interviewer who returned after about forty minutes. This procedure was chosen to guarantee that the attention of the interviewees is directed towards the sensitive topic of experiences in close relationships and to indicate that the respondents' answers will be treated anonymously and confidentially.

In the conventional face-to-face-interview two items addressed *victimization by assault* without special emphasis on a particular victim-offender-relationship. Respondents who reported at least one incident of assault with or without a weapon during the last five years were classified as victims of assault.

In the drop-off questionnaire two measures of victimization by physical violence were included. The first one was an adaptation of the *conflict tactics scale* (CTS) which is widely used in research on family violence (Straus, 1990). It contains ten different acts of physical violence by family or household members. Subjects who reported to have experienced at least one of these violent acts during the last five years were classified as victims of physical violence by a closely related offender. The second measure was a *one-item-measure of assault* (with or without a weapon). It was quite similar to the two items used in the face-to-face-interview but explicitly restricted to victimizations by closely related offenders. Here again, each respondent who reported having been assaulted during the last five years was classified as victim of assault by a closely related offender.

In face-to-face-interviews, *reporting behavior for assault* was recorded for every victim who indicated that this had been the most serious incident within the last five years. In the drop-off questionnaire, reporting behavior was recorded for the one-item measure only. Every victim who indicated that the offender of the most recent incident was a household member was asked whether this experience had been reported to the police.

A sample of 15,771 persons representative of the German speaking inhabitants of the old and new federal states of Germany aged 16 years or more was surveyed. A subsample of 5,851 participants of the face-to-face-interview was also asked to fill in the drop-off-questionnaire (for detailed information about sample characteristics see Wetzels et al., 1995). Only 2.4% of these subjects refused to participate in this additional study, resulting in a reasonably high response rate of 97.6%, i.e. 5,711 respondents, 3,255 of them aged 16 to 59 and 2,456 respondents aged 60 years or more.

Results

If differences in the social context of questioning (i.e., face-to-face-interview not restricted to a special form of victim-offender-relationship Vs drop-off-questionnaire restricted to incidents in close relationships) were in fact irrelevant with respect to recall and retrieval of victimizing experiences, those respondents reporting violent victimization in close relationships should have mentioned an assault in face-to-face-interviews too. In support of our *first hypothesis*, however, a considerable number of violent victimizations was only identified by the drop-off questionnaire (see Figure 1).

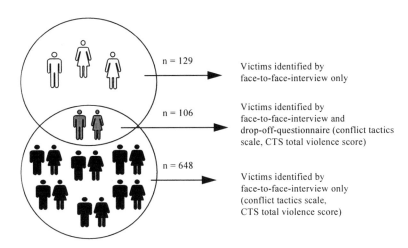

n = 129   Victims identified by
           face-to-face-interview only

n = 106   Victims identified by
           face-to-face-interview and
           drop-off-questionnaire (conflict tactics
           scale, CTS total violence score)

n = 648   Victims identified by
           face-to-face-interview only
           (conflict tactics scale,
           CTS total violence score)

Total number of victims: 883
Non-victims: 4,773
Percentage of victims of physical violence in close relationships
identified by the CTS measure of the drop-off-questionnaire only
(referring to the total number of victims of physical violence): 73.4%

Figure 1: Identification of victims of physical violence by face-to-face-interviews and drop-off-questionnaire

Figure 1 shows that 648 victims of physical violence who were identified by the CTS total violence score were not identified as victims of violence in conventional face-to-face-interviews. This amounts to nearly three quarters (73.4%) of the total number of victims identified in our study.

The possible objection that this discrepancy was nothing but a methodological artifact resulting from different numbers of items, was checked in a second step by means of the aforementioned one-item measure of assault in the drop-off questionnaire. This measure was compared to the two-item measure of assault in face-to-face-interviews. As expected, the number of victims identified additionally by the one-item-measure is in fact lower than the number of victims identified by the CTS. Nevertheless, there is still a proportion of 44.9% (n = 192) of victims who were only identified by the one-item-measure of the drop-off-questionnaire, but not during the face-to-face interview.

According to our *second hypothesis*, we expected the proportion of victims identified by the drop-off procedure only, to be higher for *women* and *elderly persons;* i.e., taking victims additionally identified by the drop-off measures into consideration, the relative increase in prevalence rates of violent victimization should have been substantially higher for women and elderly persons. As can be seen from Figure 2, both parts of this hypothesis were convincingly supported by our data when calculating the number of victims identified by both survey- and drop-off measures and comparing the respective percentages of victims identified by the drop-off measures only broken down by sex and age. There are clear differences with regard to sex and age in the rates of victims identified additionally by means of the drop-off questionnaire. Furthermore, rates also differ depending on the type of

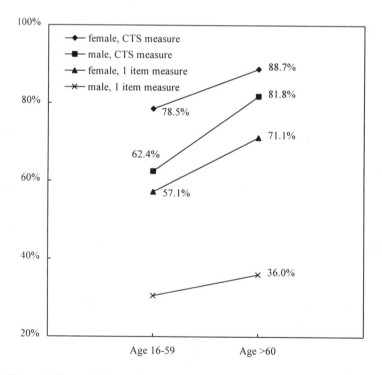

Figure 2: Victims Additionally Identified by Drop-Off Measures, by Age, Sex, and Measure

measure used. It is interesting to note that sex-related differences are more pronounced for the one-item-measure. This is in line with results from previous research, which showed that the CTS total violence score used here typically yields very similar victimization rates for men and women (see Yllö, 1993, p. 52). A closer look at the measures employed reveals that the one-item-measure is less sensitive to minor forms of physical violence than the CTS (Wetzels et al., 1995, p.164). Thus, the greater differences with regard to sex revealed by the one-item-measure indicate that victimization by physical violence in close relationships takes probably more often serious forms for women than for men.

Victimization risks are generally lower for women as compared to men if only those rates of assault are taken into account that are derived from conventional face-to-face-interviews. This result has been replicated several times by different victim surveys (cf. Gottfredson, 1986). In the KFN-survey the same results emerged when prevalence rates were computed on the basis of the face-to-face screening interview. The five year prevalence rate for assault, for instance, is 8.61% for men aged 16 to 59 years compared to only 4.3% for women of the same age group. However, when victimization experiences in close relationships as identified by the two drop-off measures are additionally taken into account, this difference is markedly diminished (men: 12.38%; women: 10.71%). This indicates that for women, a significantly greater proportion of victimization experiences takes place within close relationships. If the analysis on the basis of the one-item drop-off measure is restricted to incidents committed by offenders living together with the victim in the same household, women below the age of 60 show a higher prevalence rate of assault (4.2%) compared to men (3.0%), indicating that the home is a place of risk of victimization especially for women.

Table 1: Reporting Behavior and Dark Figure Estimates of Assault

	reported	not reported	total
Victims identified in face-to-face interviews	61 34.9%	114 65.1%	175
Victims identified by drop-off-questionnaire only	7 4.8%	138 95.2%	145
Total	68 21.3%	252 78.8%	320

Chi-square = 42.73; df = 1; p < .0001

Conforming to our *third hypothesis*, we expected that most of those experiences of physical violence in close relationships which are not reported in face-to-face-interviews but captured by the drop-off questionnaire have not been reported to the police either (forming the so-called "double dark figure" of victim surveys and police crime statistics). Our conclusions are based on data of 175 victims of assault identified in face-to-face-interviews, and 145 additional victims of assault by household members identified exclusively by the one-item measure of the drop-off questionnaire. While 34.9% of the victimizations in face-to-face-interviews were reported to the police, the respective rate for those exclusively identified by the drop-off procedure (i.e. victimizations in close relationships) is 4.8% (see Table 1). Thus, if the dark figure of assault is computed on the basis of conventional face-to-face-interviews we would end up with a ratio of 1:1.8 of reported to unreported incidents of assault. In other words, for every ten victims who reported their victimization to the police, there are eighteen additional victims who did not. If, however, victimizations identified in the drop-off were considered as well, this ratio would increase to 1:3.7. Consequently, the usual interview procedures of victim surveys lead to a clear underestimation of the amount of assaults not reported to the police.

Summary and Discussion

Research strategies and interview techniques employed in most victim surveys until today lead to a heavy underestimation of violent crimes, particularly physical violence. This underestimation is caused by the fact that victim surveys are less likely to identify violent victimizations in close relationships, although the victimizing events meet legal criteria of criminal law as well as the operational definition used by the researchers. Furthermore, most of the violent incidents within close relationships which are not reported to survey interviewers had not been reported to the police either. Finally, the results indicate that for individuals living in private households - especially for women - the risk of violent victimization by a closely related offender is far greater than that of violent victimization by a stranger or casual acquaintance. In this regard, both victim surveys and police crime statistics paint a seriously distorted picture of the amount as well as the spatial and social correlates of violent crimes against individuals. As could be shown, the drop-off method combined with instructions focusing on close relationships seems to be one means to overcome this shortcoming of previous victim surveys.

It remains unclear, however, whether the described improvement in measuring violent victimization experiences is caused by a) differences in data collection methods (oral interview Vs written questionnaire), b) the changed focus of questioning (questions about crime Vs questions about family conflicts), or c) an interaction of both. Kury (1994), who compared different methods of data collection, found that written questionnaires are less affected by social desirability. Furthermore, postally screened respondents reported more victimizing incidents than those interviewed orally. However, these results should be interpreted cautiously because of differences in return rates (written questionnaire 48.9%; oral interview 57.8%; see Kury 1994, p.26). Furthermore, these differences could be found for minor victimizations only but not for more serious incidents of personal victimization (cf. Kury & Würger 1993, p. 148). Intrafamily violence, however, is a serious form of personal victimization. Consequently, we conclude that the improvement of measuring victimization in close relationships by the drop-off questionnaire is not only attributable to differences in the mode of interviewing (orally vs. written). As comparisons of the results from the NFVR and the NCS (both conducted orally) reveal, the way a questionnaire is introduced to the respondents is of central importance for their categorizing and memorizing of victimizing events. We suppose that in the course of a survey on criminal victimization both aspects, (a) the introduction of questions on intrafamily violence as unrelated to crime but related to family conflict, and (b) a change from the oral to the written mode of questioning, will help to improve the respondents' recall and, at the same time, will increase their willingness to report the incidents recalled to the researcher. Thus, the interaction of both factors probably produced the results reported here. Only one of them might not be sufficient to adequately identify victims of violence in close relationships in a criminological victim survey.

The results described here might have considerable implications for some other areas of criminological research as well. First when correlations between *fear of crime* and *criminal victimization* are calculated on the basis of face-to-face-interviews only, they are likely to be rather low. This, however, might be attributable to a methodological artifact resulting from the fact that those forms of victimization which are typical for elderly people and for women (i.e. victimizations in close relations) more often remain undetected by this conventional research approach. Second, and in line with this, the so-called *fear-victimization-paradox* which states that women as well as elderly people have a low risk of criminal victimization while exhibiting relatively high levels of fear might be nothing but the consequence of a conceptual failure of conventional interview procedures which are not suitable to identity victims of violence by closely related offenders, thus erroneously treating them as "non victims". In the light of these considerations, we would recommend that further victimological research should adopt methods that are better suited to take all forms of violent incidents into account - whether outside or inside close relationships - in order to achieve valid conclusions about the amount and the development of crime as well as about its causes and consequences.

References

Biderman, A.D. (1975). Victimology and victimization surveys. In I. Drapkin & E. Viano (Eds.), *Victimology: A new focus. Vol. III: Crimes, victims, and justice* (pp. 153-169). Lexington, MA: Lexington.

Fattah, E.A. (1993). Research on fear of crime: some common conceptual and measurement problems. In W. Bilsky, C. Pfeiffer & P. Wetzels (Eds.), *Fear of Crime and Criminal Victimization* (pp. 139-157). Stuttgart: Enke.

Gottfredson, M.R. (1986). Substantive contributions of victimization surveys. In M. Tonry & N. Morris (Eds.), *Crime and Justice, an annual review of research, Vol. 7* (pp. 251-287). Chicago: University of Chicago Press.

Heidensohn, F.M. (1991). Women as perpetrators and victims of crime - A sociological perspective. *British Journal of Psychiatry, 158*, 1045-1058.

Kury, H., & Würger, M. (1993a). Opfererfahrung und Kriminalitätsfurcht. Ein Beitrag zur Viktimisierungsperspektive. In G.K. Kaiser & H. Kury (Eds.), *Criminological research in the 1990's*, (pp. 411-462). Freiburg: MPI.

Kury, H. (1994). Zum Einfluß der Art der Datenerhebung auf die Ergebnisse von Umfragen. *Monatsschrift für Kriminologie und Strafrechtsreform, 77* (1), 22-33.

Kury, H., & Würger, M. (1993). The influence of the type of data collection method on the results of the victim surveys. In A.A. del Frate, U. Zvekic & J.J.M. van Dijk (Eds.), *Understanding crime, experiences of crime, and crime control* (pp. 137-152). Rome: UNICRI.

Lynch, J.P. (1993). The effects of survey design on reporting in victimization surveys - The United States experience. In W. Bilsky, C. Pfeiffer & P. Wetzels (Eds.), *Fear of Crime and Criminal Victimization* (pp. 159-186). Stuttgart: Enke.

Mayhew, P. (1993). Reporting Crime to the Police. In W. Bilsky, C. Pfeiffer & P. Wetzels (Eds.), *Fear of Crime and Criminal Victimization* (pp. 139-157). Stuttgart: Enke.

Mayhew, P., & Maung, N.A. (1992). *Surveying crime: findings from the 1992 British Crime Survey.* Home Office Research and Statistics Department: Research Findings No. 2. London: HMSO.

Schneider, H.J. (1993). *Einführung in die Kriminologie.* (3. Aufl.) Berlin: de Gruyter.

Schneewind, K. A. (1991). *Familienpsychologie.* Stuttgart: Kohlhammer.

Smith, M. D. (1994). Enhancing the quality of survey data on violence against women: a feminist approach. *Gender & Society, 8 (1),* 109-127.

Sparks, R.F. (1981). Surveys of victimization - an optimistic assessment. In M. Tonry & N. Morris (Eds.), *Crime and Justice, an Annual Review of Research, Vol. 3* (pp. 1-60). Chicago: University of Chicago Press.

Straus, M.A. (1990). Measuring intrafamily conflict and violence: The Conflict Tactics (CT) Scales. In M.A. Straus & R.J. Gelles (Eds.), *Physical violence in American families* (pp. 29-47). New Brunswick: Transaction Publishers.

Straus, M.A., Gelles, R.J., & Steinmetz, S. (1980). *Behind closed doors.* Garden city: Anchor/-Doubleday.

Straus, M.A., & Gelles, R.J. (1990). How violent are American families? Estimates from the national family violence resurvey and other studies. In M.A. Straus & R.J. Gelles (Eds.), *Physical violence in American families* (pp. 95-131). New Brunswick: Transaction Publishers.

Weis, J.G. (1989). Family violence research methodology and design. In L. Ohlin & M. Tonry (Eds.), *Family violence. Crime and Justice: A review of research*, Vol. 11, (pp. 117-162). Chicago: University of Chicago Press.

Wetzels, P. (1993). Victimization experiences in close relationships: Another blank in victim surveys. In W. Bilsky, C. Pfeiffer & P. Wetzels (Eds.), *Fear of Crime and Criminal Victimization* (pp. 245-267). Stuttgart: Enke.

Wetzels, P., Greve, W., Mecklenburg, E., Bilsky, W., & Pfeiffer, C. (1995). *Kriminalität im Leben alter Menschen.* Stuttgart: Kohlhammer.

Yllö, K. A. (1993). Through a feminist lens: gender, power, and violence. In R.J. Gelles and D.R. Laseke (Eds.). *Current controversies on family violence*, (pp. 47-62). Newbury Park: Sage.

The Victim's Experience and Fear of Crime.
A Contribution to the Victimization Perspective

Helmut Kury

Introduction

Along with the rapid development of social scientifically based victim surveys, the dread of crime has emerged as a key concept richly meriting further scientific investigation. With the flourishing of national crime surveys especially in the United States but also in Europe, as for example in Great Britain, large data sets have become available for examining social scientifically not only such criminological questions as the knowledge and experience of the people regarding criminality but also their fear of offenders and other related issues (cf. *Herbert & Darwood* 1992, p. 145).

In the United States since the 1960s the discovery of the fear of crime through social scientific victims research has led to an intensive discussion of this problem, which also incidentally has stimulated an almost inconceivable outpouring of scientific publications (*Clemente & Kleinman* 1976; *Hartnagel* 1979). "Fear of crime has been a concern of national politics since the late 1960s" (*McConnell* 1989, p. 17). The fear of crime has been recognized in the course of the last 30 years as a unique and important problem (*Williams & Dickinson* 1993, p. 33). "Fear of crime has become a well-studied phenomenon. This is not to argue that it is now well understood. Some have argued that the complexities are such that it may never be" (*Herbert & Darwood* 1992, p. 150). Thus, *Garofalo* (1981) presumed from a scientific standpoint that fear of crime research will be continued indefinitely.

The origin of the fear of crime on the basis of being victimized rests on the seriousness of the victimization itself. It also depends upon the conditions in which the victims themselves live and ultimately upon their personality. The way in which victimization affects the victim cannot be determined only by victimization itself. The psychological impact of victimization is a complex psychological event whose surface up to now has barely been scratched. Even if the study of victimization and its effects on the fear of crime has only just begun, without taking into account key variables (as is very often the case), these studies as a rule have made little difference. Thus, for example the intensity of the victimization (its seriousness and frequency) has often not been assessed. But the seriousness of the victim's experience is a key factor in the development of the fear of crime. From the fact that serious victimizations are fortunately relatively rare, we can immediately conclude that urban fear of crime, which is very well established, is traceable to only a small part to the experience of becoming a victim. Conversely, however, it does not follow that serious victimization experiences have no influence on the fear of crime. Still, despite this background it is true that the victimization perspective has not been refuted.

Recent Research into the Victim's Perspective

The greatest part of the literature we have examined found a more or less moderately positive relationship between earlier victimization and a fear of crime. This connection has been proven in many empirical studies. Nevertheless, most authors still stress that this relationship should not be overestimated (cf. *Reiss* 1982; *Sparks et al.* 1977). This relationship at least between serious victimization and fear of crime is still plausible (*Marshall* 1991, p. 99).

Some researchers have found a slight to negligible relation between victim experience and fear of crime (cf. *Hartnagel* 1979; *Braungart et al.* 1980; *Smith & Huff* 1982; *Akers et al.* 1987; *Belyea & Zingraff* 1988; *Smith & Lab* 1991). *Smith* and *Hill* (1991, p. 217) found that a violent victimization alone is no predictor of offender fear but that victimization by property crimes does reveal a relationship with fear.

Other studies, however, have discovered a meaningful and even impressive relationship between previous victimization and fear of offenders. In this regard *Biderman et al.* (1967, p. 126) report overall in their investigation in Washington DC somewhat stronger fear of crime among victimized Black men, although *Lavrakas* (1982) reported only a slight effect of victimization on the fear of offenders in the same group. On the other hand, *Balkin* (1979) stresses that earlier experience as a victim is a determinant of the fear of offenders and reinforces thereby the perspective of victimization (cf. also *Clemente & Kleinman* 1976; *Lawton & Yaffe* 1980; *Lee* 1983; *Krannich et al.* 1989; *Tyler* 1980; *Lindquist & Duke* 1982; *Stafford & Galle* 1984). According to him the victims of offenders are not only more anxious than non-victims but they are also more cautious (cf. also *Yin* 1981; *Furstenberg* 1971; *Lavrakas* 1982).

According to *Maxfield* (1984, p. 7) the type of victimization generally has a particular impact on the fear of crime. Thus, several studies show a positive relationship between selected crimes and the fear of offenders.

In recent years, studies linking victimization and a general fear of crime have been distinguished by increasing methodological sophistication, which was prompted by the methodological criticism of the earlier studies. Thus, for example, the effects of intervening variables on the relationship have been taken increasingly into account. Moreover, via such refined investigations a relationship between fear of crime and previous victimizations could be shown, although in most cases the correlations were still only moderate.

Our own Investigations

Basic hypothesis

In several studies we examined the relationships between the type (for example, the seriousness and frequency) of victimization as it affected fear of crime. On the basis of the research results we formulated the following hypothesis:

Victims of criminality have more fear of crime than non-victims, although the differences are sure to be moderate. Specifically, victims of serious crimes (burglary and personal crimes, for example) have more fear of crime than victims of less serious crimes (for example, non-personal crimes). Further, victims who have had multiple victimizations have more fear of crime than those who were victimized only once. These differences remain after controlling for such intervening variables as sex, age, level of urbanization, and income.

Random samples and operationalization

We tested our hypothesis on a variety of data sets. The first worldwide International Crime Survey (ICS) was carried out in 1989 when the Criminological Research Unit at the Max Planck Institute for Foreign and International Criminal Law (MPI) headed the research in West Germany. This ICS was conducted altogether in fifteen countries scattered all over the world. Twelve countries in Europe were accompanied by the United States, Canada, and Australia. Data gathering took place in all countries during the first half of 1989. It included without exception telephone surveys and, with some exceptions, personal interviews (cf. *van Dijk et al.* 1990, p. 140). The sample size in all countries was between 1,000 and 2,000 randomly selected respondents, with the exception of Poland where only 500 people were surveyed and the questionnaire was restricted to the capital, Warsaw, and in West Germany where 5,000 interviews were attempted due to the previously discussed interest of the MPI. Detailed information of the first ICS is found in *van Dijk et al.* (1990; see also *Kury* 1991; 1993).

In order to limit the study as well as the expenses, it was only possible to gather limited information on the fear of crime. The two most important items were the questions "Please try to remember the last time you went out after nightfall. Have you ever avoided certain places or streets in order to prevent something from happening to you?" as well as "What is your estimate of the probability that during the next twelve months someone will attempt to break into your house or apartment? Is it very likely, possible or very unlikely?"

The ICS 1989 was repeated three years later (1992) by the same research unit following nearly the same method (cf. *van Dijk & Mayhew* 1992; *del Frate et al.* 1993). The procedure as well as the method of data collection were adopted almost completely. With regard to the operationalization of the fear of crime, the following standard item was included additionally in the ICS 1992: "How safe do you feel if you go out alone in your area after nightfall? Do you feel very safe, rather safe, rather unsafe, very unsafe?" Therefore, we are able to consider this item along with the two items on fear of crime from the ICS 1989 when researching the relationship between victimization experience and fear of crime.

Regarding the extent of data collection, the ICS 1992 included many more countries than the ICS 1989. Data are available from thirteen countries and, in addition, from 13 cities in various countries. In all, data from 26 different regions (countries or cities) are at hand. As in the ICS 1989, the sample size in the countries ranges between 1,000 and 2,000 persons. In eight out of the thirteen countries a minimum of 2,000 interviews were conducted. Approximately 1,000 interviews were generally carried out in the cities which, as a rule, are situated in developing nations or countries presently coping with considerable economic and social problems. Six out of the thirteen countries (ICS 1992), i.e. almost one half, were already included in the ICS 1989, thus allowing a comparison over a period of three years. These countries are Australia, Belgium, England/Wales, Finland, Canada and The Netherlands. In the ICS 1989, Poland was represented by its capital Warsaw only. In the ICS 1992, new participating countries are the states of the former Czechoslovakia, Estonia, Georgia (part of the former USSR), Italy, New Zealand and Sweden. France, Northern Ireland, Norway, Scotland, Switzerland, Spain and the United States, all of which participated in the ICS 1989, did not join in three years later, generally for financial reasons. Germany did not participate in the ICS 1992; extensive victim data from Eastern and Western Germany, however, are available from 1990 which are mostly comparable with the results of the ICS 1992, since the questionnaire of the German study was adjusted to that of the ICS 1992 (cf. *Kury* 1993). The data of the German study of 1990 are also taken into account in our evaluations.

Along with the data of the ICS, it would be well to evaluate and report on the data sets of the two German victim studies. Thus, in 1990, the MPI together with the criminalistic-criminological research team of the German Federal Bureau of Criminal Investigation (BKA) directed the first greater German-German victim study (G-G 1990) after the reunification of the two German nations (cf. *Kury et al.* 1992). This study focused on victimizations among those who were at least 14 years old regarding the same 11 criminal domains as the ICS in order to permit close comparisons of results from both studies. Data collection proceeded via personal interviews with 5,000 East German and 2,000 West German residents.

Finally, in 1991/1992, the Criminological Research Unit of the MPI, along with specialists of legal science at the University of Jena, conducted a large comparative victim study between Jena and Freiburg (FR-J 1991/92). In this study, persons aged 14 and up were questioned in detail about their victimizations regarding the same 11 crimes. Random samples were selected for each city, totalling 3,463 in Freiburg and 2,196 in Jena. Data was collected in Freiburg exclusively via mailed questionnaires, but in addition in Jena a small group also received personal interviews.

It is often argued that an influence of victimization on fear of crime can be expected especially in the case of serious and/or repeated victimizations. Thus, we examined the relationships with regard to seriousness of crime on one hand and frequency of victimizations on the other. As to seriousness of crime, we divided the victimizations indicated in our survey into three categories: 1. Non-contact crimes. They generally do not involve direct contact between offender and victim, the victimization is rather mild, or the victim is not offended personally, and the offender does not invade the victim's privacy. The following crimes belong to this category: Theft of vehicles, theft from vehicles, car vandalism, theft of motor-bicycles, theft of bicycles, theft in all other cases when the victim did not carry the stolen object with her or him (the object was not stolen violently). 2. Burglary, including attempted burglary. With regard to the impact on the development of fear of crime, burglary seems to be a serious crime insofar as the offender did invade/try to invade the victim's privacy resulting in a considerable feeling of insecurity as some studies could prove. 3. Contact crimes. Here, a direct contact between offender and victim occurred, the victim was confronted directly with assault or threats. Naturally, the victim is most likely to feel very unsafe. The following crimes belong to this category: Robbery, theft (when the victim did carry the stolen good with her or him, the object was stolen violently), sexually motivated crime/sexual assault or threats. We presume that the first crime category involves fewer feelings of insecurity and anxiety than the second or third categories. We do not expect differences between the second and third category regarding feelings of insecurity since we estimate the impact on fear of crime to be rather similar.

Statistical data evaluation

Significance tests between the single categories were obtained by multivariate variance analyses. The variables sex, age, income and size of area (level of urbanization) were always controlled.

Results

Avoiding certain places after nightfall may be considered an indicator of the dimension of the fear of crime. Persons with a great deal of fear of crime are likely to avoid places that they consider dangerous, especially when it is dark outside. No less than 11 (65%) of the 17 statistical comparisons calculated from the data of the ICS 1989 and G-G 1990 relating to the categories non-victims versus victims are statistically significant or highly significant. For the ICS 1992, a total of 26 corresponding statistical comparisons were calculated, of which no less than 21 (81%) are statistically significant and 17 (65%) even highly significant. The difference is always similar: victims more frequently avoid certain places after nightfall than non-victims. In part, there are differences by country: in France, for example, 35.6% of the victims respond in this pattern as opposed to only 22.6% of the non-victims, for Spain the figures are 34.9% and 20.4%, respectively, for Germany (former federal states) 52.2% and 37.4% and for the new federal states 50.9% and 38.8%. A comparison with the ICS 1992 reveals similarly clear differences. The statistically non-significant differences, too, with the exception of Poland (Warsaw) and Slovenia (Ljubliana) are similar: victims always show stronger tendencies to avoid certain places than non-victims.

Moreover, the statistical comparisons reveal that - with the exception of India/Bombay and Uganda/Kampala, i.e. two cities - the victimization experience does not have the heaviest impact on fear of crime in any of the countries compared. In most countries of our comparison, sex, as was expected, and often also the size of residence have a heavier impact. The city surveys - here the single comparisons naturally did not take into account the size of the place of residence, as only the data referring to a single city were compared and thus, as to size of residence, there exists no variance - revealed that, in addition to victimization experience, particularly income and partly also age influence avoidance behavior after nightfall.

As to the differentiation according to seriousness of crime, the non-victims and non-contact victims as well as the victims of burglary surveyed in the ICS 1989, with the exception of the German studies, do not reveal any statistically significant differences. In the ICS 1992, non-contact victims in Australia, Georgia and Italy show a statistically significant higher tendency to avoid certain places after nightfall than non-victims. This study revealed a statistically higher value for Finland, Italy, Poland, India/Bombay and Tanzania/Dar es Salaam regarding victims of burglary as opposed to non-victims. With respect to the comparison between non-victims and non-contact victims, the ICS 1989, however, proved nine out of the 17 comparisons (53%), i.e. more than one half, to be statistically significant (ICS 1992: statistical significance of 14 out of 26 comparisons (54%)). Again, the victims of contact crimes show stronger avoidance tendencies than non-victims.

These findings are confirmed if we look at the frequency of victimizations and their impact on avoidance tendencies. In the ICS 1989 and the G-G 1990, 12 (71%) out of 17 statistical comparisons are significant/very significant. In the ICS 1992, no less than 20 (77%) out of 26 comparisons are statistically (highly) significant. There is, again with the exception of Warsaw, also regarding non-significant differences, almost the same picture everywhere: victims are more likely to avoid certain places after nightfall than non-victims, and: The number of victimizations correlates with the tendency to avoid places which seem to be dangerous.

In six countries (Australia, Belgium, England/Wales, Finland, Canada and The Netherlands) the ICS was conducted both in 1989 and three years later; a longitudinal comparison of the relationships between victimization and avoidance tendencies here seems to be appropriate. In both studies, the rates for both non-victims and the total number of victims are surprisingly similar in all six countries.

Table 1: Findings related to: "Insecurity at Night alone Outside in the Residence Area"
(Statement: a little bit/very insecure) - Frequency of Different Categories of Seriousness
of Offense, F-and p-Values of Multivariate Variance Analysis (Each Controlled for
Sex(G), Age(A), Income(E), Size of Place of Residence(O)) - ICS 1992

Countries	Non-victims	All victims	Victims of different categories of offense (once or repeatedly/exclusively in the category below)		
			offenses without victim-offender contact	burglary offenses	offenses with victim-offender contact
	% n	% n	% n	% n	% n
Australia	31.7 (802)	34.9 (1204)	30.6 (304)	45.5 (154)	30.4 (56)
Belgium	16.9 (770)	22.5 (715)	18.0 (294)	28.3 (53)	28.2 (46)
former Czechoslovakia	40.6 (717)	45.5 (1124)	34.7 (314)	52.4 (63)	61.1 (103)
England / Wales	33.2 (765)	34.5 (1236)	28.8 (358)	41.8 (134)	36.5 (74)
Estonia	50.0 (442)	49.1 (558)	40.0 (105)	61.3 (62)	46.9 (30)
Finland	15.5 (861)	20.7 (794)	12.9 (286)	25.9 (58)	22.0 (127)
Georgia [1]	78.6 (724)	85.7 (671)	86.2 (134)	83.1 (130)	90.4 (125)
Italy	28.9 (922)	40.1 (1102)	35.4 (368)	43.1 (123)	45.3 (75)
Canada	21.0 (934)	22.1 (1218)	19.2 (354)	15.2 (79)	31.9 (66)
New Zealand	39.4 (798)	41.1 (1250)	37.8 (299)	42.7 (157)	37.3 (59)
The Netherlands	21.0 (716)	22.1 (1284)	18.0 (399)	30.0 (70)	26.3 (57)
Poland	36.3 (856)	52.0 (1177)	38.4 (276)	52.9 (172)	60.8 (204)
Sweden	12.9 (746)	14.4 (961)	11.4 (349)	11.0 (64)	17.0 (65)

[1] *Size of place of residence not included in the variance analysis, not examined*

Table 1: Continuation

Countries	Non-victims/ victims (altogether)		Non-victims / victims of different offense categories (significances)					
			non-victims/ victims of offense without contact		non-victims/ victims of burglary		non-victims/ victims of offense with contact	
	F - value p =		F - value p =		F - value p =		F - value p =	
Australia	11.596 .001	OGAE	.017 .896	OGAE	7.289 .007	OGAE	.158 .691	OGAE
Belgium	7.775 .005	OGA	.236 .627	OGA	3.661 .056	OGA	2.639 .105	OG
former Czechoslovakia	5.818 .016	OG	.020 .880	OG	3.263 .072	OGA	10.550 .001	OG
England / Wales	3.496 .062	OGAE	.104 .747	OGAE	1.474 .225	OGAE	7.217 .007	OGAE
Estonia	.394 .530	OGA	.000 .998	OGA	.742 .389	OGA	.032 .858	OGA
Finland	28.443 .000	OGAE	1.447 .229	OGAE	2.168 .141	OGAE	7.945 .005	OGAE
Georgia [1]	31.730 .000	G	16.647 .000	G	6.118 .014	G	13.256 .000	G
Italy	29.622 .000	OGA	6.806 .005	OGA	9.828 .002	OGA	5.962 .015	OGA
Canada	1.712 .191	OGAE	.056 .813	OGAE	.038 .845	OGAE	4.702 .030	OGAE
New Zealand	6.511 .011	OGAE	0.534 .465	OGA	4.649 .031	OGA	.009 .923	OGA
The Netherlands	4.832 .028	OGAE	.432 .511	OGA	4.750 .030	OGA	.491 .484	OGAE
Poland	21.848 .000	OGA	.755 .385	OGA	11.915 .001	OGA	9.676 .002	OGA
Sweden	11.623 .001	OGAE	2.849 .092	OGAE	.003 .957	OGAE	3.568 .059	OGAE

[1] *Size of place of residence not included in the variance analysis, not examined*

With regard to the relationship between seriousness and frequency of victimization as well as avoidance tendencies, the six countries clearly correspond in essential results. This confirms the fact that the derived findings have remained constant over the 3-year period.

The results mentioned above are upheld by the findings regarding the estimation of the probability of burglary within the next twelve months. It is obvious that persons who estimate the probability of being victimized by burglary as rather high feel more unsafe and fearful than persons who estimate a lower probability. After all, burglary is a serious crime generally evoking fear, since the offender invades the victim's privacy. With respect to the difference between non-victims and victims on the whole, the ICS 1989, G-G 1990 and FR-J 1991/92 revealed that no less than 17 (89%) out of the 19 calculated significance tests are statistically significant/very significant. In the ICS 1992, 24 (92%) of the 26 calculated significance tests are statistically significant. As expected, the estimation of the probability of being victimized by burglary correlates more clearly with previous victimization experience than with the tendency to avoid certain places after nightfall. The differences are of the same nature: victims estimate the probability of victimization by burglary to be higher than non-victims.

It is surprising that previous victimizations have the strongest impact on the estimation of the probability of burglary in numerous comparisons - especially in comparisons between non-victims and victims on the whole. We can say that, irrespective of sex, age, size of residence and income, a previous victimization incident represents the most distinct factor in leading victims to expect further victimizations by burglary.

This fact is confirmed if we differentiate the comparison between victims and non-victims according to the number of previous victimizations. In the ICS 1989, G-G 1990 and FR-J 1991/92, no less than 17 (89%) out of the 19 statistical comparisons are significant or very significant; in the ICS 1992, 24 (92%) out of 26 statistical comparisons are significant. With the exception of Warsaw which holds a special position in this connection, also, the differences are statistically not significant only for Switzerland and in the ICS 1992 for Belgium and South Africa/Pretoria; their tendency, however, is the same as in the remaining countries. Estimations of the probability of being victimized by burglary are surprisingly homogenous: they are higher for victims as opposed to non-victims and rise in accordance with the number of victimizations.

The two items discussed so far recorded the respondents' avoidance behavior (the avoidance of certain places after nightfall) as well as estimations of the risk of future victimization (burglary), whereas the question monitoring "feelings of insecurity alone in the dark near the place of residence" (standard item) merely records the emotional aspects of fear of crime. Even if we take into account the problematic nature of this standard item, it can be expected that some aspects of fear of crime are recorded. Accordingly, this item has been applied in research on fear of crime during the past and to this day. At the MPI in Freiburg, studies on the validity of this item with regard to the recording of fear of crime are currently being conducted. There are, however, no results available yet (cf. *Kury* 1994). The standard item was not included in the ICS 1989, but was in the ICS 1992. Thus, the results derived from this item additionally are available for this study. The results from this item confirm the findings mentioned above as far as the relationships between feelings of insecurity after nightfall in the place of residence and the (seriousness of the) victimization is concerned. Twenty-two (77%) out of twenty-six comparisons between victims and non-victims show statistical significance, and the differences meet our expectations: victims express stronger feelings of insecurity after nightfall in the place of residence than non-victims.

The correlation of the seriousness of previous victimization (non-contact victims, burglary, contact victims) with feelings of insecurity in the place of residence after nightfall could also be confirmed to a large extent. As expected, however, some country and city-related patterns can be observed. For example, in Brazil/Rio de Janeiro, India/Bombay and Slovenia/Ljubliana, victims of previous non-contact crimes express the strongest feelings of insecurity when going out after nightfall in their place of residence, which may be due to the typical structure of criminality in these cities. As is known, criminality in cities is structured differently than criminality in less urbanized regions. In general, however, feelings of insecurity increase in accordance with the seriousness of previous victimizations, in particular if we compare non-contact crimes with burglary (see Table 1). This finding is also confirmed if we take the frequency of victimization as a standard for the level of seriousness (see Table 2).

A significant difference in feelings of insecurity depending on the number of earlier victimizations can be observed in 20 (77%) of the 26 countries or cities. In this connection, we have to bear in mind that, as expected, an increase in feelings of insecurity does not hold a linear relationship with an increase in the number of victimizations. However, persons with multiple victimizations regularly express stronger feelings of insecurity.

Information on how often persons think of being victimized in the future also indicates fear of crime. As already mentioned, the corresponding item is included only in the questionnaire of the German-German survey of 1990 and the Freiburg-Jena study 1991/1992. Thus, comparisons have to be limited to these two surveys, although they are very large and representative. Both studies yielded identical results for the new federal states as well as for the former federal states: victims more frequently think of being victimized (anew) than non-victims. The differences are statistically highly significant for all comparisons. Moreover, the greater the seriousness of the previous victimization, the more frequently the respective persons think of being victimized again. Mostly victims of serious crimes (burglary and contact-crimes) more frequently think of future victimizations. It must be noted, though, that the impact of previous victimizations is not predominant. Sex, partly age, size of place of residence and income are variables with a heavier impact; with respect to their impact, earlier victimizations rank third or in part even fourth. Nevertheless, along with the above variables, they contribute to an increased preoccupation with future victimizations.

This result is backed up when compared with the number of previous victimizations. The latter obviously correlates with the thought of future victimizations. Only the variable sex has an even stronger impact throughout.

Table 2: Findings related to: "Insecurity at Night alone Outside in the Residence Area"
(Statement: a little bit/very insecure) - Frequency of Victimization, F-and p-values of
Multivariate Variance Analysis (each controlled for G, A, E, O) - ICS 1992

Countries	Non-victims	Victims (frequency of victimization)				
		1	2	3 and more		
	% n	% n	% n	% n	F - value p =	
Australia	31.7 (802)	35.0 (514)	33.8 (331)	35.7 (359)	5.825 .000	OG AE
Belgium	16.9 (770)	20.6 (393)	21.3 (192)	30.0 (130)	4.491 .004	OG A
Former Czechoslovakia	40.6 (717)	43.1 (503)	44.2 (335)	51.4 (286)	2.438 .063	OG
England / Wales	33.2 (765)	32.9 (566)	33.3 (334)	38.4 (336)	1.907 .126	OG AE
Estonia	50.0 (422)	48.0 (204)	52.0 (171)	47.6 (183)	.140 .936	OG A
Finland	15.5 (861)	17.0 (471)	21.8 (192)	32.1 (131)	17.453 .000	OG AE
Georgia[1]	78.6 (724)	86.4 (413)	84.7 (157)	84.2 (101)	10.899 .000	G
Italy	28.9 (922)	38.3 (566)	37.1 (315)	48.4 (221)	10.967 .000	OG A
Canada	21.0 (934)	20.2 (500)	19.6 (341)	27.7 (377)	2.442 .063	OG AE
New Zealand	39.4 (798)	39.2 (515)	40.2 (321)	44.2 (414)	4.563 .003	OG AE
The Netherlands	21.0 (716)	20.2 (526)	23.1 (386)	23.4 (372)	2.520 .056	OG AE
Poland	36.3 (856)	48.7 (667)	52.8 (299)	61.2 (211)	9.020 .000	OG A
Sweden	12.9 (746)	12.1 (479)	15.4 (273)	18.2 (209)	6.244 .000	OG AE

[1] *Size of residence not included in the variance analysis, not examined*

The last comparison deals with feelings of safety when going out alone in the dark. The wording of this item comes closest to that of the standard fear item. Moreover, as it was contained exclusively in the two German-German studies - with the exception of the ICS 1992 - any comparison must be restricted to these surveys. Tables 3 and 4 contain the results of the statistical analysis. All statistical comparisons between non-victims and victims are highly significant. In this connection, too, the variable sex constantly has a clearer impact than previous victimization. All victims compared have stronger feelings of insecurity than non-victims when going out alone after nightfall. A differentiation according to single crime categories regularly shows a correlation between feelings of insecurity and the seriousness of the crime, in particular with respect to burglary. Feelings of insecurity increase along with the number of victimizations (see Table 3). The differences are always highly significant statistically. These results, too, indicate an impact of victimization and its seriousness on fear of crime.

Table 3: Findings related to: "Feeling of Safety at Night Outside Alone" (Statement: quite insecure, very insecure/a little bit insecure, very insecure) - Frequency of Victimization, F-and p-values of Multivariate Variance Analysis, (each controlled for G, A, E, O; at the Freiburg-Jena-Study the Size of Place of Residence was constant)

Countries/ studies	Non-victims	Victims (frequency of victimization)				
		1	2	3 and more		
	%	%	%	%	F - value	
	n	n	n	n	p =	
Germany (former FRG) 1990	19.4 (1362)	27.6 (421)	37.9 (153)	37.6 (85)	17.852 .000	GO
Germany (former GDR) 1990	29.9 (3575)	38.4 (1010)	46.7 (285)	48.2 (110)	20.594 .000	GO
Freiburg 1991/1992 (Germany)	39.8 (1983)	43.2 (827)	46.5 (400)	51.6 (223)	14.617 .000	G
Jena 1991/1992 (Germany)	67.1 (1281)	68.0 (571)	72.7 (227)	71.1 (97)	3.484 .015	GA

Our investigations and statistical calculations yielded the essential result that the se-riousness of victimization influences the victim's feelings of insecurity and fear of crime. More serious victimizations and an increasing number (non-contact crimes, burglary, contact crimes; single or multiple victimization) usually result in higher rates of avoidance behavior, of the estimated probability of being victimized by burglary and of feelings of insecurity when going out alone after nightfall. Focusing on the crime categories we determined an increase in the indicators of fear above all from non-contact crimes to burglary, followed, in turn, by a decrease from the latter to contact crimes. This might be due to the fact that victims of burglary develop stronger feelings of insecurity and fear of crime than victims of contact crimes. This result might, however, also indicate that some victims of contact crimes are offenders simultaneously. We know from criminological research that particularly offenders in the category of contact crimes (e.g. physical injury, robbery, assault or threat) are inevitably also victimized themselves frequently. In these cases, the victimization results from the fact that the risk of being victimized is deliberately disregarded by the offending persons and/or that these persons - in general young male adults - are prepared to take risks and thus do not avoid victimogenic situations. Persons accept the risk of being victimized, e.g., if they intend to commit crimes and/or if they want to frequent certain places or crowds.

Table 4: Findings related to: "Feeling of Safety at Night Outside Alone" (Statement: quite insecure/very insecure) - Frequencies of Different Categories of Seriousness of Offense, F-and p-values of Multivariate Variance Analysis, (each controlled for G, A, E, O; at the Freiburg-Jena-Study the Size of Place of Residence was constant)

Countries	Non-victims	All-victims	Victims of different offense categories (once or repeatedly/ exclusively in the category below)		
			Offenses without victim-offender-contact	Burglary offenses	Offenses with victim-offender-contact
	%	%	%	%	%
	n	n	n	n	n
Germany (former FRG) 1990	19.4 (1362)	31.3 (659)	25.1 (307)	38.9 (36)	32.8 (61)
Germany (former GDR) 1990	29.9 (3575)	40.9 (1405)	35.2 (781)	53.6 (84)	49.1 (108)
Freiburg 1991/1992 (Germany)	39.8 (1983)	45.4 (1450)	40.0 (593)	59.3 (145)	38.2 (89)
Jena 1991/1992 (Germany)	67.1 (1281)	69.5 (895)	68.7 (489)	69.8 (43)	56.4 (39)

Countries	Non-victims/ all victims	Non-victims / victims of different offense categories (significances)		
		non-victims/ victims without contact	non-victims/ victims of burglary	non-victims/ victims of offenses with contact
	F - value p =	F - value p =	F - value p =	F - value p =
Germany (former FRG) 1990	44.275 GO .000	8.203 GO .004	11.198 GAO .001	8.163 GOE .004
Germany (former GDR) 1990	50.428 G .000	9.306 GEO .002	17.300 GOE .000	11.785 GAO .001
Freiburg 1991/1992 (Germany)	36.831 G .000	7.173 GAE .007	15.299 GA .000	1.345 GAE .246
Jena 1991/1992 (Germany)	6.978 GA .008	3.117 GAE .078	.075 GAE .784	1.282 GAE .258

As all data records exclusively concerned victim surveys, we have no information on crimes committed by the interviewed persons themselves. In the German-German victim survey of 1990 (old federal states), though, we collected information on illegal drugs as well as on the attitude towards the police. The Freiburg-Jena victim survey of 1991/1992 also yielded information on illegal drug experience, on perceptions of social factors as causes of crime and on victimization prevention strategies. We believe that this kind of information may indicate if victims are possibly involved in a crime-prone marginal group. To this end, we examined the data of both the German-German victim survey of 1990 (old federal states) and the Freiburg-Jena victim survey of 1991/1992 in an additional evaluation in order to assess the difference in these additional variables for victims of contact crimes with high fear rates on the one hand and low fear rates on the other hand. We started from the hypothesis that seriously victimized persons with low fear rates are more likely to frequent crime-prone scenes than persons with high fear rates.

For the purpose of this extra evaluation we constructed the new category "victims of serious contact crimes" by excluding victims of petty crimes. This new category includes only persons who were victimized at least once by robbery and/or assault and/or by multiple pickpocketing within the surveyed period of time. The German-German survey included only victims of *violent* robbery (i.e. not merely of threat). This differentiation could not be realized for the Freiburg-Jena study due to missing information. Pickpocketing was not included in the Freiburg-Jena victim survey, either, consequently this item was excluded from our category also. In both studies, victims of sexually motivated crimes were also excluded, because, as a rule, the level of seriousness of the victimization could not be established (serious sexual crime or simple "groping"). Due to this rigid selection of victims of serious contact crimes, only a relatively small number of persons were inevitably left, which, in turn, renders statistical comparisons rather difficult. For this reason our statistical calculations merely represent a first approach to this undoubtedly interesting issue.

All persons victimized seriously by contact crimes were categorized according to the standard fear item ("feelings of insecurity when going out alone in the area of residence after nightfall") into the two subgroups "safe" (ratings for this item: "very safe" and "rather safe") and "unsafe" (ratings for this item: "rather unsafe" and "very unsafe"). Chi^2-Tests were effected in order to examine the differences between victims of contact crimes, the remaining victims and non-victims. An examination of the differences with respect to sociodemographic variables such as schooling, training, professional status (in particular unemployment) and income did not reveal any significant differences among the categories (victims of contact crimes, the remaining victims, non-victims) except for differences which were to be expected on account of the age distribution (e.g., higher number of students among young age groups). Significance tests (chi^2) were conducted with respect to all four groups (persons seriously victimized by contact crimes expressing moderate or strong feelings of insecurity, the remaining victims, non-victims) on one hand and separately regarding the categories of persons seriously victimized by contact crimes expressing moderate or strong feelings of insecurity on the other side. Due to low case numbers with respect to persons seriously victimized by contact crimes - a problem which frequently occurs in victim surveys involving seriously victimized persons - the findings derived from our survey may therefore only be considered a first indication of relationships and ought not to be overinterpreted.

In the German-German victim survey as well as in the Freiburg-Jena victim survey the differences achieved for all variables are highly significant over all victim groups, which means that victims of serious contact crimes feeling rather safe tend to consider the acquisition of drugs easy, to know more persons acquainted with drugs, to observe drug use and trafficking more often and not to take action such as informing the police (German-German victim study), as opposed to those feeling rather unsafe, the remaining victims and non-victims. Also, as expected before the background of our results, we find the largest number of persons with their own drug experience among the "serious victims/safe" (Freiburg-Jena victim survey). Consequently, 84.2% of the category "serious victims/safe", 72.4% of the remaining victims and 60.5% of the non-victims consider it "rather easy" to procure illegal drugs. Over half (55.9%) of the "serious victims/safe" know other persons with drug experience (remaining victims: 23.9%; non-victims: 10.6%); 33.9% have observed drug use and trafficking (10.4%; 4.9%); 33.9% do not take any action upon having observed drug trafficking (18.1%; 16.3%); and 30.8% have own drug experience (16.3%; 7.5%).

A comparison between the categories "serious victims/safe" and "serious victims/unsafe" also revealed statistical significance for the majority of derived differences with regard to drug-related variables, implying that clearly more "serious victims/safe" know persons with drug experience than "serious victims/unsafe" do (55.9%: 31.8%; $p = .03$). Furthermore, more "serious victims/safe" have observed persons using or dealing with illegal drugs (33.9%: 27.3%; $p \leq .05$), with a clearly lower proportion reacting by informing the police (44.1%; 68.2%); finally, many of them are drug addicts themselves (22.0% : 4.5%; $p \leq .05$). In the above category the Freiburg-Jena study, too, contained more persons with drug experience compared to "serious victims/unsafe" (30.8% : 6.3%; $p = .000$).

It can hence be concluded that clearly more persons with their own drug experience and also drug addicts belong to the group "serious victims/safe" than the remaining victim categories, such as in particular the category "serious victims/unsafe". Problems of drug acquisition inevitably compel most drug consumers and especially drug addicts to commit further, theft and property-related crimes. As expected, this victim category seems to consist largely of persons living on the fringe of society, persons who are involved in drug and crime-related problems and are understandably likely to be victimized frequently but who simultaneously act also as offenders.

They will also inevitably develop ambivalent or negative attitudes towards the police and the authorities, a fact which our survey is able to prove. "Serious victims/safe" most clearly reject the statement that the police are friendly and helpful (37.9%; "serious victims/unsafe": 31.8%; other victims: 18.0%; non-victims: 15.3%). Simultaneously, they expressly agree that they are glad to have nothing to do with the police (81.0%; 77.3%, 73.5%; 65.4%). Finally, they mostly reject the well-known German saying "the policeman is your friend and helper" (48.3%; 36.4%; 30.5%; 20.4%).

Furthermore, the Freiburg-Jena victim survey shows that "serious victims/safe" approve least of their neighbors (55.1%; 65.6%; 78.2%; 84.4%). In consideration of what we already know about "serious victims/safe" (see above), it can be supposed that this disapproval is quite mutual.

Although the differences between the categories "serious victims/safe" and "serious victims/unsafe" with regard to the attitude towards the police are not significant, they meet our expectations without exception. "Serious victims/safe" in contrast to "serious victims/unsafe" consider the police to be less friendly and helpful, they are rather glad not to have anything to do with the police and reject the saying "the policeman is your friend and helper". With respect to approval of neighbors the differences are statistically significant for both categories ($p = .02$). "Serious victims/safe" express clearly more disapproval of their neighbors than "serious victims/unsafe" (44.9% : 34.4%).

There are also clear differences between both categories as to avoidance tendencies and mental preoccupation with victimization. Only 23.7% of the "serious victims/safe" indicate that they occasionally avoid streets and places after nightfall, whereas non-victims (32.2%) and the remaining victims (48.1%; $p \leq .001$) show stronger avoidance tendencies. The difference between "serious victims/safe" and "unsafe" (23.7%: 63.6%; $p \leq .000$) is extraordinarily striking. Also   as to mental preoccupation   with possible victimization, we found considerable differences between these two categories. Despite previous serious victimization only 5.2% of the persons belonging to the category "serious victims/safe" are very often/often mentally preoccupied with a possible further victimization. Rates for non-victims (4.5%) and other victims (7.1%) are similar. In contrast, 33.3% of the "serious victims/unsafe" are mentally preoccupied with further victimization ($p \leq .000$). These findings of the German-German study are fully corroborated by the Freiburg-Jena study, where 3.8% of the "serious victims/safe" admit being mentally preoccupied with further victimization (very) frequently (non-victims: 4.6%, remaining victims: 7.1%, "serious victims/unsafe" even 20.3%). The differences are always highly significant ($p \leq .001$). Moreover, we have to take into consideration the reverse order of identical items in both studies which guarantees independence from primacy effects. Only 15.6% of the "serious victims/safe", but 50.8% of the "serious victims/unsafe" ($p \leq .000$), 29.5% of the remaining victims and 27.8% of the non-victims ($p \leq .001$) tend to avoid certain streets when going out after nightfall. The category "serious victims/safe" is characterized by low fear rates; they are even lower than those indicated by non-victims.

The findings as to measures of self-defense when going out are also very interesting. At least 25.7% of the "serious victims/safe", but only 9.2% of the "serious victims/unsafe" ($p \leq .00$), 10.2% of all other victims and finally 6.3% of the non-victims ($p \leq .001$) are prepared for self-defense. This implies that every fourth person of the category "serious victims/safe" is prepared in self-defense or, in other words, automatically starts from a high risk of being victimized. Obviously many persons of that victim category deliberately expose themselves to victimogenic situations and thus try to protect themselves by taking defense measures.

The results on the item "how far is the attitude towards criminality dependent on one's own social experience with offending or being victimized, with delinquent neighbors etc." finally indicate the categories' characteristics. As expected, 46.9% of the "serious victims/safe" state that their attitude towards crime is predominantly or strongly dependent on social experiences, obviously because these persons are mostly either living in crime-prone and dangerous places or, as mentioned above, maintaining contact with persons belonging to this scene. The corresponding rates only equal 35.8% ($p = .02$) for "serious victims/unsafe", 28.4% for the remaining types of victims and 18.1% ($p \leq .001$) for non-victims.

Focusing on the German-German survey we note that, as expected, 81.4% of "serious victims/safe", but only 36.4% ($p \leq .001$) of "serious victims/unsafe" are men with respect to the demographic variables for the individual groups. The percentage for the remaining types of victims amounts to 51.3% and to 46.8% ($p \leq .001$) for non-victims. In the Freiburg-Jena survey, differences in sex between both categories of seriously victimized persons are not so distinct (89.0%: 53.1%; p $\leq. 000$). Victims of serious crimes who express rather strong feelings of safeness are mostly men, while those who feel rather unsafe are mostly women. We know from victimological research that women express stronger fear of crime than men. Thus the results of our study are not surprising. It can be assumed that sex also has a certain but, in our opinion not determining, moderating influence on the above-described differences. We were unable to departialize the factor "sex" on account of the low case rates. The generally uniform relationships described above cannot be solely explained by differences in sex in the individual categories. Approval of the saying "I am glad not to have anything to do with the police", e.g. constantly diminishes from the categories "serious victims/safe" to non-victims: 81.0%, 77.3%, 73.5%; 65.4%, respectively. The percentages of men within the same categories, however, clearly vary: 81.4%; 36.4%; 51.3%; 46.8%. This is not exclusively true for these variables, but also for others. There is, however, an undeniable need for larger, more differentiated, surveys of this issue. Our study can only provide some suggestions.

As already mentioned, the small sample size does not permit a final examination of the impact of sex by subdividing the groups even further. For the German-

German victim survey, however, we additionally examined the differences with respect to the individual items for the male group separately. Due to the low number of cases (particularly as concerns the subgroup "serious victims/unsafe") the findings can merely be regarded as tendencies. On the whole, these results derived with respect to the differences between the two male groups "serious victims/unsafe" and "safe" completely confirm the findings. In part, the differences derived for men are even more distinct. e.g., 81% of the monitored male victims of serious crimes who feel rather safe consider the possibility of acquiring drugs to be rather easy ("unsafe" group: 71%), 56% know persons with drug experience ("unsafe" group: 25%), 35% have observed drug use or trafficking ("unsafe" group: 29%), 40% did not take any action upon this observation ("unsafe" group: 25%), 23% judge themselves to be addicted to drugs ("unsafe" group: 13%), 17% avoid streets and places after nightfall ("unsafe" group: 63%) and 4% (very) often think of a possible victimization ("unsafe" group: 43%). Regarding attitudes towards the police, 60% of the male "serious victims/safe" agree with the statement that police officers are friendly and understanding ("unsafe" group: 63%), 83% are glad if they have nothing to do with the police (75%) and 49% consider the police a friend and helper (71%). With respect to habits of going out 31% of the male victims of serious contact crimes feeling safe state that they go out every day ("unsafe" group: 38%), 34% go out once a week (38%). Focusing on age we found that 25% of the male "safe" victims are younger than 25 ("unsafe" group: 25%), 35% are aged between 25 and 34 (25%) and 17% between 35 and 44 (13%).

This shows that the findings seem to shift only insignificantly, if at all, if the factor "sex" is left out of consideration; in part they even move towards our starting hypothesis.

With respect to age the group "serious victims/safe" consists mostly of younger persons. One quarter (23.7%), e.g., are below 25 years of age and more than one half (59.3%) are aged 34 at the most. In the Freiburg-Jena study the proportions are even more extreme: 44.3% are below 25 years of age and 69.8% are aged 34 at the most. With regard to the remaining groups we found the average age to be higher, in particular as concerns the group "serious victims/unsafe".

Given these circumstances, it is no surprise that the number of unmarried persons living alone is comparatively high within the group of "serious victims/unsafe" (40.7%; Freiburg-Jena study, unmarried: 57.4%). The same applies to the frequency of going out at night. Still one quarter (25.4%) of the "serious victims/unsafe" go out every day (Freiburg-Jena study: 22.9%).

In our view, in spite of the still open issues of this preliminary statistical analysis which suffers from low case numbers, it can be concluded from the findings that victim groups are by no means homogeneous but rather remarkably different. We tried to demonstrate this by the example of serious victims of contact crimes. With respect to the realm "fear of crime", the victims, on the one hand, clearly differentiate as expected and not surprisingly according to sex and age, two results that are known from earlier surveys. On the other hand, our findings also indicate that involvement in crimes and antisocial, criminogenic surroundings, apart from sex and age factors, reduces the fear of being victimized. Falling victim to a crime becomes calculable, at least partially, when the respective persons deliberately and consciously frequent such surroundings as they are pursuing other goals that appear attractive or important; they try to protect themselves by, for example, focusing on defensive measures. Given theses circumstances, an actual victimization incident will not evoke as much fear because the risk of falling victim to a crime was consciously taken.

On the whole we are able to regard the above hypothesis as confirmed given the above-described extensive findings.

References

Akers, R.L., LaGreca, A.J., Sellers, C., & Cochran, J. (1987). Fear of crime and victimization among the elderly in different types of communities. *Criminology, 25*, 487-505.

Balkin, S. (1979). Victimization rates, safety, and fear of crime. *Social Problems, 26*, 343-358.

Belyea, M.J., & Zingraff, M.T. (1988). Fear of crime and residential location. *Rural Sociology, 53*, 473-486.

Biderman, A.D., Johnson, L.A., McIntre, J., & Weir, A.W. (1967). *Report on a pilot study in the district of Columbia on victimization and attitudes toward law enforcement.* Washington, DC: Government Printing Office.

Braungart, M.M., Braungart, R.G., & Hoyer, W.J. (1980). Age, sex, and social factors in fear of crime. *Sociological Focus, 13*, 55-66.

Clemente, F., & Kleinman, M.B. (1976). Fear of crime among the aged. *British Journal of Criminology, 22*, 49-62.

van Dijk, J.J.M., & Mayhew, P. (1992). *Criminal victimization in the industrialized world. Key findings of the 1989 and 1992 International Crime Surveys.* The Hague: Ministry of Justice.

van Dijk, J.J.M., Mayhew, P., & Killias, M. (1990). *Experiences of crime across the world. Key findings from the 1989 International Crime Survey.* Deventer, Boston: Kluwer.

Del Frate, A.A., Zvekic, U., & van Dijk, J.J.M. (Eds.) (1993). *Understanding crime. Experiences of crime and crime control.* Rome: UNICRI.

Furstenberg, F.Jr. (1971). Public reaction to crime in the streets. *American Scholar, 40*, 601-610.

Garofalo, J. (1981). The fear of crime: Causes and consequences. *Journal of Criminal Law and Criminology, 72*, 839-859.

Hartnagel, T. (1979). The perception and fear of crime: Implications for neighborhood cohesion, social activity, and community effect. *Social Forces, 58*, 176-193.

Herbert, D.T., & Darwood, J. (1992). Crime awareness and urban neighbourhoods. In: D.J. Evans, N.R. Fyfe & D.T. Herbert (Eds.), *Crime, policing and place. Essays in environmental criminology* (pp. 145-163). London, New York: Routledge.

Krannich, R.S., Berry, E.H., & Greider, T. (1989). Fear of crime in rapidly changing rural communities. A longitudinal analysis. *Rural Sociology, 54*, 195-212.

Kury, H. (1991). Victims of crime - Results of a representative telephone survey of 5.000 citizens of the former Federal Republic of Germany. In: G. Kaiser, H. Kury & H.-J. Albrecht (Eds.), *Victims and criminal justice* (pp. 265-304). Freiburg: Eigenverlag Max-Planck-Institut.

Kury, H. (1993). Germany. In: A. Alvazzi del Frate, U. Zvekic & J.J.M. van Dijk (Eds.), *Understanding Crime. Experiences of Crime and Crime Control* (pp. 537-545). Rome: UNICRI.

Kury, H. (1994). *Zusammenhang zwischen dem psychologischen Konstrukt Angst und der in der Viktimologie erfaßten Verbrechensfurcht.* Freiburg: unpublished manuscript.

Kury, H., & Würger, M. (1993). Opfererfahrung und Kriminalitätsfurcht. Ein Beitrag zur Viktimisierungsperspektive. In: G. Kaiser & H. Kury (Eds.), *Kriminologische Forschung in den 90er Jahren. Criminological research in the 90's* (pp. 411-462). Freiburg: Eigenverlag Max-Planck-Institut.

Kury, H., Dörmann, U., Richter, H., & Würger, M. (1992). *Opfererfahrungen und Meinungen zur Inneren Sicherheit in Deutschland.* BKA-Forschungsreihe Bd.25. Wiesbaden: BKA.

Lavrakas, P. (1982). Fear of crime and behavioral restrictions in urban and suburban neighborhoods. *Population and Environment, 5,* 242-264.

Lawton, M., & Yaffe, S. (1980). Victimization and fear of crime in elderly public housing tenants. *Journal of Gerontology, 35,* 768-779.

Lee, G. (1983). Social integration and fear of crime among older persons. *Journal of Gerontology, 38,* 745-750.

Lindquist, J., & Duke, J. (1982). The elderly victim at risk: Explaining the fear-victimization paradox. *Criminology, 20,* 115-126.

Marshall, C.E. (1991). Fear of crime, community satisfaction and self-protective measures: Perceptions from a midwestern city. *Journal of Crime and Justice, 14,* 97-121.

Maxfield, M.G. (1984). *Fear of crime in England and Wales.* London: HMSO.

McConnell, E.E.H. (1989). *An examination of relationships among fear of crime, crime seriousness, crime victimization, and crime precaution behaviors.* Ann Arbor.

Reiss, A. (1982). How serious is serious crime? *Vanderbilt Law Review, 35,* 541-585.

Smith, B.L., & Huff, C.R. (1982). Crime in the country: The vulnerability and victimization of rural citizens. *Journal of Criminal Justice, 10,* 271-282.

Smith, G., & Lab, S.P. (1991). Urban and rural attitudes towards participating in an auxiliary policing crime prevention program. *Criminal Justice and Behavior, 18,* 202-216.

Smith, L.N., & Hill, G.D. (1991). Victimization and fear of crime. *Criminal Justice and Behavior, 18,* 217-239.

Sparks, R.F., Glenn, H.G., & Dodd, D.J. (1977). *Surveying victims.* Chichester: Wiley.

Stafford, M., & Galle, O. (1984). Victimization rates, exposure to risk, and fear of crime. *Criminology, 22,* 173-185.

Tyler, T. (1980). Impact of directly and indirectly experienced events: The origin of crime-related judgments and behaviors. *Journal of Personality and Social Psychology, 39,* 13-24.

Williams, P., & Dickinson, J. (1993). Fear of crime: Read all about it? The relationship between newspaper crime reporting and fear of crime. *Part. J. Criminol., 33,* 33-56.

Yin, P.P. (1981). Fear of crime as a form of chronic apprehension: The elderly in an urban setting. Unpublished doctoral dissertation, University of Minnesota/Minneapolis.

Part III
Witnesses and Expert Testimony

Child Witnesses: Lying About Something Heard[1]

Marisa Alonso-Quecuty, Estefanía Hernández-Fernaud and Laura Campos

Introduction

For centuries the law has been mistrustful of the statements offered by child witnesses (see Dent & Flin, 1992, and Goodman & Bottons, 1993 for a review). This mistrust has been justified on the grounds that a child is incapable of differentiating fact from fantasy.

In sexual abuse cases this erroneous stereotype has resulted in three new erroneous concepts:

1. The lack of confidence in the morality of children. Within this conceptual framework, children's stories about sexual abuse have usually been interpreted as conscious lies incited by immoral parents.

2. Mental disturbance. This is the second obstacle that has traditionally hindered the acceptance of child evidence. That a child should tell of having been the victim of sexual abuse was enough to consider him or her mentally ill. It was not taken into account that the abuse was precisely the cause of behavioural disorder.

3. Erotic seduction. The psychoanalytical approach of the child as a seducer was, for decades, a barrier at the moment of accepting their testimonies in cases of abuse.

The first of these arguments, that the child is capable of lying encouraged by his or her parents and other adults, is present in written works by European doctors and psychologists at the end of the nineteenth century and at the beginning of the twentieth, and is supported by anecdotal explanations of isolated cases (see: Goodman, 1984). Nevertheless there has not much research into the analysis of child witnesses' testimony when they remember an event that they did not see but only heard. We are interested in the study of this specific situation: testimonies given by children but elaborated by adults. Our *first aim* is to study the testimony about facts that our subjects did not see but only listened to an audio recording. We study the exact quantity of accurate information (accuracy) that witnesses (children and adults) provide in two types of situations: (a) when they are asked to give true statements and (b) when they are asked to give

[1]   Research supported by the Spanish Ministry of Education and Science.

false ones of a heard event. Likewise, we study the quantity of non-real information (confabulation) given spontaneously by children as well as adults in their statements.

The process of discrimination between memories derived from external experiences (reality) and memories internally generated (fantasy) has been named reality-monitoring by Johnson and Raye (1981). According to these authors, there are qualitative differences between both types of memories: On the one hand, externally generated memories contain more contextual information, more sensorial details and more semantic information about the event. On the other hand, internally generated memories possess more information about cognitive operations. Developmental research in this field shows that children are less competent than adults in two processes of reality-monitoring: a) when they are asked to discriminate between something that they have done and something that they have only imagined doing (Johnson & Foley, 1984), and b) when they must decide if they have said something or if they have only imagined saying it (Foley, Johnson & Raye, 1983). In our opinion, both situations are similar to those where children must decide if something has happened or if they only listened to others telling them that it happened.

In previous works we have connected reality-monitoring to true and false statements (Alonso-Quecuty, 1990, 1992, 1996). Indeed, we found that true statements contained more contextual and sensorial information, the criteria proposed by the hypothesis of reality-monitoring for externally generated memories, and that false statements contained more internal information, the criteria expected for internally generated memories. Our *second aim* is to determine if this pattern is followed when witnesses remember an event that they did not see but only listened to on an audio recording.

In the paper we presented at the last European Conference (Alonso-Quecuty, 1996) we compared the statements (true and false) given in a real context with those given in the laboratory context. Results demonstrated that the similarity between both types of statements (true and false) and both types of memories (real and imagined) is greater when the context is real while telling the truth or lying when a video sequence is concerned minimises the difference between the statements and both types of memories. Our *third aim* is to study the differences between these three experimental conditions: to witness a "realistic" event, to watch a video sequence of the same event in a laboratory, and to listen to an audio recording description of that event.

From the results obtained from the developmental research on reality-monitoring and also from our own results from previous research, we formulated the following *hypotheses*:

H1: There will be significant differences in reality monitoring criteria between true and false accounts in the listening condition. These differences will be affected by the experimental condition (witnessing, watching and listening).

H2: There will be significant differences between children's and adults' accounts in the listening condition. These differences will be affected by the experimental condition (witnessing, watching and listening).

Method

Subjects

The sample was composed of 50 people: 25 children (average age 9) and 25 adults (average age 21).

Material and apparatus consisted of tape recorders and audio cassettes.

Design and procedure

The subjects received instructions to listen to an audio recording description of an event. This event was the same used in our previous research (Alonso-Quecuty, 1996): A professor parked her car in the campus in front of where the witnesses were standing around. One of the windows was left half open. Minutes later, two youths approached the car, looked through the windows, opened the car through the half-open window and took out a box which had been left on the back seat. An adult witness, who was actually a confederate, questioned their right to carry the box off and, after a short argument, the situation was cleared up when the youths identified themselves as students of the car owner who, in turn, had asked them to take the box to the laboratory. This audio recorded version was elaborated from the script that had been drawn up of how the event actually appeared in the video recording.

In a second phase of the experiment, subjects were asked to give two verbal versions of what they had listened: their recall of the event listened (real/true version) and an elaborate (imagined/false) version of this event.

There were three independent variables: the Age of the witnesses (children and adults), the Truth Value of their statements (true and false), and the Experimental Condition (Real: witnessing, Video: watching and Acoustic: listening).

The dependent variables were: a) the accuracy of the statements, b) the degree of confabulation that they contained and c) the differentiating dimensions of externally/internally generated memories according to the hypothesis of reality-monitoring: contextual information, sensorial details and internal information.

Results and Discussion

The evaluation of the criteria of Accuracy and Confabulation was carried out using the script of the event as actually appeared in the audio recording. Accurate information was considered to be that given by the individual which corresponded to some of the elements in the script. Information which did not appear in the recording and which was totally elaborated by the subjects was considered to be confabulation. After carrying out the transcription of the statements, two especially trained judges classified separately, in a protocol drawn up to the effect, the content of each statement according to the criteria of reality-monitoring. The agreement between both judges was greater than 80%.

Afterwards, a series of one- and two-ways ANOVAS were carried out with the statements given by the subjects after listening to the audio recording event.

Accuracy

True statements contained more accurate information than the false ones ($F(1, 43) = 110.22$; $p < .01$). Adults demonstrated greater accuracy than children ($F(1, 43) = 6.49$; $p < .01$).

Confabulations

False statements showed more confabulated information than the true ones ($F(1, 43) = 39.59$; $p < .01$). Adults contaminated their statements with more confabulations than children ($F(1, 43) = 15.35$; $p < .01$).

Regarding the criteria of reality-monitoring:

Contextual Information

In the true statements there was more contextual information than in the false ones ($F(1, 43) = 11.48$; $p < .01$). Adults gave more contextual information than children ($F(1, 43) = 4.99$; $p < .05$).

Sensorial details

True statements presented more sensorial details than the false ones ($F(1, 43) = 22.50$; $p < .01$). Adults gave more sensorial information than children ($F(1, 43) = 8.13$; $p < .01$).

Internal information

We only found one significant effect of the Age variable ($F(1, 43) = 11.96$; $p < .01$). Adults' statements presented more internal information than those of children.

When we carried out new analyses of variance, introducing the Type of Experimental Condition: Real (witnessing), Video (watching) and Acoustic (listening) as an independent variable, both Accuracy and Confabulation were sensitive to this new variable.

Accuracy

Statements were more accurate ($F(1, 43) = 38.97$; $p <.01$) in the Acoustic condition than in the Video and the Real condition. A significant Experimental Condition x Value of Truth interaction was obtained as well ($F(1, 43) = 29.13$; $p < .01$) in the statements. While false statements were not very sensitive to this condition, true statements made in the Acoustic condition contained five times the confabulation rate obtained in a real context.

Confabulations

Statements were contaminated with more confabulations ($F(1, 43) = 12.67$; $p < .01$) in the Acoustic condition than in the Video and in the Real conditions. Furthermore a significant Experimental Condition x Age interaction was obtained ($F(1, 43) = 11.11$; $p < .01$). Adults were more sensitive to the Experimental Condition than children; their statements presented an important level of contamination in the Acoustic condition. Finally, a significant Experimental Condition x Age x Value of Truth interaction was obtained as well ($F(1, 43) = 3.94$; $p < .02$). Once more the Acoustic condition presented the highest level of contamination.

Regarding the reality-monitoring criteria, the Experimental Condition affected them in different ways.

Contextual information

The statements contained more contextual information ($F(1, 43) = 4.43$; $p < .01$) in the Acoustic and Video conditions than in the Real one. Furthermore, a significant Experimental condition x Age interaction was obtained ($F(1, 43) = 3.18$; $p < .05$). In the Acoustic condition the differences between true and false statement were significant. Finally a significant Experimental Condition x Age x Value of Truth interaction was obtained as well ($F(1, 43) = 4.76$; $p < .01$). Once again, the Acoustic condition presented the highest level of contextual information.

Sensorial details

We found a significant effect of the Experimental Condition ($F(1, 43) = 15.75$; $p < .01$). Statements made about the audio recording and about the video sequence contained more sensorial details than the others made in the Real condition. Two significant Experimental Condition x Age (F(1, 43) = 3.36; p < .05) and Experimental Condition x Value of Truth interactions (F(1, 43) = 6.50; p < .01) were also obtained. Adults gave more sensorial details in their accounts than children, especially in the Acoustic condition; furthermore, true statements contained more sensorial information than the false ones, again especially in the Acoustic condition.

Internal information

Regarding this variable, only a significant effect of the Experimental Condition was found (F(1, 43) = 6.34; p < .01). But on this occasion, the tendency was the opposite of that obtained for the previous variables. The statements elaborated by the subjects of the Acoustic condition contained less Internal information than the accounts given in the Video and the Real conditions.

Discussion

Our aims were to study two types of testimony (true and false) about facts that our subjects did not see but only listened to on an audio recording in order to determine: (a) if they followed the pattern expected by the hypothesis of reality-monitoring for externally and internally generated memories respectively, and (b) if there were differences between these statements and those obtained in our previous research carried out in two different Experimental conditions: witnessing a "realistic" event and watching a video sequence of the same event in a laboratory.

We have found that true and false statements have presented, *once again,* the pattern expected by the reality-monitoring hypothesis: true accounts contained more contextual information and more sensorial details than the false ones, which presented more references to internal processes. These results confirmed those obtained in our previous work (Alonso-Quecuty, 1990, 1992, 1996). Moreover we found that statements given by subjects about an event they only listened to were more accurate than those given after witnessing this event, but they were also more contaminated by confabulations than those obtained in more realistic conditions. At this point, we would like point out the absence of significant differences between two Experimental conditions: Video recording and Audio recording and how the significant effects were motivated for the differences between these two conditions and the Real condition, the only one where subjects could be named witnesses.

In relation to the Age, children were less sensitive to the Experimental Condition than adults. Their statements contained similar number of confabulations and had a similar level of accuracy (and contextual information and sensorial details).

These results are congruent with Kosslyn's theory that states that children think in terms of images more frequently than adults do (Kosslyn, Margolis, Barrett,

Goldknopf & Daly, 1990), with their imagination being more similar to an obvious action (Kosslyn, 1980). If they think in terms of mental images, the way they receive the information about the event is not important, because they will always transform this information into pictures. This hypothesis is congruent with our other results: children's accounts contained a low number of references to internal states. Conversely, adults could elaborate two types of memories, one more "visual" and another more "semantic", depending on what type of information they had received (visual, acoustic...). For this reason their statements were more sensitive to the Experimental Condition.

Finally only to point out - once again - the necessity of investigating memory phenomena "as they occur in everyday life instead of in the laboratory" (Hermann & Grunenberg, 1993).

References

Alonso-Quecuty, M.L. (1990). Recuerdo de la realidad percibida vs. imaginada. *Boletín de Psicología, 29*, 73-86.

Alonso-Quecuty, M.L. (1992). Deception' detection and reality-monitoring: A new answer for an old question?. In F. Lösel, D. Bender & T. Bliesener (Eds.): *Psychology and Law: International Perspectives*. Walter de Gruyter. Berlin.

Alonso-Quecuty, M.L. (1996). Detecting fact from fallacy in child and adult witness accounts. In G.M. Davies, S. Lloyd-Bostock, M. McMurray & C. Wilson (Eds.): *Psychology and Law: Advances in Research*. Berlin: De Gruyter.

Baartman, H. (1992). The credibility of children as witnesses and the social denial of the incestuous abuse of children. In Lösel, F, Bender, D, & Bliesener, T (Eds.): *Psychology and Law: International Perspectives*, Berlin: Walter de Gruyter.

Dents, H., & Flin, R. (Eds.) (1992). Children as Witnesses. New York: Johns Wiley and Sons.

Foley, M.A., Johnson, M.K., & Raye, C.L. (1983). Age-related changes in confusion between memories for thoughts and memories for speech. *Child Development, 54*, 51-60.

Foley, M.A., Santini, C., & Sopasakis, M. (1989). Discriminating between memories: Evidence for children's spontaneous elaborations. *Journal of Experimental Child Psychology, 48*, 146-169.

Goodman, G. (1984). Children's testimony in historical perspective. *Journal of Social Issues, 40*, 9-31.

Goodman, G.S., & Bottoms, B.L. (Eds) (1993). *Child Victims, Child Witnesses*. Guilford Press. London.

Hermann, D., & Grunenberg, M. (1993). The need to expand the horizonts of the practical aspects of memory movement. *Applied Cognitive Psychology, 7*, 553-565.

Johnson, M.K., & Foley, M.A. (1984). Differentiating fact from fantasy: The reliability of children's memory. *Journal of Social Issues, 40*, 33-50.

Johnson, M.K., & Raye, C.L. (1981). Reality-monitoring. *Psychological Review, 88*, 67-85.

Kosslyn, S.M. (1980). *Image and mind*, Cambridge, M.A.: Harvard University Press.

Kosslyn, S.M., Margolis, J.A., Barrett, A.M., Goldknopf, E.J., & Daly, P.F. (1990). Age differences in imagery abilities. *Child Development, 61*, 995-1010.

Instructions and Suggestions: Effects on the Amount of Details in Children's Statements

Renate Volbert and Volker Pieters

Introduction

"Suggestion" and "suggestibility" have been defined in various manners (e.g., Gheorghiu, Netter, Eysenck & Rosenthal, 1989). In most definitions, two aspects are regarded as characteristic of suggestion:

- An alteration of a position by an inadequate external stimulus (e.g., Weizenhofer, 1953), and
- a certain uncritical acceptance of the inadequate stimulus, i.e., the unwitting incorporation of information (see Pieters, 1994).

According to these criteria, neither memory errors which result from faulty processing of adequate stimuli, nor conscious deceit are defined as suggestion. Recently, however, Ceci and Bruck (1993a) argued for a more inclusive definition of suggestibility. According to their definition, "Suggestibility concerns the degree to which children's encoding, storage, retrieval, and reporting of events can be influenced by a range of social and psychological factors" (p. 404). This definition implies forms of confabulation, lying and acquiescence to social demands. The authors categorize influences by subtle suggestions, expectations, leading questions, etc., along with conscious alterations of reports induced by explicit bribes, threats, etc. Of course, due examination must be accorded to all forms of influences on children's statements. However, including unconscious memory alterations and conscious distortions of truth together in a single category may not result in a better understanding of the mechanisms underlying false statements (see Steller, Volbert & Wellershaus, 1993). It can be assumed that both groups differ in the manner of delivering their statements, and in the quality of their statements: one group is intentionally deceiving, while the other group is honestly reporting the supposed truth. Based on existing empirical research, one could postulate that misled children mainly respond incorrectly to specific questions but cannot elaborate on the topic when asked to do so (e.g., Goodman, Aman & Hirschman, 1987; King & Yuille, 1987; see also Cole & Loftus, 1987). However, recent studies by Ceci and colleagues have shown that misled children are also capable of producing highly detailed, internally coherent narratives (Ceci, 1993). Children who have been coached to intentionally deceive may try to provide as much information as possible, but children who lie without an adult having directed them to do so may not be able to fabricate a coherent statement (see Tate, Warren & Hess, 1992).

Possible differences in the quality of statements - depending on whether they are suggested, instructed, confabulated or based on real experiences - are of prime importance for assessing the validity of individual statements (see Steller & Köhnken, 1989). To date, it is the differences in statement quality between actually experienced and confabulated accounts which have chiefly been researched, whereas the quality of statements based on actual experiences versus suggested statements has not yet been subjected to comparison (for an overview, see Steller, Volbert & Wellershaus, 1993). In a study conducted to investigate differences between statements about actual experiences and accounts based on either light or heavy coaching, Joffe and Yuille (1992) found that the quality of the statement (as measured by ratings of content criteria) discriminated only between the live event and the lightly coached condition for Grade 4 children; for Grade 2 children, content-criteria scores did not distinguish reports based on experience from those based on either heavy or light coaching.

Most simulation studies which investigate the quality of statements involve children older than 6 years (see Steller, Volbert & Wellershaus, 1993). However, Ceci and Bruck (1993a) have shown that significant age differences in suggestibility appear, "(...) with preschool-aged children being disproportionately more vulnerable to suggestion than either school-aged children or adults" (p. 431). This age group has also consistently been shown to recall fewer details of actually experienced events than older children or adults (see, e.g., Cole & Loftus, 1987; Fivush, 1993). Accordingly, it seems plausible that experience-based accounts of young children are more difficult to distinguish from statements stemming from other sources than reports of older children.

In existing studies, comparisons are generally drawn between accounts based on completely self-experienced events versus completely fabricated statements. In real-life situations, however, one often deals with accounts which are without doubt partly true, but which could be partly instructed or suggested. If a child reports an instance of sexual abuse which took place in her father's bed when she was visiting him the weekend before, this child can in any event provide a vivid picture of the situation - no matter whether abuse actually took place or not. Detecting a fabricated or suggested part of a statement is possibly more complicated than detecting a completely invented or suggested account.

The following study was conducted to investigate whether differences exist in the quality of suggested and instructed parts of statements, versus accounts of the actually experienced events of preschool children. "Quality of statement" is defined here by the number of details reported for the target events. Quantity of details represents one of the general criteria applied in methods for assessing credibility which employ content criteria (Steller & Köhnken, 1989). To operationalize "quantity of details," the number of reported details are counted here, whereas this criterion is normally assessed only on a global basis. We assumed the number of reported details to be highest in the experience-based parts of statements, followed in number by instructed and, finally, by suggested accounts.

To cover "quality of statement" with a more comprehensive form of measure, we currently conduct Criteria-Based Content Analyses on the transcripts of the statements.

Method

Subjects

The participants in this study were 55 children (28 females and 27 males), ranging in age from 4 years and 3 months, to 6 years and 4 months (M = 5.6 years), from two public kindergartens in Berlin. For a number of different reasons (e.g., illness) several children were not present at one of the interview days.

Procedure

During time spent in the kindergarten, the children were shown a clown performance. Control-group children watched a 15-minute show, while children subjected to two experimental conditions saw only a shortened performance. Detailed information on the missing parts was furnished either in passing during a post-event conversation (suggestion condition), or children were provided with detailed information and instructed to claim during the following interview that certain events actually had taken place (instruction condition). It was explained to all children that a friend of the experimenter was unfortunately not able to see the show, and that the friend would come several days later and ask the children what had happened in the performance. As part of the suggestion condition, children were individually told by the experimenter after the presentation that he knew the clown very well, and that he knew that the following events were part of the clown's show. He then described elements which had not actually taken place under that condition. At the end of the conversation, the experimenter asked some misleading questions concerning the suggested elements. In the instruction condition, children were told that the friend who was coming to interview the children often teased the experimenter and that this time she wanted to turn the tables. The experimenter asked the children to fool her friend and to pretend that things happened which actually had not taken place. Afterwards, the experimenter described these elements in detail. During individual conversations, all the children were asked to repeat what they should tell the interviewer-friend. Information which children could not remember was given again.

The experiment was designed such that all children reported at least in part about actually experienced events, since some elements of the show were watched by all children (basic events). Other events were seen only by the control group children (critical events), but were supposed to be mentioned by all subjects. The critical events comprised five elements: three actions by the clown, one action in which both the clown the and children were involved, and one action by the children alone. The critical events were:

1. The clown threw a few *cartons* in the air and
2. Tied one carton with a scarf on her back and pretended that this carton was a *snail's shell*. (Cartons and pretending to be a snail played a key role in the abbreviated performance.)
3. The clown "chased" *soap-bubbles* with a pump and a ball. (In the shortened performance, the clown actually only tried to paint the soap bubbles.)
4. The clown squirted the children with water which came out of a *camera*. (In the shortened performance, the clown actually only took a picture of the children with the camera.)
5. The children themselves changed red tea into blue tea by adding a bit of lemon juice. (In the abbreviated performance, only the clown transformed the tea in this manner.)

Children were individually questioned twice by different interviewers: two days and ten weeks after the performance. Before the second interview, children under the instruction condition were directed to tell this time only what had actually happened at the clown show. Interviewers were trained in the "funnel interview technique" as described by Steller and Boychuk (1992). This interview format is designed to obtain as much information as possible in *free narrative* style; interview questions move from the general to specific as is necessary. Interviews started with a request for a free narrative (e.g., "Tell me about the clown!"), followed by *open-ended questions* (e.g., "Did the clown do anything else?"). Questions became more specific when the child did not spontaneously provide further information. At that point, *cue questions* were typically used to jog the children's memory (e.g., "Did anything happen with a carton?"), followed by more *specific questions* about the details of the event. Finally, *yes/no-questions* were asked (e.g., "Did the clown throw any cartons?"). Interviewers were not informed about the details of the clown's presentation or about the design of the experiment. However, they were instructed to ask about the carton, the snail's shell, the soap bubbles, the camera, the tea, the telephone, and the snail's song (the telephone and snail's song were of importance for the basic events). Interviewers were also provided with information about *basic* and *critical events* which they were told *might* have taken place. With regard to the soap bubbles they were told, for example, that the clown could have painted the soap bubbles, or that she could have chased them with a pump and a ball.

Analyses of data were based on the number of details children reported in the interviews for each *basic* and *critical event*. Accordingly, the number of details for accounts based on actual experience (*basic events* under all conditions and *critical events* in the control group), and for accounts based on errors of commission (*critical events* under the instruction condition and the suggestion condition) were coded. Each syntactic unit representing an action, an actor, an object or a physical trait was coded as one detail (e.g., "*I* have *swallowed* some *blue tea.*" = 4 details). Repeated information was coded only once. Information which did not cover descriptions of the performance (e.g., "I also have a camera like that at home.") was not scored.

Results

Number of details

Analyses of variance revealed no significant differences in the mean number of reported details concerning all *basic events*; this result indicates that subjects under all three conditions did not basically differ in the way in which they reported what they had watched in the performance. As expected, we found significant differences - in the mean number of reported details concerning all *critical events* - between the control condition, on one hand, and the two experimental conditions on the other, for both interviews (F(2, 46) = 22.58; p =.000 and F(2, 45) = 24.57; p = .000, respectively). The mean number of details concerning the *critical events* was higher under the instruction than under the suggestion condition, although the difference was not statistically significant (Table 1). When the mean numbers of details for all basic and all *critical events* were broken down into mean numbers for each basic and each critical event, the same pattern was found: no significant differences for each basic event, but significant mean differences for most *critical events*.

Table 1: Mean Number of Reported Details

	1st interview		2nd interview		
	basic events	critical events	basic events	critical events	
Control N = 15	41.20_a	20.00_a	34.35_a	16.41_a	Control N = 17
Instruction N = 19	36.84_a	7.79_b	29.24_a	6.71_b	Instruction N = 17
Suggestion N = 15	44.73_a	3.47_b	32.21_a	5.21_b	Suggestion N = 14

Within each column different subscripts indicate significant mean differences (p < .05)

As expected, the experimental groups were comprised of children who reported the *critical events* - as well as of children with whom experimental manipulations were not effective and who did not mention the *critical events*. If only those statements were taken into account which contained reports of *critical events*, no significant differences between groups were found (Table 2). The small number of subjects in the experimental groups under this precondition could be responsible for the lack of statistical significance, but the fact that the mean number of reported details was highest in one of the experimental groups for some *critical events* does not support this assumption. The absence of significant differences may be attributed to a floor effect, since the mean number of reported details was also quite low in the control group.

Table 2: Mean Number of Reported Details for Each Critical Event *if Inducement was Effective (Number of Children who Reported about the Event are Given in Parentheses)*

	1st interview					2nd interview					
	Car-ton	Snail shell	Soap bubble	Camera	Tea	Car-ton	Snail shell	Soap bubble	Camera	Tea	
Control	2.54	*5.08*	*3.67*	*5.73*	*5.07*	2.86	*4.00*	3.33	*4.35*	*4.07*	Control
N = 15	(13)	(12)	(12)	(15)	(15)	(14)	(16)	(12)	(17)	(15)	N = 17
Instruction	*3.00*	3.17	3.60	4.55	3.65	3.00	2.69	*4.25*	3.65	3.00	Instruction
N = 19	(8)	(12)	(5)	(11)	(5)	(8)	(13)	(4)	(9)	(2)	N = 17
Suggestion	2.00	3.00	2.33	4.80	0.00	*3.25*	2.33	3.00	3.86	2.00	Suggestion
N = 15	(3)	(5)	(3)	(5)	(0)	(4)	(6)	(5)	(7)	(2)	N = 14

p = n.s.

Time of interview

To analyze the effects of different times of interviewing, t-tests for dependent samples were calculated. T-tests revealed a significant decrease of reported details for *basic events* after ten weeks under all conditions. For the *critical events*, the following pattern was found: a significant decrease in reported details under the control condition, a slight but not statistically significant decrease under the instruction condition, and - in contrast to all other conditions - an increase of reported details under the suggestion condition after ten weeks (Table 3).

Table 3: Mean Numbers of Reported Details for Basic Events *at Both Interviews*

	Basic events				Critical events			
	1st interview	2nd interview	t-value	p	1st interview	2nd interview	t-value	p
Control N = 14	41.00	35.14	1.84	.089	20.43	16.71	2.23	.044
Instruction N = 16	36.63	28.25	3.15	.007	8.19	6.94	.056	n.s.
Suggestion N = 12	45.33	33.08	2.97	.013	3.08	5.33	-2.20	.050

This increase of reported details under the suggestion condition was found for every single critical event, although most of the differences did not approach significance (Table 4).

Table 4: Mean Numbers of Reported Details for Each Critical Event under the Suggestion Condition at Two Interviews (N = 12)

	cartons	snail-shell	soap-bubbles	camera	tea
1st interview	0.33	0.75	0.42	1.58	0.00
2nd interview	1.08	1.17	1.25	1.67	0.17
t-value	-2.02	-0.75	-2.59	-0.13	-1.00
p	.069	n.s.	.025	n.s.	n.s.

The number of children who proved to be resistant to inducements at the first interview became definitely smaller at the second interview (32% vs. 6% under the instruction condition, and 53% vs. 14% under the suggestion condition) (Table 5).

Table 5: Percentage of Children who Reported Critical Events

	Control		Instruction		Suggestion	
	1st interview	2nd interview	1st interview	2nd interview	1st interview	2nd interview
no event	0%	0%	32%	6%	53%	14%
1 - 2 events	0%	5%	21%	53%	27%	57%
3 - 4 events	33%	37%	37%	41%	20%	29%
5 events	66%	48%	11%	0%	0%	0%

Dynamics of the interview

With respect to the dynamics of the interview, we found that almost half of the reported details of the *basic events* at the first interview, and more than one third at the second interview, were provided spontaneously or in response to open-ended questions by the 4- to 6-year-old children. Under the suggestion condition, a general tendency became apparent that the children provided less information spontaneously (Table 6).

Table 6: Percentage of Details for Basic Events *Reported in Response to Different Types of Questions*

	Spontaneous or open-ended question	Cue questions	Specific questions	Yes / no questions
1st interview				
Control (N = 15)	*49.9*	32.3	12.3	5.4
Instruction (N = 19)	*43.4*	28.6	15.5	12.5
Suggestion (N = 15)	40.3	*44.1*	7.8	7.8
2nd interview				
Control (N = 17)	*38.4*	27.1	15.2	19.3
Instruction (N = 17)	*37.3*	29.7	12.4	20.6
Suggestion (N = 14)	35.7	*37.4*	12.2	14.6

Concerning the *critical events*, a similar pattern was found at the first interview (Table 7): control-group children provided about two-thirds, and instruction-group children almost half, of the information spontaneously or in response to open-ended questions - whereas children in the suggestion group recounted most details in response to cue questions. Several subjects under the instruction condition were very keen to tell about *critical events*: their accounts came spluttering out at the very beginning of the interview. No suggested information at all was produced spontaneously or in response to open-ended questions - which agrees with research which indicates that suggested information is recounted in cued form and not as free recall (Goodman, Aman & Hirschman, 1987; King & Yuille, 1987). However, most misled children did provide information in response to cue questions (e.g., "Did anything happen with a camera?") which still represents a quite open format.

Table 7: Percentage of Details for Critical Events *Reported in Response to Different Types of Questions*

	Spontaneous or open-ended question	Cue questions	Specific questions	Yes / no questions
1st interview				
Control (N = 15)	*36.7*	29.9	11.7	21.7
Instruction (N = 19)	*41.3*	28.1	4.5	26.0
Suggestion (N = 15)	0.0	*64.4*	17.8	17.8
2nd interview				
Control (N = 17)	27.6	*33.3*	8.6	30.5
Instruction (N = 17)	13.4	29.6	13.4	*43.5*
Suggestion (N = 14)	4.3	30.5	0.0	*65.2*

At the second interview, the control group produced most information about *critical events* in response to cue questions. Since control subjects were still able to provide most information on *basic events* in free recall, this trend could be an indicator for a lower level of interest among subjects in the critical compared to the *basic events*. In keeping with the studies mentioned above, details of *critical events* were mainly provided in response to yes/no questions under both experimental conditions. However, in contrast to the first interview, a small amount of suggested information was also provided in free recall. Ceci (1993) has pointed out that children who had been repeatedly misled produced errors in commission in free recall. Indications of similar results can be found in other studies (e.g., Dale, Loftus & Rathbun, 1978; Tobey & Goodman et al., 1992).

Confabulations In 17 out of 97 statements, children added extraneous information to their reports which was not related to experimental manipulation. This occurred under all conditions, and chiefly during the second interview. Five children described in free recall erroneous accounts in great detail. Included were reports of close interaction between the clown and the child. A girl under the suggestion condition, for example, reported that the clown had fallen on her lap and that all the other children had laughed. She continued by describing that the room was very crowded - to the extent that they could hardly breathe - and that they were told to crawl to the clown, who was far away in the room next door, where they were also allegedly directed to crawl. Two confabulated statements at the first interview were probably intentional fabrications, since these instruction-group children did not repeat their stories during the second interview. It is difficult to judge what underlay the other stories - possibly confusion with other similar events such as physical-education classes or theater performances.

Summary

Results show that pre-scholars are able to spontaneously provide a great deal of information about experienced events, even ten weeks after the event, but that they also reveal a vulnerability for statement alterations caused by the influence of others.

The findings support earlier results which indicate that single suggestive influences or simple instructions to provide false information do not have an impact on the statements of most, but of a substantial share, of children (e.g., Goodman & Clarke-Stewart, 1991; Haugaard & Repucci, 1992; Tate, Warren & Hess, 1992). Moreover, if only those statements were taken into account for which manipulations proved to be effective, there were no significant differences in the number of details for *critical events*. This could be an indicator that the quantity of details is not an appropriate criterion in this age-group to distinguish statements about actual experiences from accounts stemming from other sources. The absence of mean differences may be attributed to a floor effect, since pre-school children's reports generally do not contain many details. Because the number of effective experimental inducements was small in our study this hypothesis unquestionably needs further examination.

The two experimental conditions did not differ significantly with regard to the number of reported details for the *critical events*, a finding which supports the assumption of a floor effect. Several children under the instruction condition mentioned the *critical events* for the first time during the second interview, a phenomenon which could reflect non-intentional alterations of their former statements. In future studies, the following could be investigated profitably: whether young children have difficulties in differentiating between memories of what someone else has done, and memories of what someone instructed them to tell about what someone else had done. Recent studies suggest that young children may have difficulties in coping with similarity among sources (see Johnson, Hashtroudi & Lindsay, 1993).

Our results also show that erroneous post-event suggestions significantly increased the number of reported details about the non-events at the second interview, without any additional experimental manipulation between the two interviews. The increase of reported details for *critical events* under the suggestion condition is even more important if it is contrasted with the significant decrease of reported details in the control condition. These results stress the crucial importance of multiple interviews during which suggested information becomes activated and confirmed (see Ceci & Bruck, 1993b). In future studies, the importance of repeated testing in research on the suggestibility of children should always be kept in mind.

It remains an open question whether these findings can be generalized to apply to reports on personally experienced events that involve a child's own body and some degree of distress or embarrassment. However, in contrast to many assumptions, suggestibility effects have likewise been found by studies which examined stressful events and events which include bodily touching (e.g., Ceci, 1993; Peters; 1991).

Results of the Criteria-Based Content Analyses, which are currently being conducted on these interview transcripts, will reveal whether differences exist in the presence of content criteria in the statements - and whether possible differences in turn will allow valid evaluation of accounts as being experienced-based or not.

References

Ceci, S. J. (1993). Cognitive and Social Factors in Children's Testimony. Master lecture presented at the American Psychological Association Meeting, Toronto, August 20, 1993.

Ceci, S. J., & Bruck, M. (1993a). Suggestibility of the child witness: A historical review and synthesis. *Psychological Bulletin, 113*, 403-439.

Ceci, S. J., & Bruck, M. (1993b). Child Witnesses: Translating research into policy. *Social Policy Report, 7 (3)*.

Cole, C. B., & Loftus, E. F. (1987). The Memory of children. In S. J. Ceci, M. P. Toglia & D. F. Ross (Eds.), *Children's Eyewitness Memory* (pp. 178-208). New York: Springer.

Dale, P.S., Loftus, E.F., & Rathbun, L. (1978). The influence of the form of the question on the eyewitness testimony of preschool children. *Journal of Psycholinguistic Research, 7*, 269-277.

Fivush, R. (1993). Developmental perspectives on autobiographical recall. In G. S. Goodman & B. L. Bottoms (Eds.), *Child Victims, Child Witnesses* (pp. 1-24). New York: The Guilford Press.

Gheorghiu, V. A., Netter, P., Eysenck, H. J., & Rosenthal, R. (Eds.) (1989). *Suggestion and Suggestibility: Theory and Research.* New York: Springer.

Goodman, G. S., Aman, C., & Hirschman, J. (1987). Child sexual and physical abuse: Children's testimony. In S. J. Ceci, M. P. Toglia & D. F. Ross (Eds.), *Children's Eyewitness Memory* (pp. 1-23). New York: Springer.

Goodman, G. S., & Clarke-Stewart, A. (1991). Suggestibility in children's testimony: Implications for sexual abuse investigation. In J. Doris (Ed.), *The Suggestibility of Children's Recollections* (pp. 92-114). Washington: American Psychological Association.

Haugaard, J. J., & Repucci, N. D. (1992). Children and the truth. In S. J. Ceci, M. D. Leitchman & M. E. Putnick, *Cognitive and Social Factors in Early Deception* (pp. 29-46). Hillsdale: Lawrence Erlbaum.

Joffe, R., & Yuille, J. C. (1992). Criteria-Based Content Analysis: An Experimental Investigation. Poster presented at the Nato Advanced Study Institute: The Child Witness in Context: Cognitive, Social, and Legal Perspectives, May 20-31, Lucca, Italy.

Johnson, M. K., Hashtroudi, S., & Lindsay, D. S. (1993). Source monitoring. *Psychological Bulletin, 114,* 3-28.

King, M. A., & Yuille, J. C. (1987). Suggestibility and the child witness. In S. J. Ceci, M. P. Toglia & D. F. Ross (Eds.), *Children's Eyewitness Memory* (pp. 24-35). New York: Springer.

Peters, D. P. (1991). The Influence of stress and arousal on the child witness. In J. Doris (Ed.), *The Suggestibility of Children's Recollections* (pp. 60-76). Washington: American Psychological Association.

Pieters, V. (1994). *Beeinflussungen von Kinderaussagen durch Suggestionen und Instruktionen.* Unveröffentlichte Diplomarbeit, FU Berlin.

Steller, M., & Boychuk, T. (1992). Children as witnesses in sexual abuse cases: investigative interview and assessment techniques. In H. Dent & R. Flin (Eds.), *Children as Witnesses* (pp. 47-71). Chichester: Wiley.

Steller, M., & Köhnken, G. (1989). Criteria-Based Statement Analysis. Credibility Assessment of Children's Statements in Sexual Abuse Cases. In D. C. Raskin (Ed.), *Psychological Methods for Investigation and Evidence* (pp. 217-245). New York: Springer.

Steller, M., Volbert, R., & Wellershaus, P. (1993). Zur Beurteilung von Zeugenaussagen: aussagepsychologische Konstrukte und methodische Strategien. In L. Montada (Hrsg.), *Bericht über den 38. Kongreß der Deutschen Gesellschaft für Psychologie in Trier 1992. Band 2.* (S. 367-376). Göttingen: Verlag für Psychologie.

Tate, C. S., Warren, A. R., & Hess, T. M. (1992). Adults liability for children's "lie-ability": Can adults coach children to lie successfully? In S. Ceci, M. D. Leitchman & M. E. Putnick, *Cognitive and Social Factors in Early Deception* (pp. 69-87). Hillsdale: Lawrence Erlbaum.

Tobey, A. E., & Goodman, G. S. (1992). Children's eyewitness memory: Effects of participation and forensic context. *Child Abuse and Neglect, 16,* 779-796.

Weizenhofer, A. (1953). *Hypnotism: An Objective Study in Suggestibility.* New York: Wiley.

Changes in Subtle Hand/Finger Movements During Attempted Deception

Aldert Vrij

Introduction

Liars betray their lies by exhibiting different behavior than truth tellers. However, it remains unclear which behaviors indicate deception. Several meta-analyses have provided evidence that deceiving others is correlated with more speech disturbances (both "ahs" and "non-ahs") and a higher-pitched voice (DePaulo, 1992; DePaulo, Stone, & Lassiter, 1985; Ekman, 1989; Zuckerman, DePaulo & Rosenthal, 1981). But, in particular, the relationship between hand/arm movements and deception remains uncertain. According to DePaulo et al. (1985) and Zuckerman et al. (1981) an increase in hand/arm movements indicates deception, while DePaulo (1992) and Ekman (1989) suggest that a decrease in hand/arm movements indicates deception. Unfortunately, both findings could be explained theoretically. Social psychological literature reveals three main theoretical approaches concerning the relationship between nonverbal behavior and deception: that is, the emotional approach, the control approach and the cognitive approach (Ben-Shakhar & Furedy, 1990; DePaulo et al., 1985; Köhnken, 1989; Zuckerman et al., 1981).

The emotional approach (Davis, 1961; Knapp, Hart & Dennis, 1974; Köhnken, 1989; Riggio & Friedman, 1983) emphasizes that deception evokes physiological arousal. The arousal is a consequence of stress that accompanies deception. The arousal will cause nervous behavior. Indicators of nervous behavior are changes in pitch of voice (usually a high-pitched voice) and an increase in speech disturbances and liveliness (Siegman, 1985).

According to the control approach (DePaulo, 1988; DePaulo & Kirkendol, 1989; Ekman, 1989) liars tend to control their behavior, because they are afraid that their behavior will give their lies away. Although deceivers try to control all of their behaviors, some communication channels are more difficult to control than others. Those channels most difficult to control, the so-called leaky channels (Ekman & Friesen, 1974), expose deceptive intent. People are able to control their face very well. Therefore, gaze behavior, smiling and laughing will not reveal deception. But people are less able to control their voice. Therefore, deception will result in changes in pitch of voice. Finally, it is difficult to control movements. Liars believe that movements will give their lies away. Therefore, they will move very deliberately and tend to avoid those movements not strictly essentially. This results in an unusual degree of rigidity and inhibition.

The cognitive approach (Burgoon, Kelly, Newton, & Keely-Dyreson, 1989; Ekman & Friesen, 1972; Goldman-Eisler, 1968; Köhnken, 1989) emphasizes that deception is a cognitive complexity. Presumably it is more difficult to fabricate a plausible and convincing lie that is consistent with everything the observer knows or might find out than it is to tell the truth. There is evidence to suggest that people engaging in cognitively complex tasks make more speech disturbances (Goldman-Eiser, 1968) and make less hand/arm movements (Ekman & Friesen,1972). The decrease in hand/arm movements is based upon the fact that greater cognitive load results in a neglect of body language, reducing overall animation (Ekman & Friesen, 1972).

The main purpose of the present experiment was to gain insight into the relationship between hand/arm movements and deception. However, for two reasons we examined other nonverbal behavioral aspects as well. First, in that case we could investigate the relationship between hand/arm movements and deception in a broader context; based upon the approaches previously discussed, hand/arm movements seem to form part of a cluster of behaviors, that is, nervous behavior, (overcontrolled) honest behavior or a neglect of behavior. Second, it gave us the opportunity to investigate the relationship between deception and those other behaviors.

The present study differed from previous studies in two respects, that is, (a) a more detailed scoring system of hand/arm movements was used and (b) a baseline was intoduced. Those changes were necessary in order to achieve the goals of this experiment.

A. A more detailed scoring system

In the usual studies a distinction is usually made between the observation of self manipulations (scratching wrists, rubbing one's hands, etc.) and several forms of gestures (illustrators, indicative gestures, non-indicative gestures, etc.). We think that those observations are not as detailed as necessary. If for instance liars indeed behave deliberately, it is likely that they will especially avoid subtle, non-functional movements, like subtle hand and finger movements. Therefore, we decided to include those hand/finger movements as a separate category in our scoring system.

B. Introduction of a baseline

In most deception studies subjects are aware of the aim of the study, that is, to investigate their skills to make a credible impression. This means that also the honest condition is a special situation. Also in this condition people are under suspicion and will be nervous. This makes it difficult to determine if (a) being under suspicion results in honest behavior and (b) stress will cause nervous behavior by comparing the honest and dishonest interviews. More insight can be provided if subjects' behavior in these particular cases will be compared with behavior displayed in situations in which suspicion and stress are absent. By introducing a baseline we intend to create such a situation.

The three approaches previously discussed predict different behavioral differences in case of a comparison between the baseline on the one side and both "interviews" ("honest" and "deceptive" conditions) on the other side. Therefore, several competitive hypotheses are formulated. Based upon the emotional approach we expect nervous behavior in both interviews (changes in pitch of voice, and an increase in speech disturbances, gaze aversion, smiling, laughing, and liveliness, hypothesis 1A). Based upon the control approach we predict honest behavior in both interviews (looking at the conversation partner and a decrease in smiling, laughing, speech disturbances, pitch changes and liveliness, hypothesis 1B). Based upon the cognitive approach we hypothesize an increase in speech disturbances and a decrease in liveliness in both interviews (hypothesis 1C); it is likely that in both interviews subjects need to think with greater effort than in the baseline condition, since subjects have to be more aware in both interviews.

Concerning nonverbal differences between the "honest" and "deceptive" conditions, there seems to be agreement among the theoretical approaches about speech disturbances and pitch of voice. Deception will be associated with an increase in speech disturbances (cf. emotional and cognitive approach, hypothesis 2) and changes in pitch of voice (cf. emotional and control approach, hypothesis 3). With regard to liveliness two competitive hypotheses are possible; based upon the emotional approach we expect an increase in movements during deception (hypothesis 4A), and based upon the cognitive and control approach we predict a decrease in movements during deception (hypothesis 4B).

Method

Subjects

A total of 51 males and 13 females participated in the experiment. All subjects were students at the Vrije Universiteit in Amsterdam. Their average age was 22 years.

Procedure

The experiment was conducted at the university. The experimenter brought the subjects to the interview room. The interviewer (a uniformed police officer) asked the subject to take a seat and to describe their activities from the moment they were asked to participate in this study. The subjects' answer were the baseline in this study. The average length of the baseline was 26 seconds. During the baseline subjects were videotaped. The camera was installed in front of the subject, so subjects knew that they were videotaped[1]. After the answer the subject left the room and went to the experimenter. After a while the experimenter brought the subjects back to the interview room for their first interview. Before doing that he gave some subjects a set of headphones with the request to hide them carefully. In the interview room the police officer asked the subject once again to take a seat and interviewed the subject about the possession of the set of headphones. All interviews were standardized; the police officer asked five questions.

After the first interview the subject left the interview room for a short period of time to either return the set of headphones to the experimenter (if the subject was in the possession of the set of headphones during the first interview) or to receive a set of headphones (if the subject was *not* in the possession of the set of headphones during the first interview). Next the subject re-entered the interview room for the second interview. The second interview was identical to the first one. The average length of the honest interviews was 41 seconds; the average length of the deceptive interviews was 40 seconds. Both interviews were videotaped. In order to determine possible order-effects, 35 subjects received the set of headphones before the first interview, and the other 29 subjects received the set of headphones before the second interview.

Independent variables

Independent variables were (A) the three types of conversations (baseline, honest interview and deceptive interview) and (B) the order in which the honest and deceptive interviews were carried out, that is, (1) baseline, (2) deceptive interview, (3) honest interview or (1) baseline, (2) honest interview, (3) deceptive interview.

Dependent variables

The nonverbal behavior displayed by the subjects was scored in detail by one or two coders, using the videotapes. Scoring systems of gestures, self manipulations, and hand/finger movements were especially developed for this experiment: (1) *the frequency of gestures*: Hand/arm movements designed to modify and/or supplement what is being said verbally (2 coders, $r = .66$, $p<.001$), (2) *the frequency of self*

---

[1]   The baseline had to meet certain requirements. We needed to create a situation that was highly comparable to both interviews but without suspicion and stress. We believed that next to suspicion and stress a third element was inherent to both interviews: subjects knew that they were observed. Therefore, we placed, also in the baseline, the camera visible in front of the subjects in order to let them know that they were observed in this situation as well.

manipulations: scratching the head, wrists, etc. Rubbing one's hands together and fidgeting are not coded as a self manipulation but as hand/finger movements (2 coders, $r =. 65$, $p<.001$), (3) *the frequency of hand/finger movements* (also referred to as hand movements): a hand movement is a movement of a hand without the arm being moved; finger movements are movements of fingers without hands or arms being moved; simultaneous movements of more fingers were scored as one movement, and continuing movements, rubbing one's hands together and fidgeting were scored every two seconds (2 coders, $r = .90$, $p<.001$). Scoring of the other nonverbal behaviors (head movements, trunk movements, foot and leg movements, smiling, gaze aversion, ah speech disturbances, non-ah speech disturbances, pitch of voice) was based upon scoring systems developed by Vrij (1991) and Vrij and Winkel (1991) and will not be discussed here. All these behaviors were scored by two coders; the correlations between these coders varied from $r = .51$ to $r = .94$.

The behavioral scores are based on the average scores of the two coders. Then, the reported duration and frequency of all categories of nonverbal behavior were corrected for the length of the interviews or for the number of spoken words.

Results

To determine behavioral differences a 3 (conversation: baseline, honest interview and deceptive interview) x 2 (order of interviewing: baseline - honest - deceptive or baseline - deceptive - honest) MANOVA was performed. The first factor was a within-subjects factor, the second factor a between-subjects factor. Dependent variables were the eleven patterns of nonverbal behavior. At a multivariate level one significant effect emerged, that is, a main effect for the factor "conversation", $F(22, 228) = 8.78$, $p <.001$. Univariate tests and mean scores are provided in table 1.

Univariate tests (last column) revealed eight significant effects, that is, for hand/finger movements, head movements, trunk movements, foot/leg movements, smiling/laughing, gaze aversion, ah speech disturbances and changes in pitch of voice.

Tukey HSD tests were used to compare group means in determining which differences produced the eight significant univariate F-values. Results are described in superscript in table 1.

A comparison between the baseline and the honest interview (column 1 and column 3) revealed six significant effects. Mean scores indicated that being under suspicion while telling the truth resulted in a decrease in head, trunk, and foot/leg movements, smiling, and gaze aversion and in an increase in changes in pitch of voice.

A comparison between the baseline and the deceptive interview (column 1 and column 5) revealed eight significant effects. Mean scores showed that being under suspicion while lying resulted in a decrease in hand/finger, head, trunk and foot/leg movements, smiling/laughing, gaze aversion and ah speech disturbances and in an increase in changes in pitch of voice.

Table 1: Mean Scores for "Gestures" to "Smiles" Indicate the Frequency of Occurrence per Minute of Speech. Mean Scores for "Gaze Aversion" Indicates the Amount of Seconds per Minute the "Suspect" did not Look at the Police Officer. Mean Scores for "Ah Speech Disturbances" to "Changes in Pitch of Voice" Indicate the Frequency of Occurrence per 10 Spoken Words. Mean Scores (M), Standard Deviations (SD) and F-Values (F) Related to the Three Types of Conversation (Baseline, Honest Interview and Deceptive Interview)

	Baseline		Telling the truth		Deception		
	M	(SD)	M	(SD)	M	(SD)	F(2, 124)
Gestures	4.35^a	(6.9)	3.66^a	(4.5)	4.30^a	(6.4)	.39
Self manipulations	1.39^a	(4.1)	0.60^a	(1.9)	0.39^a	(1.8)	3.02
Hand/finger movements	11.96^b	(15.6)	11.24^b	(14.5)	7.48^a	(11.7)	3.61*
Head movements	28.08^b	(10.5)	20.75^a	(6.7)	21.22^a	(6.8)	34.22***
Trunk movements	9.88^b	(5.8)	6.45^a	(5.3)	6.28^a	(4.9)	16.63***
Foot/leg movements	12.71^c	(11.1)	8.02^b	(8.4)	6.36^a	(7.4)	16.36***
Smiling/laughing	5.15^b	(5.1)	2.36^a	(4.1)	2.13^a	(2.3)	20.89***
Gaze aversion	23.54^b	(10.9)	14.30^a	(9.5)	13.73^a	(9.4)	52.86***
Ah speech disturbances	0.84^b	(0.5)	0.79^b	(0.5)	0.64^a	(0.5)	4.09*
Non ah speech disturbanc.	0.50^a	(0.4)	0.46^a	(0.6)	0.33^a	(0.4)	2.85
Changes in pitch of voice	1.03^a	(1.0)	1.70^b	(1.3)	2.33^c	(1.5)	19.93***

* $p < .05$ ** $p < .01$ *** $p < .001$
Only mean scores with different superscript differ significantly ($p < .05$)

The pattern just described showed that subjects attempted to display honest behavior during both interviews. Hypothesis 1B is thus supported and hypotheses 1A and 1C are rejected.

A comparison between the honest interview and the deceptive interview (column 3 and column 5) revealed four significant effects. Mean scores showed that deception was associated with a decrease in hand/finger movements, foot/leg movements, and ah speech disturbances and with an increase in changes in pitch of voice. Results thus supported hypotheses 3 (deception results in an increase in changes in pitch of voice) and 4B (deception results in a decrease in movements), while hypotheses 2 (deception results in an increase in ah speech disturbances) and 4A (deception results in an increase in movements) are rejected.

Discussion

The behavior displayed by the subjects corresponded with the behavior predicted in the control approach. Firstly, subjects attempted to exhibit honest behavior in both interviews (hypothesis 1B), that is, compared to the baseline, both interviews resulted in a decrease in movements, smiling/laughing, gaze aversion and ah speech disturbances. Secondly, deception, compared to telling the truth, resulted in a decrease in movements (hypothesis 4B) and changes in pitch of voice (hypothesis 3).

Results seem to indicate that people by attempting to control their movements, tend to overcontrol these movements, resulting in an unusual rigidity and inhibition of movements. Overcontrol could possibly be the explanation for the unpredicted decrease in ah speech disturbances during deception. The attempted control of ah speech disturbances might result in an unusual avoidance of these ah speech disturbances.

Outcomes only partially revealed the behavioral pattern, as predicted in the emotional approach. As was hypothesized, compared to telling the truth, deception resulted in an increase in changes in pitch of voice (hypothesis 3). But the predicted increase in speech disturbances (hypothesis 2) and liveliness (hypothesis 4A) were not found, nor the nervous behavior emerged by comparing the baseline on the one side with both interviews on the other side (hypothesis 1A).

Results to some extent revealed the behavioral pattern, as predicted in the cognitive approach, that is, by comparing the baseline with both interviews, the expected decrease in movements during both interviews did occur (hypothesis 1C). Moreover, subjects displayed fewer movements during deception than while telling the truth (hypothesis 4B). Other results however, did not agree with the cognitive approach. The predicted increase in speech disturbances during deception did not occur (hypothesis 2), and the increase in changes in pitch of voice were not predicted. Finally, the increase in looking at the police officer in both interviews seems not to correspond to the cognitive approach; Burgoon et al. (1989), for instance, showed that being engaged in cognitively complex tasks results in gaze aversion.

Compared to previous deception research, two findings are remarkable, that is, the decrease in hand/finger movements and the decrease in ah speech disturbances.

The clear decrease in hand/finger movements is possibly due to the scoring system used; deception only influenced subtle hand/finger movements, which is a category of nonverbal behavior seldom utilized in previous research.

In most research an increase in ah speech disturbances was found. Possibly, the decrease in ah speech disturbances obtained in the present experiment is due to our different manipulation of deception. In the usual experiments a deception situation is created by having the subjects proclaim a counter-attitudinal opinion. To argue in favor of abortion while being against abortion is an example (Mehrabian, 1972). The procedure implies that in the deception condition subjects have to invent a response, while in the honest condition they simply can tell the truth. In this respect our manipulation was different. In the present experiment liars had to *conceal* the truth, while in other studies they had to *invent* a response. Apparently, concealing the truth results in a decrease in ah speech disturbances and inventing the truth results in an increase in ah speech disturbances.

References

Ben-Shakhar, G., & Furedy, J.J. (1990). Theories and applications in the detection of deception: a psychophysiological and international perspective. New York: Springer-Verlag.

Burgoon, J.K., Kelly, D.L., Newton, D.A., & Keely-Dyreson, M.P. (1989). The nature of arousal and nonverbal indices. *Human Communication Research, 16*, 217-255.

Davis, R.C. (1961). Physological responses as a means of evaluating information. In A.D. Biderman & H. Zimmer (Eds.), The manipulation of human behavior. New York: Wiley and Sons.

DePaulo, B.M. (1988). Nonverbal aspects of deception. *Journal of Nonverbal Behavior, 12*, 153-162.

DePaulo, B.M. (1992). Nonverbal behavior and self-presentation. *Psychological Bulletin, 111*, 2033-243.

DePaulo, B.M., & Kirkendol, S.E. (1989). The motivational impairment effect in the communication of deception. In J.C. Yuille (Ed.), Credibility Assessment. Dordrecht: Kluwer Academic Publishers.

DePaulo, B.M., Stone, J.L., & Lassiter, G.D. (1985). Deceiving and detecting deceit. In B.R. Schenkler (Ed.), The self and social life. New York: McGraw-Hill.

Ekman, P. (1989). Why lies fail and what behaviors betray a lie. In J.C. Yuille (Ed.), Credibility Assessment. Dordrecht: Kluwer Academic Publishers.

Ekman, P., & Friesen, W.V. (1972). Hand movements. *Journal of Communication, 22*, 353-374.

Ekman, P., & Friesen, W.V. (1974). Detecting deception from the body or face. *Journal of Personality and Social Psychology, 29*, 288-298.

Goldman-Eisler, F. (1968). Psycholinguistics: experiments in spontaneous speech. New York: Doubleday.

Knapp, M.L., Hart, R.P., & Dennis, H.S. (1974). An exploration of deception as a communication construct. *Human Communication Research, 1*, 15-29.

Köhnken, G. (1989). Behavioral correlates of statement credibility: theories, paradigms and results. In H. Wegener, F. Lösel, & J. Haisch (Eds.), Criminal behavior and the justice system: psychological perspectives. New York: Springer-Verlag.

Mehrabian, A. (1972). Nonverbal communication. Chicago: Aldine-Atherton.

Riggio, R.E., & Friedman, H.S. (1983). Individual differences and cues to deception. *Journal of Personality and Social Psychology, 45*, 899-915.

Siegman, A.W. (1985). Expressive correlates of affective states and traits. In A.W. Siegman & S. Feldstein (Eds.), Multichannel integrations of nonverbal behavior. Hillsdale: Lawrence Erlbaum Associates.

Vrij, A. (1991). Misverstanden tussen politie en allochtonen: sociaal-psychologische aspecten van verdacht zijn. Amsterdam: VU Uitgeverij.

Vrij, A., & Winkel, F.W. (1991). Cultural patterns in Dutch and Surinam nonverbal behavior: an analysis of simulated police interviews. *Journal of Nonverbal Behavior, 15*, 169-185.

Zuckerman, M., DePaulo, B.M., & Rosenthal, R. (1981). Verbal and nonverbal communication of deception. In L. Berkowitz (Ed.), Advances in experimental social psychology, volume 14. New York: Academic Press.

The Effects of Distraction on Police Officer Shooting Behavior

Aldert Vrij, Jaap van der Steen and Leendert Koppelaar

Introduction

When conducting a task, several distracting factors could be present, such as noise (Hockey, 1979), high temperature (Anderson, 1987) or physical tiredness (Zillmann, Katcher, & Milavsky, 1972). Psychological research has often shown that being distracted while conducting a task results in increased tension, especially if the task is difficult (Baddeley, 1972; Hockey, 1979; Loewen & Suedfeld, 1992; Smith, 1989). Conducting a difficult task requires optimal concentration. Distraction endangers such concentration and will therefore be experienced as annoying, resulting in increased tension (Hockey, 1979; Smith, 1989). Recently, a number of social-psychological studies concerning the relationship between noise (a form of distraction) and tension have been conducted (Davidson, Hagmann, & Baum, 1990; Nagar & Pandey, 1987, Nagar, Pandey, & Paulus, 1988; Tooley, Brigham, Maass, & Bothwell, 1987). However, in all these experiments "irrelevant" noise was used, such white noise (Tooley et al., 1987) or noise not very suitable in the context (for example a person talking Armenian while subjects worked on a number comparison task [Davidson et al., 1990], a cassette of a ringing alarm clock while subjects were completing anagrams [Nagar & Pandey, 1987], or noise recorded during the peak hours in a congested city market while subjects were completing anagrams [Nagar et al., 1988]). In the present experiment more "appropriate" noise was used, namely street noise at a parking-place. This enhanced the ecological validity of the results.

Several experiments have been conducted examining the effects of noise on perception and performance (see Baddeley (1972) and Smith (1989) for reviews of these studies). In these experiments subjects were asked to perform primary (important) and secondary (less important) tasks while noise was present or absent. Results showed that noise improves the performance on primary (important) tasks and impairs the performance on secondary (less important) tasks. The "cue-utilization hypothesis" formulated by Easterbrook (1959) provides an explanation. The core of this hypothesis is that an increase in tension produces a narrowing of attention (tunnel vision), with the subject concentrating more and more on the central features of the situation and paying less and less attention to more peripheral ones. As a result, noise will impair the performance on tasks which will be considered as less important (because someone will pay less attention to those tasks) but it might improve the performance on tasks which are considered as very important (because someone will be fully concentrated on those tasks).

The majority of studies concerning the tension - behavior relationship have dealt with highly artificial behavior. In most studies subjects' performance on computer games were investigated. Our experiments dealt with more real life behavior, that is, police officers' performance in simulated firearms incidents. Moreover, in most studies subjects have been students. In the present experiment patrol police officers were involved. These facts improve the ecological validity of our experiments.

Based upon the previous findings, several effects of noise on tension, perception and performance were expected. First, noise will increase tension (Hypothesis 1). Second, noise will narrow police officers' attention in such a way that they will concentrate on the central (dominant) features of the situation (Hypothesis 2). Third, noise will improve the performance on primary tasks and will impair the performance on secondary tasks (Hypothesis 3).

In the present experiment also the effects of field independence on tension, perception and performance were examined. Field independent people have the ability to understand complex situations very rapidly (Feij, 1976). In the present experiment police officers were provided with a complex situation which elapsed very quickly. Therefore, a rapid and appropriate definition of the situation was necessary. We hypothesized that field independence will result in more accurate perception and that high field independent police officers will perform better on both the primary and the secondary task than low field independent police officers (Hypothesis 4). Moreover, field independent people are less rapidly distracted by irrelevant stimuli (like noise, Feij, 1976). Therefore, also a Noise x Field Independence interaction effect was expected: the noise effects, formulated in hypotheses 1 through 3, will especially occur in low field independent police officers (Hypothesis 5).

Method

Subjects

A total of 49 patrol police officers participated in the experiment, 89% of whom were male and 11% of whom were female. The average age in the sample was 33 years (*SD* = 8 years). The average experience with police work was 11 years (*SD* = 7 years).

Procedure

The experiment was conducted among local police forces during regular shooting exercises. Police officers participated individually; participation was voluntary. All officers were willing to participate. The experimenter introduced the experiment as "an investigation of police officers' conflict handling". Subjects were brought to the experimental room in which the Fire Arms Training System (FATS) was located. FATS is an American shooting simulator, which has been recently introduced in the Netherlands. The experimenter put the subject in front of a large video screen and asked the subject to act as he or she would act in real life, such as shouting, shooting, running away, taking cover, etc. Then, by means of video and laser disc displays, a scenario was projected on the screen. The images were in full color and full size. The camera's point of view was similar to the subject's point of view. In other words "the eyes of the camera were the eyes of the subjects". As a result, what subjects saw and heard is what they would experience in reality. The weapons used were not live rounds but laser beams. Subjects' behavior was videotaped with a hidden camera. Afterwards subjects were informed about the videotapes and were asked to fill out a questionnaire related to the situation.

Scenario

The scenario took place at a parking-place. The subject (camera's point of view) and a colleague are patrolling near a parking-place. A woman walks towards the two police officers and tells them that two guys are trying to break into a car at the parking-place. Both police officers walk to the parking-place. They see two men attempting to break into a car. The two men are standing on both sides of the car. The police officers run to both men. The colleague walks to the right, out of sight of the subject. He calls both car thieves. Suddenly, both car thieves take their firearm and start shooting at both police officers (the subject and his colleague). Between two salvos they duck, protecting themselves from both police officers and making themselves invisible for the subject. The scene lasted 48 seconds; the two car thieves were shooting for 11 seconds. From the subject's point of view, one car thief (the right one) stood in the center of the visual field and was the dominant feature; the other car thief stood on the left side of the visual field.

Independent variables

Two independent variables, the amount of street noise and field independence, were introduced in this experiment. In the experimental condition ($N = 22$) additional *street noise* (the sound of a drill) was introduced. The intensity of the drill was 85 db. Subjects were randomly assigned to the control or experimental condition. *Field Independence* was determined with the Hidden-patterns Test (Feij, 1976; French, Ekstrom & Price, 1963). The items consist of simple geometrical patterns in some of which a single given configuration (lambda) is embedded. For the purpose of the analyses the variable is dichotomized: 25% of the subjects with the highest score on the test were classified as "high field independent", the remaining 75% were classified as "low field independent".

Dependent Variables

Tension was investigated with the Liebert-Morris scale (Liebert & Morris, 1967). Four questions were asked, amongst others "You were very nervous during the task" (alpha = .65). Answers could be entered on seven-point scales ranging from certainly not (1) to most certainly (7). In order to describe both car thieves ten multiple choice questions were asked, five for each car thief. An example is: "Did the man have a mustache?". Afterwards, the number of right answers was calculated. We distinguished two kinds of behavior, that is (1) shooting performance and (2) posture. Shooting performance concerns the percentage of hits (the hit rate). We determined the number of shots fired at the two men and the number of hits. The hit rate is the number of hits divided by the number of shots; posture implies whether or not the police officer took cover after the car thieves started shooting at them. Taking cover was possible, because the subjects were standing in the experimental room next to a pillar. Shooting performance was the primary task in this experiment because we expected that police officers would consider shooting performance as their main task. Posture was the secondary task.

The questionnaire concluded with background data (gender, age, position within the police, and experience).

Results

In order to test Hypothesis 1 (extra noise will result in increased tension), Hypothesis 2 (extra noise produces a narrowing attention), Hypothesis 3 (extra noise will improve the performance on the primary task and will impair the performance on the secondary task), Hypothesis 4 (field independents will give a better description of the situation, and will perform better on both the primary and secondary task) and Hypothesis 5 (Hypotheses 1 through 3 will occur especially in low field independent subjects) a MANOVA was conducted, utilizing a 2 (Street Noise: noise of drill absent or present) x 2 (Field Independence: high or low) factorial design. Both factors were between-subjects factors. The dependent variables were tension, description of the two men and shooting performance. At a multivariate level, the analysis revealed significant main effects for Street Noise, $F(4, 42) = 4.62$, $p < .01$, and Field Independence, $F(4, 42) = 3.26$, $p < .05$. The Street Noise x Field Independence interaction was not significant, $F(4, 42) = 1.58$, *ns*. The univariate tests and mean scores concerning both main effects are given in Tables 1 and 2.

Table 1 reveals that extra noise resulted in increased tension. This confirms Hypothesis 1. Extra noise did impair the description of the left car thief but did not improve, as predicted in Hypothesis 2, the description of the dominant car thief. Therefore, Hypothesis 2 was thereby only partly supported. Extra noise did not improve the shooting performance, as was predicted in Hypothesis 3.

Table 1: The Effects of Street Noise on Tension, Perception and Shooting Performance

	Extra street noise		
	absent	present	$F(1,47)$
Tension	3.70	4.35	6.17*
Description of the left man	2.96	2.23	4.48*
Description of the right man	3.26	2.95	1.15
Shooting performance	.27	.29	.05

Note. * p < .05   ** p < .01

Table 2 reveals that high field independent subjects were more able to describe the dominant car thief and had a better shooting performance than low field independent subjects. These results support Hypothesis 4.

Table 2: The Effects of Field Independence on Tension, Perception and Shooting Performance

	Field independence		
	low	high	$F(1,47)$
Tension	3.96	4.10	.71
Description of the left man	2.47	3.08	.55
Description of the right man	2.92	3.69	4.03*
Shooting performance	.22	.38	5.65*

Note. *p < .05   **p < .01

In order to test the effects of Street Noise and Field Independence on taking cover (Hypotheses 3 and 4) a loglinear analysis was conducted, utilizing a 2 (Street Noise) x 2 (Field Independence) factorial design. In agreement with Hypothesis 3, police officers were taking less cover in the experimental condition (14% versus 37%, $X^2(1) = 3.58$, $p < .05$). Altogether, Hypothesis 3 is supported concerning the secondary task and is rejected concerning the primary task. In agreement with Hypothesis 4, high field independent subjects were taking cover more frequently than low field independent subjects, (47% versus 18%, $X^2(1) = 3.28$, $p < .05$). Altogether, Hypothesis 4 is hereby supported. The Street Noise X Field Independence interaction was not significant, $X^2(1) = .02$, *ns*. Altogether, Hypothesis 5 is rejected.

Discussion

First, we examined the effects of street noise on tension, perception and performance of police officers in shooting situations. Street noise is an environmental factor, on which neither the police officer nor the offender could exert an influence. But, as results revealed, street noise did influence the police officer-offender confrontation. Hypothesis 1, stating that street noise will result in more tension, was supported. In agreement with Hypothesis 2, extra noise produced a narrowing of attention: the least dominant man was described poorer in the experimental condition than in the control condition. We had also predicted that extra noise would lead to a better description of the dominant man. This prediction was not supported by the findings. A possible explanation for the absence of this effect is that police officers did not pay very much attention to all kinds of detailed features of the man, because they were very much absorbed in shooting at this man. Another possible explanation is the "weapon-focus" effect: people concentrate their attention on a weapon during a crime, leaving less attention available for viewing other items (Loftus, Loftus, & Messo, 1990). (In the experiment we did not ask the subjects to describe the firearm but we did ask them to describe other items of the man).

In agreement with Hypothesis 3 was the impairment in performance on secondary tasks: as a result of noise police officers "forgot" to take cover. The finding implies that noise endangers police officers in shooting incidents: as a result of noise they perform less (especially on secondary tasks), thereby running the risk of getting hurt, wounded or even killed in shooting incidents.

Second, we examined the effects of field independence on tension, perception and performance in shooting incidents. As was predicted in Hypothesis 4, high field independent subjects performed better on both the primary and secondary tasks, and gave a better description of the witnessed event. This makes the recruitment of high field independent people for positions in which police officers are likely to be confronted with risky criminals (specialized arrest squads for instance) highly recommendable. Another possibility is training police officers' perception and immediate understanding of complex situations by means of a training program. The central goal of such a training program should be to train police officers (a) in making an immediate distinction between main points and matters of secondary importance and (b) in focusing themselves mainly on those main points by secluding themselves from less important points.

The Fire Arms Training System has been recently introduced in the Netherlands. The conventional firearms training for police officers in the Netherlands consists of shooting with real bullets at (non-movable) targets. Finally, we will point out the importance of the Fire Arms Training System in police officers' firearms training programs. First, FATS saves expenses, because shooting with real bullets is expensive. One bullet, for instance, costs .50 US dollar, and in the city of the Hague only 600,000 bullets are used every year during firearms exercises. Second, FATS is time-saving. Shooting with real bullets is only allowed at official rifle-ranges. So, for every shooting exercise police officers have to go to such a rifle-range. On the other hand, a FATS-simulator can easily be installed at police stations. Third, FATS makes it possible to exercise with shooting at movable targets. Our findings showed that the police officers had a rather bad shooting performance in both experiments: the hitrates (the number of hits divided by the number of shots) in the two experiments were 31% and 28% respectively. Police shooting instructors suggested that the poor performances were possible due to the fact that police officers never have the opportunity to shoot at movable targets. Fourth, the experiments showed that police officers are not used to performing under "difficult circumstances": their performances were better in the control conditions than in the experimental conditions. Other experiments (Vrij, van der Steen, & Koppelaar, 1994, 1995) revealed that police officers' shooting tendency increases with hot temperatures (Vrij et al., 1994) and that their shooting tendency declines after a physical exertion (Vrij et al., 1995). In our point of view it is important to hold shooting exercises also under less ideal circumstances. The finding that even high field independent police officers were influenced by the street noise in our experiment does emphasize the importance of such a training program. The major goal of that training program is to teach police officers to exclude themselves from environmental factors like noise and temperature.

We would not exclude altogether the importance of practicing with real bullets in fire arms training programs. Shooting with real bullets remains essential, for instance, to experience the "recoil" and the "din" accompanying a real bullet shot.

References

Anderson, C. A. (1987). Temperature and aggression: effects on quarterly, yearly, and city rates of violent and nonviolent crime. *Journal of Personality and Social Psychology, 52*, 1161-1173.

Baddeley, A.D. (1972). Selective attention and performance in dangerous environments. *British Journal of Psychology, 63*, 537-546.

Davidson, L.M., Hagmann, J., & Baum, A. (1990). An exploration of a possible physiological explanation for stressor aftereffects.*Journal of Applied Social Psychology, 20*, 869-880.

Easterbrook, J.A. (1959). The effect of emotion on cue utilization and the organization of behavior. *Psychological Review, 66*, 183-201.

Feij, J.A. (1976). Field independence, impulsiveness, high school training, and academic achievement. *Journal of Educational Psychology, 68*, 793-799.

French, J.W., Ekstrom, R.B., & Price, L.A. (1963). *Manual for kit of reference tests for cognitive factors*. Princeton, N.J.: Educational Testing Service.

Hockey, G.R.J. (1979). Stress and the cognitive components of skilled performance. In V. Hamilton (Ed.), *Human stress and cognition*. New York: Wiley & Sons.

Liebert, R.M., & Morris, L.W. (1967). Cognitive and emotional components of test anxiety: a distinction and some initial data. *Psychological Reports, 20*, 975-978.

Loewen, L.J., & Suedfield, P. (1992). Cognitive and arousal effects of masking office noise. *Environment and Behavior, 24*, 381-395.

Loftus, E.F., Loftus, G.R., & Messo, J. (1990). Some facts about "weaopn focus". *Law and Human Behavior, 11*, 55-63.

Nagar, D., & Pandey, J. (1987). Affect and performance on cognitive task as a function of crowding and noise. *Journal of Applied Social Psychology, 17*, 147-157.

Nagar, D., Pandey, J., & Paulus, P.B. (1988). The effects of residential crowding experience on reactivity to laboratory crowding and noise. *Journal of Applied Social Psychology, 18*, 1423-1442.

Smith, A.P. (1989). A review of the effects of noise on human performance. *Scandinavian Journal of Psychology, 30*, 185-206.

Tooley, V., Brigham, J.C., Maass, A., & Bothwell, R.K. (1987). Facial recognition: weapon effect and attentional focus. *Journal of Applied Social Psychology, 17*, 845-859.

Vrij, A., van der Steen, J.C., Koppelaar, L. (1994). Aggression of police officers as a function of temperature: an experiment with the Fire Arms Training System. *Journal of Community and Applied Social Psychology, 4*, 305-371.

Vrij, A., van der Steen, J.C., & Koppelaar, L. (1995). The effects of physical effort on police officers' perception and agression in simulated shooting incidents. *Psychology, Crime, & Law, 1*, 301-308.

Zillmann, D., Katcher, A.H., & Milavsky, B. (1972). Excitation transfer from physical exercise to subsequent aggressive behavior. *Journal of Experimental Social Psychology, 8*, 247-259.

Paralinguistic and Nonverbal Triggers of Biased Credibility Assessments of Rape Victims in Dutch Police Officers: An Experimental Study of "Nonevidentiary" Bias[1]

Anna Costanza Baldry, Frans Willem Winkel and Deirdre Suzette Enthoven

Introduction

A core notion expressed in many victimological analyses is that rape victims are particularly at risk of secondary victimization, of being wounded again by negative reactions from others (Burgess, 1985, 1988; Brownmiller, 1975; Greuel, 1992; Krahé, 1991). Social psychological experiments on biased attributions of responsibility have for instance documented a host of extra-legal factors (Jones & Aronson, 1973; L'Armand & Pepitone, 1982; Gerdes, Dammann & Heilig, 1988). However, only a few studies have directly examined the police interview of suspects and victims as a source of secondary victimization. In the present experiment the effects on police officers' impression formation of two extra-legal factors that might be operative during such interviews were studied, namely (a) the victim's style of self-presentation and (b) the suspect's style of denying the allegations. These factors are considered to be "extra-legal" because they merely reflect individual differences in styles of communicating about experiences, and do not , as such, convey any valid information about the actual truthfulness of a statement made.

As crime victims, individual victims react differently in many respects (Fattah, 1984; Winkel & Koppelaar, 1991), including the manner in which they inform others about their experiences. Empirical studies (Janoff-Bulman and Hanson Frieze, 1983; Kidd and Chayett, 1984) have distinguished two basic styles of self-presentation: one is a highly emotional style, in which the victim displays distress which is clearly visible to outsiders. The other style is more low-key, with feelings checked and controlled. In the first case, for instance, the experience is expressed with a trembling voice and is more often interrupted by fits of crying; while in the second case, the victim makes a more numbed and resigned impression on the observer. The latter victims will express their experiences less emotionally, at least to all appearances. With regard to rape victims, Burgess and Holmstrom (1974) and

[1] This study was supported by a VUA-USF-grant, awarded to the second author. The author is indebted to the ACHMEA-Foundation (Stichting *Achmea* Slachtoffer en Samenleving) for granting the "Kwaliteit Slachtofferhulp-Program".

Burgess (1985) were the first to observe these two styles, which they respectively labeled as expressed and numbed.

The two styles may have a differential impact on the perceived credibility of the victim. Specifically, we hypothesized emotionality to enhance, and numbness to reduce perceived credibility. This hypothesis is based on the popular conception of the rape victim as hysterical, crying and shaking and on gender role stereotyping (Brownmiller, 1975; Krulewitz & Payne, 1978) that sees emotionality as normative for women. It is also in line with the expectation formulated by Riggio, Tucker and Throckmorton (1987) that emotional individuals will generally be judged as more truthful, regardless of whether they are deceiving or telling the truth. Riggio et al. (1987) base this expectation on the "demeanor bias" (Riggio & Friedman, 1983; Zuckerman & DeFrank, 1979) and on empirical evidence indicating that expressive persons are judged as more likable speakers (Riggio & Friedman, 1983). It is thus quite clear then that equating emotionality with truthfulness is a perceptual distortion (Wortman, 1983).

Our second individual difference variable relates to suspects: they may deny the victim's allegations more or less powerfully. Erickson et al. (1978) and Lind et al. (1978) define powerless speech as a style characterized by numerous language features, including intensifiers (very, much, a lot), hesitations (eh, em, um), hedges (sort of, kind of), which means that the person hesitates to give an answer, often repeats questions that were asked and does not speak fluently. On the other hand, a powerful style is very straightforward, sure and not hesitant; for one question, one answer is given. A person who talks in a powerful way is more likely to be believed than a person who uses powerless speech. Johnson & Vison (1987) and Hosman (1989) have also examined the influence that these two speech styles have on impression formation and on the credibility of that person. They suggest that a person using powerless speech is less likely to be believed than the one who uses powerful speech: "The use of a powerful or powerless style might affect both the perceptions of the speaker and the influence of his or her communication. Listeners may see the use of a powerful style as reflecting high status and may tend to think favorably of such individuals. They may perceive powerful speakers as relatively more attractive. In addition, a powerless style, with its complex and possibly confusing features, makes attending to the communicator more difficult and psychologically costly and may decrease attraction to him for this reason. Finally, listeners may believe that a powerful style, by virtue of its succinctness and lack of hedging, indicates that the communicator is confident about the position stated in the communication. This may increase perceptions of the powerful speaker's credibility." (Erickson et al., 1978, p.268).

In summary, we hypothesized:

1. A victim reporting a rape in an emotional way is believed more and held less responsible then a victim reporting the same crime in a controlled way;
2. A suspect defending himself from rape charges using a powerful speech style is believed more than a suspect using a powerless speech style.

The Experiment

Method

Sample Subjects were 98 professional police officers attending a police academy; 56.1% were male and 43.9%, female. Their average age was 24 years. On average they were attending the police academy for 10 months.

Procedure After an oral introduction providing a general explanation of what subjects were going to see and what they were expected to do, all were exposed to a video. The video started with a short text, stating: "Christine gave a party on Saturday night. She also asked over an acquaintance of hers, Paul, who lives in the same apartment building as Christine. During the entire party they spent a lot of time together, dancing and chatting. When all the other guests had left, Paul stayed and helped Christina clean up. In the living room the sexual intercourse took place."

The video continues with the victim's testimony, in the form of answers given to the questions of a female police detective:

Question: How long have you known him?
Answer: I have known him for three months now. He says that he's been living here for six months. The first time that I talked to him was more or less three weeks ago. I was in the corridor trying to fix that thing, and he passed by: "That's no work for a woman, I'll do it for you" he told me; so he fixed the bell for me.
Q: And when did you talk to him again?
A: Well, last Saturday I had a party at my place and I had been shopping and was carrying a heavy bag and beer and so on. He came down in the elevator and offered to help me carry all the stuff. Then he asked me "Are you going to have a party?", and I said, to be polite, "Why don't you come over tonight and have a drink with us?"; and that is what he did.
Q: What time did he arrive at the party?
A: Yes, what time would it have been? Well, around ten, maybe, and there were about 25 people. I guess there were people who left early and others who arrived later in the evening.
Q: Do you think that he had been drinking when he arrived?
A: When he arrived, I think he had been drinking. Yes, he was quite cheerful, he absolutely had been drinking.
Q: Did you dance with him at the party?
A: I had been dancing quite a lot with him; in fact, he wanted to dance with me all the time and while dancing he was constantly touching me and followed me in the kitchen when I was going there. He was very obtrusive also; when we were dancing he was constantly touching my bottom. I was very ashamed towards my guests. My sister and my parents where there as well and you don't want to make a fight when everyone is watching. Actually, he had been doing this constantly.
Q: Did he dance with others as well?
A: He danced with others too, and also with my sister and after that he came up to me and told me "You have got a lovely sister".
Q: Do you think that he had been drinking during the party?
A: I think he had been drinking a lot; I saw him go into the kitchen all the time and then return with a beer; I think he was drunk.

Q: Had you been drinking yourself?

A: I had been drinking too, but not too much; you have a certain responsibility if it's your own party, you know, you want to talk to the other guests as well.

Q: How much had you been drinking?

A: I think I had drunk five glasses of wine; I wasn't drunk.

Q: And then, how did it continue?

A: Yes, at the end of the party most of the people left, I think at 2:30. There were about six people left, also my sister and my brother-in-law, and him of course. And, except for him, my sister and my brother-in-law were the last to leave and my brother-in-law asked me if my friend was staying any longer. Well, I told him that he'd better leave too since I had to do the dishes and clean up the place; and then he announced: "Well, I'll help you with it". And then, while doing the dishes, he was as obtrusive and annoying as before, while we were dancing; constantly touching me and leaning towards me and well, being very obtrusive. Yes, of course I had been trying to defend myself, *(convinced voice)* telling him to stop and I had been pushing his hands away. I just went on doing the dishes so he would understand that I didn't like it. Well, when we finished the dishes he still didn't leave, he just went to the living room and played some music, as if the party were still going on. I thought "I have to". I went to the kitchen again and made some coffee because I thought it might sober him up a little. He went and sat down in the living room.

Q: Didn't you make it clear to him that you didn't like it?

A: Yes, of course, I had been trying to defend myself, I told him to stop and I had been pushing his hands away. I just went on doing the dishes, so that he would understand that I didn't like it.

Well, and when we had finished the dishes he still didn't leave. He just went to the living room and played some music, as if the party were still going on.

I thought , "I have to...", I went to the kitchen again and made some coffee because I thought he might get sober up a little.

Q: But that didn't work?

A: No, he went and sat down in the living room. I started pacing around because I thought, "If I sit down next to him it will only get worse." So I started emptying ashtrays and wiping off tables.

At a certain point I passed by him and he grabbed me and pulled me towards him.

Q: What happened then?

A: What happened then? Then he raped me! I lost my balance and we slid off the sofa, onto the floor.

Q: Did he say something when this happened?

A: I don't remember if he said anything or not. Of course a man is much stronger in these kind of situations. Finally he covered my mouth with his hand because I was trying to scream.

The victim's testimony was followed by the testimony of the suspect, also utilizing a question-answer format:

Question: How long had you know her?

Answer: Half a year. I've been living here for half a year now. I'm living in the same corridor as she is, but my flat is further down. I used to know her just by face, when we were crossing each other and so on.

Q: When did you speak to her for the first time?

A: Two months ago; she was trying to fix her doorbell and I realized immediately that the way she was doing it wouldn't work, so I offered to do it. That was fine with her, and ever since we've been greeting each other when we meet, in the elevator for example.

Q: What about the party?

A: It was that same Saturday. It was Saturday morning and when I came down in the elevator, she was standing there with heavy bags and beer, so I offered to bring them upstairs with her and that was okay with her. Then she invited me to come over to her place and join her party that evening. So I did.

Q: What time did you arrive at the party?

A: At half-past nine.

Q: Had you been drinking before?

A: Yes, I had been drinking, at home, two beers.

Q: Did you dance with her?

A: Yes, you could say so. We were dancing the whole evening, we were dancing and having fun. It was really close dancing and I don't have any reason to believe that she didn't like it, of course I would have noticed!

Q: Did you also dance with others?

A: Yes, I also danced with other people, also with her sister, but most of the time I had been dancing with her.

Q: How much had you been drinking at the party?

A: Eight beers and I can drink beer easily without getting drunk.

Q: Had she been drinking too?

A: Yes, she was drinking wine... or sherry, no, I guess it was wine, I think at least seven glasses of wine. Yes, regularly she had her glass filled up with wine after we danced together.

Q: What happened then?

A: At the end of the party, slowly everybody had left, and at a certain moment I was the only person left. And because it was quite messy, dirty glasses and things like that, spontaneously, I offered to help her to clean things up a little and do the dishes as well; she didn't have a problem with that either. While doing the dishes, we were chatting a little bit and now and then I wrapped my arms around her waist and kissed her. If I had known that she didn't like it I would have stopped immediately. But it was all very spontaneous.

Q: And what happened when the dishes were done?

A: I went in the living room while she made some coffee. I played some music and sat down on the sofa. She came in the room and was still cleaning up, emptying ashtrays and things like that. When she came towards me I grabbed her and together we slid down onto the floor; but it happened very naturally, without any complications. It wasn't a rape at all; we were just making love.

Independent variables The independent variables were incorporated in the videos. The role of the victim and the suspect were played, in all experimental conditions, by the same actress and actor. In the emotional version the actress played a highly emotional victim. While reporting she constantly used a trembling voice and several times, during her report, she cried. Her whole appearance showed that she was shocked and agitated about what had happened. In the other version the actress played a numbed and controlled victim. We managed to manipulate this by making her report in a confident and straightforward way, telling her story as if it dealt with a daily, neutral event. She did not seem ashamed about what had happened. Because the emotional victim was constantly crying and sobbing the time length of this version was longer than that of the non-emotional one (8 minutes 20 seconds vs. 5 minutes 25 seconds).

In the powerful version the actor used powerful language, which means, according to Erickson et al. (1978), that for one question asked by the police detective, one straightforward answer was given. The style features had no hesitation forms, nor hedges and intensifiers and his whole testimony was clear.

In the second version the actor used powerless language, which means, still according to Erickson et al., that it was characterized by the frequent use of language features, such as intensifiers (very, definitely, surely), hedges (sort of, kind of), hesitation forms (uh, eh, ah, you know, let me see, etc.), repetitions (repeating the questions he was asked) and not very clear answers. The running time of the testimony of the powerless speaker was much longer than that of the powerful speaker (respectively 5 minutes 59 seconds vs. 3 minutes 38 seconds).

By combining these versions four experimental groups emerged: group 1, exposed to the emotional victim followed by the powerless suspect (time length = 20 minutes 19 seconds). Group 2 was shown the numbed victim and the powerful suspect (time length = 10 minutes 3 seconds); group 3, the numbed victim and the powerless suspect (time length = 12 minutes 24 seconds.) and group 4, the emotional victim and the powerful suspect (time length = 12 minutes 58 seconds). Two additional groups were only exposed to the victim's statements: group 5 saw the emotional, group 6 the controlled version.

Dependent variables Dependent variables were measured utilizing the 32 item multi-dimensional "Perceived Credibility Scale" (Winkel & Koppelaar, 1991). Sample items on perceived credibility of the victim and the suspect were: *"Does she make a credible impression on you?"* and *"Does she make the impression to hide the truth?"* (Cronbach's ALPHA = .83); or *"Does he make the impression to hide the truth?"* and *"Does his testimony seem trustable to you?"* (Cronbach's ALPHA = .78). Sample items on perceived responsibility include: *"Do you think the woman was responsible for what has happened?"* and *"Is the woman guilty for what has happened?"* (Cronbach's ALPHA = .68); or *"Do you think the man was responsible for what has happened?"* and *"Is the man guilty for what has happened?"* (Cronbach's ALPHA = .65). Responses were in terms of seven point rating scales. Subjects' overall impressions were also measured using a 12 (victim) and 15 (suspect) item semantic differential scale, based on the original Snider and Osgood scale. Besides, the questionnaire consisted of various open questions, and included several personal background items (such as gender, age, direct or indirect experiences with rape).

Results

Preliminary analyses

To examine the successfulness of the experimental manipulations various multivariate analyses of variance were conducted. For victim's style of self-presentation a main effect emerged ($F(2, 92) = 64.38$, $p < .001$). The analysis also revealed a main effect for suspect's style of denial ($F(3, 68) = 8.85$, $p < .001$). As to the individual items, Table 1 suggests that subjects significantly more strongly perceive the emotional victim to be shocked by the incident, and to be emotionally touched. Moreover, subjects significantly more strongly perceived the powerless suspects as talking in a hesitant way, answering questions less straightforwardly, and as repeating questions more often. Together, these analyses clearly support the successfulness of the manipulations introduced in the experiment.

Table 1: Mean Ratings on Manipulation Checks for the Victim's and Suspect's Style of Self Presentation

Manipulation check items:	Emotional victim	Controlled victim	F
Do you think the woman was shocked?	5.31	2.30	129.54*
Do you think she was emotionally touched?	5.49	3.12	70.73*
	Powerful suspect	Powerless suspect	
Did the man talk in a hesitant way?	3.10	4.37	14.46*
Did the man repeat the questions?	3.41	4.80	14.96*
Did the man answer the questions straightforwardly?	4.87	3.70	17.99*

Higher scores indicate stronger applicability of an item; *$p < .001$

Another preliminary analysis was conducted checking for the similarity of the experimental groups regarding personal background data. In groups 1 to 4 a significant gender difference emerged ($X^2 = 12.37$; $p < .05$), and a difference in being personally acquainted with a rape victim ($X^2 = 11.00$; $p < .05$). Groups 5 and 6 also slightly differed in gender composition ($X^2 = 3.88$; $p = .05$) and in the length of time at the police academy ($F(1, 22) = 4.99$; $p < .05$). In testing the hypotheses we decided to control for these differences

Main analyses

The hypotheses were tested using analyses of covariance on the basis of a 2 (emotional/numbed) x 2 (powerful/powerless) design. This analysis resulted in a main effect - supporting hypothesis 1 - for victim's style of self-presentation (see Table 2). Table 2 suggests that emotional victims were perceived as more credible. Hypothesis 2 is clearly not supported. Further support for hypothesis 1 comes from an analysis of covariance on groups 5 and 6: here, too, the perceived credibility of the emotional victim (m = 4.99) is significantly higher ($F(1, 19) = 17.08$; $p < .01$) than the credibility of the victim exhibiting a controlled style (m = 3.25).

A comparison of these latter means to the ones reported in Table 2 reveals an interesting picture, also reported in Winkel en Koppelaar (1992). Being exposed to the suspect's side of the story generally results in reducing the victim's credibility. Irrespective of the suspect's style of self-presentation, the perceived credibility of the emotional victim is significantly reduced ($F(2, 45) = 3.94$; $p < .05$).

Table 2: Mean Ratings of Victim's and Suspect's Credibility and Responsibility by Type of Self-Presentation

	Victim's style of self-presentation			Suspect's style of self-presentation		
	Emotional	Numbed	F	Powerful	Powerless	F
Victim credibility	4.21	3.59	6.58*	3.96	3.81	.89
Suspect credibility	4.43	4.25	.11	4.41	4.25	.62
Victim responsibility	3.78	3.68	.03	3.82	3.62	2.20
Suspect responsibility	3.94	3.98	.02	4.00	3.83	.29

* p < .01

Winkel and Koppelaar (1992) suggested that a police officer's need for further information - after having conducted a first interview with the victim - is negatively associated with perceptions of victim credibility. Incredibility thus stimulates further questioning. To further explore this notion in the present data, various additional analyses were performed on subjects' responses to the question as to what information they would ask for if they could interview the victim and the suspect themselves. The need for further information turned out to be rather versatile and was recorded representing the following eight more specific informational categories: (1) the defense of the woman, (2) hearing witnesses that were at the party, (3) the behavior of the man, (4) the behavior of the woman, (5) the rape itself, the evidence and what had happened afterwards, (6) the feelings of the man towards the woman, (7) the feelings of the woman towards the man and (8) the past sexual experiences of the victim and the suspect. In general, these categories were evenly distributed over experimental groups. However, a number of interesting significant differences emerged, in particular in the more "incredible" conditions. Category (3) was overrepresented in subjects exposed to the numbed victim: out of the 23 people who asked for this information 82.6% were of this group (Chi-square = 12.45, df = 1, p = .0004). Also, information regarding the behavior of the woman (category 4) was significantly more often requested by these subjects: out of the 24 people that asked for this information, 79.2% were of this group (Chi-square = 10.44, df = 1, p = .0012). Moreover, further information through hearing witnesses that were at the party - negatively associated with perceptions of victim credibility (M = 3.47 versus M = 4.01, t(73) = 1.96, p = .05) - was significantly more often requested by subjects exposed to the powerless suspect: out of the 17 people that asked for this information 76.5% were of this group (Chi-square = 7.14, df = 1, p = .007). Thus, incredibility - represented in being exposed to a controlled victim or to a powerless denial by the suspect - tends to strengthen informational needs. This outcome replicates the previous findings.

To further explore the specific pieces of information underlying the perceived credibility of the victim, responses to the pertinent open question were coded as follows: (1) non emotional, not interested, calm; (2) bad defense, submitting herself and weak; (3) emotional, touched; (4) hiding information; (5) hesitating, being insecure; (6) too confident; (7) her way of speaking, where she looked; (8) she looked sweet, innocent and honest. In the various experimental groups different mechanisms appeared to be operative.

Out of the 31 persons who based their judgment on the fact that the woman was not emotional and calm, a significant 74.2% were exposed to the numbed woman (Chi-square = 10.43, df = 1, p = .0012). For the eight subjects who based their judgment on the fact that she was emotional and touched, a significant 87.5% consisted of subjects who saw the emotional woman (Chi-square = 5.6, df = 1, p = .018). Of the seven persons who based their judgment on the fact that she was insecure, a significant 85.7% was of the subjects who saw the emotional woman (Chi-square = 4.4, df = 1, p = .036). All the 13 subjects who based their judgment on the fact that the woman they had seen was too confident had seen the numbed woman (Chi-square = 14.57, df = 1, p = .0001). Finally, of the 8 people who based their judgment on the fact that she seemed sweet and innocent, a significant 87.5% were subjects who saw the emotional woman (Chi-square = 5.6, df = 1, p = .018).

To examine the correlation between victim credibility and the kinds of information used a t-test was conducted. Data suggested that victim credibility was significantly higher for subjects using category 3 relative to not using that category (M = 4.84 versus M = 3.78, (t(73) = -2.91, p = .005). Moreover, victim credibility was significantly lower for those who utilized category (4) information (M = 3.30 versus M = 4.02, t(73) = 2.46, p = .016). Finally, victim credibility was significantly higher for subjects basing their judgment on the fact that the woman was sweet and innocent, relative to subjects who did not use this information (M = 4.91 versus M = 3.77, t(73) = -3.13, p = .003).

Responses underlying the impression formed of the suspect were also categorized: (1) nervous, ashamed; (2) confident, no hesitations; (3) hesitating, repeating questions and insecure; (4) "macho" kind of person; (5) realistic and concrete; (6) hiding information; (7) relaxed and calm; (8) nice, helpful, honest and innocent. Here too, specific pieces of information were used in specific experimental groups. Out of the 14 persons utilizing category 1 information, a significant 85.7% were exposed to the powerless man (Chi-square = 9.81, df = 1, p = .0017). For the 21 people who based their judgment on the fact that the man was too confident, a significant 85.7% saw the powerful man (Chi-square = 13.28, df = 1, p = .0003). For the 13 subjects who based their judgment on the fact that the man they saw was hesitating, repeating questions and insecure, a significant 84.6% was of the ones who had seen the powerless version (Chi-square = 8.45, df = 1, p = .0037) and finally of the 17 subjects who had the tendency to base their judgment on the fact that the man was a "macho" kind of person (Chi-square = 3.04, df = 1, p = .08), 70.6% were of the ones who saw the powerful man. Significant correlations between these judgments and suspect credibility did not emerge.

Discussion

Doubting a victim's integrity on the basis of irrelevant information no doubt constitutes a secondary victimization. The present experiment underscores the empirical validity of the notion of perceptually induced secondary victimization, that is, of secondary victimization due to biases in information processing. Through confirming our first hypothesis another "nonevidentiary bias" in police officers conducting interviews with rape victims was documented. Although styles of communicating about a negative experience merely reflect individual differences between victims, police officers wrongly tend to interpret "emotionality" as a cue to honesty and lack of emotionality as a cue to deception. Emotional victims were more easily believed than victims reporting in a more controlled way. More in general our data suggested that a rape victim's credibility is positively associated with the impression of being emotional, being touched, and of being a warm, good and "deep" person. The lack of visible emotions and being too confident reduce a victim's credibility. Moreover, our data suggested that being exposed to a suspect's denial of rape charges reduced the perceived credibility of the victim, in particular the emotional victim's credibility. Future studies should explicitly consider the issue if this constitutes another non-evidentiary bias, or merely indicates a more general tendency to become more uncertain if one is exposed to two sides of a story. The absence of differences due to a powerful or powerless style of denying the charges may be related to the fact that particularly the powerless suspect did not fit police officers' perceptions of a rapist. Our semantic differential analyses indicated that the powerless suspect made the impression of being more delicate, less cynical and less cool, while the powerful suspect was more strongly considered to be cynical, strong, cool and rugged. Future studies examining the role of paralinguistics in denying rape charges might thus profit from including more stereotyped suspects.

References

Brownmiller, S. (1975). *Against our will: Men, women and rape.* NY: Simon and Schuster.

Burgess, A.W. (Ed.). (1985). *Rape and sexual assault. A research book.* NY, London: Garland.

Burgess, A.W. (1988). *Rape and sexual assault II.* NY,London: Garland.

Burgess, A.W., & Holmstrom, L.L. (1974). *Rape: Victims of crisis.* Bowie: Brady.

Erickson, B., Lind, E.A., Johnson, B.C., & O'Barr, W.M. (1978). Speech style and impression formation in a court setting: The effects of "powerful" and "powerless" speech. *Journal of Experimental Social Psychology, 14,* 266-279.

Fattah, E.A. (1984). Victim's response to confrontational victimization: A neglected aspect of victim research. *Crime and Delinquency, 30(1),* 75-89.

Gerdes, P.E., Dammann, E.J. & Heilig, K.E. (1988). Perception of rape victims and assailants: Effects of physical attractiveness, acquaintance and subject gender. *Sex Roles, 19(3/4),* 141-153.

Greuel, L. (1992). Police officers' beliefs about cues associated with deception in rape cases.In F. Lösel, D. Bender & T. Bliesener (Eds.). *Psychology and law. International perspectives* (pp.234-239). Berlin, NY: Walter de Gruyter.

Hosman, L.A. (1989). The evaluative consequences of hedges, hesitations and intensifiers. Powerful and powerless speech style. *Human Communication Research, 15(3),* 383-406.

Janoff-Bulman, R. & Hanson-Frieze, I. (1983). A theoretical perspective for understanding reactions to victimization. *Journal of Social Issues, 39(2),* 1-17.

Johnson, C. & Vinson, L. (1987). "Damned if you do, damned if you don't ?": Status, powerful speech and evaluations of a female witness. *Womens' Studies in Communication, 10(1),* 37-44.

Jones, C. & Aronson, E. (1973). Attribution of fault to a rape victim as a function of respectability of the victim. *Journal of Personality and Social Psychology, 26(3),* 415-419.

Kidd, R.F. & Chayett, E.F. (1984). Why do victims fail to report? The psychology of criminal victimization. *Journal of Social Issues, 40(1),* 39-50.

Krahé, B. (1991). Police officers' definition of rape: A prototype study. *Journal of Community and Applied Social Psychology, 1,* 223-244.

Krulewitz, J.E. & Payne, E.J. (1978). Attributions about rape: Effects of rapist force, observer sex and sex role attitudes. *Journal of Applied Social Psychology, 8(4),* 291-305.

L'Armand, K. & Pepitone, A. (1982). Judgment of rape: A study of victim-rapist relationship and victim sexual history. *Personality and Social Psychology Bulletin, 8(1),* 134-139.

Lind, E.A., Erickson,B.E., Conley, J. & O'Barr, W.M. (1978). Social attribution and conversation style in trial testimony. *Journal of Personality and Social Psychology, 36(12),* 1558-1567.

Riggio, R.E. & Friedman, H.S. (1983). Individual differences and cues to deception. *Journal of Personality and Social Psychology, 45(4),* 899-915.

Riggio, R.E., Tucker, J. & Throckmorton, B. (1987). Social skills and deception ability. *Personality and Social Psychology Bulletin, 13(4),* 568-577.

Winkel, F.W. & Koppelaar, L. (1991). Rape victim's style of self-presentation and secondary victimization by the environment: An experiment. *Journal of Interpersonal Violence, 6,* 29-41.

Winkel, F.W. & Koppelaar, L. (1992). Perceived credibility of the communicator: Studies of perceptual bias in police officers conduting rape interviews. In F. Lösel, D. Bender & T. Bliesener (Eds.). *Psychology and law. International perspectives,*(pp.219-233). Berlin, NY: Walter de Gruyter.

Wortman, C.B. (1983). Coping with victimization: Conclusions and implications for future research. *Journal of Social Issues, 39,* 195-221.

Zuckerman, M. & De Frank, R.S. (1979). Facial and vocal cues of deception and honesty. *Journal of Experimental Social Psychology, 15,* 378-396.

Psychological Expert Testimony on Eyewitness Issues on the Basis of Case Related Field Experiments

Thomas Fabian and Michael Stadler

Introduction

Eyewitnesses are often an important if not the only evidence in court cases. They are essential but often unreliable (Loftus, 1986). This is one reason why psychologists are called as expert witnesses into courts. Psychological expert witnesses can refer to a by now large body of empirical research (comp. Ceci, Toglia & Ross, 1987; Dent & Flin, 1992; Diges & Alonso-Quecuty, 1993; Ross, Read & Toglia, 1994).

Forensic psychologists giving testimony of, for example, the credibility of a witness' statement, the culpability of a defendant or the psychosocial situation of children in divorce cases usually refer to their psychological investigation of an individual. When the accuracy of eyewitness accounts is questioned, psychological expert witnesses, however, often offer general empirical information derived from psychological research. In these cases there are three problems that may arise:

In the first place, people from the legal professions are often doubtful about whether or not research findings with students are applicable to real life events. Psychologists are also discussing questions of external validity and generalizability in the area of witness research (comp. Davies, 1992). Some carefully designed field experiments (e.g. Brigham, Maass, Snyder & Spaulding, 1982; Köhnken & Maass, 1988) may be regarded as a big step towards the actual world. However, as Yuille (1993) has pointed out, psychological research should not only concentrate on simulation studies but also study forensic eyewitnesses.

The second problem refers to the question whether findings from empirical research can be regarded as safe knowledge. Some experimental psychologists suggest abstinence from expert testimony in most cases involving questions about the accuracy of eyewitness accounts because in their view empirical data are either contradictory or trivial. The debate between McCloskey and Egeth (1983a, 1983b), who doubt the usefulness of psychological expert testimony, and Loftus (1983a, 1983b, 1986), who can look upon some 20 years of experience as an expert witness, has so far not been resolved. Loftus' arguments in favor of expert testimony have found strong support in the scientific community (e.g. Wells, 1984) and Egeth's (1993) view has now become a little more moderate. More recently Elliott (1993) has attacked the use of psychological experts on eyewitness testimony. As Kassin,

Ellsworth and Smith (1994) set out in their reply, he only repeated old arguments about the lack of sufficient research evidence.

The third problem arises when questions raised in court cases are so specific that it becomes very difficult to give expert testimony on the basis of general psychological knowledge alone. In these cases we suggest carrying out case related field experiments in which the specific conditions of observation are simulated (Stadler, Schindler & Fabian, 1992, Fabian, Stadler & Wetzels, 1994). As an example we will present the results of our experiment for the "Slab paver" case (Stadler & Fabian, 1995).

The "Slab Paver" Case

Two policemen appearing as witnesses in a penal court case reported, that while standing on a bridge they had been watching two young men. The two young men, who were about 375 meters away from the bridge, were putting concrete blocks on railway lines, presumably in order to derail the next train. The policemen claimed to have identified the men as the two defendants whom they had been observing previously almost all day because they belonged to a group of left-wing squatters in Hamburg. After the arrival of other policemen they were also able to use binoculars for the affirmation of their identification. However there had been two observational breaks: Approximately a quarter of an hour before the policemen noticed the two men near the railways, the two defendants had been out of sight because they had left their car on a parking area and the policemen had had to stay behind in order not to be noticed. A second observational break occurred when the policemen returned to the parking area in order to wait for and arrest the defendants.

The defense lawyers argued that person identification at a distance of 375 meters seems impossible and applied for the testimony of a psychological expert witness. If the two policemen had not been lying, why were they convinced that they had identified the persons near the railway lines as the two defendants? From a psychological point of view this question could be answered referring to the experiments of the Belgian perceptual psychologist Albert Michotte on the phenomenological identity of objects (Michotte, 1983): When a moving object disappears behind a screen and shortly afterwards another object appears from behind the screen people usually perceive both objects as one and the same. This may well have happened with the two policemen, since there had been two observational breaks which we will call tunnel A and tunnel B (Figure 1).

When the two defendants left the parking area, they entered tunnel A, and when they arrived at the parking area, they left tunnel B. The policemen were convinced that the two men whom they saw in the meantime between were identical to the two defendants (Figure 1a). They did not consider the more complicated possibility, that two different men may have left tunnel A and entered tunnel B, while the two defendants were out of sight (Figure 1b).

a)

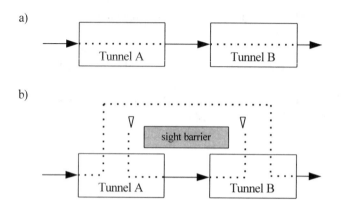

b)

Figure 1: Observational breaks

Since perception is not simply a mere reflection of our surroundings, but an active process, the policemen might have identified the two defendants because they expected to do so. In order to test the hypothesis that person identification at a distance of 375 meters is due to expectancy, we carried out a field experiment in which we simulated the conditions of the court case.

The Experiment

The experiment was carried out on the campus of the University of Bremen. The confederates came into view in a gap in a bushy hedge located at the far end of a wasteland bordering one of the buildings. The distance between the building and the hedge was about 375 meters. The subjects observed the confederates from the fourth floor of the building, i.e., an altitude corresponding to that of the bridge on which the policemen had been standing.

Confederates

Four confederates resembling the description of the perpetrators participated in the experiment: two confederates, who were very well known to the subjects, acted as targets, while another two confederates, who were not known to the subjects, acted as distracters.

Subjects

The twenty-two subjects were divided into two groups: Group 1 consisted of nine subjects, who knew both targets very well and were not informed whom they were to identify. We will call this group "naive". Group 2 consisted of thirteen subjects, who knew at least one of the targets very well. The subjects of Group 2 were introduced to the targets and told that they would be asked to identify them during the experiment ("expectant group").

Procedure

The two groups of subjects made their observations from two different rooms. They were instructed by two experimentors who were using walkie-talkies for communication with the confederates. All subjects were given printed answering forms. Subjects in Group 1 were asked if they could recognize anyone, and subjects in Group 2 were asked if they recognized the targets. The experiment included four trials: in the first trial the two distracters and in the second one the two targets appeared. The third and fourth trials were repetitions of the first two, with the difference that the subjects were given binoculars to use.

Results

Almost all subjects of the expectant group gave false alarms (92.3%) after the first trial, which means that they wrongly identified the distracters as the target persons. On the other hand, only two subjects of the naive group gave false alarms (22.2%) after the first trial. The results of the second trial correspond to these results: while only two subjects of the naive group made correct identifications, there were eleven subjects in the expectant group who correctly identified the target persons (Table 1).

Table 1: False Alarms and Correct Identifications

| | Without binoculars | | With binoculars | |
	distracters	targets	distracters	targets
"naive" group	fA = 2	cI = 2	fA = 6	cI = 8
(n = 9)	(22.2%)	(22.2%)	(66.0%)	(88.9%)
"expectant" group	fA = 12	cI = 11	fA = 8	cI = 13
(n = 13)	(92.3%)	(84.6%)	(61.5%)	(100%)
	$Chi^2 = 8.46$	$Chi^2 = 7.00$		
	$p < .01$	$p < .01$	n.s.	n.s.

Note: fA = false alarm; cI = correct identification

There are no differences between the two groups regarding the third and the fourth trial. There were less false alarms among the expectant group and more false alarms among the naive group with binoculars in the third trial compared to the first trial without binoculars. With one exception all subjects of both groups were able to make correct identifications with binoculars in the fourth trial (Table 1).

Discussion

The results of this experiment indicate that person identification at a distance of 375 meters is almost impossible. While most of the subjects among the expectant group made correct identifications in the second trial, only one fifth of the naive group could correctly identify the target persons, well-known to all subjects. Correspondingly, there were more than four times as many false alarms among the expectant group as in the naive group in the first trial. This clearly indicates the effect of expectancy on identification rates and false alarms among the experimental group. We may furthermore assume that the same may be said for the "naive" group, since the same subjects in the naive group who gave false alarms after the first trial made correct identifications after the second trial. These subjects told the experimenters later that they had assumed during the experiment that the persons to be identified should be known to all subjects. Since there weren't that many possibilities, their guesses were right. This means that in our experiment identification was not due to recognition of facial or other individual features. All subjects who made correct identifications only confirmed their perceptual hypotheses.

Correct identification seems to be possible with binoculars, since almost all subjects were able to make correct identifications of the target persons in the fourth trial. However there were more than 60% false alarms in both groups in the third trial. The astonishingly high rate of false alarms among the naive group in the third trial is probably due to the experimental situation of a group experiment where mutual influence cannot always be ruled out. It can be assumed that the subjects of the naive group also began to develop hypotheses about who the persons they were to identify could be. Even though almost all subjects could correctly identify the target persons using binoculars in the fourth trial, the high rate of false alarms in spite of the use of binoculars in the third trial is relevant to forensic practice.

On the basis of the results of this case related it may be concluded that the two policemen who appeared as witnesses in the "Slab paver" case did not identify the persons on the railway lines as the defendants because of individual features, but because they expected them to be there. Since the likelihood of false alarms according to the results of our experiment is very high, the accuracy of the two policemen's eyewitness testimony in the "Slab paver" case can therefore be doubted.

Even though the results of this experiment regarding the effect of expectancy correspond with results of a laboratory experiment by Kerstholt, Raaijmakers and Valeton (1992), who used slides as stimulus material, the specific questions raised in the "Slab paver" case made a case related field experiment necessary. Expert testimony on the basis of case related field experiments, so called "Wirklichkeitsexperimente" (reality experiments), has a long tradition in German forensic psychology: Karl Marbe, one of the pioneers of German forensic psychology, based his forensic evaluation for a court case following a railway accident on a famous case related experiment (Marbe, 1913). We strongly believe that case related field experiments in addition to basic research are a very important tool for psychological expert testimony.

References

Brigham, J.C., Maass, A., Snyder, L.D., & Spaulding, K. (1982). The accuracy of eyewitness identification in a field setting. *Journal of Personality and Social Psychology, 42*, 673-681.

Ceci, S.J., Toglia, M.P., & Ross, D.F. (Eds.) (1987). *Children's Eyewitness Memory.* New York: Springer.

Davies, G. (1992). Influencing public policy on eyewitnessing: Problems and possibilities. In F. Lösel, D. Bender & T. Bliesener (Eds.), *Psychology and Law* (pp. 265-274). Berlin: de Gruyter.

Dent, H., & Flin, R. (Eds.) (1992). *Children as Witnesses.* Chichester: Wiley.

Diges, M., & Alonso-Quecuty, M. L. (1993). *Psicología forense experimental.* Valencia: Promolibro.

Egeth, H.E. (1993). What do we not know about eyewitness identification? *American Psychologist, 48*, 577-580.

Elliott, R. (1993). Expert testimony about eyewitness identification. *Law and Human Behavior, 17*, 423-437.

Fabian, T., Stadler, M., & Wetzels, P. (1994). The "authenticity error" in real lineup procedures. Effects of suspect-status and corresponding psychological dissimilarities between target person and distractors: An experimental study. In G.M. Davies, S. Lloyd-Bostock, M. McMurran & C. Wilson (Eds.), *Psychology and Law: Advances in Research.* (pp. 29-38). Berlin: de Gruyter.

Kassin, S.M., Ellsworth, P.C., & Smith, V.L. (1994). Déjà vu all over again: Elliott's critique of eyewitness experts. *Law and Human Behavior, 18*, 203-209.

Kerstholt, J.H., Raaijmakers, J.G.W., & Valeton, J.M. (1992). The effect of expectation on the identification of known and unknown persons. *Applied Cognitive Psychology, 6*, 173-180.

Köhnken, G., & Maass, A. (1988). Eyewitness testimony: False alarms on biased instructions? *Journal of Applied Psychology, 73*, 363-370.

Loftus, E. F. (1983a). Silence is not golden. *American Psychologist, 38*, 564-572.

Loftus, E. F. (1983b). Whose shadow is crooked? *American Psychologist, 38*, 576-577.

Loftus, E. F. (1986). Ten years in the life of an expert witness. *Law and Human Behavior, 10*, 241-263.

Marbe, K. (1913). Psychologische Gutachten zum Prozeß wegen des Müllheimer Eisenbahnunglücks. *Fortschritte der Psychologie und ihrer Anwendungen, 1*, 339-374.

McCloskey, M., & Egeth, H.E. (1983a). Eyewitness identification: What can a psychologist tell a jury? *American Psychologist, 38*, 550-563.

McCloskey, M., & Egeth, H.E. (1983b). A time to speak, or time to keep silence? *American Psychologist, 38*, 573-575.

Michotte, A. (1983). *Gesammelte Werke, Band 2, Die phänomenale Beständigkeit.* Bern: Huber.

Ross, D.F., Read, J.D., & Toglia, M.P. (Eds.) (1994). *Adult Eyewitness Testimony.* Cambridge: Cambridge University Press.

Stadler, M., & Fabian, T. (1995). Der Erwartungseffekt beim Wiedererkennen von Personen, oder: Über die Tendenz, Wahrnehmungshypothesen zu bestätigen. *Zeitschrift für experimentelle Psychologie, 57*, 132-151.

Stadler, M., Schindler, H., & Fabian, T. (1992). The influence of eyewitness observation and photographic presentation on the identification of persons in lineups. In F. Lösel, D. Bender & T. Bliesener (Eds.), *Psychology and Law* (pp. 286-291). Berlin: de Gruyter.

Wells, G.L. (1984). A reanalysis of the expert testimony issue. In G.L. Wells & E.F. Loftus (Eds.), *Eyewitness Testimony* (pp. 304-314). New York: Cambridge University Press.

Yuille, J.C. (1993). We must study forensic eyewitnesses to know about them. *American Psychologist, 48*, 572-573.

Some Aspects of the Role of the Expert in Criminal Cases

J.F. Nijboer

Introduction

The involvement of experts in the investigation and adjudication of criminal cases is legally considered to be a subject that is related to procedural or adjective law rather than to substantive law. However, there are some indirect but nevertheless important connections between expertise and substantive law. An example is the adoption of technical concepts like certain "critical loads" (to measure forbidden air pollution) as elements of an offense. In recent years procedural criminal law has become the subject of international legal comparative study and interdisciplinary study as well to a much greater degree than it had been in the decades before 1970. Especially concerning the law of evidence, international comparative and interdisciplinary discussions emerged since the 1970s (Damaška, 1986; Twining, 1990).

The issues I would like to highlight at this conference are based on my earlier work. I have been researching evidence and systematics in Dutch criminal law since the mid-seventies. In 1990 I published a small book in Dutch about *Forensic Expertise*. In this book I defined forensic expertise as expertise from non-legal disciplines to be applied in concrete legal cases. Forensic experts are non-legally trained people, specializing in issues that arise in or are relevant to the investigation of and adjudication of criminal cases (Nijboer, 1990). In 1990/1991 I spent more than eight months in the United States of America (University of California, Berkeley) studying American law, especially the law of evidence related to the involvement of expert witnesses. From here I started to work on and stimulate exchange of the comparative legal and interdisciplinary study of forensic expertise.

I cannot say that I have come to very firm and clear conclusions about the subject matter as a whole. But there are two ideas which I firmly believe carry some truth in themselves.

The first derives from a comparative background. Lawyers and legal scholars in most modern legal systems are aware of some problems they have with the use of experts in investigation and adjudication. Often these problems are not perceived as general problems, but they are only connected by lawyers and legal scholars of the country to some forensic disciplines or to some experts in relation to some legal problems within their own system, for instance, the quality of forensic psychiatrists in relation to matters of the insanity of the offender. To explain problems of this kind and to search for remedies, the same lawyers and legal scholars of the country look at their own legal system and their own legal culture. Sometimes they think that the legal system and the legal culture of a neighboring country does better. So in the Netherlands we are looking at the Common Law countries and we sometimes think that a little more adversarialness in procedure might be a step to improve our system. For instance, the structural position of counter expertise in a number of cases related to, for instance, DNA-testing, dactyloscopic issues, environmental cases, etc. On the other side of the North Sea, the British, still rethinking the causes of their well known miscarriages of justice, think that the position of the police in their own country is one of the causes of bias in investigation by forensic experts; they are looking at the position of the public prosecution service in the Netherlands which they believe is a better model to control the police and to avoid highly biased police-driven forensic expertise on behalf of the police.

Within limits, both the Dutch and the British are right, insofar as one can always learn something from comparison. But still I do not think that in a more general way looking at one's neighbors and trying to transpose some elements of another system might give better safeguards in some respects as resolution for the problems, since these are perceived as too simple. I think that the contribution of this small scale import and export of legal settings, legal rules and so on is very limited, compared to the complexity of the problems involved. I say this because I am convinced that the problems that arise when we use forensic expertise are more deeply rooted at this level than on the level of the particularities of individual legal systems. I think that basically all western legal systems *share the same problems, rather than they have different problems.* And the problems they have to cope with are the increasing amount of specialists and specialties in the forensic area. Law still may be national; forensic expertise is not. As soon as forensic experts in one discipline develop new techniques or new methods, the experts and their techniques and methods spread out worldwide with the speed of planes, e-mail, and fax-machines. And where all over in the western world advocacy has become a stronger professional discipline, as well as the agencies that carry out investigation and prosecution, the professionals in these areas look for the best available knowledge, techniques, experts and so on.

So it is simply a matter of supply and demand in the field of criminal litigation. And here I get to my *second conclusion*. In my opinion it is the American legal culture with its typical adversarial advocacy where it is the norm to win the case, by settlement or in the trial, using all available tools, that accelerates the development of new forms of forensic expertise. The incentive is very clear: experts and expertise are basically seen as tools to win the case. And if one wants to win a case, one looks for the best means to achieve this. This American adversarial system is different from other western countries' systems by its almost economic principle of competition. However, as said before, in other countries legal authorities and attorneys tend to call upon the best available experts and use the best available expertise as well, but novel techniques and methods are more often available in the USA.

One other aspect related to the narrow skepticism of lawyers and legal scholars of different countries: they are not very sensitive to the circumstance that non-legal expertise derives basically from other disciplines that are no less thorough and adequate than the legal discipline. Experts assessing cases or carrying out experiments in legal settings bring with them basic evaluations from their own disciplines, from their own background. Even the paradigms involved do not automatically converge with the legal perspectives. Basically, experts from other disciplines bring with them sets of own paradigms, perceptions, norms, and values, which are not necessarily the same as the legal ones.

Experts and Expertise

Expertise suggests special abilities which contrast with general abilities. It suggests quality and reliability. In other words, expertise can be relied upon. It is the result of special education, experience or training. Arising from developments in information technology, so-called expert systems have been developed. However, in the legal context, expertise is restricted to human activity, to human expertise, although it may involve the use of tests, instruments and other special measures.

Two remarks should be made here. *First*, in the legal context, terms such as expertise, expert or expert witness are normally used to refer to specialist topics and specialists from disciplines and professions *other than the law*. But the law is a specialist topic as well (lawyers can be called as expert witnesses on the law of another country). Lawyers can be expected both to be appreciative of the importance of specialist areas of knowledge and experience and to be aware of the problems in developing and sustaining such a base from charlatans. Thus, the extent to which judges and lawyers regard themselves as able to represent another discipline's knowledge base as being common sense or unreliable is not self-evident.

Second, modern legal systems rely upon a principle of rationality in fact-finding by independent free evaluation of relevant information. This is the ideal of "free proof". This principle assumes that sound decisions about a factual dispute can be made by any unbiased person or group of people (jury) without particular skills or experience (Nijboer, in Bull/Carson, 1994). This assumption highlights the tension between fact-finding as a general lay activity and the specialist character of evidence. This tension is often reflected in discussions about and the actual assessment of expert evidence. The tension is most prominent in legal systems which have an emphasis on oral proceedings. There, as in the English criminal jury trial, expertise is represented by the expert witness, which contrasts with the mere witness as to facts and to the jury, who have to make the decision, even though it will often involve an assessment of contrasting and competing expert witnesses. Non-expert witnesses can only testify about their observations, about matters of fact deriving from their direct sensory observations/perceptions. The non-expert witness should not express an opinion, although this may prove impractical and is permitted in certain ways, such as when trying to describe a lot of information in a short manner. Another manifestation of this tension is the continuing debate in several countries over the advantages and disadvantages of *jury decision making* in criminal trials, otherwise described as lay decision making versus specialist decision making. At the heart of most of these arguments lie the very nature and quality of expertise. It has to be added that in this type of discussion, again the lawyer appears as an expert himself.

The importance of expert evidence has developed during the last century, particularly in recent years. Its role and importance is not limited to the settlement of disputes in the court. It is increasingly called upon during official inquiries into particular topics. Expertise is also increasingly important in forming new legislation and it has a major and unfortunately, frequently overlooked, role in the pre-trial investigation and in the settlement of cases. Reliance upon experience and practical skills is likely to be reduced as and where the law, reflecting a broader societal tendency, increasingly recognizes the importance of professionalism and applied forms of science in society.

Who is the Expert?

Whilst expertise covers a range of subjects, activities and techniques, the expert is an individual fulfilling a role. Who is to be recognized as an expert? Who, in legal procedures, may be called to act as an expert witness to be involved in the preparation of a report to advise lawyers and possibly give evidence during the proceedings? Most countries' legislation does not include a statutory definition of or procedure for determining who is an expert. For the Federal courts in the United States of America there is a provision within the Federal Rules of Evidence concerning the admissibility of expert witness testimony. FRE 702 defines the expert witness as "a witness qualified as expert by knowledge, skill, experience, training or education." He is allowed to testify on scientific, technical or other specialized knowledge. In a less articulated, more latent way, other jurisdictions assume a similar set of requirements. Most western legal systems rely heavily upon the discretion of the courts and of the pre-trial authorities to decide in actual cases whether or not someone is capable of acting as an expert. Recognition is not restricted to the professional or academic leaders; practitioners with sufficient experience and knowledge can and have been recognized as experts. The legal requirements for recognizing someone as an expert remain rather vague. However, the legal framework is usually supported by the professional rules and norms of the field of expertise in question. For example, chartered psychologists in the Netherlands giving an expert evidence outside of his or her area of expertise could be disciplined by the Netherlands Institute of Psychology (NIP). The merits of disciplinary norms and rules are disputed at least in the USA and in my own country. In most western jurisdictions there are special topics where legislation prescribes the nature of the expert evidence required; for example, this occurs with the taking of blood samples in drunk driving cases, or the certification that the prisoner is fit to be interviewed.

The selection of experts is one of the problematic areas which, I believe, confronts all western legal systems. At this moment it is not very regulated and practice heavily relies on haphazard information. In some areas a system of certification by the experts themselves exists; in other areas there is hardly any check on professional standards. There are almost no rules for judges, police officers, prosecutors and attorneys on how to select experts and how to select a field of expertise. Given the situation that applied scientific work in this area is sometimes very profitable, we can simply expect that amongst serious forensic expertise, "junk-science" can also slip into the legal system. This is one of the problems that I think modern countries have to cope with. This problem arises in Common Law countries as well as in Civil Law countries, since in both groups of systems there still are individuals who choose the experts from memory, lists or directories or even the phone book.

Comparing Common Law systems and Civil Law systems, it is still remarkable that the role of experts and the person who is allowed to have them participate in a case differs considerably. For instance, in England and Wales, experts are normally called to work for one of the sides in the process. Although legislation permits it, the court appointed (neutral) expert is an exception in those countries. This is clearly a consequence of or even a feature of the adversarial system. The same applies even more clearly to the United States of America. In continental European jurisdictions the situation is the reverse, not only in criminal procedure where the parties are not dominant, but also in civil procedures (where the parties litigate in a way that is not very dissimilar from the adversarial procedure in England and Wales). The court appointed or court recognized expert is the norm. And any expert appointed by one of the parties is generally considered to be an inferior kind of expert. These differences apply to the handling of cases within the courts and they also impact on the manner in which both the investigation and trial preparation are organized. However, the contrast between the Common Law countries and the Civil Law countries is less in the pre-trial stage.

Substantive Law and Probability (Criminal Law)

In substantive criminal law the principle of legality requires that crimes be well defined. Legislation normally includes sharp descriptions of behavior. The elements of the definition together form the definition of the crime. These definitions also deliver the ultimate issues that have to be proven. As we already saw, the increasing involvement of professional experts and their disciplines is a societal phenomenon that goes much further than adjudication. Also in other fields of political/legal decision making the legal system relies upon experts and their disciplines, for example in criminal legislation.

Traditionally the elements of a crime are defined in such a way that they are not too difficult to be proven. Therefore, the legislation uses, for example, the violation of a duty to care as an element of a crime, avoiding the almost impossible proof of an actual state of mind of a person. The same way certain forms of risk taking can be elements of a crime and even forms of absolute or strict liability are not unknown in criminal law. All these already traditional kinds of elements are used to facilitate the proof in criminal cases. Recently varieties emerge: certain risks are elements of newly formulated offenses in "modern" areas, but the elements are increasingly formulated in terms of expertise. And they can only be proven again by means of a specialist; for instance, so-called critical loads in environmental crimes, that can only be proven by special tests. Already more known are mandatory ways of investigation by way of fixed tests, such as blood alcohol testing. We also, in the Netherlands, know crimes where an element is disobedience to official agents, who in fact can be experts in several areas (such as in the food regulations). What we see here is a tendency to formulate the elements of crimes already in terms of other disciplines, whereas in concrete cases the fulfillment of these elements can only be proven in the way the same disciplines can do it. This may make the legal system too dependent on other disciplines. When we look at forensic psychology we have two areas where fixed tests could be used: the way identifications of persons are carried out and tests to assess someone's insanity (or even his competency to stand trial; ability to be examined).

The problems that arise here are not easy to tackle. The way crimes are formulated in legislation is a complex process. This process can not simply be reversed or altered. The only thing we can do is to be aware of the problem, especially to prevent substantial areas from being deferred to only specialists communities, instead of being kept within a broader societal, political context. Norms and values that become so important that they are enforced by criminal law must be so important that they have to be discussed in a much broader way than only by a selected forum (Hoekema, in Nijboer et al. 1993).

Methodological and Ethical Norms in the Legal and Other Disciplines

The last subject I would like to introduce here is the way the law regulates the role of the expert and to what extent. In view of the subject matter as well as the professional ethics, the law nowadays heavily depends on the disciplinary systems of the professional disciplines. Their norms, like legal norms in the area of investigation and evidence, can be divided into two groups: methodological norms and ethical norms. Of both we can ask the question whether these norms have some legal force as well. I will give an example of both:

In some recent cases involving eyewitness identification of another person in the Netherlands, the question was raised whether professional, specialist guidelines set forth for identification parades had been followed, and if not, if this should lead to exclusion of the resulting evidence gathered this way. Here the police officers setting up a parade were the forensic experts. In both cases the evidence was testimony of a witness recognizing a suspect, during the pre-trial stage, which testimony was reported by the police. In both cases in an obiter dictum, the Supreme Court of the Netherlands tends to open the door a little bit for exclusion of this kind of evidence (either as illegally obtained evidence or as unreliable evidence) (Reported in *Expert Evidence*, Vol. 1/3 and 2/2).

The other example is evidence that was the result of the work of an expert, violating *ethical* norms set forth by his own professional ethics. Should such evidence be excluded as improperly obtained? In our law of criminal procedure, illegally obtained evidence as a concept is restricted to illegal behavior of legal authorities. In other countries this is called the silver platter-doctrine: evidence improperly gathered by other people than the legal authorities is not considered as illegally obtained. When the other is a psychological expert, hired by the police authorities to "help" the police in obtaining a confession by the defendant, how would you decide?

References

Bull, R., & Carson, D. (eds.) (1994). *Handbook for Psychology in Legal Context*. Baffins Lane: Wiley and sons.

Damaška, M. R. (1986). *The Faces of Justice and State Authority*. New Haven (Yale).

Nijboer, J.F. (1990). *Forensic expertise*. Arnhem.

Nijboer, J.F., Callen, C.R. and Kwak, N. (eds.) (1993). *Forensic expertise and the law of evidence*. Amsterdam.

Twining, W.L. (1990). *Rethinking evidence*. Oxford.

Part IV
Juries and Tribunals

Models in Jury Decision-Making

Pilar de Paúl

Introduction

Final jury decision-making, the verdict, is the result of a group decision process. However, many psychological studies have not analyzed jury deliberation. Group jury studies often have been mainly concerned about the product of deliberation, without a process analysis of jury decision-making.

One of the studies of group social processes in jury decision-making is *Inside the Jury* (Hastie et al., 1983). The authors found two models of jury deliberations: the evidence-driven deliberation style and the verdict-driven deliberation style. Each style can be identified during the first stage of deliberation (which usually takes one third of the total deliberation time).

During the first stage of the verdict-driven deliberation style, the jurors take a public vote on the verdict rather than attempt to reach an agreement. This style is more habitual in decision-making by majority.

During the first stage in the evidence-driven deliberation style, the jurors pool information about their versions of the case and attempt to influence one another to reach consensus on a group story. The jury does not take a first vote in this phase.

Hastie et al. (1983), Kerr and MacCoun (1985) and Davis et al. (1988) have not found that the method and timing polling have an effect on the final verdicts reached by juries.

In this paper, the first stages of 24 jury deliberations are analyzed in order to find different styles in jury decision-making. To identify the different models, the timing polling was coded for each videotaped deliberation.

Method

The 24 mock jury deliberations come from a previous study about the influence of the size and decision rule in jury decision-making (De Paúl, 1991). In that study, the subjects listened to a real trial and were randomly assigned to 6 or 12 member juries. The juries of each size were divided into two: one-half was required to reach a unanimous verdict and the other was required to reach a two-third majority verdict. The decision-making process was videotaped without the knowledge of the subjects. The total deliberation time set was one hour.

For the present descriptive analysis, each deliberation time was divided into three stages. I analyzed if the jury took its first vote in the first third of total deliberation time in order to identify a verdict-driven deliberation style.

Results

Table 1: Timing Polling in 24 Mock Jury Deliberations

	1/3	2/3	3/3	
Six member jury	7	-	5	12
Twelve member jury	1	1	10	12
	8	1	15	24

In 8 of the 24 deliberations the jury took its first vote during the first stage. Seven of these are six-member jury deliberations (three under unanimity and four under majority). Therefore, 58.3% of six-member deliberations took a public vote that defined the opinion factions and then searched a consensus. None of these juries used the total deliberation time set. Five juries used less than 30 minutes and the other two reached a verdict after 40 minutes of deliberation.

Only one of the twelve-member jury deliberations took its vote during the first third of the total deliberation time. This jury was under majority decision rule and at the beginning of deliberation only one member thought that the accused was guilty. The total deliberation time was only six minutes.

Discussion

This descriptive analysis shows that it is more frequent for six-member juries to take their first vote at the beginning of deliberation. This event is a characteristic of the verdict-driven deliberation style.

In a previous study I analyzed the decision-making process of these mock jury deliberations (De Paúl, 1996). The jury size had a substantial effect on the number of questions asked during deliberation. It was concluded that an advantage of decision-making in larger juries is that those juries exhibit a high level of fact-finding activity. This result is consistent with the fact that the evidence-driven jury (in contrast to the verdict-driven jury) seems to have many of the desirable features of group discussion (Davis et al., 1988).

Also, the studies about verdict-driven juries found that this style is more habitual in juries under majority rule.

The Spanish jury law has established the number of members at nine and under a majority decision rule. Both factors (small jury and majority) could mean a verdict-driven deliberation.

The law also establishes a double majority decision-making rule. Seven votes are needed for a guilty verdict and five votes for not guilty. Under these conditions, the probability of a poll at the beginning of deliberation could be high because of the juries' need to know the level of agreement that they have to reach.

In order to reduce the possibility of verdict-driven deliberation in the future Spanish jury it will be necessary to instruct juries about the need to contemplate the facts, testimonies and so on before members give their personal preference for the verdict.

References

Davis, J.H., Stasson, M., Ono, K., & Zimmerman, S. (1988). The effects of straw polls on group decision-making: Sequential voting pattern, timing, and local majorities. *Journal of Personality and Social Psychology, 55, 6,* 918-926.

Hastie, R., Penrod, S.D., & Pennington N. (1983). *Inside the jury.* Cambridge, MA: Harvard University Press.

Kerr, N.L., & MacCoun, R.J. (1985). The effects of jury size and polling method on the process and products of jury deliberation. *Journal of Personality and Social Psychology, 48, 2,* 349-363.

De Paúl, P. (1991). *El proceso de deliberación en el jurado.* Madrid: Editorial de la Universidad Complutense de Madrid.

De Paúl, P. (1996). The influence of the size and decision rule in jury decision-making. In Davies, G., McMurran, M., Wilson, C. & Lloyd-Bostock, S. (Eds.) (1996). *Psychology, Law, and Criminal Justice.* Berlin • New York: De Gruyter.

Formal Pattern in Jury Decision Making

E. Inmaculada De la Fuente, Ana Ortega, Ignacio Martín and Humberto Trujillo

Introduction

In some democracies, citizens can elect executive and legislative power but cannot participate in judicial power. Such participation is not possible due to the fact that the rules that make it possible have not been developed.

In Spain, the legal framework of public participation (jury) extends from its inclusion in The Provisional Law of *Enjuiciamiento Criminal* (Criminal Procedure) of 1872 to the promulgation of the *Ley Especial del Jurado* (Special Jury Law) of April 20, 1888, after the abolition of the institution in 1875. The jury appears again in article 103 of the Constitution of 1931, in an act of 27 April that reestablishes the latter according to the law of 1888. Another act of 18 June 1931, authorizes the Geographical and Census Institute to draw up lists of possible jurors. Its abolition was decreed on September 8, 1936.

Article 125 of our current Constitution (1978) reintroduces the jury as a form of social participation in justice, and The Jury Law which sets the standard for its reestablishment has been approved recently.

The study of questions and problems concerning the jury, its origin and development, and the effect of its structure on judicial procedure are areas of great importance for its introduction. It is therefore extremely important to take into account the results obtained in the extensive research on psychological processes, the creation of the census of possible jurors, the analysis of the jury's structure, the different options that may be taken with regard to rule of resolution and any other aspect that may directly or indirectly, affect the process of decision making resulting in the issuance of a verdict.

The present paper has a twofold objective:

The theory of Behavioral Decision Making (TBD) is presented as a valid theoretical frame of reference for studying the modeling of the process that leads the jury to reach a verdict. The extensive research results in TBD on individual and collective decision making provide a broad basis to develop and contrast the goodness of the models of decision making in juries as well as its modification, should it prove to be necessary.

Similarly, a descriptive model of the issue of individual "justice" from the subjects comprising a jury is proposed. Such a model refers to the individual decision which is reached after the development of the whole judicial process, and before the initiation of the process of deliberation.

Psychology and the Jury: Origin and Development

The origin of the jury as an institution may be traced back to the 12th century (BC). Towards 900 (BC) a formula of participation in judicial processes existed in which the two parties who intervened in the lawsuit were equally represented (Nemeth, 1986). Evidence exists of its use among the Greeks (Lind, 1982). The Normans introduced it in Britain in 1066 from where it extended to the United States and to those countries under English rule. In 1791 it was introduced into France where it underwent a different evolution from that in Anglo-Saxon countries (Sobral and Arce, 1990). These brief notes establish the very early origin of the jury as an institution, even though in some cases it did not receive the name used today.

Different authors (Haney, 1984; Loh, 1981; Tapp, 1976) place the interest in different legal aspects, within the social sciences in general and psychology in particular, at the beginning of this century. The classical classification, instituted by Loh (1981) and which establishes the development of legal psychology, is presented in four stages:

An initial stage extends from the beginning of the century to the thirties. In this stage, contributions originating in experimental psychology and studies carried out on perception and memory are extended to legal phenomena and applied to the judgment of testimonies. This stage is characterized by the lack of understanding between jurists and psychologists, which caused the latter to lose their initial interest in psycho-legal research.

A second stage, extending from the thirties to the fifties, is characterized by the opening of the legal system to the social sciences and the development of empirical studies that could demonstrate the fallacies on which legal practice was based. This stage was productive in those studies applied to the area of our concern, but the academic setting was more influenced than the legal profession itself. The two major areas of investigation which characterize this period are the study of the criminal personality and the cognitive processes that affect witnesses, jurors and judges.

A third stage covers the period from the fifties to the sixties, during which forensic psychology was consolidated. Clinical psychologists and psychiatrists are required by the courts as expert witnesses in order to testify to the legal competence of the accused. At this stage, the influence of social psychology begins to be apparent in studies on civil rights and the effect of publicity on the court.

At the end of the seventies the most current stage of legal psychology commences. Psychological research in the social-legal setting centered on the study of the three principal institutions that comprise the penal system: police, correctional and treatment institutions, and courts of justice. In the literature on the subject the most outstanding initial research includes such classical papers as those of Brown (1981); Mira and López (1932), as well as the notable increment of work from that moment to the present. Examples, among others, include Bermant, Nemeth and Vidmar (1976); Saks and Hastie (1978); Sales (1977); Muñoz-Sabaté, Bayés and Munné (1980); Ker and Bray (1982); Müller, Blackman and Chapman (1984); Jiménez Burillo and Clemente (1986); Palmer (1988); Garzón (1989); Sobral and Arce (1990) and De Paúl (1991).

Within the conception of the judicial process as a social process, areas of interest for the methodologist and the social psychologist are studied. These include decision making, information processing, perception, attitudes, group dynamics, and many others that serve to exemplify aspects of the legal process which include such different areas of study as the procedure of justice in the adversarial system, the identification of witnesses, etc. In the present work some theoretical questions in the study of the jury and its members are introduced.

Study of the Jury and its Members

The aspects that are of interest to methodology and social psychology in the study of the jury are, among others, the selection of its members, decision making and the procedures of presenting evidence and instructions to the jury.

We are especially interested in the study of decision making, including both the individual decision and, after deliberation, the group decision that results in a verdict.

The task of the jury is to establish a social judgment from the existing evidence. The process that will lead a jury to reach a verdict will be, in the first place, an individual decision by each one of its members, which is the focus of the present paper. As a frame of reference for its study, we propose the theory of behavioral decision. If the entire process leading to a specific verdict is examined, a study of behavior of the dynamics of social interaction (exchange of opinion, emergence of norms and roles, etc.) must be undertaken. Finally, the individual judgments will have to be appropriately combined through the study of behavior from a group perspective, which, under a specific decisive rule, will lead to the final verdict in the process.

Theory of Behavioral Decision-Making

Thought has been an important area of study in philosophy and psychology since the time of Aristotle who, using the introspective method, concluded that the content of the mind consisted primarily of images which reproduce the sensations that the subject had experienced. Aristotle proposed that the association of ideas occurred in memory according to three principles: temporal and spatial continuity, similarity, and contrast. These principles were readopted by the English Empiricist School (Hobbes, Locke, Hume and Berkeley) for whom the elements of the mind are ideas and sensations: in association, sensations form ideas that constitute the basic material of the superior processes of the mind, that is thought. The empirical postulates provide the theoretical framework in which experimental psychology is rooted.

At the end of the last century researchers from the Wurzburg School believed that thoughts are neither sensations nor images and that, generally, people are not able to verbalize the way in which they have arrived at their answers. This subthreshold character of thought is emphasized by Gestalt Psychology in proposing the concept of "insight", or sudden comprehension of the elements of the problem confronted, and it emphasizes the importance of variables related to the task proposed to the subjects.

With the emergence of Behaviorism, the study of cognitive processes was practically abandoned for two decades. Later, under the name of "cognitive revolution" (Gigerencer and Murray, 1987), research on thought was integrated into the central line of cognitive psychology, giving rise to main areas of research related to deductive and inductive reasoning.

In natural thought induction and deduction may alternate, thus a rule that has been induced is applied deductively to a new example. In deductive reasoning the standard theory is formal and propositional logic (Wason, 1966, 1968, 1983; Wason and Shapiro,1971; Evans, 1972, 1977; Griggs and Cox, 1982; Valentine, 1985; Klaczynski, Felfand and Reese, 1989). The illogical nature of inductive inference has produced much debate in philosophy and science, given that scientific inferences are inductive in themselves, with general results inferred from specific observations. Inference is interpreted within the conceptual framework known as "Behavioral Decision Theory", an ambiguous term applied to as much of the process of decision making in humans.

The descriptive and standard foci are differentiated as much in their objectives as in the manner of understanding the way in which a person makes decisions, and his or her methods of investigation. Nevertheless, interrelations exist and, on occasions, it is difficult to place them clearly in one section or the other.

Standard focus in behavioral decision theory

The roots of the standard focus may be situated in the 17th and 18th centuries when a series of mathematicians attempted to establish models that allow maximum gains in games of chance. Since then, various models of choice with or without risk have been developed (Von Newmann and Morensten, 1944; Savage, 1954). The basic principles of these models establish that subjects construct a decision tree in order to project the consequences of the alternative actions existing in the real situation which is to be analyzed. From this position, the decision maker is the "economic man", characterized by studying the different courses of action and choosing the alternative which optimizes the decision.

Two important questions exist considering this type of investigation:
- What to use as a standard criterion.
- How to interpret the discrepancies between people's judgments and the standard criterion chosen.

Disagreement between human judgment and an accepted normative criterion may reflect an error on the part of the subject that will have to be corrected, or a legitimate disagreement between human judgment and normative criteria. This is particularly relevant when considering that the data obtained in the different investigations habitually violate some of the strong assumptions on which normative criteria are based (Wright and Murphy, 1984; Jennings et al., 1982).

Given that many decisions in the real life are made under uncertain conditions, the application of this focus has demanded a systematic approach to probability, the most usual being the "Bayesian Theory of Decision".

Research carried out in this area in the sixties indicates that, if indeed it is true that subjects use prior information in a decision making situation, it is also true that this information is not combined according to the proposed Bayesian standard (Edwards, 1968; Gigerencer and Murray, 1987). From this standpoint, only structural changes will influence decisive behavior. The task content (content of the concrete situation to be analyzed) and the form of presenting the alternatives (evidence, in form and sequencing of presentation), are not considered relevant variables which can alter the judgment made. Nevertheless, many studies have been found that the content and the way of presenting the information are relevant factors in decisions (Einhorn, 1980; Evans, 1984; Griggs, 1983; Pollard, 1982; Wason, 1983).

To state that human thought, including the emission of judgments or choices of an alternative based on prior evidence, is guided by a rule of general purpose, such as those that postulate the standard focus of the decision, implies that the context of the problem is not important. Thus, contextual variables such as concrete instructions are not considered relevant. All minds would apply the same rule to all the contents and all the contexts, which would in turn eliminate subjectivity. This would imply that aspects ranging from mere spontaneity to completely informed personal judgment are not considered, and all without considering the subjects' attitudes depending on the information content to be analyzed. Accordingly, different subjects could not reach a different conclusion in the same decision situation. This would suppose an incorrect decision which would have to be corrected (Einhorn and Hogart, 1981).

Numerous studies exist which attempt to use standard models, with the assumptions in the field of legal psychology, and centered on the individual decision making of the jury components (Grofman, 1981, 1985; Marshall and Wise, 1975; Schum, 1977; Gelfand and Solomon, 1973, 1974, 1975; Penrod and Hastie, 1979; Walbert, 1971). The results obtained show some inconsistencies between models and data. There clearly seems to be a necessity to adapt the standard position towards a descriptive modeling which utilizes relevant variables in the decision situations in humans, such as the context itself and attitudes of the subjects who will have to make the judgment.

Descriptive focus in behavioral decision theory

In contrast to the standard focus, the descriptive attempts to describe and explain how people make decisions. The decision maker is not just an "economic man", a passive subject who behaves according to the dictates of a formal rule, but an active one, who hasa limited capacity to process the information presented to him and possesses an adaptive character. This has four basic consequences:

- Perception of the information is selective and opened to influence.
- People cannot simultaneously integrate great quantities of information. Two types of processing can be carried out; in parallel, with limitation in capacity, or predominantly in sequential form.
- Information processing necessarily depends on the operations which simplify the judgment task and reduce mental effort.
- Memory capacity is limited and has a reconstructive character.

With respect to the situations that will have to be analyzed in order to make a judgment, not only their structure is considered. Content, context, method of presenting the alternatives or evidences, are variables that the researcher should take into account, since it has been shown that these may have as much influence in the ultimate choice preferences of individuals as in the strategies used by them in order to arrive at a judgment (Einhort an Hogarth, 1981; Payne, 1982).

The change of perspective assumes the development of two areas of research which are mutually supportive: on the one hand, the study of strategies used by people, based on the conception of heuristics and biases in human decision making, proposed by Tversky and Kahneman (1973, 1982, 1983); and on the other, an attempt to identify the underlying cognitive processes of judgment and choice, and the theories which allow an adequate description of subjects' behavior.

Tversky and Kahneman (1973) propose that people carry out inferences in the presence of information or evidence presented and make judgements using heuristics. In their use of the term (Kahneman and Tversky, 1973; Kahneman, Slovic and Tversky, 1982), a heuristic is a short cut and essentially simple, in contrast to the complexity of the standard theory of decision, which is very difficult to apply. In a series of papers (Tversky and Kahneman, 1973, 1974, 1982, 1983), these authors describe three types of heuristics: availability, adjustment and anchorage, and representativeness, showing at the same time that, while such heuristics may be appropriate in some contexts, they may lead to a wide range of errors and biases in others.

Subjects are using the heuristic of availability when they estimate the probability of a result in function of the ease with which they can evoke examples of it. The bias of availability may arise from the exact memory of a biased group of examples. For instance, people may overestimate the likelihood of deaths caused by accidents compared to those due to illness. The explanation given according to availability is that the media provide a high degree of selective information for deaths from violent and spectacular accidents but a low degree for deaths due to ordinary causes. It seems that information provided by the media distorts the perception of evidence presented (Lichtenstein, Slovic, Fischhoff and Layman, 1978).

The heuristic of adjustment and anchorage refers to situations in which people estimate a probability from the selection of an initial value suggested by the information presented, its form, and sequential order of presentation (Tversky and Kahneman, 1982; Einhorn and Hogarth, 1985).

The essence of this heuristic resides in the fact that the subject's response, in the form of adjustment of estimation, is biased by the initial value (anchorage) that has been chosen. The anchorage is given to the subject in presenting the information or evidence and can change with both the quantity of information presented and its form of presentation. It may be a figure already established in memory, prior to the process, being a reflection of an attitude previously indicated by the issue itself or the publicity that may have been made of it.

Representativeness is characterized by the directional relation between a model or population and an example or sample. According to this heuristic, probabilities are judged in function of the degree to which an example or sample resembles a model or population. Thus, for example, people judge the probability of a person holding a specific occupation by the degree to which the given description of this person is representative of the stereotype of the profession.

The heuristic of representativeness is consistent with the concept of likelihood of the bayesian models, with the advantage and disadvantages that such models imply.

In the attempt to obtain descriptions of subject's behavior in ambiguous situations, models have been created which either do or do not consider the different heuristics (Einhorn and Hogarth, 1985), but all of which take situations of ambiguity into account in one way or another. In these models, situations of increasing complexity have to be analyzed, in which not only the structure must be considered. The content or context and the form of presenting the evidence influences the final decision and the strategies used to reach it. The subject's attitude may also change this final decision. In obtaining models which adequately describe the situation in question, it is therefore of great importance that they incorporate the possibility of displaying individual differences, due to the personal characteristics of the subjects who will have to make the judgment.

The aim of this paper is to present a model which describes how jurors can make an individual decision regarding the probability of an event in a scale of guilt assignment. The model is constructed by the subjects faced with a situation in which they observe ambiguity. The judgment expressed is based on blocks of considered evidence coming from different sources of information with limited reliability. This model postulates that the jurors utilize a strategy of anchorage and adjustment, and that the way of combining the information is additive, directly related to the credibility of the source of information presented as evidence and inversely related to the ambiguity perceived in these sources. In the proposed model the subject's attitude is a parameter which may cause the individually expressed judgment to vary.

In order to present a useful model which may be a good predictor of the verdict in a judicial process, it is necessary to complement the present proposal with the incorporation of the elements which shape the remaining stages in the judicial process, deliberative process and combination of individual judgments. Nevertheless, in order to accept the model in its totality, a fragmented verification is necessary to indicate its shortcomings and allow for their correction.

Anchorage and Adjustment Model

The model of anchorage and adjustment (Einhorn and Hogarth, 1985) describes how the citizen makes judgments under ambiguity. In it a strategy of anchorage and adjustment is postulated in order to evaluate probabilities. According to this, subjects start with an initial value for the probability p_A on which they are asked to give an opinion. This initial value may be an account offered by experts or, simply, a number activated in memory due to previous information. If $S(p_A)$ is denominated as the judgment made with the strategy of anchorage and adjustment, we have:

$$S(p_A) = p_A + k$$

where K is the net effect of the adjustment process.

The perceived ambiguity in the situation affects the absolute size of the adjustment and is represented in the model by the parameter θ. In its turn, the attitude of the person, i.e., the tendency to give different weights to values of p that are greater or smaller than the initial estimation, are represented by β, resulting in the model:

$$S(p_A) = p_A + \theta\left(1 - p_A - p_A^\beta\right) \quad (1)$$

According to the formula, the complete model implies that the probability judged is a total weighted from p_A and $1\text{-}p_A$, and the weightings are influenced by the perceived ambiguity.

The inference considered refers to a subjective estimate which evaluates the likelihood of an event based on testimonies received from a single source of limited reliability. The results obtained by the authors of the model show that the expectations concerning *p* are influenced by the similarity of the events to which the subject is faced, the credibility that the subject herself gives to the source from which she receives the information, and the number of reports that she handles or the size of the sample.

The explicit incorporation of the size of the sample to the model assumes that if

$$\frac{\theta'}{n} = \theta$$

$$S(f,c) = p_A + \frac{\theta'}{n}\left(1 - p_A - p_A^\beta\right) \quad (2)$$

where $S(f,c)$ is the final estimate given, considering that from the total n of reports managed, f are in favor and c against, and p_A is the anchorage from which the subjects in that situation start: $p_A = f/n$.

The implications of the model presented are:

1. The effect of the quantity of judged information n is taken into account. $S(p_A) \rightarrow p_A$ when $n \rightarrow \infty$, that is, when the quantity of information increases the adjustment is minimized or, what is equivalent, $S(p_A)$ converges asymptotically to p_A.
2. The size of the sample of reports, n, also affects the activity of the complementary probabilities. The complementary probabilities are additive if $\theta = 0$ or $\beta = 1$ or $p_A = 0.1$. In any other case subaddition or superaddition exists. With the inclusion of n it must be added to the conditions discussed that additivity occurs if $n \rightarrow \infty$ and violations to it would be more likely if n were small.

A Model for Combining Sources

Introduction

The authors of the model described in point 6 consider the possibility of its extension to the case of multiple sources and different points in time.

Einhorn and Hogarth (1985) establish a matrix of evidence where each element $(f_{jk}; c_{jk})$ includes f_{jk} or number of testimonies in favor of the hypothesis produced by the source j in the period K, and c_{jk} the number of testimonies against. Evidently, a matrix of this type provides access to all the information available on the occurrence or non-occurrence of an event, but as the authors themselves point out, the challenge of explaining how people incorporate these factors into their judgments is formidable.

In real life, in general, and in the course of judicial process, in particular, the jurors will obtain information from diverse sources or blocks of evidence. Such information will be supplied to them possibly in different forms and at different times, and their sources of origin will be multiple and differentially reliabilities.

We propose to establish a function of aggregation of information for the case of multiple sources which is consistent with the strategy of anchorage and adjustment and which may be contrasted empirically by means of an experimental series.

In the construction of such a function, it is assumed that the cognitive strategies used to gather information coming from different sources must take the same elements into account as the process of adjustment undertaken to evaluate the initial probabilities p_A, and make a judgment through the mechanism of anchorage and adjustment. This assumption is based on the fact that the subjective aspects which determine the judgment of the subject, his or her perception of ambiguity and his or her aversion to or inclination towards risk, which such ambiguity involves, are not qualitatively modified by the consideration of one or several sources of information. Therefore, and in accordance to the model of anchorage and adjustment, we will consider three factors:

1. The initial evaluation of the probability obtained from different sources.
2. The amount of ambiguity perceived from the different sources.
3. The personal attitude towards ambiguity in the circumstances.

The first point leads us to consider that if we have two sources with n_1 and n_2 testimonies that provide points of anchorage p_{A1} and p_{A2}, if no other substantive element in the problem exists, the different number of testimonies in each source would lead us to establish a point of anchorage which would be the estimation obtained from the joint consideration of both sources, i. e.,

$$\frac{f_1 + f_2}{n_1 + n_2} = \frac{n_1 p_{A1}}{n_1 + n_2} + \frac{n_2 p_{A2}}{n_1 + n_2}$$

Thus, the judgment that each source would provide separately will be weighted for its relative size in a joint judgment from both sources.

Regarding the second point, it seems evident that the sources which generate the greatest ambiguity will have a smaller assessment at the time of making a judgment than those others which are assessed as less ambiguous. Therefore, each source will be considered with the inverse of this ambiguity with respect to the mean ambiguity of the sources.

The third element to assess, the personal attitude towards perceived ambiguity, will be considered initially depending on the intrinsic characteristics of the subject making the judgment, and for this reason it will be considered unvarying from one source to another.

Two sources of information

Let f_1, c_1, f_2, c_2, be the reports in favor and against an event of interest proceeding from two sources of information F_1 and F_2. The total number of observers who report from both sources is called n_1 and n_2, and θ_1 y θ_2 the components of the total perceived ambiguity corresponding to F_1 and F_2 respectively.

The judgment that results in such a situation is a combination weighted from the resulting judgments of a simple situation, in that the sources F1 and F2 are considered separately. For reasons already discussed in the introductory section, a direct proportionality with the total number of favorable reports has been used in the weightings, and an inverse proportionality with the component of ambiguity related to the source. According to this, the following expression is proposed for the assessment of the probability of an event from two sources.

$$S(f_1, c_1; f_2, c_2) = \sum_i \frac{n_i}{\Sigma_i \theta_i} \frac{\Sigma_i \theta_i}{2\theta_i} S(f_i, c_i) \quad (3)$$

Taking into account the form of $S(f_1; c_1)$ y $S(f_2; c_2)$, which appears in (2), it follows that:

After a reorganization appropriate for a simpler presentation

$$S(f_1, c_1; f_2, c_2) = \frac{\Sigma_i \theta_i}{2\Sigma_i n_i} \Sigma_i \left(\frac{n_i p_{A_1}}{\theta_i} + \frac{n_i \theta_i}{\theta_i n_i} \left(1 - p_A - p_{A_i}^\beta \right) \right)$$

of the equation, we obtain:

$$S(f_1, c_1; f_2, c_2) = \frac{\Sigma_i \theta_i}{2\Sigma_i n_i} \Sigma_i \left(\frac{n_i p_{A_1}}{\theta_i} + 1 - p_{A_1} - p_{A_i}^\beta \right)$$

K sources of information (K>2)

The equation (2) is generalizable to the situation in which K sources of information intervene with $n_1, n_2,..., n_k$ reports respectively. If a combination of the judgments estimated from each one of the sources is established, in terms of equation (4), a final assessment results which, suitably developed, has the following form:

$$S(f_1, c_1,..., f_k, c_k) = \frac{\Sigma_i \theta_i}{K\Sigma_i n_i} \left(\Sigma_i \frac{n_i p_{A_i}}{\theta_i} + K - \Sigma_i p_{A_i} - \Sigma_i p_{A_i}^\beta \right)$$

Properties of the model

a) θ affects the absolute size of the factor o adjustment, i.e., $\theta = 0$ y $S(p_A) = p_A$.
b) $S(p)$ is regressive with respect to p.
c) The conditions under which the probabilistic judgments of complementary events are additive reflect those in which our generalization is based, i.e. if $\theta = 0$ or being θ_1

= θ_2, with $\beta = 1$ or $p_A = 0.1$. In the other case, subadditivity exists if β is less than 1 and superadditivity if β is greater than 1.

d) If the resulting equation $S(f_1,c_1;f_2,c_2)$ is analyzed in the situation in which two sources with identical reliability are considered, the conclusions reached partially coincide with those that would result from considering both sources as one only. The result, after comparing the corresponding equations, leads us to conclude that the existence of two sources with identical reliability gives us a point of anchorage identical to the situation resulting from considering both sources as only one. The same does not occur with the parameter of ambiguity of the model; the fact of considering two sources even with identical reliability assumes an increment or decrease of the parameter depending on the parameter β. Thus, for example in situations in which $\beta = 1$ the ambiguity in the situation of two sources diminishes.

Conclusions

The proposed model predicts probability judgments which could be established in terms of scales of guilt. It allows for the prediction of individual judgments, combining the testimonies presented in multiple reports. It takes into account that the credibility of different blocks of evidence influences the ambiguity perceived by the subjects. It also takes into account that the attitude of the subject is a parameter which can cause the judgment made by the jurors to vary, and it postulates that the cognitive strategies used by the subjects are those which are proposed in the model for combining sources. It is necessary to establish an experimental series which tests the goodness of the model proposed.

References

Bermant, G. Nemeth, C. & Vidmar, N. (1976) *Psychology and the law. Research Frontiers* Lexington: Lexintong Books.

Brown, M.R. (1981) *Legal Psychology*. New York: Dacapo Press

De Paúl, P. (1991) *El proceso de deliberación en el jurado*. Tesis doctoral. Universidad Complutense de Madrid. Madrid.

Edwards, W. (1968). Conservatism in human information processing. In B.Kleinmuntz (Ed.), *Formal representation of human judgment*. New York: Wiley Press.

Einhorn, H.J. (1980). Learning from experience and suboptimal rules in decision making. In T. Wallsten (Ed.), *Cognitive processes in choice and decision behavior*. Hillsdale, New York.: Lawrence Erlbaum.

Einhorn, H.J. & Hogarth, R.M. (1981). Behavioral decision theory: Processes of judgment and choice. *Annual Review of Psychology*, 32, 53-88.

Einhorn, H.J. & Hogarth, R.M. (1985) Ambiguity and uncertainty in probabilistic inference. *Psychological Review*, 92, 433-461.

Evans, J.St.B.T. (1972). Interpretation and matching bias in a reasoning task. *British Journal of Psychology*, 24, 193-199.

Evans, J.St.B.T. (1977). Toward a statistical theory of reasoning. *Quarterly Journal of Experimental Psychology*, 29A, 297-306.

Evans, J.St.B.T. (1984). Heuristic and analytic processes in reasoning. *British Journal of Psychology*, 75, 451-468.

Garzon, A. (1989) *Psicología y Justicia*. Valencia. Promolibro.

Gelfand, A.A. & Solomon, H.(1973). A study of Poisson's models for jury veredict in criminal and civil trials. *Journal of American Statistical Association*, 68, 241-278.

Gelfand, A.A. & Solomon, H.(1974) Modeling jury verdicts in American legal system. *Journal of the American Statistical Association*, 69, 32-37.

Gelfand, A.A. & Solomon, H.(1975) Analizing the decision making process of the American Jury. *Journal of the American Statistical Association*, 70, 305-310.

Gigerencer, G. & Murray, D.J. (1987). *Cognition as intuitive statistics*. Hilldale, New York: Lawrence Erlbaum.

Griggs, R.A. (1983). The role of problem content in the selection task and the THOG problem. In J.St.B.T. Evans (Ed.), *Thinking and reasoning: Psychological approaches*. London: Rutledge and Kegan Paul.

Griggs, R.A. & Cox, J.R. (1982). The elusive thematic-materials effect in Wason's selection task. *British Journal of Psychology*, 73, 407-420.

Grofman, B. (1981) Mathematical models of juror and jury decision-making: The state of the art. In B.D. Sales (ed). *Perspectives in law and psychology: The trial process*, New York: Plenum Press, vol. 2., 305-351.

Grofman, B. (1985) Research note. The Accuracy of group majorities for disjunctive and conjunctive decision task. *Organizational behavior and human decision processes*, 35, 119-123.

Haney, C. (1984) Social factfinding and legal decision-making. In D.J. Muller, D.E. Blackman & A.J. Chapman (Eds). *Psychology and law*, 33-54. Chichester. Wiley Press.

Jennings, D.L.; Amabile, T.M. & Ross, L.(1982). Informal covariation assesment: data-based versus theory-based judgements. In D. Kahneman, P. Slovic & A. Tversky (Eds.). *Judgement under uncertainty: Heuristics and biases*. New York: Cambridge University Press.

Jiménez-Burillo J.F. & Clemente, M. (1986) *Psicología Social y Sistema Penal*. Madrid: Alianza.

Kahneman, D.; Slovic, P. & Tversky, A. (1982). *Judgment under uncertainty: Heuristics and Biases*. New York: Cambridge University Press.

Kahneman, D. & Tversky, A. (1973). On the psychology of prediction. *Psychological Review*, 80, 237-251.

Kerr, N.L. & Bray, R.M. (1982) *The psychology of the courtroom: An introduction*. New York: Academic Press.

Klaczynski, P.A.; Gelfand, H. & Reese, H.W. (1989). Transfer of conditional reasoning: Effects of explanations and initial problem types. *Memory and Cognition*, 17, 208-220.

Lichtenstein, S.; Slovic, P.; Fischhoff, B. & Layman, M. (1978). Judged frequency of lethal events. *Journal of Experimental Psychology: Human Learning and Memory*, 4, 551-578.

Lind, E.A. (1982) The psychology of courtroom procedure. In: N.L. Kerr & R. M. Bray (Eds.) *The psychology of the courtroom*. New York Academic Press.

Loh, W. (1981) Perspectives on Psychology and Law. *Journal of Applied Social Psychology*, 11, 314-355.

Marshall & Wise (1975) Juror decisions and the determination of guilt in capital punishment cases: A bayesian perspective. In D. Wendt & C. Ulek (Eds). *Utility, Probability and Human Decision Making*. Dordrecht, Holland. Reidel.

Mira y López, E. (1932) *Manual de psicología jurídica*. Barcelona: Salvat.

Müller, D.J., Blackman, D.E. & Chapman, A.J. (1984) *Psychology and law*. Chichester. Wiley Press.

Muñoz-Sabate, L., Bayes, R. & Munne, F. (1980) *Introducción a la psicología jurídica*. Mexico: Trillas.

Nemeth, CH.J.(1986) Procesos de grupo y jurados: Estados Unidos y Francia. In S. Moscovici (Comp.) *Psicología Social I*. Buenos Aires: Paidos.

Palmer, A. (1988) *El jurado y la Psicología Social*. Barcelona. PPU.

Payne, J.W. (1982). Contingent decision behavior. *Psychological Bulletin*, 92, 382-402.

Penrod, S. & Hastie, R. (1979) Model of jury decision making process of the American jury. *Journal of the American Statistical Association*, 86, 462-492.

Pollard, P. (1982). Human reasoning: Some possible effects of availability. *Cognition*, 12, 65-96.

Sales. B.D. (1977) *The criminal justice system. Perspectives in law and psichology, vol. 1.* New York: Plenum Press.

Sanks, B.D. & Hastie, R.C. (1978) *Social Psychology in Court*. New York. Van Nostrand Reinhold.

Savage, L.J. (1954). *The foundations of statistics*. New York: Wiley Press.

Schum, D.A.(1977). The behavioral richness of cascaded inference models: examples in jurisprudence. In N. Castellan, D. Pijoni & G. Potts (Eds). *Cognitive Theory (vol 2)* Hillsdale. Erlbaum.

Sobral, J, & Arce, R.(1990) *La psicología social en la sala de justicia*. Barcelona: Paidos.

Tapp, J.L. (1976) Psychology and the law: An overture. *Annual Review of Psychology*, 27, 359-404.

Tversky, A. & Kahneman, D.(1973). Availability: A heuristic for judging frequency and probability. *Cognitive Psychology*, 4, 207-232.

Tversky, A. & Kahneman, D. (1974). Judgment under uncertainty: Heuristics and biases. *Science*, 185, 1124-1131.

Tversky, A. & Kahneman, D. (1982). Evidential impact of base rates. In D. Kahneman,; P, Slovic & A. Tversky (1982). *Judgment under uncertainty: Heuristics and biases*. New York: Cambridge University Press.

Tversky, A. & Kahneman, D. (1983). Extensional versus intuitive reasoning: The conjunction fallacy in probability judgment. *Psychological Review*, 91, 293-315.

Valentine, E.R. (1985). The effect of instructions on performance in the Wason selection task. *Current Psychological Research and Reviews*, 4, 214-223.

Von Neuman, J. & Morgenstern, O. (1944). *Theory of games and economic behavior*. Princeton, New York: Princeton University Press.

Walbert (1971) The effect of jury size on the probability of conviction: an evaluation of Williams v Florida. *Case Western Reserve Law Review*, 22, 529-554.

Wason, P.C. (1966). Reasoning. In B.M. Foss(Ed.), *New horizons in Psychology. I*. Harmondsworth: Penguin.

Wason, P.C. (1968). On the failure to eliminate hypotheses - A second look. In P.C.Wason & P.N. Johnson-Laird (Eds.), *Thinking and reasoning*. Harmondsworth, Middlesex, England: Penguin.

Wason, P.C. (1983). In J.St.B.T. Evans (Ed.), *Thinking and reasoning: Psychological approaches*. London: Routledge and Kegan Paul.

Wason, P.C. & Shapiro, D. (1971). Natural and contrived experience in a reasoning problem. *Quarterly Journal of Experimental Psychology*, 23, 63-71.

Wright, J.C. & Murphy, G.L. (1984). The utility of theories in intuitive statistics: The robustness of theory-based judgment. *Journal of Experimental Psychology: General*, 113, 301-322.

Inquisitorial Jury Selection through Scientific Support

Ramón Arce, Francisca Fariña, Carlos Vila and Santiago Real

Introduction

Recently, through the mass media, we witnessed how an American citizen of African-American descent, Rodney King, was brutally assaulted by the police. The videotape presented as evidence by the prosecution, in which both the victim and the aggressors are clearly visible, did not seem to be decisive for the jury. The result was a verdict of not guilty, which was regarded as incomprehensible by many Americans, and resulted in four days of violent rioting. Such an episode could be regarded as purely anecdotal. However, the results from many studies do not support this view and suggest this was not an exception; that is, socially unacceptable jury verdicts and similar phenomena are more frequent than is commonly believed.

Current Procedures

There are a variety of models for the selection of juries, e.g., stand-by, voir dire, random selection and through legal commissions. Although the precise applications of jury selection procedures vary from one country to another and even within the same country, we may divide these into two main groups: the inquisitorial and the adversarial. In the former the aim is not to select a good jury but rather to avoid selecting a bad one. Essentially it is based on lists or a census of citizens, usually the electoral census from which the corresponding judges or other representatives of the legal community "eliminate" those citizens who they feel are unsuitable for jury service. From this filtered list, a random jury panel is obtained. Thereafter, the inquisitorial procedure applies another "filtering" mechanism for the formation of specific juries in order to avoid kinship or economic ties and *legal* prejudices relevant to any of the parties concerned. This procedure is based on, mutatis mutandis, the inquisitorial system of administering justice in the selection of a jury.

In contrast, the adversarial system, using procedures such as stand-by or voir dire, searches for the perfect jury by means of confrontations among the parties in order to eliminate jurors from the panel who are regarded as unsuitable. Under these circumstances, the search for an impartial jury depends on the lawyers' abilities to reject adverse jurors and retain those who are favourable. The adversarial system permits rejection of jurors by both parties on the grounds that this will avoid the formation of biased juries. A further detailed analysis of the underlying factors reveals that the reasoning used by some of the more prestigious lawyers, based on their common sense and their experiences, is not substantiated when compared with the empirical data. Therefore, it would be interesting to determine the impact of the adversarial selection system on the outcome of a trial (Hastie, 1991).

The Impact of Selection Procedures

If the view that current selection procedures are objective and thus avoid the selection of biased juries is correct, one would expect to find a faithful cross-section of society in a large number of juries. However, previous studies do not seem to support such a conclusion, particularly if we bear in mind that these studies were undertaken when selection procedures were subject to greater limitations. Van Dyke (1977) and the Academy of Lyon (1975) have reported considerable discrepancies in the ratio between the participation of certain social groups in jury service and the percentages of the population which they represent. Thus, in France, 50.1% of the population are women, yet they only constitute 7% of the preparatory lists for jurors. This percentage is even smaller if we consider that women are only responsible for 4.1% of judging juries. Likewise, Van Dyke reported similar findings: only 44.4% of Hispanics were included in the jury lists and 58.1% of younger citizens under the age of 25. Recent legal measures designed to check these deviations have not proven to be effective (Fukurai et al., 1991). The constant rejections and peremptory challenges have a final, substantial effect on jury composition. Thus, Van Dyke found that in the United States the prosecution rejected, without any reason, 25% of the black population while the defence rejected 10%. In contrast, the defence and the prosecution rejected 26.7% and 6.2% of Anglo-Europeans respectively. These figures bring into question the lawyers' true objectives when using the voir dire procedures. Several authors have suggested that these procedures serve to obtain biased jurors and hence a favourable jury (verbi gratia, Kuhn, 1968). A review of the literature confirms this view. Van Dyke has reported that in the United States the prosecution avoids selecting blacks, Hispanics and young people on the grounds that these groups emit fewer guilty verdicts. Therefore, the data do not appear to substantiate the view that the voir dire procedure is effective in the selection of unbiased juries, but rather that juries are not representative of a wide cross section of society (Van Dyke, 1977; Academie de Lyon, 1975).

Furthermore, it appears that the suggestions of various prestigious lawyers are still in force today; for example, Belli (1954) recommends avoiding agricultural workers in criminal cases and accepting them for civil cases, Appleman (1952) states that the young favour the accused in certain cases, and Adkins (1968-1969) points out that the elderly are more lenient except in murder cases. These are but mere examples of a long list of recommendations, some of which are even clearly contradictory as well as lacking any empirical basis.

As for the latent objectives of voir dire procedures, field studies undertaken by Broeder (1965) indicate that voir dire procedures are neither effective in the search for unfavourable jurors nor in the search for useful data for determining which individuals might be unfavourable. An in depth analysis undertaken by Fulero and Penrod (1990), revealed that, after reviewing the recommendations of lawyers concerning the selection of jurors, their judgements were based mainly on racial, sexual and ethnic stereotypes as well as on their own idiosyncratic experiences rather than on any criteria indicative of any particular judgement. Moreover, Olczak and colleagues (1991) reported that lawyers used stereotypes similar to those used by lay people when selecting juries. Thus, paradoxically, the defence tended to accept more pro-guilty than pro-innocent jurors. Furthermore, as to the content of the voir dire procedures, Balch and colleagues (1976) found that lawyers spent 43% of their time indoctrinating juries and 36% inquiring about the personal and biographical details of jurors. The extent to which jurors are honest under the voir dire procedures remains unclear. The anxiety produced by these types of procedures used for the evaluation and the demand of characteristics has been reported to have an effect on the honesty of jurors, whereas the expectations of lawyers and judges do not affect their honesty (Marshall & Smith, 1986).

The selection procedures under the inquisitorial system consists of four possible options: pure random selection; selection by judges; by commissions or experts; or based on legal criteria. It is well known that pure random selection is not viable since it gives rise to a large number of anomalous juries; consequently, this has led to the introduction of rejections and peremptory challenges. Voir dire selection procedures undertaken by judges under inquisitorial conditions exhibit similar problems as those undertaken by lawyers under the adversary system, as well as being ineffective. In fact, lawyers are much more efficient than judges in eliciting candidate self-disclosure from potential jurors. The presence of a judge, however, implies pressure towards conformity in a set of perceived judicial standards among jurors (Jones, 1987). Selection from lists by Commissions or experts has also given rise to biased juries, thus this method has been rejected given the prevalence of certain social groups in detriment of others (Sobal & Hinrichs, 1986). Alternatively, if selection is based on legal principles designed to check attitudinal, personality and other bias, this may lead to grave social injustice. Thus, in the USA those against the death penalty ("excludables") have been excluded by law from cases involving the death penalty (Witherspoon v. Illinois). However, bias still arises since those in favour of the death penalty ("non-excludables") are more inclined to accept aggravating circumstances in these types of cases (Luginbuhl & Middendorf, 1988). Under these circumstances a more objective jury could be obtained if each case were considered individually, given that 65% of those against the death penalty would be willing to reconsider their position in specific cases (Cox & Tanford,

1989). These types of juries would offer a guarantee to the accused. However, the interaction between the jurors and each case would be difficult to evaluate given the infinite number of possible situations, and that each case would have to be individually assessed.

Safeguards

It is assumed that though jurors may be biased in their individual decision, the group decision would be more objective since would it counteract any prejudices. This is particularly true when dealing with dispositional variables (Kaplan & Miller, 1978; Penrod, 1990). The pooling of the diversity of opinions is one of the fundamental cornerstones of the jury as an institution (i.e., Van Dyke, 1977). Consequently, homogeneity in the jury's points of view, whether at a socio-demographic or psychological level, should be avoided. Historically, socio-demographic heterogeneity has evolved, with "good juries" approaching a nearly representative level; the current trend towards greater inclusion of women is one of many examples. In order to assess the effects of demographic variables, i.e., gender homogeneity, we have undertaken a study in which juries composed of only men or only women reached a unanimous verdict in an authentic rape trial recorded on videotape. The results show that, in homogeneous groups, women were more inclined to emit guilty verdicts than men $[X^2(1) = 6.35; p < .01]$.

The effect of psychological homogeneity in certain judicial cases was also evaluated using statistically designed profiles (based on discriminant analysis) that could lead to biased judgements, namely ideology and attribution (refer to Arce 1989; Arce et al., 1992a for further information concerning methods and procedures). With juries that were homogeneous in these psychological profiles, we have observed jury verdicts where the influence of these profiles was statistically predictable in some cases (Arce et al., 1992a). The bias produced by group homogeneity influenced not only the verdict (see Arce et al., 1992a), but also the style of the deliberation (Arce, Fariña & Real, in press) and the content of the deliberation, since certain evidence was either considered or ignored depending on whether it was cognitively in conflict with the final decision (Arce, Fariña & Vila, in press). For example, for the same case of burglary, a progressive jury reached a verdict of not guilty, whereas a homogeneously conservative jury a guilty verdict (for further examples see Arce at al., 1992b). Cowan et al. (1984) observed similar effects with homogeneous juries, in which homogeneity was measured with reference to the juror's attitudes (pro- or con-) towards the death penalty. Thus we may conclude that juries sharing homogeneous values, socio-demographic groupings or socio-psychological factors should be controlled in order to avoid biased deliberations. These biases had been previously rejected on the grounds that they were of little value in terms of prediction and were not consistent from one case to another (Penrod, 1990). Likewise, Lennox (1990) has observed that some jurors base the evaluation of information on irrelevant, non-rational artefacts. Thus the deliberation process, by a jury composed of jurors whose evaluation of the evidence has been non-rational, entails many risks. It appears, therefore, that the standard selection procedures are not designed to deal with such anomalies, unless one of the parties involved resorts to scientific measures in an attempt to obtain a favourable outcome.

With reference to specific instances, the first Rodney King trial led to a verdict of not guilty by a jury who, according to the press, was composed of only upper middle class whites. We suggest that the jury's socio-demographic homogeneity explains the verdict. In contrast, the jury in the second trial was composed of nine whites, two blacks and one Hispanic who reached a verdict of guilty.

It would be interesting to determine whether these psychosocial variables are predictors of biased verdicts at the individual juror level. However, at a group level, homogeneity multiplies the effects of a bias. For details of how and when this effect is produced see Arce et al. (1992b). It is impossible to accurately estimate the number of homogeneous or quasi-homogeneous juries in actual trials, but we would suggest that they are the norm rather than the exception (bearing in mind that nine out of ten juries reach a post-deliberation verdict similar to the pre-deliberation majority verdict; Kalven & Zeisel, 1966), this effect is even greater if there is a bias in favour of acquittal (MacCoun & Kerr, 1988). Occasionally, we find contra-natura verdicts which could be based on a supposed homogeneity. Though homogeneous juries may reach a just verdict on some occasions (Arce et al., in press), heterogeneous juries are more efficient at problem solving (Zeisel, 1971; Lempert, 1975).

A New Approach to Selection

Currently, selection procedures do not appear to guarantee heterogeneous juries, either in the majority of cases or in specific instances. Moreover, the procedure known as scientific selection (i.e., Schulman et al., 1973) of the jury has been criticised by the legal or scientific communities on the grounds that it is biased towards one of the parties. Furthermore, it has been criticised on the grounds that it undermines the legitimacy of the jury by reducing the representation of a cross-section of society. Other critics have argued that it does not fulfil the claim which is often attributed to it, i.e., it cannot even guarantee a *biased* selection that will ensure the success of the party in question. An objective evaluation of the data reveals that the so-called scientific selection procedure does not always produce a favourable verdict, though in many instances favourable results are obtained. These include the exclusive use of verdict predictors such as: the attitude towards the crime and the legal system, the evaluation of the probability of guilt for a given crime and demographic variables, which increase the number of correct predictions of individual verdicts from 50% to 78% (Moran et al., 1990). Likewise, Horowitz

(1980), who instructed students in the detection of bias according to empirical observations of the social sciences, observed that these students performed better than the students who did not receive instruction and whose detection of biased juries was based on intuition.

The question now arises concerning which is the most impartial alternative, the inquisitorial or the adversarial system. The former implies a selection under the auspices of the judiciary, which would be the same for everybody. The latter involves leaving the procedures as they are, thus enabling those who can afford to apply the scientific selection procedures for their own benefit. Bearing in mind that the controlled selection procedures have inherent limitations, our approach consists of a combined selection procedure which would guarantee the representation of a wide cross-section of society and would obtain the most impartial jury as possible. Thus, scientific advances would serve to promote justice and not the partial interests of a specific party. Therefore, we propose that selection should be based on scientific advances applied by experts in the social sciences who, under an inquisitorial system, would be responsible for the selection of the most objective jury without rejecting social requirements and equal opportunity which would be guaranteed by the random selection of a jury panel from lists of jurors.

Representation of a cross-section of society and the equal opportunity to participate in the jury would be attained by the random selection of jurors from the electoral census as well as from income tax and social security lists, etc. The jury panel would be scrutinised by experts in order to avoid any dangerous homogeneity of the jury. Socio-demographic homogeneity is easily dealt with but psychological variables are not, since they can not be detected without using psychometric devices. Demographic considerations also have to be taken into account to assess whether the demographic proximity of the accused leads to jury bias, in which case demographic diversity would be convenient (Golash, 1992). A viable procedure to check such bias would be the statistical method proposed by Press (1992). To assess psycho-social variables in the formation of juries, a psychometric instrument was designed in order to evaluate attribution, ideology and attitudes towards justice and crime as well as the probability of guilt in a specific case. The avoidance of homogeneous juries in relation to the above mentioned variables together with others of a socio-demographic nature will help to prevent some evidence from being only partially considered and other evidence being overweighed, hence, aiding juries to deliver verdicts more impartially. We do not propose to eliminate jurors who only process part of the information or give greater weight to certain evidence in detriment to other evidence as has been suggested by Graziano and colleagues (1990). Our aim is to ensure that not all of the jurors process the evidence in the same way and focus their attention on certain pieces of evidence at the expense of others which would be appraised by other juries. In fact, juries composed of certain elites, as in the period of "good juries", are not representative in their capacity to process. With reference to the group deliberation it is well known that almost all the evidence is considered, among it the most relevant, though individual jurors only recall 70% of it (Hastie et al., 1983). If the information that is individually recalled is the same as that which receives most attention by all the jurors, i.e., a homogeneous jury, the group judgement will be predetermined, given that the jurors will disregard certain information if it is considered to be incongruent with the final decision (Wyer & Srull, 1989). On the other hand, if there is a diversity in the recollections and in the weight of different evidence, the deliberation will be much more rigorous and objective. Reference to the content of homogeneous group deliberations and the consequent bias in group judgement making can be found in Arce, Fariña and Vila (in press).

Postscript

Objections may be raised by certain members of the judiciary concerning the selection of the jury with the assistance of psychometric assessment methods, since these procedures may be said to limit the equal rights of citizens to participate in juries. However, this is not so since jurors are randomly chosen from a variety of lists of citizens and the inclusion of all citizens would guarantee equal opportunity. The attempt to avoid a homogeneous jury, contrary to what is often argued, would be aimed at providing the fairest trial possible. However this can not be obtained using either random selection or ordinary procedures such as stand-by or voir dire. Furthermore, if selection is not undertaken by means of the inquisitorial procedure, this will only serve to benefit one party at the expense of another (e.g., the attempts to apply "scientific selection" procedures in order to favour a particular party are described by Hans and Vidmar, 1986).

References

Academie de Lyon (1975). *Jury criminal l'Ain: Enquête de sociologie judiciaire*. Institut d'Etudes Judiciaires.

Adkins, J. C. (1968-1969). An art? A science? Or luck?. *Trial, December-January*, 37-39.

Appleman, J. A. (1952). *Sucessful jury trials: A symposium*. Indianapolis:Bobbs Merrill.

Arce, R. (1989). *Perfiles psicosociales, veredictos y deliberación en jurados legos*. Doctoral thesis, University of Santiago de Compostela.

Arce, R., Fariña, F., & Real, S. (in press). Perfiles psicosociales y estilos de deliberación. *Cognitiva*,

Arce, R., Fariña, F., & Sobral, J. (1992a). Verdicts of psychosocially biased juries. In F. Lösel, D. Bender, & T. Bliesener (Eds.). *Psychology and law.International Perspectives*, 435-439. Berlin: De Gruyter.

Arce, R., Fariña, F., & Sobral, J. (1992b). *From juror to jury decision making. A non model approach*. Third European Conference on Law and Psychology, Oxford.

Arce, R., Fariña, F., & Vila, C. (in press). Análisis de contenido en la interacción de jurados legos. *Análisis y Modificación de Conducta*,

Balch, R. W., Griffiths, C. T., Hall, E. L., & Winfree, L. T. (1976). The socialization of jurors. The voir dire as a rite of passage. *Journal of Criminal Justice*, *4*, 271-283.

Belli, M. M. (1954). *Modern trials*. Indianapolis: Bobbs-Merrill.

Broeder, D. (1965). Voir Dire examination: An empirical study. *Southern California Law Review*, *38*, 503-528.

Cowan, C. L., Thompson, W. C., & Ellsworth, P. C. (1984). The effects of death qualification on jurors predisposition to convict and on the quality of deliberation. *Law and Human Behavior*, *8*(1/2), 53-79.

Cox, M, & Tanford, S. (1989). An alternative method of capital jury selection. *Law and Human Behavior*, *13*(2), 167-183.

Fukurai, H., Butler, E. W., & Krooth, R. (1991). Where did black jurors go? A theoretical synthesis of racial disenfranchisement in the jury system and jury selection. *Journal of Black Studies*, *22*(2), 196-215.

Fulero, S. M., & Penrod, S. D. (1990). Attorney jury selection folklore: What do they think and how can psychologists help? *Forensic Reports*, *3*(3), 233-259.

Golash, D. (1992). Race, fairness, and jury selection. *Behavioral Sciences and the Law*, *10*(2), 155-177.

Graziano, S. J., Panter, A. T., & Tanaka, J. S. (1990). Individual differences in information processing strategies and their role in juror decision making and selection. *Forensic Reports*, *3*(3), 279-301.

Hans, V. P. & Vidmar, N. (1986). *Judging the jury*. New York: Plenum Press.

Hastie, R. (1991). Is attorney conducted voir dire an effective procedure for the selection of impartial juries. *American University Law Review*, *40*, 703-726.

Hastie, R., Penrod, S., & Pennington (1983). *Inside the jury*. Cambridge, Mass.: Harvard University Press.

Horowitz, A. (1980). Juror selection: A comparison of two methods in several criminal cases. *Journal of Applied Social Psychology*, *10,1*, 86-99.

Jones, S. E. (1987). Judge-versus attorney-conducted voir dire: An empirical investigation of juror candor. *Law and Human Behavior*, *11*(2), 131-146.

Kalven, H., & Zeisel, H. (1966). *The American jury*. Boston: Little Brown.

Kaplan, M. F., & Miller, J. H. (1978). Reducing the effects of juror bias. *Journal of Personality and Social Psychology*, *36*, 1443-1455.

Kuhn, R. S. (1968). Jury discrimination: The next phase. *Southern California Law Review*, *41*, 235-328.

Lempert, R. O. (1975). Uncovering "nondiscernible" differences: Empirical research and the jury-size cases. *Michigan Law Review*, *73*, *4*, 643-708.

Lennox, R. D. (1990). Applications of structural equation methodologies to jury-selection research. *Forensic Reports*, *3*(3), 349-360.

Luginbuhl, J., & Middendorf, K. (1988). Death penalty beliefs and jurors' responses to aggravating and mitigating circumstances in capital trials. *Law and Human Behavior*, *12*(3), 263-281.

MacCoun, R. J., & Kerr, N. L. (1988). Asymmetric influence in mock jury deliberation: Jurors' bias for leniency. *Journal of Personality and Social Psychology*, *54*(1), 21-33.

Marshall, L. L., & Smith, A. (1986). The effects of demand characteristics, evaluation anxiety, and expectancy on juror honesty during voir dire. *Journal of Psychology*, *120*(3), 205-217.

Moran, G., Cutler, B. L., & Loftus, E. F. (1990). Jury selection in major controlled substance trials: The need for extended voir dire. *Forensic Reports*, *3*(3), 331-348.

Olczak, P. V., Kaplan, M. F., & Penrod, S. D. (1991). Attorneys' lay psychology and its effectiveness in selecting jurors: Three empirical studies. *Journal of Social Behavior and Personality*, *6*(3), 431-452.

Penrod, S. D. (1990). Predictors of jury decision making in criminal and civil cases: A field experiment. *Forensic Reports*, *3*(3), 261-277.

Press, J. S. (1992). La estadística en la selección de jurados: Cómo evitar jurados adversos. In J. M. Tanur (Ed.). *La estadística: Una guía de lo desconocido*. Madrid: Alianza Editorial.

Schulman, J., Shaver, P., Colman, R., Emrick, B., & Christie, R. (1973). Recipe for a jury. *Psychology Today*, 37-44, 79-84.

Sobal, J. & Hinrichs, D. W. (1986). Bias against "marginal" individuals in jury wheel selection. *Journal of Criminal Justice, 14*(1), 71-89.

Van Dyke, J. M. (1977). *Jury selection procedures: our uncertain commitments to representative panels*. Cambridge, Mass. Ballinger Publishing Company.

Wyer, R. S. Jr., & Srull, T. K. (1989). *Memory and cognition in its social context*. Hillsdale, N.J.: LEA.

Zeisel, H. (1971). ... And then there were none: The diminution of the federal jury. *University of Chicago Law Review, 38 (4)*, 710-724.

Influence of the Prosecutor's Plea on the Judge's Sentencing in Sexual Crimes: Hypothesis of the Theory of Anchoring by Tversky and Kahneman

Eugenio Garrido Martín and Carmen Herrero Alonso

Introduction

The problem of the perception of reality is not new; on the contrary, throughout the history of human thought we see good examples of it in the explanations of universal ideas in the illumination of Plotinus or Aristotle's abstraction, Descartes' doubt, or the proposals of idealism. But, while the positive sciences have advanced, philosophical solutions have been abandoned. This has happened, and is accepted, because of what are referred to as cosmological questions. The same criterion must be kept in questions of philosophical anthropology or rational psychology. Psychology has tried to give scientific answers to the ancient questions about truth and knowledge.

Leaving this solemn affirmation aside, when we observe the answers that psychology has given to the ancient questions about knowledge, it should be stated that with more objective, more verifiable, and more quantitative methods, we have reached the same relative conclusions or perspectives that a good part of those philosophical theories defended.

In our own cultural arena, Ortega y Gasset's (1970) theory on perspective is well know: "Things in their reality are somewhat more o less, they are only approximately themselves (...) The precision of things is precisely what is unreal, that which is legendary of them" (p. 652). Examples of this psychological perspectivism are the theories of social perception, causal attribution, studies on memory or decision making. Compare Ortega's statement with this one by Tversky and Kahneman (1981): "Because of imperfections of human perception and decision, however, changes in perspective often reverse the relative apparent size of objects and the relative desirability of options" (p. 453). Everything depends on the perspective from which things are observed, says Ortega; everything depends on the framing of the perception and of the choices, say Tversky and Kahneman.

The present study is framed within the theory of framing (the redundancy is purposeful) by Tversky and Kahneman in reference to decision making (Kahneman & Tversky, 1973; Tversky, 1977; Tversky & Kahneman, 1974; 1981; 1983). According to these authors, the decisions we make in life are not directed by pure rationality, but by the frame from which the probabilities, contingencies, results, etc., of such decision are presented. For example, Tversky and Kahneman (1974) recall how in a debate which dealt with the passing on to clients some of the costs involved in the manufacture of credit cards, the managers preferred announcing the decision as a "deduction" in their (the clients') passbooks, rather than as an additional cost, because, based on the neutral hypothetical situation (that of receiving the credit cards free of charge), adding costs is perceived as having to pay more than having a small amount deducted from their accounts, even though the amount in both cases was the same. Rodrigo (1985) gives us an example of framing to explain why the Spanish Armed Forces collaborated or were not opposed to the transition to the democracy: during the years of peace an image had been created of a professional army which had set needs and democratic means of negotiation: "(...) worried about improving their professional opportunities, they preferred adapting their way of intervening in politics to that which is proper of a democracy, using negotiation and pressure to receive larger budgets and more influence in the legislature" (p. 62).

Among the ways of framing an event or outcomes that determine one decision over another is the strategy of "anchoring", borrowed from the metaphor of the anchor that secures ships in a fixed place, permitting only a minimal possibility of movement. In decision making, anchoring is a point, a quantity from which one parts, and which requires that the subject move around it. Within the theory by Tversky and Kahneman, it can said that anchoring can be considered either that simplified fact that induces one to make decisions without keeping in mind the complexity of other intervening factors, or as that apparently neutral point, in comparison with which other outcomes are evaluated as gains or losses. If a person in a negotiation begins by asking for a sizable sum, we know that that is not what he or she wants, but that the person is indicating the point from which he or she is willing to negotiate. Consider an example by Tversky and Kahneman: if we tell a group of people that 25% of the population is mentally ill, they will think that is quite high, but might accept 17%. On the other hand, if we start by telling another group of people that the percentage of mental illness is 17%, they too, will think it is high and accordingly, lower that percentage. The starting point is an anchoring point around which posterior decisions are made and around which the negotiation will be carried out. Precisely, in situations of negotiation anchoring theory is well known, even though, as Ross and Stilling (1991) say, this can become a barrier of conflict that impedes the negotiation.

Seeking explanations in more comprehensive psychological processes, the anchoring hypothesis can be seen as a solidification of the motivation of self-evaluation and a social comparison with like models. Anchoring is possible and believable when we lack objective norms, whether these be sensory measures or laws (Festinger, 1954; Gerard, 1954; Schachter, 1959). From this perspective of the communion between social comparison and anchoring, psychology in general, and social psychology in particular, has always counted on the theory of anchoring, has given it its approval, and has used its hypotheses to generate, for, example, the sensation of self-efficacy in patients who lacked it

(Schunk & Hanson, 1989), to instill self-referent judgments (Cervone & Peake, 1986), managerial behavior (Bandura & Jourden, 1991), and to maintain secondary control when reality tells us that primary control is failing due to illness or aging (Heckhausen, 1992). In general, all possible participation of modeling in behavior modification is anchored in social comparison (Bandura, 1994; Garrido, 1993c).

But it is Fitzmaurice and Pease (1986) who bring together a systematic exposition of Tversky and Kahneman's hypothesis of anchoring in judicial sentences. Concretely, and using the judicial system of the United Kingdom, the authors propose two types of applications: the first refers to the tariff model, that is, if some day we are able to admit the possibility of avoiding disparities among judges when sentencing the same cases by using computer programs that weigh each one of the intervening elements in the sentence against each other, without a doubt it will be with anchoring, using sentences other judges have give in similar cases. In a previous work, Garrido (1993a) has reviewed the theoretical suppositions of the tariff method. It is not difficult to understand that in this way the discriminatory bias found in given sentences is perpetuated (Lovegrove, 1989).

The second application that Fitzmaurice and Pease (1986) make for the anchoring hypothesis refers to the appeals courts to explain certain types of sentences. In these cases the sentences that reach the court have been assessed and have a concrete punishment. This assessment and punishment could serve as an anchoring for those who would judge the case in superior courts.

Another circumstance that can confirm that the anchoring hypothesis exists in our penal system or penal process is the relationship between what is solicited by the district attorney (public prosecutor) and the final sentence handed down by the judge. This relationship between the prosecutor and judge lends itself to even further psychological research. In principle, even though they have different roles, they both are judging the same case with the same evidence. Only this fact would allow us to analyze the discrepancy or disparity among professionals of justice regarding the same matter. Sometimes, psychologists who research the problem of disparity have to make use of experimental operationalization by writing up one sentence that must be judged by many judges (Palys & Divorski, 1984; Sobral & Prieto, 1993). On the other hand, in real life, we have the same cause with the same evidence and in absolutely the same conditions that must be judged by two criminal justice professionals: the public prosecutor and the judge.

The present study attempts to test, specifically, the anchoring hypothesis between the punishment the prosecutor solicits and that which the judge gives in cases of sexual offenses. It is believed that each and every one of the required conditions for Tversky and Kahneman's anchoring, when making risk-taking decisions, is found in this circumstance: for example, the behavior in sentencing. What the prosecutor solicits is what should have influence over the actual sentence the judge dictates. But in this relationship between what the prosecutor solicits and what the judge decrees, there is an exceptional condition, as was mentioned above, that is found implicit in Tversky and Kahneman's theory: social comparison. But it is a social comparison with a social representation or stereotype: the prosecutor's office tends, by definition, to solicit exaggerated punishments.

The final scene now set for anchoring between the prosecutor and judge is the following: by law, for sex offenses, there is not necessarily a link between the sentence the judge hands down and that which the prosecutor solicited, which is different from what occurs in other trials (civil trials). However, habit and the definition of functions have made the social representation and the role of the prosecutor appear to be more salient, more demanding of the defendant than the same function of the judge. To give an anecdote as an example, when, in a trial, the police are asked whom they should look at when they are speaking, they say the prosecutor because he is on "their side". In the culture surrounding the police (Garrido, 1993b), chase and confession are essential functions. At first, it seems the judge would be on the accused's side, while the prosecutor would be on the victim's side in a representation where the law of "an eye for eye" prevails (Box-Grainger, 1989).

The prosecutor and the judge share this vision and that is why, even though they judge using the same canon, one exaggerates and the other tends to reduce the sentence. If this is so, the correlation between the two must be as high and positive for the type of crime as it is for the sentence. If in addition to this correlation, the hypothesis that the prosecutor's social representation of asking for stiffer sentences than the judge is confirmed, in the prosecutor's conclusions or plea there should appear, in statistical analysis, higher means in years of punishment than for the sentences imposed by the judge. Of course we are conscious of the fact that agreements and high correlations can be explained by the fact that they are both judging the same case using the same canon. But this should lead to agreement, not to correlation and should be the same for any type of crime and in any circumstance.

Prior studies (De Elena & Garrido, 1990) have demonstrated that in traffic accidents the judge coincides more often with the Guardia Civil of Traffic than with the local police; that is, judging similar cases, the judge anchors part of the time. The aforementioned research which makes reference to the discrepancy among judges who judge the same case would indicate the same outcome. Therefore, even while judging the same case, the judge and the prosecutor can disagree and show a high level of agreement in the assessment of the crime and, furthermore, a high coincidence in the sentence (punishment) would favor the anchoring hypothesis such as Fitzmaurice and Pease (1986) proposed. Perhaps it would be more precise, while inferring, to affirm that the high agreement insofar as assessment of crimes and the high positive correlations between the sentence asked for and that handed down do not disqualify the anchoring hypothesis. If the difference in means is significant, the existence of a stereotype would also be confirmed.

Method

This study is framed within a much larger endeavor which for the last three years now has been carried out by the Department of Social Psychology of the University of Salamanca on judicial sentences for sex offenses. In order to do that the judicial sentences were photocopied from the courts in Badajoz, Salamanca, and Orense and were submitted to a qualitative and quantitative content analysis.

The dependent variable by definition is the verdict the judge hands down in the sentence. The more than 400 independent variables refer to the crime, the characteristics of the aggressor and victim, the described behavior in the sentence, legal considerations, the aforementioned articles of the penal code, and even the impression the sentence has on the person who evaluated it, and so on.

One of the quantitative variables which was coded is the prosecutor's plea in reference to the assessment, as well as to the length of punishment. Keeping in mind the petitions and sentences, we find, in this study, agreements in assessment, correlations and difference in means.

Analysis and Results

It could be said that the hypothesis of anchoring would be confirmed in judicial sentences, in this case for sex offenses, or even better, that it would not be disqualified if we were to find a greater coincidence than expected between the prosecutor's assessment of the crime and that handed down by the judge. In those cases in which the judge accepts the prosecutor's assessment, and therefore, they both assess the crime in the same manner, we should find high correlations between the length of prison term solicited by the prosecutor and that handed down by the judge. Another optimal condition under which we could see our hypothesis confirmed would be the existence of differences between the months of prison solicited by the prosecutor and that given by the judge. According to our proposal, such differences should be that the length of prison term solicited by the prosecutor would be greater than that given by the judge.

Let us examine the analyses carried out with each one of the aforementioned aspects. The initial analyses revealed that in 81.7% of the cases the judge accepts the assessment of the prosecutor, that is, judge and prosecutor coincide in the assessment of the crime. We could ask what happens in the remaining 18.3 % of the cases in which the judge and prosecutor do not coincide. This question will be addressed further on.

In order to examine the relationship between the different crimes under consideration (dishonest abuse, estupro**[see note 1], attempted rape and rape) and the agreement or disagreement between the prosecutor and the judge in the assessment of the crime the chi-square test were carried out. The agreement between the prosecutor and the judge in the assessment of the crime was expected not to depend on the crimes under consideration. Nonetheless, our expectations were not verified. The agreement between the judge and prosecutor was significantly related to the type of crime ($\chi^2 = 12.19$; $p = 0.0067$). Examining the contingency table reveals that the crimes of dishonest abuse and rape were responsible for the observed outcomes. The proportion of agreement between the prosecutor and judge for these crimes is different from that which would be expected under the hypothesis of independence.

Table 1: Frequencies and expected values (in parenthesis) of agreement or disagreement between prosecutor and judge in each of the crimes.

Crimes	Non agreement	Agreement
Estupro	1	9
	(1.8)	(8.2)
Attempted rape	1	10
	(2.0)	(9.0)
Dishonest abuse	5	48
	(9.7)	(43.3)
Rape	12	18
	(5.5)	(24.5)
Total	19	85

As can be observed from Table 1 there is greater agreement than theoretically expected between the assessment of the prosecutor and that of the judge in the case of dishonest abuse. This pattern is reversed, however, when we are dealing with rape, where there is less agreement than expected. Therefore, the results indicate that there may well be a greater percentage of cases in which the prosecutor and judge coincide, but the difference between the percentage of agreement and disagreement is not the same for each crime; it reduces notably in the assessment of rape (See Fig.1).

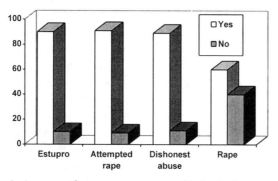

Figure 1: Agreement between prosecutor and judge in the assessment of each crime.

Previously we asked what had happened in the 18,3% of the cases in which the prosecutor and judge did not coincide. The results in respect to this question demonstrate that as regards the assessment of dishonest abuse or rape, in general the disagreement is not due to the fact that the judge does not accept the assessment of the prosecutor and proposes another. The disagreement stems, fundamentally, from the fact that in the majority of the cases, especially in rape, the judge acquits the defendant.

On the other hand, the Pearson Correlation Coefficient was used to analyze the relationship between the months of prison solicited by the prosecutor and those handed down by the judge in cases in which both assessed the crime in the same way. In Table 2 the magnitude of the coefficient can be appreciated when the crimes are taken as a whole as well as when they are observed separately.

Table 2: Correlation between months in prison solicited by the prosecutor and those given by judge for crimes taken as a whole and separately.

Crimes				
1- Whole (n = 85)	2-Estupro (n = 9)	3- Attempted rape (n = 10)	4- Dishonest abuse (n = 48)	5- Rape (n = 18)
.587 ***	.997 ***	.22 (ns)	.191 (ns)	.939 ***

Note: * $p < 0.05$; ** $p < 0.01$; *** $p < 0.001$; ns: non-significant

As can be seen from the preceding table (Table 2), when prosecutor and judge coincide in the assessment, the months of prison dictated by the judge for the crimes taken as a whole (1) were significantly and highly related to those solicited by the prosecutor. The higher the prison term solicited by the prosecutor, the higher the term dictated by the judge. The detailed analysis of each crime separately manifests a very high and positive correlation between the prison term solicited by the prosecutor for estupro (2) and rape (5) and that handed down by the judge for the same crimes. On the other hand, the prison terms dictated by the judged when dealing with crimes of dishonest abuse (4) or attempted rape (3) are not related at all to what the prosecutor solicited for the same crimes.

Finally, t-tests were used to find out if there would be differences between the months of prison solicited by the prosecutor and those handed down by the judge in the cases where they coincided on the assessment. The results appear in Table 3.

Here, it can be seen that, except in the case of attempted rape, the punishment (in months) solicited by the prosecutor for the rest of the crimes tends to be greater than that dictated by the judge. The differences, however, did not reach an acceptable level of significance for the analysis of the whole, nor in separate analyses. It should be noted that, in general, the variability in months of prison dictated by the judges for the same crime tends to be higher than that observed for the prosecutors.

Table 3: Means scores of punishment in months solicited by the prosecutor and dictated by judge for crimes as a whole and separately. (The standard deviations appear in parenthesis).

Crimes	Prosecutor	Judge	t Value	p
As a whole	72.1059	69.1647	.23	0.818
(n = 85)	(106.237)	(142.450)		
Estupro	10.8889	10.1111	1.67	0.133
(n = 9)	(16.205)	(16.647)		
Attempted rape	129.6000	170.9000	-0.39	0.703
(n = 10)	(187.919)	(317.851)		
Dishonest abuse	32.0833	23.6042	1.20	0.238
(n = 48)	(30.450)	(44.816)		
Rape	177.5000	163.6667	1.27	0.222
(n = 18)	(119.049)	(133.586)		

Discussion and Conclusions

The results obtained demonstrate that if, in general, the percentage of agreement in assessment of crimes given by the prosecutor and the judge is high, said percentage varies, contrary to what was expected, depending on the crimes considered (see Fig.1). Therefore, for the first condition, the anchoring hypothesis in judicial sentences is not confirmed for all crimes. In the case of rape the percentage of agreement between the assessment of the prosecutor and that of the judge is less than that for the rest of crimes. For dishonest abuse, however, the percentage of agreement between assessments is higher than what was theoretically expected. Contrary to what happens insofar as rape is concerned, in dishonest abuse the judge seems to accept the assessment of the prosecutor more easily.

How to interpret these results? If the prosecutor and the judge are guided by the same laws, by the same penal code, and if they are both faced with the same facts, then why is the agreement between them for rape less than that for other offenses such as dishonest abuse? To answer this question we must examine what happens in the cases where the judge does not accept the prosecutor's assessment and therefore they do not coincide. The data indicate that in such cases and fundamentally when dealing with rape assessment, the judge does not propose a different assessment of the cases, rather he or she acquits the accused. These results seem to indicate that, for the judge to accept the prosecutor's assessment of rape, he or she must have extremely clear evidence. On the contrary, if the judge is not absolutely sure of the facts constituting a crime of rape, the option will be to acquit the defendant. This, however, does not appear to be as accentuated in crimes of dishonest abuse.

The data suggest that the differences to which we have referred between crimes of dishonest abuse and rape could be due to the greater punishment associated with rape. If this were the most adequate explanation, and the data seem to demonstrate it, such results have important repercussions in legal circles. They indicate that the higher the punishment for the crime, the less probability there will be of the judge convicting, unless he/she is absolutely sure, beyond a doubt, or unless the facts prove, beyond a doubt, that there has been a penal infraction. This lead us to believe that, contrary to what is being said in different social and legal sectors, to increase the punishment for crimes such as rape would bring with it nothing less than additional problems and surely, unexpected, or at least, not sought after effects. We believe that the judges would hand down even fewer convictions than they presently do.

Other relevant results of the research we carried out refer to the relationship that exists between the prison term (in months) solicited by the prosecutor and that which the judge hands down in those cases in which the judge accepts the prosecutor's assessment of the crime. When these results are examined as a whole, the data indicate the existence of an important relationship between the punishment solicited by the prosecutor and that dictated by the judge. The greater the number of months in prison solicited by the prosecutor, the greater the prison term dictated by the judge. These results support the anchoring hypothesis proposed in this study. However, when we examined such relationship for each one of the crimes separately, depending upon the crime, different results appeared again. While there were high and positive correlations between the months of prison solicited by the prosecutor and those handed down by the judge for estupro and rape, for the rest of the crimes there way no relationship at all between the punishments for both the prosecutor and the judge, that is, for the crimes of dishonest abuse and attempted rape. Therefore, this means that the judge anchors with the prosecutor only for the crimes of estupro and rape and sentences thus or acts independently of prosecutor (more "on his or his own") for the rest of the crimes.

Having arrived at this point, we must ask ourselves again the reason for these differences. Why are there high correlations for estupro and rape and none for the rest of the sex offenses? What is it about crimes of estupro and rape that makes them different from dishonest abuse and attempted rape? In our opinion, the key difference that helps to explain the obtained results is in the social perception of the seriousness of the sex offenses considered in this study. That is , we believe that in a social context rape and estupro (for the lay person, rape of a minor) are considered much more serious crimes than a "simple" case of dishonest abuse, or a "mere" attempted rape. When the judge, who, like all "mortals" is immersed in the social context surrounding these crimes (Herrero, 1993), faces cases of estupro and rape, he/she can feel immensely pressured by "society", by the strong demands associated with these crimes and not so pressured when faced with other crimes socially not so seriously perceived. For the crimes socially perceived as more serious - rape and estupro - the judge seems to want to hand over more readily the responsibility of the decision to the prosecutor. For crimes considered less serious, however, the judge assumes all responsibility and dictates the sentence without taking into consideration, in the same way he/she does for crimes of estupro and rape, the punishment solicited by the prosecutor.

In light of these results we can say that the judge anchors with the prosecutor to sentence those cases which suppose a certain risk on his or her part: in those cases where the sentence could be questioned more severely by the public, if, for example, the sentence were not as severe as the "society" would demand or expect. If this is so. if the explanation for preceding results lies in the different perception of the seriousness of crimes, and if we assume that estupro and rape have in common the seriousness that society attributes them, another question arises for which we must find an explanation. We are referring to the fact that the judge seems less ready to accept the prosecutor's assessment of rape than that of estupro. For the latter also, the agreement between the prosecutor and the judge in the assessment of the crime (estupro) should have been less. One possible explanation for these facts arises when we look closely at the pertinent articles of our penal code (Art. 429 in the case of rape and Arts. 434 and 435 in the case of estupro). It can be seen that, even though rape and estupro are considered socially as very serious, and are considered as very serious in the same way (a question to be verified), in the Spanish penal code, the crime of estupro, whatever type, carries with it much less punishment than rape. What we definitely want to say with this is that in the case of estupro, given that the punishment is not as severe, it can be less inconvenient for the judge to accept the prosecutor's assessment. In the case of rape, however, to accept such an assessment automatically implies imposing a severe sentence. Again, these results abound in the idea we spoke of earlier regarding the consequences that increasing the punishment for crimes such as rape would bring about.

We must say, on the other hand, that the results of the differences in means between the months of prison solicited by the prosecutor and those handed down by the judge do not allow us for the moment to completely verify our hypothesis regarding a stereotype. If, except in the case of attempted rape, the punishment (in months of prison) solicited by the prosecutor tends to be greater than that dictated by the judge, the differences did not reach an acceptable level of significance. The absence of these differences, however, does not invalidate our proposal on the stereotype of the prosecutor. Further studies will have to be done in which the number of sentences is greater in order to see if this tendency can be considered significant. Finally, we do not want to overlook the observed variability in years of prison dictated by the judge for all crimes. These results suggest that the punishments handed down by different judges for the same crime can be greater than those found that were solicited by different prosecutors, also for the same crime. These and other questions must receive empirical support and will be the object of study on further occasions.

Notes

1. We use term *estupro* which in Spanish Penal Code is define as follows: The person who has sexual intercourse with another who is older than twelve and less

than eighteen, availing himself of his superiority which originates in whatever relationship or situation, will be punished for estupro with six months and one day to six years. The punishment will be of maximum degree when the crime is committed by parents or brothers. Estupro is also committed when the person who used deception has sexual intercourse with another older than twelve and less than sixteen. In this case the punishment will be from 1 month and one day to six months.

References

Bandura, A. (1994). *Self-Efficacy. The Exercise of control.* New York: Freeman.

Bandura, A., & Jourden, F. J. (1991). Self-regulatory mechanisms governing the impact of social comparison on complex decision making. *Journal of Personality and Social Psychology ,60,* 941-951.

Box-Grainger, J. (1986). Sentencing rapists. In R. Mathews and J. Young (Eds), *Confronting crime.* (31-52). London: Sage Publications.

Cervone, D., & Peake, P. K. (1986). Anchoring, efficacy and action: The influence of judgmental heuristics on self-efficacy judgments an behavior. *Journal of Personality and Social Psychology, 50,* 492-501.

De Elena, J., & Garrido, E. (1990). Peritaje policial y decisión judicial: estudio psicosociológico. In I. Balaguer (Ed.) *Psicología Política y Procesos Judiciales.* Barcelona: PPU.

Festinger, L. (1954). A Theory of Social Comparison Process. *Human Relations, 7,* 117-140.

Fitzmaurice, K., & Pease, K. (1986). *The Psychology of judicial sentencing.* Manchester: Manchester University Press.

Garrido Martín, E. (1993a). Psicología de las sentencias judiciales en materia de delitos sexuales. In M. García Ramírez (Comp.), *Psicología social aplicada en los procesos jurídicos y políticos.* (15-31). Sevilla: Eudema.

Garrido Martín, E. (1993b). La policía en la sociedad actual a la luz de la ley Orgánica 2/86. *Policía científica, 23,* 65-81.

Garrido Martín, E. (1993c). La comparación social origen de autoeficacia personal percibida, *Revista de Psicología Social Aplicada, 3,* 5-23.

Gerard, H. B. (1954). The anchorage of opinions in face-to-face groups, *Human Relations, 7,* 313-325.

Heckhausen, J. (1992). Adults expectancies about development and its controllability: Enhancing self-efficacy by social comparison. In R. Schwarzer (Ed), *Self-Efficacy: Thought control of action,* Washington, D.C.: Hemisphere.

Herrero, C. (1993). Percepción Social de la Violación y Reacciones Hacia sus Víctimas. Doctoral Thesis. University of Salamanca.

Kahneman, D., & Tversky, A. (1973). On the psychology of prediction. *Psychological Review, 80,* 237-251.

Lovegrove, A. (1989). *Judicial decision making, sentencing policy, and numerical guidance.* New York: Springer Verlag.

Ortega y Gasset, J. (1970). Introducción a Velázquez. *Obras Completas,* Vol. 8. Madrid: *Revista de Occidente.*

Palys, T. S., & Divorski, S. (1984). Judicial decision-making: an examination of sentencing disparity among Canadian Provincial Court Judges. In D.J. Müller, D.E. Blackman and A.J. Chapman (Eds), *Psychology and law.* Chichester: John Wiley and Sons.

Rodrigo, F. (1985). Las fuerzas armadas y la transición. *Revista de Occidente, 54,* 57-67.

Ross, L., & Stilling, C. (1991). Barriers to conflict resolution. *Negotiation Journal, October*, 389-404.

Schachter, S. (1959). *The Psychology of affiliation.* Stanford, Ca.: Stanford University Press.

Schunk, D.H., & Hanson, A.R. (1989). Self-modeling and children's cognitive skill learning. *Journal of Educational Psychology, 81*, 155-163.

Sobral, J., & Prieto, A. (1993). Racionalidad, formaciones ideológicas y disparidad en las decisiones judiciales. In M. García Ramírez (Comp.), *Psicología social aplicada en los procesos jurídicos y políticos.* (115-131). Sevilla: Eudema.

Tversky, A. (1977). Features of Similarity. *Psychological Review , 84*, 327-352.

Tversky, A., & Kahneman, D. (1974). Judgement under Uncertainty: Heuristics and Biases. *Science, 185,* 1124-1131.

Tversky, A., & Kahneman, D. (1981). The framing of decisions and the psychology of choice. *Science, 211,*4 53-458.

Tversky, A., & Kahneman, D. (1983). Extensional versus intuitive reasoning: The conjunction fallacy in probability judgment. *Psychological Review, 90*, 293-315.

An Enquiry into Judicial Decisions

Jorge Sobral Fernández

Judges and Their Decisions

Judges as viewed by citizens: their social representation

In modern democratic societies, justice has slowly lost the holy halo drawn round it in times of greater obscurantism. Nowadays its values, procedures and protagonists are right in the middle of social and political debates.

The mere intuition of any casual observer is that judges and their decisions encounter more and more disapproval these days. That is why we would like to refer to some partial results, the outcome of research that we have been conducting at the University of Santiago. This research examines the social representation of justice and, especially, of judges.

A representative sample from our university assessed judges more favorably than offenders ($t = 9.65$; $p = .000$) and more favorably than prosecutors ($t = 4.90$; $p = .000$), but much worse than the stimulus "justice" ($t = 14.87$; $p = .000$) and the stimulus "police" ($t = 16.80$; $p = .000$). Taking this into account, it seems reasonable to conclude that the judges do not "enjoy a good press".

Perhaps one of the more powerful reasons why this representation has grown is one that is related to the perception of judges as people who apply the law in an exceedingly "personal" way, that is to say, in a way too partial to their own interests, values and ideological education. People often perceive that the result of the trial process depends too much on the "personal" variables of the judge as opposed to on what is judged. The chart of contingencies between the deviant behavior and the punishment imposed, in which the social regulation of the conflict is supported, is threatened in two of its basic requirements: its clarity and regularity.

But this problem also directly impinges on a question central to any democratic system; citizens' equality before law. If similar people who have committed similar crimes, under similar circumstances do not receive similar sentences, equality before the law would only be a chimera typical of a somewhat moral and legal philosophy.

Citizens as viewed by judges: the problem of sentencing disparity

The problem is far from simple in its analysis and solutions. The question has been raised in different historical moments and countries (Sellin, 1928; Green, 1964; Palys and Divorski, 1984; Lovegrove, 1984; Oswald, 1992; Konecni and Ebbesen, 1992; Sobral, 1993). In all of these countries the question is reaching the dimension of a "social problem" and therefore, turning into a topic for social and political debates. This may be one of the contexts in which decision making is even more crucial, socially speaking, in the sense that such decisions can dramatically affect the lives of other people.

Let us consider the matter from the point of view of verdicts and sentences taken as decisions.

There have been many people who have stated that justice tries to adjust the reality to the juridical world, that is to say, to the rule, and not the other way round. From this point of view we should consider the juridical reality as something new that pulls through and transforms the natural reality with which it deals. That's why it could be said that any judicial decision "puts up" reality (the reality is different before and after a sentence) and it also "puts it down" (Munné, 1994). The psychosocial perspective seems to be especially privileged in order to analyze that process of putting up and down reality. Far from consisting of the use of juridical and established elements, this process embodies extrajuridical factors with an overriding force that comes from its capacity to function as an "arranging" or "reducing" element of reality, sheltering it under the concept of juridical purity (Bierhoff, Buck and Klein, 1989).

Psychology can play a major role, when getting to the bottom of this bundle of relationships between the legal and extralegal points, in order to establish the level and origin of the influence of the extralegal upon the legal one. The idea is to explain in a comprehensive way the process of adjustment between two highly complicated systems: the juridical rationality and the subjective one of the person who applies it (for further detail, refer to Sobral and Prieto, 1994).

The clashes between both patterns of rationality (Bruner, 1984), could be the source of results such as those found out by Hommers and Anderson (1989) when they analyze the present determinations between what could be called "a legal thought" generic for the judges, and the cognitive processing of the evidence in a specific case, especially emphasizing the role of the values involved in both cases. Those clashes would also be the source of the results of Schüneman and Bandilla (1989), when they show that German judges enter the courtroom with such knowledge of the case to judge that their decision is nearly always made in advance. This previous knowledge is due to the great anchoring bias produced in the previous inquiry. The clash of rationalities would also apply to the results of Margit Oswald (1992), when she extensively shows that in the final sentences of German judges there are extralegal characteristics such as the "attributional styles" apart from the strictly legal or juridical consideration and these styles are also related to the ideological orientation of each judge. In this way we could also understand the results found by Partridge and Eldrige (1974), when a number of New York judges differed in 16 out of 20 cases on something so important as whether the defendant should go to jail or not. We could also understand the results of Diamond and Zeisel (1975), when they analyzed the data relating to the Sentencing Council of Chicago District and found that 30% of individual sentencing suggestions differed in the same basic decision: whether to send the offender to prison or not.

The same scheme would allow us to understand better the results of Diamond's research (1981), where he finds that a number of North American judges differ in their sentences for similar cases depending on the offender's sex, race, education, age, etc. He also finds out that the more complicated the case is, the greater the discrepancies.

But this is not all. There are yet several more cases that could be analyzed from the point of view of confronted rationalities. Some results show that, basically, the judges' orientation over the deterrent effect of punishment explains the great differences in harshness of two courts from the same Australian city.

In a study promoted and financed by the Canadian Administration of Justice, Palys & Divorski (1984), find that the great disparity observed in the judges from that country was due especially to differences in values (that is to say, to extralegal differences) to the extent that the judges believed that their sentences should help to maximize deterrence, to protect public security and to defend society, contrasted to the extent to which such sentences could have the aim of rehabilitating the offender.

This research is reminiscent of what Hogart had found out in 1971, that is, that a number of "moral", legal and sociopolitical attitudes of the judges were shaping, in an important way, the "output" of the given sentence.

We could quote many other studies on the topic; confronted rationalities include one which requires the juridical established consideration of the evidence and of the adjustment to specific codes, and one which every individual has when, in his or her professional activity, he or she makes use of his or her psychological styles, beliefs, ideological and political orientation, etc.

It should be noticed that all the above-mentioned research comes from geographical areas, different juridical systems and traditions different from ours. It could be claimed that things would be different in our country, that the disparity would lessen, that the relatively closed specification of the characteristics of a certain crime in our Penal Code would function as a vaccine against this phenomenon, etc. Taking this into account it seemed especially interesting to carry out similar research with Spanish judges. The objective is to check the level of disparity among our professional judges and to find some of the sources for these disparities. These were our aims when designing the research that we carried out at the University of Santiago. The research was complex and quite exhaustive and so, we will only show here some of the more important conclusions (for further detail refer to Sobral & Prieto, 1994).

If Spanish judges were prisoners of "legal" and "extralegal" forces, how would they react? To answer this question we made use of the cooperation of 32 judges specialized in penal cases in Spain. All of them studied the summary of five real crime investigations where they had the necessary information to give a sentence. The facts were taken as proven in the hearing and all of the 32 judges were asked to sentence in each of the cases.

We should point out that the cases were selected taking into account that they had to be simple and daily, that is, common. After sentencing, the judges answered a questionnaire where we tried to find out the relative influence of both the "legal" and "extralegal" elements when sentencing.

Case number 1 The defendant caused a fight in a bar resulting in the permanent loss of vision in one eye of the victim. These were the sentences given by our judges:

% Judges	Sentences
43.75%	From 7 to 28 months imprisonment
28.12%	From 29 to 50 months imprisonment
18.75%	From 51 to 72 months imprisonment
9.37%	From 121 to 144 months imprisonment

The importance of this disparity can be clearly seen.

Case number 2 A heroin addict attacked an elderly couple without causing physical harm. The sentences were the following:

% Judges	Sentences
6.25%	From 7 to 28 months imprisonment
59.37%	From 29 to 50 months imprisonment
31.25%	From 51 to 72 months imprisonment
3.12%	From 97 to 120 months imprisonment

Once more the disparity is alarming. Whether this heroin addict is sent to prison for 7 months or for 120 depends on the judge who, by chance, is in charge of his case.

Case number 3 A woman gambling addict commits a robbery in order to finance her gambling debts. The sentences, once more worrisome, were the following:

% Judges	Sentences
3.12%	From 0 to 1 months imprisonment
13.63%	From 5 to 6 months imprisonment
15.62%	From 7 to 28 months imprisonment
59.37%	From 29 to 50 months imprisonment
8.25%	From 51 to 72 months imprisonment

Case number 4 A woman cashier constantly steals money from the department store. The sentence disparity was incredibly high.

% Judges	Sentences
3.12%	From 0 to 1 months imprisonment
6.25%	From 1 to 2 months imprisonment
8.12%	From 3 to 4 months imprisonment
18.75%	From 5 to 6 months imprisonment
31.25%	From 7 to 28 months imprisonment
9.37%	From 29 to 50 months imprisonment
3.12%	From 51 to 72 months imprisonment

As can be seen, any sentence was possible depending on the judge who made the decision.

Case number 5 Sexual abuse under threat, without resulting in rape. Let's see the sentence disparity.

% Judges	Sentences
15.62%	From 5 to 6 months imprisonment
56.25%	From 7 to 28 months imprisonment
6.25%	From 29 to 50 months imprisonment
21.90%	From 51 to 72 months imprisonment

Once more, we find a great disparity: the sentences of our judges vary from six months to six years imprisonment.

To sum up, it is obvious that the level of disparity among the judges of our research is high enough so as to require deep thought. In some of the cases this disparity turns out to be quite shocking and flagrant; the sentence, whether to go to jail or not, whether to go for a short spell or a long one, can strictly depend on the judge you come across rather than on the type of crime and the legal prescription for it.

From our point of view, we are far from achieving a balance between, on one hand, a reasonable disparity resulting from practicing the judicial function independently and from the margins of the interpretation of the law, and, on the other hand, the need to establish a feeling of juridical security as regards the penal consequences of certain behavior. All this can lead to a situation where both clients and lawyers would "choose" a judge "à la carte".

But, it is also true that the different decisions made by the judges, and also by those from our research, both by the strictest ones and by the most lenient ones, can not be the results of a simple arbitrary act. We are not dealing with judges who improperly transgress their duties but, on the contrary, with judges who impose that sentence which, in their moral sense and regarding the law, they consider to be the fairest one. So then, there must be a rational explanation for that great disparity. Obviously, we are dealing with judges who know the law and its rules, the lists of anticipated aggravating and mitigating circumstances, etc. The problem, thus, seems to lie in the process where each individual judge tries to fit each specific case into the legal models. And so, it seems reasonable to presume that the "extralegal" characteristics of that process, that is, the judges' beliefs, values, ideological orientation, etc., are the ones which can be the origin of that disparity. This was the hypothesis that we wanted to test in the second part of our research.

The judges had to answer a number of items where they had to point out the level of importance they usually give to a series of facts when making a decision on a certain sentence. They had to give their opinion about a number of elements which belonged to two different worlds: on one hand, what we could call "legal characteristics of the case" (seriousness of the crime, whether the individual had been previously sentenced or not, how long ago he or she was previously sentenced, etc.) and, on the other hand, what we call "extralegal characteristics" or rather "sociolegal and ideological objectives" of our judges' thought (the way they consider that a sentence contributes to: compensate the harm caused to the victim, protect citizens' property and security, preserve social values, serve as a deterrent or hold exemplary character, etc.).

To sum up, let us say that both groups of variables (both the legal and extralegal one) were put to a factor analysis to obtain the basic factors which will hold up for groups of sentences. These factors would also be used afterwards as predictor variables in multiple regression equations regarding the magnitude of the sentences. The objective was clear: to check which of those factors better predicts or explains the sentence disparity. The careful reader is likely to presume which were the results of the surveys; obviously those factors related to the extralegal world better explained the range of sentences. The judges who imposed harsher or ligther sentences differed from one another in the way they confessed: a) to have included in their sentences a greater or lesser orientation towards "the protection of the victim and the society"; b) to have included in their sentences a greater or lesser orientation towards "the offender and his or her possibilities for rehabilitation"; and c) to have included in general a more or less "conservative and punitive" orientation regarding the social function of justice.

Earlier in our work we have referred to rationality models, different juridical philosophies, specific deep conceptions which turn out into concepts that involve a high level of pre-judgment (in its literal sense) and that end up by being "proto-decisions". In the conflict between rules, facts and values where the judges of our research operate, values seem to score the most goals. More or less harsh sentences are determined by the judges' beliefs about the deterrent, exemplary, conservative role of justice and its punishment.

Such beliefs are not present in our codes, neither are they studied in our faculties of law. They are simply possessed, kept and changed or not. In short, the disparity clearly seems to be explained by what have been called "extralegal" or "extrajuridical" elements, which have been used to refer to an ideological influence. Therefore, as it has already been said (cfr. Sobral, 1993), we are dealing with the influence of several models of political rationality upon the juridical world; models of humans and of society: and so, the judge is an unavoidable political agent.

What has been said so far has an inexorable result. We can start by asking ourselves: how can we establish if it is "better", that is, fairer on one hand to sentence an individual to probation who has harmed another one causing him or her serious injury, being that the first time he or she has committed such a crime, and so, avoiding introducing him or her to the vicious cycle of prison; or on the other hand, to punish harshly, with imprisonment, some antisocial behavior which resulted in a harmed innocent person, aiming to exemplify or maximize the protection of society? Both alternatives can be equally rational, internally coherent and legally defensible. When facing dilemmas like these, the judges respond by making use of their ideological options.

We think that the whole society should be the one to make a pronouncement about these dilemmas; society should be the one to choose the risk and solidarity levels it is willing to assume. It is society itself which, anywhere and anytime, chooses a model or image to follow. In order to make society play its role, there are two possible solutions: to increase the responsible social action of the citizens or, as a consequence, to make civil society to play its own role in the administration of justice. And this has only been attempted so far through the establishment of a jury, with all its problems and contradictions.

Some Practical Implications and Some Final Comment

We could point out many practical implications of what has been said so far. Let us see some of them.

First, there is an obvious need for judges, in their training process, to be exposed to a certain amount of psychological knowledge, the research available on bias in the processing of social information, heuristics, prejudice, stereotypes, the role of values in social categorization, decision making, etc. This would allow the judges to have a certain knowledge of their possible sources of error and distortion.

Second, all the things that we have pointed out in this work can obviously be useful for specific professional practice. For example, we have already talked about the fact that certain actors in the trial process can try to "choose" the judge. In fact, the choice of the time when an appeal or an accusation should be made and the arguments used often depend on the knowledge of the judge or judges who will be in charge. We have previously written about the amount of psychological intuition used by lawyers in their professional activity (Sobral, 1991). In his or her job a lawyer could obviously profit from good psychological knowledge. Let us take a lawyer in the moment when he or she has to make a decision on the uncertain lines of a defense or prosecution. The knowledge the lawyer may have about certain characteristics of the judge (his or her more or less punitive conservative or rehabilitating orientation, etc.) together with knowledge about the psychology of persuasion (for instance, the use of "peripheral routes") can put him or her into a privileged position when defending the interests he or she represents.

Diamond (1981) perfectly showed, for example, how the fact of emphasizing one or another aggravating or mitigating circumstance in a specific case can make the judicial resolutions differ in an outstanding way (at least those resolutions of American judges).

Knowledge about a judge's personal characteristics can also be used when making a decision about the moment or the way of presenting specific evidence, in the preparatory activity of the witnesses (in order to increase their credibility and influence), in the establishment of arguments, etc. Although in order to put this into practice we need more information, apart from our intuition, the idea is as simple as this: by knowing the variables which rule the decisions we are nearer to knowing the variables which contribute to persuasion.

The courtroom is the place where a past reality is remembered, rebuilt and categorized. The courtroom is what we could call a context for an "architecture of the truth". The point is to influence, in a more or less important way, the design of that reconstruction, to make one or another vision of the reality prevail. In this process the psychological element is essential for those who want and know how to make use of it.

References

Bierhoff, H.W., Buck, E. & Klein, R. (1989). Attractiveness and respectability of the offender as factors in the evaluation of criminal cases. In H. Wegener, F. Lösel & J. Haisch (Eds.). *Criminal behavior and the justice system: psychological perspectives.* New York: Springer-Verlag, 193-207.

Bruner, J. (1984). *Narrative and paradigmatic modes of thought.* Annual Convention of APA. Toronto.

Diamond, S.S. (1981). Exploring sources of sentence disparity. In B.D. Sales (Eds.). *The trial process.* New York: Plenum Press, 387-411.

Diamond, S.S., & Zeisel, H. (1975). Sentencing councils: A study of sentence disparity and its reduction. *University of Chicago Law Review, 43,* 109-149.

Green, E. (1964). Inter and intra-racial crime relative to sentencing. *Journal of Criminal Law, Criminology and Police Science, 55,* 348-358.

Hogart, J. (1971). *Sentencing as a human process.* Toronto: University of Toronto Press.

Hommers, W. & Anderson, N.H. (1989). Algebraic schemes in legal thought and in everyday morality. In H. Wegener, F. Lösel & J. Haisch (Eds.). *Criminal behavior and the justice system: Psychological perspectives.* New York: Springer-Verlag, 136-150.

Konecni, V.J. & Ebbesen, E.B. (1992). Methodological issues in research on legal decision-making with special reference to experimental simulations. In F. Lösel, D. Bender & T. Bliesener (Eds.). *Psychology and law: International perspectives.* Berlin: Walter de Gruyter, 413-423.

Lovegrove, S.A. (1984). Structuring sentencing discretion. In D.J. Müller, D.E. Blackman & A.J. Chapman (Eds.). *Psychology and law: Topics from an international conference.* New York: Wiley.

Munné, F. (1994). Reduccionismos y decisiones implícitas en las decisiones judiciales. In J.Sobral, R. Arce & A. Prieto (Eds.). *Manual de psicología jurídica.* Barcelona: Paidós.

Oswald, M.E. (1992). Justification and goals of punishment and the attribution of responsability in judges. In F. Lösel, D. Bender & T. Bliesener (Eds.). *Psychology and law: International perspectives.* Berlin: Walter de Gruyter, 424-434.

Palys, T.S. & Divorski, S. (1984). Judicial decision making: An examination of sentencing disparity among Canadian Provincial Court Judges. In D.J. Müller, D.E., Backman & A.J. Chapman (Eds.). *Psychology and law: Topics from an international conference.* New York: Wiley.

Partridge, A. & Eldridge, W.B. (1974). *The second circuit sentencing study: A report to the judges of the second circuit.* Washington, D.C.: Federal Judicial Center.

Schüneman, B. & Bandilla, W. (1989). Perseverance in courtroom decisions. In H. Wegener, F. Lösel & J. Haisch (Eds.). *Criminal behavior and the justice system: Psychological perspectives.* New York: Springer-Verlag, 181-192.

Sellin, T. (1928). The negro criminal: A statistical note. *Annals of the American Academy of Political and Social Science, 140,* 52-64.

Sobral, J. (1991). El abogado como psicólogo intuitivo. *Anuario de Psicología Jurídica, 1,* 17-29.

Sobral, J. (1993). Sobre la disparidad de sentencias judiciales. In P. Puy (Ed.). *Análisis económico del derecho y la política.* Santiago: Fundación Alfredo Brañas.

Sobral, J. & Prieto, A. (1994). *Psicología y ley. Un examen de las decisiones judiciales.* Madrid: Eudema.

Is the Judge's Role to be Reformulated?
A Socio-Psychological Approach to Office and Practice

Raimund Jakob

Judicature as Performance

The image of the judge, as it corresponds to common notions in most of the Western countries of the European continent, goes back to the 19th century. It is molded by the liberal rule of law which the French Revolution made possible. The principle of public procedure as well as the realization of the idea of the separation of powers are important elements of it. This development reached its climax with the promulgation of written constitutions, which comprised rights of liberty for the citizen and special provisions for the judge. Thus the role of the judge became a central one for the state and an important one for society.

The role of the judge is determined by the legal order, especially by the judicial office and its practice. The practice of this office together with other persons according to a certain succession of events and according to a certain program reminds one of the performance in a theater. If we accept the prevailing juridical doctrine it is not important which person performs this role. This would not affect the result of theprocess. Experienced lawyers take another point of view - not only when asked by their clients about the prognosis. Thus the person in question who carries out the office seems to influence essentially the shaping of the role - similar to an actor - and in this way the result. Under these circumstances, for the explanation of the judge's actions it makes sense to include in the considerations his social and political background, personal attitudes, even the psycho-physical disposition of the day. In fact hardly any research exists in this regard. An explanation for this might be the lack of cooperation by the judicature (Kette, 1987, p. 233).

There are especially two types of classic plays where the judge stands in the center; on the one hand, the civil procedure as a small play of intrigues and on the other hand, the criminal procedure as a great world theater (Rasehorn, 1980). According to the citizens' sense of justice, civil procedure sometimes is quite immoral. This may be due to the influence of Roman Law on civil law. The audience of the play of intrigues consists of insiders; a wider audience lacks understanding of the matter and of the performance. As far as the great world theater is concerned, things are different. It should communicate to the broad audience that criminality does not pay. A part of this goal is to stabilize society; a possible cathartic effect is not undesired.

The last time that the continental judge's role was formulated was in the 19th century. In spite of this, the results of jurisdiction have not become more rational (cf. Ehrenzweig, 1973, pp. 342-348). The goal of the following considerations is to look closer into the problem by means of selected present phenomena and practices that do not represent only peculiarities of special nations. The following considerations are based on in-depth psychological as well as legal theoretical findings.

The Nearness to God

As far as the particular expectations of men are concerned, they are older than the judge's office and go back into human phylogenesis. Also in the psychic development of the individual person they take place at the beginning. Here it is a question of the subjective demand to be accepted by its human surroundings and to gain affective attention (cf. Erikson, 1971, p. 242). From these roots the life-long strive for the ius suum cuique, for justice is developed (Jakob, 1987, pp. 9-11). This is a demand which reality cannot fulfill.

Only religious offers are able to mediate in the resulting psychic conflicts. Thus for instance in Christian religions God is the judge of the world and the last judgment will provide for ultimate justice. The judge's function, which consists essentially in jurisdiction, can be seen in this way as a replica of God's, which is derived from the divine being and is transmitted into human affairs. Seen from a psycho-analytical viewpoint the judicial function of God the Father is to be understood as a projection of a deep seated human need - the need for a just father - in the religious dimension. In contrast to the more secular arbitrator, who mostly is in an equal position, the judge is seen as one who presides above the dispute (Jakob, 1984). As far as the German speaking countries are concerned linguistic findings indicate a notional nearness to God for the person of the judge (cf. Klappenbach, IV, p. 3044).

Influenced by scientific positivism, the 19th century brought changes also here. Changes first of all concern the legal order, where legal positivism gains influence in the second half of the bygone century. Judicature where the role of the judge is secularized only conditionally is not so strongly influenced. The reason for this may be that this role is as old as civilization itself. Judges under the influence of the reception of Roman Law at the end of the Middle Ages adopted the goddess Justitia as the symbol for their work. Already before this time the Roman and the Christian symbols mingled (cf. Kissel, 1984, pp. 26-45). Under this symbol of a magna mater with all of its helping, granting, healing, but also devouring aspects, jurisdiction is performed until today.

The Image in Society

Justitia not only has several faces but this is also true for her functionaries. At a closer look we find evidence already in the 19th century where the ideal type of the just and unbribable judge is contrasted to the type of a judge who is primarily concerned with his own advantage or worse if he is not directly corrupt. We are reminded of Honoré Daumier who in his graphic artworks often reprimands judges who became kind of a caste demanding power. Furthermore, Jean J. Grandville shows us sights of a judicature ignorant of the world. In the first third of this century the reproach of class justice is expressed (cf. Fraenkel, 1927). We all know the part of judicature in the Fascist society. After World War II the judges disappeared from political discussion. Traditionally here Switzerland is an exception.

The polarization of the judge's image seems even stronger in our days; in any case the feeling for it is more widely spread in a better informed society. There are judges in the Italian Republic who have sacrificed their lives in the struggle against criminality and at the same time presidents of courts who are bribed by organized criminals. Judges of the German Federal Republic are criticized because of indolence as the motivation for choosing this career and laziness in the exertion of their duties (Der Spiegel, September 20, 1993). This enumeration could be continued for a number of other countries. The low rating of judges by youth (14 to 19 years) is remarkable. Only 33 percent consider the judge's image positively. This fact was published on the occasion of the Austrian "Richterwoche 1994" (Salzburger Nachrichten, June 15, 1994).

A well-known phenomenon from court practice is people's fear in the search for justice. In former times it was the fear of social contact, fear of authority, of the alien milieu and the unusual language of judicature that played a role in this context. An example is an old woman who as a witness stresses the fact that never in her life had she had anything to do with judicature. Today the fear of the uncertain outcome or in civil cases the fear of a possible economical loss prevails - even if one thinks he or she has good arguments.

An example of a case of damage shall illustrate this: let us presume that none of the parties to the conflict has entered the process fraudulently, that no compromise is reached and that also the judge's decision contains no element of compromise. That means that only one person has to pay completely for the damage. This happens in spite of the fact that both parties have entered the process convinced of their right and thus endorsed by their lawyers. The party who was condemned will feel this to be highly unjust. In former times the authority's decision would have been more convincing. Possibly one would have not understood the decision but would have accepted it as the product of a higher authority, quasi as a fate. In a secular world with authorities who prove daily to be defective, if not corrupt, those persons affected by such a decision lose their believe in judicature. Thus mistrust involves more and more persons. Apart from this the disparity of courts' decisions in comparable penal causes, known from the mass media, strengthens the feeling of citizens' discomfort.

Collective Identity and Fear of Provocation

Throughout history judges have developed a strong feeling for their class together with a strongly developed collective identity. The basis for this is the privileged status and the function transmitted by the state to achieve justice and to protect legal peace. One of the preconditions for such an activity is a corresponding closeness to the value-system existing in a society. This is possible only conditionally. Furthermore, this value-system is not homogeneous any more. To an increasing degree judges are exposed to the conflict that on the one hand they should promote the economy and on the other hand they should show social solidarity.

The independence from a direct authority is a privilege; however, it can create insecurity concerning evaluating decisions. Especially authoritarian personalities have the feeling of a deficit here. This need of a lacking authority from above can be coped with by the view to right and left, by closeness to their colleagues - by the identification with persons of the same standing respective to those who are equally weak (cf. Freud, XVIII, pp. 120-121). A visible sign is that judges like to spend their free time together and like to go to the same restaurants. For third persons the intensity of inside communication between judges is noticeable. This is also true for information of a quite trivial character.

Awareness of status and the feeling of identity can make judges hyper-sensitive and at the same time helpless in view of provocations; for example when fellow-players forget their role. Examples of this are when in the so-called Hamburg "Strip-Tease-Case" female sympathizers in the auditorium took off their clothes or in an Italian terrorist-process during the procedure two of the accused copulated. Such events strengthen the judicature's desire for protection. That in Italy, France, Germany and other European countries security controls similar to those in airports are performed at higher courts has its justification in the exposure of such institutions to terrorist attacks. Such measures exist in Austria only since 1995. In March of that year a man who had lost in a civil procedure shot some people, among them the judge. Before this time such measures were discussed more or less in terms of keeping notorious troublemakers away from the courts (cf. Salzburger Nachrichten, March 2, 1994).

The Withdrawal from the Public

Where there is an opportunity judges withdraw from the public. This is especially true for civil procedure. Proceedings regularly take place in the judge's office, where there is place only for a clerk and for the parties with their lawyers.

Somewhere in the courthouse there is a schedule which informs the public that a certain judge performs proceedings in his office. This way of procedure might be formally correct but in fact the public is excluded.

To justify this, it is normally said that it is so in the interest of the parties and so-to-say progress. In a relaxed situation - without symbols of justice, without robes and without the presence of uninvolved persons - the parties could argue more unbiased, and this again would be in the interest of an adequate decision. Moreover, an audience would be interested only in spectacular cases. The economic argument that in wintertime one should not unnecessarily heat a hall for only a few people is not known in this context. In any case this would be a more apt argument. If no audience is to be expected what would hinder the judge then to perform the process in a court-hall? In Austria such an attitude is in any case against the idea of the Federal Constitution, where in Art. 90 a public procedure is explicitly demanded. In the Law on the Judiciary (Richterdienstgesetz) the two existing commentaries also contain the constitutional provisions concerning judges. In one of these commentaries Art. 90 is missing. By the way: both editors of this book are judges (Faseth & Markel, 1995).

Everybody acquainted with the court's customs knows that the argument in favor of a relaxed atmosphere in the interest of the parties is only a pretended argument. If this atmosphere favors somebody then it is the judge himself who in this way can cope with the parties and the witnesses in a more shirt-sleeved and intimidating manner. The argument that parties confronted with such a behavior are protected by their lawyers proves to be fictitious. That lawyers usually do not react to a vehement behavior of the judge is due to the fact that they daily have to get along with the court and that the client, who normally is a casual one, is not in such contact with the lawyer (cf. Rasehorn, pp. 336-340). This is especially true for places where lawyers and judges live in a face-to-face-relationship. The limit is 70-80 judges at one place. Where there are larger courts the situation becomes slightly better.

How is the judges' withdrawal from the public to be understood? It is to be regarded as an indication of the judge's fear towards a citizen who is better informed and who is more critical? The judge's attitude is to be understood as a reaction in the sense of a repulsion of fear and aggression, similar to the case of parents whose children reach puberty and become more and more intelligent and ask more and more questions. Frequently the parents are inclined to react aggressively.

This fear is connected with their vanishing authority. Against this one could argue that this can not be true, because otherwise the services of judicature would not be requested so frequently. This demand still remains unchanged; it even increases. Against this one could again argue that this demand is not to be regarded as a proof of confidence but even more as a sign of ambivalence. This means that in spite of the mistrust the desire for order is not to be eliminated. We also have to think here of the value of experience of a "state in action" (Rasehorn, pp. 331-332).

The Problem of the Evaluation of Evidence

Until now we have referred to judges in general. We shall now deal in more detail with one of the judge's main functions, namely with the evaluation of evidence. Apart from the fixing of the penalty the evaluation of evidence comprises one of the most important activities of a judge from a psychological point of view. One matter of concern is the so-called free evaluation of evidence. Here we are faced with the question whether in view of the offered evidence according to free conviction a fact is to be regarded as proven or not. In the realm of the juridical doctrine this is an activity of reason and not of subjective feeling. When settling the "truth for the court" the judge has to proceed logically - not bound to any rules of evidence.

Especially problematical in this connection is the questioning of the parties and the evidence by witnesses, because the evidence is not only evaluated according to its contents but also according to its presentation. For a certain purpose a testimony might be excellent as far as its contents are concerned and still might be useless or detrimental if the judge received a bad impression of the person who gave testimony. Identifications and prejudices play a not unimportant part for the personal impression; for example, in the case of a judge who takes all his children say for liars and who then has to evaluate the testimony of a youth. But also the condition of the day or a dispute before the process could be factually of importance. The evaluation of evidence itself is subject to a later control by appeal. Exempt from this is the evaluation of the credibility of a party or a witness according to personal impression. Thus in Austria there does not exist the duty to found such impressions in regard of the contents - this being strengthened by the jurisdiction of the highest courts (for instance OGH, March 23, 1982, 9 Os 38/82; July 27, 1982, 10 Os 86/82 and VfGH December 1, 1982, B376/82; September 24, 1983, B 128/83). This way of procedure is not only pragmatical; it forms at the same time a taboo by which personal evaluations of the judge are not subject to a questioning and thus are protected from desecration. What shall society think about a being similar to God who evaluates the testimony of a sexually attractive person more favorably than that of an old woman? Whoever would discover something like this would be frustrated about justice forever. Above that the world of juridical fictions then would no more be sound.

The possibility of an expert opinion on the credibility of a person means a mitigation and at the same time a switch of the problem into another sphere. To a greater extent these are children, young and growing persons, who in a criminal procedure are put to this test (cf. Arntzen, 1983, p. 129). Otherwise such opinions are the exception. And this is not so because of reasons of economizing the procedure.

Whereas in occidental judicature it is more or less denied that the judge's decision is influenced by factors which are based on psychic processes which occur in the judge's personality, the Islamic judicature traditionally proves to be aware of this problem (Schneider, 1990, pp. 60-68 and passim). Islam has besides procedural law special rules of behavior for judges which bear normative character. These prevent the judge from entering into a procedure as long as he is in a unbalanced psychic or physical status. This is so in spite of a strong religious background, where there exists a divine judge as well as a last judgment. The difference might be explained by the fact that the judge in the Islamic world is a man who like all other men is able to realize the truth only to a limited extent and that Islamic judicature - in contrast to occidental judicature - does not comprise a worldly possibility of appeal.

Attempt of an Answer

The role of the judge is as old as civilization itself. This role has been reformulated for the last time in the 19th century. The process of secularization began shortly before this. In the last decades provocations occur against the judicature which judges face helplessly because they are not prepared for them. Wherever possible judges react by retreat. Experiments with new forms of procedure provide for a destabilization of the traditional role. In the judge's activities additionally problems in connection with the evaluation of evidence and the fixing of penalty arise. Especially in regard of the latter, judicature finds itself exposed to the reproach to act irrationally. How can this role become more attractive and acceptable again for the actors and for society? Have we to rewrite this role or what can be done to adapt this role to our times and to the expectations connected with it?

Measures in two directions seem to be necessary. First of all it is necessary to bring the judge back to the publicity of the court-room. Considering the judge's privileged status this will not be so easy. Where it is not provided for until now, the free evaluation of evidence should be accompanied by an equivalent duty of founding it; this is especially true for the meta-level.

Forensic psychology obviously aims at the disparity of criminal judges' decisions and discerns here a need for reform. Special training programs are offered as well for the individual judge's decision as well as for the group decision. Moreover in some Western European countries deliberations were made to install a system of presumptive punishment. The presumptive punishment is a standardized punishment that a perpetrator committing a typical crime for the first time receives. For a perpetrator who repeatedly does wrong the presumptive punishment is increased to an extent which is fixed already in advance (cf. Kette, pp. 240-246). These measures seem to be problematic in various regards, not in the least because only a symptom is dealt with.

For all persons involved it makes more sense to cope with the personality of the judge. To reach this aim possibilities of self-experience should be offered obligatorily to trainees, be it individually or in groups. Afterwards in the judge's professional life a supervision in the manner of Balint-groups should take place to help the judge clear and disentangle his involvement in the relations of a case (cf.

Stucke, 1990, pp. 67-76). Moreover here the motivation of the individual judge can be questioned. These necessities are also realized by the judges themselves and in single cases such groups are organized privately. Reports of this kind make us feel optimistic in regard to the actors and to their role.

References

Arntzen, F. (1983). *Psychologie der Zeugenaussage. System der Glaubwürdigkeitsmerkmale.* 2nd ed. München: C.H. Beck.

Ehrenzweig, A.A. (1971, German transl. 1973). *Psychoanalytische Rechtswissenschaft.* Berlin: Duncker & Humblot.

Erikson, E. (1963, German transl. 4th ed. 1971). *Kindheit und Gesellschaft.* Stuttgart: Ernst Klett.

Faseth, E., & Markel, E., Eds. (2nd 1995). *Richterdienstgesetz.* Wien: Staatsdruckerei.

Fraenkel, E. (1927, repr. 1968). Zur Soziologie der Klassenjustiz. In: E. Fraenkel: *Zur Soziologie der Klassenjustiz und Aufsätze zur Verfassungskrise 1931-1932*, pp. 1-41. Darmstadt: Wissenschaftliche Buchgesellschaft.

Freud, S. (1953 onwards). *The Standard Edition of the Complete Psychological Works* (ed. by J. Strachey), XXIV vols. London: The Hogarth Press & The Institute of Psycho-Analysis.

Jakob, R. (1984). Iudex oder Arbiter? In W. Krawietz & Th. Mayer-Maly & O. Weinberger (Eds.), *Objektivierung des Rechtsdenkens*, pp. 605-614. Berlin: Duncker & Humblot.

Jakob, R. (1987). Rechtspsychologie. In R. Jakob & M. Rehbinder (Eds.), *Beiträge zur Rechtspsychologie*, pp. 9-23. Berlin: Duncker & Humblot.

Kette, G. (1987). *Rechtspsychologie.* Wien: Springer.

Kissel, O. (1984). *Die Justitia.* München: C.H. Beck.

Klappenbach, R., ed. (1961 onwards). *Wörterbuch der deutschen Gegenwartssprache, VI vols.* Berlin: Akademieverlag Berlin (GDR).

Rasehorn, Th. (1980). Die Justiz als Theater. In E. Blankenburg & E. Klausa & H. Rottleuthner (Eds.), *Alternative Rechtsformen und Alternativen zum Recht*, pp. 328-343. Opladen: Westdeutscher Verlag.

Salzburger Nachrichten. (newspaper) Salzburg.

Schneider, I. (1990). *Das Bild des Richters in der "Adab Al-Qadi"-Literatur.* Frankfurt Main: Peter Lang.

Der Spiegel. Das deutsche Nachrichtenmagazin. (weekly magazin) Hamburg.

Stucke, W. (1990). *Die Balint-Gruppe.* 2nd ed. Köln: Deutscher Ärzte-Verlag.

Part V
Child Development and Delinquency

Delinquency Prevention in the First Few Years of Life

David P. Farrington

Introduction

In my plenary address to the Second European Conference on Law and Psychology in Nuremberg (Farrington, 1992b), I reviewed psychological contributions to the explanation, prevention and treatment of offending. I reviewed knowledge about the link between offending and individual difference factors such as intelligence and neuropsychological deficit, personality and impulsivity; and about family, peer, school and situational influences on offending. I also reviewed methods of preventing and treating offending based on this knowledge, including cognitive-behavioural skills training, parent training, peer and school programmes, and situational prevention. My focus was very much on prediction and prevention in childhood and adolescence. In contrast, in this plenary address to the Fourth European Conference on Law and Psychology in Barcelona, I want to focus on much earlier prediction and prevention - in pregnancy, the perinatal period, and the first few years of life.

In this paper, I will review methods of preventing juvenile delinquency that are targeted on the development of children and families and that can be implemented between conception and age 5-6. Zigler et al. (1992) and Yoshikawa (1994) have provided more detailed reviews of these programmes. I have termed these methods "early developmental prevention" to distinguish them from situational prevention (which focuses on reducing opportunities for crime by increasing physical security and surveillance), social prevention (which focuses on community-based programmes, such as providing better leisure facilities for youth living on deprived housing estates) and prevention through criminal justice system measures (which focuses on detection, retribution, deterrence and incapacitation). I will emphasise knowledge about early developmental prevention obtained in randomised experiments, since these yield the most convincing demonstration of causal and preventive effects (Farrington, 1983; Farrington et al., 1986).

Methods of preventing delinquency should be grounded in knowledge about the causes of delinquency, or at least in knowledge about risk and protective factors that predict delinquency (Coie et al., 1993). Hence, before reviewing each prevention method, I will briefly summarise knowledge about causes. I will focus especially on prenatal and perinatal factors, on the individual factors of impulsivity and low intelligence and on parental child-rearing techniques. Generally, early child-bearing (teenage pregnancy), substance use during pregnancy, and perinatal complications are associated with poor child-rearing and with hyperactivity, impulsivity, low intelligence and low attainment of the child, which in turn predict childhood behaviour problems and later delinquency and crime. Since this chain of events begins at the child's conception, it is important to implement delinquency prevention programmes as early in a child's life as possible.

The most adequate knowledge about causes, risk factors and developmental sequences has been obtained in prospective longitudinal surveys, which make it possible to establish causal order and to avoid retrospective bias in measuring risk factors. Few surveys have begun during the prenatal or perinatal period and followed up children to investigate their juvenile and adult offending. In fact, there seem to be only four prospective longitudinal surveys of this type that included personal contacts with the subjects (as opposed to data collection only from records).

In the British National Survey of Health and Development, Wadsworth (1979) tracked a nationally representative sample of over 5,000 children from their birth in 1946 and studied offending up to age 20. Similarly, in the Newcastle Thousand-Family Study, Kolvin et al. (1988, 1990) followed over 1,000 children from Newcastle-upon-Tyne from their birth in 1947 and studied offending up to age 32. In Kauai (Hawaii), Werner (1989) tracked about 700 children from their birth in 1955 and studied offending up to age 32. Finally, in Dunedin (New Zealand), Moffitt and Silva (1988b) followed over 1,000 children from their birth in 1972-73 and studied offending up to age 15.

While very few prospective longitudinal surveys have spanned the full period from birth to adulthood, useful conclusions can often be drawn by combining results from surveys spanning segments of the full period. For example, in a study of nearly 200 children from Outer London, Richman et al. (1982) found considerable continuity in behaviour problems between ages 3 and 8. In our Cambridge Study in Delinquent Development, which is a prospective longitudinal survey of over 400 Inner London boys, we found considerable continuity in antisocial behaviour between ages 8 and 18 (West & Farrington, 1977) and between ages 18 and 32 (Farrington, 1991a). It is plausible to deduce from these two surveys that there is likely to be significant stability in antisocial behaviour from age 3 to age 32.

Delinquency and Antisocial Personality

Juvenile delinquents are predominantly versatile rather than specialised in their offending (e.g. Klein, 1984; Farrington et al., 1988). In other words, people who commit one type of offence have a significant tendency also to commit other types.

For example, 86% of convicted violent offenders in our Cambridge Study also had convictions for non-violent offences (Farrington, 1991b).

Just as offenders tend to be versatile in their types of offending, they also tend to be versatile in their antisocial behaviour generally. In the Cambridge Study, convicted delinquents tended to be troublesome and dishonest in their primary schools, tended to be frequent liars and aggressive at age 12-14, and tended to be bullies at age 14. By age 18, delinquents tended to be antisocial in a wide variety of respects, including heavy drinking, heavy smoking, using prohibited drugs and heavy gambling. In addition, they tended to be sexually promiscuous, often beginning sexual intercourse under age 15, having several sexual partners by age 18, and usually having unprotected intercourse (Farrington, 1992a). Because of this versatility, any prevention method that succeeds in reducing delinquency is likely also to reduce these associated social problems.

West and Farrington (1977) argued that delinquency (which is dominated by crimes of dishonesty) is only one element of a larger syndrome of antisocial behaviour which arises in childhood and usually persists into adulthood. In trying to measure this syndrome, I developed scales of "antisocial personality" at ages 10, 14, 18 and 32, based on offending and on other types of antisocial behaviour (Farrington, 1991a). For example, the scale at age 18 included convictions, high self-reported delinquency, high self-reported violence, drug-taking, heavy smoking, heavy drinking, drunk driving, heavy gambling, promiscuous sexual intercourse, an unstable job record and anti-establishment attitudes. All these measures tended to be inter-related.

These results are consistent with findings obtained in numerous other studies. For example, in a St Louis (Missouri) survey of over 200 black males, Robins and Ratcliff (1980) reported that juvenile delinquency tended to be associated with truancy, precocious sex, drinking and drug use. In the literature on childhood psychopathology, it is also customary to identify a single syndrome of "conduct disorder" (Robins, 1991) or "externalising problems" (Achenbach et al., 1987), including stealing, lying, cheating, vandalism, substance use, running away from home and truancy.

Continuity in Antisocial Behaviour

Numerous studies also show that conduct problems in infancy and childhood predict later offending and antisocial behaviour (e.g. Loeber & LeBlanc, 1990). For example, Spivack et al. (1986) in Philadelphia discovered that troublesome behaviour in Kindergarten (age 3-4) predicted later police contacts; and Tremblay et al. (1988) in Montreal showed that ratings of aggressiveness by teachers and peers in the first grade (age 6) predicted self-reported offending at age 14-15.

As already mentioned, in the Cambridge Study there was evidence of continuity in antisocial behaviour from childhood to the teenage years. The antisocial personality scale at age 8-10 correlated .50 with the corresponding scale at age 14 and .38 with the scale at age 18 (Farrington, 1991a). Half of the most antisocial boys at age 8-10 were still among the most antisocial at age 14, and 43% of them were still among the most antisocial at age 18. In regard to specific types of antisocial behaviour, troublesomeness (rated by peers and teachers) at age 8-10 was the best predictor of truancy, bullying and aggressive behaviour at age 12-14 in the secondary schools (Farrington, 1980, 1989, 1993).

There is also continuity in antisocial behaviour at younger ages. For example, Rose et al. (1989) in New York City found that externalising problems on the Achenbach Child Behaviour Checklist, completed by parents, were significantly correlated (r = .57) between ages 2 and 5. Furthermore, a mother's ratings of her boy's difficult temperament at age 6 months significantly predicted (r = .31) his externalising problems at age 8 in the Bloomington (Indiana) longitudinal survey (Bates et al., 1991). As already mentioned, Richman et al. (1985) in Outer London reported that behaviour problems tended to persist between ages 3 and 8, and in New Zealand White et al. (1990) showed that externalising problems and being difficult to manage at age 3 predicted antisocial behaviour at age 11. The fact that antisocial behaviour in the first few years of life predicts later antisocial behaviour and delinquency is a strong argument for concentrating prevention efforts around the time of the child's birth.

Prenatal and Perinatal Factors

At least in Western industrialised countries, early child-bearing, or teenage pregnancy, predicts many undesirable outcomes for the children, including low school attainment, antisocial school behaviour, substance use and early sexual intercourse (Furstenberg et al., 1987a, 1987b). The children of teenage mothers are also more likely to become offenders. For example, Morash and Rucker (1989) analysed results from four surveys in the United States and England (including the Cambridge Study) and found that teenage mothers were associated with low income families, welfare support and absent biological fathers, that they used poor child-rearing methods, and that their children were characterised by low school attainment and delinquency. However, the presence of the biological father mitigated many of these adverse factors and generally had a protective effect. In Newcastle-upon-Tyne, Kolvin et al. (1990) reported that mothers who married as teenagers (a factor strongly related to teenage childbearing) were twice as likely to have sons who became offenders by age 32 (49% as opposed to 23%). Baker and Mednick (1984) in Copenhagen also concluded that children of teenage mothers tended to be more aggressive and to have low school attainment.

Substance use (smoking, drinking and drug use) in pregnancy is also associated with the later undesirable development of children. For example, Streissguth (1986) showed that smoking in pregnancy was associated with low birth weight, small height and low school attainment. Excessive alcohol consumption in pregnancy predicted poor physical growth, low intelligence and hyperactivity of children. Of course, none of these results necessarily prove causal effects; for example, smoking and low school attainment could both be caused by a deprived background. Prevention experiments trying to change a risk factor are the best means of proving causal effects.

A low birth weight, a relatively small baby, and perinatal complications (such as forceps delivery, asphyxia, a long duration of labour or toxemia in pregnancy) also predict later conduct problems and delinquency of children, although the low prevalence of such complications in representative community samples makes it difficult to establish their effects. For example, in Cleveland (Ohio), Breslau et al. (1988) found that males with low birth weight were more aggressive, hyperactive and delinquent at age 9 (on the Achenbach Child Behaviour Checklist) than other males, independently of differences in intelligence. In Ontario (Canada), Szatmari et al. (1986) reported that pregnancy and birth complications were more common in antisocial adolescents than in their siblings. However, perinatal complications were rather weak predictors of offending in the surveys by Werner (1986) in Hawaii and Denno (1990) in Philadelphia.

It seems likely that the effects of perinatal complications may vary with other factors such as the quality of the home environment. For example, Kolvin et al. (1990) in Newcastle-upon-Tyne found that neonatal injuries significantly predicted offending up to age 32 only for boys who were in deprived families (low income or disrupted) at age 5. In Dunedin (New Zealand), McGee et al. (1984) reported that children who were small at birth for their gestational age significantly tended to be badly behaved at age 7, especially if they were also exposed to family adversities. In later research on the same survey, Moffitt (1990) showed that perinatal complications predicted delinquency, but only among boys who were also hyperactive.

The most extensive studies of the link between perinatal complications and later delinquency have been carried out in Copenhagen. Kandel and Mednick (1991) and Brennan et al. (1993) showed that delivery complications significantly predicted later violent offending for males (12% as opposed to 3% had recorded offences up to age 21), but only if the males had a psychiatric (psychopathic or schizophrenic) parent. Pregnancy complications tended to predict property offences. Baker and Mednick (1984) found that "medical risk" (a combination of physical health at birth and motor development at 12 months) predicted later aggression and bullying in school, but only for children from broken families. As Morash and Rucker (1989) also suggested, coming from an intact family (having the biological father present) may act as a protective factor. The key link in the chain between perinatal complications and delinquency may be injury to the brain and neurological dysfunction; Rivara and Farrington (1996) have extensively reviewed the effects of brain injury on delinquency and violence.

Delinquency Prevention in Pregnancy and Infancy

Adolescent pregnancy prevention programmes have been reviewed by Hayes (1987). Most focus on imparting knowledge (e.g. in sex education classes), improving decision-making skills (e.g. through peer counselling), enhancing a girl's life options (e.g. in education or employment) and providing access to contraception (e.g. in school-based clinics). Unfortunately, while many programmes have been developed and implemented, it is hard to find randomised experiments with rigorous evaluations of effectiveness.

Problems in pregnancy and infancy can be alleviated by home visiting programmes designed to help mothers. For example, in New York State, Olds et al (1986a, 1986b) randomly allocated 400 mothers either to receive home visits from nurses during pregnancy, or to receive visits both during pregnancy and during the first two years of life, or to a control group who received no visits. Each visit lasted about one and a quarter hours, and the mothers were visited on average every two weeks. The home visitors gave advice about prenatal and postnatal care of the child, about infant development, and about the importance of proper nutrition and avoiding smoking and drinking during pregnancy.

The results of this experiment showed that home visits during pregnancy led to teenage mothers having heavier babies. Also, women who had previously smoked decreased their smoking and had fewer pre-term deliveries. In addition, the postnatal home visits caused a decrease in recorded child physical abuse and neglect during the first two years of life, especially by poor unmarried teenage mothers; 4% of visited versus 19% of non-visited mothers of this type were guilty of child abuse or neglect. This last result is important because of the common observation that being physically abused or neglected as a child predicts later violent offending (Widom, 1989).

Similar results were obtained by Larson (1980) in a similar experiment in Montreal with over 100 lower-class mothers. The mothers were randomly allocated to receive either home visits both before and after the child's birth, or home visits only after the child's birth, or no visits. The home visitors (child psychologists) provided advice about taking care of the infant and about infant development. The home visits had beneficial effects, since the children of visited mothers sustained significantly fewer injuries in the first year of life. The children of mothers visited both before and after birth (the category with the best outcome) had only half as many injuries as the children of non-visited mothers. Also, the mothers visited both prenatally and postnatally were rated by observers as the most skilled in taking care of the child.

One of the largest early prevention projects was the Infant Health and Development Programme, which was carried out with nearly 1000 low-birth-weight infants in 8 sites across the United States (Brooks-Gunn et al., 1993). Children were selected at birth and randomly allocated to experimental or control groups. The experimental families received about three home visits per month up to age 3, providing family support and information about health and development. Also, the experimental infants received a free child care programme in their second and third years. This treatment had beneficial effects, since the experimental infants had higher intelligence and fewer behaviour problems at ages 2 and 3.

Few early prevention experiments have included a long-term follow-up of the children. However, in Houston (Texas), Johnson and Walker (1987) carried out a home visiting programme when children were aged between 1 and 3 and then followed up about 140 children to age 11. Low-income Mexican-American families with one-year-old children were randomly assigned to receive home visits or no visits. The home visitors advised the mother about child development and parenting skills, tried to help her develop an affectionate relationship with her child, and also aimed to develop the cognitive skills of the child. At the end of the programme at age 3, the visited mothers were rated as more affectionate, as using more praise and less criticism, and as providing a more stimulating home environment. At age 11, teachers rated the visited children as less aggressive than the controls. Therefore, the early home visits led to improved child behaviour.

One of the very few prevention experiments beginning in pregnancy and collecting outcome data on delinquency was the Syracuse (New York) Family Development Research Programme (Lally et al., 1988). The researchers began with a sample of pregnant women and gave them weekly help with child-rearing, health, nutrition and other problems. In addition, their children received free day care, designed to develop their intellectual abilities, up to age 5. This was not a randomised experiment, but a matched control group was chosen when the children were aged 3. The treated children had significantly higher intelligence than the controls at age 3 but were not different at age 5. Ten years later, about 120 treated and control children were followed up to about age 15. Significantly fewer of the treated children (2% as opposed to 17%) had been referred to the juvenile court for delinquency offences, and the treated girls showed better school attendance and school performance. Hence, this prevention experiment agrees with others in showing that early home visits providing advice and support to mothers can have later beneficial outcomes, including the reduction of offending.

Intelligence and Attainment

As Hirschi and Hindelang (1977) showed in their review, low intelligence is an important predictor and correlate of offending: at least as important as social class or race. For example, in a prospective longitudinal survey of about 120 Stockholm males, intelligence measured at age 3 significantly predicted officially recorded offending up to age 30 (Stattin & Klackenberg-Larsson, 1993). Frequent offenders (with 4 or more offences) had an average IQ of 88 at age 3, whereas non-offenders had an average IQ of 101. Official offending was also significantly predicted by language development at 6, 18 and 24 months. All of these results held up after controlling for social class. Also, in the Perry pre-school project in Ypsilanti (Michigan), Schweinhart et al. (1993) concluded that intelligence at age 4 significantly predicted the number of arrests up to age 27. However, intelligence at age 4 was a weak predictor of offending in the Philadelphia survey of Denno (1990).

In the Cambridge Study, West and Farrington (1973) found that twice as many of the boys scoring 90 or less on a non-verbal intelligence test (Raven's Progressive Matrices) at age 8-10 were convicted as juveniles than of the remainder. Low non-verbal intelligence was highly correlated with low verbal intelligence (vocabulary, word comprehension, verbal reasoning) and with low school attainment, and all of these measures predicted juvenile convictions to much the same extent. In addition to their poor school performance, delinquents tended to be frequent truants, to leave school at the earliest possible age (which was then 15) and to take no school examinations.

Low non-verbal intelligence was especially characteristic of the juvenile recidivists and those first convicted at the earliest ages (10-13). Furthermore, low non-verbal intelligence predicted juvenile self-reported offending to almost exactly the same degree as juvenile convictions (Farrington, 1992a), suggesting that the link between low intelligence and delinquency was not caused by the less intelligent boys having a greater probability of being caught. Also, measures of intelligence predicted measures of offending independently of other variables such as family income and family size. Similar results have been obtained in other projects (Lynam et al., 1993; Moffitt & Silva, 1988a; Wilson & Herrnstein, 1985). Just as low intelligence is a risk factor, it has also been argued that high intelligence is a protective factor against offending for children from high-risk backgrounds (Kandel et al., 1988; White et al., 1989).

Intelligence may lead to delinquency through the intervening factor of school failure, as Hirschi and Hindelang (1977) suggested. However, a more plausible explanatory factor underlying the link between intelligence and offending is the ability to manipulate abstract concepts. Delinquents often do better on non-verbal performance tests, such as object assembly and block design, than on verbal tests (Walsh et al., 1987), suggesting that they find it easier to deal with concrete objects than with abstract concepts. People with a poor grasp of abstract concepts tend to do badly in intelligence tests such as the Matrices and in school attainment, and they also tend to commit offences, probably because of their poor ability to foresee the consequences of their offending and to appreciate the feelings of victims (i.e. their low empathy).

Pre-School Intellectual Enrichment Programmes

If low intelligence and school failure are causes of offending, then any programme that leads to an increase in school success should lead to a decrease in offending.

One of the most successful delinquency prevention programmes has been the Perry pre-school project carried out in Ypsilanti (Michigan) by Schweinhart and Weikart (1980). This was essentially a "Head Start" programme targeted on disadvantaged black children, who were allocated (approximately at random) to experimental and control groups. The experimental children attended a daily pre-school programme, backed up by weekly home visits, usually lasting two years (covering ages 3-4). The aim of the programme was to provide intellectual stimulation, to increase cognitive abilities, and to increase later school achievement.

About 120 children in the two groups were followed up to age 15, using teacher ratings, parent and youth interviews, and school records. As demonstrated in several other Head Start projects, the experimental group showed gains in intelligence that were rather short-lived. However, they were significantly better in elementary school motivation, school achievement at 14, teacher ratings of classroom behaviour at 6 to 9, self-reports of classroom behaviour at 15 and self-reports of offending at 15. Furthermore, a later follow-up of this sample by Berrueta-Clement et al. (1984) showed that, at age 19, the experimental group was more likely to be employed, more likely to have graduated from high school, more likely to have received college or vocational training, and less likely to have been arrested.

By age 27, the experimental group had accumulated only half as many arrests on average as the controls (Schweinhart et al., 1993). Also, they had significantly higher earnings and were more likely to be home-owners. More of the experimental females were married, and fewer of their children had been born out of wedlock. Hence, this pre-school intellectual enrichment programme led to decreases in school failure, to decreases in offending, and to decreases in other undesirable outcomes.

The Perry project is admittedly only one study based on relatively small numbers. However, its results become more compelling when viewed in the context of 10 other similar American Head Start projects followed up by the Consortium for Longitudinal Studies (1983) and other pre-school programmes such as the Carolina Abercedarian Project, which began at age 3 months (Horacek et al., 1987). With quite impressive consistency, all studies show that pre-school intellectual enrichment programmes have long-term beneficial effects on school success, especially in increasing the rate of high school graduation and decreasing the rate of special education placements. The Perry project was the only one to study offending, but the consistency of the school success results in all projects suggests that the effects on offending might be replicable.

Hyperactivity and Impulsivity

Hyperactivity is an important psychological construct that predicts later delinquency. It usually begins before age 5 and often before age 2, and it tends to persist into adolescence (Taylor, 1986). It is associated with restlessness, impulsivity and a short attention span, and for that reason has been termed the "hyperactivity-impulsivity-attention deficit" or HIA syndrome (Loeber, 1987). HIA may be an early stage in a causal or developmental sequence leading to offending. For example, in the Cambridge Study, Farrington et al. (1990) showed that HIA at age 8-10 significantly predicted juvenile convictions independently of conduct problems at age 8-10. Related concepts include a poor ability to defer gratification (Mischel et al., 1989) and a short future time perspective (Stein et al., 1968). Pulkkinen (1986) has usefully reviewed the various concepts and measures of hyperactivity and impulsivity.

Hyperactivity is often treated using drugs such as Ritalin (Whalen & Henker, 1991). However, I will focus on psychological techniques designed to increase self-control. Hyperactivity and impulsivity might be altered using the set of techniques variously termed cognitive-behavioural interpersonal skills training, which have proved to be quite successful (e.g. Michelson, 1987). Also, if risk factors have additive or cumulative effects, a combination of interventions may be more effective than a single method.

One of the most important prevention experiments was carried out in Montreal by Tremblay et al. (1991, 1992). They identified about 250 disruptive (aggressive/hyperactive) boys at age 6 for a prevention experiment. Between ages 7 and 9, the experimental group received training to foster social skills and self-control. Coaching, peer modelling, role playing and reinforcement contingencies were used in small group sessions on such topics as "how to help", "what to do when you are angry" and "how to react to teasing". Also, their parents were trained using the parent management training techniques developed by Patterson (1982) in Eugene (Oregon). Parents were trained to notice what a child is doing, to monitor the child's behaviour over long periods, to state house rules clearly, to reward prosocial behaviour, to punish behaviour consistently and contingently, and to negotiate disagreements so that conflicts and crises did not escalate.

This prevention programme was quite successful. By age 12, the experimental boys committed less burglary and theft, were less likely to get drunk, and were less likely to be involved in fights than the controls. Also, the experimental boys were higher in school achievement. Interestingly, the differences in antisocial behaviour between experimental and control boys increased as the follow-up progressed.

Another important prevention experiment was carried out in Seattle by Hawkins et al. (1991, 1992). This combined parent training, teacher training and skills training. About 500 first grade children (aged 6) in 21 classes in 8 schools were randomly assigned to be in experimental or control classes. The children in the experimental classes received special treatment at home and school which was designed to increase their attachment to their parents and their bonding to the school, on the assumption that offending was inhibited by the strength of social bonds. Their parents were trained to notice and reinforce socially desirable behaviour in a program called "Catch them being good". Their teachers were trained in classroom management, for example to provide clear instructions and expectations to children, to reward children for participation in desired behaviour, and to teach children prosocial methods of solving problems.

In an evaluation of this programme 18 months later, when the children were in different classes, Hawkins et al. (1991) found that the boys who received the experimental programme were significantly less aggressive than the control boys, according to teacher ratings. This difference was particularly marked for white boys rather than black boys. The experimental girls were not significantly less aggressive, but they were less self-destructive, anxious and depressed. By the fifth grade, the experimental children were less likely to have initiated delinquency and alcohol use. It might be expected that a combination of interventions might in general be more effective than a single technique, although combining interventions makes it harder to identify the active ingredient.

Conclusions

The stability of antisocial behaviour from childhood to adulthood suggests that delinquency prevention efforts should be implemented as early in a child's life as possible. Teenage pregnancy, substance use in pregnancy, and perinatal complications (including low birth weight) are risk factors for a variety of undesirable outcomes, including low intelligence and attainment, hyperactivity and impulsivity, and child conduct problems, aggression and delinquency. Hence, it is important to mount delinquency prevention programmes targeting these risk factors, and to follow up the children into adolescence and adulthood to establish the long-term effects on delinquency and crime. Home visiting programmes, attempting to improve child-rearing methods and parental knowledge about child development, seem to be quite effective.

High impulsivity and low intelligence are important risk factors in the first few years of life that predict later delinquency and crime. Both of these may be linked to a poor ability to manipulate abstract concepts, which may also be related to other individual factors such as egocentricity and low empathy. Since the roots of crime lie primarily in individual and family factors, methods of reducing crime should attempt to tackle these factors. Cognitive-behavioural interpersonal skills training to improve self-control, pre-school intellectual enrichment programmes to develop cognitive skills, and parent management training all seem to be effective methods of preventing offending.

Because of the link between offending and numerous other social problems, any measure that succeeds in reducing crime will have benefits that go far beyond this. Any measure that reduces crime will probably also reduce alcohol abuse, drunk driving, drug abuse, sexual promiscuity, family violence, truancy, school failure, unemployment, marital disharmony and divorce. It is clear that problem children tend to grow up into problem adults, and that problem adults tend to produce more problem children. Major efforts to tackle the roots of crime are urgently needed, especially those focusing on early development in the first few years of life.

References

Achenbach, T.M., Verhulst, F.C., Baron, G.D., & Althaus, M. (1987). A comparison of syndromes derived from the child behaviour checklist for American and Dutch boys aged 6-11 and 12-16. *Journal of Child Psychology and Psychiatry, 28*, 437-453.

Baker, R.L., & Mednick, B.R. (1984). Influences on human development. Boston: Kluwer-Nijhoff.

Bates, J.E., Bayles, K., Bennett, D.S., Ridge, B., & Brown, M.M. (1991). Origins of externalizing behaviour problems at 8 years of age. In D.J. Pepler & K.H. Rubin (Eds.) The development and treatment of childhood aggression (pp. 93-120). Hillsdale, NJ: Erlbaum.

Berrueta-Clement, J.R., Schweinhart, L.J., Barnett, W.S., Epstein, A.S., & Weikart, D.P. (1984). Changed lives. Ypsilanti, Michigan: High/Scope.

Brennan, P.A., Mednick, B.R., & Mednick, S.A. (1993). Parental psychopathology, congenital factors and violence. In S. Hodgins (Ed.) Mental disorder and violence (pp. 244-261). Newbury Park, California: Sage.

Breslau, N., Klein, N., & Allen, L. (1988). Very low birthweight: Behavioural sequelae at nine years of age. *Journal of the American Academy of Child and Adolescent Psychiatry, 27*, 605-612.

Brooks-Gunn, J., Klebanov, P.K., Liaw, F., & Spiker, D. (1993). Enhancing the development of low-birthweight, premature infants: Changes in cognition and behaviour over the first three years. *Child Development, 64,* 736-753.

Coie, J.D., Watt, N.F., West, S.G., Hawkins, J.D., Asarnow, J.R., Markham, H.J., Ramey, S.L., Shure, M.B., & Long, B. (1993). The science of prevention: A conceptual framework and some directions for a national research programme. *American Psychologist, 48*, 1013-1022.

Consortium for Longitudinal Studies (1983). As the twig is bent...Lasting effects of pre-school programmes. Hillsdale, N.J.: Erlbaum.

Denno, D.W. (1990). Biology and violence. Cambridge: Cambridge University Press.

Ensminger, M.E., Kellam, S.G. & Rubin, B.R. (1983). School and family origins of delinquency. In K.T. Van Dusen & S.A. Mednick (Eds.) Prospective studies of crime and delinquency (pp. 73-97). Boston: Kluwer-Nijhoff.

Farrington, D.P. (1980). Truancy, delinquency, the home and the school. In L. Hersov and I. Berg (Eds) Out of school: Modern perspectives in truancy and school refusal (pp. 49-63). Chichester: Wiley.

Farrington, D.P. (1983). Randomized experiments on crime and justice. In M. Tonry & N. Morris (Eds.) Crime and justice, vol.4 (pp.257-308). Chicago: University of Chicago Press.

Farrington, D.P. (1989). Early predictors of adolescent aggression and adult violence. *Violence and Victims, 4,* 79-100.

Farrington, D.P. (1991a). Antisocial personality from childhood to adulthood. *The Psychologist, 4*, 389-394.

Farrington, D.P. (1991b). Childhood aggression and adult violence: Early precursors and later life outcomes. In D.J. Pepler & K.H. Rubin (Eds.) The development and treatment of childhood aggression (pp. 5-29). Hillsdale, N.J.: Erlbaum.

Farrington, D.P. (1992a). Juvenile delinquency. In J.C.Coleman (Ed.) The school years (2nd ed.) (pp. 123-163). London: Routledge.

Farrington, D.P. (1992b). Psychological contributions to the explanation, prevention and treatment of offending. In F. Lösel, D. Bender & T. Bliesener (Eds.) Psychology and law: International perspectives (pp. 35-51). Berlin: De Gruyter.

Farrington, D.P. (1993). Understanding and preventing bullying. In M. Tonry (Ed.) Crime and justice, vol. 17 (pp. 381-458). Chicago: University of Chicago Press.

Farrington, D.P., Loeber, R., & Van Kammen, W.B. (1990). Long-term criminal outcomes of hyperactivity-impulsivity-attention deficit and conduct problems in childhood. In L.N. Robins & M. Rutter (Eds.) Straight and devious pathways from childhood to adulthood (pp. 62-81). Cambridge: Cambridge University Press.

Farrington, D.P., Ohlin, L.E., & Wilson, J.Q. (1986). Understanding and controlling crime. New York: Springer-Verlag.

Farrington, D.P., Snyder, H.N., & Finnegan, T.A. (1988). Specialization in juvenile court careers. *Criminology, 26*, 461-487.

Furstenberg, F.F., Brooks-Gunn, J., & Morgan, S.P. (1987a). Adolescent mothers and their children in later life. *Family Planning Perspectives, 19*, 142-151.

Furstenberg, F.F., Brooks-Gunn, J., & Morgan, S.P. (1987b). Adolescent mothers in later life. Cambridge: Cambridge University Press.

Hawkins, J.D., Catalano, R.F., Morrison, D.M., O'Donnell, J., Abbott, R.D., & Day, L.E. (1992). The Seattle social development project: Effects of the first four years on protective factors and problem behaviours. In J. McCord & R. Tremblay (Eds.) Preventing antisocial behaviour (pp. 139-161). New York: Guilford.

Hawkins, J.D., Von Cleve, E., & Catalano, R.F. (1991). Reducing early childhood aggression: Results of a primary prevention programme. *Journal of the American Academy of Child and Adolescent Psychiatry, 30*, 208-217.

Hayes, C.D. (1987, Ed.). Risking the future. Washington, D.C.: National Academy Press.

Hirschi, T., & Hindelang, M.J. (1977). Intelligence and delinquency: A revisionist review. *American Sociological Review, 42*, 571-587.

Horacek, H.J., Ramey, C.T., Campbell, F.A., Hoffmann, K.P., & Fletcher, R.H. (1987). Predicting school failure and assessing early intervention with high-risk children. *Journal of the American Academy of Child and Adolescent Psychiatry, 26*, 758-763.

Johnson, D.L., & Walker, T. (1987). Primary prevention of behaviour problems in Mexican-American children. *American Journal of Community Psychology, 15*, 375-385.

Kandel, E., & Mednick, S.A. (1991). Perinatal complications predict violent offending. *Criminology, 29*, 519-529.

Kandel, E., Mednick, S.A., Kirkegaard-Sorenson, L., Hutchings, B., Knop, J., Rosenberg, R., & Schulsinger, F. (1988). IQ as a protective factor for subjects at high risk for antisocial behaviour. *Journal of Consulting and Clinical Psychology, 56*, 224-226.

Klein, M.W. (1984). Offence specialization and versatility among juveniles. *British Journal of Criminology, 24*, 185-194.

Kolvin, I., Miller, F.J.W., Fleeting, M., & Kolvin, P.A. (1988). Social and parenting factors affecting criminal-offence rates: Findings from the Newcastle Thousand Family Study (1947-1980). *British Journal of Psychiatry, 152*, 80-90.

Kolvin, I., Miller, F.J.W., Scott, D.M., Gatzanis, S.R.M., & Fleeting, M. (1990). Continuities of deprivation? Aldershot: Avebury.

Lally, J.R., Mangione, P.L., & Honig, A.S. (1988). Long-range impact of an early intervention with low-income children and their families. In D.R. Powell (Ed.) Parent education as early childhood intervention (pp. 79-104). Norwood, N.J.: Ablex.

Larson, C. (1980). Efficacy of prenatal and postpartum home visits on child health and development. *Pediatrics, 66*, 191-197.

Loeber, R. (1987). Behavioural precursors and accelerators of delinquency. In W. Buikhuisen & S.A. Mednick (Eds.) Explaining criminal behavior (pp.51-67). Leiden: Brill.

Loeber, R., & LeBlanc, M. (1990). Toward a developmental criminology. In M. Tonry & N. Morris (Eds.) Crime and justice, vol.12 (pp. 375-473). Chicago: University of Chicago Press.

Lynam, D., Moffitt, T., & Stouthamer-Loeber, M. (1993). Explaining the relation between IQ and delinquency: Class, race, test motivation, school failure or self-control? *Journal of Abnormal Psychology, 102*, 187-196.

McGee, R., Silva, P.A., & Williams, S. (1984). Perinatal, neurological, environmental and developmental characteristics of seven-year-old children with stable behaviour problems. *Journal of Child Psychology and Psychiatry, 25*, 573-586.

Michelson, L. (1987). Cognitive-behavioural strategies in the prevention and treatment of antisocial disorders in children and adolescents. In J.D. Burchard & S.N. Burchard (Eds.) Prevention of delinquent behaviour (pp.275-310). Beverly Hills, California: Sage.

Mischel, W., Shoda, Y., & Rodriguez, M.L. (1989). Delay of gratification in children. *Science, 244*, 933-938.

Moffitt, T.E. (1990). Juvenile delinquency and attention deficit disorder: Boys' developmental trajectories from age 3 to age 15. *Child Development, 61*, 893-910.

Moffitt, T.E., & Silva, P.A. (1988a). IQ and delinquency: A direct test of the differential detection hypothesis. *Journal of Abnormal Psychology, 97*, 330-333.

Moffitt, T.E., & Silva, P.A. (1988b). Neuropsychological deficit and self-reported delinquency in an unselected birth cohort. *Journal of the American Academy of Child and Adolescent Psychiatry, 27*, 233-240.

Morash, M., & Rucker, L. (1989). An exploratory study of the connection of mother's age at childbearing to her children's delinquency in four data sets. *Crime and Delinquency, 35*, 45-93.

Olds, D.L., Henderson, C.R., Chamberlain, R., & Tatelbaum, R. (1986a). Preventing child abuse and neglect: A randomized trial of nurse home visitation. *Pediatrics, 78*, 65-78.

Olds, D.L., Henderson, C.R., Tatelbaum, R., & Chamberlain, R. (1986b). Improving the delivery of prenatal care and outcomes of pregnancy: A randomized trial of nurse home visitation. *Pediatrics, 77*, 16-28.

Patterson, G.R. (1982). Coercive family process. Eugene, Oregon: Castalia.

Pulkkinen, L. (1986). The role of impulse control in the development of antisocial and prosocial behaviour. In D. Olweus, J. Block & M.R. Yarrow (Eds.) Development of antisocial and prosocial behaviour (pp. 149-175). New York: Academic Press.

Richman, N., Stevenson, J., & Graham, P. (1982). Pre-school to school. London: Academic Press.

Richman, N., Stevenson, J., & Graham, P. (1985). Sex differences in the outcome of pre-school behaviour problems. In A.R. Nicol (Ed.) Longitudinal studies in child psychology and psychiatry (pp. 75-89). Chichester: Wiley.

Rivara, F.P., & Farrington, D.P. (1996). Head injury and criminal behaviour. In D. Johnson, B. Pentland & E. Glasgow (Eds.) Head injury and litigation. London: Sweet and Maxwell, in press.

Robins, L.N. (1991). Conduct disorder. *Journal of Child Psychology and Psychiatry, 32*, 193-212.

Robins, L.N., & Ratcliff, K.S. (1980). Childhood conduct disorders and later arrest. In L.N. Robins, P.J. Clayton & J.K. Wing (Eds.) The social consequences of psychiatric illness (pp.248-263). New York: Brunner/Mazel.

Rose, S.L., Rose, S.A., & Feldman, J.F. (1989). Stability of behaviour problems in very young children. *Development and Psychopathology, 1*, 5-19.

Schweinhart, L.J., Barnes, H.V., & Weikart, D.P. (1993). Significant benefits. Ypsilanti, Michigan: High/Scope.

Schweinhart, L.J., & Weikart, D.P. (1980). Young children grow up. Ypsilanti, Michigan: High/Scope.

Spivack, G., Marcus, J., & Swift, M. (1986). Early classroom behaviours and later misconduct. *Developmental Psychology, 22*, 124-131.

Stattin, H., & Klackenberg-Larsson, I. (1993). Early language and intelligence development and their relationship to future criminal behaviour. *Journal of Abnormal Psychology, 102*, 369-378.

Stein, K.B., Sarbin, T.R., & Kulik, J.A. (1968). Future time perspective: Its relation to the socialization process and the delinquent role. *Journal of Consulting and Clinical Psychology, 32*, 257-264.

Streissguth, A.P. (1986). Smoking and drinking during pregnancy and offspring learning disabilities: A review of the literature and development of a research strategy. In M. Lewis (Ed.) Learning disabilities and prenatal risk (pp. 28-67). Urbana: University of Illinois Press.

Szatmari, P., Reitsma-Street, M., & Offord, D.R. (1986). Pregnancy and birth complications in antisocial adolescents and their siblings. *Canadian Journal of Psychiatry, 31,* 513-516.

Taylor, E.A. (1986). Childhood hyperactivity. *British Journal of Psychiatry, 149,* 562-573.

Tremblay, R.E., LeBlanc, M., & Schwartzman, A.E. (1988). The predictive power of first-grade peer and teacher ratings of behaviour: Sex differences in antisocial behaviour and personality at adolescence. *Journal of Abnormal Child Psychology, 16,* 571-583.

Tremblay, R.E., McCord, J., Boileau, H., Charlebois, P., Gagnon, C., LeBlanc, M., & Larivee, S. (1991). Can disruptive boys be helped to become competent? *Psychiatry, 54,* 148-161.

Tremblay, R.E., Vitaro, F., Bertrand, L., LeBlanc, M., Beauchesne, H., Boileau, H., & David, L. (1992). Parent and child training to prevent early onset of delinquency: The Montreal longitudinal-experimental study. In J. McCord & R. Tremblay (Eds.) Preventing antisocial behaviour (pp. 117-138). New York: Guilford.

Wadsworth, M. (1979). Roots of delinquency. London: Martin Robertson.

Walsh, A., Petee, T.A., & Beyer, J.A. (1987). Intellectual imbalance and delinquency: Comparing high verbal and high performance IQ delinquents. *Criminal Justice and Behaviour, 14,* 370-379.

Werner, E.E. (1986). A longitudinal study of perinatal risk. In D.C. Farran & J.D. McKinney (Eds.) Risk in intellectual and psychosocial development (pp. 3-27).

Werner, E.E. (1989). High-risk children in young adulthood: A longitudinal study from birth to 32 years. *American Journal of Orthopsychiatry, 59,* 72-81.

West, D.J., & Farrington, D.P. (1973). Who becomes delinquent? London: Heinemann.

West, D.J., & Farrington, D.P. (1977). The delinquent way of life. London: Heinemann.

Whalen, C.K., & Henker, B. (1991). Therapies of hyperactive children: Comparisons, combinations and compromises. *Journal of Consulting and Clinical Psychology, 59,* 126-137.

White, J.L., Moffitt, T.E., Earls, F., Robins, L.N., & Silva, P.A. (1990). How early can we tell? Predictors of child conduct disorder and adolescent delinquency. *Criminology, 28,* 507-533.

White, J.L., Moffitt, T.E., & Silva, P.A. (1989). A prospective replication of the protective effects of IQ in subjects at high risk for juvenile delinquency. *Journal of Consulting and Clinical Psychology, 57,* 719-724.

Widom, C.S. (1989). The cycle of violence. *Science, 244,* 160-166.

Wilson, J.Q., & Herrnstein, R.J. (1985). Crime and human nature. New York: Simon and Schuster.

Yoshikawa, H. (1994). Prevention as cumulative protection: Effects of early family support and education on chronic delinquency and its risks. *Psychological Bulletin, 115,* 28-54.

Zigler, E., Taussig, C., & Black, K. (1992). Early childhood intervention: A promising preventative for juvenile delinquency. *American Psychologist, 47,* 997-1006.

Self-Reported Delinquency in Spain and Castilla-La Mancha: A Comparison of National and Subnational Samples

Juan Montañés-Rodríguez, Cristina Rechea-Alberola and Rosemary Barberet

Introduction

Officially reported delinquency data provide criminologists with an insufficient knowledge of the quantity, etiology and development of criminality. This in turn brings into question the efficacy of any conventional social or penal measure used to control crime. Therefore it is necessary to turn to alternatives that help us understand predelinquent and delinquent behavior - not in order to substitute, but to complement official statistics. This is the objective of the self-report method.

The participation of the Criminology Unit at the University of Castilla-La Mancha in the International Self-Report Delinquency Project has resulted in the completion of a nationwide self-report delinquency study, financed by the Ministry of Justice, and a second study at the regional level of Castilla-La Mancha, financed by the Social Welfare Department of the autonomous government of Castilla-La Mancha and by the City of Albacete.

What follows is a comparative study between the national and regional samples, with some general results. Further analyses will allow more elaboration of these analyses.

The Regional Research Setting: Castilla-La Mancha

Castilla-La Mancha is located on the southern plain of the Iberian peninsula. It occupies third place among the seventeen Spanish regions in terms of area, with 79,230 square kilometers, which corresponds to 15.7% of Spain. It is composed of 5 provinces: Albacete, Ciudad Real, Cuenca, Guadalajara and Toledo. Its total population numbers 1,698,392, or 4.3% of the national population (38,425,679). There are no great urban concentrations in Castilla-La Mancha. Only six cities surpass 50,000, and only one, Albacete, has more than 100,000. The population density of the region, 21.3 inhabitants per square kilometer, is far lower than the national average of 77.6 inhabitants per square kilometer.

According to the first annual report of Castilla-La Mancha (Bisagra, 1993), the five provinces of Castilla-La Mancha fall into the bottom half of all the lists of indicators that are used to measure wealth, in absolute and relative terms.

Nevertheless, Castilla-La Mancha tops the list of all the autonomous regions in terms of economic growth. In the last four years in particular, it has witnessed an annual growth rate of 0.75% greater than the national rate, which means that the average growth rate of the regional gross domestic product was 5%. In 1993, the year of economic crisis, Castilla-La Mancha registered a recession of -0.46%, less than the national average (-1.13%).

At any rate, this region's economy is still marked by a low level of development. It is still a strongly rural region which depends on agriculture for subsistence. Twenty percent of the active workforce is engaged in agriculture, compared to the European average of 4% and the Spanish average of 13%. Furthermore, the agricultural features of the region include 84.7% dedicated to grain, grapes and olives - dry crops - with serious diversification, complementary industry, and commercialization problems.

The industry of the region is characterized by a majority of small and medium level businesses, whereas large businesses are few in number; those that exist are tied to foreign or public investment. Construction has been one of the sectors that has generated most employment. Construction has grown 11.2%, compared to the national rate of 8.9%.

Due to its geographical position - situated between the center of the peninsula and the South and the Spanish levante area, it occupies a strategic area in terms of communication among these regions. Consequently, in the last few years the National Highway Plan is improving the 14,533 kilometers of highways in the region. Railways have also improved with the addition of the high speed train (AVE) and other faster trains.

As regards public health there is a network of 14 hospitals with a total of 3,681 beds. In education there are two hundred thousand primary school students, fifty thousand secondary school students, 30,000 vocational school students and twenty thousand university students. It is one of the regions in Spain, along with Extremadura and Andalusia, with low newspaper distribution rates.

The ISRD Questionnaire

The questionnaire (Questionnaire for the International Study on Self-Report Delinquency), in its final version had 574 items grouped into three parts[1]:
1. Sociodemographic questions or items regarding the youth's experiences with his or her family, with school and work, with his or her peer group, with leisure time and with his or her community.

---

[1]   The ISRD questionnaire, too long to reprint in this volume, appears in Junger-Tas, Terlouw and Klein (Eds.), *Delinquent Behavior Among Young People in the Western World* (Amsterdam, Kugler, 1994).

2. General questions about deviant or delinquent behavior. These items are classified into the following categories:
- Problem behavior and youth-related behavior
- Vandalism
- Property offenses
- Violent offenses
- Drug Use and Trafficking

3. Specific follow-up questions about each of the previously mentioned behaviors, in the cases where the youth admitted participation in these behaviors over the last year.

The Sample

Given that juvenile delinquency is primarily an urban phenomenon, the decision was made to limit the cities under consideration for the sample to those over 50,000[2]. Within Castilla-La Mancha the following cities met this requirement and were chosen for the sample: Albacete, Ciudad Real, Guadalajara, Puertollano, Talavera and Toledo. Cuenca, with a population of slightly less than fifty thousand, was also added in order to gain representation from all five provinces of the region.

Table 1: Sample Distribution for Castilla-La Mancha

Sampling Site	Total N	Base N	Marginal N
Albacete	140	140	-
Ciudad Real	161	139	22
Cuenca	162	141	21
Guadalajara	201	177	24
Puertollano	165	140	25
Talavera	160	143	17
Toledo	160	139	21
Total	1,149	1,019	130

Regarding sample selection within each municipality, different options were considered. Since the study deals with juvenile delinquency, a special "at risk"[3]

---

2   This same criteria was used for the national sample.

3   The "at risk" population in this study was defined as that which resides in areas or neighborhoods termed "marginalized" or of "high conflictivity", which, from a theoretical

subsample was considered convenient. Therefore, out of the total 1,149 subjects in the sample, 130 "at risk" subjects were included, spread out proportionately in each of the selected cities, as Table 1 indicates. The reader can note that 1,149 total interviews were conducted in seven different cities with 130 of the interviews in marginalized neighborhoods, as defined through consultation with municipal social service agents and police forces.

In Table 1 the reader can see that except at two sampling sites (Albacete and Guadalajara) there is uniformity in terms of the number of subjects included in the sample, in both in the base sample and the marginalized sample. The differences that appear in the base sample in Guadalajara are due to the fact that since this city was also selected for the national ISRD study, for which the fieldwork was conducted a month earlier, for methodological and financial reasons the sample obtained for the national study was used. As regards Albacete, for similar reasons the sample obtained for the pilot study was used. At the time of the pilot study in Albacete there were no intentions of obtaining a marginalized subsample, although the sample was obtained in a random manner from all the neighborhoods of the city. These discrepancies in subsample size were reconciled using appropriate weighting matrices, which also corrected for the oversampling from marginalized neighborhoods.

In comparison, the national sample, as detailed in Table 2, is composed of six cities of over 50,000 inhabitants. Of these cities, one was of over one million inhabitants (Madrid) and another was of slightly less than one million inhabitants (Valencia). We can thus say that the national sample is more urbanized and cosmopolitan than the regional sample.

The sampling method was designed to select respondents in a way that all sorts of youths would form part of the sample. The best way to achieve this is a random sample, where all subjects have an equal probability of being selected. But in order to carry out this kind of sampling method correctly, one should possess a complete and correct census list, which is extremely difficult to obtain. Therefore, we decided to used a multi-staged cluster sampling method in which the cluster or unit of the first stage were census sections. These census units were stratified according to the different types of habitats established and the type of sample desired (base or marginalized). Therefore, there was a random sampling of census sections within each habitat, in the case of the base sample, and a purposive selection of the marginalized areas. One must remember that, according to random sampling, marginalized areas could also fall into the base random sample of areas. The final units of analysis (individuals) were selected according to age and sex quotas covering various stages (within each census section a group of buildings were selected randomly, and within these buildings a group of households, and finally the subject was selected within the household).

---

point of view, have been considered areas where youth are characterized by factors associated with juvenile delinquency.

Table 2: Sample Distribution for National Spanish Sample

Sampling Site	Total N	Base N	Marginal N
Madrid	500	440	60
Valencia	400	352	48
Badajoz	400	352	48
Dos Hermanas	200	176	24
Cornellà	200	177	23
Portugalete	200	177	23
Guadalajara	200	176	24
Total	2,100	1,850	250

Field Work

Fieldwork for the regional study was subcontracted to the same survey research company that had undertaken the national study, one specialized in sociological research which was chosen for having already conducted a certain number of studies related to social issues. Fieldwork took place from January to April of 1993. We will focus on the regional study here because the results of the national level study have already been presented in another paper (Barberet, Rechea-Alberola & Montañés-Rodríguez, 1994). We will only allude to the national study where we mention the comparison of results.

Data collection

The interview was administered in a personalized and individualized manner. Once the interviewee was selected, within the corresponding census section, he or she was located in his or her home. The interview could be carried out at home or outside of the home, in cases where it was necessary to avoid non response or the possible bias introduced by the presence of the family.

The interview was divided into two parts for data collection purposes. The first part was self-administered and corresponds to the second part of the questionnaire (offense prevalence), which was handed to the interviewee at the beginning of the interview for him or her to complete. This was intended to avoid the subject's tendency to increasingly deny or not admit his or her delinquent behavior with the passing of the interview, given that each time behavior is admitted, a fairly long series of follow-up questions must then be asked with the consequent tiring of the interviewee. The second part, composed of the items in the first and third parts of the interview, was directly administered by the interviewer to the interviewee.

To obtain the number of interviews planned (1,149), there were 1,658 attempted interviews, of which 196 were rejected by the interviewer due to filled age and sex quotas. The rest of the attempted but unsuccessful interviews (313), were composed of incomplete, refused, impossible to locate and moved or absent interviews. This amounts to a non-response rate of 21%. In comparison, at the national level, 4,187 interviews were attempted, with 1,032 rejected by the interviewer due to filled age and sex quotas. Other unsuccessful interviews amounted to 1,055, which leads to a non-response rate of 33% for the national sample. This implies that the youthful population of Castilla-La Mancha was generally more cooperative, in spite of the nature of the interview.

Reliability

Reliability was measured in both the national and subnational studies by repeating six questions at the end of the interview to see if answers were consistent with the first time the question was asked. In the national study, consistent responses were the case for 84.1% to 98.8% of the sample, for the six questions; in the subnational study, the range was from 75.7% to 96.6%.

Results

Sample Description

The sample obtained is composed of equal numbers of young men and women, with a homogeneous distribution by age among the four age groups (14-15, 16-17, 18-19, and 20-21), in spite of the fact that the 20-21 age group appears to be slightly smaller. This aspect is the only major difference between the two samples.

As regards education (grouped into high, medium and low levels), both samples are similar in that 47% of each sample falls into the middle range, and are different in that in the national sample the high and low categories are almost the same (27% and 26%, respectively), whereas in the Castilla-La Mancha sample the lower category (31.7%) is clearly greater than the higher category (20.8%). In the case of socioeconomic status, the two samples are concentrated in the middle-lower class category with 43.3% for Castilla-La Mancha and 47% in the national sample. Nevertheless, both samples have 83% of the sample concentrated in three levels, middle, middle-low and low. These results could be due to possible socioeconomic and cultural differences that we mentioned in the introduction.

Total prevalence

Comparing the total prevalence of delinquent behavior for the two samples (Table 3). one can observe minimal differences between both although the prevalence level is higher for the national sample.

Table 3: Total Prevalence of Delinquent Behavior

Total Prevalence of Delinquent Behavior	National Sample (N = 2,100)		Castilla-La Mancha Sample (N = 1,149)	
	Ever	Last year	Ever	Last year
	1,704 81.1	1,214 57.8	909 79.1	626 54.5

This similarity is also observed when the prevalence levels for different offenses are rank ordered for each sample (Table 4). For this comparison we have selected, out of the 33 behaviors in the questionnaire, those with a prevalence of more than 5% in the last year, although the similarity is also given for those behaviors that do not appear in the table.

Table 4: Rank Ordering of Most Prevalence Offenses, "Last Year"

Rank order	Delinquent or problem behavior	National sample	Regional sample
1	Alcohol consumption	79.3	79.8
2	Driving without a license/ insurance	22.5	20.5
3	Truancy	20.5	20.0
4	Fights/ Riots	17.2	16.2
5	Vandalism	16.3	16.0
6	Soft drug use	15.0	15.4
7	Fare dodging bus/metro	13.4	6.2
8	Graffiti	9.5	8.4
9	Carrying a weapon	8.4	8.8
10	Burglary	6.9	4.3
11	Shoplifting	6.6	5.7
12	Fare dodging train	5.9	5.7
13	Buying stolen goods	5.9	3.7

The six first behaviors that appear in the table have the sample order in both samples and have similar percentages. The only important difference that is observed is regarding behavior Number 7, "fare dodging in bus/metro", which is fairly logical given that the national sample includes large cities (with metros) such as Madrid and Valencia, whereas in Castilla-La Mancha bus transportation is not the most frequent form of transportation within the cities sampled, and there is no metro in any city in the region.

Analysis of categories

Given the overall prevalence results for the last year, the following commentary focuses on those behaviors, within each category, which have a prevalence level (ever) of more than 5% - that is, offenses or behaviors admitted by more than 5% of the sample. With this approach we do not wish to imply that the other behaviors with smaller prevalence levels are not important, but simply that they are less representative of behaviors that youths engage in routinely. Concretely, this cut-off of 5% means that of the 1,149 subjects in Castilla-La Mancha, only 58 subjects admitted to the behavior "ever". The selection of the 5% cut-off was made because it is the traditional percentage that is used in statistical hypothesis testing.

In tables where we compared the prevalence percentages from the two samples for the behaviors included in each of the established categories, no great differences are observed. Z scores from a difference of proportions test yielded significant differences ($p < .01$) for only three behaviors: burglary, buying stolen goods and fare dodging bus/metro.

In the case of property offenses (Table 5), there is only a significant difference between regional and national samples in burglary and buying stolen goods.

Table 5: Prevalence of Property Offenses

Self-reported Behaviors	National sample (N = 2,100)				Castilla-La Mancha sample (N = 1,149)			
	Ever		Last year		Ever		Last year	
Shoplifting	487	23.2	138	6.6	302	26.3	65	5.7
Burglary*	456	21.7	145	6.9	235	20.5	50	4.3
Stealing at school	303	14.4	45	2.1	157	13.7	21	1.9
Buying stolen goods*	270	12.8	124	5.9	91	7.9	43	3.7
Stealing at home	190	9.0	72	3.4	107	9.3	44	3.9
Stealing something else	96	4.6	20	0.9	62	5.4	19	1.6

Nevertheless, it is important to note that there are differences by gender. In the national sample there are significant differences in favor of the young men in the sample in all behaviors except "stealing at home", whereas in the Castilla-La Mancha sample these differences disappear in all cases except for the total and for "burglary". Regarding other variables, such as age and SES, there are no relevant differences between the two samples.

In violent offenses (Table 6) there are slightly greater prevalence levels for these behaviors in the Castilla-La Mancha sample, most notably in the total of violent offenses against persons and in "carrying a weapon", while in the case of "vandalism" there are identical prevalence levels in both samples. The case of "carrying a weapon" can be explained by the fact that the weapons are mainly knives, and that a knife is not considered purely a weapon in Castilla-La Mancha (seat of cutlery manufacturing for all of Spain), but rather a commonly used tool.

Table 6: Prevalence of Violent Offenses

Self-reported behaviors	National sample (N = 2,100)				Castilla-La Mancha sample (N = 1,149)			
	Ever		Last year		Ever		Last year	
Vandalism	1,050	50.0	342	16.3	575	50.0	184	16.0
Fights & riots	630	30.0	361	17.2	363	31.6	187	16.2
Graffiti	497	23.6	199	9.5	283	24.6	96	8.4
Carrying a weapon	341	16.3	176	8.4	226	19.7	102	8.8
Beating up non-family	118	5.6	49	2.3	56	4.9	23	2.0
Total violence against objects	1,152	54.8	461	21.9	638	55.5	234	20.3
Total violence against persons	814	38.8	476	22.7	477	41.5	246	21.4

* z = 2.99, z = 2.71 respectively, p < .01

Regarding drug-related offenses (Table 7), although the prevalence levels for both samples are relatively similar, in this case the national sample has higher levels compared to the regional sample. Nevertheless, although the characteristics of soft drug users (mostly men with an initiation age of 15.8) are different between samples in that in the national sample they are marked by a high educational level and a medium-high SES, whereas in the regional sample bothy variables are associated with the lower levels of the same. Among the characteristics associated with hard drug use, we have not found significant differences betweend the two samples, except that the age of iniciation for this behavior is 16.9 for the national sample and 17.2 for the regional sample. In both cases the behavior is associated with low SES and education. The significant age group for hard drug use is 20-21, for both samples.

Table 7: Prevalence of Drug Offenses

Self-reported Behaviors	National sample (N = 2,100)				Castilla-La Mancha sample (N = 1,149)			
	Ever		Last year		Ever		Last year	
Soft drug consumption	444	21.2	315	15.0	232	20.2	177	15.4
Hard drug consumption	94	4.5	53	2.5	44	3.8	33	2.8

Among the youth-related offenses (Table 8), the prevalence for "fare dodging in bus/metro and train" is significantly lower for the regional sample, since in the national sample there are cities with metros and commuter trains. The opposite occurs for "driving without a license/insurance", where the subjects in the regional sample have higher prevalence levels. This is also the only behavior engaged in significantly more by young men than by young women in Castilla-La Mancha, but not in the national sample. Regarding age, higher prevalence levels occur between 14 and 17 years of age in both samples (still not able to obtain a license). Also due to age, the educational level of those admitting this behavior is split between low and medium.

Table 8: Prevalence of Youth-Related Offenses

Self-reported Behavior	National sample (N = 2,100)				Castilla-La Mancha sample (N = 1,149)			
	Ever		Last year		Ever		Last year	
Driving without license	886	42.2	472	22.5	508	44.2	235	20.5
Fare dodging bus/metro*	709	33.7	282	13.4	226	19.7	72	6.2
Fare dodging train	346	16.5	125	5.9	142	12.4	66	5.7

The most striking result in the area of problem behaviors (Table 9) is the high prevalence levels of alcohol consumption in both samples. Although we have not mentioned incidence levels yet in this paper, we consider it important to mention that the average incidence for this behavior for the national sample is 79.6 (135.1) and 63.9 (97.9) for the regional sample. Nevertheless, the distribution of incidence is very similar for both samples; 20.7% of the national sample admitted never consuming alcohol, and 20.2 of the regional sample. Another 20% (21.3% of the national sample and 32.4 of the regional sample) consume alcohol sporadically (1 to 10 times a year), whereas habitual use (11 to 50 times a year) is a feature of 26.9% of the national sample   and   27.1% of the regional sample. Finally, 31.1% of the national sample and 29.4% of the regional sample consumed alcohol more than 50 times in the last year.

Table 9: Prevalence of Problem Behaviors

Self-reported Behaviors	National sample (N = 2,100)				Castilla-La Mancha sample (N = 1,149)			
	Ever		Last year		Ever		Last year	
Alcohol consumption	1,801	85.7	1,666	79.3	967	84.2	917	79.8
Truancy	1,004	47.8	430	20.5	520	45.3	230	20.0
Running away from home	116	5.5	35	1.6	73	6.4	24	2.1

* z = 6.30, p < .01

Conclusions

In spite of the fact that the comparisons that appear in this paper have been very global, we can tentatively state that:
1. In spite of the differences that could be foreseen "a priori", due to differences between the contexts of the two samples (in population density, income per capita, SES, levels of industrialization, etc.), the national and Castilla-La Mancha samples are similar regarding their age, gender, education, and SES distributions.
2. The fact that the two contexts are different does not result in significant differences in terms of prevalence levels or the rank ordering of prevalence levels within each category.
3. Consequently, we can conclude that apart from the context where these behaviors occur, the behaviors admitted by youths tend to be similar. The common variables of historical moment, of the economic, political and educational situation and the influence of the mass media tend to homogenize the population of a country.
4. Given the similarities found in the comparison, we can say that the regional study serves as a validation of the results found at the national level, besides the fact that

the results from both samples serve to confirm the success of the adaptation of the instrument to the Spanish context.

5. It is our intention to conduct more extensive analyses of the comparison of both samples once the regional report is finished. These will permit more definitive conclusions. It would also be interesting to conduct subanalyses of cities that are similar demographically.

References

Barberet, R., Rechea-Alberola, C., & Montañés-Rodríguez, J. (1994). "Self Reported Juvenile Delinquency in Spain". In Junger-Tas, Terlouw and Klein (Eds.), *Delinquent Behavior Among Young People in the Western World*. Amsterdam: Kugler.
Bisagra (1993). *Primer Anuario de Castilla-La Mancha*. Toledo: Bisagra.

Adoption and Murder

Philip D. Jaffé

Adoption clearly represents an opportunity for many well-meaning couples to constitute families, as well as a chance for thousands of children to be cared for beyond unfortunate birth circumstances. In the vast majority of instances, adoption works and improves the quality of life of all those involved. However, adoption is not an easy task. On the contrary, more often than not it is a traumatic event for the adopted child, the adoptive parents, as well as for the biological parents.

In this article, the dark side of adoption will be examined.

I. The links between adoption, psychopathology, and crime are considered.

II. The case of David, a young man who killed his adoptive father and almost did the same to his adoptive mother, illustrates how the psychodynamics of adoption are easily overlooked in forensic mental health evaluations.

III. While adoption homicide is a rare event, there are some indications it may be more frequent than commonly believed.

Is Adoption Pathogenic?

In adoption, as with all traumatic events, psychological issues must be worked through. Biological parents who give up their child for adoption often deal with a painful sense of loss despite all the rationalisations that they are acting responsibly for the child they are unable to care for. As for the adoptive parents, they often mourn their inability to procreate on their own and must deal with deep narcissistic injuries. Above all, the adopted child faces, even in the best possible scenario, a lifelong task of integrating complex issues regarding his or her identity. He/she must deal with the unavoidable feelings that the biological parents abandoned him or her, and often desperately tries to answer the unanswerable questions of "Why did this happen to me?", "What if it had not happened?" and "What would it be like had I not been adopted?"

Perhaps the fact that so many psychological issues must be worked through partially explains why adoptive families and adopted children are such great consumers of psychotherapy and psychiatric treatment services. In the United States and in the Netherlands some estimates put the rate of help-seeking adopted children at double the rate of the population as a whole or more. Adoptees represent only about 2% of the total US population, but they constitute about 4% of the total number of clients in one form of treatment or another. This represents a highly significant figure that implies that adopted children experience distress and psychopathological states more frequently than many other segments of the population.

In this context, three groups of adopted children can be described: higher functioning adoptees, adoptees with behavioural problems and lower functioning psychiatrically disordered adoptees.

With regard to the higher functioning group, it seems that one of the reasons most adopted children and their families seek counselling services more frequently that the population at large stems from the fact that their life course has, on the whole, made them more sophisticated psychologically. Indeed, in dealing with adoption related crises, these non biologically related families probably become more aware of their intense feelings, anxieties and longings. They are thus more likely to seek professional help.

A second group of adopted children is characterised in several studies (e.g., Brodzinski, Radice, and Hufman, 1987) as suffering from a wide range of non-specific behavioural symptoms: pathological lying, stealing, truancy, underachievement, firesetting, promiscuity, running away, learning difficulties, etc. Some research supports that adoptees as a whole demonstrate higher levels of antisocial behaviour.

Finally, a third group of adoptees shows marked signs of psychiatric disorder, typically various psychotic and schizophrenic pathologies.

These three groups appear to be fairly fluid, with a number of adoptees in the higher and lower range of functioning troubled at one point or another by transient behavioural problems and acting out.

What then is the relationship between adoption, mental illness and crime? Two influential studies make a case for genetic factors weighing in on the behaviour of adoptees. First, on the link between adoption and crime, research by Mednick, Gabrielli, and Hutchings (1984) demonstrates that if neither the biological parents nor the adoptive parents are criminal (as defined by court convictions), 13.5% of adopted sons turn out to be criminals. If the adoptive parents qualify as criminal but the biological parents do not, this figure rises slightly to 14.7%. However, if the biological parents, but not the adoptive parents, qualify as criminal, 20% of their sons turn out to be criminal. Not surprisingly, the rate is even higher, about 24% if both the biological parents and the adoptive parents qualify as criminal. One major caveat regarding these results is that the relationship between adoption and crime is only significant for property crimes and not for violent crimes.

Using the same adoption data, Moffit (1987) investigated adoptees whose biological parents suffered from a mental disorder and had been convicted of criminal acts as well. Results are similar to Mednick, Gabrielli, and Hutchings' (1984) study: adopted sons demonstrate a significantly elevated rate of multiple recidivistic non-violent criminal behaviour when mental illness and criminal involvement characterises the adoptees' biological families. However here again, the relationship with regard to physical violence is not significant despite being elevated.

It would appear for now at least that genetic factors do not seem to play a convincing role in terms of the violent acting out of adoptees although there seems to be some degree of genetic predisposition as well as perinatal factors that have yet to be more fully researched.

Other explanations come from individual and family dynamics. There is however a dearth of literature dealing specifically with the dynamics of adoptees who commit parental homicide. Kirschner (1992) published one of the rare articles on this subject. Reviewing several cases, he proposes an Adopted Child Syndrome (ACS) which he considers to some degree common to all adopted children. Some of the main traits of the ACS are: extreme dissociation of rage, painful identity confusion, marked hypersensitivity to rejection, and antisocial behaviour. In addition, an aspect of the self, experienced as "bad" and usually identified with the fantasised biological parents, is dissociated. Under conditions of stress, and in particular when dealing with perceived or real loss or rejection, the dissociated portion of the self may erupt in murderous violence against the adoptive parents or others. Many of these traits appear extremely relevant to the case that will follow.

Adoption Overlooked: the Case of David

I met David in 1988 while working in a maximum security psychiatric hospital in Massachusetts (USA). At the time, he was 20 years old and showed all the classic signs of a schizophrenic disorder. A year earlier, he had killed his adoptive father and almost succeeded in doing the same to his adoptive mother. The facts were the following: David's parents returned home from early evening food shopping and placed grocery bags on the kitchen table. David, with whom nobody had spoken during the day, rummaged through the bags, took out hamburger meat, prepared a few patties for himself and started cooking. His father told him his mother was going to prepare a meal for the whole family. David answered "no" by waving his finger. His father instructed his wife to go ahead anyway, but David seized a kitchen knife, kicked his father in the groin and then stabbed him to death. His mother fled through the kitchen door out into the street and was stabbed several times in the back as she escaped.

When I met David, he was undergoing a forensic mental health evaluation to determine his competency to stand trial and his criminal responsibility (he was later found Not Guilty by Reason of Insanity). In many ways, his case is prototypical of adoptees: hardly any attention is given to their adoption status and to the role it plays in their pathology (and ultimately as in some cases in the killing of a family member). In reality, adoption is a crucial but unacknowledged component of their violent acting out.

The most striking element in David's otherwise fairly complete medical chart is what is missing. Indeed, even though it is mentioned that he was adopted, there is no additional information or discussion regarding this all important issue: no mention of when he was adopted, when and how he was told that he was adopted, no mention of his feelings on the issue.

The same absence of information is evident in David's criminal responsibility evaluation report, written by an experienced senior forensic psychologist and, in all other aspects, an excellent assessment. After mentioning in passing that David is an adopted child, the forensic psychologist sets out to develop criminal responsibility arguments based on David's symptoms of schizophrenia. Towards the end of the report, he mentions that David suffers from a peculiar olfactory delusion, specifically that his body generates a bad odour, that other people can smell this distinctive odour but that they refuse to acknowledge it. If the forensic evaluator had been attuned to the issue of adoption, he may have speculated that this olfactory delusion smelled like a primitive form of identity preoccupation. Indeed, in his bizarre way, David seems to be saying I am different and bad, and nobody wants to acknowledge this difference.

Elsewhere in the report, the forensic evaluator again fails to make the important connection between David's symptomatology and adoption. He writes: "David's childhood is filled with instances of bizarre behaviour which could be easily overlooked but which in retrospect seem indicative of his illness. For instance, his mother reports that *as a child David always thought that people should be 'perfect' and worried that he himself was not perfect*" (emphasis added). In hindsight, what better way for a child to communicate his feeling of being a defective offspring, a very common fantasy among adopted children which explains why their biological parents had to get rid of them.

Again, the main point is that adoption as a factor in the dynamics of homicide was overlooked in David's case as it usually is in similar cases. This was reinforced over the several years I followed David clinically and testified in court on numerous occasions regarding his need for continued involuntary hospitalisation.

For example, David's preoccupation with perfection is further revealed by an almost trivial piece of data. His adoptive mother reports that, as an adolescent, David enjoyed looking at the images of naked women in Playboy magazines (a behaviour not necessarily unusual nor even unhealthy in adolescent boys). However, in David's case, his interest apparently lied in the notion that the magazine women were "perfect" when compared to his adoptive mother. Here again, we may speculate that perhaps unresolved identity issues, and not David's emerging age-appropriate libido, may be at the heart of his curiosity. Later on, David's mother also recalled that her son began expressing the belief that he was of Jewish heritage and thus differed from his Italo-American adoptive parents. Once again we notice his intense preoccupation with his origins.

David was adopted shortly after birth. His parents later adopted a second child, a girl. No information is available on David's sister other than she reached adulthood without any significant problems. The adoptive parents came from a working class background and had modest financial means. They had been trying to have children for quite some time and adopted David when they were already in their 40s. According to David's mother, both children were aware of their adopted status "from the beginning".

While this may be the case, this type of statement should always be investigated further with adoptive parents. Indeed, parents sometimes give surprising explanations to children on the subject of their adoption. For example, one set of parents that consulted me stated that they had told their three year old child that he had been adopted, but never again discussed this with him because it did not seem to bother him and because he did not ask. This situation is quite frequent because it allows the adoptive parents to live with the illusion that they are the real parents and that their adopted child accepts them as such. Something similar may have occurred in David's case.

In any event, he reportedly showed no signs of abnormal psychological development until age 15. He was a good student in high school and had many friends. Suddenly, he became withdrawn, his grades plummeted, he retired to his room and spent his time watching television. His withdrawal gradually became almost complete, he barely talked with his parents or sister and no longer took meals with them. At the same time, he became more and more entitled, acting like a dictator in the home. Major behavioural problems started to appear. When contradicted he would become violent. Once, he forcefully shoved his mother out of a bathroom she had been occupying and struggled with his father when he intervened. Several revealing verbal outbursts took place. David for example yelled at his parents that they were beneath him and, mocking their modest background and means, belittled them for not having completed high school and not having made anything of their lives.

This incident led to a series of short hospitalisations interspersed with violent outbursts directed at his parents. Hospitalisations were always involuntary and David strenuously struggled in court to avoid treatment.

Two very interesting events took place during the year before David killed his father. The first followed a hospitalisation during which the treatment team had done a good job mediating between David and his adoptive parents. Upon discharge, David was to look for a job. To the surprise of all, in particular his mother's, it was discovered that instead of looking for a job, David was spending most his time trying to retrace his biological origins. In fact, he was arrested at Massachusetts' main adoption agency after reacting violently to the staff's refusal to provide him with any information regarding his origins.

The second event followed yet another hospitalisation. Considering that David was uncontrollable, complex legal manoeuvres were undertaken to appoint David's adoptive father as his legal guardian, place him in an institution for difficult juveniles and obtain court-ordered psychiatric treatment. In looking back on this episode, it is striking that David's worst fears were becoming reality. David, the adopted son who looked down on his adoptive parents, who was trying to figure out his identity by violently confronting his adoptive parents and to piece together his biological origins, was stripped all of a sudden of his individual rights and faced rejection by his adoptive family which was seeking to institutionalise him. Paradoxically, the control of his existence was placed in the hands of his adoptive father, of all people. The events that followed brutally speak for themselves. His institutional placement was delayed, he remained at home and he killed his father.

Adoption Homicide: A Rare Event Too Often Ignored

Regardless of the method of computation, killing adoptive parents is a rare event. Indeed, even parental homicide by biological children is a very rare form of what sociologists call family nonintimate homicide. In the United States, killing of a parent amounts to only 1.5 to 2.5% of all homicides, slightly more frequent than sibling homicide. In 1989, out of 21,500 homicides, only 344 matricides and patricides by children of all ages were reported (Mones, 1991). In the vast majority of cases, matricide and patricide take place in the context of very abusive family situations.

It appears however that patricide and matricide by adopted children is a more frequent phenomenon than suspected. While no statistics exist to back this up, I conducted an informal survey via electronic discussion groups in the field of mental health and the law. Over a dozen recent cases of adoptive patricide and matricide were reported.

The most famous case was the Menendez brothers, taken to trial in California for killing their adoptive parents. Allegedly, the two brothers had been sexually abused by their father and their mother failed to protect them. However, it seems that part of the motive was to obtain the parents' wealth. The case is now in appeal stages and the prosecution is attempting to obtain a conviction for murder.

In another case dating back to 1985, Steve Benson, the heir to Benson & Hedges cigarette fortune, was convicted for the bombing murder of his adoptive mother.

In his article on adoptees who kill, Kirschner (1992) gives details of three cases out of the seven he is personally familiar with. One of the cases he reports on bears a striking resemblance to David's. Patrick DeGelleke at age 14 set a fire that killed his adoptive parents. Shortly before the murder, his parents had threatened to petition the court to have him taken from the home and put in an institution.

Kirschner (1992) also implies that a disproportionate number of adoptees commit generic homicides. He also contends that a disproportionate number of multiple and serial killers are adopted, among them the well-known David "Son of Sam" Berkowitz, Gerald Eugene Spano who killed 32 people in Florida, and Kenneth Bianchi, also known as the "Hillside Strangler", who raped and strangled 10 young women in Los Angeles back in the late 1970s.

If in fact adopted children commit murders more frequently than suspected, the question then becomes why is this not common knowledge?

One simple reason may be that nobody, including the killer knows of his adoptive status. While this appears farfetched at first, extreme secrecy does often surround many cases of adoption. Even if the family secret is known to the killer or to a family member, it is often a piece of information not easily volunteered.

Another reason may be that adoption is a piece of demographic information that is often overlooked by the criminal justice system. For all practical purposes, the difference between parental murder by an adopted child and parental murder by a non adopted child is irrelevant. Indeed, from a legal standpoint, an adopted child is simply the child of his parents.

Another explanation may have to do with society's benevolent attitude towards adoption and denial when it goes sour. Adoptive parents are commonly perceived as altruistic adults who perform a positively sanctioned act by adopting a child. By revealing the dark side of adoption too much, social values would need to be transformed.

To conclude, murdering adoptive parents is but one form of intrafamilial violence. Killing family members is an old business, the stuff that makes up countless Greek tragedies and myths around the world. Husbands kill wives, wives kill husbands, parents mistreat, sexually abuse and kill their children, and every now and then a child kills one or both his parents. What is curious is that, whenever you read about parenticide, everyone talks about Oedipus and the killing of his father Laius. Rarely does anyone mention that Oedipus was an adopted child...

References

Brodzinski, D. M., Radice, C., & Hufman, L. (1987). Prevalence of clinically significant symptomatology in a non clinical sample of adopted and non adopted children. *Journal of Clinical Child Psychology, 16*(4), 350-356.

Kirschner, D. (1992). Understanding adoptees who kill: Dissociation, patricide, and the psychodynamics of adoption. *International Journal of Offender Therapy and Comparative Criminology, 36*(4), 323-333.

Mednick, S. A., Gabrielli, W. F., & Hutchings, B. (1984). Genetic factors in criminal behaviors: Evidence from an adoption cohort. *Science, 224* (891-893).

Moffit, T. E. (1987). Parental mental disorder and offspring criminal behavior: An adoption study. *Psychiatry, 50*, 346-360.

Mones, P. (1991). *When a child kills.* New York: Pocket Star.

A Descriptive Preliminary Study of the Long Term Effects of Divorce on the Psychological Adjustment Process of Children

Adolfo Jarne, Elena Requena, Josep Moya and Mónica Timón

Introduction

In the last four decades there has been an increasing interest in studies of the psychological effect of divorce on children, and this interest has been spurred by the problems generated by the growing increase in separations and matrimonial break-ups. A good example of this is the important amount of research devoted to the topic, nearly all in the context of Anglo-Saxon culture (Wallerstein, 1990).

Such an interest is not strange if one contemplates the worry that the break-up situation generates in parents regarding their children and in the many conferences and mental health resources that exist on the topic.

In the specialized literature, two well differentiated research phases can be identified. The first encompasses until the seventies with its zenith in the decade of the fifties and sixties and that was centered on the comparison of the psychological adjustment in children with a single parent and intact family children. Within groups of children with a single parent the levels of contentment were the same as for the children of divorced parents as well as for children in which one of their two progenitors had died. In these studies the sort of relationship of the couple of the intact family was not controlled for generally. The results were too heterogeneous and scattered so as to allow one to arrive to some definitive and clear conclusions.

Due to the methodological problem derived from comparing two groups that they were not homogeneous either inter or intra groups, this area of research was abandoned. In the eighties efforts have been geared toward the study of the structure and familiar process of those couples that are separated, under the basic assumption that not always can a psychopathological or abnormal reaction to the separation be verified, and so it is preferable to speak of the adjustment process of the children to the new situation.

Furthermore, there is an increasing acknowledgment of the fact that it is not the phenomenon of the separation from which psychological problems are derived, but rather from the internal processes that accompany each separation concretely, that is to say, of those variables that intervene in the marital break. Shaw (1991) has systematized a way to understand clearly the variables that play an important role in the adjustment process of the child to the separation of his or her parents and that encompass the following areas: (a) interparental conflict; (b) the separation from an attachment figure; (c) the time factor; (d) the age of the children at the moment of the divorce; (e) the sort of relationship of the children with the residential parent; (f) the relationships of the children with the non residential parent; (g) the new marriages and affective relationships of the parents; (h) economic aspects; and (i) the sex of the child. In spite of the abundance of studies in this line, there is no unanimity in the results of the different studies.

Almost the only point of agreement is that separation itself does not constitute a risk factor for psychopathological disorders, with the child response being very individualized. In addition to this, traditionally the immediate or short term effects of the separation have been researched in cross-sectional designs. However, lately we have seen the need for longitudinal designs which permit us to observe the effects in the long term, which are extremely difficult to evaluate (Wallerstein, 1990). It is considered important to know what is the effect of the separation of the parents on their children, at the moment of separation and 20 years afterwards. In fact, differences have been found among the effects immediately after the separation, that would follow a crisis model or by adjustment to the stress and the observed years afterwards. Another point of agreement is the existence of a group of children where one can observe a psychopathological response to the separation of their parents that transcends beyond the logical adjustment process. This sort of response has been studied generally along two key variables: sex and the age.

The differential effects of separation in boys and girls has been studied, with a great number of studies demonstrating less psychological maladjustment in boys than in girls (Shaw, 1991; García et al., 1986). Also there is agreement in that for boys more psychopathological maladjustment of the type that has been qualified as external has been appreciated and that encompasses conduct disorders, aggressive behavior, scholastic problems, discipline problems, etc. On the contrary, in girls disorders designated as internal prevail such as depression problems, anxiety and isolation (García et al., 1986; Bouchard & Drapeau, 1991; Shaw, 1991).

Concerning the influence of the age, there is less consensus. There is perhaps a greater effect of maladjustment in small children (six less than years) that in older children (Shaw, 1991).

However, there is no unanimity among the different studies, in such a way that still it can not be said that the age of the child will be an important determinant concerning the effects of interparental conflict (García et al., 1986). Finally, we wish to point out that most of the research on the effect of divorce in children have been carried out with extracted samples from the general population, since the interest in the field has been limited to the prototypical response expected for most of the affected child population. However, this seems improper when there is a particular interest in studying specifically psychopathological responses, since in the general population these will not be, presumably, observable, and a good adjustment process is seen in most cases. From this point of view there is a special interest in studying that group of the population that offers an abnormal response or a wrong adjustment.

Our Research

The data that are presented here constitute the preliminary results of a research program that has as its general objective the study of the psychopathological response of children before the separation of their parents. As the primary interest of this research is to study maladaptative responses and not the adjustment, the sample is comprised of boys and girls attended to in a CAPIP (Center of Infantile Primary Psychiatric Assistance), of the metropolitan area of Barcelona.

Thus, our study is undertaken with a sample as peculiar as many in this research area: children that present psychological problems and that are engaged in a psychotherapy process in the CAPIP of L'Hospitalet of Llobregat (Barcelona). All of these children have in common the fact of originating from families in which the parents have separated. In all the cases the demand for psychological intervention holds a more or less direct relationship with the timing of the separation of its parents. The data relating to the family and separation process have been extracted from the clinical history of each child, while the first psychopathological exploration is carried out upon the initiation of this research.

Thus, this investigation intends to study prospectively and in an evolutionary way the presence, characteristic, type and evolution of the psychopathology presented by the children of the sample throughout the psychotherapeutic process, and here we present the initial results of the first evaluation.

Subjects

Our sample is composed of 25 subjects of which 68% were boys and 32% girls. The principal characteristics concerning the age of the children, age at the time of separation and age upon acceptance to the center, are presented in Table 1. As can be observed, there is a difference of almost 2.5 years between the age of the children at the moment of their parents' separation and the request for a first consultation, a period that corresponds to the manifestation of psychopathology.

Also, there is a small difference in age at the moment of the treatment request and upon the actual delivery of the same, which is due to a waiting list.

Material

In this investigation three different types of data have been collected: relative to the family and separation process, to the clinic that refers the child and to a psycopathological and systematized exploration. The first and second groups were collected through a protocol of data elaborated by the authors and organized in the form of closed items. The first group of data includes three different areas:

a.- Data related to the separation motives, psychopathology of the spouses, mistreatment and new couple's formation.

b.- Social data of the couple: couple modality, social and cultural level of the spouses.

c.- Data related to the semiology of the separation: sort of separation, current situation of each parent, economic problems, fulfillment of the paternal and maternal roles at some point beyond the separation, return to the family of origin of the separate spouses, new couple's formation and custodian and custody regime, and of visits.

In the second block of the protocol data were collected related to the clinic of the child: sex, age at the moment of separation, age at the moment of acceptance in the CAPIP, age at the moment of first visit, consultation motive, person that attends to the consultation, symptoms, temporary relationship symptoms - separation, repercussions in daily life, evolution during the treatment of the child and therapeutic bonding of the family.

Finally, the psychopathological exploration is carried out with a version of the CBCL (Child Behavior Checklist) according to a Spanish version by Dr. Toro and his team of the Provincial Clinical Hospital of Barcelona. As is known, the CBCL is a questionnaire elaborated to evaluate the presence of psychopathology in the child. The questionnaire consists of 113 items that are organized in nine factors: withdrawn, somatic complaints, anxious/depressed, social problems, thought problems, attention problems, delinquent behavior and aggressive behavior. For each factor, a T score is obtained that if it is equal to or greater than 70 is considered a pathology index. Furthermore, the questionnaire organizes the different factors in two more general factors: psychopathology type (internal and external).

In our case, the questionnaires were answered by the parents with whom the child lives.

Results

The number of completed CBCL questionnaires was 25, of those which for only 14 of these subjects data relative to the process were procured.

As can be consulted in Table 1, of the total of 25 subjects, 17 (68%) were boys and 8 (32%) girls. The mean age of the children when their parents were separated was 5.75 years (s.d. 2.3). The mean acceptance age in the psychotherapy center was 8.27 years (s.d. 2.8); the first visit was effected at a mean of 8.68 years (s.d. 2.74); and at the current moment of the investigation the mean age of the sample is of 9.38 years with a s.d. of 2.96. In 14 of our subjects some data could be collected related to the history of the couple (see Table 2).

In the parents there is a presence of psychopathology, which is mainly alcoholism. In the case of the mothers, depression and/or anxiety prevails. Also, the fathers had formed a new couple to twice the extent of the mothers though the

Table 1: Sample Characteristics

Sex	Male - 17 (68%) Female - 8 (32%)	
Separation age	x 5.75	S.D. 2.99
Acceptance age CAPIP	x 8.27	S.D. 2.80
Age at 1st visit	x 8.68	S.D. 2.74
Current age	x 9.38	S.D. 2.96

Table 2: Data of the Couple and Separation

Pathology presence	Father 41.7%	Mother 16.7%		
New couple	Father n = 2	Mother n = 6		
Modality of separation	Abandonment by the father 1 (6.7%)	Abandonment by the mother 2 (13.3%)	Agreement 4 (26.7%)	Conflict 8 (53.3%)
Custody	Father 2 (18.2%)	Mother 9 (81.8%)		
Emotional separation	Father Yes 8 (77.8%) No 2 (22.2%)	Mother Yes 7 (57.1%) No 6 (42.9%)		
Agreement on economic aspects	Yes 5 (33.3%) No 10 (66.7%)			
Visits regime compliance	Yes 3 (23.1%) No 10 (76.9%)			
Economic pension compliance	Yes 5 (38.5%) No 8 (61.5%)			

majority had not a new couple. With respect to the semiology of the separation, data were collected regarding separation modality, custody, emotional separation, agreement in economic aspects, visits and fulfillment of economic obligations. The data referring to these variables are also shown in Table 2. Note the low percentage of cases in which the separation was made by mutual agreement and consequently the high percentage of conflict (more than half, 53.3%), which is reflected in the inability to agree on economic aspects (66.7% in disagreement). With these data it does not seem strange that in 61.5% of the cases the payment of the economic pension does not occur. Stranger perhaps is that in 76.9% of the cases the visits regime is not carried out. Since in most cases it is the woman who has custody, we can deduce that the contact of these children with their fathers is scarce.

The scores obtained upon administering the CBCL are summarized in Figure 1 and in Table 3.

Table 3: CBCL Scores

	x	S.D.
Withdrawn	7.8	4.4
Somatic complaints	0.8	0.5
Anxious/depressed	3.4	2.6
Social problems	5.6	3.2
Thought problems	2.9	2.1
Attention problems	11	4.5
Delinquent behavior	4.5	3.1
Aggressive behavior	17.7	8.8
Internal score	21.5	11.0
External score	22.3	10.4

In Table 3, the average and the standard deviation of the direct scores are presented for each factor. In Figure 1 the averages of the group for each area of the CBCL, in T scores, are presented.

As can be observed, solely in the case of withdrawal and in attention problems do the scores surpass the cut-off point of the appraisal of psychopathology. Withdrawal is considered of the internal type and attention problems of the external type. The thought problems approach the cut-off point but do not surpass it.

A general appraisal of this would be that our sample does not present an important level of psychopathology since in only two scales a certain increase is observed. In summary, this pilot study forms part of a wider investigation that intends to study the long term effect of divorce in the psychological adjustment of children. The data that we handled refer to variables of a different nature that we have grouped in three areas that have been indicated earlier. In the present work we have included only two areas of data out of three areas. We offer some results that serve as a guide for projects where a statistical contrast would be sought

In the first area, (the results in Tables 2 and 3), a high percentage of separations is observed whose motive is the presence of a psychopathological disorder in the father, and the high incidence of new couples in the case of the male parents is also noted.

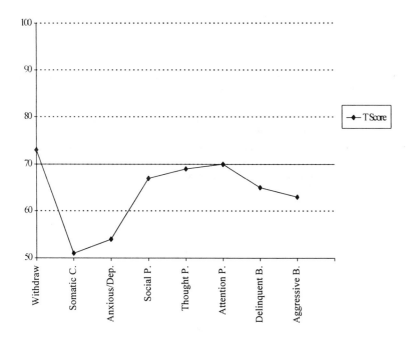

Cut Point = 70

Figure 1: Child Behavior Checklist (CBCL): General Profile

With respect to the semiology of the separation, we want to indicate the following outstanding data:

1. In more than half of the sample, the separation was conflictive;
2. As compared to 57.1% of the mothers, 77.8% of the fathers have accomplished an emotional separation;
3. There is no agreement on economic aspects in most cases;
4. There is a very high percentage of visit regime noncompliance on the part of the parents; and
5. The economic pension is not complied with in more than half of the sample.

Overall, of our sample the profile of a child that undergoes psychotherapy and whose parents are separated is the following: male, whose parents have been separated in a conflictive way, the mother has the custody, the father has accomplished the emotional separation and the mother perhaps not, there is no agreement in economic aspects, the visits regime is not kept nor the economic pension on the part of the fathers, and the maladjustment is expressed preferably by inhibition and attention problems, and secondarily for thought problems.

References

Bouchard, C., & Drapeau, S. (1991). The psychological adjustment of children from separated families: The role of selected social support variables. *Journal of Primary Prevention, 2 (4),* 259-276.

García, A., Cervera, S., Bobes, J., Bousoño, M., & Lemos, S.(1986). Hogares disociados y psicopatología infanto-juvenil. *Anuario de Psiquiatría, 2 (5),* 201-209.

Shaw, D.(1991). The effects of divorce on children's adjustment. *Behavior Modification, 15 (4),* 456-485.

Wallerstein, J. (1990). The long-term effects of divorce on children: To review. *Journal of the American Academy of Child Adolescent Psychiatry, 30 (3),* 349-360.

Custodian's Gender and Disorders in the Psychical Development of Children

Alicja Czerederecka and Teresa Jaskiewicz-Obydziñska

Introduction

While investigating the mutual relations in broken families and their influence on the psychic development of a child, authors frequently have observed important associations between explored phenomena and the gender of the custodian (Czerederecka and Jaskiewicz-Obydziñska, in press; Czerederecka and Jaskiewicz-Obydziñska, 1994). These observations sometimes confirmed and others times contradicted the social stereotypes and ascertainments of the psychological literature (Chassegnet-Smirgel, 1986; Hodges, 1991; Matyjas, 1993; Rembowski, 1972; Ziemska, 1988). At the same time in recent years fathers in our country again and again have fought for the rights of custody, fathers' rights defence committees are founded, etc. An idea arose from this to separate two groups according to the custodian's gender from the investigated population of parents fighting for custody and to explore their influence on the psychic development of a child.

The Method

The research included 50 children from 36 families. The population was divided into two equal groups: children under the mother's custody and children under the father's custody. The aim of the work was to establish to what extent disorders in the psychic development of children depend on custodian's gender. Disorders were estimated on the basis of the effects of a psychological investigation of the child: observation, interview and tests - CAT (44 children) or TAT (6 children), Gille's Film (34 children) and Rotter's.

Quantitative and qualitative analyses were undertaken. Three degrees of the disorders were separated by means of the competent judges method:

0 - no disquieting changes in development
1 - light disorders
2 - considerable disorders.

In the same way, disorders in the form of self-image, emotional and social development were estimated.

Furthermore, the psychic state of the child at the moment of taking custody over him or her was established. A comparison of disorders which occurred at that time and disorders ascertained at the time of examination was a base of estimation of changes in the psychic state of the child. The competent judges method was also used and three degrees were separated:

+ - changes for the better
0 - no important changes
− - changes for the worse

The following hypotheses have been put forward:

1. The level of disorders in the psychical development of a child differs depending on the custodian's gender.
2. There are qualitative differences between children in their father's custody and children in their mother's custody.

The influence of child's gender and age on the emotional ties between children and different genders of custodians was also established. The evaluation of the emotional ties with parents was taken from the previous work of the authors conducted on the same population (Czerederecka and Jaskiewicz-Obydzińska, 1994). A simplified division of emotional ties was used in the current study:

P - mutual positive tie between parent and child
A - ambivalent, but not negative tie
N - negative attitude at least on one side.

Characterisation of the Examined Population

All children were in the custody of only one parent at least for one year. In 20 cases (10 fathers and 10 mothers) the period of the custody was no longer than 1.5 years, in 10 cases (4 fathers and 6 mothers) it ranged from 1.5 to 3 years and in 20 cases (11 fathers and 9 mothers) it exceeded 3 years.

A scope of custody also differentiated the population: 4 fathers and 2 mothers had assumed care almost from birth and contacts with the second custodian were very seldom; 15 fathers and 13 mothers, who had assumed a care for at least 1.5 year, had an equally dominant influence on custody; some greater influence of a second parent in custody (frequent contacts or lack of participation in custody no longer than 1.5 years) were stated in the cases of 6 children in their father's custody and 9 children in their mother's custody.

Examined groups were differentiated considering the age of the children as well as the time of taking over custody as in the time of the investigation. Fathers more often than mothers took custody over children under 3 years old (6 fathers and 3 mothers) and more rarely over children of early school age (4 fathers, 8 mothers). At the time of investigation more children of early school age were in their father's custody (13 fathers, 6 mothers) than those in early adolescence (4 fathers, 11 mothers).

Boys were more frequently in their father's custody (16 boys, 9 girls), girls, in their mother's custody (9 fathers, 16 mothers).

The signs of psychic pathology were found in the cases of 11 mothers (3 of them were main custodians) and social pathology in 3 cases (1 main custodian). Among fathers psychic pathology was found in 9 cases (4 main custodians) and social pathology in 6 cases (4 main custodians).

A strong tie between the custodian's gender and his or her attitude towards contacts of the second parent with the child was observed. Women had not shown prejudice against children's contacts with the second parent in 7 cases. These mothers even tried to stimulate fathers to contact with their children. In the case of fathers, this kind of attitude was not observed at all; on the contrary, they did not allow meetings between children and the former spouse (8 men, 4 women) or actively impeded their mutual contacts. The reason for this phenomenon can be on one side a greater uncertainty and the lack of sense of social support for men as custodians and the satisfaction of being a "good mother" in women, on the other side in stereotyped coping methods. In cases of men it was a radical way of problem solving, especially aggression; in cases of women it was a way of seeking help and support (Chassegnet-Smirgel, 1986; Czerederecka and Jaskiewicz-Obydzińska, in press; Hodges, 1991; Kluck, 1992).

Results of the Research

First a general level of disorders in the psychic development of children being in custody of parents of different sexes was examined. Results are shown in Table 1. It turned out that there were significant differences between both groups. Children in their mother's custody manifested much lower levels of disorders than children in their father's custody.

Table 1: Custodian's Gender and Disorders in the Psychical Development of a Child

Level of disorders	Together		Girls		Boys	
	Fathers	Mothers	Fathers	Mothers	Fathers	Mothers
0	1	7	-	5	1	2
1	16	14	9	8	7	6
2	8	4	-	3	8	1
Total	25	25	9	16	16	9
r_p	0.4		0.56		0.52	

0 - no important disorders   1 - light disorders   2 - considerable disorders

The relation between custodian's gender and disorders in the psychic development of a child becomes still more visible when the sex of the child was also taken into consideration. It was found that all girls in their father's custody showed light disorders, whereas among girls in their mother's custody a third did not show disorders, but a fifth had considerable disorders. A different relation was found with regard to boys: as many as half of them with their father as the main custodian showed considerable disorders, whereas the analogous phenomenon in cases where the mother was the main custodian, was found in only one case. These results contradict the stereotyped opinion that it is better for men to take care of boys than of girls (Hurlock, 1984; Matyjas, 1993).

The next step of the examination was to compare disorders of a particular sphere of personality. The results referring to self-image proved to significantly differentiate the examined population. Detailed results are shown in Table 2. The children in their mother's custody manifested much fewer disorders in self-image than children whose custodian was the father: almost half of them (as in girls as in boys) did not show any disquieting symptoms, whereas there were only three such cases (two girls and one boy) among children in their father's custody.

Table 2: Custodian's Gender and Disorders in Children's Self-Image

Level of disorders	Together		Girls		Boys	
	Fathers	Mothers	Fathers	Mothers	Fathers	Mothers
0	3	12	2	8	1	4
1	16	11	7	7	9	4
2	6	2	-	1	6	1
Total	25	25	9	16	16	9
r_p	0.43		0.4		0.53	

0 - no important disorders   1 - light disorders   2 - considerable disorders

A qualitative comparison of the results (see Table 3) shows that among children in their father's custody the fluctuation of self-esteem was shown much more often (11 fathers, 4 mothers).

Disorders in emotional development occurred most frequently in the examined population and they differentiated both groups much more, to the father's disadvantage, as well. Detailed results are shown in Table 4. Only one child (a boy) in his father's custody had not shown disorders in this sphere and as many as 10 (also boys) revealed considerable disorders. When mothers were custodians, the proportions were almost reversed (8 children without disorders, 3 with considerable disorders). Among children whose custodian was the mother, girls developed correctly more often than boys.

Table 3: Custodian's Gender and Disorders in Children's Self-Image - Qualitative Estimation

Qualitative estimation of disorders	Fathers	Mothers	r_p
disorders in forming self-image (psychosexual identification in it)	3	1	
fluctuations of self-esteem	11	4	0.41
lowered self-esteem	6	6	
heightened self-esteem	3	3	

Table 4: Custodian's Gender and Children's Emotional Disorders

Level of disorders	Together		Girls		Boys	
	Fathers	Mothers	Fathers	Mothers	Fathers	Mothers
0	1	8	-	6	1	2
1	14	14	9	8	5	6
2	10	3	-	2	10	1
Total	25	25	9	16	16	9
r_p	0.5		0.56		0.58	

0 - no important disorders   1 - light disorders   2 - considerable disorders

Within the group of children in their father's custody, the unfulfilment of the need for emotional support and love or even the need for safety was observed much more often. Emotional liability and impulsiveness were noticed a little more often. In the majority of cases the origin of this state was the keeping of traditional rules of upbringing, showing girls more affection and warmth as well as harshness and distance towards boys. In effect, boys avoiding the directional participation of mother in custody had many more difficulties in fulfilling fundamental psychic needs (Ziemska, 1973; 1988). Among the children whose custodian was the mother a denial of conflicts was observed in as many as in 5 cases (see Table 5).

Table 5: Custodian's Gender and Children's Emotional Disorders - Qualitative Estimation

Qualitative estimation of disorders	Fathers	Mothers	r_p
anxiety	4	2	
emotional lability	8	4	0.28
impulsiveness	8	4	0.28
emotional immaturity	2	-	
painful emotions	5	5	
superficial emotions	1	-	
emotional inhibition	3	3	
dependency	2	4	
denial of conflicts	-	5	0.45
unfulfilment of the need for safety	8	1	0.48
unfulfilment of belonging and love needs	16	5	0.57

The social development of children in their father's custody followed a much more unfavourable path. Detailed results are shown in Table 6. In this sphere, as in others, considerable disorders were shown most of all by boys whose custodians were their fathers, while the development of the girls in their mother's custody in considerable majority was correct. The children whose custodian was their father showed a lack of self-dependence or inadequacy in coping; they also more often sought help in the environment or isolated themselves from other people (see Table 7).

Table 6: Custodian's Gender and Disorders in Children's Social Development

Level of disorders	Together		Girls		Boys	
	Fathers	Mothers	Fathers	Mothers	Fathers	Mothers
0	4	12	2	9	2	3
1	13	10	7	5	6	5
2	8	3	-	2	8	1
Total	25	25	9	16	16	9
r_p	0.42		0.5		0.46	

0 - no important disorders   1 - light disorders   2 - considerable disorders

Table 7: Custodian's Gender and Disorders in Children's Social Development - Qualitative Estimation

Qualitative estimation of disorders		Fathers	Mothers	r_p
in behaviour	aggression	11	8	
	negativism	10	5	
	seeking help	10	4	0.36
	manipulation	1	2	
in attitude	inhibition	4	2	
	isolation	5	1	0.33
	lack of distance	4	2	
in coping	lack of self-dependency or inadequacy	10	3	0.43
	avoiding responsibility	2	1	
	overresponsibility	0	1	
in position	dominance	7	7	
	submission	2	2	

The next step of exploration regarded the relation between custodian's gender and the changes in children's development from the time of taking custody over them. The results are shown in Table 8. It proved that much more often beneficial changes were observed among children whose custodian was their father than among children in their mother's custody. This relationship is especially visible in reference to girls. In almost half of the daughters whose custodian was their father, the improvement of their psychic state was noted, whereas among the daughters in their mother's custody only one manifested changes for the better. In reference to boys, differences are not significant, although changes in development proved to be more advantageous when the father was the main custodian.

Table 8: Custodian's Gender and Changes in Psychic State of a Child

Changes	Together		Girls		Boys	
	Fathers	Mothers	Fathers	Mothers	Fathers	Mothers
+	9	2	4	1	5	1
0	9	15	2	10	7	5
-	7	8	3	5	4	3
Total	25	25	9	16	16	9
r_p	0.42		0.54		0.28	

+ - for the better   0 - the same state   - - for the worse

The results put the previous information in a new light. That the majority of children remaining with the father manifested more serious disorders does not necessarily mean that fathers committed more serious upbringing errors, but that at the moment of taking over custody, their children (especially boys) had already shown more serious disorders and although fathers had visible childrearing successes, they had not been sufficient to lead to a radical improvement in the psychic state of the child (Ry, 1993).

Available material does not allow us to unequivocally answer the question as to what was the reason for such a significant difference in the state of the children in the moment of taking custody over them by mother or father. However, the hypothesis arises that the children remaining in their father's custody had not fulfilled basic psychic needs from the mother's side and these deprivations created such serious disorders in development that the father's custody was not sufficient to eliminate them.

To indirectly verify this hypothesis it proved helpful to examine the relationship between the child's age, his or her emotional tie with the non-custodian parent and the psychic development of the child.

Concerning the age of children, it turned out that beneficial changes occurred in the psychic state of those children remaining with father, who at the moment of taking over a custody were under 3 years of age or of early school age, while at the time of investigation in pre-school age. At the same time the younger children showed most frequently considerable disorders in each sphere of psychic development, whereas the development of the children of early school age was similar in the mother's and father's home. Among children remaining with the father, who were of early school age in the time of the investigation, advantageous changes were found as often as disadvantageous ones. These children most frequently showed light disorders in each sphere of psychic development.

Among children remaining with the mother, the less unfavourable changes in development were observed when at the moment of taking over custody they were of early school age, whereas at the time of investigation, between early school age and early adolescence. The same children showed a lighter level of disorders, especially in social development. Considerable disorders were found only in the youngest children.

The problem examined further was the influence of emotional ties on the psychic development of children remaining in different sexes' custody. The emotional tie with the direct custodian did not differentiate the explored group significantly, especially because it was always positive. However, we concentrated on the problem of to what extent the relation with the second parent not directly participating in custody can determine his or her child's development.

It turned out that if the mother was not the direct custodian, the relationship was high, and in reference to the formation of self-image even very high. Children whose tie with their mother was positive did not show considerable disorders and the improvement of their psychic state was observed. Ambivalent attitudes usually went together with light disorders, and negative ties accompanied disorders in all spheres; positive changes in their psychical state were not observed either.

If the main custodian was the father, a positive relation with him accompanied the lack of significant changes in the psychic state of the child. Incorrect emotional ties led mainly to disorders in the emotional development of the child. The results mentioned before seem to confirm the hypothesis that disorders in the psychic development of the child are determined by the unfulfilment of basic needs from the mother's side in early childhood. Fathers more often than mothers took custody over younger children in the examined population. The fact that the most considerable disorders occurred in children of this age both in the fathers' and mothers' houses, clearly shows the destructive and pervasive influence of the wrong socialisation atmosphere on the early development of the child. If the lack of positive relation with the mother goes together with it, the consequence is the consolidation of a considerable number of disorders in the psychic development of the child.

Conclusions

The hypotheses put forward at the beginning have been confirmed.

1. The children remaining in their father's custody showed many more considerable disorders in forming self-image, and in emotional and social development. These disorders were more significant for boys than for girls. The most considerable disorders have been found in all children in emotional development. Among children remaining in their mother's custody the correct development was observed

much more frequently, especially in the social sphere. The last result is a bit surprising, because the important role of father in forming correct social development is underlined in the psychological literature.

2. The children whose main custodian was their father much more frequently show a fluctuation of self-esteem, unfulfilment of the emotional support and love need or even the safety need, lack of self-dependence or inadequacy in coping, isolation from the social life or seeking for help. The children remaining in their mother's custody show an intensive tendency to deny of conflicts.

In the father's custody much more frequently than in the mother's childrearing progress has been found, especially if they have taken care of girls. However, this progress has not often resulted in a satisfying state for the child.

A lack of considerable disorders was found only in those cases in which fathers had taken custody over children after pre-school age and whose contact with the mother as the second custodian was correct.

This leads to the conclusion that in the cases of the break-up of a family, fathers can potentially be the main custodian as well as mothers. However, they should incorporate a striving for the establishment of better mutual contacts between a child and a mother into their childrearing activities much more than they do, and not concentrate on a conflict with former spouse, seeking social support for such forms of behaviour.

The last postulate, although to a lesser degree, refers also to mothers. The children remaining in their custody manifested disorders too, especially in the emotional development, if the mutual relations with their father were unfavourable.

References

Czerederecka A., and Jaskiewicz-Obydzińska, T. (1994). *Emotional ties between parents and children and their influence the expert's opinion concerning the parents custody. (Printing in:* Z zagadnien nauk sadowych. Problems of forensic sciences, 30)

Czerederecka, A., and Jaskiewicz-Obydzińska, T. (in press). *Factors neutralising development disorders in children from broken-up families.* Materials from the III European Conference "Law and Psychology", Oxford).

Chassegnet-Smirgel, J. (1986). *Sexuality and mind. The role of the father and the mother in the psyche.* New York: University Press.

Hodges, W. F. (1991). The unique problems of single parents. In: *Interventions for children of divorce.* New York: John Willey and Sons, Inc.

Hurlock, E. B. (1984). *Rozwój dziecka.* Warszawa: PWN.

Kluck, M. L. (1992). Diagnostic judgement on parental custody as decision-making process. In: F. Lösel, D. Bender and T. Bliesener (Eds.) *Psychology and Law.* Berlin: Walter de Gruyter.

Matyjas, B. (1993). Opiekuńczo-wychowawcza rola ojca w rodzinie (w wietle wypowiedzi dziecka. *Problemy Rodziny, 3,* 23-26.

Rembowski, J. (1972). *Wiêzi uczuciowe w rodzinie.* Warszawa: PWN.

Ry, M. (1993). Poziom zaspokojenia potrzeb w dzieciństwie a zaspokojenie potrzeb w maceństwie. *Problemy Rodziny, 1,* 20-23.

Ziemska, M. (1973). *Postawy rodzicielskie.* Warszawa: Wiedza Powszechna.

Ziemska, M. (1988). *Ksztatowanie ról rodzicielskich po rozwodzie.* Prace Instytutu Profilaktyki Spoecznej i Resocjalizacji UW, t.10.

Part VI
Psychological Factors Related to Crime

Mental Illness and Criminality: A Study of a Sample of Psychiatric Out-Patients

Salvatore Luberto, Patrizia Zavatti and Giorgio Gualandri

Introduction

The many studies carried out all over the world on the dangerousness of the mentally ill have documented the absence of a direct correlation between mental pathology and criminality, showing an incidence of the phenomenon that is not significant with regard to that found in the general population (Rubin, 1972; Boker, Hafner, 1973; Guze et al., 1974; Steadman & Cocozza, 1978; Canepa & Traverso, 1980; Goppinger & Boker, 1980).

Although this is an acquired fact, a stereotyped vision remains of the mentally ill to whom serious and brutal crimes tend to be attributed.

Various factors undoubtedly affect the perception of dangerousness:

- In the first place, the emotional empathy aroused both by mental illness and by particularly serious and violent crimes, which, being phenomena that are difficult to understand and strongly induce anxiety, favour mechanisms of negation and projection;
- In the second place, the attitude of the mass media, which not only widely publicise brutal crime, but also frequently tend to place it in connection with the presence of mental disorders, often without any elements of proof;
- Finally, the methodological approach of many studies which have shown the prevalence of serious crimes among subjects affected by mental disorders.

Referring to this last point, it should be stressed how most of the work concerning the criminality of the mentally ill has been carried out on samples of subjects interned in special institutes because they had already committed a crime, or institutionalised for years in psychiatric structures because they are affected by serious pathologies (Goppinger & Boker, 1980; Traverso, 1980).

Such a connotation of the samples may affect both the entity of the phenomenon and the identification of the typology of the crimes committed by the mentally ill.

Indeed, since these studies were carried out on preselected samples, they discount a high dark figure by not pointing out petty offences and by drawing attention only to more serious and violent crimes. There is a consequent strengthening of the stereotype of dangerousness of the mentally ill.

So as to evaluate the real incidence of deviant behaviour among psychiatric patients, we studied, in a previous work (Luberto et al., 1993), the incidence of unlawful behaviour in a sample of the mentally disordered undergoing treatment at local psychiatric centres in two North Italian towns. The data found were broadly consistent with information unquestionably consolidated in the literature, and documented a low incidence of the phenomenon, especially of the prevalent typology of petty offences committed by patients suffering from serious psychiatric pathology who have been undergoing treatment over a long period.

In this second work it has been our aim to verify the previously found data on control samples, conducting an in-depth examination of any differential factors in the group of patients who have committed offences compared with the greater number of those who, with the same pathology, have not.

Method

The study was carried out on a sample made up of patients in care at the local psychiatric centres of the city of Bologna on 1991.

On a methodological basis, the same technique as that of the previous study was used, i.e., a structured questionnaire divided into three sections.

The data were collected through consultation of case sheets and/or direct interview with the psychiatric operators who had knowledge of the cases.

Besides biographical elements (first section of the questionnaire), data on the pathology and the relative course of each single case (second section) were recorded, and, finally, the unlawful conducts and successive legal procedures taken (third section). With reference to this last point, we would underline that we took into account all conduct qualifiable as crime, since it implies the effective violation of a penal law, independently of its being reported and of its seriousness.

We are obviously aware of the anomalous means of recording the conduct as crime, but our aim was to reduce as much as possible the dark figure and to show the real incidence of deviant criminal behaviour in a wide sample of psychiatric patients in normal therapy, not preselected in any way.

The data obtained were used at first comparatively with those of the previous study so as to verify the degree or lack of consistency.

The present sample was then broken down into two groups according to the presence or absence of at least one unlawful behaviour, to analyse any differences between them.

In order to control the statistical significance of the differences between the two groups examined, we used the chi-square test (X^2).

Results

The sample analysed is made up of 326 patients followed throughout 1991 at the out-patient and residential psychiatric centres of the Bologna Local Health Authority which has a catchment area of 200,000 residents. Among these, 63 subjects (19.3 %) had committed crimes (Table 1).

Table 1: The Sample Examined

Catchment area	Patients in care	Perpetrators of crime	%
200,000	326	63	19.3

Taking into consideration only the subjects who had committed a crime in one year (12 subjects in 1991), and with reference to the resident population (catchment area: 200,000 persons) the annual ratio of mental patient perpetrators of crimes out of 100,000 residents was calculated.

This rate was 6 subjects per 100,000 inhabitants; it is a rather low annual ratio, lower even than the rate founded in the previous study carried out at the Psychiatric Services of Modena and Reggio Emilia, and confirms the slight incidence of deviant behaviour in the mentally ill.

First of all, the biographical and socio-personal data were examined.

As can be seen in Table 2, among the mental patient perpetrators of crimes, males (65.1%) prevail, just as occurred in the previous study.

Table 2: Sex

	Mental patient offenders		Non mental patient offenders	
Male	41	65.1	114	43.3
Female	22	34.9	149	56.7
Total	63	100.0	263	100.0

$X2 = 9.6258$ d.f. = 1 $p < 0.01$

Concerning age (Table 3), mental patient perpetrators of crimes prevailed in the group between 36 and 45 years (38.1 %) and, on the whole, in the young adult group (76 %), while in the older groups, crime perpetration is less frequent. This result, too, is similar to that of the previous study.

To be precise, the patients who are perpetrators of crimes are mostly in the younger range, up to 25 years (12.6 % vs. 7.6 %), in the ranges between 26 and 35 years (25.3 vs. 15.6 %) and between 36 and 45 years (38.1 % vs. 21.7%); while those who have not committed any crime are mostly in the older groups.

Thus, a consistency can be seen in these data with sane perpetrators of crimes who show deviant behaviour mostly in the same age range, in agreement with data reported in the literature.

Table 3: Age Classification

	Offenders		Non offenders	
Up to 25 years	8	12.6	20	7.6
26-35	16	25.4	41	15.6
36-45	24	38.2	57	21.7
46-55	8	12.7	59	22.4
56-65	4	6.4	45	17.1
Over 66 years	3	4.7	41	15.6
Total	63	100.0	263	100.0

$X2 = 20.4952$ d.f. = 4 $p < 0.01$

Marital status (Table 4), with all the socio-relational implications it involves, seems to affect the commission of deviant behaviour since, among perpetrators of crime, unmarried subjects (60.3 %) prevail, while in the group of the widowed, probably in relation to age, the frequency is definitely lower (4.7%).

Table 4: Marital State

	Offenders		Non offenders	
Single	38	60.3	138	52.5
Married/cohabitant	11	17.5	82	31.2
Divorced/separated	11	17.5	19	7.2
Widow/er	3	4.7	24	9.1
Total	63	100.0	263	100.0

$X2 = 4.9348$ d.f. = 2 $0.1 < p > 0.05$

From a comparison of the two groups, it emerges that among single subjects there are no significant differences; among married/cohabiting subjects, those who have not committed a crime prevail (31.2% vs. 17.5%), while in the divorced/separated group, perpetrators prevail (17.5% vs. 7.2%); in the widowed group those who have not committed crime prevail (9.1% vs. 4.7%).

These figures reflect the importance of family integration in the process of control and of restraint of deviant behaviours.

A confirmation can be derived from the analysis of different states of cohabitation (Table 5). The subjects suffering from mental illness who live with an acquired family show a lower incidence of deviant behaviour (34.6 % vs. 14.3 %), while the mental patients living alone or with their original family show a higher percentage of deviance (34.9 % vs. 26.6 % and 36.5 % vs. 22.8 % respectively).There seem to be no significant differences among subjects living in welfare institutions.

Table 5: Type of Cohabitation

	Offenders		Non offenders	
Alone	22	34.9	70	26.6
Original family	23	36.5	60	22.8
Acquired family	9	14.3	91	34.6
Other	-	-	7	2.7
Welfare institutions	8	12.7	28	10.6
Not known	1	1.6	7	2.7
Total	63	100.0	263	100.0

$X2 = 13.4863$ d.f. = 3 $p < 0.01$

On the one hand, this confirms the difficulty in self-management of psychiatric patients who, if left to themselves, often live in conditions of greater alienation and are less likely to follow therapeutic courses, with consequently greater behavioural disorders and deviant acts; on the other hand, it seems to stress the frequent inadequacy of the original family, which is often expulsive, compared to the acquired one.

Table 6: Schooling

	Offenders		Non offenders	
No certificate	5	7.9	12	4.6
Primary school	14	22.3	75	28.5
Middle school	21	33.3	51	19.4
High school certificate	15	23.9	81	30.8
University degree	3	4.7	22	8.4
Not known	5	7.9	22	8.4
Total	63	100.0	263	100.0

$X2 = 10.2036$ d.f. = 3 $p < 0.01$

The analysis of the educational level (Table 6) of the mental patients emphasises a greater incidence of perpetrators of crime among subjects holding a middle school certificate (school leaving age 14 years) (33.3 %), while a higher education seems to guarantee a lower incidence of deviant behaviours. From a comparison of the two groups, patients who have not committed crimes in the main hold a high school diploma (30.8 %), just as graduates are more frequently represented (58.4 % vs. 4.7 %).

As can be seen from Table 7, the perpetrators of crimes are mostly unemployed (79.4 %).

This datum can be superimposed both on that of the general population of perpetrators of crimes, and on that of the general population of mental patients (regarding the latter it is confirmed by our study). This seems to be indicative of poor social integration, not only of the psychiatric patient who commits a crime but also of mental patients in general.

Table 7: Employment

	Offenders		Non offenders	
Yes	13	20.6	75	28.5
No	50	79.4	188	71.5
Total	63	100.0	263	100.0

X2 = 1.6023   d.f. = 1   p n.s.

In short, the analysis of socio-personal characteristics of subjects in care at the psychiatric out-patient and residential services of the Bologna Local Health Authority leads to conclusions that do not diverge from those found in the previous, above-mentioned study carried out on subjects treated at the Modena and Reggio Emilia Local Psychiatric services.

As we have already shown, there are, however, significant differences in a comparison between patients who are and those who are not perpetrators of crime, especially with respect to sex, age, marital status and living conditions.

With regard to clinical data, as shown in Table 8, among mental patient perpetrators of crime, those affected by borderline personality disorders (36.5%) or dissociative syndromes prevail (over half of the sample).

The comparison between the two groups of patients (perpetrators and non-perpetrators of crime) shows, first of all, that dissociative syndromes are at about the same level (31.9% vs. 33.4%). Moreover, patients affected by affective disorders rarely commit crimes (only 4.7%), and the datum regarding organic disorders appears to be barely significant.

Referring to subjects affected by borderline disorders (which were distinct from other personality disorders due to the obvious criminological implications involved in this disorder) it is interesting to note that as perpetrators of crime, they represent 36.5% of cases against only 5.3% of those who have not committed any crime (p < 0.01).

This situation is reversed when we consider the group of other personality disorders and neuroses. This group rates at 17.5% among offenders and 30.8 % of non-offenders.

Table 8: Psychiatric Diagnosis

	Offenders		Non offenders	
Dissociative syndromes	21	33.4	84	31.9
Dysthimic syndromes	3	4.7	73	27.8
Organic psychoses	5	7.9	11	4.2
Border-line disorders	23	36.5	14	5.3
Personality disorders/neuroses	11	17.5	81	30.8
Total	63	100.0	263	100.0

X2 = 54.1471   d.f. = 3   p < 0.01

Table 9 reports the distribution by typology of crimes committed. The slight incidence of serious or violent crimes (only 3.2% of the total) is evident, while not so serious crimes, particularly bodily harm (31.7%) distinctly prevail. It is interesting to note the data on theft/robbery and drug-related crimes (23.8 % and 15.8% respectively), probably strictly related to each other and with the typology of the sample examined (high incidence of borderline patients).

Table 9: Crime Typology

Bodily harm	20	31.7
Attempted murder/murder	2	3.2
Duress	1	1.6
Slander-libel	1	1.6
Theft/robbery	15	23.8
Damage	5	7.9
Sexual crime	5	7.9
Insulting a public officer	4	6.3
Drug abuse	10	15.8
Total	63	100.0

The procedure following the committing of crime shows that of the 63 mental patients perpetrators of crime, 29 (46 %) were reported to the legal authorities and 9 (14.3 %) were not prosecuted. The phenomenon of "depenalisation", shown in the previous work is at a lower rate in this sample, perhaps in relation to the type of subjects followed and, in particular, to the greater number among them of drug addicts. Of the 29 subjects reported and prosecuted, 15 (23.8% of the total) were convicted and only 2 (3.2 % of the total) acquitted on grounds of insanity. Of these two cases, the safety measure of the penal Psychiatric Hospital was applied to one, while no safety measure was applied to the other as he was held to be not dangerous.

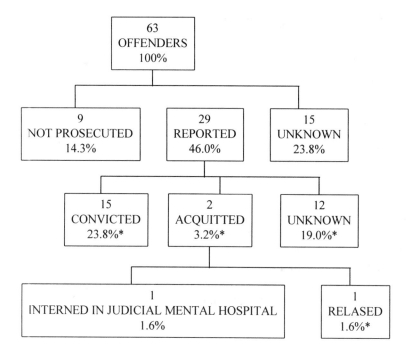

* Percentages refer to total number of cases

Figure 1: Procedure after Crime

Discussion

The results of the research carried out on a small, though sufficiently representative sample may be quite indicative of the reality of the phenomenon and enable us to make some important considerations on the incidence of criminality, the various cases of crimes and the typology of mental illness.

In the first place, our study has confirmed the data that emerged from previous studies, emphasising not only the low incidence of criminality among psychiatric patients, but also the distinct prevalence of petty crimes. It confirms the random nature of the persistent stereotype concept of the dangerousness of the mental patient.

Secondly, the subdivision of the sample into offenders and non-offenders has enabled us to show significant differences according to sex, marital status, living conditions and, in particular, psychiatric diagnosis. Offenders are mostly male, younger, single, and they mainly live alone in conditions of isolation and alienation, or with their original family. Together with the data on employment, this has confirmed the importance of social and family integration in the control of deviant behaviour among mental patients (Traverso, 1980).

As far as the connection between criminality and typology of mental disorder is concerned, the most important point that has emerged from our study is the high incidence of deviant behaviour, which takes on juridical relevance, among subjects affected by borderline personality disorders. Among the perpetrators of crime 36.5% of the subjects are affected by this mental disorder. Compared with this figure, among those who have not committed crime, only 5.3 % were classified as borderline.

This is probably imputable to the criminological implications relating to such a disorder; these are subjects who, as shown by DSM III-R diagnostic criteria (APA, 1988), present a marked instability of personal identity and of interpersonal relationships, with a tendency to solve intrapsychic conflicts in an alloplastic manner (Grinker et al., 1968; Bergeret, 1984; Kernberg, 1987; Dutton, 1994). From this derives a high incidence of self and/or heteroaggressive behaviours and frequent drug abuse (Guze et al., 1974; De Fazio & Luberto, 1987).

Another significant incidence of criminality emerged among patients affected by dissociative syndromes (33.4 %), but it must be pointed out, on the one hand, that of the total number of psychotics, only a quarter committed crimes and, on the other, that among offenders and non-offenders, dissociative syndromes were present to the same extent.

Finally, we would point out how the data relative to the typology of crime have shown a very low incidence of murder and attempted murder (3.2 %) with a distinct prevalence of petty crimes, in the expression of which, besides the clinical elements, also factors of maladjustment and of alienation linked with the mental illness are likely to play a significant role.

To conclude, it can essentially be affirmed that patients affected by mental illness present the risk of deviance but to quite a low degree if compared to the rest of the population, and they often commit crimes that are not very serious.

This fact calls our attention to the criminological values inherent in psychiatric activity, often acted upon, more or less consciously by the territorial health workers (Luberto, 1991). This confirms the preventive potential of adequately putting into effect the above-mentioned values, since it is quite clear that the better handling of such situations has a positive repercussion on prevention.

In such a prospective also the few cases of violent crime could be handled better and thus destined to further reduction thanks to this hypothesised preventive activity.

If we bear in mind the prescriptive definition of social dangerousness - in our country grounded on the probability of generic recidivism - most subjects acquitted on account of mental insanity should be held socially dangerous, owing to the greater likelihood that a psychotic or a borderline case, in care, may relapse into analogous behaviours. Such a conclusion leads to internment of the subjects in a penal Psychiatric Hospital for a minimum of two years, with a consequent interruption of treatment that may have been going on for some time, loss of contact with the subject's own environment and a possible, if not probable, increase in difficulties in adaptation. The only way out of this situation is to consider the subject not dangerous while he is undergoing treatment. We are dealing with a broader interpretation, at the limit of what is allowable in the notion of dangerousness which, in its extreme, presents serious inconveniences as it does not foresee any kind of treatment obligation, or any serious suggestion of undergoing it, either for the patients or for the Services.

Adaptation of this law would be desirable through the introduction of a greater articulation of sanctioning and legal provisions which would take into account the necessities of treatment of single cases, along the lines of regulations provided for in other countries.

References

American Psychiatric Association (1988). *DSM-III-R. Manuale diagnostico e statistico dei disturbi mentali*. Ed.Italiana. Milano: Masson.

Bergeret, J. (1984). *La personalitá normale e patologica*. Ed.Italiana. Milano: Raffaello Cortina Ed.

Boker, W., & Hafner, H. (1973). *Gefalltaten Geistesgestorter. Eine psychiatrische-epidemiologische Untersuchung in der Bundesrepublik Deutschland*. Berlin: Springer-Verlag.

Canepa, G., & Traverso, G.B. (1980). Mental disease and criminality. An introduction. *Rassegna di Criminologia*, 407-414.

De Fazio, F., & Luberto, S. (1987). Problematica psichiatrico-forense delle sindromi marginali: imputabilitá ed ipotesi di trattamento. *Psychopathologia*, 25-31.

Dutton, D.G. (1994). Behavioural and affective correlates of borderline personality organization in wife assaulters. *International Journal of Law and Psychiatry, 17 (3)*, 265-277.

Goppinger, H., & Boker, W. (1980). On delinquency of the mentally ill. *Rassegna Italiana di Criminologia*, 451-477.

Grinker, R.R., Werble, B., & Drye, R. (1968). *The borderline syndrome. A behavioural study of Ego functions*. New York: Basic Books.

Guze, S.B., Woodruff, R.A., & Clayton, P.J. (1974). Psychiatric disorders and criminality. *Journal of American Medical Association, 227 (6)*, 641.

Kernberg, O. (1987). *Disturbi gravi della personalitá*. Ed.Italiana. Torino: Bollati Boringhieri.

Luberto, S. (1991). Attualitá e prospettive degli interventi criminologici territoriali. *Rassegna Italiana di Criminologia, 2-3*, 259-270.

Luberto, S., Zavatti, P., & Gualandri, G. (1993). Tipologia di reato e malattia mentale. Indagine campionaria su pazienti in trattamento psichiatrico. *Quaderni di Psichiatria Forense, Vol. II (1)*, 78-103.

Rubin, B. (1972). Prediction of dangerousness in mentally ill criminals. *Archives of general Psychiatry, 27*, 397.

Steadman, H. J., & Cocozza, J. (1978). Psychiatry, dangerousness, and the repetitively, violent offender. *Journal of Criminal Law and Criminology, 69 (2)*, 226-231.

Traverso, G.B. (1980). Social control of abnormal law-violation: preliminary findings of a research on the relations of mental illness to crime. *Rassegna Italiana di Criminologia*, 533-560.

Outcome Expectancies: An Important Link between Substance Use and Crime?

Mary McMurran

Introduction

That there is a relationship between substance use and crime is by now well established (Collins, 1981; Nurco, Hanlon, & Kinlock, 1991). The nature of the relationship may be addressed within two broad frameworks, relating to systems and individuals. Where *systems* are concerned, there is the truism that crime is created by legislation, and drug use is a crime *per se*. Additionally, the law creates situations where criminal activities flourish as the operational methods of the underground drug economy. The topic of interest in this paper, however, concerns how the use of alcohol or drugs affects *individuals* to produce criminal behaviour.

Whilst drinking and drug use are associated with crime, it is obvious that, alcohol- and drug-defined crimes aside, much substance use occurs without resulting in any crime, and crime often occurs without being preceded by drinking or drug use. In order to further our understanding of the nature of the relationship between substance use and crime, we must determine for *whom* under what *circumstances* will what kind of *substance use* alter the probability of which *criminal behaviour* (Lang & Sibrel, 1989). This challenge to researchers in the field of substance use and crime requires examination of the following areas: (1) *Person variables* including physical status, cognitive abilities, personality factors, and previous experiences; (2) *Situation variables* including culture, social context, and the immediate environment; (3) *Substance variables*, including types of substance used, dosage, and method of administration; and (4) *Crime variables*, that is the nature of the criminal behaviour.

This multifactorial model, which includes a wide variety of interdependent and interactive factors, can be studied through cognitive processes. With reference to the explanation of drinking behaviour, Goldman, Brown, Christiansen, and Smith (1991) suggest that "Because of their potential for tying together a host of psycho-social and biological/genetic variables, and carrying forward the influence of these variables over extended time periods, memory processes (information storage) are now being considered by researchers of all types as one possible 'final common pathway' for drinking decisions" (p. 138). They place outcome expectancies in the context of cognitive research: "Research during the past decade on alcohol-reinforcement expectancies has been consistent with cognitive approaches to the study of memory processes, and has provided a new research 'window' from which the emergence of the incentive patterns that influence lifelong alcohol decision making may be studied" (p.138).

Outcome expectancies may be defined as knowledge about the relationships between events, with an anticipatory "if-then" component; that is, *if* a certain event is registered, *then* a certain event is expected to follow (Goldman, Brown, & Christiansen, 1987). Outcome expectancies are *mediational mechanisms* which operate to influence the independent variable (Goldman, Brown, Christiansen, & Smith, 1991). The effect of alcohol outcome expectancies on behaviour is most clearly demonstrated in balanced placebo design experiments, where half the subjects are given a drink containing alcohol and the other half are given a drink without alcohol. Half the subjects in each group are led to believe that their drink contains alcohol, and the other half are led to believe they are not drinking alcohol. Those who think they are drinking alcohol, but are not, report feeling cravings for more alcohol, drink more alcohol in subsequent "taste-tests", behave more aggressively, and show more sexual arousal (see review by Goldman, Brown, & Christiansen, 1987). Clearly, these effects cannot be explained by a drug effect, and so the *expected* effects of alcohol may be seen as variables mediating behavioural outcomes after drinking.

Outcome expectancies are learned through instructional messages from parents, peers, and media figures, and modified by drinking experiences. In alcohol research, outcome expectancies have been shown to differ depending upon a number of factors: the cultural roots of the drinker (Teahan, 1988); the gender of the drinker (Brown, Goldman, Inn, & Anderson, 1980); drinking experience (Brown, Creamer, and Stetson, 1987; Brown, Goldman, and Christiansen, 1985; Southwick, Steele, Marlatt, & Lindell, 1981); the type of beverage (Lindman & Lang, 1986); the amount drunk on a specific occasion (Connors, O'Farrell, Cutter, & Thompson, 1987); and the context of drinking (Sher, 1985).

One way of representing the complex field of substance use and crime is in terms of outcome expectancies, that is outcome expectancies may mediate between substance use and crime. Outcome expectancies are *important* in that they predict behaviour in relation to substance use. They are *relevant* to the study of crime in that specific outcome expectancies can be risk factors (e.g. alcohol makes me violent) or protective factors (e.g. alcohol makes me mellow). Expectancies are *representative* in that they can take into account the complexities of person x substance x situation interactions which explain criminal behaviour. The study of expectancies is also *useful* in that changing an individual's outcome expectancies may present a direction for developing interventions with offenders whose crimes are related to alcohol or drug use so that the likelihood of crime is reduced.

In this paper, data will be presented from two studies into alcohol-related expectancies held by offenders. The first is a study of male young offenders conducted in Her Majesty's Young Offender Centre Glen Parva (McMurran, Hollin,

& Williams, in press). The second is a study of sex-related alcohol expectancies in rapists conducted in Rampton Hospital (McMurran & Bellfield, 1993).

Study 1

The first study aimed to collect normative data for male young offenders on an alcohol expectancy questionnaire, and to assess the reliability of the questionnaire with this subject group. These results will not be presented here, except to say that the questionnaire showed high test-retest reliability. The main aim, which is of greater interest to report, was to explore the relationships between alcohol expectancy scores and offence type, measures of alcohol consumption and dependence on alcohol, and self-reported alcohol-related crime.

Subjects

The research was conducted in a Prison Service institution for male young offenders between the ages of 15 and 21. The centre contained approximately 360 convicted offenders living in six accommodation units. Three of these units were randomly selected for the study, giving a total population of 177 young offenders. Of these, only those scoring a reading age of 12 or more on the NFER-NS6 Reading Test (National Foundation for Educational Research, 1972) were selected to ensure comprehension of the expectancies questionnaire. This gave a potential sample of 116, of whom 85 comprised the final sample (26 were discharged before the questionnaire could be administered; two refused to take part; and three returned incomplete questionnaires). The mean age of the sample was 19.53 years (SD = 1.32) with a mean sentence length of 25.33 months (SD = 10.45).

Measures

1. *Record check*. Each subject's prison record was checked to identify the type of current offence(s). For analysis, these were categorised as (1) against property only; (2) against property and against the person; and (3) against the person only.
2. *Alcohol Expectancies Questionnaire - Adolescent Form (AEQ-A)*. The AEQ-A (Goldman, Christiansen, & Brown, 1987) is a 90-item questionnaire designed to measure positive and negative alcohol-related expectancies in adolescents. Factor analysis of the AEQ-A has revealed seven scales: (1) Global positive changes; (2) Changes in social behaviour; (3) Improved cognitive and motor abilities; (4) Sexual enhancement; (5) Cognitive and motor impairment; (6) Increased arousal; (7) Relaxation and tension reduction.
3. *Short Alcohol Dependence Data Questionnaire (SADD)*. The SADD is a 15-item questionnaire designed to measure dependence on alcohol (Davidson & Raistrick, 1986; Raistrick, Dunbar, and Davidson, 1983). Norms for young offenders have

been reported and the questionnaire has been reworded for ease of understanding by young offenders (McMurran & Hollin, 1989).

4. *Structured Interview*. Each subject was interviewed about his drinking and the relationship between his drinking and offending. This comprised a quantity-frequency assessment of a "typical" week's alcohol consumption prior to imprisonment; direct questioning about whether or not the offender considered his offending to be alcohol-related; and presentation of a cue card containing seven possible relationships between drinking and offending from which the offender could choose those relevant to him. For analysis, these items were grouped into (1) direct relationship, e.g. "I do things after drinking that I would not do when sober", "I offended so that I could drink"; (2) indirect relationship, e.g. "I drank after I offended"; or (3) no relationship.

Results

Because the scores on expectancy scales were highly interdependent (i.e. they did not measure discrete factors), a factor analysis of the expectancy data was carried out. This showed a three factor solution to fit the data, accounting for 81.7% of the variance. These three factors were labelled:

Factor 1. *Global positive change* -- the sum of scores on
    scales 1, 4, 6, and 7.
Factor 2. *Change in cognitive and motor abilities* -- the
    score of scale 3 minus the score on scale 5.
Factor 3. *Change in social behaviour* -- the equivalent of the
    score on scale 2.

A stepwise multiple regression analysis was carried out. This revealed that Factor 1 (Global positive change) was predicted by the relationship between drinking and offending as identified by the cue card; Factor 2 (Change in cognitive and motor abilities) was not predicted by any variable; and Factor 3 (Change in social behaviour) was predicted by the relationship between drinking and offending as identified by the cue card, *plus* offences against the person (that is, a *combination* of how strongly the offence is alcohol-related and offence against the person). SADD scores and quantity-frequency drinking estimates did not predict any factor.

Conclusions

Those offenders whose offences are alcohol-related expect more global positive change (Factor 1). This factor contains items relating to *increasing self-confidence* (e.g. alcohol makes people more sure of themselves, less worried about what other people think of them, better able to talk to the opposite sex), *easing tension* (e.g. alcohol makes people worry less, loosen up), and *increasing assertiveness* (e.g.

alcohol helps people stand up to others, talk more easily to others). Overall, these components suggest that offenders who admit to alcohol-related offending are reinforced by the immediate social benefits of alcohol and would gain from social skills training in order to help them cope with their insecurities without relying on alcohol to give global positive change.

Amongst those who report alcohol-related offending, most positive social change (Factor 3) is expected by those who offend against the person. Factor 3 contains items relating to feelings of friendliness, joining in and having fun. It seems logical to assume that people who wish to be gregarious will drink in social settings, such as bars and clubs, and such venues are frequently scenes of violent conflict. Offences against the person occur, in all probability, as a result of the influence of individual expectancies, of the setting, and an interaction between the two. For this group, interventions combining social skills training and rule-setting to avoid contexts where trouble is likely to occur might prove effective in reducing both drinking and related crime.

Study 2

One specific expectancy common in Western cultures is that drinking alcohol facilitates sexual behaviour. Leigh (1990) suggested that this expectancy should lead to drinking in sexual or potentially sexual situations, particularly for those who have more need of an excuse for their sexual behaviour. She surveyed 844 men and women to collect information about their drinking, sexual behaviour, sex-related alcohol expectancies, and attitudes to sex. She found that the stronger a person's beliefs in alcohol's ability to enhance sexual experience, the more likely was that person to drink and drink in larger amounts in conjunction with sexual encounters, particularly if the person felt guilty and/or nervous about sex.

This raises some interesting questions about the role of alcohol in sexual offences. In the second study, three hypotheses were tested:

(1) That rapists whose offences were alcohol-related would be heavier drinkers and more dependent on alcohol than rapists whose offences were not alcohol-related;
(2) That rapists whose offences were alcohol-related would hold stronger positive sex-related alcohol expectancies than those whose offences were not alcohol-related; and
(3) That rapists whose offences were alcohol-related would hold more negative attitudes to sex than those whose offences were not alcohol-related.

Subjects

The research was conducted in Rampton Hospital, which contained at the time 424 male patients. Of these, 29 had an index offence of rape and 17 were selected for the research (permission to interview was refused by the responsible medical officer for 7 patients; 3 were on trial leave; and 2 were intellectually unable to complete the questionnaires). Rape was alcohol-related for 9 subjects, and not alcohol-related for 8 subjects.

Measures

1. *Record check.* Records were checked for details of the offence, particularly drinking around the time of the offence.
2. *Structured interview.* Subjects were interviewed to access information about alcohol consumption around the time of the offence, and the subject's perceptions of the role of alcohol in the offence. Subjects were asked to complete a quantity-frequency chart for a "typical" week's drinking around the time of the offence, and to classify themselves as abstainers, light, moderate or heavy drinkers.
3. *Short Alcohol Dependence Data Questionnaire (SADD).* This was described earlier.
4. *Sex-related alcohol expectancies.* Leigh (1990) designed a 13-item questionnaire on which subjects are asked to rate their agreement, using a four-point rating scale, with the possible effects of alcohol on sexual behaviour. Leigh's (1990) research with the general population revealed three factors: (1) enhanced sex; (2) decreased nervousness; and (3) increased riskiness.
5. *Sexual beliefs.* Again, Leigh (1990) designed a questionnaire to measure attitudes to sex. This is a 13-item questionnaire, on which subjects rate their agreement using a five-point scale. It contains four factors: (1) nervousness; (2) guilt; (3) sex without love; and (4) fun.

Results

1. *Drinking and alcohol dependence.* Results show that more of the alcohol-related crime group reported themselves to be heavy drinkers, and their level of self-reported alcohol consumption is significantly higher than the non-alcohol-related crime group. SADD scores are also significantly higher for the alcohol-related crime group. (See Table 1).

Table 1: Mean Scores on Drinking Measures

	Self-classification				Weekly consumption (units)**	SADD score
	A	L	M	H*		
Drinking and offending related (N = 9)	0	0	6	3	90.55	11.33
Drinking and offending not related (N = 8)	1	5	2	0	12.62	3.00
					$p < .01$	$p < .05$

* A = Abstinent L = Light drinker M = Moderate drinker   H = Heavy drinker
** 1 unit = 8 grammes of alcohol

2. *Sex-related alcohol expectancies.* The mean scores of the two groups are presented in Table 2. Only scores on increased riskiness are significantly different: higher for the alcohol-related crime group.

Table 2: Mean Scores on Sex-Related Alcohol Expectancies

	Factor 1. Enhanced sex	Factor 2. Decreased nervousness	Factor 3. Increased riskiness
Drinking and offending related (N = 9)	5.11	8.11	3.00
Drinking and offending not related (N = 8)	2.75	6.50	1.13
	ns	ns	p < .05

3. *Sexual beliefs.* Mean scores on the sexual beliefs questionnaire are presented in Table 3. No significant differences were found between the two groups.

Table 3: Mean Scores on Sexual Beliefs Questionnaire

	Factor 1. Nervousness	Factor 2. Guilt	Factor 3. Sex without love	Factor 4. Fun
Drinking and offending related (N = 9)	15.78	9.33	3.89	5.22
Drinking and offending not related (N = 8)	13.63	11.00	5.37	10.00
	ns	ns	ns	ns

Conclusions

Results show that rapists who say their offence was alcohol-related are very heavy drinkers, whereas rapists whose offence was not alcohol-related drink in quantities comparable with general population norms. Alcohol-related rapists are moderately dependent on alcohol, as indicated by SADD scores.

Rapists whose offence was alcohol-related scored significantly higher on an expectancy of increased riskiness after drinking. There are only two items in this factor: (a) After drinking alcohol I have sex with people that I wouldn't have sex with when I was sober; and (b) After drinking alcohol I am more likely to do something that is sexually risky. Faced with the evidence from past events, it is hardly surprising that rapists whose offences were alcohol-related score high on this factor. Sex-related alcohol expectancies may be construed as representations of prior experience, but expectancies also *predict* future behaviour. That is, if offenders believe that they are likely to do something that is sexually risky after drinking alcohol, then this may become a self-fulfilling prophecy. Clearly, drinking alcohol is a high-risk situation for some rapists. Whilst abstinence may be a suitable goal for some people, high rates of relapse from abstinence must influence our interventions. We need to design cognitive-behavioural interventions which address outcome expectancies.

General Conclusions

The findings presented here indicate that alcohol outcome expectancies do differentiate offender groups. In the first study, offenders whose crimes were alcohol-related expected more global positive change, and those who offended against the person expected more positive social change. In the second study, rapists whose offences were alcohol-related expected drinking to lead to risky behaviour. Obviously, both research studies were conducted after the event, and drinking experiences change expectancies. It cannot be said, therefore, that these expectancies existed prior to offending. Nevertheless, these expectancies may well predict future behaviour after drinking, and alcohol outcome expectancies may, therefore, be valid targets in interventions to reduce alcohol-related crime.

A range of interventions are relevant for offenders in reducing substance use and related crime. These include motivational interviewing, behavioural self-control training, social skills training, relapse prevention, and lifestyle modification (McMurran & Hollin, 1993). Interventions such as these may take effect in part by changing outcome expectancies, and there is evidence that expectancies correlate with treatment outcome (Connors, Tarbox, & Faillace, 1993; Guydish & Greenfield, 1990). However, interventions may be augmented with a direct expectancy challenge component. Expectancy challenge used with male college students in an experimental situation has been shown to reduce alcohol consumption significantly more than alcohol education, or an assessment-only control (Darkes & Goldman, 1993). The expectancy challenge intervention consisted of giving subjects either alcohol or a placebo, then requiring them to participate in group tasks (a word game and a debate). Subjects were then asked to identify those who had consumed alcohol and those who had not. All subjects made some errors in identification. Information about the role of alcohol expectancies was then given. The purpose was to challenge and break down misleading alcohol expectancies.

Positive outcome expectancies appear to hold greater predictive power for drinking than do negative outcome expectancies. That is, heavier drinkers hold more positive outcome expectancies than do lighter drinkers, whereas negative outcome expectancies do not differ significantly (Brown, Creamer, & Stetson, 1987).

Goldman, Brown, Christiansen, and Smith (1991) suggest that in heavy drinkers, drinking behaviour is an overlearned behaviour, and controlled by automatic processing (as opposed to controlled processing which is evident in novel situations). In automatic processing, expectancy elements relating to reinforcement are more retrievable than those relating to punishment. The clinical direction suggested by these findings is that positive outcome expectancies relating to substance use should be modified; that is the aim should be to attenuate positive expectancies rather than strengthen negative expectancies.

Lang and Sibrel (1989) have criticised research investigating the relationship between alcohol and crime as having become stagnant, owing to the persistent pursuit of a single simple causal relationship. They state unequivocally that we must recognise the complexity of human social behaviour and, where alcohol-related crime is concerned, the study of interactions among drinking, the person, and the situation will offer better insights. Outcome expectancies may be an important link between drinking and crime in that they represent these interactions. Pihl and Peterson (1993) acknowledge the role of outcome expectancies in alcohol- and drug-related crime, and point out that our knowledge about the effects of drugs other than alcohol is poor, since research in this area is made difficult by bureaucratic restrictions. Whilst there is obviously much work yet to be done, the research findings presented here make a modest contribution to our understanding of the interaction between alcohol expectancies, drinking, and crime.

References

Brown, S.A., Creamer, V.A., & Stetson, B.A. (1987). Adolescent alcohol expectancies in relation to personal and parental drinking patterns. *Journal of Abnormal Psychology, 96*, 117-121.

Brown, S.A., Goldman, M.S., & Christiansen, B.A. (1985). Do alcohol expectancies mediate drinking patterns in adults? *Journal of Consulting and Clinical Psychology, 53*, 512-519.

Brown, S.A., Goldman, M.S., Inn, A., & Anderson, L.R. (1980). Expectations of reinforcement from alcohol: Their domain in relation to drinking patterns. *Journal of Consulting and Clinical Psychology, 48*, 419-426.

Collins, J.J. (Ed.) (1981). *Drinking and Crime*. New York: The Guilford Press.

Connors, G.J., O'Farrell, T.J., Cutter, H.S.G., & Logan, D. (1987). Dose-related effects of alcohol among male alcoholics, problem drinkers, and nonproblem drinkers. *Journal of Studies on Alcohol, 48*, 461-466.

Connors, G.J., Tarbox, A.R., & Faillace, L.A. (1993). Changes in alcohol expectancies and drinking behavior among treated problem drinkers. *Journal of Studies on Alcohol, 53*, 676-683.

Darkes, J., & Goldman, M.S. (1993). Expectancy challenge and drinking reduction: Experimental evidence for a mediational process. *Journal of Consulting and Clinical Psychology, 61*, 344-353.

Davidson, R. & Raistrick, D. (1986). The validity of the Short Alcohol Dependence Data (SADD) questionnaire. *British Journal of Addiction, 81*, 217-222.

Goldman, M.S., Brown, S.A., & Christiansen, B.A. (1987). Expectancy theory: Thinking about drinking. In H.T. Blane and K.E. Leonard (Eds). *Psychological Theories of Drinking and Alcoholism*. New York: The Guilford Press.

Goldman, M.S., Brown, S.A., Christiansen, B.A., & Smith, G.T. (1991). Alcoholism and memory: Broadening the scope of alcohol-expectancy research. *Psychological Bulletin, 110*, 137-146.

Goldman, M.S., Christiansen, B.A., & Brown, S.A. (1987). *Alcohol Expectancy Questionnaire - Adolescent Form*. Odessa, Florida: Psychological Assessment Resources, Inc.

Guydish, J., & Greenfield, T.K. (1990). Alcohol-related cognitions: Do they predict treatment outcome? *Addictive Behaviors, 15*, 423-430.

Lang, A.R., & Sibrel, P.A. (1989). Psychological perspectives on alcohol consumption and interpersonal aggression. *Criminal Justice and Behavior, 16*, 299-324.

Leigh, B.C. (1990). The relationship of sex-related alcohol expectancies to alcohol consumption and sexual behaviour. *British Journal of Addiction, 85*, 919-928.

Lindman, R., & Lang, A.R. (1986). Anticipated effects of alcohol consumption as a function of beverage type: A cross-cultural replication. *International Journal of Psychology, 21*, 671-678.

McMurran, M. & Bellfield, H. (1993). Sex-related alcohol expectancies in rapists. *Criminal Behaviour and Mental Health, 3*, 76-84.

McMurran, M., & Hollin, C.R. (1989). The Short Alcohol Dependence Data (SADD) questionnaire: Norms and reliability data for male young offenders. *British Journal of Addiction, 84*, 315-318.

McMurran, M., & Hollin, C.R. (1993). *Young Offenders and Alcohol-Related Crime: A Practitioner's Guidebook*. Chichester: Wiley.

McMurran, M., Hollin, C.R., & Williams, M. (in press). Alcohol expectancies in male young offenders.

Nurco, D.N., Hanlon, T.E., & Kinlock, T.W. (1991). Recent research on the relationship between illicit drug use and crime. *Behavioral Sciences and the Law, 9*, 221-242.

Pihl, R.O., & Peterson, J.B. (1993). Alcohol/drug use and aggressive behavior. In S. Hodgins (Ed.) *Mental Disorder and Crime*. Newbury Park, Ca.: Sage Publications.

Raistrick, D., Dunbar, G., & Davidson, R. (1983). Development of a questionnaire to measure alcohol dependence. *British Journal of Addiction, 78*, 89-95.

Sher, K.J. (1985). Subjective effects of alcohol: The influence of setting and individual differences on alcohol expectancies. *Journal of Studies on Alcohol, 46*, 137-146.

Southwick, L., Steele, C., Marlatt, A., & Lindell, M. (1981). Alcohol-related expectancies: Defined by phase of intoxication and drinking experience. *Journal of Consulting and Clinical Psychology, 49*, 713-721.

Teahan, J.E. (1988). Alcohol expectancies of Irish and Canadian alcoholics. *The International Journal of the Addictions, 23*, 1057-1070.

Socio-Cognitive Skills and Female Crime: A Study of Institutionalized Women Offenders

Ana M. Martín-Rodríguez and Ana M. Rodríguez-Rodríguez

Criminological theories have dealt almost solely with offenses committed by men. The main interest of criminologists has been centered on the study of the idiosyncratic nature of crime committed by women and the differential involvement in offending by men and women. The few works about women offenders have viewed them as personally accountable for their criminal behavior and their deviation because of individual pathologies (Brown et al., 1991). Although women offenders are fewer than men offenders, they are also in need of effective psychosocial interventions and, in this sense, a deeper knowledge about their characteristics as a group is essential (Palmer, 1983/1992).

It is of particular interest to observe to what extent women offenders share a series of peculiarities that would allow us to differentiate them from men offenders. Our purpose is not to defend the need for a Feminist Criminology as proposed by Daly and Chesney-Lind (1988), but to stress the opportunity for the study of those characteristics of women offenders that have not been reflected in traditional criminological analyses.

The study of women's offending behavior started at the beginning of the last century. Since then, some biological and psychological theories of scarce explanatory power have followed (Clemente, 1987). It was during the 1960s that the rise in the rate of offending by women and the sexual revolution, among other factors, produced a significant increase of interest in women's criminality. During this time a group of criminologists began to study offenses and socialization processes in women, favoring a change in the emphasis from individual to environmental factors that intervene in women's offending (Brown et al., 1991). Among the theories generated those of sex role socialization and equal opportunity stand out.

The theory of sex role differentiation has been developed by Hoffman-Bustamante (1973). She explained the lower rate of offending by women by emphasizing the assigning of different roles to boys and girls during the socialization process. The nature of the feminine role would also determine less violence and less use of strength in women's offending, in comparison to men's.

The equal opportunity theory as applied to female criminality can be seen as closely related to the theory of sex role differentiation and has in Figueira-

MacDonough (1982) its main representative. The fundamental thesis of this author is that the increase in misbehavior by women is due to the growth of opportunities given to women as a result of their increased participation in society. Under similar alienating pressures and with the same access to legitimate opportunities, individuals who are supposed to have similar characteristics would engage in the same right or wrong behavior, irrespective of gender.

Both explanations are reasonable and could be combined quite easily, to the extent that the second involves the first. The final product could be then integrated with Platt and Prout's (1987) formulations, in which Bandura's (1973) social learning theory has been explicitly applied to crime and delinquency. From their point of view, the acquisition of misconduct by either men and women could be explained using learning mechanisms, among which observational learning especially stands out. Real or symbolic models to which individuals are exposed to within the socialization process play a fundamental impact on the kind of behaviors they display. These models would obviously be different depending on the gender role individuals have to adopt.

Platt and Prout's (1987) explanation also borrows from Bandura (1973) the idea that individuals play an active role in the learning process, in the sense that they can create their environment in different ways. This reality perceptive construction is mediated by cognitive factors in such a way that a defective development of socio-cognitive skills underlies differences in offending behavior, not only between women and men but among other social categories.

This relationship between offending behavior and cognition has been analyzed by different authors during recent years. Many of them agree in asserting that there is enough empirical evidence to conclude that offending and non offending individuals are different in their level of socio-cognitive skills. Similarly, it has been said that not only offenders are defective and that not all of them are (Ross and Fabiano, 1985), but in practice these warnings have not been as stressed as the possibilities that this framework has for rehabilitation.

Research on socio-cognitive deficits has been seldom centered on women offenders, nor has it analyzed different types of offenders very often. In this context, it is common to talk about offenders as if they were a homogeneous group, converting what in origin was a critical element for rehabilitation of some groups of offenders into an unanswerable criminogenic factor. Therefore it is not surprising that many works inform more about the effectiveness of socio-cognitive skill training than about previous differences between offenders and non offenders, and/or differences among types of offenders.

Socio-cognitive skills can be classified in two broad categories, although many authors refer to both indistinctly: social skills and interpersonal problem-solving skills.

In relation to social skills, some deficiencies in male offenders compared to male non offenders have been shown by several studies (Freedman et al., 1978; Oyserman and Seltz, 1993). The works in which women offenders are explicitly analyzed are rare and many are limited to the implementation of training programs, taking for as granted that previous deficits exist (e.g., Spence, 1979). Research comparing women offenders to women non offenders is more the exception than the rule, but when conducted such research points to less ability in the former (Gaffney, 1984; Gaffney and McFall, 1981; Ward and McFall, 1986). Also there are some data suggesting that violent (Hains and Herrman, 1989) and sexual (Valliant and Antonowicks, 1991) offenders are more deficient than others.

In relation to interpersonal problem-solving skills, four categories can be differentiated: alternative thinking, consequential thinking, means-end thinking, causal thinking and perspective taking. Several works suggest that offenders have deficient alternative thinking (e.g., D'Zurilla and Goldfried, 1971; Platt et al., 1973) but without comparing them to non offenders. The only work in which this differential analysis is made (Ollendick and Hersen, 1979) shows that non offenders are the most lacking. Data about women or other groups of offenders are not available.

Concerning consequential thinking, means-end thinking and causal thinking, Spivack and Levine's (1963) work stands out. These authors verified that non offenders are less faulty than offenders but also that middle class offenders are more lacking than the rest. In a study carried out in Spain, Báguena, Beleña and Díaz (1993) have shown that drug addicted women offenders are more deficient in consequential thinking than non addicts. Likewise, more recently Higgings and Thies (1981) have confirmed Spivack and Levine's (1963) results on means-end thinking.

The study of causal thinking in the offender population has received attention mainly from Spivack and his colleagues (Spivack and Levine, 1963; Spivack et al., 1973; Spivack et al., 1976). Conclusions they have reached suggest that offenders are more deficient than non offenders in this skill. In a second study carried out in our country, Báguena and Beleña (1993) have observed that recurrent women offenders are more skilled in causal thinking than non recurrent. Likewise, in the study by Báguena, Beleña and Díaz (1993) cited above, it was confirmed that drug addicted women offenders score less on this skill than non addicts.

Perspective taking is perhaps the interpersonal problem-solving skill that has received most attention. Many authors conceptually identify a defective development of this skill with social deviation. However, this relationship has been verified only in some research (e.g., Ellis, 1982; Deardoff et al., 1977), whereas in others it has been found that offenders score higher than non offenders (e.g., Kurtines and Hogan, 1975). More detailed analyses have shown that the most violent offenders are also the most deficient (Ming and Prentice, 1988). In a third study carried out in Spain, Díaz and Báguena (1989) found that a group of adolescent girl delinquents scored higher on a factor of feeling identification than a group of badly socialized adolescents, and the latter more than a group of non problematic adolescents. The pattern is reversed for adolescent girls. Non problematic adolescent girls score the highest, followed by badly socialized adolescent girls and lastly by delinquent girls.

Differences between non offending men and women are not clear either. Bethencourt (1989) carried out research with 601 subjects of an average age of 34 years and showed that there were no significant differences between men and women in any of the five skills analyzed. Differences due to gender were again not found in relation to perspective taking by Bengtsson and Johnson (1992), Platt et al. (1987) and Sprinthall and Burke (1985). However women are presented as more empathic than men as studies by Adams et al. (1979), Bryant (1982), Hoffman (1977), Hoffman and Levine (1976), Mehrabian and Epstein (1972) and Sagi and Hoffman (1976) have shown.

Given the lack of consistency among previous studies, this work has the aim of analyzing the role of socio-cognitive skills in explaining female offending in particular, and crime in general. With this purpose we examine to what extent offending women differ from non offending women in several interpersonal problem-solving skills, comparing them to offending and non offending men. Skills under study are perspective taking, alternative thinking, causal thinking, consequential thinking and means-end thinking.

It was suggested that in relation to these five skills: (a) there are no differences between offending and non offending women; (b) offending men are more deficient than non offending men; and (c) in general women score higher than men.

Results from this analysis could be specially useful in designing and implementing future training programs for offenders. Underlying this statement is the conviction that a deeper knowledge of the characteristics and typology of subjects whom such programs are focused on could have favorable effects on their success (Palmer, 1983/1992).

Method

Subjects

116 subjects participated in this study. All of them had Spanish citizenship and were included in one of four groups of 29 persons each: offending women, non offending women, offending men and non offending men. These groups were similar in age, socio-cultural level and place of residence. Subjects' ages were between 20 and 30 years and their academic levels were in general Certificado de Estudios Primarios (4-year level) and Graduado Escolar (8-year level). Also, they lived in marginal neighborhoods, located on the periphery of the city of Santa Cruz de Tenerife.

The female offender group was composed wholly of inmates with Spanish citizenship in the women's unit of the Centro Penitenciario Tenerife II. The group age average was 25.86 and the standard deviation 3.07. Offenses that caused their imprisonment were: drug trade, (58.7%), prostitution (20.7%), drug use (10.4%), robbery (3.4%), possession of weapons (3.4%) and murder (3.4%). Male offenders were selected to be similar to women offenders in age and socio-cultural level. The average age of the men was 24.86, with a standard deviation of 3.73. Offenses that caused their imprisonment were: robbery (73.1%), drug use (20.1%), possession of weapons (3.4%) and drug trade (3.4%).

Both groups of non offenders were selected from the participants of several courses given by the Instituto Nacional de Empleo (INEM, Employment Office) in Santa Cruz de Tenerife. The average age of the men was 23.96, with a standard deviation of 3.16. The average age of the women was 24.40 and the standard deviation 3.93.

Design

This research follows a 2x2 factorial design, with two independent variables, gender and criminality, with two levels each. Dependent variables number five: perspective taking, alternative thinking, causal thinking, consequential thinking and means-end thinking. Controlled variables are age, educational level, citizenship and place of residence.

Instruments

The five questionnaires applied in this study were elaborated by Bethencourt (1989) to measure socio-cognitive skills, following Spivack et al.'s (1976) formulations. Each of these instruments was composed of 15 problem situations about which subjects have to give their opinion.

The means-end thinking questionnaire is used to measure the ability to orient oneself and to conceptualize means to reach a goal, step by step. The alternative thinking questionnaire assesses the ability to elicit alternative solutions to a complex interpersonal situation. The causal thinking instrument involves the degree to which subjects think spontaneously in terms of possible causal elements of a problematic situation. The perspective taking instrument measures the capacity to adopt the point of view of the persons who take part in a particular problem situation. Lastly, the questionnaire to assess consequential thinking considers subjects' capacity to anticipate behavior consequences.

In coding subjects' answers to the questionnaires, norms given by Bethencourt (1989) were closely followed. His suggestion concerning the intense training of people who do the coding to facilitate a high level of agreement was especially taken into account. This training was successful to the extent that final levels of agreement oscillate between 94.5% and 91.0%. Crombach's Alpha values for each questionnaire were also adequate, between .96 and .90.

Procedure

The procedure followed was similar in the four groups. The five questionnaires were assembled in a booklet that was given to each subject following the standard procedure for paper and pencil tests. In a few cases, however, subjects' problems with reading and/or writing made individual interviews necessary. These subjects were in both offender groups.

Results

To test whether gender and criminality were related to the five socio-cognitive skills studied, data were analyzed using five ANOVAs. Results are as follows.

The perspective taking skill was not related significantly to gender or criminality (see Figure 1), although the probability associated with gender was close to significant ($p = .07$). The interaction between both variables had an acceptable level of significance ($F(1, 114) = 6.12$; $p = .015$). But offending men ($M = 67.76$) did better ($t(56) = 2.42$; $p = .019$) than non offenders ($M = 52.64$). On the contrary, non offending women ($M = 68.73$) rated higher than the offenders ($M = 65.33$), but the difference was significant at a 0.052 level ($t(58) = .81$). Men offenders did not differ significantly from women offenders. In relation to the non offenders ($t(56) = 3.40$; $p = 0.001$), women scored higher ($M = 68.73$) than men ($M = 52.64$).

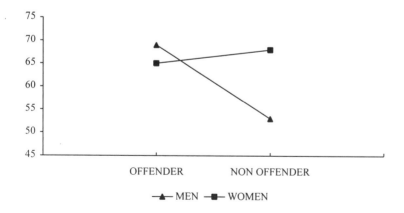

Figure 1: Mean Scores in Perspective Taking as a Function of Gender and Criminality

Consequential thinking was significantly related to gender ($F(1, 112) = 4.17$; $p = .043$) (see Figure 2), with women ($M = 32.74$) at a higher level than men ($M = 27.82$). Also, neither criminality nor its interaction with gender was significant, but the difference between offending men and women was (t(57) = 3.25; p = .003). In this case women offenders (M = 34.03) score higher than men offenders (M = 30.06). No significant differences between offending and non offending women, or offending and non offending men, were found.

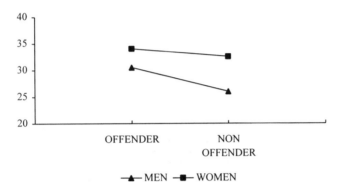

Figure 2: Mean Scores in Consequential Thinking as a Function of Gender and Criminality

Causal thinking was not related significantly to gender, but was to criminality (F(1, 113) = 8.15; p = 0.005) (see Figure 3). Offenders scored higher in this case (M = 38.27), when compared to the non offenders (M = 29.36). Differences between men and women were not significant in either of both groups, but women tended to score higher than men here also.

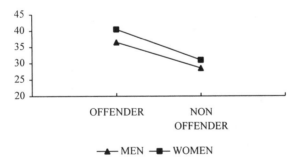

Figure 3: Mean Scores in Causal Thinking as a Function of Gender and Criminality

Regarding alternative thinking (see Figure 4), a significant association with gender was found (F(1, 113) = 10.23; p = 0.002). Again women (M = 33.26) did better than men (M = 26.47), irrespective of their criminological status. In the same way offenders were more skilled than non offenders, though not at a significant level.

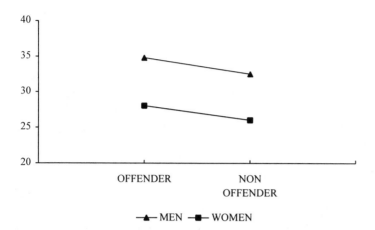

Figure 4: Mean Scores in Alternative Thinking as a Function of Gender and Criminality

Lastly, gender was significantly related to means-end thinking (F(1, 113) = 9.39; p = 0.003) (see Figure 5); women (M = 35.39) were more competent than men (M = 28.15). When we compared both genders as a function of subjects' criminological status, we observed that the difference between offending men and women was not significant, but that it was between non offending men and women (t(55) = 3.83; p = 0.00). Additionally, offenders were shown to be more skilled than non offenders, although the significance level was trivial.

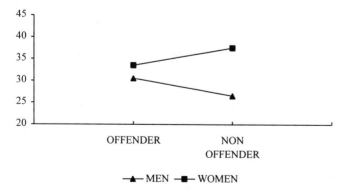

Figure 5: Mean Scores in Means-Ends Thinking as a Function of Gender and Criminality

Discussion

In general terms, we have found, first, that offending women scored significantly higher than non offending women on causal thinking and, although not at a significant level, in consequential thinking and alternative thinking. They were less skilled in perspective taking and in means-end thinking, but not significantly.

These results suggest that we should look for other factors that are more important in relation to the social rehabilitation of women offenders, at least as far as the group under study is concerned. This group, however, was composed of all the Spanish women inmates in the institution when the research was carried out. Thus, it seems that the socio-cognitive skill level is not a crucial factor in explaining the criminological status of these women, to the extent that the comparison group had a similar level and they were not in prison. Perhaps their ability in means-end thinking, and especially in perspective-taking should be analyzed in detail before making more general conclusions, basically because they were asked to say what were the feelings of a person who appeared in a story, but not to adopt different perspectives around a specific situation. Moreover, the task is predominantly cognitive, and no emotional or affective mechanisms were favored.

Another result to emphasize was the fact that offending men scored significantly higher than non offending men in perspective taking and, although not to an appropriate significance level, in causal thinking, consequential thinking, means-end thinking and alternative thinking; that is, in all the five skills being studied. In introducing this study it was stated that there was some research whose conclusions point to this direction. However, it is still interesting to confirm that the relationship between criminality and cognition is complex. Again it is important to emphasize that our conclusions are limited to the group under study, and that the possibility of finding deficits in other offender groups should not be rejected. But from a pragmatic point of view, the offenders that were assessed corresponded to the types of male inmates most frequently found in Spanish prisons.

In relation to differences between women and men offenders, our results show that the former have a significantly higher level than the latter in consequential thinking and in alternative thinking, and a higher but not significant level in causal thinking and means-end thinking. Men scored higher but not to a significant level in perspective taking. Again perspective taking is a skill that deserves future research efforts. But in dealing with the present research we can conclude that, with the exception of perspective taking, if male offenders do not seem to need training in socio-cognitive skills, women offenders need this training even less.

Lastly, in general women scored significantly higher than men in alternative thinking, consequential thinking and means-end thinking. Also they were more skilled in causal thinking, but not at a significant level. Results on perspective taking suggest that among non offenders, female superiority is maintained, whereas among offenders, it is men who score highest but not significantly.

In short, our results seem to show that the fact of being a man or a woman is more relevant than being an offender or a non offender, at least with regard to socio-cognitive skills.

References

Adams, G., Schvaneveldt, J. and Jenson, G. (1979). Sex, age and perceived competency as correlates of empathic ability in adolescence. *Adolescence, 14*, 811-818.

Báguena, M. & Beleña, M. (1993). Pensamiento causal: Efecto de un programa de entrenamiento en mujeres delincuentes institucionalizadas. In M. García (Comp.) *Psicología social aplicada en los procesos jurídicos y políticos* (pp. 135-144). Madrid: Eudema.

Báguena, M., Beleña, M. & Díaz, A. (1993). Habilidades interpersonales y consumo de drogas en mujeres delincuentes. In M. García (Comp.) *Psicología social aplicada en los procesos jurídicos y políticos* (pp. 153-158). Madrid: Eudema.

Bandura, A. (1973). *Aggression: A social learning analysis*. Englewood Cliffs, NJ: Prentice-Hall.

Bengstsson, L.G. and Johnson, L. (1992). Perspective Taking, empathy and prosocial behaviour in late childhood. *Child Study Journal, 22*, 11-22.

Bethencourt, J. (1989). *Evaluación de habilidades sociales en adultos*. Unpublished doctoral dissertation, Universidad de La Laguna.

Brown, S., Esbensen, F. & Geis, G. (1991). *Criminology. Explaining crime and its context*. Cincinnati, OH: Anderson.

Bryant, B.K. (1982). An index of empathy for children and adolescents. *Child development, 53*, 413-425.

Clemente, M. (1987). *Delincuencia femenina: Un enfoque psicosocial*. Madrid: UNED.

Daly, K. & Chesney-Lind, M. (1988). Feminism and criminology. *Justice Quarterly, 5*, 497-538.

D'Zurrilla, T. & Goldfried, M. (1971). Problem-solving and behaviour modification. *Journal of Abnormal Psychology, 78*, 107-126.

Deardoff, P., Kendall, P. & Finch, A. (1977). Empathy, Locus of Control and anxiety in college students. *Psychological Reports, 40*, 1236-1238.

Díaz, A. & Báguena, A. (1989). Factores personales. Análisis estructural en adolescentes delincuentes y no delincuentes. *Delincuencia, 1*, 277-306.

Ellis, P. (1982). Empathy: A factor in antisocial behaviour. *Journal of Abnormal Child Psychology, 2*, 123-133.

Figueira-MacDonough, J. (1982). *Female delinquency: A review*. Michigan: University of State of Michigan.

Freedman, B., Rosenthal, L., Donahoe, C. & Schudt, D. (1978). A social behaviour analysis of skills deficits in delinquents and non-delinquents. *Journal of Consulting and Clinical Psychology, 46*, 1448-1462.

Gaffney, L. (1984). A multiple-choice test to measure social skills in delinquents and non delinquents adolescent girls. *Journal of Consulting and Clinical Psychology, 52*, 911-912.

Gaffney, L. & Mc Fall, R. (1981). A comparison of social skills in delinquents and non-delinquents girls using a behavioral role-playing inventory. *Journal of Consulting and Clinical Psychology, 49*, 959-967.

Hains, A. & Herrman, L. (1989). Social cognitive skills and behavioral adjustment of delinquent adolescents in treatment. *Journal of Adolescence, 12 (3)*, 323-328.

Higgings, J. & Thies, A. (1981). Social effectiveness and problem-solving thinking of reformatory inmates. *Journal of Offender Counselling Services and Rehabilitation, 5 (314)*, 93-98.

Hoffman, M.L. (1977). Sex differences in empathy and related behaviours. *Psychological Bulletin,* *84*, 712-722.

Hoffman-Bustamante, D. (1973). The nature of female criminality. *Issues in Criminology, 8 (2),* 117-136.

Hoffman, M.L. and Levine, L.E. (1976). Early sex differences in empathy. *Developmental Psychology, 84*, 557-558.

Kurtines, W. & Hogan, R. (1975). Sources of conformity in un-socialized college students. *Journal of Abnormal Psychology, 80*, 49-51.

Mehrabian, A. and Epstein, N.A. (1972). A measure of emotional empathy. *Journal of Personality, 40*, 525-543.

Ming, L. & Prentice, N. (1988). Interrelations of empathy, cognition and moral reasoning with dimensions of juvenile delinquency. *Journal of Abnormal Child Psychology, 16 (2)*, 127-139.

Ollendick, T. & Hersen, M. (1979). Social skills training for juvenile delinquents. *Behavioral Research and Therapy, 17*, 547-554.

Oyserman, D. & Seltz, E. (1993). Competence, delinquency and attempts to attain possible selves. *Journal of Personality and Social Psychology, 65*, 360-374.

Palmer, T. (1992). The "effectiveness" issue today: An overview. In L. Travis III, M. Schwartz and T. Clear (Eds.), *Corrections. An issues approach* (pp. 257-271). Cincinnati, OH: Anderson. (Original work published in 1983)

Platt, M.W., Golding, G. and Kevig, P. (1987). Lifespan differences in adult thinking about hypothetical and personal moral issues: Reflection or regression? *International Journal of Behavioral Development, 10*, 359-375.

Platt, J. & Prout, F. (1987). Cognitive behavioral theory and interventions for crime and delinquency. In E. Morris & C. Braukmann (Eds.), *Behavioral Approaches to Crime and Delinquency Handbook of Application*, (pp. 27-60). New York: Plenum, 477-497.

Platt, J., Scura, W. & Hannon, J. (1973). Problem-solving thinking of youth incarcerated heroin addicts. *Journal of Community Psychology, 1*, 278-281.

Ross, R. & Fabiano, E. (1985). *Time to think: A cognitive model of delinquency prevention and offender rehabilitation.* Johnston City, Canada: Institute of Social Sciences and Art.

Sagi, A. and Hoffman, M.L. (1976). Empathic distress in the newborn. *Developmental Psychology, 12*, 175-176.

Spence, S. (1979). Social skills training with adolescents offenders: A review. *Behaviour Psychology, 7*, 49-57.

Spivack, G. & Levine, M. (1963). *Self regulation in acting-out and normal adolescents.* Washington D.C.: National Institute of Health.

Spivack, G., Platt, J., Altman, D. & Peizer, S. (1973). Adolescent problem-solving thinking. *Journal of Counselling and Clinical Psychology, 42*, 787-793.

Spivack, G., Platt, J. & Shure, M. (1976). *The problem-solving approach to adjustment: A guide to research and intervention.* San Francisco, CA: Jossey-Bass.

Sprinthall, N.A. and Burke, S.M. (1985). Intellectual, interpersonal and emotional development during childhood. *Journal of Humanistic Education and Development, 24*, 50-58.

Valliant, P. & Antonovicks, D. (1991). Cognitive behaviour therapy and social skills training improves personality and cognition in incarcerated offenders. *Psychological Reports, 68*, 27-33.

Ward, C. & Mac Fall, R. (1986). Further validation of the problem inventory for adolescent girls: Comparing caucasian and black delinquents and non-delinquents. *Journal of Consulting and Clinical Psychology, 54 (5)*, 732-733.

An Empirical Approach to Offender Profiling

J.L. Jackson, J.C.M. Herbrink and P. van Koppen

What is Offender Profiling?

Over the last few years there has been an upsurge in public and media interest as well as scientific research in the area of crime analysis known as offender profiling. The basic motivation underlying the development of this type of analysis is the desire to apply scientific methods to police investigations and thereby increase the likelihood of successful detection of criminals. Whilst the actual methods being explored by various research groups vary considerably, they share a common goal in that all attempt to facilitate detection by objectively predicting characteristics of offenders such as age, personality and life style.

Several methods are available which tackle offender profiling from an analytic bottom-up approach. This profiling has mainly involved using statistical analysis - such as cluster techniques or multivariate analysis - on large data bases to see whether it is possible to classify offenders with respect to aspects of the crime and personal characteristics. As is the case in several other countries, such data bases exist or are in the process of being assembled in the Netherlands. Another method which is currently being used in our institute to develop an offender profiling system for domestic burglaries is based on AI techniques. Using data collected from analyses of police files, transcripts of observations made by the police at the scene of the crime, structured interviews with detectives and interviews with convicted burglars, a computer-based "profiler" is being developed which should be able to assist the police in their investigations.

A further approach to profiling, and the one which we will consider in more depth in this chapter, is that adopted by the American FBI. It is a more top-down oriented approach which is based on in-depth interviews with a restricted number of convicted murderers plus the extensive experience of detectives in the homicide field. It is an investigative technique which seeks to objectively identify the major personality and behavioural characteristics of serious offenders based on an analysis of the crimes he/she has committed. This emphasis means that not all types of crime are suitable for this particular type of profiling. For example, cases involving destruction of property, assault or murder during the commission of a robbery are generally unsuitable since the personality of the criminal is frequently not revealed in such crime scenes. Contact crimes, on the other hand, particularly those where the criminal has demonstrated some form of psychopathy, seem to offer the best chance of useful information relating to personality characteristics being disclosed. Although obviously an oversimplification, the basic blueprint for the FBI approach involves considering the available aspects of the crime scenes; the nature of attacks; forensic evidence; information related to the victim; then classifying the offender and finally referring to the appropriate predicted characteristics. Results from such investigations are incorporated in a framework which basically classifies serious offenders according to whether they are "organised" (which implies that murderers plan their crimes, display control at scene of crime, leave few or no clues and the victim is a targeted stranger) or "disorganised" (which implies that murders are not planned and crime scenes show evidence of haphazard behaviour), or a mixture of the two. This approach represents an educated attempt to provide law enforcement agencies with detailed information about the personal characteristics of an unknown individual who has committed a violent crime (Geberth, 1981). The information is obviously not summarised and given to the police in the form of the name, address and phone number of the guilty person but is a psychological profile describing the personality of the killer. This profile should then be used by detectives working on the case to reduce the potential search area and to direct their further investigations.

Effectiveness of FBI Profiling Techniques

As readers of *"The Silence of the Lambs"* as well as viewers of numerous television programmes will no doubt be aware, profiles based on the FBI methodology are portrayed as producing a high success rate. Although this may indeed be the case, the claim is not easy to verify independently since, in the main, there is not much published data about FBI cases available. Although the basic blueprint of the approach is clearly described in the training manuals, more detailed descriptions of how specific profiles actually develop from the information available does not appear in the FBI research literature (e.g. Sexual Homicide of 1988). For the reader many explanations no doubt underlying the deductions remain vague and unclear and the processes involved in reaching a personality profile are not revealed. This paucity of information has given rise to the view that profiling may have more elements of an art form than a science: that success is based on educated intuitions resulting from experience rather than on applying scientific measures. Moreover, the lack of a corpus of published studies makes it very difficult to establish how effective profiling techniques actually are. Some members of the Behavioral Science Unit of the FBI are aware of this problem as is indicated by McCann (1992, pp. 479). He wrote, "Another area of potential value is the design of so-called 'consumer satisfaction' studies (...). Under this research paradigm, resulting profiles can be assessed for their accuracy and validity by those who make use of the profiles, namely criminal investigators and police agencies." He did not, however, refer to any studies that had actually explored consumer satisfaction.

Experimental Questions

In 1988-89, crime analysis became an important issue in the Netherlands and this interest led to a Dutch detective, experienced in homicide cases, taking part in a one-year training course in profiling techniques at the FBI Academy in Quantico, Virginia. On his return to the Netherlands, he was seconded to the National Criminal Intelligence Division (CRI) of the National Police Agency where, together with a forensic psychologist, he began offering profiling and investigative assistance to police colleagues who requested help. From the beginning of the contact with the FBI, members of the CRI have been aware of the necessity of objectively evaluating the efficacy of such a project for the Netherlands and of understanding the processes involved in the technique. This has led to collaborative research which is initially exploring three basic questions:

- How do police investigative teams view the advice given by a professional profiler?
- What are the processes involved in criminal personality profiling?
- Are there substantial differences (quantitative and/or qualitative) between the processes used by a professional profiler, an intelligent novice and an experienced detective?

A Consumer Report

The first experimental question focuses on an issue that has a direct bearing on the professed goal of profiling: If the aim of profiling is to objectively predict characteristics of offenders in order to assist the police in their investigations, then surely how the police evaluate the effectiveness of the profiles they are given should be of prime importance. Only by asking the consumers themselves can researchers ever ascertain what, if any, specific profiling information and which particular details are of most assistance in guiding their investigations.

From the very beginnings of the Dutch venture with profiling, the stated desire to objectively evaluate the efficacy of the service as it developed included approaching the consumers. A consumer evaluation study was therefore carried out early in 1993 to gauge police satisfaction with the service (for a full report of the study, see Jackson, van Koppen & Herbrink, 1993). Although almost forty cases had been presented to the CRI team by this time, they were in various stages of completion. In order to achieve some level of conformity, the cases selected for evaluation had to meet several selection criteria. These included the following: the complete set of case papers (i.e., the police files, forensic reports, crime scene photographs, etc.) had to be available to the CRI team; a final report (or profile, if made) had been completed and delivered to the police force; and sufficient time had elapsed for the investigating team to act on the advice given. Twenty cases met these criteria. They varied from sexual homicide to threat and were not only spread geographically over different regional police forces in the Netherlands but also included two cases in Belgium. The actual breakdown of the cases was as follows: 8 sexual homicides; 4 murders; 4 rapes; 1 disappearance; 2 threat cases and 1 child sexual abuse series. One prominent member (e.g. head of the investigating team) from each case was contacted and an interview was arranged. The questions guiding the interview included the following:

- How did the team know about the services offered by the profiling group?
- Why did the team decide to get in contact with the profiling group?
- What were the team's expectations in contacting the profiling group and what sort of help/advice were they hoping to get?
- How did the team experience the contact at a personal level?
- How did they rate the usefulness of the advice/help they were given - did it meet their expectations or were they disappointed or surprised that the help was in a different direction than they had anticipated?
- Would they ask for similar help in the future or did they have ideas about other sorts of support/advice systems that would be either equally or more beneficial to officers in the field?

The approach adopted to collect answers to these types of question was as unstructured and non-directive as possible although a back-up procedure in the form of a checklist was used in the final stages of the interview to ensure that all of the relevant questions had actually been discussed.

Advice Offered

While it may be assumed that a profiling team's basic task is to produce a profile, such a job description would hide both the depth and breadth of support that such an independent team can actually offer. Trained profilers have high demands in relation to the amount of information they require to produce a profile and when this is not available, no profile is forthcoming. This was also the case in our study: of the 20 cases examined, only six were found by the CRI team to be suitable for profiling. As far as the other 14 were concerned, in some, there was already a suspect in custody: in others, there were simply not enough data available; and in yet another, a disappearance case, there was no crime scene. This lack of suitable information for profiling did not mean, however, that no assistance could be offered. On the contrary, our interviews showed that a whole package of help was available - help of the sort subsumed under the broader label of "criminal investigative analysis" as used by the FBI. This includes advice such as investigative suggestions, personality assessment and interview techniques which may often be as useful to the investigating team as an actual profile. Moreover, the assistance given was seldom simply of one type. Apart from one instance of threat assessment, all the cases we examined resulted in a combination of assistance being offered (e.g. profile + investigative suggestions + advice on interviewing techniques).

Evaluation of Advice Received

The evaluations of the interviewees were divided into three categories: very useful, reasonably useful and not very useful. The broad conclusion to be drawn from the ratings was that the majority of detectives interviewed could be viewed as satisfied customers: of the 42 evaluations made, only two were viewed in a completely negative light. Of the 7 respondents who had received help on interviewing techniques, all judged the advice to be very useful; of the 8 personality assessments given, 6 were rated as being very useful and 2 as reasonably useful; 12 of the 17 investigative suggestions given were rated as being very useful, 4 as reasonably useful and only 1 as not very useful. In summary, therefore, the great majority of advice falling under the broader label of criminal investigative analysis was rated very highly indeed. Moreover, transcripts of the interviews revealed another important function of the expert team: that of teaching. Irrespective of the crime they had been investigating, the majority of those interviewed remarked spontaneously that the contact with the crime analysis group had been something of a *general learning experience*. They described how much they had learned from the experience of simply discussing the case with experts who were not directly involved in the case, how many new ideas and work strategies they had acquired and how useful these would be in future investigations. While hard to quantify, this teaching role is an important measure of consumer satisfaction and this type of help should be available to police forces who request it.

But what of profiles? Did the positive satisfaction with other types of advice extend to profiles? How successful were they? We have already mentioned that only 6 of the 20 cases studied actually resulted in a profile being produced. Four of these six related to sexual homicides, one to a rape case and the other to a child sexual abuse series. Judgements in relation to the six profiles were mixed with two being judged as positive, three as intermediate and one as negative. Drawing conclusions from such judgements is therefore difficult. Another means of evaluating profiles of course would be to look at success rate. Did the profiles that were made actually help the police to the extent that the perpetrator was found? In the first instance, the answer to the question seems to be negative with no criminal yet being caught as a direct result of the profiles made. We must not be too quick to censure profiles, however. A further investigation of the possible reasons for lack of success given by the interviewees themselves revealed that in 4 of the cases the profile as such was not actually used. In two cases, the reasons appear to be of a financial or organisational kind. Another reason for the lack of acceptance in a couple of cases related to differences of opinion between the police investigation team and the CRI team that resulted in little use being made of the profiles. Given that this evaluation study was carried out retrospectively and the subjective views of all those interviewed may therefore be confounded with both memory and hindsight bias problems, it is difficult to do more than simply state these differing views. At present, we have no way of evaluating whether the profile was indeed inadequate or wrong or whether we are dealing with a case of inflexibility in the teams involved.

Another type of criticism that was expressed by the persons involved in a number of the cases was more fundamental and therefore also more worrying. The criticisms related to the generality of the profile and thus to the lack of specific detail. Perhaps the teams who made such criticisms were dissatisfied because their high expectations were not met. A number of those interviewed did certainly indicate that they had expected far more detailed information, perhaps not at the level of a name, address and telephone number, but certainly more than the generalities they thought they were given. Such criticisms bring us round to the other basic question we are interested in, namely the processes involved in producing a profile.

The FBI approach has developed over the years into a systematic process that follows a sequence of widely accepted stages. These are data assimilation; crime classification; crime reconstruction and finally, profile generation. This latter stage includes hypotheses about demographic and physical characteristics, behavioural habits and personality dynamics of the perpetrator. Moreover, as can be seen in the left-hand column of Table 1, the profiles generated in this way tend to follow a standard format. Though one may attempt to defend the choice of uniformity in terms of cognitive economy, at the same time this uniformity tends to detract from the dynamism and impulse of the final product and may account for the dissatisfaction expressed by a number of the detectives we interviewed. It is at present difficult to make many quantitative judgements on this issue. Apart from the small number of successes explicitly described by Canter (1994), it is difficult to find published literature (other than autobiographical accounts) that independently compare a profile with the characteristics of a perpetrator once he is caught.

Another way to try to understand why the profiles that were made were so general would be to explore in more depths the processes involved in the production of a profile. This leads us to a consideration of the second and third basic questions we formulated earlier in the chapter.

Detection as Problem Solving

In our daily lives, both at home and in the workplace, we are continuously being faced with problems that require to be solved: these may vary from trying to determine why the vacuum cleaner will not function properly, to scheduling our teaching, research and appointments in such a way that sufficient time is still available for reading. Problem solving is therefore a major human activity and the work of crime investigators is no exception but can easily be fitted into the same framework: detectives are presented with a problem, for example a murder, and their task is to solve the problem, namely to find the murderer. As with most other types of problem, the correct solution will frequently only be reached as a result of exploring different paths - many of which may turn out to be dead-ends. While trained profilers may be presented with a similar murder case, their task appears to be somewhat different: their aim is not to find the murderer per se, but instead, based on behavioural knowledge, to produce a description of the type of person the murderer may probably be and to offer this to the police to assist them in their hunt for the murderer. In other words, profilers aim to offer detectives an extra set of search heuristics that will suggest more targeted, and hopefully more fruitful, paths to follow.

Table 1: The Standard Format of an FBI Profile is Shown in the Left-Hand Column; The Summary of the Profiler, Translated into the Same Format is Presented in the Middle Column; The Right-Hand Column Shows the Same Format for the Detective's Profile.

Standard Format	Profiler	Detective
1. Demographic information: age, race, occupation, marital & socio-economic status	1. White male, 30 years or older. Functions reasonably well in society. Possibly has partner - woman may look like a child	1. Male, 18 years or older. Not physically strong. Hair not blond
2. Educational level, intellectual functioning	2. Average intelligence	2. ---
3. Legal & arrest history	3. Has prior record	3. Probably first offence and possibly the last
4. Military background	4. ---	4. ---
5. Family characteristics	5. ---	5. ---
6. Habits & social interests	6. Occupation possibly related to children, enjoys driving	6. ---
7. Evidence in relation to crime scene	7. Knowledge of geographical area	7. Knowledge of geographical area
8. Age and type of vehicle	8. Car in the middle range. Car in good condition	8. Type of car not clear
9. Personality characteristics, possible forms of psychopathology	9. Normal fuctioning, not mentally disturbed. Socially adept. Sexually competent. Not sadistic	9. Friendly, normal behaviour. Has sexual problems
10. Suggested interview techniques	10. ---	10. ---

If we accept the assumption that crime detection is simply another example of human problem solving then it should be possible to use some traditional methods of cognitive psychology to explore the processes used by experienced profilers as well as experienced detectives and try to understand how these differ - if they indeed do differ. We can then seek answers to empirical questions such as: What do trained profilers actually do? How do they infer offender characteristics from offence characteristics? How do experienced detectives go about solving a complex sexual crime? Do their methods differ significantly from a professional profiler or do they intuitively use a sequence of steps that is in fact similar to those listed in FBI manuals?

Human Expertise

One method used by cognitive psychologists to explore expertise in specific domains has been to utilise verbal protocols to compare expert and novice (or learner) behaviour. Before examining the specific domain of crime investigation in some detail, let us first consider one stable finding which has emerged from various studies comparing the performance of experts and novices (e.g. VanLehn, 1989).

• In general, strategy differences are found with experts adopting a top-down and novices a bottom-up strategy
• In general, experts perform faster than novices

Since it is particularly relevant for our further discussions let us consider the first finding in some more detail. A top-down approach implies that the processing of information is guided by information already stored in memory; i.e. by the prior knowledge, expectations determined by context, and concepts acquired from past experience. This is in contrast to novice behaviour which is predominantly bottom-up in nature, in other words, since the knowledge base relating to the particular domain under consideration is still so limited, processing is directly and almost solely affected by the information input.

Since expert detective skills have seldom been considered within an expert/novice paradigm, let us speculate on how these strategy differences might apply in the criminal investigation domain. As an expert in crime, we would expect the experienced police detective to adopt a top-down approach. In other words, when he comes to examine a crime scene, his knowledge of previous crimes as well as of the ways and workings of criminals allows him not only to organise his thinking and actions within a particular framework or scenario but also to fill in gaps in his information. As an expert, the detective has at his command a large portfolio of scripts and episodes from which to construct a scenario that fits the critical events of the crime; he will then use this scenario as a basis for actively searching for further evidence which, by inference, should exist if the chosen scenario is to have validity. In short, a detective's skill may rely less on the processes he uses but more on the depth and breadth of his specific knowledge base.

Somewhat earlier in the paper we described the FBI approach as being top-down oriented. If expert detectives also use top-down strategies, where, if anywhere, does the strength of the FBI approach lie? Do differences lie in quantitative measures of domain specific knowledge and/or are there genuine qualitative differences in approach? These are obviously empirical questions which can only be answered satisfactorily by experimental investigation.

An Empirical Study

The way we have attempted to explore the processing of profilers and detectives is to carry out an exploratory, in-depth study using three subjects: a professional FBI trained profiler; an experienced detective from the Rotterdam police force; and a colleague who is a psychologist used to reading police files but mainly for civil offences. We have been fortunate in being allowed to use all the documentation relating to the sexual murder of a young boy (H) which took place seven years ago but still remains unsolved. The three subjects were given access to all the available information and were asked to "think aloud" as they worked through the files and attempted to develop a profile of the perpetrator. In cases where they remained silent too long they were prompted. They were filmed as they worked through the files (which took each of them almost a full working week).

Results

These will only be described briefly and will be based solely on the analyses of the profiler and detective (a more comprehensive article including the data of the psychologist is in preparation).

Data assimilation

The first stage for both participants was the gathering of information relating to the case. The time that each participant spent on collecting information of different types is shown in Table 2. Whilst accepting that any conclusions based on these data must be tentative in the extreme, let us nevertheless attempt to fit them within the general findings of the novice/expert paradigm.

From the table, it is clear that there are two types of police files: the main files including all written statements; and a more extensive set of files which are more in the nature of a log book and include all the tips and information that is gathered on a daily basis from all possible sources. There was a large difference in the amount of time the profiler (17h 23m) and the detective (9h 01m) spent reading these reports. If, as we had predicted, the profiler adopts a top-down strategy this was certainly

Table 2: The Amount of Time Spent by Both Profiler and Detective in Data Assimilation

	Profiler	Detective
Police reports (main)	4h 54m	6h 28m
Police reports (tips)	12h 29m	2h 33m
Forensic report	14m	16m
Photos of crime scene	26m	1h 9m

coupled with an extremely precise reading of all available information and this took a long time. The reading strategy adopted by the detective, on the other hand, was based on his own high standards of police practice. In his view, in any well conducted investigation, the main files should always contain all the important information relating to the case and therefore, he need not spend too much time reading the various "tips" that had been received. In this respect, he differed fundamentally from the profiler who expressed a somewhat more cynical view of general standards of police reporting. In his opinion, investigative "bookkeeping" was frequently inadequate[1] and log books frequently contained important information that did not reappear in the official files. For this reason, it was important that everything was read.

Differences were also found in the time spent by both in studying the photos of the crime scene. These time differences may be explained by the particular task situation: the profiler has been explicitly trained to study photos in order to pick out relevant features and can therefore be viewed as an expert at this particular task. He therefore performs it relatively quickly. The normal work pattern of the detective on the other hand, is to either visit the scene of the crime personally or, at least, to have some local knowledge of the location of a crime he is investigating. He had therefore much less experience of the task he was asked to perform and, as a result, took longer. He returned to studying the photos on several occasions and spontaneously reported that he picked up new information and ideas on each occasion.

Reconstruction of the crime

Both the profiler and the detective used the data they had assimilated to reconstruct the crime. The main points of each reconstructions is summarised in Table 3. An inspection of this table shows that, while certain similarities exist, differences are also apparent (e.g. location of crime scene 1). Until the perpetrator is found, it is impossible to judge which of these reconstructions is the correct one. They are,

---

[1]   A view that was subsequently endorsed by the detective at the debriefing session.

however, closely related to the profiles that are made. For example, an examination of item 3 in Table 1 (legal and arrest history) shows that the profiler who stated in his reconstruction that the offender is cruising around looking for victims, described the perpetrator as having a prior record. For the detective, on the other hand, the meeting with the victim was more of a chance encounter and he assumed that the crime was probably the first and possibly the last the offender would carry out.

Table 3: A Summary of the Most Important Elements of the Reconstruction for Both the Profiler and Detective

	Profiler
*	Offender is cruising, looking for victims
*	Unexpected encounter with H. - uses ruse - H. goes willingly
*	Crime scene 1 - somewhere outdoors
*	Partially undressed (top half)
*	Oral sex - sperm in mouth
*	During or shortly after sexual encounter strangled - with hands
*	Redressed
*	Transportation to crime scene 2 (known to offender) - to prevent discovery of body
*	Offender leaves scene quickly
*	Discard garment
	Detective
*	Offender uses ruse (e.g. ask directions) to get H. into car. H. goes willingly
*	Crime scene 1 = car
*	Garment off
*	Forced to have oral sex - sperm found in mouth
*	H. escapes
*	Offender catches him - face down in the dirt - kills him probably with rope
*	Transportation to crime scene 2 (known to offender) - to prevent discovery of identity
*	Interrupted - escapes in panic
*	Throws garment away

Problem solving strategies

Having described several differences in outcomes, let us now consider briefly how the differences came about. In what ways did the problem solving strategies of the profiler differ from that of the detective. For both, the starting point was the data itself (the WHAT). The processes they used to analyse these data, however, were rather different. From the transcript of the profiler's protocol, it was clear that, as he read the information, he was trying to build up a picture of the type of person the perpetrator was. While he read everything very carefully, his analyses were guided in a top-down fashion by a mental checklist which included domain-specific knowledge based on probability judgements. This related to factors such as knowledge of different offender types, generating selection rules, matching current crime with previous crimes and predicting post-crime behaviour. He used this knowledge to interpret and structure the data he was assimilating. A working hypothesis was then made and an initial reconstruction of the crime was developed. Further reading of the file resulted in refinements being made to his working hypothesis and an elaboration of the reconstruction. Based on these, he developed an initial summary of the case listing some of the characteristics of the probable offender (the WHO). A brief overview of a few of the statements taken from the summary are shown in the middle column of Table 1 written in a format similar to the FBI standard. The profiler then took this summary to Quantico. This is in line with the normal methods employed at the FBI Academy. The actual preparation of a profile is seen as being essentially a group process: the trainees are first taught to work through a number of well defined stages such as we have discussed earlier and must then present their case to their colleagues in what is called a brainstorming session. (The brainstorming session around this case was tape recorded and analysed. The final profile will be discussed elsewhere, Jackson et al, in preparation).

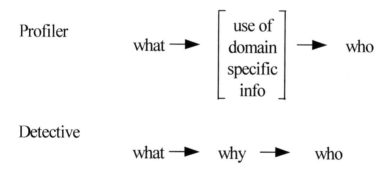

Figure 1: General Processing Strategies Used by Profiler and Detective in Solving the Problem

The starting point for the detective was the crime itself. This was the problem that had to be solved and as he studied the files, he focused on details (the WHAT) that could be used as evidence to convict the perpetrator (the WHO). Unlike the profiler, he constructed a picture of the crime very quickly and only then did he formulate working hypotheses which he then sought to confirm. From his transcripts, it was clear that his reading of the autopsy reports and study of the crime scene pictures was guided by a search for the motive for the crime (the WHY) and that this variable was important in arriving at a possible WHO. While he did produce a description of the possible suspect (the profile which we have summarised in an FBI fashion in the right hand column of Table 1), his main concern was with matching the evidence he had acquired to possible suspects. His goal was clearly to find the offender and to produce enough corroborating evidence to convict him.

Conclusion

The expert/novice paradigm we have used to examine differences between a detective, a profiler and a psychologist has proved to be very time consuming. Progress has been made, however, and process models for all three are reaching the final stages of completion. What the short description of the results has hopefully shown, however, is that the approach is indeed a viable one and that we can learn a lot about the processes underlying specific profiling techniques from its use.

The profiler and detective whom we researched tackled the case very differently: they had different goals and used different strategies to reach them. While the detective worked in a more bottom-up fashion assimilating more and more details and attempting to corroborate and weigh up their value as evidence at each step, the profiler brought with him a wide range of experience of similar cases and used this knowledge in a top-down fashion to analyse and interpret the case information. While our detective had many years of general experience and came to us with high recommendations, his experience with this specific type of case was quite limited and this lack of probabilistic knowledge resulted in more novice-like bottom-up strategies being applied.

References

Canter, D. (1994). Criminal shadows: Inside the mind of the serial killer. London: Harper Collins.

Geberth, V.J. (1981). Psychological profiling. Law and Order, 29, 46-49.

Jackson, J.L., van Koppen, P.J., & Herbrink, J.C.M. (1993). Does the service meet the needs? Technical Report, NSCR 93-05.

McCann, J.T. (1992). Criminal personality profiling in the investigation of violent crime: recent advances and future directions. Behavioral Sciences and the Law, 10, 475-481.

VanLehn, K. (1989). Problem solving and cognitive skill acquisition. In M.I. Posner (Ed). Foundations of cognitive science. Boston, MA: MIT Press.

The Criminal Psychologist: Between Tradition and Utopia

Vicente Garrido Genovés

Introduction

Each time I have discovered that I have made a mistake, or that my work has been less than perfect, and when I have been contemptuously criticised and even over-estimated to the point of my own mortification, my greatest consolation has been to tell myself time and again that "I have worked to the best of my ability, and nobody can do more than that." (Darwin, 1993, p.73).

These are the words of Charles Darwin, extracted from his autobiography. They illustrate, with the greatest simplicity, the scientist's tenacity in laying, stone by stone, an accessible path towards knowing reality, and, eventually, towards the improvement of this reality for the greater welfare of the human race.

At the onset of contemporary scientific criminology initiated by the discoveries of Darwin, there is a general spirit of this same genre, a desire to discover how to improve society. This, in fact, is an important path originating from the utopia of liberalism and positivism. Psychology, impelled by the same sources (where canons of utilitarianism and functionalism triumph), also participated in the impetus to achieve a more scientifically organised society, which would be, in those times, the aim of a greater welfare for all. Criminal psychology was then born in the very heart of one particular utopia: that of comprehending human beings and designing methods of prevention and treatment to lead us towards a crime-free society. Independently from the way in which some of these initial proposals manifest themselves, the reformist movement for criminals and young offenders is an attempt to develop a science which may improve the human condition.

The tradition held in the field of legal psychology is the result of over one hundred years of scientific research. It consists of a significant heritage of knowledge, the sum of efforts of the previously mentioned utopias, with the addition, after the 1930s, of works driven by another utopia: socialism - with its ideals of egalitarianism and social justice (Young, 1992).

This progress has earned psychology recognition as an important science in the twentieth century. Although legal psychology took more time in gaining its position in the market of rendering services to society, it would probably be quite correct to say that today no modern state can disregard the services of the psychologist in the administration of criminal or civil justice. In other words, it may be asserted that psychologists have shown our benefit to the world, and proven ourselves of use.

Judges, in fact, need to consult us when dealing with a minor, or when deciding who should take custody of a child in a case of divorce. Likewise, victims receive support and comfort from us when they have to restore their lives, altered by the impact of the suffered offence. Society also relies upon psychologists for the elaboration of programmes for offenders, whether in prison or in the community. Our work helps to impede new offences, or a least, our diagnosis and classification facilitate this process. Furthermore, this contributes towards the objective of a safer and fairer coexistence, including for the offenders themselves within this society.

More than one hundred years after psychologists began to attempt to comprehend and predict human behaviour, we can conclude the following: we are useful to society, and we contribute towards the reduction of human suffering and towards the increase in the quality of life. The problem is that concepts such as "quality of life" and "welfare" are used all to often in discussions without any real meaning, when what is really relevant is the appearance of what is desired, rather than what is actually done. However, although politics often thrive on the language of appearances, what is less justifiable is that psychologists should sympathise with such a "laissez faire" social policy, where the importance of the discourse lies in utility rather than effectiveness; i.e. the fulfilment of objectives which advance towards solving the problems defined by society, whether concerning the prevention of child and woman abuse, juvenile delinquency, or drug abuse.

The fundamental argument of this paper is that the psychologists working in the field of law have made huge efforts to try to show society that we are of use. These efforts are apparent when considering our previous lack of social penetration, which has now given way to the moment when we try to prove our effectiveness in problem-solving. When defending our claim to be beneficial, we wanted to show that we could be of service, that it was important to accept directly the fact that the psychologist has much to say about many of the law-related areas: the dispute of child custody, the diagnostics of criminals and young offenders, counselling to judges when passing sentence, assistance to a rape victim, etc. It would appear that society and institutions have accepted this presence, although to a varying degree depending on the country or the sphere in question. It is also clear that although we cannot be dormant in the struggle to obtain an even greater representation (or utility, if I may be allowed to use this expression as a synonym of social relevance), the end of the millennium must witness the initiation of the struggle towards effectiveness in legal psychology.

We cannot simply be satisfied with pursuing the priority of showing our utility; we must climb onto the next and important rung - that of proving our effectiveness. In other words, it is not enough just to "be there" performing a role which, no doubt, achieves its aims. We must make society and its rulers see that our intervention is essential for the solving of important social problems.

Consequently, I propose that we take advantage of the tradition we enjoy, and return once again to utopia as the main supervisor of our efforts. We cannot continue in a tradition which has already lost much of its initial thrust provided by

19th century utopias. The new motor of our re-emergence must be effectiveness, understood as a structured strategy to obtain the desired objective. More generally speaking, we must channel our labours, in both theory and application, towards devising and testing models of analysis and accomplishment, focusing on specific social problems and contributing to their solutions.

Issues to be Considered

With regard to these fundamental concerns, this paper will attempt to emphasise which are to be the objectives and conditions to govern the transition of legal psychology from utilitarian tradition to the utopia of effectiveness - an effectiveness oriented towards resolving human problems and not towards economic achievement or other deceitful ends. In particular, I will concentrate on criminal psychology, although many of my comments can be equally applied to all branches of psychology applied to law. The reason for this is that I believe that the most important challenge for the legal psychologist is the prevention and control of human violence within the boundaries of the laws in society. The task of the criminal psychologist, therefore, is the elaboration of theoretical and applied models impeding the development of antisocial subjects, or, at least, "curing" them of this kind of behaviour in the shortest time possible. Likewise, the criminal psychologist has an important responsibility in the sphere of victimology. The domain here should be amplified - within the broad framework of prevention and control of antisocial violence - to create assistance networks and support programmes for crime victims. Of course, not to be forgotten is the psychologist's excellent relations of recent years with the police and social agents of the community to obtain a greater solidarity and conscious activity in crime prevention in neighbourhoods.

However, I am also aware that psychologists employed in the counselling of disputes at family tribunals or in the area of civil justice help to alleviate situations which could place a subject in a position of social disadvantage or incompetence. Likewise, the psychologists in the courtroom itself studying witnesses and the behaviour of the judge and jury also help to obtain a fairer and more efficient proceeding. I intend to develop this argument throughout my paper, which will be divided into various sections. First, I will show how criminal and legal psychology are now in need of the strength of a new utopia, since the 19th century utopias have accomplished their mission. Then, after pausing to consider some preliminary questions concerning the project of an effective criminal psychologist, we will proceed to the third section to determine the priorities of this new agenda for the 21st century. Fourth, I will explain the strong need of spreading a fundamental belief, essential in this new stage; this is the belief of being able to and wanting to have a less violent society. Fifth, we will consider how the criminal and legal psychologist must be sensitive to social issues, and, as certain authorised present-day scientists in this field have pointed out, they must struggle to establish themselves in a psychology of commitment.

The Strength of Utopia

For Horkheimer (1974, p.211), conformity in thought and action lead to the relinquishing of thinking and acting. To combat inertia, critical thought must be asserted: criticism should be the consequence of knowledge, an example of progress and a constant aspect of all disciplines and social system (cited in Fernández-Ríos, 1994). Elsewhere (Garrido, 1990) we have defined the role of the professional working in criminal behaviour as founded on a "critical opitmism", or, to put it another way, based on a non-conformist ideology with the "status quo" but committed to the consistent progress towards an ideal. Critical optimism seeks the approach to a utopia, endeavouring day by day to use the knowledge of science and technology as productively as possible. Its principal aim is not destruction but the creation of a reality forming the foundations of the following stage.

My recommendation is that we must not lose sight of the sense of progress in our discipline, or its ultimate aims which should be impregnating our daily chores. Tradition is important, but we must not remain stagnant, contemplating ourselves in the mirror of achievement, as the image soon fades and we become disoriented. We must gather together the purest aspects of this tradition, and go forth. As Young confirms (1992), in the evolution of criminology (also implying criminal psychology and therefore ourselves) utopias have played a highly significant role. Utopias must not to be confused with theories, even though we refer to these theories as having a certain element of utopia. On the contrary, utopian thought is intimately related to the future, directed outwards; it has a clear temperamental streak. In the words of Young (1992 p. 429):

Most significantly of all, utopias are intimately connected with hope. Utopias are inherently optimistic and continually argue for a brighter future. (...) they are a manifestation of imagination, faith, and belief and the best of them spark off these same qualities in those who read or otherwise gain experience of them (...) Because of these connections with the passions, however, the utopian mentality does itself continually generate schemes and plans of an opposing nature. There are as many dystopias as there are utopias (...) Just as utopias express hope and faith, dystopias express melancholy and despair.

Thus, utopian thought does not relinquish the attainment of an ideal, encouraged by the obvious incongruity between what it is and what it should be. It is clearly opposed to realism, which is influenced by what circumstances allow.

So, which have been the most important utopias to influence the development of criminology? Without a doubt, the three utopias constituting "a type of 'profound structure' upon which rests everything we do and think" (Young, 1992, p.432), are liberalism, positivism and socialism. The predominant focal points of research in criminology, as the causes of crime, can only be explained by its development throughout the years, if we search for the conceptual peculiarities found in these utopias. In the area of causes of crime, exactly the same emergence of positivism can be witnessed (Young, 1992, p. 433):

Within classicism, the question of the causes of crime is insignificant (which does not deny the importance ascribed to the idea of responsibility), but within positivism this quest is all-embracing. It provides the "raison d'être" of the discipline; it was the characteristic which was seen to differentiate a positive scientific approach to the study of crime of from all others, including classicism (...) Hence, upon the foundation of the search for causes it was proposed to build a wider edifice of control; the positivist project, at its purest, was to establish both a science of causes and a science of control.

Criminology, therefore, emerges and develops in the context of liberal and positivist utopias, and the research programme set in these origins to a great extent still survives today. Even the theories denying the validity of liberal-positivist criminology have to be referred to in the light of these predominant areas of research, as if unable to progress without actively opposing such models.

For Young (1992), the existence of "a feasible criminological project profoundly influenced by utopias" rejects the criticism frequently made to this discipline, i.e., that criminology has always been at the service of the dominant powers, as if an addition to the penal system. On the contrary, criminology has generally provided a strong critical sense and drive, although certain schools and criminologists were acritical with regards to power. This, however, has been considered more as the product of professionalisation, that often establishes a considerable distance with the discipline's origins; or rather, as the result of being concerned with highly restrictive aspects, which can actually cause the loss of impartiality demanded by the original utopian thought.

Consequently, it is important to accept, in the near future, that the utopian dream is not to be detained but rather expanded. This is true especially when considering that there are more than just a few socio-cultural and economical queries hovering over man and woman.

This warning note is, we believe, now quite opportune, since, from various different sources arise rumbles of intellectual threat and abandon of knowledge in favour of conserving a secure feeling based on punishment. Opposing the argument that "nothing can be done about crime" (Wilson, 1983), and the progressively "justicialism" ideologies - in the terms used by Santiago Redondo, 1993 - our responsibility will continue to be to declare, and more importantly, prove that we are able to obtain changes to benefit everyone.

Preliminary Questions

What preliminary questions are to be considered for this great new horizon in criminal psychology? I will deal with three: the first is to generalise the belief that the battle now is set in terms of effectiveness; the creation of an impatience to qualitatively surmount this stage, and aim at more and ambitious objectives. The second question to be considered is the definition of certain limits, which, in their turn, assume an awareness that psychology is not alone in the task of solving social problems. And the third preliminary question, complementary to the former, is to generate a confidence in the technology psychology has accumulated thanks to its scientific tradition.

First, and with regard to the diffusion of the utopia of effectiveness, we must remember that legal psychologists have, fortunately, enjoyed a certain success. This success can be attributed to effectiveness, in other words, to a project oriented towards solving a problem. For instance, psychologists advise judges in cases of minors in Spain before passing sentence. This has resolved to a great extent the problem of excessive legal intervention, i.e., the only criteria of the law as a response of society confronted with a juvenile delinquent. If this can be defined as a problem, which for me doubtlessly it is, then we, as psychologists, have solved a problem. However, if we go a little beyond this, and we define as a problem the case where serious young offenders do not become criminals, then obviously, we have yet to achieve effectiveness in this sphere; and concern about these projects is precisely what would allow psychology to advance, impelled by the utopia of effectiveness.

Another preliminary question is deciding which are the tasks to be legitimately borne on our shoulders without exceeding our strength, or rather, simply because we are incapable. Evidently, many criminological problems do not depend exclusively on psychologists for their solution, and, in my opinion, no sensible psychologist should, furthermore, claim the credit for psychology in such cases. In fact, the great challenges for the criminal psychologist are the great challenges of society. So, we want to prevent criminal behaviour, and have very good ideas to carry out prevention programmes, but we are all in agreement that this prevention demands an extensive social policy involving many social sectors. Thus, it becomes a problem and a objective for everyone.

This, however, does not eliminate our responsibility, because we do not easily inconvenience ourselves in our daily chores, thinking that something "needs a total change", or that "it is not my concern". What criminal psychology is considering now, along with other areas of psychology, is that we have important reasons not to be sitting with our arms crossed. A specific example of this is the magnificent recent work of Lipsey and Wilson (1993) where they analyse 302 meta-analyses carried out over the last fifteen years in the sphere of psychological, educative and behavioural treatments aimed at solving social problems or practical problems of the individual. The conclusion of this analysis was that there are abundant reasons to affirm the utility of these treatments; in other words, the employment of these psychological programmes contributes significantly towards the solution of the problems. Thus, psychology is an instrument to rely upon. The following question must then be: Towards what objectives must we direct our vision in the search for programmes which are increasingly effective?

Priority of objectives

In what follows, I will refer to the objectives that, in my opinion, we as criminal psychologists should consider within our scheme of achieving effectiveness (now I will restrict myself specifically to criminal issues .) I will allude to the necessities of my own country, mentioning some of the most important challenges - although it is impossible to be extensive - with the certainty that many of the proposals are perfectly applicable in many other locations.

Crime prevention Previously, I have said that the question of prevention is of a very wide spectrum, involving many social agents and institutions. Fine - but I believe that we can still do a lot more in this sphere, and prove that we are effective in prevention, that we really are able to deter certain youths from committing offences when entering adolescence, or becoming involved in a life replete with crime. Nowadays, we are aware of many of the key aspects of this task, the benefit of which will be felt by all. A recent preventive study (Yoshikawa, 1994) has calculated, with great accuracy, the possibilities of psychology and other related disciplines in confronting the classic (and enormous) problem of crime prevention. In short, Yoshikawa reviewed some 300 studies discussing the prevention of violence, and found that programmes combining family support and early education of children help to prevent juvenile violence and delinquency (see also Zigler, Taussig and Black, 1992). Such programmes (including the Yale child welfare project, the Houston parent-child development centre, the Syracuse family development research project, and the Perry preschool programme) allow the state to save money, and also obtain a greater economic independence for the families participating, as well as less need for the compensatory education and reduction in child abuse and neglect (Barnett, & Escobar, 1990).

So, how do these programmes work? On the one hand, the component of family support reduces the risk of violence within the family, such as a punitive up bringing, lack of supervision, abuse and a very poor level of education. On the other hand, early education reduces the risk of these problems found in the child: premature behavioural problems and low school performance. The combination of the two programmes is, in the author's opinion, essential to crime prevention.

To be more specific, programmes of this type should be carried out over a period of at least two years - preferably three or five - and give best results if begun very early on in the child's life. Visits to the parents are recommended once a week or fortnight, offering emotional help, information about raising children and their development, and support for the objectives set by the parents themselves. Finally, these programmes affirm that the children should attend play-schools or pre-school centres of a high quality.

I believe that our responsibility is to demand, in all possible circles, that programmes of this nature be carried out; and that new experiences allow the further development of a field already abundant in very real possibilities.

The prevention of child abuse and neglect (including sexual abuse) Although on many occasions, child abuse and neglect in infancy and infant-juvenile delinquency go hand in hand, it is vital to recognise that they are different problems sharing the same important causes (Garrido & Marín, 1992). Likewise, nobody can deny the urgency of confronting the insidious phenomenon of the sexual abuse of minors, although legal and social origins make it a delicate issue to undertake (Ammerman & Hersen, 1991). Be that as it may, the violence *suffered by children* is as significant as the violence shown by them; and the present programmes available to us (Wolfe et al., 1991) are a permanent reminder that psychologists have still to unearth these weapons in order to confront this conflictive situation. In other words, we have still not been able to stir the awareness and the means of society sufficiently (cf. Salter, 1988).

Complementary to this, it is important to remember that due to the significant link between the origins of criminal behaviour, child abuse and neglect and drug abuse, (see Hawkins, Catalano & Miller, 1992) it would seem likely that the consumption of addictive substances will be affected considerably by these above-mentioned prevention programmes.

The community context of rehabilitation The development undergone in Spain in terms of community intervention of offenders has been extremely limited. What is worse is that we have not even achieved that the future penal code - except with last minute rectification - contemplate the possibility of probation as an alternative to imprisonment. This deficiency has prevented alternative sentences to prison from being found within the usual catalogue of penal execution. Thus, many prisoners are robbed of the possibility whereby they could accelerate their return to a non-criminal life, and society is deprived of the possibility of different groups taking part in this rehabilitation. We psychologists have to be very stubborn on this issue, and begin our work. The first step is to prove, without room for doubt, that we can handle offenders within the community, and successfully. Our possibility focuses today on the designing of studies in open prisons and on the treatment of juvenile delinquents, where such intervention in the community is possible, and suitably diffuse the results (supposing they are good results!). What is meant here is the following: if we want probation and other community alternatives to imprisonment to become reality, we must begin by showing that we are effective with the offenders in those community contexts where we are already at work. In Spain, at least, this is yet to be achieved.

The development of the organisational perspective in the management and concept of prisons The majority of psychological research carried out in prisons has been related to treatment programmes, i.e., to a clinical perspective dealing with the rehabilitation of the offender. Lösel and Bliesener (1989) claim that such an orientation is complemented by an approach derived from organisational psychology. In Spain, Redondo also suggested this necessity some years ago (see

Redondo, 1993). Psychological tasks understood thus can be included in different spheres, such as a diagnostic strategy (including information about the real states and processes within the organisation, of its individuals and groups, such as attitudes and personality of the correctional officers, levels of stress, role problems, organisational climate, etc.), development and training strategies for the staff, and strategies of work organisation and environmental design. There appears to be no risk in saying at this stage that classic prisons are outdated with regards to organisational qualities developed by psychology.

On the other hand, I would like to make known a worry of mine which has concerned me for some time: that prison psychology in Spain runs the risk of confining itself to the eternal tasks of classification, and, at best, to treatment programmes for special groups, such as sexual offenders, inmates infected with AIDS, etc. Evidently, it as important to be concerned with these groups, but not at the cost of the majority of the other prisoners. Furthermore, I believe that the prison policy of recent years is actually neglecting, the elaboration of ambitious intervention programmes, where doubtless psychology is to play a leading role, in favour of "activities". This is an strange philosophy where many activities without any logical connection to bind them are to supplant an integrated model of intervention. In this philosophy, "socio-cultural vitality" is the central dogma and the combination of hundreds of trivial activities such as radio transmission, tiling, Spanish dancing or transcendental meditation become the greatest ambition. Occasionally even psychosocial activities such as social skills and relaxation are added to the menu, lending to the issue a greater appearance of scientific respectability. As my kind readers will no doubt have understood, I am showing a slight but deliberate irony here in order to emphasise, not that socio-cultural programmes are unimportant, but that prisons should not fall into the trap of appearances. Once again, these appearances profess the image of utility, which, at the end of the day proves to be limited. The image's background message is "have everybody constantly occupied" precisely to prevent us from channelling our efforts towards something more effective: I repeat: a comprehensive programme linking prison management to generalised activities of what is learnt in the stage of conditional release in the community.

The prevention and attention for battered and sexually assaulted women It is true that in many countries as well as in Spain, in recent years we have witnessed an important increase in the awareness and attention paid to these phenomena. Additionally, we have developed significant models for its treatment (Calhoun & Atkeson, 1991), but our great pending failure has been prevention. This objective of preventing physical and sexual assault on women has, for me, a special significance, since, through its relation to education, mass media, and the institutions of penal justice, it reveals the entire functioning of society. In other words, the attitudes and tendencies of society clearly show , by way of its demands and possibilities, the restraint in changing the social conditions that encourage the relation of coercion and contempt which always underlie in such assaults.

I am certain that we could add more objectives here, all of doubtless importance. Those above are mentioned simply to reflect the urgency of such projects, without diminishing the significance of others.

A Fundamental Belief: We Can and Want a Less Violent Society

No diligent observer can deny the tremendous extent to which violence is accepted in our society. What is worse, an extreme uneasiness is felt upon sensing the belief, so often implicitly portrayed with resignation, that human beings "are simply like that and nothing can change us". And yet, like other researchers (Lore & Schultz, 1993), I refuse to accept this theory that asserts that violence cannot be and must not be controlled. It is affirmed that the culture providing the environment of an individual plays a substantial role in the shaping of his aggressiveness, and that such control can only be beneficial. In order to consider this issue, it helps to reflect upon the well-established theory that the human being is the only gratuitously aggressive species (as proposed by Lore and Schultz, 1993), explained in the works of Lorenz (1966), with the conclusion that this theory can no longer be substantiated today. In fact, Lorenz assured us that virtually all species - except man and by the way the Norwegian rat - are able to restrain and control their aggressive instincts. In the western world, especially in the United States, it is firmly believed that imposing controls on this aggressiveness demands the high price of the loss of liberty.

However, recent research discloses only too well the existence of gratuitous aggression in chimpanzees, various types of monkey and other mammals. The number of animals killed by aggressive acts of the same species increases with the number of hours spent observing them in their natural habitat (Marler, 1976). And, as with humans, the deaths may be few, but we must remember that a slight injury can be fatal for many animals.

However, if evolution has preserved its aggressiveness due to its adaptability, it is also true that mechanisms of control and restraint have been established where the results depend basically on social experience and the present context in which the man or animal lives. Research in children shows that they are perfectly able to employ mechanisms to restrain their aggression as circumstances demand: the experiment of Besevegis and Lore (1983) shows that children unsupervised by adults are more capable of controlling their aggressiveness than those accompanied by adults. This is due to the fact they exhibit that aggression in circumstances that could have more serious consequences because of the absence of adults (to stop the fight).

Lore and Schultz (1993) agree with the teaching of the control of aggression to children, without negative consequences being produced. They quote the experiment of Olweus (1991) who showed a significant reduction in violence of school children towards their fellow students in the Norwegian school system after a programme of intervention was carried out.

Generally speaking, the control of aggression in our society can be exercised, according to Lore and Schultz, using different methods. For instance, with regards to the problem of wife battering, research carried out by Sherman and Berk (1984) showed that those husbands arrested by the police repeated this offence less than those who had only been warned, or those receiving the suggestion that they remain away from home for several hours. Therefore, occasionally the use of sanction imparted by society can have positive effects on the reduction of violence.

Now, we all know that punishment as a fundamental tool for confronting criminal behaviour is no great strategy, although there exists a certain faith in its effectiveness in the developed world on the part of society in general and numerous sectors of the political circle (a good example being the merely transitory effects in the reduction of homicides as a consequence of applying capital punishment, as compared to the consequence of life imprisonment; see Phillips and Hensley, 1984). For this reason, other recommendations would appear to be of more use, such as the control of firearms, the reduction of over-exposure to violence in mass media, prevention programmes aimed at multi-problematic families and finally the treatment of subjects previously suffering from a personal history of violence.

What is certain is that, as in other species, aggression is only one of the available options for the human being, since we have developed powerful mechanisms both for the expression and the control of violence. As Lore and Schultz correctly declare (1993, p.24):

Were we to accept the simple assumption that a great deal of human violence could be inhibited, we might then begin to develop governmental policies and societal traditions to encourage large numbers of people to learn more constructive ways to cope with life's multiple frustrations. Long ago we accepted governmental regulation of automobiles for the common good. Virtually all of us now stop for red lights and not many of us would want to drive in an area where unlicensed cars and drivers are permitted. We are also beginning to implement relatively gentle policies designed to curb other forms to destructive behaviour, such as drug abuse and smoking. Current levels of violence in American society are probably as costly - and even more amenable to change - as these addictive behaviours.

Consequently, it would seem unreasonable to assume that generalised violence is to be with us forever. We legal psychologists would do well to contend the contrary (i.e., that violence can and must be substantially reduced), as a prerequisite for the project of the new utopia of effectiveness.

A Psychology of Commitment

Criminal psychology cannot be distanced from the relentless evolution occurring in the world of science of today. One of the axes of this substantial change has been the end of the dichotomy between "what" and "what for", otherwise known as the myth of absolute neutrality in the scientific task, so far removed from the aim of research. To the contrary, nowadays, even renowned physicists are pursuing an active commitment to confront major social problems. For instance, the Nobel Prize Winner of Physics, Leon Lederman, recently declared (EL PAÍS, March 9, 1994):

I believe that, in the United States, and perhaps in other industrialised countries, a certain frustration has been aroused because we have a very strong and dynamic organisation. Yet, there are social, economic and environmental problems which are very serious. Some believe that science is to blame, the planet cannot live without a growing scientific activity. Until now, we have created science to be used by industry (obtain profits), by governments (for their proposals, whether military or otherwise), and we have been very careless in this issue. As a result, the world has some serious problems yet to be solved (...) each will have his own list.

Science currently feels a certain commitment towards the improvement of life of the human race and of the planet. The problems troubling society are defined to a great extent by that society itself. As Popkewitz asserts (1988, p.54):

Far from being isolated from society, research activity confirms certain social values, beliefs and hopes...

And not only can science not lay dormant with what it has achieved, but it cannot allow itself the luxury of accumulating more knowledge without some clear ideas of action. It must be a science with an aim. And an important priority must be to rely upon suitable technology: there is a need for more science, but this science must be effective, and at the disposition of programmes conceived to solve specific problems. Lederman again states (EL PAÍS, March 9, 1994):

Many of the problems that people complain about can be solved because we have sufficient knowledge to do so. We know how to eliminate the ghettos in our cities, how to have clean air, and clean water. We understand many of these things, but we need support.

On this issue, Paul Scott, a researcher in aggressiveness commented, after reviewing the research of the last 50 years, that "scientific research can solve the problems of destructive human violence" (1992, p.12).

However, the power of our discipline may be doubted upon taking on, along with others, a task of this magnitude. In particular, certain eminent psychologists have indicated their despondency on this issue due to the lack of unity in our discipline. As for example, Leahey (1987, p.548) assures us: "Psychologists have never agreed seriously on anything, whether defining psychology, its methods or even its theories." Jaspers pointed out (1977, p.20): "In psychology (...) the fact is that very few affirmations, perhaps none at all, can be made, that aren't objectionable somewhere along the line" (see Fernández-Ríos, 1994). Staats (1983) also spoke of the confusion existing in psychology and recommended achieving a unity to overcome this obstacle in various fields: experimental, theoretical, methodological, philosophical, organisational and in publications.

We must also consider, nonetheless, if such a unification would be desirable supposing it were possible. The position of researchers is not clear at all. As an example, Fernández-Rios (1994, p.15) at first affirms that:

(...) theoretical diversification can be useful, since it allows scientific practice to be guided in a multitude of socio-cultural contexts, to observe different problems, and consider a problem from various perspectives.

However, further on :

In prevention, tribalism shows itself in various different theoretical perspectives. For example, the model of competitiveness instead of deficit; blaming the victim for his health problems or circumstances; adopting an ecological or transactional perspective (...) this, instead of helping to describe, explain and modify the social problem to be prevented, can contribute to dividing research teams and masking a reality objectively equal for all, but apprehended under discourses which linguistically aren't incompatible, but simply different.

It would seem that Fernández-Ríos, in this last text, is against simply employing variations in language - perspectives which only differ coincidentally - in order to study this phenomenon. In the previous paragraph, nevertheless, he defended an authentic plurality of methods and focus with which to embark upon the issue to be studied. But, even so, the problem prevails, because it is difficult to define "variations" and "focuses". There is more than one author who would disagree with disregarding terms and variables which are cherished by him or her, with the only justification that there are other terms, perhaps more accurate and popular, which carry out the same function. But I can see no way of evading this task; without a common vocabulary and method, the progress of being acquainted with and modifying a reality becomes irritating and ineffective. Different focal points on a certain area to be researched are advantageous and even necessary, but only when they throw light on specific areas in the studying of a phenomenon, and do not reject the aspects we do not want to see because they interfere with our preconceived ideas of this phenomenon.

In Spain, we have witnessed this process recently, as to the polemic of whether rehabilitation was a goal and a recommendable plan of action in our prison system (see Garrido and Redondo, 1993; Redondo, 1993). It has become customary, in the heat of the debate, for some psychologists and legal scholars to pronounce that apart from constituting a debatable - if not doomed - objective, "clearly" treatment programmes could never bring about positive results, treating such a failure as an accepted fact. It cannot be denied that the most valuable contributions of legal scholars to the rehabilitation debate were their sensitivity towards individual rights and their possible abuse, (which, in the name of offender resocialisation, could have occurred), and other very general affirmations about rehabilitation as a goal. But it was also unfair that, in order to support their thesis that rehabilitation was ethically incorrect (because it implied moulding the personality of the inmate, obliging him or her to conform to the status quo), they chose to ignore the results of empirical research, which has clearly shown that certain intervention programmes achieve positive results with a great number of offenders.

Regarding the comments above, it becomes evident that presently we must promote a significant effort in order to achieve a greater unity within psychology. This, without sacrificing the plural richness of perspectives, would permit a fruitful path towards the utopia of effectiveness, and towards the solution of the different objectives mentioned in previous pages. Some authors, such as Sperry (1993), assure us that unity has been achieved under the protection of cognitive psychology, while others, such as Friman et al., (1993), testify that behavioural psychology and psychoanalysis still enjoy good health. Be this as it may, we believe that the dispute can only be settled when considering the facts, where the superiority of cognitive and behavioural models in the prevention and treatment of criminal behaviour is indubitable (Redondo, 1993; Yoshikawa, 1994; Lipsey, 1992).

Epilogue

In reply to the question whether the American Psychological Association, or any other institution, could survive another one hundred years, Skinner once commented "the more I learn about human behaviour, the less promising seems the future" (cited in Sperry, 1993, p.878). On the contrary, with the new effort of criminal psychology, sheltered by the utopia of effectiveness, we are unable to agree with this eminent psychologist. We cannot be stagnant if we want to exert a significant influence in solving social problems, nor can we maintain an aseptic position, free of values. In fact, we have already begun this in our country: the criticism that, in many parts of Spain, psychologists offered regarding draft of the penal code of 1993, or the majority's support of the penal age at 18, are both worthy considerations, a product of our reflections that we believe serve to improve society. We must embark upon rigorous research within the framework of certain confessed interests, objectives based on the physical and psychological welfare of individuals and society. Even though there may be a dispute as to what this welfare is, we would do well to adhere to the values and recommendations of the Human Rights Charter of the United Nations, recommendations of international humanitarian societies, and the values of a humanist society.

I am aware that this transition from the tradition of utility to the utopia of effectiveness cannot be achieved in every country at the same time, nor be carried out in the same fashion in all the fields of action of legal psychology. For instance, in Spain, our own country, the acquisition of our image of utility is very recent, and although it has been created in a surprisingly short period of time, - scarcely twenty years - there are still important terrains left to conquer.

Essentially, I believe, however, that opting for the utopia of effectiveness supposes a new impetus, a new form of conceptualising the application of psychology which does not mean too long a delay. Time presses on, and perhaps it would be a good idea to embrace the utopia of effectiveness as a cover letter, even in those locations where we have yet to reach the status of utility. It is true that I maybe wrong here since, before reaching effectiveness in a certain area, it is vital to research and promote the fundamental principles of knowledge. I have nothing against this, except that I believe psychology should investigate to attain effectiveness. Furthermore, in the area of criminal psychology and legal psychology, the fundamental orientation must be towards analysing and acting in order to elaborate programmes in their own right: of a social necessity, and of a defined objective, whether it is to reduce the number of delinquent families in a particular district, or the rate of adoptions which are inappropriate. The psychologists charged with applied tasks, but not directly related to the execution of the programmes, such as those carrying out tasks of diagnosis, should maximise their interventive implications, exerting themselves to show to the system their ultimate aim is that something be done with the person diagnosed; and this "something" should be carried out to the point of the appropriate effectiveness.

Recently, the case of the rape and murder of a little girl was on trial. The following is a fragment of the account in the press (EL PAÍS, March 18, 1994):

Scarcely a hundred people were present at the arrival of the alleged murderer at the provincial High Court in Lugo. José María Real entered the building with his head covered by a leather jacket. The public timidly rebuked him and asked the Civil Guard to let them see his face. "We want to see the face of the monster", they said. When the president of the tribunal of Lugo asked him what his profession was, the alleged rapist and murderer (of a nine year old girl) answered: "I don't know". From among the crowd, a woman murmured: "that of a murderer!".

This paper has deliberately been generic and theoretical. I know full well that behind my lines there is an underlying stark reality, as illustrated in these words: the offender guilty of an atrocious crime, an angry and indignant society, justice called upon to punish without mercy. However, an important part of my message originates precisely in this, in remembering that we, criminal and legal psychologists make up a force of reflection and action, beyond everyday occurrences. This means undertaking a huge responsibility: the responsibility of progressing, undetained, with the heritage of tradition, towards the hope of utopia.

References

Ammerman, R. T., and Hersen, M. (Eds.) (1991). *Case studies in family violence*. NY: Plenum.

Barnett, W. S., and Escobar, C. M. (1990). Economic costs and benefits of early intervention. In S. J. Meisels and J. P. Shonkoff (Eds.), *Handbook of early childhood intervention* (pp. 560-582). Cambridge: Cambridge University Press.

Besevegis, E., and Lore, R. (1983). Effects of an adult's presence on the social behavior of preschool children. *Aggressive Behavior*, 9, 243-252.

Butler, S. (1980). Incest: Whose reality, whose theory. *Aegis*, Summer.

Calhoun, K. S., and Atkeson, B. M. (1991). *Treatment of rape victims. Facilitating psychosocial adjustment*. NY: Pergamon.

Darwin, C. (1993 (1876)). *Autobiografía*. Madrid: Alianza.

Fernández-Ríos, L. (1994). *Manual de Psicología preventiva*. Madrid: Siglo XXI.

Friman, P. C., Allen, K. D., Kerwin, M. L. E., and Larzelere (1993). Changes in modern Psychology. A citation analysis of the Kuhnian displacement thesis. *American Psychologist*, 48(6), 658-664.

Garrido, V. (1990). *Pedagogía de la delincuencia juvenil*. Barcelona: CEAC.

Garrido, V., and Redondo, S. (Eds.) (1993). *La intervención educativa en el medio penitenciario. Una década de reflexión*. In Madrid: Diagrama.

Garrido, V., Marín, J.M. (1992). Infancia en riesgo: Violencia familiar y desviación social. *Revista Española de Pedagogía*, september-december num. 190, 563-606.

Hawkins, J. D., Catalano, R. F., and Miller, J. Y. (1992). Risk and protective factors for alcohol and other drug problems in adolescence and early adulthood: Implications for substance abuse prevention. *Psychological Bulletin*, 112(1), 64-105.

Horkheimer, M. (1974). *Teoría crítica*. Buenos Aires: Amorrortu.

Jaspers, K. (1977). *Psicopatología general*. Buenos Aires: Beta.

Leahey, T. (1987). *Historia de la psicología*. Madrid: Debate.

Lipsey, M. W. (1992). The effect of treatment on juvenile delinquents: Results from Meta-analysis. In F. Lösel, D. Bender and T. Bliesener (Eds.), *Psychology and Law. International perspectives* (pp. 131-143). Berlin: De Gruyter.

Lipsey, M. W., and Wilson, D. B. (1993). The efficacy of psychological, educational and behavioral treatment. Confirmation from meta-analysis. *American Psychologist*, 48(2), 1181-1209.

Lore, R. K., and Schultz, L. A. (1993). Control of Human Aggression. A comparative perspective. *American Psychologist*, 48(1), 16-25.

Lorenz, K. (1966). *On aggression*. NY: Harcourt, Brace and World.

Lösel, F., and Bliesener, T. (1989). Psychology in prison: Role assessment and testing of an organizational model. In H. Wegener (Eds.), *Criminal Behaviour and the justice system* (pp. 419-440). NY: Springer-Verlag.

Marler, P. (1976). On animal aggression: The role of strangeness and familiarity. *American Psychologist*, 31, 239-246.

Olweus, D. (1991). Bully/victim problems among school children: Basic facts and effects of a school-based intervention program. In D. Pepler and K. Rubin (Eds.), *The development and treatment of childhood aggression* (pp. 411-448). Hillsdale, NJ: Erlbaum.

Phillips, D. P., and Hensley, J. E. (1984). When violence is rewarded or punished: The impact of mass media stories on homicide. *Journal of Communication*, 34, 101-116.

Popkewitz, T. S. (1988). *Paradigma e ideología en investigación educativa*. Madrid: Mondadori.

Redondo, S. (1993). *Evaluar e intervenir en las prisiones. Análisis de conducta aplicado*. Barcelona: PPU.

Salter, A. C. (1988). *Treating child sex offenders and victims*. Newbury Park, CA: Sage.

Scott, J. P. (1992). Aggression: Functions and control in social systems. *Aggressive Behavior*, 18, 1-20.

Sherman, L. W., and Berk, R. A. (1984). The specific deterrent effects of arrest for domestic assault. *American Sociological Review*, 49, 261-272.

Sperry, R. W. (1993). The impact and promise of the cognitive revolution. *American Psychologist*, 48(8), 878-885.

Staats, A. W. (1983). *Psychology's crisis of desunity*. NY: Praeger.

Wilson, J. Q. (1983). *Thinking about crime*. NY: Basic Books.

Wolfe, D., Kaufman, K., Aragona, J., and Sandler, J. (1991). *Programa de conducción de niños maltratados. Orientación para padres intolerantes* . México.: Trillas.

Yoshikawa, H. (1994). Prevention as cumulative protection: Effects of early family support and education on chronic delinquency and its risks. *Psychological Bulletin*, 115(1), 28-54.

Young, P. (1992). The importance of utopias in criminological thinking. *British Journal of Criminology*, 32(4), 423-437.

Zigler, E., Taussig, C., and Black, K. (1992). Early childhood intervention: A promising preventative for juvenile delinquency. *American Psychologist*, 47, 997-1006.

Part VII
Drug Addiction Interventions

Drug Addiction Among Inmates

Serge Brochu and Louise Guyon

North-American research clearly highlights the high prevalence of psychoactive substance use among incarcerated individuals. A recent literature review (Brochu, 1995) indicates that up to 80% of North American inmates present a history of illicit psychoactive substance use.

One of the present authors directed three years ago a research project on psychoactive substance use among offenders in Québec (Brochu et al., 1992). For this research, 453 individuals under custody in detention centers of the province of Québec were interviewed (54 girls and 175 boys, under 18 years old; 94 women; 130 men). The average participation rate was 82%. Among other things, subjects were approached in order to evaluate illicit drug use in the year preceding detention. From this, it appeared that cannabis was the most popular drug for most groups except for women who preferred cocaine. Forty-seven percent of women, 54% of girls, 63% of men, and 63% of boys reported using cannabis in the 12 months preceding detention. Cocaine was second best for the groups that did not make it their first choice: 59% of women, 57% of men, 38% of boys, and 33% of girls reported having used cocaine in this period.

Let's take another example in order to better illustrate this point. In the course of his Master's degree in criminology, one of our research assistants conducted a study on drug use among inmates at Montréal's detention center. Results of this survey (Forget, 1990) indicated that *more than thre e quarters* of inmates had used illicit psychoactive substances at least five times in their lives. More than half reported having used at least one such drug in the last month before detention. These results contrast sharply with those from the general population survey "Santé Québec" (1988) which indicated that *less than 20%* of Quebecoises aged 15 to 44 had used illicit psychoactive substances at least five times in their lifetime.

Forget (1990) also interviewed the inmates concerning the drug-criminality link. More than a third of interviewed individuals reported increasing their income by engaging in criminal activities in order to pay for illicit drugs. Also, about a third mentioned "drug debts". It is therefore not surprising that many American authors establish a link between drug use and repeat offending (see Wish & O'Neil, 1991).

However, drug use does not equal addiction. Studies limited to tracking down drug use prevalence among offenders do not inform about the true nature of the addiction related problems experienced. It is therefore necessary to assess addiction using fully proven specialized techniques.

Given our experience with the Addiction Severity Index (ASI) (McLellan, Luborsky, Woody, & O'Brien, 1980) through previous studies and our understanding of the prison setting, we were inclined to believe that this index could allow a deeper recognition of the addiction-related problems experienced by inmates.

The aim of this paper consists of comparing the psychosocial adaptation of addicted versus non-addicted inmates at Montréal's detention center using the Addiction Severity Index. This comparison will give an indication of the addiction treatment needs of inmates in prison.

Method

Subjects

The study was conducted on a sample of 304 inmates admitted at Montréal's detention center during the summer of 1993 and chosen through the daily admission list on a random basis[1]. The participation rate was 85.9%.

Montréal's detention center is a provincial prison admitting those sentenced to less than two years of detention. Offenders sentenced to two years or more of detention are sent to a federal penitentiary.

The addiction severity index

A validated French translation of the Addiction Severity Index (ASI) adapted for the correctional setting was used in order to diagnose addiction and to obtain a psychosocial profile of the inmates admitted at Montréal's detention center (internal consistency ranging from .55 to .82; test retest reliability ranging from .46 to .97) (Bergeron, Landry, Ishak, Vaugeois, & Trépanier, 1992; Brochu and Guyon, 1995).

The ASI consists of a psychometric inventory measuring clusters of problems often observed among addicts (including alcoholics). It is made up of seven scales: Drug; Alcohol; Medical Status; Family/Social Relationships; Psychological Status; Employment/Support Status; and Legal Status.

A composite score can be computed for each of the scales using a predetermined set of items. Each of these scores is obtained using mathematical calculations which weigh the item's relative worth. These scores are expressed in decimals on a scale ranging from zero to one. Comparisons between addicts and non-addicts were made on these scores using appropriate statistical tests.

---

[1]   The authors are aware that this procedure of using the "flux" of inmates rather than the "stock" could underestimate addiction problems among offenders.

Results

Addiction profile

It was first determined that one-third (102) of the inmates participating in the study presented an addiction profile according to the norms developed by Brochu and Guyon (1955) (Alcohol composite score greater than 0.34 and Drug composite score greater than 0.12; these norms were developed in accordance with scores obtained by clients admitted to an addiction treatment center in Montreal).

Sample characteristics

There was no significant difference (chi-square = 1.90; p = .60) for mean age between the addicted (31.2) and non-addicted samples (30.2), both groups presenting a similar distribution, peaking between 25 and 34 years of age. The same went for schooling, presenting similar distribution curves for both groups with the bulk of subjects dropping out during high school (see Table 1).

Both groups differed on living arrangements (chi-square = 20.51; p = .009). Addicted individuals were more isolated than their non-addicted counterparts with only 16% of addicted individuals living in couple arrangements (vs. 28% for non-addicted) and 37% reporting living alone (vs. 23% among non-addicted). We notice however that addicted individuals were proportionately more numerous in reporting living with friends (13% vs. 7%). Here, we recognize the tendency for addicts to cut down on expenses so they can maintain drug use. However, if we add the number of subjects reporting living with family or friends for both groups, the difference disappears with 27% of addicted individuals and 26% of non-addicted individuals living in a setting allowing cost reduction. It then appears that this type of lifestyle may just as well be adopted by both groups (see Table 1).

The socio-demographic profile also indicated that non-addicted individuals were more active when it came to employment with 64% having a job, being in school, or being actively seeking a job (receiving unemployment benefits) as compared to 51% for addicted individuals. On the other hand, 27% of addicts and 19% of non-addicts were on welfare (social security), an indication that they had been out of work for a long period of time (see Table 1).

There is no marked difference in the grounds for custody of both groups. Most inmates were incarcerated for minor offenses against the law (e.g., unpaid parking tickets...) or parole/probation misconduct. In second place were theft and robbery. Drug crimes represented grounds of only 5% of all incarceration for both groups.

A history of prior detention was reported for 82.4% of addicts and 70.3% of non-addicts. Addicted individuals' grounds for prior detention were primarily related to offenses related to the Canadian drug law (addicted = 27.5%; non- addicted = 5.4%). The most common grounds for prior detention among non-addicted

Table 1: Socio-demographic data

	Addicts		Non-addicts		Total	
	N	(%)	N	(%)	N	(%)
Age group						
18-24 years	25	(25.0)	55	(27.4)	80	(26.5)
25-34 years	43	(43.0)	95	(47.3)	138	(45.8)
35-44 years	25	(25.0)	42	(20.9)	67	(37.4)
45 and over	7	(7.0)	9	(4.5)	16	(5.3)
Mean	31.2		30.2		30.5	
Life conditions						
Couple	14	(14.0)	55	(27.4)	69	(23.0)
Single parent	--	--	2	(1.0)	2	(0.6)
Parents	9	(9.0)	27	(13.4)	36	(12.1)
Family	5	(5.0)	12	(6.0)	17	(5.5)
Friends	13	(13.0)	14	(7.0)	27	(9.5)
Alone	38	(38.0)	46	(22.9)	84	(28.0)
Institution	17	(17.0)	44	(21.9)	61	(20.2)
Other/unstable	2	(2.0)	1	(0.5)	3	(1.0)
Civil status						
Married	12	(12.0)	55	(27.4)	67	(22.2)
Separated/ divorced	17	(17.0)	22	(10.9)	39	(13.0)
Single	71	(71.0)	124	(61.7)	195	(64.8)
Others	--	--	--	--	--	--
Activity status						
Work	50	(49.0)	122	(60.7)	172	(56.5)
Student	--	--	3	(1.5)	3	(1.0)
Pension	2	(2.0)	4	(2.0)	6	(2.0)
Unemployment	3	(3.0)	4	(2.0)	7	(2.3)
Institution	1	(1.0)	4	(2.0)	5	(1.7)
Social Security	28	(27.0)	38	(18.9)	66	(21.6)
Home	3	(3.0)	8	(3.5)	11	(3.6)
Unstable	15	(15.0)	19	(9.5)	34	(11.3)
Studies						
1-7 years	9	(8.0)	14	(7.0)	23	(7.5)
8-11 years	68	(67.0)	127	(63.2)	194	(64.1)
12 and over	25	(25.0)	61	(29.9)	86	(28.4)

individuals were minor offenses (e.g., unpaid parking tickets...) or parole/probation misconduct (addicted = 6.9%; non-addicted = 23.8%). Theft was second in both groups (addicted = 11.8%; non-addicted = 10.9%). Violent crimes such as assault or robbery were more characteristic of non-addicted individuals (addicted = 1.0% and 2.0%; non-addicted = 9.9% and 4.0%). These facts support in part the hypothesis that addicts are not violent offenders but rather are individuals who repeatedly commit crimes in order to acquire drugs.

Psycho-social profile of addicted and non-addicted inmates

The psycho-social profile was obtained using the composite scores of the ASI scales. Given the way the groups were formed, it is understanding that composite scores for the Alcohol and Drug scales were significantly different between the two groups. However, it is interesting to note in Table 2 that the addicts' profiles were systematically more severely impaired than those of other inmates.

For the Legal Status scale, we found that addicts were more prone to be accused of other offenses in addition to those for which they were currently under custody, compared to non-addicts (addicts = 50%; non-addicts = 35%; chi-square = 6.22; p = .01). When asked to rate the severity of their legal problems, 41% of addicted inmates rated them as considerably or extremely important versus 21% for non-addicts (chi-square = 19.17; p < .001). Furthermore, one quarter of addicted inmates reported it was either considerably or extremely important to get help for their legal problems versus only 8% of non-addicts (chi-square = 21.86; p < .001). It also appears that addicts have a longer history of incarceration than other inmates (t-test = 2.12; p = .04) (see Table 3). Indeed, addicts had been incarcerated for a mean of 18.36 (s.d. = 29.36) months compared to 11.42 (s.d. = 21.34) for non-addicts.

The psychological profile was also more severely impaired among addicts. Systematically more of them reported severe depression, severe tensions, hallucinations, attention deficits, or lack of anger control. During the month preceding the interview, 20% of addicts reported suicidal ideation versus 5% among other inmates with 3% of addicts having attempted to end their lives and none of the other inmates. Following this, it was not surprising to see that 47% of addicts compared to 26% of non-addicts reported being considerably or extremely preoccupied by their psychological problems (chi-square=23.41; p< .001) (Table 3).

Concerning the Family/Social Relationships scale, it appears that addicts generally reported more serious conflicts with their environment than other inmates. Only conflicts with children were less often reported by addicts. Once again, they are proportionately more numerous in considering their family and social problems as considerably or extremely severe (addicts = 28.5%; non-addicts = 12.3%; chi-square = 19.82; p < .001) and to demand some help accordingly (addicts = 15.7%; non-addicts = 3.5%; chi-square = 21.90; p < .001) (see Table 3).

It comes as no surprise that addicts also reported a more severely impaired Medical Status. They had been hospitalized more days in the month preceding the interview (addicts = 8.35; non-addicts = 6.05; t-test = 1.71, p = .09) and a greater number of them thought they required medical intervention (addicts = 23.5%; non-addicts = 11.3% for the considerably and extremely rating level) (see Table 3).

As we mentioned earlier, inmates usually do not represent a very active group; however, addicted inmates really top the mark when it comes to inactivity on the job market. The pattern repeats itself with addicts more often considering their employment situation as highly problematic and demanding help for this problem area proportionately more often (see Table 3).

Table 2: ASI Scores according to the addiction diagnosis

Scale	Addicts			Non-addicts			T Test
	Mean		Standard Deviatio	Mean		Standard Deviation	
Alcohol	.3584	N = 102	.256	.0960	N = 201	.094	10.02***
Drugs	.1735	N = 102	.114	.0231	N = 202	.033	13.05***
Medical status	.2480	N = 102	.114	.0231	N = 202	.270	2.09*
Employment/ support status	.7938	N = 100	.242	.7120	N = 200	.286	2.59**
Family/social relationships	.2466	N = 101	.214	.1391	N = 201	.151	4.52***
Psychological status	.2920	N = 102	.230	.1469	N = 202	.157	5.72***
Legal status	.4019	N = 95	.224	.2182	N = 188	.195	6.78***

Discussion

Drug addiction among inmates represents a troublesome and very real problem. Not only do inmates present an addiction profile, but they are also conscious of the importance of their drug-related problems and ask for help. For the time being, there is no addiction treatment program in the large majority of Quebec's provincial prisons. The reason given to explain this situation is the short sentences of these convicts.

Drug addiction hinders the hope of rehabilitation praised by some professionals working within the prison setting. How can we hope to diminish an individual's repeat offending without giving help to solve drug addiction?

The study of this problem area is now beyond simple prevalence inquiries. These efforts have appropriately demonstrated that inmates use drugs more often and in greater quantities than the general population (Brochu, 1995; Lipton, Falkin, & Wexler, 1992). The scope of problems related to drug use must now be investigated. We are at a stage where psychometric assessment of addiction problems is required. Of course, drug use does not necessarily equal addiction. Indeed, in this study, although about 80% of inmates reported ever having used an illicit drug, one-third presented an addict profile. Yet, it is still a very high rate: one inmate in three suffers from drug addiction.

Table 3: Self-evaluation of importance of the problem and need of treatment according to the scales

Scale		Addicts (N = 102)					Non-addicts (N = 202)				
		0	1	2	3	4	0	1	2	3	4
Alcohol	Importance	56 (54.9%)	5 (4.9%)	10 (9.8%)	20 (19.6%)	11 (10.8%)	185 (91.6%)	14 (6.9%)	2 (1.0%)	1 (0.5%)	---
	Needs	50 (49.0%)	13 (12.7%)	10 (9.8%)	9 (8.8%)	20 (19.6%)	183 (91.0%)	9 (4.5%)	7 (3.5%)	2 (1.0%)	---
Drugs	Importance	33 (15.0%)	13 (12.7%)	14 (13.7%)	19 (18.6%)	23 (22.5%)	187 (92.6%)	10 (5.0%)	3 (1.5%)	2 (1.0%)	---
	Needs	40 (39.2%)	10 (9.8%)	15 (14.7%)	15 (14.7%)	22 (21.6%)	181 (89.6%)	12 (5.9%)	6 (3.0%)	2 (1.0%)	1 (0.5%)
Medical status	Importance	63 (61.8%)	13 (12.7%)	9 (8.8%)	8 (7.8%)	9 (8.8%)	133 (65.8%)	29 (14.4%)	12 (5.9%)	15 (7.4%)	13 (6.4%)
	Needs	65 (63.7%)	10 (9.8%)	3 (2.9%)	13 (12.7%)	11 (10.8%)	162 (80.2%)	10 (5.0%)	7 (3.5%)	11 (5.4%)	12 (5.9%)
Family relationship	Importance	61 (59.8%)	2 (2.0%)	10 (9.8%)	11 (10.8%)	18 (17.6%)	159 (78.7%)	10 (5.0%)	8 (4.0%)	13 (6.4%)	12 (5.9%)
	Needs	72 (70.6%)	8 (7.8%)	6 (5.9%)	7 (6.9%)	9 (8.8%)	183 (60.2%)	6 (3.0%)	6 (3.0%)	4 (2.0%)	3 (1.5%)
Social relationship	Importance	72 (70.6%)	9 (8.8%)	11 (10.8%)	6 (5.9%)	4 (3.9%)	175 (86.6%)	10 (5.0%)	6 (3.0%)	3 (1.5%)	8 (4.0%)
	Needs	76 (74.5%)	10 (9.8%)	8 (7.8%)	5 (4.9%)	3 (2.9%)	181 (89.6%)	4 (2.0%)	8 (4.0%)	5 (2.5%)	4 (2.0%)
Psychological status	Importance	26 (25.5%)	12 (11.8%)	16 (15.7%)	28 (27.5%)	20 (19.6%)	108 (53.7%)	21 (10.4%)	20 (10.0%)	31 (15.4%)	21 (10.4%)
	Needs	49 (48.0%)	13 (12.7%)	5 (4.9%)	9 (8.8%)	26 (25.5%)	170 (84.2%)	9 (4.5%)	7 (4.5%)	6 (3.0%)	10 (5.0%)
Employment/support status	Importance	60 (59.4%)	8 (7.9%)	6 (5.9%)	7 (6.9%)	20 (19.8%)	140 (69.3%)	8 (4.0%)	12 (5.9%)	23 (11.4%)	19 (9.4%)
	Needs	62 (61.4%)	6 (5.9%)	6 (5.9%)	11 (10.9%)	16 (15.8%)	148 (73.3%)	6 (3.0%)	14 (6.9%)	13 (6.4%)	21 (10.4%)
Legal status	Importance	21 (20.6%)	17 (16.7%)	22 (21.6%)	26 (25.5%)	16 (15.7%)	69 (34.3%)	57 (28.4%)	33 (16.4%)	27 (13.4%)	15 (7.5%)
	Needs	53 (52.0%)	14 (13.7%)	8 (7.8%)	15 (14.7%)	12 (11.8%)	151 (74.8%)	20 (9.9%)	14 (6.9%)	11 (5.4%)	6 (3.0%)

0 = Not at all   1 = Slightly   2 = Moderately   3 = Considerably   4 = Extremely

Furthermore, these addicted inmates present an impaired psycho-social profile when compared to other inmates. Their lifestyle puts them more at risk of experiencing numerous disorders. These are the reasons for wanting to provide help. The challenge is to know how. After the dark years that followed Martinson's (1974) "Nothing works", a new day is dawning with a more optimistic perspective about treatment interventions within the prison setting. It is time to make our mark and demonstrate the benefits of treatment.

All of this wishful thinking being done, let's drift back a few moments into the everyday reality of the correctional services employees working inside the walls at the Montréal's detention center. The latter usually have a good understanding of criminology or of some related field while at the same time have developed an expertise of the prison setting. With a little luck, their training included one or two introductory classes on drugs. They are usually less familiar with the psychoactive effects of drugs than most inmates are. However, many have learned just enough to know that the rates of success with addicts hardly exceed 40% in one year follow-ups. What will then be their reaction to the addicted inmate encountered? They may well try to ignore symptoms indicative of the presence of addiction or deafen themselves to the calls of help coming from the addicts. Hopefully, the most likely scenario will be the one in which the addict is identified (often by means of a cursory assessment) and referred to a specialized treatment facility outside the jail after conditional or final release. This way, the correctional services will be rid of the addict by means of referral to the "utmost skillful" authority, or so perceived, in the form of the addiction treatment specialist.

In return, we can well imagine the way in which these addiction specialists will receive this "reckless rebel" who is just out and is still acting according to the norms he learned "inside". Chances are that this ex-convict referred to an addiction treatment center will drop out quite quickly if he is not under explicit pressure from the judicial system.

We are in the presence of two professional "solitudes", both acting on troubled areas conceived as independent: delinquency and addiction. The truth is not that simple. One-third of the inmates of the sample interviewed in the course of this study experienced addiction-related problems. As a parallel, numerous addicts in rehabilitation centers present a criminal history (and often a current state of legal troubles too) (Guyon & Brochu, 1994). The welfare of these individuals should not be conceived through the lens of restricted professional expertise anymore. Quite the contrary, the future of rehabilitation lies in mixed disciplines and mixed milieu interventions. Professionals within the delinquency field must do more than discuss with the addiction worker; concrete mixed settings and collaborative efforts must be conducted. There has to be a two-way movement of criminologists towards addiction treatment centers and addiction specialists towards prison and other restricted environments. At the dawning of a new "passion" for treatment intervention and recovery, this inter disciplinary collaboration appears essential or else nothing will work for society's most deprived individuals.

References

Bergeron, J., Landry, M., Ishak, A., Veaugeois, P., & Trépanier, M. (1992). *Validation d'un instrument d'évaluation de la gravité des problèmes reliés à la consommation de drogues et d'alcool. L'indice de gravité d'une toxicomanie (IGT)*. Montréal: RISQ.

Brochu, S. (1995). *Drogues et criminalité*. Montreal: Presses de l'Université de Montréal.

Brochu, S., Desjardins, L., Douyon, A., & Forget, C. (1992). Drug Use Prevalence among Offenders. In F. Losel, D. Bender, & T. Bliesner (Eds.), *Psychology and Law: International Perspectives*, (pp. 105-110). Berlin: Walter de Gruyter.

Brochu, S., & Guyon, L. (1995). An Addiction Severity Index for Inmates. *International Medical Journal, 2 (1)*, 54-58.

Forget, C. (1990). *La consommation de substance psycho-actives chez les détenus du centre de détention de Montréal*. University of Montreal: Master theses.

Guyon, L., & Brochu, S. (1994). Addiction and Criminal Background in a Public Rehabilitation Center for Drug and Alcohol Abusers. Fourth Conference on Psychology and Law. April 1994.

Lipton, D.S., Falkin, G.P., & Wexler, H.K. (1992). Correctional Drug Abuse Treatment in the United States: An Overview, in NIDA Research Monograph Series, *Drug Abuse Treatment in Prisons and Jails*, (pp. 8-30). Rockville: U.S. Department of Health and Human Services.

Martinson, R. (1974). What Works? Questions and Answers about Prison Reform. *The Public Interest, 35*, 22-54.

McLellan, A.T., Luborsky, L., Woody, C.E., & O'Brien, C.P. (1980). An Improved Diagnostic Evaluation Instrument for Substance Abuse Patients. The Addiction Severity Index. *The Journal Of Nervous and Mental Disease, 168*, 26-33.

Santé Québec. (1988). *Et la Santé, ça va?* Quebec: Quebec Government.

Wish, E. D., & O'Neil, J. (1991). Cocaine Use in Arrestees: Refining Measures of National Trends by Sampling the Criminal Population. *National Institute on Drug Abuse Research Monograph Series: the Epidemiology of Cocaine Use and Abuse, 110*, 57-70.

Addiction and Criminal Background in Rehabilitation Centers for Drug and Alcohol Abuser Clientele

Louise Guyon and Serge Brochu

Introduction

This paper is part of a series of studies on the relationship between psychoactive substance use and criminality. Literature on the subject reports relationships between these two phenomena, without however establishing, with any certainty, the significance and sense of the relationship.

It is generally accepted that drug use is quite high among persons who have been in a prison environment. Studies carried out on this subject report a high proportion of persons under the influence of drugs amongst individuals arrested for various misdemeanors. Studies conducted in the United States have pointed out that up to 80% of arrested men had traces of drugs present in their urine (Brochu, 1993; 1994). Even though similar studies have not been possible in Quebec up to now, it is known, however, from self-reported statements that a relatively high proportion of convicts have drug problems. Thus, one of these studies, (Hodgins & Côté, 1990) reports a 36% rate of abuse or dependence to at least one psychotropic drug.

Is addiction a result of or a prerequisite to delinquency? Are the two phenomena mutually linked? Whatever the link between the two, it is obvious that the presence of both problems within an individual does constitute a factor of severity, especially regarding to his social reintegration possibilities.

Most studies dealing with this double problem have been carried out on prison populations. However, convicts present only one aspect of the whole spectrum in relation to drug and crime. These studies have certain limits inherent to the data collection process itself. For example, it is not possible to ensure totally the reliability of the responses in such an authoritative context; the possibility of over-representation of drug addict offenders cannot be ignored. Finally, the results of these studies cannot be generalized to all prison populations because of the specific context of each of them. For all of these reasons, it appeared interesting to determine how this double problem is present in another population whose main characteristic is its dependence on a psychoactive substance; these are persons admitted for treatment in a public rehabilitation center for alcohol and drug abusers. Since some of these individuals are offenders, the object was to find out how they differed from other drug addicts, what their specific needs were and whether or not they received a different treatment than the other clients in the institution. Moreover, on a more practical level, we wanted to measure the effect of the implementation of a new clientele rating instrument on the treatment approach and on the range of services offered to this clientele.

The basic assumption was that the socio-sanitary profile of alcohol and/or drug addicts who have a criminal background is more deteriorated than others, resulting in decreased chances of rehabilitation. This hypothesis is supported in part by the fact that since certain drugs are illegal, involvement with the delinquent subcultures promotes living on the fringe of society and contributes to the deterioration of the social and familial context. Also, indebtedness and violent behavior, often associated with the use of these substances, increase the likelihood of the rupture of a favorable environment to social reintegration. It was assumed that the instrument used, the Addiction Severity Index (ASI), could account for this deterioration and contribute useful elements to rehabilitation activities.

Methodology

A French version of the Addiction Severity Index (McLellan et al., 1980), validated by our research team, is used to rate the severity of the clientele's problems. The validation included: an evaluation of the translation, reliability tests (internal consistency analysis and Cronbach's alpha coefficient), test-retest reliability, analysis of variance and examination of individual items, face validity as evaluated by three experienced clinicians, and finally, a test of internal validity. The results of the analyses of the psychometric qualities of the French version were judged satisfactory and allow us to consider it equivalent to the original ASI (Bergeron et al., 1992). This instrument is comprised of seven scales, each dealing with a specific type of problem often observed in drug or alcohol abusers (Guyon & Landry, 1993). These scales include: "Drugs", "Alcohol", "Medical Status", "Family and Social Relationships", "Psychological Status", "Employment and Resources" and "Legal Status".

The ASI is administered by an interviewer, during a semi-structured interview lasting from one to one and one-half hours, to all clients when they are admitted to the treatment center. It has been used routinely by the Center in the evaluation of its clients since 1990. The instrument is used to establish two rating measures: 1) a *severity* rating carried out by the interviewer based on elements dealing with the individual's lifestyle (on a scale ranging from one to nine), and 2) a *composite* score, objectively calculated for each type of problem, based on a combination of weighted items related to the current situation. This last score is expressed in decimals on a scale ranging from zero to one.

In this study, 1,054 subjects representing the whole of the male clientele admitted for treatment between May 1, 1991 and April 31, 1992 were studied. The subjects were divided into two groups: "offenders" (i.e. those who had been convicted of a criminal offense at least once) and "non-offenders" (i.e. all other subjects, whether they had been charged or not). The results obtained by these two sub-groups were compared as to socio-demographic characteristics, composite scores and the severity of their situation. Certain statistical tests were performed (Chi Square and Student's t-test) in order to see if the differences observed between the two groups were significant.

Results

Description of study population

Quebec's population is approximately 6.8 million people. Among the adult population (15 years of age and more), 6 to 10% are considered heavy drinkers, according to the General Health Surveys (Santé Québec, 1995). As for illegal drug users, there is no accurate data available on their importance. The health care system provides free services to individuals who have addiction problems. About fifteen public rehabilitation centers across the country treat more than 15,000 people each year.

One of these centers, Domrémy-Montréal, deals with the Greater Montréal Area population (3 million people). Approximately 1,700 people use its services on an annual basis. Men represent 70% of the institution's clientele; the majority of these men are between 25 and 44 years of age, and two-thirds are employed. Their education level is low and they lead rather unstable lives. They very often use several substances together with alcohol, more often than not cocaine. Finally, 45% have been convicted of a criminal offense at least once in their lives.

Age

Offenders are younger (mean age 31.1 vs. 34.4 years for non-offenders). This difference between the two groups increases with age. After 45 years of age, the number of offenders drops by almost half.

Activity status

Only 55% of the offenders have remunerated employment, compared to 73% of the other drug abusers. Almost a third are on welfare, which is 2.5 times higher than the non-offenders. Offenders have a significant non-employment record: 26% state that their longest employment period was 1 year or less, this being the case for only 15% of the non-offenders. All these differences are statistically significant.

Table 1: Socio-demographic Characteristics Among Offenders and Non-Offenders

	Offenders (N = 534)	*Non-offenders* (520)
Mean age	3.11 Years	34.4 Years
Occupation		
Work	55.3% (275)	73.2% (379)
Social Welfare	30.5% (163)	12.0% (62)
Unemployment	4.7% (25)	5.8% (30)
Others	9.6% (51)	9.1% (47)
-----> $x^2 = 56.2$	dl = 3 p < .001	
Education (Years)		
1 - 7	12.6% (67)	8.5% (44)
8 - 11	61.2% (326)	46.1% (239)
12 +	25.5% (136)	45.4% (235)
-----> $x^2 = 44.5$	dl = 2p < .001	
Actual Living Arrangements		
Couples	29.7% (159)	36.2% (187)
Alone	28.8% (154)	33.8% (175)
Parents	12.7% (68)	15.1% (78)
Family	6.9% (37)	3.7% (19)
Friends	8.6% (46)	5.8% (30)
Institution	9.9% (52)	2.7% (14)
Others	3.3% (18)	2.7% (14)
-----> $x^2 = 36.7$	dl = 6 p < .001	

Education

Offenders are also significantly less educated. Nearly three-fourths have not completed high school (vs. 46% for the non-offenders). These figures are even more significant in a context where education is state-provided up until the end of college.

Living arrangements

For this item, the questionnaire considers two points in time: a mean of the past three years and the present situation. Typically, 46% of the offenders are living as a couple and 24% say they live alone. On the whole, their living conditions are much more varied than those of the other drug addicts. What is of particular interest is the deterioration of their lifestyle when they are admitted to the institution: the percentage of those living as a couple falls to 30%. This seems to be a worsening of their situation; indeed, if it is accepted that living with a spouse ensures some degree of emotional and financial security, the break-up of the union and the change to another lifestyle may trigger a crisis situation, particularly serious if it occurs in an addiction context. Individuals who have both problems (substance abuse and criminal background) seem especially vulnerable in that area. It must be noted that at the time of the survey, 10% said they were usually living in an institution.

Composite scores

The composite score, as previously mentioned, is the result of the combination of items in each of the seven ASI scales. These items were selected because they reflect changes which occurred in the thirty day period prior to the interview and because they can provide a more reliable general estimate of the severity of the problems presented in each of the areas dealt with by the ASI. They are expressed in decimals from 0 to 1 and are completely independent of one another. They should not, therefore, be compared without standardization but rather observed to see how they vary according to the other variables, or by comparing various populations. It is impossible to calculate a global score that would synthesize the seven composite scores.

Offenders have higher scores in 5 out of 7 items and these differences are all statistically significant (see Table 2). As for the other two scores, differences are not significant. Among the scales that show a significant difference between offenders and non-offenders, it is the "Employment/Support Status" and "Legal Situation" scales in which one observes the largest differences.

In the employment situation, this difference can be explained by the fact that addicted offenders have been less employed and have had lower income in the month prior to the interview. Moreover, few of them have a valid driving license and a car; this poses a problem when looking for employment.

All the legal score items are higher for the offenders: a greater number of them are in the process of being charged, tried or sentenced (hence a higher level of chronicity among them). In fact, they perceive their situation in this regard as being much more serious, and a higher number of them are seeking specialized help. Finally, their illegal activities, as well as the earnings they gain from these, are clearly higher than those of the other clients at the center.

Offenders are also different as far as the "Family/Social Relationships" score is concerned. In this case, serious conflicts with their spouse or father are involved.

Drug abuse, for the offenders, is marked by a greater variety of products used and by a longer consumption period.

Chronicity

According to the therapists, the clients they see are often characterized by the chronicity of their drug abuse situation. Moreover, it was observed that the same is true for other aspects of their lives. Indeed, a significant proportion have at one time or another in their lives been treated for drug abuse, as well as for psychological and legal problems.

Table 2: Composite Scores Among Offenders and Non-Offenders

Scale	Offenders		Non offenders		T Test
	$\overline{x}$	(S.D.)	$\overline{x}$	(S.D.)	
Alcohol	.4268	(.270)	.4289	(.288)	1.14
Drug	.1647	(.117)	.1496	(.121)	1.07*
Medical	.1270	(.223)	.1346	(.229)	1.05
Employ/support status	.6819	(.316)	.5220	(.325)	1.06***
Family/soc.	.3666	(.206)	.3320	(.205)	1.01**
Psychological	.3746	(.102)	.3491	(.187)	1.06*
Legal	.1880	(.237)	.0919	(.185)	1.64***

*   P < .05
**   P < .01
***   P < .001

Note: All composite scores are entirely independent and therefore cannot be compared to each other.

In all those cases, offenders have the highest levels of chronicity. These differences are not surprising as far as the legal situation is concerned. But the results of substance abuse treatment are notable; almost half have previously been treated for alcoholism and 42% for drug abuse.

Table 3: Chronicity Among Offenders and Non-Offenders

	Offenders		Non-offenders		X^2
	%	(N)	%	(N)	
Treatment					
Alcohol	49.2	(262)	38.0	(197)	13.6***
Drug	42.0	(222)	25.2	(129)	33.0***
Psychological Tx.					
Hospital	15.2	(81)	11.7	(61)	3.9
Clinic	30.6	(163)	25.9	(134)	5.8*
Legal					
Probation/					
Cond. Discharge					
and/or	48.3	(258)	14.6	(76)	138.2***
Appearance					

*   P < .05
**   P < .01
***   P < .001

Treatment

It seems obvious that the situation of addicts who have a past and present criminal background is more deteriorated than that of the other addicts in the institution. The question is: can this affect the rehabilitation activities proposed to them by the institution?

First, there is no difference in the basic orientation of the treatment. Almost two-thirds of the clients are offered out-patient activities, whereas a little more than a third will at first go through an intensive stay in residence. The existence of a criminal background problem does not account for the latter measure; this means is more appropriate for individuals who have serious psychological or addiction problems, which is not necessarily the case with offenders.

Rating

Three items comprised in the ASI were considered: *first*, the rating carried out by the substance user of his condition's severity (question: "How serious do you feel your present legal problems are?" or "How troubled or bothered have you been by these employment problems in the past 30 days?"), *second*, the evaluation of his treatment needs ("How important to you now is counseling or referral for these legal problems?") and *third*, the rating carried out by the therapist, i.e. *the severity rating*. It should be noted that this last rating confirms the need for *additional* treatment or support over and above the treatment the client is presently receiving ("How would you rate the patient's need for legal services or counseling?").

In general, offenders say they are more disturbed by the problems they face in the various aspects of their lives, and their request for treatment is consistent with that statement. With the exception of the medical situation, therapists evaluate them more strictly, especially in terms of drug use, employment situation and, of course, legal situation. Do they differ in the treatment *persistence*, or the *length of time* they follow treatment? The presence of past criminal records will influence treatment persistence. On the one hand, offenders will remain in treatment for shorter periods of time; however, this situation will be inversed when the treatment has been requested by the legal system as opposed to the client himself. In other words, when the request is made by a third party, treatment persistence will be better.

Discussion

The ASI, when used in a clinical context, has helped highlight the specificity of the "Drug Abuse/Criminality" double problem clientele. The results of the analysis not only provide a better knowledge of their socio-sanitary profile, but also help identify their needs in terms of services and therapeutic approach. These needs are varied. They are particularly urgent in terms of job market reintegration, the need to

Table 4: Patient and Interviewer's Severity Rating Scale

	Offenders		Non-offenders	
	X̄	(S.D.)	X̄	(S.D.)
Alcohol				
Patient Problems *	2.2	(1.49)	2.0	(1.51)
Patient Tx.**	2.6	(1.52)	2.4	(1.60)
Int. Tx.***	4.8	(2.67)	4.5	(2.67)
Drug				
Patient Problems *	2.3	(1.60)	2.0	(1.64)
Patient Tx.**	2.6	(1.61)	2.2	(1.72)
Int. Tx.***	4.7	(2.80)	3.9	(2.91)
Medical				
Patient Problems *	0.7	(1.17)	0.7	(1.25)
Patient Tx.**	0.4	(1.01)	0.4	(1.01)
Int. Tx.***	0.7	(1.53)	0.7	(1.63)
Family/Social relationship				
Patient Problems *	2.1	(1.47)	2.0	(1.51)
Patient Tx.**	2.3	(1.47)	2.1	(1.54)
Int. Tx.***	5.2	(2.11)	4.7	(2.32)
Psychological				
Patient Problems *	2.7	(1.13)	2.7	(1.13)
Patient Tx.**	3.0	(1.13)	3.0	(1.13)
Int. Tx.***	5.5	(1.84)	5.3	(1.91)
Employment/Support status				
Patient Problems *	1.4	(1.53)	1.4	(1.58)
Patient Tx.**	1.1	(1.46)	0.9	(1.42)
Int. Tx.***	2.2	(2.64)	1.9	(2.52)
Legal				
Patient Problems *	0.9	(1.37)	0.4	(1.10)
Patient Tx.**	0.6	(1.19)	0.2	(0.80)
Int. Tx.***	1.3	(2.24)	0.5	(1.48)

Patient's Rating   Interviewer's Rating
 Problems * (0 - 4)   Needs for Tx. ***(0 - 9)
 Importance of Tx. **(0 - 4)

reduce dependence on illegal drugs and the involvement in the delinquent sub-cultures associated with drug use. They also address the problem of rebuilding family and social environments, more often than not destroyed by a long career of addiction and criminality.

Recently, the same analyses were carried out with the clientele of two other rehabilitation centers in different Quebec regions (Laflamme-Cusson et al., 1994). Similar results were found in spite of differences in the socio-geographic contexts.

The results were presented to the therapists and the program team of these centers. The clientele's profile provided to the treating staff was found extremely useful on a clinical level.

An in-depth review of the rehabilitation activities program is currently under way at Domrémy-Montréal. The importance of criminality-related problems, as evidenced by the ASI analysis, has led to a reflection on the need to develop specific approaches aimed at the double-problem clientele.

These analyses have contributed to the development of a model which, based on a delinquency background, has helped identify a profile that will guide eventual treatment. (Desjardins & Germain, 1994). This model is based on the developmental approach of misdemeanor mechanisms (Leblanc & Fréchette, 1988; 1989). According to the level of delinquency (persistent, intermittent or low) specific objectives will be targeted: persistence in treatment, improvement of the social integration level by taking charge of the main aspects of one's life, personal support in aggressiveness control, basic social skill development and job market integration for the more serious cases. Cognitive and behavioral strategies will be preferred for other subjects.

References

Bergeron, J., Landry, M., Ishak, A., Veaugois, P., & Trépanier, M. (1992). *Validation d'un instrument d'évaluation de la gravité des problèmes reliés à la consommation de drogues et d'alcool. L'indice de gravité d'une toxicomanie (IGT)*. Montréal: Cahiers de Recherche du RISQ.

Brochu, S. (1993). *Drogues illicites et questions criminelles*. Montréal: International Center for Comparative Criminology, Université de Montréal.

Brochu, S. (1994*). Drogues illicites et criminalité, Traité des problèmes sociaux*. Montréal: Institut québécois de la recherche sur la culture.

Desjardins, L., & Germain, M. (1994). *Profil criminologique de la clientèle de Domrémy-Montréal en début de traitement*. Montréal: Cahier de Recherche du RISQ.

Guyon, L., & Landry, M. (1993). *Analyse descriptive de la population en traitement de Domrémy-Montréal à partir de l'IGT (ASI)*. Montréal, Cahiers de Recherche du RISQ.

Hodgins, S., & Côté, G. (1990). Prévalence des troubles mentaux chez les détenus des pénitenciers du Québec. *Santé mentale au Canada, 38*, 1-5.

Laflamme-Cusson, S., Guyon, L., & Landry, M. (1994). *Analyse comparée de la clientèle de trois centres de réadaptation pour personnes alcooliques et toxicomanes, à partir de l'IGT (ASI)*. Montréal: Cahier de Recherche du RISQ.

Leblanc, M., & Fréchette, M. (1988). Les mécanismes de développement de l'activité délictueuse. *Revue internationale de criminologie et de police technique*.

Leblanc, M., & Fréchette, M. (1989). L'analyse de l'activité délictueuse: description, délimitation et comparaison. *Revue internationale de criminologie et de police technique*.

McLellan, A. T., Luborsky, L., Woody, C.E., & O'Brien, C.P. (1980). An Improved Diagnostic Evaluation Instrument for Substance Abuse Patients. The Addiction Severity Index. *The Journal of Nervous and Mental Disease, 168*, 26-33.

Drug Addiction Intervention Programmes Using Agonists and Antagonists Opiates in Catalonian Prisons

Andrés Marco

Introduction

Heroin is the drug which provokes the greatest number of requests for assistance in drug dependent assistance centres throughout Spain. In Catalonia, in the third quarter of 1993, 50.4% of cases attended (79.6% male and 20.6% female) reported this substance as the main cause of their need for assistance (Organ Tècnic de Drogodepèndencies, 1993). The administration of the drug is largely intravenous, as occurs with 72.3% of heroin addicts treated in Catalonia, although other studies have observed a tendency for this mode of consumption to decrease (Plan Nacional sobre Drogas, 1994; Comisionado para la Droga, 1993; Megías, 1993).

In the European Economic Countries (EEC), 25% of the prison population has a background of illegal drug use. Spain has a figure of 45-48% (Martín Sánchez, 1990; Marco, 1991), with the largest proportion that of intravenous drug users (IDU). The high presence of this group in the prison population responds to, on one hand, the lack of alternative measures to prison in our country for convicted drug users. It is also estimated that the high number of IDU admissions could have been influenced (up until the publication of the Royal Decree 75/1990 by the Health and Consumption Ministry, which relaxes the inclusion in treatments with agonist opiates) by the poor assistance available to patients who dropped out of or rejected "drug free" assistance programmes. It has been stated that a greater application in previous years of methadone maintenance programmes (PMM) might have reduced the number of drug dependents sent to prison, given the effectiveness of these treatments in reducingthe consumption of opiates (Des Jarlais, 1992; McLellan, 1993; Magura, 1990) and even a fall in criminality (Battejes, 1988), although the latter aspect is still quite controversial (Strang, 1989).

The high number of heroin addicts sent to prison has meant that the majority of resources and projects regarding attention to drug addicts carried out in Catalan prison centres has been consequently directed at addressing this type of patient, without supposing the exclusion from treatment of those users of other types of substances.

Socio-Sanitary Profile of the Drug Dependent Inmate

From a sociological viewpoint the profile of the drug dependent inmate in a Spanish prison corresponds to that of a male patient, with elementary education possibly completed, unemployed, but with an unskilled occupational background, living with his parents, or, more rarely, with his own independent family unit (Martín Sánchez, 1990). He or she is a young adult, younger than the average age of the IDU groups in other countries such as the United States (New York City Department of Health AIDS Surveillance, 1986), with a slight representation of immigrant inmates (mainly North Africans, Central Africans and South Americans) with a low drug consumption profile and, with the consumers, a greater incidence of nasal or inhalation administration methods.

On a sanitary level, the UDVP usually present a background of infectious diseases mainly associated with a lack of hygiene and/or the habit of sharing hypodermic material. Of these diseases we must make mention of viral hepatitis, tuberculosis and HIV infection.

It has been seen that, for example, the level of tuberculosis is higher in inmates than in the general population of the same age group, as well as the fact that in prisons one sees epidemic outbreaks occurring with relative frequency and that the incidence of tuberculosis is on the increase, as much in Spain as in other developed countries (Centers for Disease Control, 1986). This is owing to, basically, the origin of the inmates, in many cases preceding from hyperendemic areas of tuberculous infection, the closed nature of the institution which favours the transmission via air of the sickness, and the high number of inmates infected with both tuberculosis and HIV.

It is calculated that furthermore, the HIV infection rate in the Spanish prison population reaches a figure of 30-40% (Martín Sánchez, 1990; Martín, 1990), much higher than the average European (10%) (Harding, 1987), American (1-17%) (Vlahov, 1990; 1991; Patel, 1990; Salive, 1990; Smith, 1991; Bellin, 1993) or Australian figure (1%) (Gaughwin, 1991). Moreover, the prevalence of HIV infection in Catalan prisons is as high as 59%, being less among women and among inmates from lower age groups (18-21) (Guerrero, 1993).

Assistance for Drug Dependents in Catalan Prison Centres

As has already been mentioned, drug consumption by intravenous means and the commonly associated pathologies with this consumption (hepatitis, tuberculosis and HIV infection, generally) constitute the main health problem in prison centres. Thus, the Health and Justice Departments have implemented, together, specific programmes aimed at prevention, diagnosis and treatment of these illnesses. Therefore in January, 1990, in the area of assistance to drug dependents, a "drug free" programme - in collaboration with prison body outside the prison - was set up in the Barcelona Male Prison Centre, an establishment containing at that time over 40% of the Catalan prison population. Towards the end of that same year in the Quatre Camins prison a Department for Drug Dependence Specialised Attention was created, which - with its therapeutic structure and organisation located within the prison itself, although working on an independent basis - made a second step towards helping this kind of patient. At present the offer of assistance has increased with the generalisation of drug free programmes, either in form of day centres or residential centres, and the introduction of programmes with treatment with agonist and antagonist opiates. Also, the collaboration with the public assistance network outside of prison has increased in such a way that this complements the in-prison assistance (day centres and social re-insertion resources, basically) or carries out the therapeutic process itself, either through applying the present prison legislation (Art. 57 of the Spanish Penitentiary Law) or through the referral of inmates interned only within the prison at night.

Programmes with Antagonist Opiates

Historically, different antagonist opiates have been used in the treatment of drug dependents although presently only naltrexone is the antagonist in clinical use. The use of naltrexone in prisons is quite surprisingly, still scarce in our country even today, even though it is the drug that adapts best to the conditions of the prison centre. It seems generally accepted that, in this case, successful results have been obtained with this treatment on patients who present external coercive situations (parole or probation, prison permits, inmates with open or semi-open prison status) (Greenstein, 1983) as well as those who come from a therapeutic prison or community (Kleber, 1985), although also it also has been mentioned that those users with a high rate of criminality show the worst results (Parwatikar, 1976).

There are experiences with naltrexone use in Catalan prison centres, generally as a complement to the present "drug free" assistance programmes, but these are often sporadic and irregular. Naltrexone treatment, applied in a controlled way and following evaluation parameters (Blanco, 1993), is at present carried out in the Quatre Camins Prison Department of Specialised Attention, a therapeutic centre located within the prison itself. The basic objective is to encourage abstinence, especially in risk situations. Its application in therapeutic centre conditions, with a previous selection of patients, use of auxiliary therapies and family support, leads one to expect satisfactory results.

Treatment Programmes with Agonist Opiates

The elaboration and management of agonist opiate treatment programmes for application in prisons has corresponded to a inter-departmental Justice-Health Commission. The agonist opiate chosen, as usually occurs outside prisons in Spain, was methadone. The maintenance programme with this drug (Marco, 1992) was begun in a Catalan prison in 1992 on an experimental basis.

The experience was initiated, on one hand, in order to avoid the interruption of methadone treatment for those inmates previously involved in methadone maintenance programmes outside prison. On the other hand, the idea was to incorporate the experience within the harm reduction (George, 1991) programmes; interventions which, without discarding abstinence, present intermediate objectives, obtainable on a short term basis, that aim at reducing the harm caused by drug consumption in the patient and in society. Therefore, admission criteria did not only include those who maintained the treatment outside the prison but also those psychotic opiate consumers who might be unable to handle abstinence and those affected by illnesses which could worsen with drug use, especially those affected with acquired immunodeficiency syndrome (AIDS).

Initially it was feared that the application of this kind of programmes inside prisons could bring about a search for the drug or desires for escape, which would lead to an increase in the demand for treatment by those persons who did not meet insertion criteria. However, the evaluation of the programme (Marco, 1993) did not confirm these fears, with the attainment of a satisfactory response from the prison inmates, as well as good acceptance of the intervention by prison staff. It must be mentioned that less social conflictiveness was observed in those inmates included in the treatment, a fact which had already been mentioned in similar studies (Magura, 1993). Moreover, emphasis must be given to the fact that a drop in opiate consumption was noted which was also greater for those who followed a methadone dose higher than 50 mg ($p < 0.04$), a circumstance already noted in other international works (Caplehorn, 1991, 1993) as well as a decrease in the habit of sharing injection material ($p < 0.005$), above all in those in treatment for periods of over 6 months. It is also worth mentioning that significant statistical differences were observed regarding the use of condoms in HIV infected users ($p < 0.001$), an aspect which, like the previous ones, is especially important and would be worthwhile looking at in more longer term studies.

The good results obtained in the programme evaluation have confirmed that this treatment method should form part of the drug dependence assistance offer of the Justice Department. At present three prison institutions are prescribing and issuing methadone, with the goal of having all prisons being able to issue this drug by the end of 1995.

References

Battejes, R. J. (1988). El síndrome de inmunodeficiencia adquirida y el consumo de drogas por vía endovenosa. *Boletín de estupefacientes, 1*, 23-38.

Bellin, E. (1993). Abnormal Chest X-rays in Intravenous Drug Users: Implications for Tuberculosis Screening Programs. *American Journal of Public Health, 83*, 698-670.

Blanco, X.R. (1993). *Antagonistas opiáceos. Utilización de antagonistas opiáceos en una Comunidad Terapéutica de un Centro Penitenciario.* León: I Congreso Nacional de Sanidad Penitenciaria.

Boletín Oficial del Estado (1990). *Real Decreto 75/1990, por el que se regulan los tratamientos con opiáceos de personas dependientes de los mismos. Boletín n° 20.* Madrid: Ministerio de Sanidad y Consumo.

Caplehorn, J.R. (1991). Methadone dosage and retention of patients in maintenance treatment. *Medical Journal Aust, 154,* 195-199.

Caplehorn, J.R. (1993). Methadone dose and heroin use during maintenance treatment. *Addiction, 88,* 119-124.

Centers for Disease Control (1986). Prevention and Control of Tuberculosis in correctional institutions: Recomendations of the Advisory Committee for the Elimination of Tuberculosis. *MMWR, 18,* 313-321.

Comisionado para la Droga (CD) (1993). *Memoria 1992.* Sevilla: Consejeria de Asuntos Sociales de la Junta de Andalucia.

Delegación del Gobierno para el Plan Nacional sobre Drogas (PND) (1994). *Sistema Estatal de Información sobre Toxicomanias (SEIT). Informe año 1992.* Madrid: Ministerio de Sanidad y Consumo.

Des Jarlais, D.C. (1992). Crack cocaine use in a cohort of methadone maintenance patients. *Journal of Substance Abuse Treatment, 9,* 319-325.

Gaughwin, M.D. (1991). HIV prevalence and risk behaviours for HIV transmission in South Australian prisons. *AIDS, 5,* 845-851.

George, M. (1991). Methadone screws you up. *International Journal of Drug Policy,* 24-25.

Greenstein, R.A. (1983). Predictors of favorable outcome following naltrexone treatment. *Drug Alcohol Dep, 12,* 173-180.

Guerrero, R.A. (1993). *Marcadores serológicos de hepatitis B en la población penitenciaria catalana.* León: I Congreso Nacional de Sanidad Penitenciaria.

Harding, T. (1987). AIDS in Prison. *Lancet, ii,* 1260-1263.

Kleber, H.D. (1985). Naltrexone. *Journal of Substance Abuse Treatment, 2,* 117-122.

Magura, S. (1990). Variables influencing condom use among intravenous drug users. *American Journal of Public Health, 80,* 82-84.

Magura, S. (1993). The Effectiveness of in-Jail Methadone maintenance. *Journal of Drug Issues, 1,* 75-99.

Marco, A. (1992). *Programa Piloto de Mantenimiento con Metadona en el Centro Penitenciario de Hombres de Barcelona.* Barcelona: Departament de Justicia de la Generalitat de Catalunya.

Marco, A. *Tratamientos con sustitutivos opiáceos. Evaluación de un programa aplicado en instituciones penitenciarias.* León: I Congreso Nacional de Sanidad Penitenciaria.

Marco, A. (1991). *Drogodependencias e ingreso en el centro penitenciario de hombres de Barcelona.* Barcelona: IV Jornadas Droga-Delincuencia.

Martín Sánchez, M. (1990). Programa de Prevención y Control de Enfermedades Transmisibles en Instituciones Penitenciarias. *Revista de Estudios Penitenciarios. Monográfico de Sanidad Penitenciaria, extra 1,* 51-67.

Martín, V. (1990). Seroepidemiology of HIV-1 infection in a Catalonian penitentiary. *AIDS, 4,* 1023-1026.

McLellan, A.T. (1993). The effects of psychosocial services in substance abuse treatment. *Journal of the American Medical Association, 269,* 1953-1959.

Megias, E. (1993). *Toxicomanias: Situación actual e impacto en instituciones penitenciarias.* León: I Congreso Nacional de Sanidad Pernitenciaria.

New York City Department of Health AIDS Surveillance (1986). The AIDS epidemic in New York City, 1981-1984. *American Journal of Epidemiology, 123*, 1013-1025.

Organ Tècnic de Drogodepèndencies (OTD) (1993). *Sistema d'Informació sobre drogodependències a Catalunya. Informe trimestral nº11.* Barcelona: Generalitat de Catalunya.

Parwatikar, S. (1976). Narcotic antagonist: Naltrexone. In D. Julius, P. Renault (ed). *Factors influencing succes in a antagonist treatment program.* Washington: NIDA Monograph.

Patel, K.K. (1990). Sentinel surveillance of HIV infection among new inmates and implications for policies of corrections facilities. *Public Health Report, 105*, 510-514.

Salive, M.E. (1990). Coinfection with Tuberculosis and HIV-1 in Male Prison Inmates. *Public Health Report, 105*, 307-310.

Smith, P.F. (1991). HIV infection among women entering the New York State correctional system. *American Journal of Public Health, 5*, 845-851.

Strang, J. (1989). "The British System": Past, present and future. *International Review of Psychiatry, 1*, 109-120.

Unknown (1994). *Management of drug addicts in prison.* Athens: Commission des Communautés Européennes.

Vlahov, D. (1990). Seasonal and annual variation of antibody to HIV1 among male inmates entering Maryland prisons: repdate. *AIDS, 4*, 345-350.

Vlahov, D. (1991). Prevalence of antibody to HIV-1 among entrants to US correctional facilities. *Journal of the American Medical Association, 4*, 345-350.

A Therapeutic Community for Incarcerated Drug Offenders: Three Years in the Specialised Attention Department (DAE) of Quatre Camins Penitentiary Centre

José R. Sanchis, Immaculada Ibern, Montserrat Soto
and Paula Montero

Introduction

The DAE program, a specialised care unit for the treatment of addictive behaviour, was created in 1990 (Pleite & Pardo, 1990). It is a residential programme aimed at Catalan prison inmates with an addiction problem, who can not resort to an external outpatient department because of their sentence/criminal circumstances, i.e. inmates sentenced and classified in the second category of treatment - the ordinary regime.

The DAE is a "therapeutic community", which in this case refers to a Spanish legal concept, that allows specific and differentiated intervention for particular problems of inmates in a prison. The program's general goals are :

1. Abstinence from the use of drugs,
2. Improvement in the quality of life.

The DAE is inside Quatre Camins Penitentiary Centre, 25 kilometers from the city of Barcelona.

Organisation

Staff

The staff responsible for the programme is composed of: a director, an assistant director, a physician, two psychologists, a social worker, two educators, eight officers, an administrative assistant and two teachers (adult education and professional training).

The DAE has its own decision making organ, the "Junta d'Equip i Règim", which is independent from the penitentiary centre in which it is located.

Subjects

The inmates of all Catalan prisons can voluntarily request to be admitted to the DAE. The different treatment professionals in the centre of origin file the petitions.

Then, the inmates are assessed by the DAE professional staff. The only requirements to be admitted to the DAE are:

1. To have a history of drug addiction,
2. That the time corresponding to three-fourths of his sentence be between one and three years, and
3. Not to be unable, due to health problems, to attend and take part in the DAE activities.

The DAE can admit up to 35 inmates.

The DAE user's profile in 1993 was as follows: male, unmarried (68%), 27.6 years old (average, ranging from 21 to 41), having had his first contact with heroin at the age of 16.9 (average, ranging from 11 to 25), having been 5 times remanded in prison and residing in the province of Barcelona (86.6%, 10% living in Barcelona city). As for his penitentiary situation, he has been sanctioned several times and comes from lower treatment phases, which is an indicator of poor adaptation to prison, basically because of problems related to drug abuse.

Methodology

Theoretical background

The program's theoretical model is based on social learning theories with reference to the works of Büringer (1976), Ross and Fabiano (1985) and Marlatt and Gordon (1985). The intervention emphasises positive reinforcement of prosocial and alternative-to-drug-abuse behaviours. The DAE regime favours an educative interaction based on the adoption of new behavioural patterns, including correctional officers assigned to the DAE without the regulation uniform, and disciplinary reports replaced by behaviour observation records.

Evaluation

Previous information about the cases has been collected from reports written by the staff in the penitentiary centre of origin. If a case fulfils the minimum requirements mentioned above, this information is completed with a structured interview, an abridged version, adapted to prison, of the Addiction Severity Index (ASI) (McLelland et al., 1980) and ten group sessions aimed at defining the addiction problem in terms of function analysis (evaluation group). In order to see which inmates need detoxification, the physician administers naloxone and evaluates the symptoms produced by this drug. This information is used to prepare the individual treatment programme.

The evaluation during the programme is based on the three following instruments:

a. Fact report records (Pleite & Ibern, 1991). The staff of the DAE write down in these records the relevant behaviour that they observe. The relevant behaviour is defined in categories, there existing two different forms, one for the patterns of behaviour to be increased and another one for the patterns to be reduced. At the end of these forms there is a space in which to describe the observed behaviour in a detailed and operative way, as well as to indicate the type of immediately administered consequence. The reports from each subject are assessed by a group in the weekly treatment sessions, thus serving as an orientation on the specific interventions to be performed.

b. Analysis of urine samples. The possible drug consumption detection is done by analysis of the different drugs present in urine samples. The urine samples are collected between two and four times a week following a random system. The urine samples are then sent to an external laboratory for their analysis. The substances that are usually analysed are: opiate, cocaine, cannabioids, buprenorfine, benzodiacepines and amphetamines. In certain moments reagents are also used for the immediate detection of opiate or cocaine consumption. These reagents are mainly used in the last phases of the programme, when it is more frequent for the inmates to leave the prison, and the results of the samples sent to the laboratory to be analysed are not yet received when they leave. The results of the reagents may cause provisional measures to be taken while awaiting the confirmation of the results by the laboratory.

c. Self-record forms. When the inmates leave prison it is always according to a plan drawn up together by the inmates and the treatment staff. On their return they must submit a self-record form, stating the fulfilment of the goals previously planned, the situations of consumption risk they lived through and how they coped with them, as well as their use of free time. These self-record forms are assessed in individual sessions and the support of the family and the external outpatient department is sought to confirm the facts.

Monitoring of the programme once the treatment has ended is done by means of an interview based on the previously mentioned abridged version of the ASI, converting the answers afterwards into the following three ratings: 0 - goal not achieved, 1 - goal partly achieved and 2 - goal achieved, in seven areas: drug consumption, alcohol consumption, health, work, interpersonal relationships, legal matters and resorting to therapeutic assistance.

Procedure and specific goals

The DAE programme intends:

a. to teach inmates with an addiction problem the necessary skills to cope with it in order to gain self-control over their behaviour. Programmes implemented to achieve this goal are as follows: cognitive restructuring (Beck, 1976), relaxation (Jakobson, 1974), interpersonal problem solving - TIPS - (Platt and Duome, 1981), decision making - CORT - (DeBono, 1985), social skills (structured learning therapy by Goldstein, 1973), discussion of moral dilemmas (Galbraith & Jones, 1976), emotional control, critical reasoning and negotiation abilities (see Ross & Fabiano, 1985), relapse prevention (Marlatt & Gordon, 1985) and life-skills training.

b. to provide basic education and professional training: permanent adult education and occupational training courses (plumbing, electricity, gardening).

c. to stimulate and reinforce activities alternative to drug consumption, such as sport, music, hiking, drawing, painting, etc., attempting to turn them into positive addictions and to increase contacts with groups of non drug users who carry out such activities.

d. to improve relations with the family of the inmates: through individual interviews and group sessions with relatives (family programme).

e. to give more importance to health: individual medical attention by the doctor in the Department, prophylactic programmes (mainly tuberculosis, hepatitis and HIV) and health education group.

Structure

The programme is structured in progressive periods that gradually confer greater autonomy, in order to achieve a change in lifestyle that favours their giving up drug consumption and improving their quality of life. These periods are:

- Initial period. Voluntary request on the part of the inmate and study of the case (assessment of the admission criteria).
- Preparatory period. Evaluation and detoxification (only when considered necessary after having carried out the naloxone test).
- Period of intense learning. Individualised programme: intense skill learning, stress control, learning strategies to cope with their wish for drug use (minimum contact outside the DAE).
- Test period. Characterised by the fact that it includes programmed visits outside the prison, aiming at the practice of the learned skills, under the observation and assistance of the DAE staff.
- Semi-controlled period. Characterised by the fact that it includes ordinary permits to leave the prison (usually from two to seven days), in order to favour self-control and to prepare them for the subsequent life upon release.
- Semi-open period. It means progressing to the superior category of treatment, spending more time outside the prison (open prison) and being referred to therapeutic outpatient departments for ambulatory monitoring of their addiction problem, and to other social assistance facilities. In many cases, if they have fulfilled three-fourths of their sentence, it means being put on parole.

Community unit

The programme includes a unit that allows contact between the users of the DAE and social assistance facilities that could help them improve the quality of life of the inmates in different areas, such as work, education, sport, health, free time, family, etc. The families of the inmates take part in weekly group sessions (10 weeks duration), in which they are given information on the evolution of their relative, as far as the treatment and basic skills learned for coping with the problems associated with addiction are concerned.

Results

Development of the programme

From September 1990 until December 1993, 143 inmates have been admitted to the DAE out of the 593 who filed their petitions. The three main reasons for not being admitted to the programme are:

1. The time they have left to finish their sentence is under 12 months (they could not complete the programme).
2. The time they have left to fulfill three-fourths of their sentence is above three years (in this case are included in a waiting list until they have fulfilled this requirement, and included in other treatment programmes).
3. Their health conditions do not allow them to follow the programme with a minimum of regularity (in this case are sent to hospital care and oriented toward maintenance programmes with opiate agonists).

During this period, the results referring to the use of the programme on the part of the admitted inmates are as follows:

The average duration of the stay in the Department for those that complete the programme is of 12 months.

Table 1. Results of Programme Implementation

	Therapy discharge	Expulsions	Renunciations
1990 (Oct-Dec)	0	4	2
1991	8	3	6
1992	19	19	3
1993	20	20	4
Total	47	46	15

Monitoring data

The evaluation of the monitoring data of the inmates having finished the treatment up until December 31,.1993 is shown in Table 2. The most notable results are:

a. Drug consumption: 67% achieved the goals of the treatment, i.e. maintained abstinence; 28% achieved the goals only in part, i.e. they had some relapse and resorted to an outpatient department for treatment; and only 6% failed in this area, i.e. they returned to regular drug abuse.

b. Legal area: in this area we have information about all the subjects, as there is a computer program covering the whole country with information about all subjects remanded in prison (SIGMA 60). From this program we know that only 7% of the inmates had returned to prison for a new sentence, 39% were in prison for a sentence prior to completing treatment or as preventive detention, and 55% were still in the community.

c. Occupational area: In this area we should point out the great difficulty the subjects have to find employment upon finishing the treatment; 67% did not have a regular job at the moment in which the monitoring interviews were carried out.

d. Resorting to therapeutic outpatient departments: a large number of subjects were being treated in the therapeutic departments outside the penitentiary centre to which they had been directed to upon ending treatment in the DAE; 50% had regular contact with them and 17% in a sporadic way.

e. Interpersonal relationships: they are satisfactory in a good number of cases (67%), referring mainly to the family and friends who are not drug users.

f. Alcohol consumption: from the information obtained we could say that a regular alcohol consumption prevails (67%), which could be considered as social consumption (in parties, with friends and during meals), but which is still worrisome in people with an addiction problem.

Health area: Because of the delicate health condition of many of the subjects, it would have been desirable to keep good, constant medical monitoring in a greater proportion than the 39% of cases shown in the results.

Table 2. Monitoring results

N = 47	Without data	Deceased	No data	0: No goals achieved	1: Goals partly achieved	2: Goals achieved
Drug abuse	26	3	18	1 (6%)	5 (28%)	12 (67%)
Alcohol use	26	3	18	0	12 (67%)	6 (33%)
Work	26	3	18	1 (6%)	10 (56%)	7 (39%)
Interper. relation.	26	3	18	3 (17%)	9 (50%)	6 (33%)
Legal matters	0	3	44	3 (7%)	17 (39%)	24 (55%)
Therap. assistance	26	3	18	6 (33%)	3 (17%)	9 (50%)

It must also be taken into account that at the moment when this assessment was conducted 3 subjects had died.

Discussion

The experience of the DAE, an ambitious project for treating drug abuse inside a prison, in a regime similar to that of therapeutic communities outside the prison, can be considered to be offering very important results. First, one should note the continuity of the experience in an environment in which drug use is usually seen as a problem of order, security and discipline rather than a behavioural problem that can change with adequate intervention. Second, it is important to note the results obtained with a population that shows important problems to progress in the penitentiary system, who have been sanctioned several times and are frequently hopeless. Third, because it shows an important application of solid psychological models: the effective conjunction of the Psychosocial Competence Programme of Ross' group and the relapse prevention model of Marlatt and Gordon. To sum up, the fact that an experience like the DAE has already been running for four years, with an educational therapeutic approach to cope with an important problem of today's penitentiary centres, means a new reinforcement of the rehabilitation model, transferring again the problem to politicians and their financial priorities, rather than to a supposed limitation of psychosocial science.

References

Beck, A. (1976). *Cognitive Therapy and the emotional disorders.* Scarborough: New American Library.
Bühringer, G. (1976). Terapia de conducta en la adicción a drogas. *Análisis y Modificación de Conducta, 2,* 57- 69.
DeBono, E. (1986). *The CORT Thinking Program.* Oxford: Pergamon Press.
Galbraith R.E., & Jones, T.M. (1976). *Moral Reasoning.* Minn, MN: Greenhaven Press.
Goldstein, A.P. (1973*). Structured Learning Therapy: Toward a psychotherapy for the poor.* New York: Academic Press.
Jakobson, E. (1974). *Progressive Relaxation.* Chicago: University of Chicago Press.
Marlatt, G.A., & Gordon, J. (Eds.) (1985). *Relapse Prevention: maintenance strategies in addictive behavior change.* New York: Gudford Press.
Martínez Serrano, M.C. (1991*). Programa de habilidades de vida del DAE.* Unpublished document.
McLellan, A. T., Luborsky, L., Woody, C.E., & O'Brien, C.P. (1980). An improved Diagnostic Evaluation Instrument for Substance Abuse Patients. The Addiction Severity Index. *The Journal of Nervous and Mental Disease, 168,* 26-33.
Platt, J.J., & Duome, M.J. (1981). *TIPS: Training in Interpersonal Problem-solving Skills.* Philadelphia, Penn.: Hahnemann Medícal & College Hospital.
Pleite, A., & Pardo, C. (1990). *Programa d'atenció especializada per al tractament de les conductes addictives dels interns dels centres penitenciaris de Catalunya.* Direcció General de Serveis Penitenciaris i de Rehabilitació. Unpublished document.
Pleite, A., & Ibem, I. (1991). Registro de notificación de hechos. Paper presented at the 11th International Congress "Latini Dies". Societat Catalana de Rercerca i Teràpia del Comportament. Sitges.
Ross, R. R., & Fabiano, E. A. (1985). *Time to think: A cognitive model of delinquency prevention and offender rehabilitation.* Johnson City: Institute of Social Sciences & Arts.

Part VIII
Correctional Treatment and Prison Initiatives

Children Imprisoned With Their Mothers: Psychological Implications

Philip D. Jaffé, Francisco Pons and Hélène Rey Wicky

Introduction

The number of incarcerated men and women is rising in most countries. Many are fathers and mothers, and several studies (e.g., Bouregba, 1992; Fishman, 1982; Gabel, 1992; Hannon, Martin, & Martin, 1984; Lowenstein, 1986; Sack, 1977; Sack, Seidler, & Thomas, 1976) clearly show that parental imprisonment has a dramatic effect on the remaining family members, particularly on children.

As for female prisoners, they have doubled in the past decade. In Western Europe, they represent between 3% and 7% of the total adult prison population. Estimates of incarcerated mothers vary between 5% and 60% of the female prison population. The imprisonment of mothers, more so than fathers, is an extremely destabilizing event for young children and for the family as a whole (Kiser, 1991; Hale, 1988; Sarradet, 1992). In addition, it raises legal, penal, social and ethical questions to which no society has found satisfactory answers.

One solution is to allow young children to live in prison with their mothers for a period of time. Until recently, this co-detention only took place when placing the child proved difficult. However, it occurs more and more frequently and is sometimes considered a progressive solution in the child's best interest. On the plus side, it recognizes the important bonds between mother and child and the crucial role their relationship plays in the child's development. However, this solution is also criticized. On the minus side, some argue that a child should never be placed in a prison environment and that his best interest is better served by traditional alternatives such as foster care, adoption and parenting by another family member.

In this article, we explore four themes:

I. We briefly compare how various countries apply penal sanctions to pregnant women and to their young offspring;

II. We describe how the peculiar prison setting may affect the mother-child dyad;

III. From the point of view of the prototypical child, we speculate on some of the cognitive and emotional developmental consequences that can be expected;

IV. We propose various pragmatic changes designed to avoid detrimental consequences and to promote the child's, but also the mother's mental hygiene.

Incarcerated Mothers: An International Panorama

World-wide, the diversity of solutions is striking. These seem to only partially reflect cultural variations and indicate rather that numerous jurisdictions are confronted by a lack of satisfactory solutions in the face of a growing phenomenon.

With regard to detained pregnant women, several countries go out of their way to welcome their children in the best possible conditions. Usually, the mother gives birth in a civil maternity ward and returns to prison after a short period, sometimes to a special prison section partially adapted to the child's needs. Hungary, for example, offers one of the most progressive policies. Professing a hesitation to incarcerate pregnant women, prison sentences can be delayed up to a year so that a female offender may give birth and/or care for her child at home.

In some countries, no rules exist. Prison authorities act as they wish, often inconsistently. In a few developing countries, women give birth in prison with no external help.

Other countries not too subtly encourage female offenders to abort (Tomasevski, 1986) and, if this fails, act to separate the child from its mother as soon as possible whether placement is sought in the biological family, foster care, an institution or via adoption.

When the new born or the young child is tolerated in prison, the length of co-detention varies considerably across national jurisdictions, from the breast feeding period into the teen years. Most Western European countries have set a 1 to 3 years co-detention period.

How can the situation of female offenders and their children be explained? Firstly, it would appear that, in a majority of jurisdictions, the evolution of criminal justice is to incarcerate women more frequently regardless of their circumstances. On the one hand, this results from reduced tolerance in the face of rising female crime rates. On the other hand, profound social changes have altered representations of women in general, and of mothers in particular. Gone are the times when motherhood conferred a sacred status and could not be violated until offspring reached total adult autonomy. Illustrating this change, consider for example the state of Utah, USA. If a mother commits a crime that entails a prison sentence, the prevailing legal philosophy is that the criminal act itself demonstrates that she is an unfit parent and withdrawal of parental authority is made easier.

Secondly, co-detention provokes a social malaise and a policy-setting paralysis. Indeed, even in jurisdictions where laws and regulations exist, considerable decision power is left to prison or judicial authorities to establish and change the conditions and length of co-detention. In practice, this lack of predictability generates a lot of anxiety for the mother which in turn may affect the child.

In summary, the lack of clear guidelines on co-detention suggests that the larger issue of how to "punish" female offenders while respecting their children's best interest is not resolved. This seems the case despite the recent evolution of international law, exemplified by the Convention relative to children's rights (United Nations, 1989) which requires that children be taken into account as subjects of law with specific rights.

Penal Sanction, the Mother's History and Prison Constraints

It is beyond the scope of this article to describe material detention conditions around the world and how they impact on the child. The media and various non-governmental organizations (e.g., Observatoire International des Prisons, 1993; Défense des Enfants - International, 1993) have reported on chilling local situations. In some countries, the danger comes from horrendous hygiene conditions. Sometimes, sufficient food is not available for detained, be they male or female, adult or children.

We chose to focus on Western Europe and on the prison setting per se reduced to its simplest reality, that is an institution that places constraints on freedom. How do these constraints on freedom, the mother and child's freedom (even in prisons specially designed for mother-child dyads), affect the child?

To our knowledge, there is an absence of empirical studies on this question and but a few conceptual publications. Two variables seem particularly relevant: 1) the mother and her history, 2) the prison structure itself.

The mother and her history

According to several schools of thought, criminal populations differ from the population as a whole. The differences commonly described are constitutional, psychological and/or socio-economical. In this view, incarcerated mothers also differ from the general population of mothers and this influences how the child is cared for. For example, a majority of incarcerated women are often ex-addicts sentenced for drug-related crimes. Maternal drug use is also generally considered a risk factor for the offspring and many young female drug users are not psychologically prepared to care for young children.

A prison sentence may also alter a mother's attitudes towards her child. She is confronted to the social perception that she is a "bad" mother and sometimes this image takes hold. She may then brutally or gradually disinvest her child, abandoning him/her psychologically. In some cases, incarcerated mothers tend to overinvest their child, be it by guilt or for other reasons. One additional reason is status during incarceration. Material conditions are sometimes better for detained mothers than for common prisoners, mothers being perceived and treated more humanely.

The constraining effects of prison

Prison is by definition a very constraining institution. Spatial, temporal and social constraints abound, impact on the mother-child relationship, and in turn on the child's emotional and cognitive development.

Spatial boundaries are the most obvious. There are security perimeters that impede free movement. Living space is reduced and children often share small cells with their mothers. This spatial shrinking is in contradiction with a child's needs to move, to discover his environment and to be surrounded by a rich and diversified milieu.

Prison also imposes strict temporal constraints. Activities take place in rigid and regulated sequences. Institutional routine excludes temporal discontinuity and spontaneity. While regularity is a good thing for a child, it goes too far in prison and imposes the unadorned cadence of a metronome.

Social deprivation is evident in the rarefied and homogeneous human milieu. Cut off from the outside world, human exchanges are limited to the same people, prisoners and guards, most of whom are women. The hierarchical prison structure also imposes restrictions. Prisoners are at the bottom of the ladder and stay there. Personal autonomy is discouraged and various controls discourage responsible behavior. A mother is generally not allowed to freely care for her child. On the one hand, she earns little or no money and relies on prison authorities for almost everything the child needs. On the other hand, she is dependent on prison personnel who monitor her continuously, including her maternal performance. Not only are her maternal responsibilities reduced, but surveillance per se generates stress and anxiety.

Psychological Implications for the Co-Detained Child

Having identified some factors peculiar to the incarcerated mother and her history, and to the prison world, how is the mother-child relationship altered and are there any repercussions for the child's cognitive and affective development?

The emotional sphere

Maternal presence has been postulated to be crucial for a child's development and its absence during the key early years of a child's development can cause indelible consequences. Classical contributions (Spitz, 1968; Bowlby, 1952) describe the pathogenic effect of maternal abandon on a child, whether this abandon is voluntary or not.

At birth, the child is in a state of dependency and the relationship to the mother is merged, undifferentiated and symbiotic. During the early stages of the child's life, the mother plays an essential protective role, filtering and organizing stimuli. Living conditions in prison, where stress levels are high both in the milieu as well as in the mother's subjective world, diminish her protective capacities and her ability to set aside the vicissitudes of her personal life, her mood variations, her anxieties, etc. As Bouregba (1992-1993) points out, this constitutes a serious risk factor for the child.

As they are condemned to share limited physical space, locked for long periods of time in single prison cells, mother and child are stuck to one another. Neither can escape the other's frustrations and mood swings, perhaps contributing to what Duché and Gransac (1982) view as simultaneous apathy and nervousness.

Of course, various safety valves set up by correctional authorities (e.g., day nurseries) help reduce the time mother and child are stuck to one another. However, even these essential contributions are derisory in the face of the early creation of a particularly strong symbiotic link in the imprisoned mother-child dyad.

Later, under normal circumstances, children gradually undertake a process of individualization leading to ever greater personal autonomy. In addition to maturational factors, children are subjected to unavoidable frustrations due to their mothers' inability to be continuously gratifying. Slowly, the symbiotic dialogue characterized by symbiotic love evolves towards differentiation.

This process of psychological differentiation begins very early and gathers speed towards 18 months along with the child's increasing locomotion capacities. The child leaves the protective maternal sphere and undertakes exploring the outlying environment. However, the child frequently returns to the maternal soothing presence for reassurance and to gather momentum for future excursions (Mahler, Pine, & Bergman, 1975). If the maternal base is solid and reassuring, the non-imprisoned child can successfully negotiate the separations of nursery and elementary school.

Yet, mother-child proximity in prison is much more accentuated than for non-imprisoned dyads and acts as a brake in the child's autonomization process. The exaggerated and prolonged symbiotic state to which mother and child are subjected in prison implies a longer and more delicate period of psychological differentiation. The 2-3 years period of co-detention permitted in most Western European countries seems insufficient for autonomization to get significantly under way before the inescapable separation must take place. Under co-detention conditions, this separation appears much more traumatic for the child since it takes place in the context of a more symbiotic relationship than the norm and since it is amplified by the well understandable anxiety the mother experiences during several years at the very idea of severing ties with the child.

The cognitive sphere

Heuristically, two types of cognition can be distinguished. The first relates to the universal or specific knowledge that the subject gathers from the environment (e.g., space, time, causality, etc.), and the second to the instruments of acquisition (e.g., different forms of memory, intelligence, language). Therefore, cognitive development can be described along two axes: a) the development of knowledge the subject has of his/her world, and b) the development of underlying instruments.

With regard to the knowledge a subject gathers from the environment, prison differs from the outside world in that it offers a limited set of potential stimuli. In other words, co-detention has an incidence on the quality and quantity of information that a child can construct and thus, for example, on his/her capacities to produce behaviors that are as varied as in a non-prison situation.

Beyond the limitations to the variety of objects the child may be confronted to in prison, the interactions with these objects are also unusual. This influences for example the construction of object permanence, a universal and fundamental form of knowledge.

The first forms of permanence appear normally towards 5 months for animate objects (among which, the mother) (Spitz, 1958) and towards 12 months for inanimate objects (Piaget, 1937). In our view, the prison environment can produce lags in both these forms of object permanence.

With regard to the construction of the animate object, prison impedes the elaboration of the object permanence of "mother" and thus the representation of the mother by the child during her absence. Indeed, constraints imposed on their relationship limits the possibility of separation and the emergence of symbolic representation which is one of the basic instruments of cognitive development. It is for example a precondition for the emergence of language. Developmental language delays alter the child's capacity to communicate and his/her styles of social interactions, also crucial elements for cognitive development after 2 years old. For example, the passage from egocentric and individual thinking to decentered and social thinking may be affected (Piaget, 1923).

Other aspects of cognitive and emotional development could be examined from the unique viewpoint of the co-detained child. The above illustrations of the risks entailed bring us to examine alternatives to co-detention as it is practiced with the stated goal of minimizing its immediate and long term impact on the child's development.

Promoting the Co-Detained Mother-Child Dyad's Mental Hygiene

Various pragmatic and mostly simple changes could enhance the child's healthy development while preserving the unity of the mother-child dyad. Several of the following suggestions are already practiced sporadically in different jurisdictions. Others, more original, await implementation by criminal justice and correctional authorities.

Perhaps the most obvious alternative would be to restrict imprisonment only to childless female offenders who have committed violent acts and thus fulfill a dangerousness clause. The remainder could serve some form of sentence on an extra-institutional basis. For example, pre and post-trial detention of a female offender responsible for a child could take place at home under a system of incremental restrictions. In the most serious cases, the offender would not be allowed to leave the premises of her home except under supervision from social services staff. Day programs could be developed for groups of female offenders in similar situations. In less serious cases, the accused or sentenced mother could manage her life and her child's with some degree of autonomy. This solution is technically feasible with the use of electronic bracelets that record a person's proximity to a specific object (generally the home phone). In addition to the consideration this option grants to the child by avoiding a period of prison detention, it offers the financial advantage of reducing the number of incarcerated female offenders. Indeed, while it is true that the number of violent criminal acts by women is increasing, the vast majority of offenses committed are relatively minor (i.e., drug or prostitution related for the most part) and do not require heavy security measures.

In the event that criminal justice authorities estimate that some categories of female offenders must be incarcerated and allow a period of detention with their children, special prison structures staffed by trained personnel are required to support the mother and to make sure children are exposed to an enriched prison milieu as well as to life beyond prison. Several countries, notably France, have set up well-designed programs of this type.

In addition, borrowing on the practice in Switzerland, prison authorities should consider allowing co-detention periods to extend beyond the typical 2-3 years period. Indeed, at this age, the mother-child break up takes place during a developmentally delicate stage that can be exacerbated by the unique circumstances of life in prison leading up to it.

Another option favors smoothing the traumatic effect of a brutal separation. Well before a child reaches the designated age for separation from his/her mother, social services, in co-ordination with correctional authorities as well as with the mother herself should prepare a progressive plan leading up to a gradual separation. The advantages of this preparation are manifold: a more foreseeable evolution for the mother, the possibility of confronting and getting used to new environments for the child, the availability of fallback plans if the separation is problematic, etc.

One source of inspiration for a scheme involving careful preparation of the mother and child can be drawn from the practice in the state of New York, USA. (even though co-detention does not take place in this jurisdiction). In this state, a significant number of children are allowed to visit their incarcerated mothers for extended periods of time. For example, once a year, they may spend a "vacation" of up to several weeks duration in prison with their mother. By inverting this model and adapting it to co-detention, social staff could early on recruit foster families who are in close geographical proximity to the prison. Children of incarcerated female offenders could spend increasing amounts of time in these foster families. At some point and in accordance with their individual developmental tempo, the children would graduate to full time living with these families. In turn, as in the state of New

York, they could then spend "vacation" time with their mothers under conditions of co-detention. In this way the important ties between mother and child are acknowledged and maintained.

A complementary proposal, in line with the doctrine of "therapeutic jurisprudence" (Wexler, 1991), would be to grant furloughs as well as credits towards lower sentences to mothers who remain responsibly involved with their children. Their child would thus benefit from the mother's active interest and she would be encouraged to assume maternal responsibilities in preparation for an eventual release. The elegance of this solution holds in the therapeutic influence the State can exert on its citizens, not by imposing constraints, but by encouraging persons to change by providing them with psycho-social incentives.

Conclusions

For many (e.g. Bonin, 1990), the words "prison and child" are antinomical. Despite this commonly shared view, in a plurality of countries around the world, ever-increasing numbers of mothers are incarcerated and their children co-detained. Often this co-detention results from an absence of solutions for the placement of the child. However, this practice is also growing under the influence of child development theories and due to new conceptions on children's rights.

Given the reality of this evolution, co-detention must be critically examined to identify any risk factors that may impact on the child's well-being and development. We have underscored that in prison mother-child dyads relate under unusual circumstances if compared to non-imprisoned dyads. Furthermore, these differences must be taken into account to minimize potential traumatic effects to the child of incarcerated female offenders. While these differences are identified conceptually, it is necessary for well-designed research projects to identify the factors that may impact negatively on the child's well-being.

Even if difficult to envision from a methodological perspective and raising complicated ethical questions, research results would go a long way towards shaping the important political, legal and psychological debate that surrounds co-detention and what constitutes the child's best interest. In the meantime, various short term pragmatic changes in the practice of co-detention could significantly improve the child's well-being and promote his or her rights as set forth in the International convention relative to children's rights (United Nations, 1989). The psychological benefits for co-detained children and mothers as well as the financial savings for society as a whole would be substantial.

References

Bonin, Y. (1990). Enfant et prison: deux images difficiles à réconcilier. In Y. Bonin (Ed.), *Enfants et prison* (pp. 16-20). Paris: Eshel.

Bouregba, A. (1992). De la rupture au maintien des liens. *Transition*(31), 80-85.

Bouregba, A. (1992-1993). Dans les ténèbres de l'enfance: L'enfant de moins de dix-huit mois vivant avec sa mère en détention. *Enfance Majuscule*(8), 15-17.

Bowlby, J. (1952). *Maternal care and mental health.* Geneva, Switzerland: World Health Organisation.

Défense des Enfants - International (1993). Enfants en prison: La situation dans 12 pays. *Tribune internationale des droits de l'enfant, 10*(4), 15-17.

Duché, N., & Gransac, A. (1982). *Prison de femmes.* Paris: Denoël.

Fishman, S. H. (1982). The impact of incarceration on children of offenders. *Journal of Children in Contemporary Society, 15*(1), 89-99.

Gabel, S. (1992). Children of incarcerated and criminal parents: Adjustment, behavior, and prognosis. *Bulletin of the American Academy of Psychiatry and Law, 20*(1), 33-45.

Hale, D. C. (1988). The impact of mother's incarceration on the family system: Research and recommendations. *Marriage and Family Review, 12*(1), 143-154.

Hannon, G., Martin, D., & Martin, M. (1984). Incarceration in the family: Adjustment to change. *Family Therapy, 11*(3), 253-260.

Kiser, G. C. (1991). Female inmates and their families. *Federal Probation, 55*(3), 56-63.

Lowenstein, A. (1986). Temporary single parenthood: The case of prisoners' families. *Family Relations Journal of Applied Family and Child Studies, 35*(1), 79-85.

Mahler, M., Pine, F., & Bergman, I. (1975). *The psychological birth of the human infant: Symbiosis and individuation.* New York: Basic Books.

Observatoire international des prisons (1993). Les conditions de détention des prisonniers ordinaires. Lyon.

Piaget, J. (1923). *Le langage et la pensée chez l'enfant.* Neuchâtel, Switzerland: Delachaux & Niestlé.

Piaget, J. (1937). *La construction du réel chez l'enfant.* Neuchâtel, Switzerland: Delachaux & Niestlé.

Sack, W. H. (1977). Children of imprisoned fathers. *Psychiatry, 40,* 163-174.

Sack, W. H., Seidler, J., & Thomas, S. (1976). The children of imprisoned parents: A psychosocial exploration. *American Journal of Orthopsychiatry, 46*(4), 618-628.

Sarradet, J.-L. (1992). L'enfant de moins de 18 mois vivant en détention avec sa mère. In Fondation de France (Ed.), *Enfants, parents, prison, 4* (pp. 80-83). Paris.

Spitz, R. (1958). *La première année de la vie de l'enfant: Genèse des premières relations objectales.* Paris: Presses Universitaires de France.

Spitz, R. (1968). *De la naissance à la parole: Les premières années de la vie.* Paris: Presses Universtaires de France.

Tomasevski, K. (1986). *Des enfants en prison avec des adultes.* Paris: Fayard.

United Nations (1989). *The Convention of the Rights of the Child.* Geneva.

Wexler, D. B. (1991). Introduction to therapeutic jurisprudence. In D. B. Wexler & B. J. Winnick (Eds.), *Essays in therapeutic jurisprudence* Durham, N.C.: Carolina Academic Press.

Organizational Assessment of a Prison

Miguel Clemente

Introduction

In the majority of cases, research on subjects related to crime has focused on the offenders themselves. Accordingly, in a recent review of the role of psychologycal research and intervention in the legal system, Munné (1987) points out that legal psychology has over-emphasized the penal aspects, and not paid sufficient attention to those of a purely civil, administrative, political or fiscal nature. This does not, however, imply that social psychology should neglect the study of all matters related to the penal institution, rather, that these other aspects should be given greater emphasis.

Taking these facts into account, and focusing on one organization within the criminal justice system, we will henceforth refer to the prison, and more specifically to the impact it has on those within it (whether they be staff or inmates), but in this case the analysis will concentrate on the organizational, rather than the individual aspects. The knowledge which may be obtained in this sphere will contribute to what Munné (1987) considers to be two of the most important aspects of the legal psychologist's professional role: guidance in the development of more appropriate laws for the individual and for human groups, and guidance towards more suitable organization of the justice administration system.

This first section, consisting of a theoretical review of the subject, analyzes certain organizational and occupational psychologycal variables which have been studied within penal institutions, with the main emphasis being on studies about prison staff.

An important work by Lombardo (1981) highlighted the stress which characterizes the work of custodial staff, to such an extent that at times the staff involved in this task can end up themselves feeling "imprisoned", displaying a state of uncertainty and lack of command of the situation. Some key explanations (at least in the United States) are provided by Crouch (1984), who argues that two decades earlier the perspective was very different. In fact, important changes did occur during that period, not least of these being the rise to prominence of the philosophy of rehabilitation and the increase in prison population. For the staff involved, dealing with prisoners creates a series of problems, normally labeled under the term stress.

In the study of organizations, systematic analytical techniques commonly have been used when developing techniques for intervention in the organization. Organizational analysis has been applied to various levels and facets, both for theoretical purposes (development of models) and for evaluative and diagnostic purposes (McCormick et al., 1979; Hackman and Oldham, 1975; Alderfer, 1983; Fuertes, 1983; Pérez, 1988). On the other hand, it has been used relatively often in developing rational and empirical taxonomies of organizations, as can be seen in Fleischman and Quaintance (1984).

From the applied point of view, the rise of organizational analysis and diagnosis in a holistic sense began with the Organizational Development movement, in which it assumed considerable importance (Schein, 1980; Friedlander and Brown, 1974; Lawrence and Lorsch, 1969). This movement, which currently concentrates on addressing the problems of complex organizations using a systematic globalizing approach, began in the forties with the introduction of laboratory training methods ("T Groups") and Lewin's (1946) "Action Research" model, into the processes of organizational change, giving rise to the school of human relations and to the philosophy based on the active participation of members and groups as agents of change (Friedlander, 1980; Petit, 1984; Beer, 1983).

After the necessarily brief analysis of the important theoretical elements in approaching a prison from an organizational point of view, we will now describe the research carried out.

Research

Problem, determination of objectives, and research hypothesis

On the basis of the theoretical review carried out, it is possible to establish in what ways the Organizational Assessment Instruments are appropriate for diagnosing organizations, detecting possible problem areas, and also indicating the appropriate ways of intervening to resolve deficiencies which may be detected in the organization.

However, it is equally true that these instruments have a limited applicability, in so far as they are primarily intended for application in private organizations, where the profit motive is fundamental, the hierarchy of the structures is so arranged that the formal level of the organization chart predominates over the informal level, and where certain concepts acquire different dimensions from those they have in organizations of a public nature.

Thus, whilst acknowledging the value of the organizational assessment tests, it must also be recognized that it is necessary to find another set of instruments better suited to organizations of a public nature. Thus, the problem of this research is as follows: to create a suitable assessment system for the organizational diagnosis of public administration organizations, based on the theoretical concepts of organizational development and assessment.

Method

Sample First, the pilot study was undertaken on representative samples of the organization in which the research was to be conducted. Ten subjects were used in the pilot study: two of them were employees from penal institutions, working in offices in the headquarters of the General Directorate. The other eight were from the Foncalent Penitentiary Center (Alicante, Spain). With regard to the definitive

Table 1: Definition of the Sample

Length of service with the institution:	
6 months to 2 years:	37.5 %
3 to 5 years:	22.9 %
Over 5 years:	35.4 %

Income level:	
75,000 to 100,000 Ptas. a month:	4.2 %
100,000 to 125,000 Ptas. a month:	8.3 %
125,000 to 150,000 Ptas. a month:	29.2 %
150,000 to 200,000 Ptas. a month:	54.2 %
Over 200,000 Ptas. a month:	4.2 %

Sex:	
Female:	29.2 %
Male:	70.8 %

Age:	
Very wide range, with an average age of 32.	

Marital status:	
Single:	29.8 %
Married:	68.1 %
Divorced:	2.1 %

Level of Education:	
Graduates:	63.6 %
Skilled training:	13.6 %
Secondary education:	22.7 %

sample, and bearing in mind that this was organizational research, the study was applied to all members working in the Alcalá-Meco Center for Young Offenders (Madrid, Spain). Ninety-one people took part, which was somewhat less than half of all the employees. The characteristics of this sample were as follows (see Table 1).

Instruments used This research was conducted using the Organizational Assessment Instruments created by Van De Ven et al., a set of scales developed since 1972. Since that date, three versions of the instrument have been developed. In recent years there has been an abundance of literature published on the metric properties and applications of the Organizational Assessment Instrument (e.g. Van De Ven, Delbecq & Koening, 1976; Van De Ven, 1976a, 1976b, 1976c, 1980a, 1980b; Van De Ven & Walker, 1984; Van De Ven, Walker & Liston, 1979; Van De Ven & Drazin, 1985; Drazin & Van De Ven, 1985; Mark, 1985; Jacobsen et al, 1986).

Research design and data analysis procedures The design corresponds to a correlational methodology, in which all variables act as dependents. The following statistical tests of data analysis were used.

* Univariate descriptive statistics for all the assessment systems questions.
* Factorial analysis of the items in each of the questionnaires, determining the Cronbach "alpha" coefficient to establish the reliability of the questionnaires on the basis of their consistency. In all of the factorial analyses, the procedures of factorization of the main components and rotation of maximum variance were used.

Results

The factorial analyses are dealt with, allowing the variables to be grouped into significant factors, and two new questionnaires to be constructed, adapted to the populations dealt with in this study, as being of particular interest. The results of the descriptive analysis are discussed in the next section.

We will now give information regarding the name of each factor, and its definition. The respective tables show the mathematical characteristics of the factors, the Cronbach "alpha" coefficient, and the items of the new questionnaire created, together with the relevance factors. Information on specific saturations of each item in the initial questionnaire has been removed in cases where they were below the level of 0.50.

FACTOR I: Perceived influence of the unit as a group.
The element which best defines this factor is perceived influence. From the employees' viewpoint, it implies the existence of the unit as a cluster, in such a way that its components are as much members of the said unit as are the supervisor or supervisors of the same. As regards the areas encompassed in this, they are

extensive, focusing mainly on norms and procedures, performance, and on all matters relating to decisions about the work of the unit itself.

FACTOR II: Coordination.

This factor refers to the need to coordinate with others when carrying out the task. From an internal viewpoint, within the unit itself, it concerns everything relating to the need to discuss, communicate, support and suggest in order to be able to carry out the task. From an external viewpoint, it refers to the influence on the work of the unit of people and bodies from outside. Finally, at a personal level, it implies the attainment of satisfaction.

FACTOR III: External dependence in completion of the task.

This involves the existence of bodies outside the unit which to a great extent determine the system of norms and procedures, of task completion, and of all matters related to the activities of the work unit itself. This external dependence refers to the supervisor as well as to people from outside the unit. It implies that the employees develop their career within the organization at the expense of others, that there is a low degree of responsibility in the completion of tasks, and that there is little advance knowledge of the work to be done.

FACTOR IV: Personal control over the work.

This relates to the extent to which the unit members are autonomous when determining procedures for carrying out tasks, deciding what tasks need to be done, and even when specifying the working rhythm to be followed. This autonomy is due to the existence in the centers of instructions and procedures which are, to a great extent, unspecific, and this in turn implies that the influence on the daily work of the unit of people and bodies within the organization of the center, but outside the base unit itself, is very small. This in turn implies low exchangeability of roles (each person has his own specific tasks, which cannot be done by other people from the unit), great repetitivity of the said tasks (very high specification), as well as an increase in personal satisfaction for completing the tasks (being something which only that particular person can do).

FACTOR V: Task feedback.

This relates to the extent to which the employee obtains information from the actual task he is performing (not from colleagues or other people) on whether his or her work is well done. This factor implies finding satisfaction and personal self-esteem in the completion of the task, as well as putting more effort into doing the job, and having a preference for jobs involving stability (this stability concerns both the component of the task itself - which is more related to monotony - and that of an economic kind - preference for working in an organization where economic problems do not arise, namely, one dependent on an official organism, rather than a private company).

FACTOR VI: External dependence of the post.

Whereas the previous external dependence factor was focused on the completion of tasks, this one relates to the unit member's lack of power to establish, in the long term, the characteristics of his or her post and his or her position within public organizations. It is a factor of uncertainty, of being aware of the influence of elements outside his own unit and work place on determining his future activities, and, therefore, the significance of his position in the organization. The consequence of the existence of this factor is the employees' preference for a good salary, even if it means sacrificing the possibility of being innovative in the post.

Table 2: Items of the New Questionnaire on Characteristics of the Work and Determination of Relevance Factor

ITEM	F.I	F.II	F.III	F.IV	F.V	F.VI	F.VII
1				*			
2					*		
3		*					
4				*			
5				*			
6				*			
7				*			
8		*					
9					*		
10			*				
11					*		
12	*						
13						*	
14					*		
15					*		
16				*			
17			*				
18	*						
19	*						
20	*						
21			*				
22		*					
23							*
24							*
25							*
26		*					
27							*
28	*						
29						*	
30		*					

FACTOR VII: Communication.

This factor relates to the necessity for the existence of formal, as well as informal communication in the organization. At a formal level, this communication is revealed in the normal functioning of the unit; whereas at an informal level, it is revealed by the need for it when resolving conflicts which may arise. The aspects involved in this factor are the influence of the unit from an internal viewpoint, and the routine (limited innovative capacity of the unit).

On the basis of these results, a new questionnaire was created, consisting of seven factors and 30 items (Table 2).

Factorial analysis of the general questionnaire on technology and procedures, and construction of the new questionnaire The information provided with regard to this questionnaire will be similar to that given for the previous one. We will begin by defining each factor.

FACTOR I: Need to modify, re-check or re-complete the work.
This factor is defined as the production of sub-standard work, which therefore has to be modified, re-completed or re-checked. This factor is closely linked to the general functioning of the organization, covering a great number of aspects. Thus, it is influenced by variables of the workers themselves (lack of appropriate preparation and training, lack of motivation and satisfaction, etc.), by variables of coordination and authority (relationships with supervisors, poor coordination, etc.), as well as the general organization of the center. It involves significant or excessive delays in the work, slow flow of work, etc. In general, it involves poor performance.

FACTOR II: Sense of poor preparation and training for the post.
This relates to a perceptive aspect, not to a reality. Although the staff think that they perform their tasks adequately due to their personal commitment and sense of responsibility in the post, they think that they have scarcely received any training for it, which may cause problems, particularly with reference to the delay in the normal flow of work.

FACTOR III: Autonomy and personal independence in the post.
This is defined as the impossibility of turning to others, whether they be work colleagues or supervisors, with whom they can discuss, express doubts, or try to resolve problems encountered in their work. Thus, although the increase in personal fulfillment and satisfaction may be a positive aspect, it is also problematic with respect to the lack of support, solutions to problems and co-ordination.

FACTOR IV: The need for education, training and information.
Whilst acknowledging that the work does get done, albeit with delays, it is recognized that it could be done better, and in this sense performance could be improved, if the members of the organization received more education, training and information. It is again a question of a factor of a perceptive type, and one which has great repercussions on the reality of the job.

FACTOR V: Deficiencies in job materials.
This relates to available materials or tools being in bad conditions, or to them not being available often enough. This lack of appropriate materials for completing the job in turn implies the importance of re-doing, re-checking or modifying the job, as well as considerable wastes of time. This is a factor related to the materials themselves, and not to the opinions of the workers.

FACTOR VI: Performance of official duties.

This factor reveals that the workers are usually assigned official tasks, although normally these assignments do not relate to important productive tasks, nor to doing no tasks, but to performing merely routine tasks. To a large extent, the existence of the previously mentioned conditions which affect the work flow, leads to the staff always performing productive activities. Given that this factor can be regarded as being included in the referents to the questionnaire about the characteristics of the work of the members of the units, questions about this will not appear in the definitive questionnaires.

Table 3: Items of the New Questionnaire on Technology and Determination of Relevance Factor

ITEM	F.I	F.II	F.III	F.IV	F.V
1				*	
2		*			
3		*			
4				*	
5		*			
6		*			
7		*			
8				*	
9			*		
10	*				
11	*				
12	*				
13	*				
14					*
15	*				
16	*				
17	*				
18	*				
19		*			
20					*
21		*			
22	*				
23			*		
24			*		
25			*		

Conclusions and Discussion

Any methodological study invariably involves two aspects: on the one hand, there is the achievement of the technical objective, which in this case was the construction of a system of assessment in accordance with the declared objectives. We believe that this technical objective has been achieved in this study; moreover, the system of assessment fulfills the relevant statistical requisites and its application is simple and of short duration.

As regards the second question, it must be pointed out that any methodological study deals with a specific population and with specific samples. In this case, the population was that of the employees of a public organization; namely, the employees of a penal center.

Since the first of these aspects has already been discussed at length, we will comment on the second of these, namely the aspect concerning the specific samples which were chosen as an approach to a particular population.

Firstly, it is important to point out that to speak about employees of public organizations is something extremely diverse and varied. Such has proved to be the case in this study. An employee of a prison forms part of an organization which has certain characteristics because it is of a public type, but also because it is a prison. Although, as has been proved here, it is possible to construct a general instrument, which is only of use in detecting those aspects which characterize an environment common to all organizations of a public nature, but it will also be necessary to detect other more specific characteristics, according to the type of activity of the organization.

However, returning to the general characteristics common to all organizations of a public nature, the data gathered in this study sheds light on a series of points which allow us to pass from the realm of assessment into that of intervention. Thus, some data which may assist subsequent intervention programs are as follows:

* All the employees of public organizations interviewed feel demotivated. They have a total lack of interest in their work, and as a general rule it does not make any difference to them whether they do it well or badly.

* Moreover, there is commonly a performance norm which either subjectively or agreed on by the group, pressurizes individuals into low performance. Thus, anyone performing better than the agreed minimum finds himself with adaptation problems, is isolated from the rest of the group, and excluded from informal circles.

* Despite the parameters mentioned, employees of public organizations generally feel satisfied with their jobs, and have no intention of looking for alternative employment or accepting any other offers. Although this is in part explained by the fact many people have invested a great deal of time in order to obtain their post, there must be more to this explanation, related to the advantages of an informal nature already mentioned, and to others specified below.

* The employees of a public organization totally separate their personal lives from their work. Thus, the arguments, problems, etc. which arise at work are restricted and confined to this work space and time. This allows them to develop other more fulfilling activities in their leisure time or time outside work. Thus, many of them acknowledge that it is in their interest to continue working for an institution they do not like, but which allows them to have free time and to be able to enjoy their hobbies at leisure.

* One fundamental characteristic of public organizations is that they involve a structure which implies that in reality nobody is responsible for anything. Thus, when faced with a job badly done, errors, etc., the fact that the job has to be re-done

is seen as perfectly normal, and is nobody's responsibility. It is interesting to note that this chain of lack of responsibility means that situations arise in which nobody is responsible for anything, and it is impossible to ascertain where an error has been committed.

* Related to the previous aspect we discover a shocking fact: that time wasted, together with time lost in re-doing work, in the case of some organizations, affects up to 50 per cent of the total time. Particularly serious is the existence of a time every day when it is acknowledged that absolutely no work is being done in the post.

* On the other hand, the greatest problems from which these organizations suffer are evident, and relate to communication: there is a generalized lack of communication at all levels, except the informal. Thus, supervisors do not usually specify to their workers whether or not the work is well or badly done, nor do the workers do so to their colleagues in the unit, and at no time are there clear and precise instructions which would allow any unusual doubts to be resolved.

* In addition to the communication flow, which clearly affects coordination, the second great problem lies in the allocation of tasks. Those workers who can see the fruits of their labors are much more satisfied than those who perform a merely bureaucratic task, without at any time perceiving what is achieved by their "small contribution".

To deal with problems of this sort, an intervention program should be set up, which could be based on the guiding principles of organizational development, and which would involve the implementation of a series of changes, at a general organizational level, as well as in the units, in each post itself, and in the workers in each post.

One final point: we have been intentionally pessimistic, assuming a role which has allowed us to detect possible faults in organizations of a public nature. Although in some organizations it is not necessary to adopt a negative point of view in order to detect the great problems they have, it is important to recognize, and we think that everyone would agree, that public organizations have made great advances over the years. This research is intended to assist in making greater progress in the current situation; progress which can be achieved, albeit in a simple way.

References

Alderfer, C.P. (1983). Change Processes in Organizations. En M.D. Dunnette (ed.). *Handbook of Industrial and Organizational Psychology*. New York: John Wiley and Sons (2nd ed.).

Beer, S. (1983). The Technology of Organization Development. En M.D. Dunnette (ed.). *Handbook of Industrial and Organizational Psychology*. New York: John Wiley and Sons (2a ed.)

Crouch, B. (1984). *Prison Guards on the Line*. New York: Academic Press.

Drazin, R., and Van De Ven, A.H. (1985). *An Examination of Alternative Forms of Fit in Contingency-Theory*. New York: McGraw Hill.

Fleishman, E.A., and Quaintance, M.K. (1984). *Taxonomies of Human Performance*. New York: Academic Press.

Friedlander, F. (1980). The Facilitation of Change in Organizations. *Professional Psychology*, 11 (*3*), 520-530.

Friedlander, F., and Brown, L.D. (1974). Organization Development. *Annual Review of Psychology, 25*, 313-341.

Fuertes, F. (1983). *Correlatos Cognitivos del Rendimiento en Tareas Administrativas*. Tesis Doctoral. Barcelona: Universidad Autónoma de Barcelona.

Hackman, J.R., and Oldham, G.R. (1975). Development of the Job Diagnostic Survey. *Journal of Applied Psychology*, 60 (*2*), 159-170.

Jacobson, M.D., Gattiker, U.E., and Piccini, C.L. (1986). *Organizational Assessment in a Non-Profit Health Care Organization*. Chicago: University of Illinois.

Lawrence, P.R., and Lorsch, J.W. (1969). *Developing Organizations: Diagnosis and Action*. Reading: Addison Wesley.

Lewin, K. (1946). Action research and minority problems. *Journal of Social Issues, 2*, 34-64.

Lombardo, L. (1981). *Guards Imprisoned: Correctional officers at work*. New York: Elsevier.

Mark, B. (1985). Task and Structural Correlates of Organizational Effectiveness in Private Psychiatric Hospital. *Health Services Research*, 20 (*2*), 199-224.

McCormick, E.J., Denisi, A.S., and Shaw, J.B. (1979). Use of the Position Analysis Questionnaire for Establishing the Job Component Validity of Test. *Journal of Applied Psychology*, 64 (*1*), 51-56.

Munne, F. (1987). La Investigación y la Intervención Psicológicas en el Sistema Jurídico. *Papeles del Colegio; Psicólogos*, 5 (*30*), 5-9.

Perez, F. (1988). *Evaluación Organizacional de un Hospital*. Tesis Doctoral Inédita. La Laguna: Universidad de La Laguna.

Petit, F. (1984). *Psicología de las Organizaciones*. Barcelona: Herder.

Poole, E., and Monchick, R. (1976). The Effects of Incompatible Organizational Goals Upon Correctional Officers. Reunión Anual de la *Asociación de Sociología del Pacífico*.

Schein, E.H. (1980). *Organizational Psychology*. New York: Prentice Hall (2ª ed.).

Van De Ven, A.H. (1976a). Equally Efficient Structural Variations Within Organizations. En R.H. Kilmann, L.R. Pondy and D.P. Sleven (eds.). *The Management of Organization Design: Research and Methodology*. New York: North-Holland-Elsevier, 155-170.

Van De Ven, A.H. (1976b). A Framework for Organization Assessment. *Academy of Management Review*, 1 (*1*), 64-78.

Van De Ven, A.H. (1976c). *Group Decision Making and Effectiveness*. Ohio: Kent State University Press.

Van De Ven, A.H. (1980a). Problem Solving, Planning and Innovation: Part I, Tests of the Program Planning Model. *Human Relations*, 33 (*10*), 614-654.

Van De Ven, A.H. (1980b). Problem Solving, Planning and Innovation: Part II, Speculations for Theory and Practice. *Human Relations*, 33 (*11*), 757-779.

Van De Ven, A.H., Delbecq, A.L., and Koening, R. (1976). Determinants of Coordination Modes within Organizations, *American Sociological Review*, 4 (*41*), 322-338.

Van De Ven, A. H.; Walker, G., and Liston, J. (1979). Coordination Patterns Within and Inter-Organizational Network. *Human Relations, 32* (1), 19-36.

Van De Ven, A.H., and Drazin, R. (1985). The Concept of Fit in Contingency Theory. *Research in Organizational Behavior*, 7, 333-365.

Van De Ven, A.H. and Koenig, R. (1976). A Process Model for Program Planning and Evaluation. *Journal of Economics and Business*, 28 (*3*), 161-170.

Van De Ven, A.H., and Walker, G. (1984). The Dynamic of Interorganizational Coordination. *Administrative Science Quarterly*, 29 (*4*), 598-630.

Prison and Feelings: Suicide Attempts

Júlia Behar, Anna Cordomí and Jordi Bajet

Introduction

An approximation to the psychological aspects relating to any self-aggression is always complex, whether this be self-injury, a suicide attempt or actual suicide, because it results in the negation of the most basic instinct: self-preservation. When this type of event occurs in prison, there is the possibility that the milieu could be one of the factors which set it off, as a result of its negative influence on the subject's emotional balance.

Backett (1988) believes that there is a connection between the degree of stress and suicide; and given that the period spent in prison increases stress, it cannot be denied that prison itself plays an important role in the crisis leading to suicide. This author lists the following as factors of stress specific to prison: *loss of freedom*, including separation from the family circle, from friends, and the fear of losing one's wife or girlfriend; *loss of autonomy*, that is to say, restriction of movement and the impossibility of choosing how to spend one's time or whom one is with; and *loss of personal security* in the face of the constant threat of physical aggression.

Welch (1991) and Zupan (1991) agree with the assumption that various aspects of prison life could influence the likelihood of suicides occurring; and Wooldredge and Winfree (1992) indicate that suicides among prisoners are less common in prisons with more humane conditions of confinement as these cause less stress. These authors' research shows that varying the ratio of prison officers to prisoners, and as a result the greater availability of prison personnel, is a significant predictor of the decrease in the ratio of suicides among the latter.

Withdrawal of freedom, overcrowding, social isolation, loss of peer group, absence of sexual and recreative satisfaction, and for many, the consumption of toxic substances - all aspects of the prison milieu - can cause feelings of frustration, guilt, low self-esteem and defenceless conduct. These factors may increase the risk of self-aggression (Berheim, 1987).

Other authors do not share this view on the importance of the environment. Achille-Delmas (1932) associated suicide with a particular state of mind, cyclothymia in the depressive phase. Freud, in his duality theory (1920) referred to the life impulse and the death impulse, without referring directly to suicide. More recently, Baechler (1975) conducted an exhaustive study of the previous concepts, and rejected them, before setting out his views on suicide. This author believes that suicide is above all a way of resolving an existential problem whose only solution can be found in death. As a result, he considers suicide and attempted suicide the same.

Given that suicidal conduct is not found in prison conditions alone, but that it occurs in the general population too, we can infer that it is not the prison environment alone that brings the prisoner to this extreme form of self-aggression, and that we should consider the interaction between the negative environment and emotional, psychosocial and family factors. Focusing on the prison milieu, Topp (1979) attributes the greater proportion of suicides in this environment to clinical, behavioural and social factors.

Davidson, Facy, Philippe and Laurent (1981) supply data on the characteristics of suicides in the 20 to 25 age group among the general population, and show that suicide is less frequent among those with a higher level of education and among the more qualified professional classes. If it is considered that prisoners are generally from very low social classes, with virtually no professional training, this is a relevant point and must be taken into account, along with the prison environment, in explaining the higher proportion of suicides in prison. These authors carried out an epidemiological study of those who attempted to commit suicide in Lyons and in the department of Bas Rhin over the course of a year. Statistical analysis of the data obtained brought to light the presence of a series of negative factors among these people: mental pathology and psychosocial and family factors.

A study in Catalonia (Direcció General de Serveis Penitenciaris i Rehabilitació, 1993) on death by suicide in this region's correctional institutions (18 cases in the period 1987 to 1992,) listed the following as risk factors, by order of frequency: entering prison for crimes of sexual aggression and against the person, entering on remand, the period following sentencing, being under 26 years of age, having a psychiatric record, and showing symptoms of depression.

As far as suicide attempts are concerned, there were 25 of these in Catalan prisons during 1992. These attempts are counted in such a way that a single prisoner could have done so on more that one occasion, and so the number of prisoners behaving in this way could have been less than 25.

According to Topp (1979), 50% of prisoners who committed suicide in England between 1958 and 1971 had a previous history of self-injury or suicide attempts. Especially in prison, suicide attempts are frequently genuine suicides which do not succeed as a result of the speedy intervention of a prison officer or another prisoner. In other cases, just as in the outside world, the wish to do away with oneself is not so clear. Other authors, such as Hawton (1986) state that in general, self-injury and suicide attempts are considered to be unrelated to one another.

This study considers both environmental and psychological aspects relating to both types of self-aggression to be relevant in themselves, because they could be the early warning signal for an actual suicide. A more thorough study of the various environmental and psychological aspects of prisoners who have injured themselves or attempted suicide can give a better understanding of the process that drives prisoners to harm themselves, and at the same time supply information for designing preventative strategies, in so far as possible. In order to do this, an 18-item questionnaire was formulated on affective relations with family and friends inside and outside prison, and on experiences relating to entry into prison and the time spent there. A final question referred to the reason for the self-injury or suicide attempt. This article supplies information on the analysis of only two of these questions, specifically those referring to prisoners' feelings and emotions relating to prison.

Procedure and Material

All subjects in the sample were given a questionnaire with 18 questions to find out the prisoners' feelings about family and friends, and about their entry into and stay in prison. This work analyses the two questions about entry into and stay in prison only.

- State what struck you most and what you felt on your first entry to prison.
- State what you feel about your stay in prison.

The questionnaire was given individually in each of the correctional institutions (Barcelona Youth, Barcelona Men's, and Quatre Camins Prisons), by one of the research team's psychologists, who was not attached to any of the mentioned correctional institutions.

Personal contact, with the resulting attention given to the prisoners, led to better co-operation.

The Sample

The sample consisted of a total of 85 prisoners who, at the time the questionnaire was given, were imprisoned in Barcelona Youth, Barcelona Men's and Quatre Camins prisons, all in the province of Barcelona. Of these 85, 8 had attempted suicide on at least one occasion, 32 had intentionally injured themselves, and 45 had neither injured themselves nor attempted suicide, and thus form the control group; the two groups had been checked to ensure the prisoners were of the same age (see appendix).

Table A (see appendix) details age, type of crime and situation (remand or sentenced) for the individuals who had attempted suicide. Table B (see appendix) gives the same information for the group of self-injured prisoners, and Table C (see appendix) does so for the control group.

Problems arose in setting up the sample, as in some cases the statistical data of the General Administration of Prison and Rehabilitation Services do not agree with the actual prison's data. In order to obtain reliable data where there was disagreement between the two sources, the participation of the doctor who attended the prisoner at the time was asked for in each prison.

Codifying the Data

The prisoners' answers to the two questions being treated here were analysed using a semantic content analysis. Once the texts had been read, codification was carried out by establishing a list of distinctive characteristics, allowing a system of classes to be created for each of the questions.

Each of the two resulting systems is exhaustive and mutually exclusive. Some of the classes appear in both systems, while others appear only for some of the groups and for each of the questions put.

The systems of classes were established from the answers to the questions put. This procedure allowed information on the prisoners' impressions, feelings, and emotions relating to prison to be obtained without any sort of intermediate manipulation. The words have in no case been altered; they have only been brought together in classes.

The classes of each of the systems are set out below, along with their definitions as well as some of the codified phrases by way of illustrating the content of each class.

First entry into prison

Lack of freedom. Refers to absence of liberty.
   "Not being free"
   "I felt that I lacked something, freedom"

Emotional reaction. Refers to various emotional reactions shown in prison, such as sadness, loneliness, fear, anger, powerlessness, etc.
   "I felt that the world had collapsed on me"
   "All I felt was a huge emptiness inside"
   "I felt a bit afraid"
   "A huge grief and loneliness inside"

Prison structure and society. Aspects inherent to prison life, the physical and human environment, prisoners and prison officers who live in prison.
   "The people, the space"
   "The sordidness of the wings in the Model (prison) struck me"
   "The looks of all who you met"

Family. Any sort of reference to the family or to people whom they feel very close to, such as a girlfriend.

"The situation regarding the family"

"Leaving my family hurt me"

"I'd leave my family alone, and my daughter"

The unknown. References to not knowing what life would be like in prison.

"At first, I was frightened by the unknown"

"I felt a great fear of the unknown"

No impression. A manifestation of the lack of any sort of reaction or impression on entering prison.

"I didn't feel anything"

"Nothing, because it's nothing special"

Prison violence. References to violence that happens among prisoners.

"Men stabbed and daily occurrences"

"Seeing how three mates buggered a guy in the landing toilet, with others queuing up"

The stay in prison

The following classes from "First entry into prison" are repeated here, so their definition is not repeated: *lack of freedom, emotional reaction, prison structure and society,* and *family.* However, the other classes are defined.

Lack of freedom

"Let them just give me back what is mine, that is, freedom"

"Thinking of the day I'll be free"

"I'm not free"

Emotional reaction

"I feel sorry for myself"

"It's sickening"

"Above all, powerlessness and defencelessness regarding the wrongs I see every day"

Prison structure and society

"Prison is a waste of time and makes people worse than they already are"

"Prison isn't the best place to live"

Family

"I regret not seeing my family"

"I hope nothing happens to my family"
"I want my father, but can't hug him"

Overcoming the present situation and future projects. Efforts towards improving the present situation, whether from the legal or the personal point of view.
"I hope to change when I get out"
"I want to get out and I'll fight for it day by day, working"

Self-aggression. References to harming oneself.
"Sometimes I cut my wrists to let off steam, it harms nobody"

Drugs. Any sort of reference to drugs.
"Facing up to drugs"

Acceptance. Acquiescing to the present situation although it is negative.
"It's not the best place to live, but it has to be done"

Guilt. Assuming responsibility for previously committed mistakes.
"I understand all the mistakes I made when I was free"
"I did something really stupid"

Results

Table 1 gives information on the frequencies of the classes relating to the question on entering prison, and Table 2 on the frequencies of the classes relating to the question on the stay in prison for each group of prisoners. Both tables have a greater number of classes than subjects in the group as some of the replies involved more than one piece of meaningful information.

An analysis of the data in Table 1 shows that for the prisoners who attempted suicide, the classes *prison structure and society*, which is present only for the group who attempted suicide, and *prison violence* stand out. This result agrees with the views of Backett (1988), Welch (1991) and Zupan (1991) on how the actual prison environment, with all its associated factors, affects the prisoner in a negative manner. Furthermore, the fact that the control group gives greater importance to the class *emotional reaction* than the attempted suicide and self-injury groups do is relevant. It seems that the self-aggression groups have a certain difficulty in working out their feelings, as if the impact of the environment was so strong that the prisoners were unable to go beyond their actual perception of the environment. What must also be taken into account is that the suicide attempt group makes no codifiable reference to the class *lack of freedom*, and the control group makes relatively few *references to the family*, as if they had not as much of a need for affective contact.

Table 1: First Entry into Prison. Frequencies and Percentages for Each of the Classes Relating to the Question on Entry into Prison

	Suicide attempt (n = 8)	Self-injury (n = 32)	Control group (n = 45)
Lack of freedom	-	5 (13.51%)	7 (11.6%)
Emotional react.	2 (16.6%)	9 (24.32%)	27 (45%)
Prison structure and society	7 (58.3%)	11 (29.72%)	21 (35%)
Family	1 (8.3%)	7 (18.91%)	2 (3.3%)
The unknown	-	3 (8.1%)	2 (3.3%)
No impression	-	2 (5.4%)	1 (1.66%)
Prison violence	2 (16.6%)	-	-
Total	*12*	*37*	*60*

Table 2: Stay in Prison. Frequencies and Percentages for Each of the Classes Relating to the Question on Time Spent in Prison

	Suicide attempt (n = 8)	Self-injury (n = 32)	Control group (n = 45)
Lack of freedom	1 (6.25%)	5 (11.90%)	6 (9.20%)
Emotional react.	8 (50.00%)	25 (59.50%)	25 (39.50%)
Prison structure and society	2 (12.50%)	2 (4.75%)	11 (17.00%)
Family	3 (18.75%)	6 (14.30%)	8 (12.50%)
Overcome sit. & future projects	2 (12.50%)	1 (2.40%)	8 (12.50%)
Self-aggression	-	3 (8.10%)	2 (3.30%)
Drugs	-	2 (5.40%)	1 (1.66%)
Acceptance	-	-	2 (3.10%)
Guilt	-	-	4 (6.20%)
Total	*16*	*42*	*64*

Such conspicuous differences between the groups do not appear in Table 2 on the stay in prison as in the earlier table. There has been a certain adaptation to the environment. All the same, we only notice *feelings of guilt* among the control group, albeit infrequently, while few expressions that could be included in the *emotional reactions* class are produced, as if in spite of an awareness of the mistakes made, the degree of depression and sadness is less. However, for the self-injured group the *emotional reactions* class forms 60% of the replies, but references to *overcoming the present situation* are virtually nil. This group of prisoners are overcome by negative emotions and lack hope for the future. However, this group contains the only prisoners - although few - who refer to self-injury and to drugs.

We can make a comparison of the two tables and in this way find the change in the prisoners' view of the correctional institution. Here, the most notable aspects would be an increase in the frequency of the *emotional reactions* class in the two groups who injure themselves; a decrease in all three groups in references to *prison structure and society*, as if they had adapted to the environment, and finally the appearance of codified replies such as *overcoming the present situation*, which seems to mean that some of the prisoners were able to formulate plans for dealing with the future.

Conclusions

From the results commented on, we can deduce the existence of differences between the three groups studied, allowing us to draw a generalised profile for each of them.

The group that attempts suicide can be characterised by the strong impact that all they see on entering prison has upon them, both the physical environment and the people, both prisoners and prison officers, as well as the violence that exists there. These two classes make up 75% of the replies. It could be considered that at first these prisoners have a block, and hardly refer to emotional aspects. A considerable proportion of suicides and attempted suicides happen during the first days of stay in prison; Backett (1988) indicates that 20% of prison suicides happen during the first 48 hours, and Gibbs (1983) mentions that during the initial phase of the stay in prison prisoners undergo a greater degree of stress, as a result of the impact caused by prison life, and because it is when the greatest effort has to be made to adapt to the environment. Perhaps the incapability of verbalising their emotions brings them to express them through aggressive action towards themselves. After some time in prison, *emotional reactions* come to the fore, reaching 50% of replies, and sadness, depression and emptiness are present; as are mentions of the absence of the *family*, which is again a reference to emotional links.

Although the self-injury group reacts similarly in the *prison structure and society* class, the values are much lower. They also show a growth in *emotional reactions*, but have a higher score in both tables. Therefore, these prisoners are very prone to mention emotional aspects, and this can be said to be their predominant characteristic. References to *lack of freedom* are made on entry, and continue during their stay in prison. These prisoners would seem to be characterised by poor control of their emotions, and are increasingly frustrated by their lack of freedom. As such, self-injury in this group does not occur during the first days, but in the course of their sentence, and according to Bajet, Behar and Cordomí (1993), on some 40% of occasions it is to call attention to their plight and to try to improve it. In other words, in these cases, self-injury is the method used to express their demands.

Finally, the control group shows the least difference in the replies on entry and during their stay in prison. In both situations the emotions are to the fore, as if the prisoner were literally overrun by feelings of fear, desperation, sadness, etc. Although forming a very small proportion, we must mention references to an acceptance of the situation and feelings of guilt about their previous actions. The ability to use words to express their emotions may explain this group's lack of a need to behave aggressively towards themselves. At the same time, they would seem to have a tendency to adapt better to prison life.

When psychologists in institutions belonging to the Justice department become aware of this sort of data about groups of individuals who tend to injure themselves, to a greater or lesser extent, they should act preventively in such a way as to transform the thought of self-aggression into words rather that into deed. Some experiments provide information on the efficacy of this type of preventative task (Ramsay, Tanney & Searle, 1987, and Sánchez Hernández, 1991).

Appendices

Table A: Prisoners with One or More Suicide Attempts

Number	Date of birth	Crime	Situation	Sentence y/m/d
0002	09.10.68	Homicide	Sentenced (in detention)	4/5/0
0006	09.30.67	Parricide	Remand	-
0010	07.18.69	Robbery	Sentenced (in detention)	9/7/2
0011	04.30.66	Robbery with violence	Sentenced (unclassified)	12/0/0
0016	04.12.62	Robbery	Sentenced (in detention)	5/2/1
0021	05.14.66	Rape	Remand	-
0022	01.01.63	Robbery	Sentenced (in detention)	4/2/1
0033	06.09.61	Robbery with violence	Sentenced (unclassified)	0/6/1

Table B: Prisoners with One or More Self-Inflicted Injury

Number	Date of birth	Crime	Situation	Sentence
0001	04.11.50	Rape	Sentenced (open prison)	30/0/0
0003	05.19.72	Homicide	Remand	-
0004	12.29.66	Robbery with violence	Sentenced (in detention)	6/75/2
0005	05.26.60	Robbery with violence	Sentenced (in detention)	37/24/4
0007	07.19.55	Robbery	Sentenced (in detention)	15/4/0
0008	03.02.73	Robbery	Remand	-

Table B: (Continuation)

Number	Date of birth	Crime	Situation	Sentence
0009	09.30.63	Robbery with violence	Sentenced (in detention)	20/10/3
0012	07.09.65	Robbery with violence	Remand	-
0013	01.26.69	Robbery with violence	Remand	-
0014	03.04.60	Robbery with violence and sexual abuse	Sentenced (high security)	11/16/4
0015	12.24.71	Robbery	Sentenced (in detention)	13/16/1
0017	08.05.67	Robbery with violence	Sentenced (in detention)	8/17/5
0018	10.09.65	Robbery	Remand	-
0019	02.16.71	Robbery with violence	Sentenced (in detention)	2/4/1
0020	01.03.68	Robbery with violence	Remand (unclassified)	-
0023	02.08.68	Homicide	Sentenced (in detention)	12/0/1
0024	07.24.59	Robbery with violence	Remand	-
0025	01.01.64	Robbery	Sentenced (in detention)	20/29/41
0026	04.03.75	Robbery with violence	Remand	-
0027	05.12.55	Robbery	Remand	-
0028	07.12.69	Robbery	Sentenced (unclassified)	4/2/1
0029	06.13.66	Robbery	Remand	-
0030	02.03.64	Robbery with violence	Remand	-
0031	12.23.62	Rape Homicide	Sentenced (in detention)	34/16/3
0032	02.17.53	Robbery	Sentenced (in detention)	Triple life
0034	05.17.72	Robbery	Sentenced (in detention)	4/7/1
0035	12.17.65	Robbery with violence	Sentenced (in detention)	15/37/3
0036	11.11.60	Robbery with violence	Remand (unclassified)	-
0038	04.03.72	Robbery	Sentenced (unclassified)	0/6/1
0039	04.03.62	Robbery with violence	Sentenced (in detention)	10/6/0
0040	08.16.69	Robbery with violence	Remand	-
0041	05.29.73	Robbery	In liberty	0/4/1

Table C: Prisoners who Have Neither Attempted Suicide nor Injured Themselves. Control group

Number	Date of birth	Crime	Situation	Sentence
0002	09.17.73	Robbery	Sentenced	4/0/0
0003	06.17.72	Murder	Remand	-

Table C (Continuation)

Number	Date of birth	Crime	Situation	Sentence
0004	11.11.67	Robbery	Sentenced	15/2/1
0005	06.11.73	Against the public order	Remand	-
0007	03.24.66	Robbery	Sentenced	2/4/1
0008	01.11.68	Robbery with violence	Remand	-
0012	09.24.67	Robbery	Remand	-
0013	05.11.63	Robbery	Remand	-
0015	09.12.74	Robbery	Remand	-
0016	12.21.59	Robbery	Sentenced	19/12/4
0018	09.21.68	Robbery	Remand	-
0021	06.15.70	Homicide	Remand	-
0022	04.21.62	Robbery with violence	Sentenced	14/6/3
0023	02.26.55	Robbery	Remand	-
0024	07.14.59	Robbery	Sentenced	0/4/1
0026	04.30.74	Against the public order	Sentenced	3/0/0
0027	04.08.66	Robbery	Sentenced	0/5/0
0028	02.16.72	Homicide	Remand	-
0029	06.14.68	Murder	Remand	-
0030	02.08.70	Robbery	Sentenced	4/2/1
0033	05.20.75	Robbery	Remand	-
0034	12.10.67	Robbery	Remand	-
0035	02.26.62	Assault	Sentenced	17/0/0
0038	10.31.64	Robbery	Remand	-
0039	03.02.66	Robbery	Sentenced	30/8/4
0040	06.29.72	Robbery	Sentenced (high security)	0/14/2
0041	08.02.73	Murder	Remand	-
0042	12.20.74	Murder	Remand	-
0043	12.02.68	Homicide	Sentenced	16/0/0
0044	01.05.72	Not stated	Remand	-
0045	01.15.63	Robbery	Sentenced (high security)	17/21/1
0046	07.09.70	Robbery	Sentenced (high security)	2/6/2
0047	03.18.66	Not stated	Remand	-
0051	08.14.64	Robbery with violence	Sentenced	20/26/4
0053	08.30.63	Robbery	Sentenced	10/2/1
0055	02.16.55	Robbery	Sentenced	8/4/1
0056	02.28.67	Robbery	Sentenced	6/6/1
0058	09.01.73	Against the public order	Sentenced	2/4/1
0062	06.29.69	Robbery	Sentenced	8/16/2
0064	04.04.73	Robbery	Sentenced	8/4/2
0065	01.03.68	Robbery	Sentenced	18/6/3

References

Achille-Delmas, F. (1932). *Psychologie pathologique du suicide*. Paris: Alcan.

Backett, S. (1988). Suicide and stress in prison: implications for a preventative strategy. In S. Backett, J.McNeil and A. Yellowlees. *Imprisonment today: Current issues in the prison debate.* London: The MacMillan Press Ltd. 70-84.

Baechler, J. (1975). *Les suicides*. Paris: Calmans-Levy.

Bajet, J., Behar, J., & Cordomí, A. (1993). *Incidencia del suicidio en las prisiones de Cataluña.* Address to the VI Jornada de Suicidiología. Barcelona.

Berheim, J.C. (1987). *Les suicides en prison*. Montreal: Editions du Meridien.

Davidson, F., Facy, F., Philippe, A., & Laurent, F. (1981). Comparaison entre facteurs psychopathologiques et facteurs socioeconomiques dans les tentatives de suicide. In J.P. Soubier and J. Vedrinne, *Depression et suicide*. Paris: Pergamon Press, 61-67.

Direcció General de Serveis Penitenciaris i Rehabilitació (1993). *La incidència del suïcidi i les autolesions a les presons de Catalunya.* Barcelona: Departament de Justícia de la Generalitat de Catalunya.

Freud, S. (1920). Au-delà du principe du plaisir. In *Essais de Psychanalyse*. Paris: Payot. Ed. (1973), 7-81.

Gibbs, J.J. (1983). The first cut is the deepest: Psychological breakdown and survival in the detention setting. In R. Johnson and H. Toch (Eds.). *The Pains of Imprisonment*. Beverly Hills: Sage Publications.

Hawton, K. (1986). *Suicide and Attempted Suicide amongst children and adolescents*. London: Sage.

Liebling, A. (1986). *Sucide in Prison.* London: Routledge.

Ramsay, R.F., Tanney, B.L., & Searle, C.A. (1987). Suicide prevention in high-risk prison population. *Canadian Journal of Criminology*, 29, 3, 295-307.

Sánchez Hernández, C. (1991). Programa general de prevención de suicidio en el centro penitenciario de cumplimiento de jóvenes de Monterroso (Lugo). *Revista de Estudios Penitenciarios, 245*, 95-106.

Smalley, H. (1991). Report by the medical inspector. In *Report by the Prison Commissioners.* London: HMSO.

Topp, D.O. (1979). Suicide in prison. *British Journal of Psychiatry, 134*, 24-27.

Welch, M. (1991). The expansion of Jail capacity: Makeshift Jail and Public Policy. In J.A. Thompson and G.L. May (Eds.), *American Jails: Public Policy and Issues*. Chicago: Nelson-Hall.

Wooldredge,J.D., & Winfree, L.T. (1992). An aggregate-level study of inmate suicides and deaths due to natural causes in U.S. Jails. *Journal of Research in Crime and Delinquency, 29, 4*, 466-479.

Zupan, L.L. (1991). *Jails: reform and the new generation philosophy*. Cincinnati, Oh: Anderson.

Therapy Motivation in Prisons: Towards a Specific Construct for the Motivation to Enter Psychotherapy for Prison Inmates

Klaus-Peter Dahle

Therapeutic work with offenders has to deal with a lot of resistance, particularly under the specific circumstances of a prison environment. Salient topics thereby are institutional problems: the "therapy hostility" of correctional institutions; problems arising from the inconsistent tasks of correction and punishment; and methodological problems - the question of the right therapeutic technique for delinquent patient-groups. The main difficulties, however, are usually seen to be located in the person of the offender himself. References to the extent, the complexity and the seriousness of the psychic disturbances are made, but first of all a lack of fundamental therapy motivation is complained, which is usually said to be not sufficient for successful therapeutic work. The motivation to undergo psychotherapy is supposed to be a basic requirement. The importance given to that construct stems from the assumption that all therapeutic methods are based on any kind of social interaction and are therefore in vain without sufficient co-operation. There is some empirical evidence for that point of view, although - especially concerning particular patient-groups - the existing studies are not completely consistent (see e.g. Schneider, 1986).

The "Classical" Construct of Therapy Motivation

Complaints about the lack of motivation to undergo therapy are not only described for delinquent groups. Offenders as well as other "problematic" patients - e.g. patients with psychosomatic disturbances or patients addicted to substances - normally show quite little therapy motivation, if they are looked at in a "classical" way. This classical understanding estimates the individual's motivation essentially by looking at the subjective suffering from internal problems and corresponding feelings of pressure in connection to a frankly expressed readiness for therapy. Clinical praxis with the above-mentioned patient groups however has brought that kind of understanding more and more into question. In the last one or two decades many modifications have been made, taking the particular circumstances and prerequisites of the respective patient group into account - e.g. Riedel (1989) and Schneider (1986) for psychosomatic patients, or Krampen (1989) for patients with substance abuse. The underlying cause of this development seems to be the understanding that the classical concept - which originally was developed regarding to neurotic patients - does not really meet the reality of these clients. A lot of conflicts between the assumptions of the classical model and the psychopathology of these patients required specific modifications. Sufficient motivation turned out to be a partial target of therapy, instead of being a prerequisite. According to that, the main objective of the modifications is to improve the "guidelines" for these first steps, by precisely describing, "where the therapist has to pick up his patients".

Concerning the treatment of offenders, however, few efforts in this direction can be seen. Existing studies confirm a prevailing use of the classical concept of therapy motivation in practice in prisons (e.g. Ortmann, 1986). However, this practice is also often criticised, unfortunately mostly without empirical evidence. Therefore, our first step was an examination of the usefulness of this classical construct for work with prison inmates. The sample consisted of about 400 randomly chosen prisoners, whom we asked for self-ratings regarding their therapy motivation, operationalised in the described classical manner. Figure 1 illustrates the distribution of the resulting four possible groups:

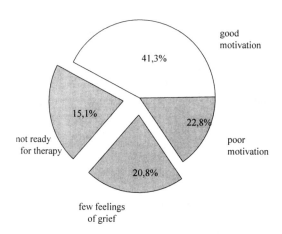

Figure 1: The Distribution of a Sample of Prison Inmates (N = 397) Using a "Classical" Understanding of Therapy Motivation

About 41% of the sample were "well-motivated" in that classical sense while about 23% were not. The remaining 36% however - more than one third of the sample - did not fit the model. Some were ready for therapy without realising too many problems (21%), others showed a high degree of suffering from internal problems but refused therapeutic help - at least within the prison setting (15%). It is important to see that this result is not (only) an artificial effect of poor methodological validity nor an effect of a possible "moderate degree" of motivation of these two groups (between the implicit poles of "good" or "bad" motivation). It was rather some kind of specific "ambiguity" of the non-fitting groups that the classical construct failed to clarify. All groups showed multiple specific coherences with other variables - concerning socialisation, former imprisonment, specific personality traits and so on - so that a discriminant analysis was able to re-identify the groups in more than 90% (for more details see Dahle, 1994). Obviously the classical conception neglected some influencing factors, which seem to be necessary for an adequate description and explanation of the motivational ambiguity of some of the prison inmates.

The Development of a Specific Construct

The resulting task was the design of an adequate concept of therapy motivation, explicitly regarding imprisoned offenders. Looking at the heterogeneity of different offender groups, we did not strive for a "total construct", which includes all possible individual eventualities. This would obviously lead to a complexity which excludes any practicality. In contrast to former modifications, we also could not orientate by the psychopathology of diagnostically homogeneous patient groups. Our aim was a construct however, which explicitly takes the influences of relevant characteristics into account that definitely affect prison inmates - e.g., the experience of the actual (or former) imprisonment or implications of the social origin of most of the prisoners. Furthermore we intended to describe motivational conditions through the eyes of the offender (because motivation is definitely a subject-related construct). This means that we tried to avoid looking at the demands of specific therapeutic schools, which surely enclose desirable attributes of the offender from the point of view of the therapist, but do not really meet their motivational conditions. The background for this explicit decision was the experience of an increasing tendency to mingle motivational terms with other promising prognostic factors when assessing therapy motivation (e.g., verbal intelligence, or social skills [Raskin, 1961]). In our opinion, this practice leads to a dilution of the construct and decreases its contribution to a comprehensive insight of subjective conditions, by attributing all therapeutic problems to the patient's responsibility.

Guidelines for the development of the construct were theoretical assumptions concerning motivation, knowledge from the literature about prisonisation and offender groups and - last but not least - the already mentioned critique of the classical motivational concept regarding delinquent persons. Table 1 shows a selection of the most important - as defined by the most frequently mentioned - points of critique.

A closer look at the specific arguments shows that the focus of the critique mostly does not refer to an insufficient extent of the individual's insight of the need to change. It does not seem to be the question of "*why*", but rather more instrumental questions concerning the basic availability of therapy as a proper expedient. In other terms, the question of "*how*" (... to succeed in solving my problems) appears. It is remarkable that the classical construct of therapy motivation only asks the question of "why" and not of "how". The possibility that there may be insecurities or specific fears concerning the instrument of therapy, or doubts regarding specific circumstances under which an intended therapy has to take place, are not taken into consideration.

Table 1: Frequent Criticisms of the "Classical" Construct of Therapy Motivation as Regards Imprisoned Offenders [a]

Reference	Objection	Focus
1. Regarding the prison environment	• decrease of trust in the therapeutic intentions of the prison	⇒ therapy as an expedient (valence)
	• increase of therapy-resistant behaviour	⇒ therapy as an expedient (availability)
	• hope for privileges as the "real" motive	⇒ questionable reason (viewpoint of the therapist)
2. Regarding the social origin	• little familiarity with therapy	⇒ therapy as an expedient (availability/valence)
	• social distance to the therapist	⇒ therapy as an expedient (availability/valence)
	• therapy-incompatible habits and attitudes	⇒ therapy as an expedient (availability/valence)
3. Personality factors	• tendency to externalise internal problems	⇒ questionable reason (viewpoint of the client)
	• traumatic social experiences implying social distrust	⇒ therapy as an expedient (availability/valence)

[a] *For details concerning particular objections see e.g. Rauchfleisch, 1990; Dahle, 1993; Dahle & Steller, 1989*

The most elementary step towards the development of an offender-specific understanding of therapy motivation was therefore to distinguish between these fundamental components: factors regarding the aims of an intended therapy on one hand and factors regarding relevant attitudes concerning the instrument and its context-specific conditions on the other. Concerning the aims it is in general a matter of the individual's perception and evaluation of relevant problems. Important elements are questions about the realised extent of problems, the nature of them, anticipated responsibilities, the question of the expected changeability and the perceived locus of control and so on. These factors show similarities to the classical understanding, although we tried to define the different aspects in a more open way, to take possible attributional characteristics into consideration (e.g. a possibly increased tendency to externalise internal problems). The instrumental side of the motivational construct on the other hand distinguishes between attitudes concerning therapy as a way to cope with problems (the general value of therapy and its specific value under the conditions of the prison environment) and the question of the anticipated availability of expected necessary competencies. Examples for such expectations are abilities to cope with the stigma of being in need of help, anticipated behavioural prerequisites - e.g. a minimum of eloquence - or a minimum of social and self confidence to run the risk of joining a therapy in prison in spite of remaining incertitude.

So far, components with a direct relation to therapy and their implications have been described. Regarding the singularlity of the prison environment, the whole conception also includes aspects with a more indirect relation to therapy and its purposes. On the side of the aim-related motives these are anticipated outcomes of therapy, which have at the first sight nothing to do with the intrinsic purpose of it. That means there are specific expectations of consequences concerning the environment which need attention. In the case of an actual imprisonment, such desirable outcomes could be the hope for a forced relief from restrictions within prison (by signalling readiness for co-operation); or the hope for climatic improvements in the case of a special social-therapeutic ward. On the instrumental side of the construct, alternative individual chances to cope with internal problems, beyond the possibilities of a therapy, need inclusion. Relevant concepts for the individual's abilities to deal with problems are the amount of anticipated self-efficacy and the extent of external support. Figure 2 comprises a summary of the whole conception[1].

By including the specific characteristics of the target group and implications of the prison environment, the construct of therapy motivation had become quite complex. This was an expected consequence as all modifications (in regard to specific patient groups) showed this tendency. However the increasing complexity has an important disadvantage. While not only one dimension needs attention, simple judgements as "good", "insufficient" or "bad" motivation do not make much sense any more. Particularly in case of lacking motivation, the construct requires more precision: it is necessary to describe whether there is a low degree of realised problems, whether there are reservations concerning therapy at all or concerning therapy through prison staff or whatever. We believe, however, that this precision meets the reality of imprisoned offenders better than an oversimplification, especially as it allows a further look at the often noted "ambiguity" of the offender's therapy motivation.

Evaluation Studies

Several evaluation studies have been conducted to examine the structure of the factors and to test the construct's capability to explore and predict the motivational behaviour of the target group. Two of them are described as follows. The basis of the study was an investigation of a sample of 120 inmates in a special prison ward,

---

[1] For more details about the model, its theoretical background and its evaluation see Dahle (1995).

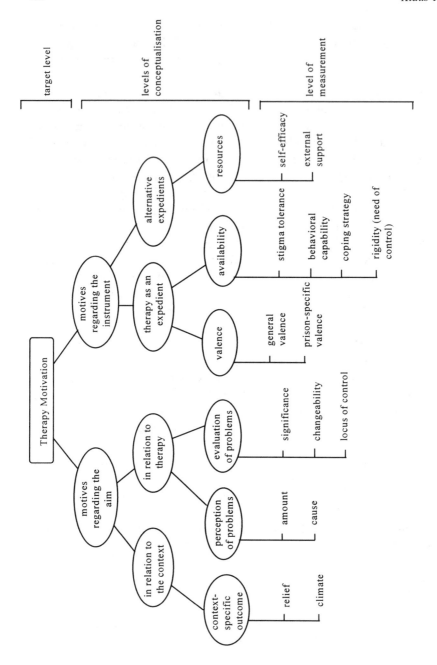

Figure 1: The Development of an Offender-Specific Construct of Therapy Motivation

which was designed for doing a first psychological "check-up" of all new prisoners in Berlin before sending them to different institutions. Therefore all inmates were at the beginning of their individual sentence under similar circumstances and the sample was relatively unselected.

Table 2 encloses some discriminant analysis with different criteria variables and the elements of our construct as predictors:

Table 2: Discriminant Analysis with the Construct of Therapy Motivation and Some External Criteria

Criteria variables	Significant predictors[1] (p < .01)	Hit rate
therapy readiness (65%)	• amount of problems (positive) • general belief in therapy (positive) • existence of expected necessary competencies (pos.) • trust in therapeutic intention of the prison (positive) • hope for climatic improvement (negative)	94.9%
active search for therapy (13%)	• amount of problems (positive) • prevalence of internal conflicts/problems (positive) • attribution to internal causes (positive) • internal locus of control (positive) • hope for privileges in prison (negative)	93.1%
social therapy (14%)	• trust in therapeutic intention of the prison (positive) • hope for privileges in prison (negative) • *problem orientation* as dominant coping style (neg.)	89.4%
therapy advice (21%)	• amount of problems (positive) • trust in therapeutic intention of the prison (positive) • *social-orientation* as dominant coping style (positive)	89.9%

[1] Predictors in order of their importance

Therapy readiness stands for a positive answer to the simple question, whether the prisoners were ready for therapy, if there existed an adequate offer (65% agreed). The relevant predictors can be seen from Table 2. Using these variables, the rate of correctly predicted therapy readiness was about 95%. The second criteria - *active search for therapy* - means that the person showed any further interest in therapy, before our investigation started - e.g. he acquired information from external institutions (13%). With the variables identified as important for prediction (see Table 2), about 93% were classified correctly. This selection shows some correspondence to the assumptions of the classical construct, because all selected variables refer to the aim of therapy (and not to the instrument) and confirm the need of an internal perception of problems by the offender. It appears that in case of predicting active searching behaviour, both conceptions have similar assumptions.

The other two criteria were not defined by the offenders themselves, but by the decisions of the prison staff. *Social therapy* indicates that the prisoners were sent to a social therapeutic ward half a year after our investigation (14%). It was important that the offenders themselves expressed their will for a therapy and the staff agreed on a sufficient indication[2]. Using the relevant predictor variables (see Table 2), about 89% of the sample could be classified correctly. Surprisingly, the extent of reported problems had no significant effect in the analysis (although there was a correlation). The included variables appear to equalise the influence of the extent of reported problems, so that they did not contribute any more to the prediction. The last criteria - *therapy advice* - indicates a corresponding hint in the report of the diagnostical ward where we did our investigations (21%). This criteria could be predicted correctly in 90% of all cases.

Two points are worth mentioning. At first it is remarkable, that those criteria, that were defined by the offenders themselves could be predicted with a (slightly but constantly) higher precision than those that were defined by the staff. This could mean that the decisions of the professionals were influenced by additional factors which are not described by the construct. Empirical studies imply that these additional criteria may be their evaluations of the institutional therapeutic capabilities to deal with particular offenders. This interpretation however would indicate institutional deficits more than eventual shortcomings on the side of the offenders, so that this factor should not be mingled with motivational terms. However it is astonishing that the decisions of the staff could be best predicted by the extensive use of instrument-related attitudes, where the offender's trust in the honesty of therapeutic intentions of the prison staff played a major role. The second point is that the analysis consistently found more influencial factors to be relevant in case of offender-defined criteria. This fact underlines the complexity of the motivational background structure and emphasises the demand that the individual degree of suffering from problems needs more attention.

In the course of the report of our first study, four groups were mentioned which resulted from a classical operationalisation of therapy-motivation: a motivated, a non-motivated and two non-fitting groups. Since we were interested in the question of how the new construct fits these groups, we rebuilt them the same way as already described. Table 3 shows those variables of the construct which discriminated significantly between the four groups.

Those groups who already matched the classical construct also met plausible expectations of our new model quite well. The motivated group indicated more problems and showed prevailing internal attributions; concerning the instrumental side of therapy motivation, their view of therapy was a quite positive one, whereas the availability of possible alternative instruments was rather poor. On the other side the non-motivated group formed an almost perfect counterpart to this figuration of motivational structure.

---

[2]   During the course of our investigation, the social therapeutic ward was not fully utilised, so that organisational shortcomings or needs were not essential factors.

Table 3: Differences between Some Motivational Unequivocal and Ambiguous Groups

	bad motivation (n = 26)	little grief (n = 28)	no readiness (n = 15)	good motivation	p (ANOVA)
1. Motives regarding the aim:					
1.1 Problem-specific:					
quantity	8.4	10.7	18.3	18.7	•••
internal cause[a]	48%	54%	29%	60%	••
changeability[b]	56%	68%	34%	58%	•
internal control[c]	48%	56%	30%	52%	•
1.2 Context specific:		no significant differences			
2. Motives regarding the expedient:					
2.1 Therapy:					
expected effectiveness	-.72	.09	-1.31	.34	•••
stigma-fear	12.8	9.8	13.7	11.5	•
capability	.04	.22	-.37	.15	•
rigidity	35.0	30.1	38.4	29.6	•••
2.2 Alternative resources:					
self-efficacy	1.04	.48	.43	-.76	•••
- int. LOC	38.4	35.4	39.7	34.8	•
- capability	49.2	48.1	40.8	37.9	•••

All measures are group means; the problem-specific attributions (a-c) are mean percentages concerning the individual number of realised problems; • p <.05, •• p <.01, ••• p < .001

The non-fitting groups, however, produced particular profiles which may contribute to clarify their ambiguity. Group 2 (which was ready for therapy without too much distress) showed a moderate level of problems. Like the motivated group, they believed them to be internally caused and controlled and therefore changeable. On the whole, their attitudes concerning therapy were quite positive. Besides a lower amount of realised problems, the main difference to the motivated group was a higher degree of realised personal resources. The other non-fitting group showed a high degree of distress caused by their problems, but they did not feel responsible for that - either in regarding the anticipated causes or regarding the specific locus of control. Consequently, they did not believe the problems to be changeable. Regarding the instrument-related variables, this group showed very unfavourable conditions. They indicated very negative attitudes concerning therapy and did not believe meeting anticipated requirements. Their *rigidity* - defined as the general need to control life and its circumstances - was very high, compared to the other groups. Another interesting difference between the non-fitting groups, concerning their perception of personal resources, is worth mentioning. While no differences in regard to their anticipated self-efficacy could be noticed in general, the assembly of this construct is a completely different one. The group who resisted therapy showed a very high degree of a generalised internal locus of control but realised very little necessary competence for that. In case of the other non-fitting group, exactly the reverse is true. The fitting groups, however, once again showed a homogeneous composition.

Conclusion

The studies exemplify the expediency of a specific construct of therapy motivation for the situation in prisons. Such a construct improves the understanding of the origins of the often noticed ambiguity of the offender's motivation, by specifying particular fears and resentments caused by the actual imprisonment or by other (e.g. social) offender-specific circumstances. It also improves our predictive capacities concerning defined subgroups by identifying relevant factors that may influence their reactions to offers of help in prison. For these reasons, it seems to be appropriate for scientific purposes as well as for practical therapeutic needs.

The classical construct - as it was originally developed in regard to neurotic patients - appeared to be an essential conception which is adequate in special cases where there are no further complications besides the existence of psychic (and definitely intrinsic) conflicts. In this case, all other possible influencing factors can be assumed as sufficiently given and therefore irrelevant (i.e., the patient has a sufficient idea about therapy and its possibilities, he trusts in the integrity and professionality of the therapist, etc.). In cases, however, in which the kind of problems, the therapeutical setting or specific characteristics of the target group themselves contradict this postulate, appropriate extensions are necessary. Above all in prison environments the confinement to the "essentials" of the classical construct seems to meet an interest in selecting appropriate sub-groups concerning therapeutic prognosis rather than being suitable for evaluating the complexity of motivational structures. The question of selection (i.e. indication) however needs to be considered as an interaction between characteristics of the patient (where motivation is only *one* dimension) on one side and institutional, personal and methodological capabilities to meet these requirements on the other (e.g. Steller, 1993).

References

Dahle, K.-P. (1994). Therapiemotivation inhaftierter Straftäter. In M. Steller, K.-P. Dahle & M. Basqué (Eds.) *Straftäterbehandlung - Argumente zur Revitalisierung in Forschung und Praxis,* (pp 227-246). Pfaffenweiler: Centaurus.

Dahle, K.-P. (1995). Therapiemotivation hinter Gittern. Zielgruppenorientierte Entwicklung und Erprobung eines Motivationskonstrukts für die therapeutische Arbeit im Strafvollzug. Regensbrug: Roderer.

Krampen, G. (1989). Motivation in the Treatment of Alcoholism. *Addictive Behaviors, 14,* 197-200.

Ortmann, R. (1986). Resozialisierung im Strafvollzug - Eine vergleichende Längsschnittstudie zu Regelvollzugs - und sozialtherapeutischen Modellanstalten. In H.-J. Albrecht & U. Sieber (Eds.), *Zwanzig Jahre Südwestdeutsche Kriminologische Kolloquien,* (239-278). Freiburg: Selbstverlag Max-Plack-Institut.

Rasch, W. (1994). Mit differenzierter Optik sich dem Gegenstand Kriminaltherapie nähern. In M. Steller, K.-P. Dahle & M. Basqué (Eds.) *Straftäterbehandlung - Argumente zur Revitalisierung in Forschung und Praxis,* (pp 250-253). Pfaffenweiler: Centaurus.

Raskin, A. (1961). Factors Therapists Associate with Motivation to Enter Psychotherapy. *Journal of Clinical Psychology, 17,* 62-65.

Riedel, W. (1989). *Therapiemotivation und Therapieerfolg - Prädiktoren des Inanspruchnahmeverhaltens und deren Bedeutung für das Therapieergebnis in einer stationären Psychotherapie.* Regensburg: Roderer.

Schneider, W. (1986). *Zum Begriff der Psychotherapiemotivation - Konstruktvalidierung und Entwicklung eines Meßinstrumentes.* Marburg: unveröff. Dissertation.

Steller, M. (1993). Über Unbelehr - und Unbehandelbare. In N. Leygraf, R. Volbert, H. Horstkotte & S. Fried (Eds.). *Die Sprache des Verbrechens - Wege zu einer klinischen Kriminologie.* Stuttgart: Kohlhammer.

The Treatment of Aggressive Prisoners.
A Closed Regime Programme

Joan P. Queralt, Judith Caballero, Alícia Casals, Joan C. Navarro and Silvia Serra

Introduction

The Spanish Penitentiary Law of 1979, with its regulations contained in decree 1201/81 of the 8th of May 1981, sought to construct a flexible, progressive and humane penal system. It was drawn up taking into account the most modern developments in penal practice world-wide, and was inspired by the Minimum Rules for the Treatment of Prisoners dictated by the United Nations in 1955, by the Council of Europe in 1973, the international agreements on human rights and the penal legislation adopted by the most advanced nations (Sweden, Germany, Italy, etc.).

Spain's penal legislation embodies a philosophy oriented towards encouraging a penitentiary treatment directed at the reeducation and reinsertion into society of the prisoner. In this respect, and within this legal framework, the legislation seeks to establish that the prisoner continue to be a person that forms part of society and is not isolated from it. In line with this principle, the potentiality of the open regime was declared, with the *limitation of the closed regime to exceptional circumstances*. This established that sentences would be served according to a system of scientific individualisation, structured in three separate grades or stages. The second and third grades were to be served, respectively, in centres operating an ordinary and an open regime. Those classified in the first grade, the subject of this study, would serve their sentences in institutions with a closed regime or in a special section. This regime is applied to those prisoners classified as extremely dangerous, or to cases of failure to adapt to the ordinary and open regimes. Before it is applied, there must exist a series of circumstances defined by law, these being: membership in a criminal organisation, participation in collective disorder or physical violence towards other prisoners or staff, and unwarranted refusal to comply with legal orders or sanctions. Continuance in this regime must be reviewed within a maximum period of three months where it is the consequence of a regression from a higher grade.

The operation of penitentiaries with a closed regime is governed by the principles of security, order and discipline, determined by the need to avoid infractions of the system of order, but without neglecting the fundamental orientation which is to facilitate treatment.

The Centre Penitenciari Brians, which runs an ordinary regime, was opened in May 1991. However, in May 1991 a closed regime department was brought into service. The staff of the treatment team were given the task of organising and applying the appropriate treatment, but they were not subject to a defined and structured programme in terms of objectives and content. Thus, the results relating to the prisoners' periods of stay and to indices of discipline during their stay in the closed regime did not meet expectations.

With the idea of classifying these prisoners in terms of treatment requirements, a closed regime programme was drawn up, based on a system of progressive phases, but at the same time including:

- A clear definition of objectives;
- The figure of a tutor, who would provide the prisoner with feedback and keep him continually informed as to what was expected of him;
- A treatment based on techniques of self-control, a programme of physical activities and sports, adjustment of the educational activities to the needs of the prisoner and definition of the functions of the staff assigned to the department (creation of a multidisciplinary team).

Description of the Programme

Objectives

The programme thus designed pursues two basic objectives:

- Reduction of the period of stay of prisoners in the closed regime;
- Decrease in the index of discipline problems through a decrease in sanctionable behaviours, and reincorporation into the ordinary regime.

Theoretical model

Our model is that of Bandura's Psychology of Social Learning (1969, 1980), the bases of which consist in operant conditioning and observational learning. This model seeks to underline the active role of the subject in his interaction with the environment. Organismal and environmental variables and the subject's own conduct all interact with one another.

The model also postulates that the consequences of a behaviour influence that conduct, creating expectations of similar results on future occasions. There is a contingent relationship between the conduct and the environment in which it is produced, there is an environmental stimulus which precedes and propitiates the conduct and, on a second level, the environmental effects which reach the subject when the conduct is displayed control its display in the future.

In this way, we established which conducts were to be potentiated and which were to be eradicated (problem behaviours), and a system of contingent reinforcements. Thus, desirable conducts were followed up with positive consequences (reinforcements), while problem conducts were followed by negative consequences (punishments). By this means we sought to augment the probability of the production of desirable conducts and diminish undesirable or problem behaviours.

Programme of progressive phases

The programme of progressive phases (Redondo, Roca & Portero, 1986; Redondo, 1993) is a dynamic-motivational system in which prisoners are placed in accordance with the behaviours displayed, and in which the number of reinforcers increases in relation to the level attained by the prisoner.

The basic characteristics of this type of programme are: the *progressive scale* of both the objectives and the available lifestyles and reinforcements; the clear and evident *differentiation* between the phases, perceptible to the prisoner; a clear *operationalization* of conducts, available reinforcers and criteria of application for each of the phases; and a *contingency of reinforcement* to the display of both desirable and undesirable conducts.

A programme of three successive phases with a minimum duration of three months (12 weeks) was established, with the following characteristics:

Phase 1. This is the phase to which the prisoner is assigned on regressing to a closed regime or first grade. The minimum duration is three weeks, with the prisoner occupying an individual cell. He receives attention from the staff in his cell, is allowed one hour a day in the exercise yard, and may make one telephone call a month. The absence of serious or very serious misconduct results in progress to Phase 2.

Phase 2. The minimum duration is four weeks, and the prisoner may share his cell with another inmate. He engages in 2.5 hours of programmed activities in the classroom and two hours daily in the exercise yard. During the last two weeks he eats in the refectory, may make two telephone calls per month, may receive a "face-to-face" visit of one hour, and is allowed to have a television set in the cell. Absence of serious misconduct, participation in 90% of the activities and a score of 27 points or more on a questionnaire of normalised conducts designed to evaluate the generalisation of behaviour will result in progress to Phase 3.

Phase 3. The minimum duration is five weeks. In this phase the prisoner is provided not only with the Phase 2 reinforcers, but is also permitted two hours of "face-to-face" visits and one hour each day of leisure activities in the refectory-lounge. Absence of serious misconduct, participation in 90% of the activities, a score of 45 points or more and the attainment of the objectives set for the individual at the start of the programme will result in cessation of the closed regime.

Table 1: Progressive Phases System

	Phase 1	Phase 2	Phase 3
System of life	1 h. a day in the exercise yard. Individual cell. Meals in the cell. One telephone call a month.	2 h. a day in the exercise yard. A cell for two. The third and fourth week meals in the refectory except breakfast. 2.5 h. of programmed activities in the classroom. Two telephone calls a month. 1 h. visit "face to face". Television in the cell if there are not serious misconducts.	2 h. a day in the exercise yard. A cell for two. Meals in the refectory except breakfast. 2.5 h. of programmed activities in the classroom. Two telephone calls a month. 2 h. visit "face to face". Television in the cell if there are no serious misconducts.
Minimum duration	Three s weeks	Four weeks	Five weeks
Progression	Absence of serious or very serious misconduct.	Absence of serious or very serious misconduct. Participation in 90% of the programmed activities. Obtaining 27 points.	Absence of serious or very serious misconduct. Participation in 90% of the programme activities. Obtaining 45 points. Having obtained the objectives of the programme set at the beginning.
Maintenance	One very serious misconduct. One serious misdeed: 2 weeks. Another serious or very serious misconduct: one week for each.	One serious misconduct: two weeks. Not participating in 90% of the programmed activities: two weeks. Not obtaining 27 points: two weeks.	Not participation in 90% of the programmed activities: two weeks. Not obtaining 45 points: two weeks. Two light misconducts: two weeks. Not obtaining the objectives set in the beginning of the programme: until obtained.
Regression		One very serious misconduct. Two serious misconducts.	One very serious misconduct: phase 1. One serious misconduct: phase 2. Not participating in 50% of the programmed activities for two weeks: in phase 2.

Staff

The following staff were assigned to the application of the programme:

- A jurist-criminologist responsible for informing the prisoner of his legal, penal and prison situation.

- A psychologist responsible for evaluating and intervening in techniques of self-control (Wessiger, 1985).
- An educator, with the role of tutor, responsible for carrying out the educational and sports activities.
- A teacher responsible for basic adult education.
- A unit leader in charge of the organisation and allocation of tasks to the prison staff responsible for maintaining control and order in the department.

Results

The results were obtained on the basis of comparison of two groups with the following characteristics:

- Control group: composed of 14 prisoners who had been in the center for at least six months before their regression to the first grade, who progressed without the application of the programme, and who remained in the centre for at least six months after their progression.
- Experimental group: composed of 17 prisoners who were in the centre for at least six months before their regression, who progressed on the basis of the application of the programme, and who remained in the centre for at least six months after their progression.

Homogeneity of variances

The homogeneity of the variances was assessed using the Snedecor test, obtaining an observed value of $F = 2.77$, lower than the theoretical value for $F(14, 17, 0.05) = 2.87$, which defines the region of rejection. Accordingly, the hypothesis of equality of variances between the two groups in relation to the index of discipline problems three months prior to the application of the programme is accepted.

Duration of stay

The average number of days spent in the first grade was established for each of the groups, this being 137.93 days (with a minimum stay of 90 days and a maximum of 247) for the control group, and 115.93 days (ranging between a minimum of 85 days and a minimum of 181) for the experimental group. The two averages were compared by means of the Student-Fisher significance test, which confirmed the experimental hypothesis of reduction of the period of stay in the first grade. (Observed value $t = 1.85$; theoretical value $t(0.05) = 1.69$).

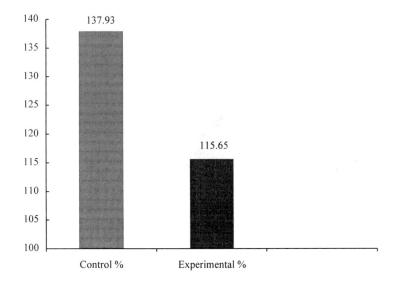

Average number of day spent in the first grade was established for each of the groups; control group: 137.93; experimental group: 115.65

Figure 1: Duration of Stay

Distribution by intervals

We show a distribution of frequencies by intervals of 21 days (three weeks) on the basis of the minimum observed period of stay (85 days), and observed that in the control group the highest percentage of prisoners was found in the interval 129-150 (35.71%), while in the experimental group this corresponded to the interval 85-106 (64.71%). The control group presented greater dispersion, while in the experimental group there was less, and concentrated in the first interval (Table 2).

Table 2: Distribution by Intervals

	Control %	Experimental %
85-106	28.6	64.7
107-128	14.3	5.8
129-150	35.6	11.8
151-172	7.1	11.8
173+	14.3	5.8

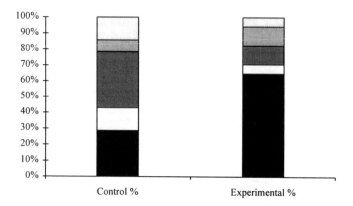

Distribution of frequencies by intervals of 21 days (three weeks), on the basis of the minimum observed period of stay (85 days)

Figure 2: Distribution by Intervals

Reduction of discipline problems during the first grade

The level of discipline problems was evaluated by means of an index which weighed the seriousness of the breaches of discipline in terms of the classification applied by the current penal norms. Thus, each very serious infringement committed was assigned a value of 3, with a value of 2 for serious infringements and one for minor infringements. This procedure gave an average score for discipline problems by months of stay in the first grade equivalent to 2.44 for the control group and 1.5 for the experimental group. Application of the Student-Fisher significance test revealed a significant difference in the level of confidence of 10%, so that the experimental hypothesis of reduction of indiscipline during the period of stay in the first grade is accepted (observed value t = 1.32; theoretical value t(0.10) = 1.30).

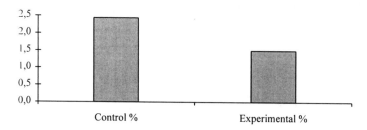

Average score for indiscipline by months of stay in the first grade; control group: 2.44; experimental group: 1.5

Figure 3: Reduction of Indiscipline during the First Grade

Distribution of frequencies

We present a distribution of frequencies by intervals of two points of discipline problems, observing that in both groups the highest percentage of prisoners was concentrated in the interval 0-2. Nevertheless, in the control group this interval represented 50% of the prisoners, while in the experimental group the percentage rose to 82.36%, accompanied by the observation of a greater dispersion in the control group. At the same time it is worth emphasising that while in the control group 7.14% of the prisoners had no infringements during the period of application of the first grade, in the experimental group this percentage rose to 29.41% of prisoners.

Table 3: Distribution of Frequencies

	Control %	Experimental %
0-2	50.0	82.3
2.1-4	28.6	5.9
4.1-6	14.3	0
6.1+	7.1	11.8

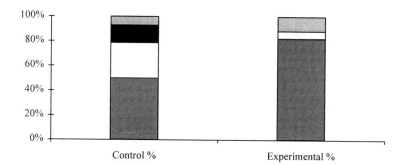

Distribution of frequencies by intervals of two points of indiscipline

Figure 4: Index of Indiscipline (during the Application in the First Grade)

Evolution of indiscipline

A study of discipline problems was conducted six months before and after the application of the first grade at intervals of three months in order to observe the evolution of the indices of discipline problems with reference to the generalisation of behaviours after application of the programme. Although the differences between the two groups were not statistically significant in this respect, it was possible to observe that the experimental group manifested greater discipline problems than the control group prior to the application of the first grade, while it subsequently manifested less discipline problems during the period of application (where there were indeed significant differences), and discipline problems in this group continued to be lower in the two ensuing three-month periods.

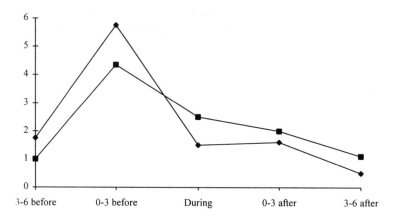

Discipline problems were measured six months before and after the application of the first grade at intervals of three months in order to observe the evolution of the discipline problems scores

Figure 5: Evolution of Discipline Problems (before/during/after the First Grade)

Conclusions

The application of the programme of progressive phases reduced both the length of stay in the first grade and the indices of discipline problems during the stay in a significant manner.

It is therefore possible to carry out an intervention oriented towards positive change in the conduct of prisoners classified as dangerous or maladapted to penitentiary norms who have to be assigned to maximum security departments.

Improvements were obtained in the generalisation of behaviour and in the reduction of indices of discipline problems following application of the programme, although these differences are not statistically significant.

In spite of these findings, we consider that the results may be mediated by the characteristics of the samples available. If these had been larger, it is possible that the results would have presented higher indices of significance (especially in the index of discipline problems), given that the variances prior to the application of the programme would be compensated (even accepting the hypothesis of homogeneity of variances with a risk of error of 0.10).

References

Bandura, A. (1969). *Principles of behaviour modification.* New York: Holt, Rinehart & Winston.

Bandura, A. (1980). Análisis del aprendizaje social de la agresión. In A. Bandura & E. Ribes. *Modificación de conducta. Análisis de la agresión y la delincuencia,* cap. 11. México: Trillas.

Redondo, S., Roca, M. and Portero, P. (1986). Aproximación conductual en un centro penitenciario de jóvenes: un sistema de fases progresivas. *Revista de Estudios Penitenciarios,* n. 236, pp. 127-140.

Redondo, S. (1993). *Evaluar e intervenir en las prisiones.* Barcelona: PPU.

Weisinger, H. (1985). *Técnicas para el control del comportamiento agresivo.* Barcelona: Martínez Roca.

Organization Program of the Barcelona Women's Prison: Six Years of Evaluation

José M. Montero, Jesús Martínez, Miguel Angel Esteban, Ana Alonso and Carles Soler

Introduction

The prison environment has been, historically, a reluctant setting for planned and evaluated intervention. There are rare references to concrete works in the literature. In Catalonia, with the only exception of Redondo and a few other authors (Redondo, 1983; Redondo, Roca, Pérez, Sánchez & Deumal, 1990), who have played key roles in management as well as in divulgation of intervention, there have few serious efforts overall to dote the organization of penitentiary centers with effective programs for ameliorating their functioning.

Perhaps the only area that has been developed systematically in the last ten years has been that related to prison classification programs. The results obtained (Redondo, et al., 1990) support their continuity. Nowadays, these programs are adopted generally at all Catalonian centers.

In all the centers where they have been implemented, improved hygienic behaviors, increased participation in activities and a reduction of violent behaviors have resulted.

This work tries to respond to the following questions: if the introduction of a support program (Redondo, 1993) such as classification produces positive results in the evaluation of different behavioral areas of the inmate population, what would happen if we added to this support program another one: educational orientation or personal tutoring and the design of a program of contents (Redondo, 1993) such as the educational-modular program (Direcció General de Serveis Penitenciaris i de Rehabilitació, 1990).

Our hypothesis is that continuos implementation of these three programs during five years will have produced an important improvement in the following evaluated behavioral areas:

- Personal hygiene and self-care.
- Individual conflictivity.
- Social climate.
- Participation in educational programs.

Thus, we hope to obtain significant statistical differences in all of those areas when we compare the results of this work with that described in preceding ones (Redondo et al., 1986).

Subjects

The Barcelona Women's Prison is a center for convicted women and those in preventive detention. During the period of study, this center had a maximum of 355 inmates and a minimum of 245, with a mean of 300. The program tested in this study was applied to all members who were in the center since its progressive application. The program of classification, initiated in 1989, has been applied to a total of 6,420 inmates. In 1991 we started the modular education program and tutoring. Of the total of 6,420, 3,233 inmates participated in these last programs. During the evaluated period, time spent by the inmates in the center was as follows: 42% remained a period inferior to 30 days, 32% from one to five months, and 26 % more than five months. Following are some additional data, obtained from a sample of 300 inmates: medium age: 26 years old (ranging from 17 to 68 years old); education level as follows: 30% low level, 30% medium level, 40% high level.

At the moment of reception into the center, 37% of the inmates were addicted to some kind of drug.

Instruments

The instruments used to obtain the results were as follows: systematic registers of behavioral observation, a behavioral evaluation scale, the register of disciplinary infractions, notifications of positive behaviors made by prison officers, reports made by educators and tutors of the center, protocol to inform the inmates about extraordinary sentence reductions, activity and institutional conflictivity cards. The Moos Social Climate Scale (Moos, 1975) was also used in penitentiary centers.

Methods

The basic components of the classification program, from 1988 (when we began to apply it) to 1991, are the following:

- Four classification units were established at the center. At the residential level, the units had different locations, although most of activities were held in common areas. The difference among those units consisted of an increase of demand in different behavior areas and of active participation. At the behavioral level, the program basically is based on hygiene and personal self-care, order in rooms, the degree of adaptation to center rules and improvements in inadaptative behavior, such as isolation and self-injury. Concerning participation in activities, we had been obliged to guarantee the participation in the basic training program, which involved a minimum activity of 15 hours per week. The maximum established, following a demanding gradient, was 40 hours of activity per week.

Following a qualitative and quantitative increase of level, we assigned some benefits and reinforcements to each level. There were different kinds of benefits, most of them based on elements that are inherent to the prison regime (number of communications, time spent in these, schedules, sentences reductions, etc.):

- At first we assigned one of the four units to inmates, based on an initial review of misbehavior and the capacity to achieve behaviors demanded in each unit. This first evaluation was done by professionals that belong to the observation and treatment group of the center (psychologists, jurist-criminologist, teachers, etc.).
- Establishment of a periodic revision system of inmate evaluation. We analyzed the evolution of inmates in the areas described before, based on data obtained from the indicated registers and reports . The movement of inmates to superior or inferior units was based on this evaluation, their behaviors and participation in activities.
- Other basic components of this Program were: improvement of programs and activities that belong to the educational training planning of the center, clarification of behavior and life , norms to follow, information for staff and inmates about the operation of the classification program.

During 1991 we introduced into the Center the Modular Educational Program, the Tutoring Program and we revised the Classification Program.

After the revision of the classification program we adapted the following components:

- All the inmates were evaluated monthly and a system of notification of results to the inmates was established.
- A notification system of positive behaviors to everybody in the center was applied when the positive behavior defined previously was exhibited. In the notification to inmates some benefits were included.
- We made individual behavior contracts with the inmates. The inmates more reluctant to change and who had no adaptive behavior were subject to individual behavior contracts.
- In addition to the above-mentioned components, we introduced more systematic behaviors, tests and a card system of activity to supervise the evaluation systems of behavior and the participation of inmates. Also, we increased levels of behavior demand and the participation in all classification units in the center.

The modular educational program consisted of the following basic components:

- An evaluation of the mean time spent by the inmates in the center. This allowed us to adjust the offer of basic training in the Center to real temporal possibilities of inmate training.
- An evaluation of training contents adjusted to inmates' deficiencies in each area (Coll C., 1986; García Carrasco, 1991) and established norms about adult training (Llei Parlament Catalunya, 1991).

We arranged the offer of training programs to the inmates in three groups depending on their content and duration. The training groups are the following:

1. A shock program with a curriculum for inmates that spend a short time in the center. The characteristics of this program are the following: mean duration of four weeks; the program is divided in units that have an independent content, and it is taught by people from different collectives of the center, which are flexible and open. This program tries to transmit useful habits that will improve the return to a crime-free life outside the center (health, family planning, etc.).

2. Short-term programs, maximum time of three months. These programs are applied to homogeneous groups and have more special contents.

3. Medium and long-term programs. These programs give specialized knowledge and are taught by docent staff.

The Tutoring Program had the following components:

- A collective of professional people, that belong to any of the center areas, who serve as tutors. The number of tutors depends on the number of inmates assigned to each tutor, ranging from 15 to 20 inmates.
- Tutors' training in specific techniques, interviews, personal evaluation, design programs and education paths, and information techniques.
- Definition of basic activities of tutors. These are:
  . To inquire about the needs, interests and aptitudes of assigned inmates.
  . To facilitate integration and participation of inmates in everyday life in the center.
  . To design programs and education steps for inmates, based on previous programs. The designed programs are transferred to other specific programs (methadone, prevention of suicides, leaves, etc.). The first evaluation is made at the moment when the inmates enter the center and then after a month of having been in it.
  . To review inmates' evolution and progression in achieving the aims that are defined in programs assigned to each inmate.
  . To create a system to assign inmates to tutors.
  . To define a system to attend to the inmates (schedule and meeting place, etc.).

Results

The results obtained from the indicator variables of prison behavior and the level of participation in activities are the following:

The behavioral data refer to hygiene aspects, conflictivity (evaluated by number of disciplinary infractions, recorded as "slight", "serious" or "very serious") and the evaluation of classification (regarding a high degree of inadaptation to basic norms of living together). Referring to the participation level in different activities, we evaluated the hours spent in planned activities and the amount of extra sentence reduction obtained with these activities. We also applied the "Moos Social Climate Scale", for which data will be presented.

The data show the evolution of different behaviors during the period of study (1991-1994).

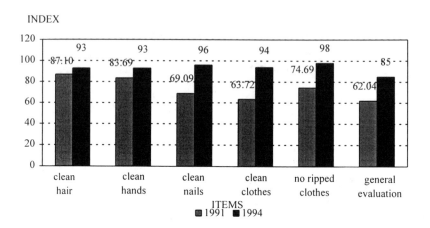

In the graph the mean scores obtained in the respective observational register are presented. They are presented at two different moments: before the implementation of the classification program (1991) and now at (1994).

Figure 1: Self-Hygienic Register (1991-1994)

Figures 1 and 2 show an improvement of hygiene since 1991, when the classification program was applied, until 1994. This improvement is reflected in the hygiene indicators evaluated during this period.

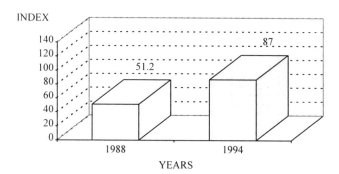

Global scores for all the inmates that scored correct on all the items of the scales. In the x axis are the time periods. In the y axis are the percentages.

Figure 2: Self-Hygienic Register 1988-1994

num. of infractions

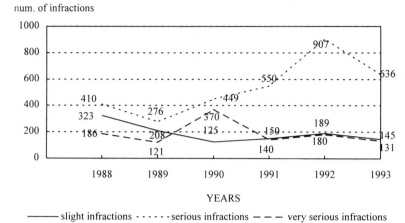

YEARS

——— slight infractions · · · · · · serious infractions — — — very serious infractions

In the y axis are the total number of disciplinary infractions, recorded as "slight", "serious" and "very serious". In the x axis are the six years of the period evaluated.

Figure 3: Individual Conflictivity 1988-1993

TOTAL

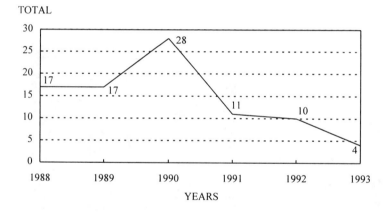

YEARS

In the y axis is the total number of applications of the first degree and art. 10, motivated by the high degree of indaptation to norms. In the x axis are the years of the period evaluated.

Figure 4: Statistics of 1st Degree and Art. 10

In figures 3 and 4 we present the evaluation of conflict in the center, during the evaluated period.

a) Figure 3 shows the conflictivity degree by the number of disciplinary infractions. These results indicate a decrease in the number of very serious and slight disciplinary infractions. Although the decrease is not continuous during the evaluation period, we observe fewer infractions during 1993 that in 1988. The number of serious infractions was increased during that period, and the greatest number took place in 1992. However, in 1993 the number of serious infractions decreased.

b) We also show the degree of conflictivity by the number of classifications in indication of a high degree of inadaptation to basic norms of living together. We can observe an important decrease in assigning these classifications. These results, with the decrease of serious disciplinary infractions, indicate an improvement in inadaptive behavior and an achievement of basic communal living norms that demonstrate a qualitative modulation of inmate behavior.

Figure 5 shows the results obtained in the *Moos Social Climate Scale*. All evaluated scales show an important improvement during the evaluation period. The improvement is related to organizational aspects in the center (organization, clarity, etc.) and to the helping role of the institution (help, expression, implication, etc.). We should point out that the only area that shows no improvement is that about perception of control; this result is related to an increase in autonomy.

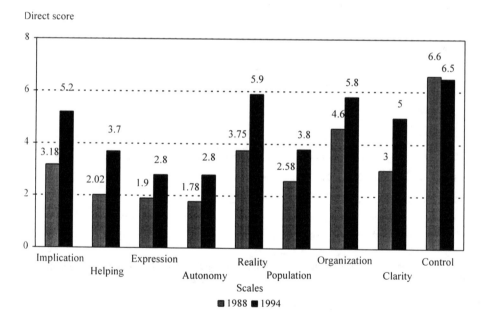

In the y axis are the direct scores obtained in the Moos Social Climate Scale. In the x axis are the years (1988-1994) when the scale and the elements of the scale were implemented.

Figure 5: Social Climate (Barcelona Women's Prison)

In Figure 6 and Table 1 we show results about the level of participation in activities. The means of extraordinary sentence reduction days obtained yearly due to participation in different activity programs are shown in Figure 6. These data indicate a significant increase in the number of days and reflect the degree of participation in activities since 1989. In Table 1 we present the occupation index of inmates in the center. We observe a significant increase of this index throughout the evaluation period.

Table 1: Index of Inmate Occupation

Total	Number of inmates (corrected * 1)	X Hours per week occupied by inmates	Occupation index * 2
Nov 15, 1991	205	32.17	61.20%
Feb 15, 1992	246	30.09	54.55%
Nov 15, 1992	186	34.40	64.36%
Feb 15, 1993	201	38.36	74.44%
Nov 15, 1993	232	36.29	71.64%
Feb 15, 1994	251	37.52	73.24%

(* 2) Equivalent to:

Total of occupied inmates x n° hours of activity

Total number of inmates in the Center x Maximum number of hours that inmates can dedicate to activity (50 h./week)

(* 1) Corrected number of inmates = total number of inmates - inmates in open section, infirmary and admissions.

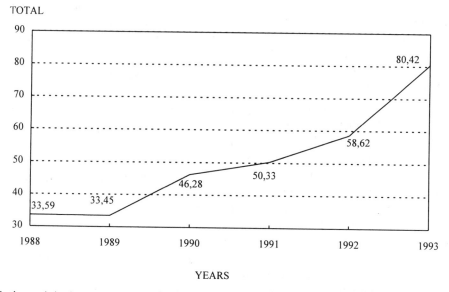

In the y axis is the mean number of days obtained for extraordinary sentence reduction. In the x axis are the years of the period evaluated.

Figure 6: Extraordinary Sentence reductions

Discussion

The results obtained show us the way for ameliorating the organization of Penitentiary Centers.

The implementation of the first generation of classification programs represented a landmark in the "technological history" of Catalonian prisons. In the Centre Penitenciari de Dones (penitentiary center for women) the evolution led to complement the classification program with a positive behavior notification system (since April, 93 until January, 94 there were 1,493 notifications that affected 45% of inmates, with a mean of 150) and with a system of behavioral contracts for those inmates more reluctant to change (inmates in the first phase).

At the same time we implemented two new programs:

1. Tutoring, with the objective of motivating and orienting the individual assignment to those activity programs considered necessary for the inmate.
2. Educational-modular, that start from the theoretical principles of Adult Education (García Carrasco, 1991; Puigdellívol, 1993; Martínez Tuya, 1993). It is structured innovatively:

- form: offering a curricular design based on days in prison (programs for inmates with only one month in prison, 45% of all the population, three-monthly and annual). These programs are drawn up by the tutors themselves after a detailed evaluation.

- content: offering educational contents as a function of the evaluated needs of the inmates. The assignment to a Principal Training Program (Basic Training, Occupational Courses, Professional Training, etc.) and to another complementary one (Psychosocial Competence, Communication, Physical Training, Artistic Expressions, etc.) is obligatory. There is the possibility of individual curricular design because all the programs are conformed by independent modules.

We understand these results as conclusive ones:

1. Substantial improvement in all the scales of the Hygienic Register. Comparing the results, in 1994 there is an increment of almost 40 percentage points compared to 1990 in those inmates with positive scoring on all behaviors of the scale.
2. Substantial improvement in conflictivity. The evidence is not as strong for the decrease in disciplinary infractions (decrease of very serious and slight infractions) as in the great decrease of the application of first degrees and art. 10.
3. Social climate. There is a statistically significant improvement in all the evaluated scales, except in perceived control, that diminished. This last scale reaffirms the thesis that inmates perceived less conflictivity.
4. Participation in activities. The increment can be considered spectacular. We can not really visualize the difference because we have no results before 1991 (when activities were computerized). In any case, the difference with other Catalonian penitentiary centers is more than double (DGSPIR, 1994). The occupation index is a mean of 37 hours per week and 97% of participation of the inmates in the designed educational programs. These can be considered, really, important results.

References

Coll, C. (1986*). Marc curricular per a l'ensenyament obligatori.* Barcelona: Departament d'Ensenyament de la Generalitat de Catalunya.

Direcció General de Serveis Penitenciaris i de Rehabilitació (1990). *Model organitzatiu d'educació d'adults als centres penitenciaris de Catalunya.* Not published. Barcelona: Departament de Justícia de la Generalitat de Catalunya.

Direcció General de Serveis Penitenciaris i de Rehabilitació (1992). *Programa d'orientació educativa.* Not published. Barcelona: Departament de Justícia de la Generalitat de Catalunya.

Direcció General de Serveis Penitenciaris i de Rehabilitació (1994). *Estudi estadístic d'activitats 1r trimestre 1994.* Not published. Barcelona: Departament de Justícia de la Generalitat de Catalunya.

García Carrasco, J. (1991). *La formación básica de adultos.* Barcelona: CEAC.

Llei 3/1991 de 18 de març de Formació d'Adults. Parlament de Catalunya. *Diari Oficial de la Generalitat de Catalunya, 1424.*

Martínez Tuya, M.(1993*). Trabajar con el curriculum.* Málaga: Agora.

Moos, R.H. (1975). *Evaluating Correctional and Community Settings.* New York: Wiley.

Puigdellívol, I. (1993). *Programación del aula y adecuación curricular.* Barcelona: Graó.

Redondo, S. (1983). "Una aplicación de la economía de fichas en la prisión de Madrid". *Revista Española de Terapia de comportamiento, 1* (3), 303-327.

Redondo, S., Roca, M., & Portero, P. (1986). Aproximación conductual en un Centro Penitenciario de jóvenes: un sistema de fases progresivas. *Revista de Estudis Penitenciaris, 236,* 127-140.

Redondo, S., Roca, M., Pérez, E., Sánchez, A., & Deumal, E. (1990).Diseño ambiental de una prisión de jóvenes: cinco años de evaluación. *Delincuencia/Delinquency, 2* (3), 331-357.

Redondo, S. (1993). *Evaluar e intervenir en las prisiones. Análisis de conducta aplicado.* Barcelona: PPU.

Part IX
Correctional Evaluation

Methodological Advances in the Assessment of Correctional Programs

M. Teresa Anguera

Introduction

Correctional evaluation is an in-depth investigation of a program's characteristics and merits. Its purpose is to provide information on the effectiveness of projects so as to optimise the outcomes, efficiency, and quality of correctional programs.

Correctional program evaluations require diligence in the choice and application of methods. One of the major tasks of an evaluation is to judge the program's merits and to analyse its relation with available resources.

As Redondo (1993) states, besides diverse objectives of an evaluative nature, the aim corresponding to synchronic / diachronic analysis of implemented programmes can be found in the penitentiary area, which implies knowledge of the operational adaptation of interventions at distinct critical moments (synchronic analysis), or by permanently evaluating the programmes (diachronic analysis). One question which certainly represents progress in the evaluation of correctional programmes is the progressive introduction of lag-log (or synchronic/diachronic) designs, without overlooking the incomplete variations of synchronic and diachronic designs.

This new methodological perspective on the empirical aspect of evaluation of correctional programmes makes it necessary to solve a number of methodological difficulties, many of which depend on the development and execution of decisions which are modulable, based on established feedback in accordance with the forecasts of the non-linear models in programme evaluation.

The task is not at all easy due to the inherent complexity derived from the specific characteristics of the internment context (Redondo, 1989a; 1989b), as well as the convergence of different coordinates: on the one hand, conceptual frameworks exert a decisive and broadly diversified effect; on the other hand, the different situations in penitentiary centres where interaction takes place are so varied that the empirical problems for which solutions are sought do not allow for specific criteria; furthermore, the difficulty differs depending on the approaches inspired by each case, from trivial solutions to the persistence of unresolved problems.

It cannot be denied that, given the dominant role of interactive behaviour (Redondo, Pérez, Agudo, Roca & Azpiazu, 1990), different levels of analysis enter into play and the one which should probably be considered first is social behaviour, because interaction has properties which are not relevant when the behaviour of the subjects in question is studied separately; thus, for example, the behaviour of the members of a vocational training group at a penitentiary centre may or may not be coordinated and may be cooperative, competitive or may occupy an area which can be described with some of the many intermediary terms. A second level is that of interpersonal relationships, which imply a number of interactions over time between dyads, triads, tetrads, etc., and where all of the interactive behaviour is influenced by prior behaviour. Moreover, we can not overlook relationships of undeniable complexity, such as those which are derived from a certain group structure, with all the emerging properties this implies.

A crucial initial question is the choice of units in the context of the type of communicative or interpersonal function to be analysed. A second decision relates to the level of response or communicative behaviour, bearing in mind the multifunctional nature of the latter and the relationship between the various possible levels. And thirdly, the decision which derives from the very purpose of the study will have its effect on one data-analysis technique or another, given the fact that the researcher may or may not take into account the temporal aspect, the co-occurrence of response levels, synchrony between the interactors, asymmetry, cyclicity (Fogel, 1988), expansivity of the social networks (Iacobucci & Wasserman, 1987), branching out into minimal dyadic units (Iacobucci, 1990), dominance in the interactive relationship (Budescu, 1984), etc.

Therefore, only after solving the problems just described can the researcher set out to analyse the data. Data analysis, in turn, requires meeting requisites of a methodological nature, such as inter- or intrasessional homogeneity insofar as no exogenous or endogenous elements that may influence interactors' responses exist and there is no problem with the aggregation of data from different subjects, dyads, sessions, etc. (depending on the individual case).

Elaborating a Design for Program Evaluation

After these questions have been resolved, the structure or framework which empirically controls the evaluation process is the design. An apparently simple, yet far-reaching definition of design is that proposed by Judd and Kenny (1982, p. 25), when they affirm that "in its most basic form, research implies the observation of diverse units under diverse conditions". This definition, of course, requires further specification of the number and type of units and an outline of the questions relating to temporalisation conditions, implementation modalities and the dominance exerted by the objective(s) of the programme.

Besides the need to differentiate between standard and non-standard designs (Anguera, 1989; 1995), no overall approaches have been implemented to date which unify the reference axes or criteria to enable the designs to be generically structured regardless of the methodology used.

We will start from the premise of the differentiation between standard and non-standard designs, which shares a logical parallelism with the existence of greater or lesser dominion or control of the situation. The result is a limited number of standard designs, but not limited to the rest, since in each case they can be configured according to the needs and characteristics of the programme, understood in its broadest sense, and therefore, according to the users, temporality and other modulating elements.

The resulting skeleton or framework of joint consideration of these referents is organised based on the two orientational axes:

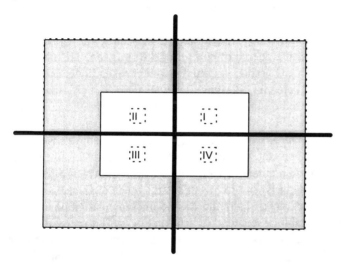

Vertical axis: Users
Horizontal axis: Temporality
White areas (Quadrants I, II, III and IV): Non-experimental designs
Shaded areas (Quadrants I, II, III and IV): Varying degrees of experimentation

Figure 1: Guiding diagram for the configuration of designs in correctional-programme evaluation

The vertical axis refers to the programme users or involved audience (units) and the upper section of this axis refers to the idiographic or individual character of the programme, with the understanding that the consideration of one unit does not necessarily imply that there is only one subject for example, in individualised attention programmes for inmates with special psychological problems. The lower section of the axis refers to the nomothetic character, where the users as a group are placed, since the essential thing is the consideration of a multiplicity of units, whether they are users (as in personal hygiene programmes) or behaviour levels where treatment occurs (cognitive programmes of discrimination of licit acts and social skills in inmates in penitentiary centres, regardless of whether they are applied individually or collectively).

The horizontal axis is assigned to the temporality of the design and, therefore, to the moments or periods of data collection. The segment on the left represents the specific moment of data collection, which is referred to as accumulative or results evaluation when it takes place at the end of programme implementation (such as an evaluation of the visit to an exhibition made by inmates with the right to make programmed excursions); and the segment on the right corresponds to data collection performed throughout the monitoring process and is referred to as training or process evaluation performed parallel to programme implementation, and with the possibility of subsequent monitoring once implementation has ended (for example, an assertiveness training programme as a free time activity during an entire quarter).

In addition to these very important axes, a number of planes are superimposed which are organised based on the degree of control of the situation. The number of planes depends on the established gradation, which can be broken down in different ways. The option chosen here for designs in evaluation of programmes in correctional institutions is based on only two planes, but there are, of course, other alternatives:

The first plane (white areas in Figure 1) symbolises the absence of experimentation, understood as the naturalness of the situation, despite the fact that a programme is being implemented (for example, in a sports programme in which the participants regularly perform this and other physical activities). When evaluating programmes it is common for the implementation of treatment to be carried out in the habitual context of life and/or activities of the users involved, in this case, the inmates. These are apparently observational designs, but while all of the other defining features are fulfilled, one of them is not, i.e., the study of the spontaneous behaviour of the subjects (Anguera & Redondo, 1991). In the strictest sense, the methodology is not observational, but the special arrangement or structure of the designs considered here coincides with that of observational designs.

Non-experimental designs are more flexible, making it possible to adapt them to each specific case. Their non-standard nature increases their versatility and, as a result, the variations which can modulate them.

The second plane (shaded areas in Figure 1) corresponds to the existence of experimentation, which can act with various degrees of intensity based on the degree to which control of the situation is exerted and the characteristic methodological restrictions in each case; for example, literacy programmes for inmates who never received schooling or whose schooling was deficient. However, as Riecken and Boruch (1974, p. 87) have stated, "the limits between quasi-experiments and correlational studies or descriptive evaluations are difficult to define", and there is a marked lack of consensus in this group of designs.

A treatment is implemented in the quasi-experiments, but it lacks at least one of the two additional properties which characterise true experiments: random samples and a control group. The main difficulty is its weakness in relation to experimental designs, which makes it difficult to formulate random inferences. Consequently, the results must be considered with a great deal of caution.

It is interesting to point out the need for various designs to complement one another in order to combine their respective advantages. Thus, it is very common to evaluate social skills, training or self-esteem programmes, etc. using diachronic, synchronic or lag-log designs and survey designs and to compare these to quasi-experimental designs. It is possible to use, for example, programmes to detoxify heroin users implemented in specialised departments of penitentiary centres, etc.

Guidelines for Resolving Basic Designs

Figure 1 shows the four resulting quadrants and given the predominance of non-experimental designs in correctional programmes due to its specific characteristics (Redondo, 1989a, 1989b; Redondo & Garrido, 1991), we have channelled the analytical possibilities of each one, which we describe as follows:

Quadrant I (synchronic designs)

Quadrant I relates to *diachronic designs*. Here, I consider the following two data-analysis techniques:

1. *Search for behaviour patterns*, in interactive dyads, tryads or tetrads, etc. at a specific response level. This would enable the researcher to detect the existence of regularity in the interactive sequence. Such regularity would be characterised by the alternation of responses between the interacting subjects, e.g. in a conversation between inmates about choosing a videotape.

There are various data-analysis techniques relating to quadrant I. Essentially, the following ones can be highlightedy: The calculation of coefficients of change with reference to panel analysis, regression, time series analysis and lag sequential analysis.

The last case is, to my mind, the most appropriate data-analysis technique in the context of interactive behaviour when observational methodology is being applied. The technique of lag sequential analysis was developed by Sackett (1978; 1980; 1987) on the basis of previous work performed by Bakeman and Brown (1977). Those evaluators used one-way conditional probabilities. The technique is as follows. The data are recorded and assembled according to the order of occurrence of the series of categories (*type I data*); or the data also include the duration (Griffin & Gardner, 1989) - in standard time units - of each one of the occurrences of interactive behaviour (*type III data*). From these, the researcher obtains values of self-contingency and also hetero-contingency as between the behaviour events manifested by the interacting subjects. From such a record of data, the researcher achieves a more or less stable configuration (the *behaviour pattern*) of interactive behaviour that can then be interpreted. This configuration is a highly condensed extract of the information obtained. Such a configuration is very useful for the purpose of objective knowledge about the interactive behaviour under study and also with a view to analysing the evolution of such behaviour, if this is desired.

In the foregoing data-analysis technique, the evaluator starts out from the null hypothesis that there is no dependence between the sequential events and, for this reason, the various behaviour events have a random order, i.e. they are not sequenced in any way.

In a lag sequential analysis, in order to make calculations with *type I data*, the researcher starts out from a type of behaviour hypothesised as a possible beginner of a stream of behaviour. This is called the *"criterion-behaviour"*. A table of matching frequencies in lag[1] series is elaborated and the corresponding conditional probabilities are also calculated, based on the frequency of each one of the categories of behaviour in the record (conditional or observed probabilities are dependent on the order of occurrence of the behaviour-events; unconditional or expected probabilities depend on their frequency during the entire session).

In this way, the evaluator can determine the excitatory behaviour-events in each lag, once their conditional probability has exceeded the unconditional one. As a result, the evaluator can consider that, between the behaviour events involved, there exists an intensity of association that is greater than mere random linking. Thus, patterns of behaviour are obtained which are composed of a series of "links in a chain" (such patterns relate to the various lags). These patterns can be given a name, defined and studied in great detail as regards their constancy or variability from one session to the next. This can also be done as far as concerns the parts which are different in a session, the subjects involved, the various behaviour-events considered to be "criterion-behaviour", etc.

In order to find out whether the difference between observed and expected match probabilities is statistically significant, the evaluator uses the binomial tests (providing that N - the number of behaviour-events which make up the record - is greater than 30 and p_{exp} is less than or equal to 0.1).

At present, the GSEQ-SDIS programme (Bakeman & Quera, 1995) is particularly useful for performing any of the lag sequential analysis modalities.

2. *Interlinking analysis between all the behavioural categories and one of them* (the focal behaviour). These include prospective and retrospective perspectives, using the polar graph technique proposed by Sackett (1980). This analysis technique is especially useful in those cases where the evaluator seeks only one response from the interacting subjects, such as, for example, a person asking for his or her turn to speak in a sports debate between experts, who make up the interacting subjects.

The primary aim of this analysis technique is data reduction. The evaluator ends up with a few indicative parameters that have arisen from the possible versatility of the

---

[1]   *Lag* is the order number of each behaviour event recorded as from the occurrence of the "criterion behaviour" (whenever it appears in the record).

situation. It is on these parameters that the weight of interpretation will be laid. The most basic of the foregoing parameters is z_{sum}. This parameter was described by Cochran (1954) and applied by Bobbitt, Gourevitch, Miller and Jensen (1969) in the study of interactive relationships between mothers and offspring in primates. It was also applied by Sackett (1980) in the case of the occurrence of one single behaviour event (speaking/not speaking) in a group of subjects attending a series of meetings.

Therefore, the evaluator starts out from the values of the conditional probabilities in the number of lags considered. From these values, the appropriate z_{sum} parameters can be found. Using a graph called a scattergram, the researcher can ascertain whether excitatory or inhibitory dependence exists and whether the nature of the latter is symmetrical or asymmetrical. In this way, data can be greatly reduced.

Finally, it is possible to reduce data to an even greater extent by representing the scattergram values in the form of a polar graph, using vectors, and by calculating the value of the vector length or module and the value of their angle.

The vector length or module relates to the intensity of the interactive relationship (whether statistically significant or not), whilst the angle enables the researcher to ascertain the quality or type of interactive relationship being studied:

- An *angle from 1^0 to 90^0* --> "Criterion behaviour" and "matching behaviour" that are mutually excitatory, i.e. reciprocal and symmetrical activation between the focal subject and the interactor(s).
- An *angle from 91^0 to 180^0* --> "Criterion behaviour" that is inhibitory and "matching behaviour" that is excitatory. Therefore, the focal subject inhibits behaviour events of interactive subjects who, on their part, asymmetrically activate such behaviour in him or her.
- An *angle from 181^0 to 270^0* --> "Criterion behaviour" and "matching behaviour" that are mutually inhibitory. As a result, there is reciprocal and symmetrical inhibition between the focal subject and the interactor(s).
- An *angle from 271^0 to 360^0* --> "Criterion behaviour" that is excitatory and "matching behaviour" that is inhibitory. This implies that the focal subject activates behaviour events in the interactive subjects, which asymmetrically inhibit such behaviour in the focal subjects themselves.

Here we are dealing with a technique of data analysis that is highly sensitive and very useful when the researcher is studying one level of response in a group of interactive subjects.

Quadrant II

Quadrant II cannot produce any research design, because there is insufficient empirical basis.

Quadrant III (synchronic designs)

Quadrant III is of a specific, nomothetic type. Because of this, it is especially advantageous when there are a number of interactive subjects, or when the researcher is interested in several response levels from which to obtain a specific record, e.g. interaction between teacher and inmate during the class or part of the class. The technique of data analysis used in a large number of studies is that of $\_^2$. However, there are limitations to this technique of data analysis which militate against its use. One such limitation is that this technique of data analysis is only possible where the evaluator has only two levels of response to analyse. The other limitation is that the evaluator is not only interested in ascertaining whether or not a statistically significant relationship exists, but also, how intense the association is.

In many cases it is useful to establish various systems of categories in accordance with criteria that are deemed relevant. The result is that the same behaviour event is simultaneously categorised from different perspectives. In this way, data are obtained relating specifically to one or various sessions. Such data can cross in a contingency table, in response to the various systems of categories considered.

According to Bakeman and Gottman (1989), the most suitable technique of recording data in the study of interactive behaviour is that of events classified in crossed form in a contingency table. Thus, there is no need for any continuity between events that follow upon one another. It is the result of taking down sequences of behaviour (Castellan, 1979) and such sequences are classified from various dimensional perspectives. The key elements are the systems of categories applied concurrently. Let us suppose that the evaluator is interested in assessing episodes of behaviour where quarrels arise between a group of three subjects. In principle, one evaluator might suggest calculating the frequency of the quarrels. However, evaluators could also be asked to note down what each boy had been doing immediately before the quarrel began; what behavioural manifestations were involved; and how the quarrels were resolved. If a series of exhaustive, mutually exclusive categories were defined for each one of these three perspectives, evaluators could classify the quarrels in crossed form in a contingency table.

Recording events in crossed form is always very simple. Data are presented in the form of contingency tables. From these, the evaluator ascertains whether or not there exists any relationship between the variables and the intensity of such association. Until just over two decades ago, analysis of qualitative/categorical data was limited to the context of two-dimensional tables. $\_^2$ was applied in the study of such data.

However, thanks to the pioneering efforts of Fienberg (1977) and Goodman (1970; 1971; 1978) - later publicised by Kennedy (1983) among others - *analysis of contingency tables using linear logarithmic models, otherwise called "log-linear" analysis,* has been developed. Such analysis has been applied in symmetrical types of association between the variables, and not in the question of causality between those variables). On the other hand, a different technique of analysis needs to be applied (*"logit" analysis*), if the research being performed is asymmetrical. Thus, one variable adopts the role of an explanatory or independent variable, whilst the other takes on the role of a variable of response or a dependent variable.

Log-linear analysis is very simple and flexible. The restrictions imposed on data are few and the results can be expressed using the familiar terminology of variance analysis. Evaluators define a series of hierarchical models ("hierarchical" in the sense that the simplest models constitute subgroups of other, more complex ones) with the number 2^k, where k represents the number of dimensions or category systems considered.

Whatever the number of models (four in the case of the two-dimensional model, eight in that of the three-dimensional one, etc.), the simplest model - the null or equiprobable model - generates the same expected value for each cell in the table of contingencies. The most complex model - the saturated model - contains enough terms to generate expected values for each cell which are identical to those observed in reality. The aim is to find the least complex model that can nevertheless generate expected values which are not too different from the values observed, values that are determined by how good the fit is. In general, the evaluator begins with the null hypothesis of a given simple model. If the data generated do not fit the data already held, more complex models need to be tried out. Even if all the models fail to meet requirements, the saturated model will always make a fitting possible, because it generates values that are identical to those observed.

The simplest example can be found - subject to the previously mentioned limitations - in the χ^2 test (Bakeman & Gottman, 1989). This is so because the model that is usually tried out first - the model of "non-interaction" - consists of two terms, one for the row variable and the other for the column variable. To put it another way, the row and column totals with respect to the data generated by the model are forced to agree with the row and column totals observed in reality. In the case of a 2 x 2 table, the only "non-interaction" model is the saturated one, which includes a term of interaction in addition to the effects of row and column. That is to say that the expected frequencies calculated for the χ^2 test of independence are in fact generated by a model without interaction. If χ^2 is significantly large, then this model does not work in the fitting of the data. The evaluator needs a term of interaction, which means that the row and column variables are not independent of one another, although in fact they are in association.

At this point, all that I am trying to do is to highlight the interest that exists in this analysis technique, which characterises transversal designs in social interaction studies. For example, consider a dyadic interaction between two inmates in an observation session based on the criteria of the exchange of looks and sounds.

inmates in an observation session based on the criteria of the exchange of looks and sounds.

Quadrant IV (diachronic / synchronic designs)

In *quadrant IV* observation of a group of subjects constitutes a complex problem for breaking down into parts:

1. On the one hand, because of this quadrant's relationship with quadrant I, the evaluator would have to study the sequentiality in parallel of each member of the group. On some occasions, this could lead to the designation of a "prototype-subject" which could be considered representative of all those subjects having the attributes or characteristics of membership with respect to the group initially defined.

2. It would be much more interesting to look at quadrant IV in the light of its relationship with quadrant III. This gives rise to *diachronic/synchronic designs (lag-log designs)*. In these designs, the previously mentioned crossed form of data is not only considered on one occasion (Bakeman, Adamson & Strisik, 1987), but also in a series of activities that are close in time to each other. This would imply quasi-continuous observation for the duration of the period under consideration. This design can be considered the optimum design for studying interactive behaviour.

The complementation of both perspectives, which makes diachronic/synchronic or lag-log designs very powerful and leads one to think of other designs as incomplete variants of lag-log designs, does not lack complexity as regards the way it is treated. The main difficulty lies in joint consideration of different category systems due to the existence of relevant criteria (synchronic perspective) over time (diachronic perspective).

One problem that remains unsolved is that of the internal dynamics of each of the category systems involved during the study over time. It is, of course, useful to study the associative relationship between the respective categories of different systems, but it is also beneficial to know the relative behaviour of each one of the categories in each system.

The *polar-coordinate technique* suggested for lag-log designs is a reducing technique, as mentioned above, but its main point of interest is that it develops a map of relationships that link a specific category - focal behaviour - with all the categories of the system. To this end, there is a complementary linking of the prospective and retrospective perspectives, relative to the sequentiality implicit in the empirical situations to which the lag-log design is applied.

One great advantage of this (Anguera, Blanco & Losada, 1995), is that it offers interpretable results that show how, in successive programmed moments - whether periodic or not, but which correspond to the diachronic perspective - a vector representation is obtained which provides a map (corresponding to the synchronic perspective) of relationships between the focal behaviour and the other categories.

interrelationship between said focal category and each of the others, bearing in mind that the vector representation makes it possible to interpret both the nature of each one of the relationships on the map (based on the vector angle) and the intensity (based on the radius or modulus).

With this aim, the incorporation of this analytical treatment into lag-log designs definitely increases their development because it strengthens their diachronic perspective by incorporating into all desired points in time the intercategory dynamic analysis for each of the relevant criteria established at the commencement of the evaluative task.

Epilogue

The range of possible methodological advances in the evaluation of correctional programmes is very broad but, in any case, revolves around the design since it organises the empirical aspect of evaluation. The preparation of the design shows the versatility of which they are capable and the many possibilities they offer the evaluator, especially in the absence of experimentation, given that it is dependent on the specific characteristics of the penitentiary environment.

Specifically, in designs created for each correctional programme, following only a few guidelines, there are specified and certain data-analysis techniques are implemented in an attempt to be as rigorous as possible.

References

Anguera, M.T. (1989). Innovaciones en la metodología de evaluación de programas. *Anales de Psicología, 5,* 13-42.

Anguera, M.T. (1995). Diseños. En R. Fernández Ballesteros (Dir.). *Evaluación de programas sociales: Una guía práctica en ámbitos sociales, educativos y de salud* (pp. 149-172). Madrid: Síntesis.

Anguera, M.T., Blanco, A., & Losada, J.L. (1995, April). *Aportación de la técnica de coordenadas polares en diseños mixtos.* Paper presented at IV Congreso de Metodología de las Ciencias del Comportamiento. La Manga del Mar Menor (Murcia).

Anguera, M.T., & Redondo, S. (1991). La evaluación de la intervención penitenciaria. *Delincuencia/Delinquency, 3* (3), 245-289.

Bakeman, R., Adamson, L.B., & Strisik, P. (1987). Lags and logs: Statistical approaches to interaction. In M.H. Bornstein & J. Bruner (Eds.) *Interaction in human development* (pp. 241-260). Hillsdale, N.J.: Lawrence Erlbaum Associates.

Bakeman, R., & Brown, J.V. (1977). Behavioral dialogues: An approach to the assessment of mother-infant interaction. *Child Development, 48,* 195-203.

Bakeman, R., & Gottman, J.M. (1989). *Observación de la interacción: Introducción al análisis secuencial.* Madrid: Morata.

Bakeman, R., & Quera, V. (1995). *Analyzing Interaction: Sequential Analysis with SDIS and GSEQ.* New York: Cambridge University Press.

Bishop, Y.M., Fienberg, S.E., & Holland, P.W. (1975). *Discrete multivariate analysis*. Cambridge, Mass.: The M.I.T. Press.

Bobbitt, R.A., Gourevitvh, V.P., Miller, L.E., & Jensen, G.D. (1969). Dynamics of social interactive behavior: A computerized procedure for analyzing trends, patterns, and sequences. *Psychological Bulletin, 71*, 110-120.

Budescu, D.V. (1984). Tests of lagged dominance in sequential dyadic interaction. *Psychological Bulletin, 96*, 402-414.

Castellan, N.J. (1979). The analysis of behavior sequences. In R.B.Cairns (Ed.). *The analysis of social interactions: Methods, issues, and illustrations* (pp. 81-116). Hillsdale, N.J.: Lawrence Erlbaum Associates.

Cochran, W.G. (1954). Some methods for strengthening the common χ^2 tests. *Biometrics, 10*, 417-451.

Fienberg, S.E. (1977). *The analysis of cross-classified categorical data*. Cambridge, Mass.: M.I.T. Press.

Fogel, A. (1988). Cyclicity and stability in mother-infant face-to-face interaction: A comment on Cohn and Tronick (1988). *Developmental Psychology, 24* (3), 393-395.

Goodman, L.A. (1970). The multivariate analysis of qualitative data: Interactions among multiple classifications. *Journal of the American Statistical Association, 65*, 226-256.

Goodman, L.A. (1971). The analysis of multidimensional contingency tables: Stepwise procedures and direct estimation methods for building models for multiple classifications. *Technometrics, 13*, 33-61.

Goodman, L.A. (1978). *Analyzing qualitative/categorical data. Log-linear models and latent structure analysis*. Cambridge, Mass.: Abt Books.

Griffin, W.A., & Gardner, W. (1989). Analysis of behavioral durations in observational studies of social interaction. *Psychological Bulletin, 106* (3), 497-502.

Iacobucci, D. (1990). Derivation of subgroups from dyadic interactions. *Psychological Bulletin, 107* (1), 114-132.

Iacobucci, D., & Wasserman, S. (1987). Dyadic social interactions. *Psychological Bulletin, 102* (2), 293-306.

Iacobucci, D., & Wasserman, S. (1988). A general framework for the statistical analysis of sequential dyadic interaction data. *Psychological Bulletin, 103* (3), 379-390.

Judd, Ch.M., & Kenny, D.A. (1982). Research Design and Research Validity. In D. Brinberg & L.H. Kidder (Eds.), *Forms of validity in Research* (pp. 23-39). San Francisco: Jossey-Bass.

Kennedy, J.J. (1983). *Analyzing qualitative data. Introductory log-linear analysis for behavioral research*. New York: Praeger.

Redondo, S. (1989a). Reflexiones sobre la intervención penitenciaria. *Papers d'Estudis i Formació, 5*, 157-170.

Redondo, S. (1989b). El ambiente penitenciario: Su análisis funcional y aplicaciones. *Delincuencia/Delinquency, 1* (2), 133-161.

Redondo, S. (1993). *Evaluar e intervenir en las prisiones. Análisis de conducta aplicado*. Barcelona: P.P.U.

Redondo, S., & Garrido, V. (1991). Diez años de intervención en las prisiones españolas. *Delincuencia/Delinquency, 3* (3), 193-243.

Redondo, S., Pérez, E., Agudo, F., Roca, M., & Azpiazu, M. (1990). *Programes de rehabilitació a les presons*. Barcelona: Departament de Justícia de la Generalitat de Catalunya.

Riecken, H.W., & Boruch, R.F. (Eds.)(1974). *Social Experimentation. A method for Planning and Evaluating Social Intervention*. New York: Academic Press.

Sackett, G.P. (Ed.) (1978). *Observing Behavior: Data collection and analysis methods*. Baltimore: University Park Press, vol. II.

Sackett, G.P. (1980). Lag sequential analysis as a data reduction technique in social interaction research. In D.B. Sawin, R.C. Hawkins, L.O. Walker & J.H. Penticuff (Eds.) *Exceptional infant. Psychosocial risks in infant-environment transactions* (pp. 300-340). New York: Brunner/Mazel.

Sackett, G.P. (1987). Analysis of sequential social interaction data: Some issues, recent developments, and a causal inference model. In J.D. Osofsky (Ed.) *Handbook of infant development* (pp. 855-878). New York: Wiley.

Young Offenders and Alcohol: Relative Merits of Institutions and Community Prevention Initiatives

Clive R. Hollin

The Relationship Between Alcohol and Crime

This paper was presented in a symposium concerned with alcohol and crime, two topics that are often seen to have a close association. Is there any evidence, however, to support this suggestion of a link between alcohol and offending? Several studies, principally with convicted young offenders, suggest strongly that there may be an association.

At an English Young Offender Centre, Sleap (1977) noted a "problem drinker" rate of 40% in the institution's population. In Wales, with a similar population, Fuller (1979) reported a rate of 30% "problem drinkers". In Scotland, Heather (1981, 1982) found that of admissions to a young offender institution, 63% of the sample reported that they had been drunk when committing their present offence. Hollin (1983), with a sample from an English young offenders' institution, found that 38% said they had been drinking immediately before offending; with a problem drinker rate of around 40% of the sample. More recently, McMurran and Hollin (1989) from a survey of an English young offender institution, found that 43% of the sample were "heavy drinkers" - that is they consumed over 50 units of alcohol per week. (The "safe" level of consumption, recommended by the Royal College of Physicians (1987), is 21 units per week).

One advantage for the researcher of convicted offenders held in institutions is that he or she has, so to speak, a captive population to study. In the community, however, it is not so simple but there is ample evidence to suggest that alcohol and crime are related. In the 1983 British Crime Survey (Hough & Mayhew, 1983) it was clearly shown that physical assault and other violent crime were associated with drinking. A state of affairs that remains largely unchanged today: the 1992 British Crime Survey makes the observation that "The vast majority of pub assaults involved offenders said to be drunk. But many other incidents of violence were also committed by drunken offenders" (p. 99, Mayhew, Maung & Mirrlees-Black, 1993). An inquiry by the Association of Chief Police Officers in England noted 250 incidents classed as "mass public disorder" in 1987: alcohol was implicated in 90% of these incidents. Indeed, to look further at the extremities of crime of violence, it is well established that alcohol plays a role in a disproportionately high number of murders (e.g. Berkowitz, 1993).

Thus, from research both with imprisoned offenders and in the community, it appears that there that there are substantial numbers of offenders with drink problems and for whom drink and crime are associated. However, an association or correlation between two variables does not in itself prove that there is a casual relationship between the two.

The nature of the association

Three possible types of association between alcohol and criminal behaviour can be defined: i) drinking directly leads to offending; ii) offending leads to drinking; iii) the two coexist but are not causally related.

In the previously noted study, McMurran and Hollin (1989) explored these possibilities among convicted young offenders. They found that the young offenders had no difficulty in deciding the nature of the relationship in their own case. Overall, almost half the sample claimed that their drinking and offending were not related. In other cases drinking was seen as leading to crime: typically, either because alcohol leads to behaviour that the individual claims would not take place if they were sober, or because the idea for an offence took place while drinking with friends. Fewer offenders said their drinking was a result of crime, although some did say that they drank heavily either to celebrate or to alleviate anxiety.

When it comes to the design and evaluation of prevention programmes for offenders who drink, exact knowledge of the nature of the relationship between drink and criminal behaviour is crucial. Andrews et al. (1990) have argued for the need to separate clinical/health change outcome variables from criminogenic outcome measures. The force of this argument is that while it may be possible to bring about significant changes in drinking behaviour, this may take place without having a similar impact on criminal behaviour. Unless offenders are selected for programmes on the basis of their *risk* for reoffending if alcohol consumption is unchanged, then the chances of programmes failing to impact on criminal behaviour are increased. As happened with social skills training (Hollin & Henderson, 1984), unless this risk principle is followed drinking programmes for offenders will raise false expectations of what they can achieve in terms of changing criminal behaviour. Again, as with social skills training, it will then become more difficult to evaluate programmes and to interpret fully the findings of the outcome literature.

Tackling Alcohol Related Crime

There are, broadly speaking, three styles of prevention: *primary prevention*, which seeks to prevent completely a behaviour across the whole population; *secondary prevention*, which specifically directs preventive programmes at identified at risk groups; and *tertiary prevention* that aims to prevent future occurrences of a behaviour from those who have already acted in a given manner. Primary prevention in this area needs cultural and social change on an unlikely scale. Secondary prevention becomes a possibility when the variables used to predict at risk individuals are finely defined. However, it is with tertiary prevention that most knowledge has accumulated and to which attention is paid here.

A common response to the problem of the drinking offender is to offer some form of intervention that will help the offender to overcome his or her drink problems and, hopefully, help him or her to give up a life of crime. What are the relative merits of institutions and community settings as the location for such individualised preventive strategies?

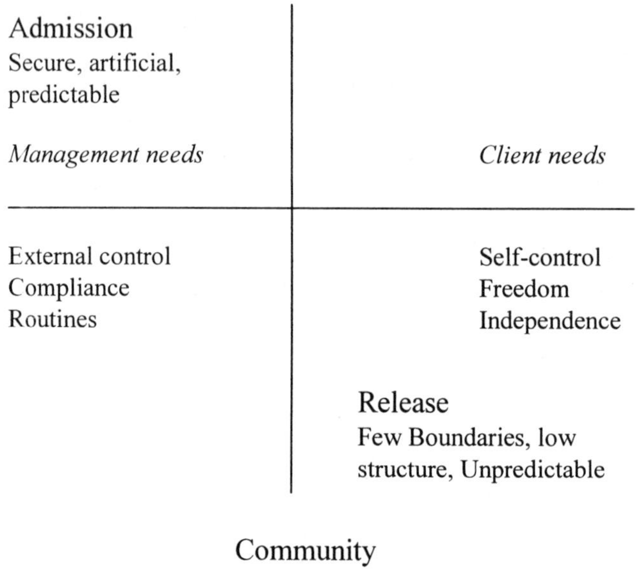

Admission
Secure, artificial,
predictable

Management needs   *Client needs*

External control   Self-control
Compliance   Freedom
Routines   Independence

                            Release
                            Few Boundaries, low
                            structure, Unpredictable

Community

Figure 1: Client versus Organisation Needs

Institutional programmes

For many reasons, including legal requirements, protection of the individual, protection of the public, safety of staff and other inmates or residents, and the establishment of a safe working environment, institutions are characterised by both *security* and *predictability* of routines. Of course this, in turn, produces a highly artificial environment when compared to real-life community settings. The community is in many respects the opposite of an institution: it lacks structure, fails to define boundaries, and is often unpredictable.

Overlaying the continuum between institutions and community, we can also distinguish between management needs and client needs. Management needs, reflected in the characteristics of many organisations, include effective means of control to ensure compliance, effective containment, and adherence to institutional routines. These management needs contrast with client needs for effective functioning in the community: such client needs include self-control, freedom, and independence. The task of managers and practitioners is to move the individual from admission to release, moving from institutional control to self-control (Hollin et al., 1995).

If we concentrate upon the institution, what are the advantages and disadvantages of this type of environment for the treatment of young offenders with alcohol-related problems? The advantages are that the clients are immediately accessible and some may even be motivated towards tackling their drink problem. Certainly some studies have reported that many young offenders with drink problems said they would accept the offer of treatment if it was forthcoming (e.g. Hollin, 1983). Further, the meta-analyses of the offender treatment literature have suggested that structured behaviour change programmes are advantageous in working with offenders (e.g. Lipsey, 1992). Such a structured approach might fit more easily into institutional routines - with the additional advantage of the ready availability of young people to participate in programmes - rather than into less-structured community settings.

The types of specific intervention, known to be effective with problem drinker populations, which would sit comfortably with a structured approach includes educational programmes, skills training, cognitive skills training, self-control programmes, and relapse prevention programmes (McMurran & Hollin, 1993).

The disadvantages of institutional treatment are many: the emphasis on security and rules may prohibit any type of intervention, such as controlled drinking, which involves the use of alcohol; the client's motivation to enter treatment may be to comply with perceived institutional demands rather than for the sake of personal change, so that any treatment gains that do take place may fail to generalise from the artificiality of the institution to the unpredictability of the real world. In practice, the balance between these advantages and disadvantages usually tilts in favour of maintaining the institutional status quo, which means little in the way of organised treatment for offenders with alcohol-related problems.

Community programmes

In the community the advantages and disadvantages of institutional attempts at treatment are reversed. In the community the practitioner can use the full range of techniques, including those that incorporate the use of alcohol; it is easier for the client to consent to treatment for genuine reasons rather than feel pressured to remain in treatment to satisfy institutional demands; and as the treatment is taking place in the real world there are fewer problems with generalisation.

The types of technique that might be more successful here are those used successfully with problem drinkers such as marital/partner work, family work, lifestyle modification programmes, employment counselling, and leisure counselling.

The disadvantages, on the other hand, are that without external control and an accompanying failure to develop self-control, real-world contingencies might counter any effects of intervention. In other words, if the reasons for drinking are stronger than pull of treatment so that the chances of success are much reduced.

Strategies for Maximising Effectiveness

Linking institutions and communities

There are several strategies that can be adopted to maximise the effectiveness of programmes aimed at offenders who drink, particularly for those who face the difficulty of transition from institution to community. If work on alcohol related problems is tackled in an institution, using whatever techniques are possible, it is obviously to everyone's advantage that any gains and advantages continue and are built on when the offender returns to the real world. This demands some continuity between institution and community, in effect to "hand over" the offender to the neighbourhood. This might be achieved by a period of graded or special release before discharge, or a similar period in a pre-release hostel. This would allow a semi-structured and managed movement back into the community to test the robustness of treatment gains, set new targets, and give professionals from the institution and the neighbourhood time to ease the offender from one setting into the other, and, of course, giving families and the offender time for readjustment.

Generalisation, the transfer of behaviour change from the treatment setting to the real world, is a litmus test of any programme. The same principles apply here as elsewhere, basically working for as great a similarity as possible between treatment setting and the natural environment (Hollin, 1990). In practice, this may mean a co-ordinated approach in which the flow of preventive methods moves from structured, focused programmes (education, skills training, relapse prevention), to more open-ended, community-relevant programmes (marital/partner/family work, lifestyle modification, employment counselling, leisure counselling).

Resistance to Intervention

While there are distinct advantages and disadvantages to treatment of alcohol-related problems among offender groups according to institutional or community setting, also resistance to treatment will be common to both. This resistance can come from three sources - the individual client him or herself, the local environment (institution or community), or on a broader societal level.

Client resistance

Client resistance, especially among problem drinker populations, is well documented in the literature and must be part of the experience of any practitioner who has worked with drinkers. However, this client resistance may be heightened still further for the offender with a drink problem. Some offenders see little need to change either their drinking or their offending and may be part of a subculture that reinforces both drinking and offending. In the community this subculture may be the counter to any therapeutic change, and when we look to institutions the same may be the case. Indeed, the ethos in many institutions, perhaps particularly penal institutions, is not treatment-orientated, but emphasises austerity and containment.

What can be done with the reluctant client? The offender with a drink problem who refuses to admit to a problem and is opposed to any attempt at intervention. Whatever the setting, be it institution or community, it is difficult if not impossible to conduct any intervention that is going to be successful if the offender him or herself is resistant to change. However, advances in the use of motivational interviewing (Miller & Rollnick, 1991) have opened new possibilities with respect to working with both offending and drinking behaviour.

Organisational resistance

Within an institution staff at all levels can do a great deal to counter the effects of any therapeutic endeavour. Staff resistance may come from management who see the use of treatment as a threat to the stability and smooth-running of the institution; from staff who are opposed to any "soft" options for offenders; and even across professions, it is not unheard of for professional staff of different persuasions to sabotage each other's therapeutic efforts. These manifestations of resistance can occur in the community as in institutions, but it does seem that there is something about institutions that fosters such professional discord.

What can be done with organisational resistance?: the local forces that may counter treatment initiatives. There are several reasons why local resistance is found: these include a rejection of something not understood, misperceptions of the purpose of intervention, and hostility to a treatment-orientated approach to offender problems. To an extent this can be countered through training and education with the primary aim of engaging others - institutional staff, other disciplines, family - in your way of viewing the problem. To train staff to participate in treatment - rather than an élitist approach in which treatment can only be done by the psychologist, social worker, or whatever - can have enormous benefits.

The purpose of treatment is often poorly understood, and therefore a clear statement of intent from practitioners is helpful. If the reason for a programme is to help offenders overcome problems with their drinking, clear arguments in defence of that *clinical* goal must be articulated to justify the work. If the reason for a programme is to help offenders overcome problems with drinking to prevent future *offending*, then that *criminological* goal must also be justified. (Which demands that, in an individual case, assessment has shown a causal link between drinking and offending: i.e. the risk principle as discussed previously.)

Public resistance

Finally, there may be public resistance, most typically manifest in the popular media, to treatment initiatives with offenders. To counter public resistance to work of this type, it is necessary to articulate a response that takes the line of sparing future victims from the behaviour of drunken offenders. It needs to be made clear that it is in the *public* interest to assist efforts to work with offenders: not least because the measures being used at present are harmful, expensive, and of little use in reducing recidivism.

A second strand to changing public opinion is to direct efforts at those who hold political, financial, and administrative power. Burchard (1987) draws the distinction between therapeutic contingencies and political contingencies. Practitioners are concerned with the former, politicians and administrators with the latter: it goes almost without saying that the latter, the politicians and administrators, are more powerful politically than the former: decisions about funding, hiring and firing of personnel, allocation of resources and so on are made by administrators not by practitioners. Therefore, like it or not, if we want to advocate treatment oriented policies for offenders who drink, we must have the politicians and administrators on our side. Strategies are needed to engage the attention of policy makers - which is an unlikely task for the individual clinician. A concerted, properly managed, strategy by professional bodies seems more likely to meet with success. In addition, several studies have used the tactic of costing in financial terms the price of clinical interventions that prevent future offences and reduce recidivism (e.g. Prentky & Burgess, 1990).

Conclusion

Overall, we are left with a situation in which while we can see a clear association between alcohol and offending, the environmental pressures - be they from the institution or the community - work against tackling the problems. While there are no easy answers, with the right strategies it may be possible to counter resistance. Indeed, the re-emergence of a rehabilitative ethos in offender services has been a feature of the 1990s (Palmer, 1992); in a similar vein there is a growing body of work on effective programmes for problem drinking (e.g. Hester & Miller, 1989); while both academics and practitioners are working towards an integration of these two bodies of knowledge (McMurran & Hollin, 1993).

References

Andrews, D. A., Zinger, I., Hoge, R. D., Bonta, J., Gendreau, P., & Cullen, F. T. (1990). Does correctional treatment work? A clinically relevant and psychologically informed meta-analysis. Criminology, 28, 369-404.

Berkowitz, L. (1993). *Aggression: Its causes, consequences, and control*. NY: McGraw-Hill.

Burchard, J. D. (1987). Social policy and the role of the behavior analyst in the prevention of delinquent behavior. Behavior Analyst, 10, 83-88.

Fuller, J. R. (1979). Alcohol abuse and the treatment of young offenders. *Directorate of Psychological Services Report*, Series I, No. 13. London: Home Office.

Heather, N. (1981). Relationship between delinquency and drunkenness among Scottish young offenders. British Journal on Alcohol and Alcoholism, 16, 50-61.

Heather, N. (1982). Alcohol dependence and problem drinking in Scottish young offenders. British Journal on Alcohol and Alcoholism, 17, 145-154.

Hester, R. K., & Miller, W. R. (Eds). (1989). *Handbook of alcoholism treatment approaches*. Elmsford, NY: Pergamon Press.

Hollin, C. R. (1983). Young offenders and alcohol: A survey of the drinking behaviour of a Borstal population. Journal of Adolescence, 6, 161-174.

Hollin, C. R. (1990). *Cognitive-behavioral interventions with young offenders*. Elmsford, NY: Pergamon Press.

Hollin, C. R., Epps, K. J., & Kendrick, D. J. (1995). *Managing behavioural treatment: Policy and practice with delinquent adolescents*. London: Routledge.

Hollin, C. R., & Henderson, M. (1984). Social skills training with young offenders: False expectations and the "failure" of treatment. Behavioural Psychotherapy, 12, 331-341.

Hough, M., & Mayhew, P. (1983). *The British Crime Survey: First Report*. London: HMSO.

Lipsey, M. W. (1992). Juvenile Delinquency Treatment: A Meta-Analytic Inquiry into the Variability of Effects. In T. D. Cook, H. Cooper, D. S. Cordray, H. Hartmann, L. V. Hedges, R. J. Light, T. A. Louis, and F. Mosteller (Eds.), *Meta-analysis for explanation: A casebook* , pp. 83-127. NY: Russell Sage Foundation.

McMurran, M., & Hollin, C. R. (1989). Drinking and delinquency: Another look at young offenders and their drinking. British Journal of Criminology, 29, 386-394.

McMurran, M., & Hollin, C. R. (1993). *Young offenders and alcohol-related crime: A practitioner's guidebook*. Chichester: Wiley.

Mayhew, P., Maung, N. A., & Mirrlees-Black, C. (1993). *The 1992 British Crime Survey*. London: HMSO.

Miller, W. R., & Rollnick, S. (1991). *Motivational interviewing: Preparing people to change addictive behavior*. NY: Guilford Press.

Palmer, T. (1992). *The re-emergence of correctional intervention*. Newbury Park, CA: Sage.

Prentky, R., & Burgess, A. W. (1990). Rehabilitation of child molesters: A cost-benefit analysis. American Journal of Orthopsychiatry, 60, 108-117.

Sleap, H. (1977). *Problem drinkers at Glen Parva: A survey of the drinking habits and alcohol-related problems of a delinquent male population*. Unpublished manuscript, HM YOI, Glen Parva, Leicester.

Royal College of Physicians. (1987). *The medical consequences of alcohol abuse: A great and growing evil*. London: Tavistock Publications.

Methodological Issues in the Meta-Evaluation of Correctional Treatment

Julio Sánchez-Meca

Introduction

The great social importance of criminality has generated a research field named *crime treatment evaluation*. Several decades ago, it was intended to clarify whether the rehabilitation of offenders was possible. Currently, the number of empirical evaluations on correctional programs is so huge that is practically impossible to revise and integrate all the literature without using systematic and quantitative procedures of research synthesis. This is precisely the objective of meta-analysis: to integrate quantitatively the results of empirical studies on a topic (Cooper, 1989; Cooper & Hedges, 1994; Glass et al., 1981; Hedges & Olkin, 1985; Hunter & Schmidt, 1990; Rosenthal, 1991; Sánchez-Meca & Ato, 1989; Wachter & Straff, 1990; Wolf, 1986).

Meta-analytic studies, usually performed to study the outcome of intervention programs, start from a basically descriptive position: to determine the mean effect of a program and the possible influence of certain moderator variables on the results of such program. But meta-analyses can provide a more explanatory than merely descriptive approach, can and should propose explanatory models of why a program is effective and under what conditions it works better, and also prove the possible influence of methodological factors in the results of the primary studies. Thus, it is necessary to apply statistical models adapted to meta-analysis focusing on explanation rather than description.

Stemming from ideas recently proposed by authors such as Lipsey (1992a, 1992b, 1992c, 1994; Durlak & Lipsey, 1991), Cook, et al., (1992), and Rubin (1990, 1992), the advantages of meta-analysis to detect the influence of methodological aspects on correctional program evaluation are presented. First, a brief description of meta-analysis is presented; second, a conceptual framework that permits us to classify and identify the susceptible methodological variables of study in a meta-analysis is explained; several examples from existing meta-analyses at present on correctional evaluation follow; and finally, a meta-analysis model is outlined in which the effects of methodological variables can be controlled and the results of the program evaluations can be explained.

Meta-analysis: conceptualisation

To carry out a meta-analysis the result of each study is measured in a standard way through some index of the magnitude of the effect (for example, the standardised mean difference, the Pearson correlation coefficient, the *Phi* coefficient, the odds ratio, etc.) and the most relevant study characteristics are coded aiming at ascertaining their possible moderating influence on the effect magnitude. In this way, the review process of a topic turns into an investigation in which the analysis unit is the empirical study, the dependent variable is the effect magnitude of each study, and the independent variables are the characteristics coded in the studies. From this perspective, the meta-analysis applied to program evaluation allows one to: (a) obtain a global index of the program outcome; (b) test whether the results of the studies are homogeneous vis-a-vis the global index, and, otherwise, (c) search for those study characteristics that could explain the heterogeneity of the results.

Since Glass in 1976 coined this term, there have been countless quantitative syntheses in the behavioural and social sciences, and, particularly, in the evaluation of psychosocial intervention programs (Glass, 1976; Glass et al., 1981). The field of correctional program evaluation has not been detached from the arrival of this new research methodology. In fact, since the 1980s, several meta-analytic studies on this topic have been published, which point out the existence of certain positive results, in general terms, contradicting the conclusions reached by previous traditional reviews (Andrews et al., 1990; Garrett, 1985; Gensheimer et al., 1986; Gottschalk et al., 1987a, 1987b; Lipsey, 1992a; Lösel & Köferl, 1989; Mayer et al., 1986; Whitehead & Lab, 1989).

Meta-Analysis as a Meta-Evaluation Tool

Although determining the global efficiency of an intervention program is a suggestive issue, the advantages of meta-analysis go further. Thanks to meta-analysis it is possible to determine *the state of the art* of any research field, that is to say, it is possible to study how it is being investigated, what methodological deficiencies the primary studies contain, and how they can be eliminated. In this way, meta-analysis is a powerful tool for the meta-evaluation of intervention programs.

In order for a meta-analysis to carry out this function, meta-analysts as well as meta-analytic study consumers should be aware of the fact that the results of a program evaluation can be affected not only by substantive factors such as type of treatment, subject characteristics or setting, but also by methodological factors and experimental procedure, such as subject assignment type, design type, or attrition. Thus, following Light and Pillemer (1984), and most recently Rubin (1990, 1992), it is possible to formulate a simple functional model, in which the result of an intervention program evaluation is a function of substantive and methodological aspects:

$$Y = f(X, M),$$

where Y is the result of the empirical evaluation; and X and M represent substantive and methodological characteristics, respectively.

Starting from this simple model, meta-analysis, through the integration of the studies, can determine the influence of substantive as well as methodological variables on the effectiveness of a given program.

A conceptual framework of study characteristics

Thus, it is necessary to elaborate a conceptual framework that permits us to classify the study characteristics attending to the distinction between methodological and substantive variables. The proposed framework is shown in Table 1.

Following Lipsey (1994), together with the methodological and substantive characteristics, a new variable type that may be referred to as extrinsic variables is included.

(a) *Substantive characteristics* refer to the nature of the treatment provided (e.g., treatment modality, underlying theoretical model, treatment duration, number of sessions, etc.), the characteristics of the subjects included in the study (e.g., gender, age, offence type, cultural status, etc.), or even aspects related to the setting in which the treatment has been implemented (e.g., geographical, cultural, temporal, or political setting). Usually, substantive characteristics are considered the most important in meta-analyses; therefore meta-analyses of correctional evaluation have been centred on the study of their influence on the effect magnitude of the evaluations.

(b) *Methodological characteristics* include aspects related to the design and the research procedures used to evaluate the program such as, design type (experimental, quasi-experimental, pre-experimental), subject assignment type to the groups, control group type (not treated *versus* placebo), attrition, design quality, quality and nature of outcome measures, sample size, etc. Of course, not all these variables will necessarily influence the results of a program evaluation, but a central aspect in any meta-analysis should be to test their possible moderator effects.

(c) Finally, following Lipsey (1994), Table 1 includes a third variable category called *extrinsic characteristics*; they are not directly related to program implementation and in previous classifications were included within the category of methodological variables. Although extrinsic variables would not influence the results of a program evaluation, it has been shown that these variables are correlated with the effect magnitude in many meta-analyses. Of particular mention are the publication source (published *versus* unpublished studies), researcher characteristics (e.g., gender, disciplinary affiliation, etc.), nature of research sponsorship, and accuracy of empirical studies to present any relevant information about the measures used, experimental procedure, treatment features, etc.

Table 1: A Conceptual Framework to Characteristics of Studies

Methodological characteristics	Nature of treatment provided	Type of treatment Dosage / Intensity Duration Therapist experience
	Characteristics of subjects	Age Sex Offence type
	Setting / context	Cultural Geographic Temporal
	Design type	Experimental Non-equivalent groups Pretest-postest Normative group Other
	Data analysis (statistical tests) Sample size (n) Attrition (%) Design quality Quality of measures Assignment (random vs. non-random) Pretest measures (present vs. absent)	
Extrinsic characteristics	Characteristics of the researcher/s	Gender Affiliation Training
	Research circumstances	Nature of study Sponsorship
	Form of publication	Journal article Chapter or book Thesis Unpublished manuscript Other
	Accuracy of reporting (details of procedures, method, measures, treatments and results)	

The influence of methodological characteristics in correctional evaluation

In the field of psychosocial program evaluation and especially in crime treatment evaluation, it is very difficult to apply experimental designs whose principal requirement is the random assignment of the subjects to the groups. On the contrary, as Lipsey reported (1988; Lipsey et al., 1985), the evaluation of intervention programs is most represented by the use of quasi-experimental methodology, particularly designs with non-equivalent control groups and, less frequently, pretest-postest designs with one group. From Cook and Campbell's research validity framework (1979), when the intention is to obtain an index of treatment effectiveness, the main problem in the quasi-experimental designs is the differential selection of the subjects that receive the program compared to the subjects that do not receive it. If at the beginning of the program the two groups are non-equivalent in the relevant variables, then the postest comparison of the two groups can produce a biased estimate of the effect size. But the use of an experimental design in correctional evaluation does not assure us that the effect size estimate will not be biased. As Wortman (1992, 1994) emphasised, experimental designs present the problem of attrition; thus, two groups of subjects formed through random assignment can become non-equivalent at the postest due to the differential loss of subjects in both groups.

Consequently, to obtain an unbiased estimate of the effect size will require controlling for the possible research validity threats, whatever the research design. This is possible to accomplish in a meta-analysis, provided that the relevant methodological features of the studies can be codified. Although meta-analyses on correctional evaluation mainly have been centred in substantive variables, they have analysed the influence of several methodological variables too. Examples to illustrate it are presented.

Table 2a: Average Effect Size by Outcome Measure

Outcome	ES	N
Recidivism	0.13	34
Institutional adjustment	0.41	41
Psychological adjustment	0.52	60
Community adjustment	0.63	12
Academic improvement	0.78	30
Vocational adjustment	0.001	5
Other	0.71	11

ES: Mean effect size (standardised mean difference)
N: Number of studies
(Adapted from Garrett, 1985, p. 299)

Table 2b: Average Effect Size by Type Measure

Type of measure	ES	N
Behavioural observation	0.57	58
Peer-rating sociometric	0.37	19
Expert rating	0.98	8
Normed measures	0.29	51
Unnormed measures	0.51	74
Achievement-intellectual test	0.59	20
Cognitive-performance measure	0.67	78
Objective performance measure	0.37	4

ES: Mean effect size (standardised mean difference)
N: Number of studies
(Adapted from Durlak, 1991, p. 208)

First, meta-analytic studies on correctional evaluation show that different outcome measures produce different effect sizes (e.g., recidivism, psychological adjustment, interpersonal adjustment, occupational adjustment, etc.). Table 2a shows the results of the meta-analysis of Garrett (1985) on the treatment programs for adjudicated offenders in residential / institutional settings. As a general rule, the recidivism measures tend to have the lowest effect sizes. Another example is shown in Table 2b from Durlak et al., (1991) on the effectiveness of cognitive behavioural therapy with dysfunctional children. In this case the effect sizes varies as a function of the type of measure.

Second, it seems that evaluation studies with higher sample sizes present the lowest effect sizes. In their meta-analysis review on the efficacy of psychological, educational, and behavioural treatment, Lipsey and Wilson (1993) showed similar results. Table 3 shows how the mean effectiveness diminishes when sample size increases. Probably this is due to the interaction of this variable with other methodological and substantive variables (for example, type of treatment, setting). Also it could be explained by the greater care and control when performing evaluations with reduced groups.

Table 3: Comparison of Effect Sizes Based on Studies with Different Sized Samples

Sample size	ES	N
N less than 50	0.58	39
N 51 to 100	0.52	39
N more than 100	0.35	39

ES: Mean effect size (standardised mean difference)
N: Number of meta-analyses
(Adapted from Lipsey and Wilson, 1993, p. 1195)

Third, it is a clearly demonstrated fact that pretest-postest designs overestimate effect size in comparison with between-group designs. For example, in their meta-analysis on the efficacy of community-based interventions for juvenile offenders Gottschalk et al., (1987a) showed how pretest-postest designs present a mean effect size higher than between-group designs. Lipsey and Wilson (1993) obtained similar results (see Table 4). This could be explained by the influence of some validity threats in pretest-postest designs such as maturation. Also it could be put down to some artefact in the calculation of the indices of the effect size because of the correlational nature of the data.

Table 4: Average Effect Sizes as a Function of Design Type

| | Design type | | | |
| | E/C | | Pre-post | |
Source	ES	N	ES	N
Gottschalk et al., (1987a)	0.36	66	0.93	35
Lipsey and Wilson (1993)	0.47	45	0.76	45

ES: Mean effect size (standardised mean difference)
N: Number of meta-analyses or studies
E/C: Experimental versus Control design
Pre-post: Pretest-Postest design

Fourth, follow-up time is a relevant variable in program evaluation. In this way, Lösel and Köferl (1989), and Lipsey (1992a, 1992b, 1992c) have shown lower effect sizes with longer follow-up times.

Subject assignment to the groups has been considered essential in research design, distinguishing basically between random (experimental designs) *versus* non-random assignment (quasi-experimental designs). Several meta-analyses of correctional evaluations have approached this factor and observed ambiguous evidence. The meta-analyses of Andrews et al., (1990), Whitehead and Lab (1989) and Lipsey (1992a, 1992b, 1992c), as well as the meta-analysis review of Lipsey and Wilson (1993), have not found a clear influence of subject assignment type on effect magnitude. Nevertheless, in the meta-analysis on community-based interventions, Gottschalk et al., (1987a) found higher effectiveness in the studies with random than those with non-random assignment.

Finally, the design quality integrates, somehow, the aforementioned aspects. But there are no clear results in meta-analyses on correctional evaluation. Thus, Garrett (1985) has found that the less rigorous studies present the higher effect sizes, and vice versa; while Andrews *et al.* (1990) and Lipsey and Wilson (1993) have not found relevant differences as a function of design quality (see Table 5).

Table 5: Average Effect Sizes as a Function of Methodological Quality

| | Methodological quality | | | |
| | High | | Low | |
Source	ES	N	ES	N
Gottschalk et al., (1987a)	0.36	66	0.93	35
Lipsey and Wilson (1993)	0.47	45	0.76	45

ES: Mean effect size (standardised mean difference)
N: Number of meta-analyses or studies

The situation is aggravated since the existence of interrelationships between some methodological and substantive characteristics is very common. In the meta-analysis on institutional treatment of juvenile delinquents, Garrett (1985) includes a clear example shown in Table 6. Taking their results globally, behavioural treatment seems to be more effective than psychodynamic and life skills treatments. However, when the most rigorous studies are selected, no differences among behavioural therapy and life skills are observed. Furthermore, within those presenting recidivism outcomes, only life skills treatment seems to be effective. This is a clear example of interaction among design quality, treatment type, and outcome measure.

Table 6: Average Effect Sizes for Different Delinquency Treatments in Relation to Study Design and Outcome Measure

| | Overall | | Rigorous designs only | | Rigorous designs, recidivism outcome only | |
Treatment category	ES	N	ES	N	ES	N
Psychodynamic	.17	164	.17	141	-.01	84
Behavioural	.63	149	.30	62	-.08	17
Life skills	.31	57	.32	35	.30	19

ES: Mean effect size (standardised mean difference)
N: Number of studies
(adapted form Garrett, 1985)

Consequently we agree that the effect of methodological variables should be examined before studying the influence of substantive variables in a meta-analysis (Hedges, Shymansky, & Woodworth, 1989; Lipsey, 1992a, 1992b, 1992c, 1994; Wortman, 1992, 1994). Otherwise, the obtained mean effectiveness might be biased.

Explanatory Meta-Analysis

How can the influence of methodological variables be controlled? The answer to this question implies a step forward in the configuration of a meta-analysis: it is necessary to outline statistical models to explain the variability of the effect sizes as a function of a set of preselected study variables. The approach that Lipsey (1992a, 1992b, 1992c) proposes and, in fact, is applied in his recent meta-analysis on juvenile offender treatment, starts from an explanatory model of the effect size variability through hierarchical regression analysis by weighted least-squares. Table 7 shows the basic structure of the model. The main aspects of the model are the following:

Table 7: Statistical Model: Hierarchical Regression Analysis by Weighted Least Squares

$$Y_i = x_{i1}{}^{b}{}_1 + x_{i2}{}^{b}{}_2 + ... + x_{ip}{}^{b}{}_p + x_{ip+1}{}^{b}{}_{p+1} + x_{ip+2}{}^{b}{}_{p+2} + x_{iq}{}^{b}{}_q + e$$

Y: Vector of effect sizes

X_M: Submatrix of methodological variables

X_S: Submatrix of substantive variables

B: Vector of regression coefficients

E: Vector of random errors

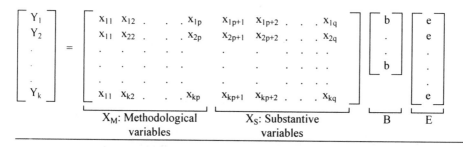

1. The dependent variable is the effect size of the study.

2. The predictor variable matrix is composed of two submatrices, that is, methodological and substantive variables.

3. The estimation method is *by weighted least-squares* because each effect size proceeds from studies with different sample sizes; consequently, it is convenient to weight the variables by the inverse of the variance of the effect sizes (Hedges, 1994; Hedges & Olkin, 1985).

4. Since there will be numerous potential predictor variables, the selection must be guided by conceptual and theoretical criteria.

5. Furthermore, if we take into account that interrelationships among substantive and methodological variables exist, the entry order of these will have to be

determined beforehand and attending to theoretical criteria; but methodological variables will enter first in the model, and then the substantive variables. In this way, it is possible: (a) to determine the percentage of variance explained by methodological variables, and (b) to determine the percentage of variance explained by substantive variables *once the influence of methodological variables is eliminated.*

An example of this can be seen in Table 8 in which the results of a hierarchical regression analysis applied in the meta-analysis of Lipsey (1992a, 1992b, 1992c) are presented. The set of methodological variables explain 25% of the variance of effect size, a not negligible percentage. In addition, one can observe how the set of substantive variables still explained 22% of the remaining variance, once the influence of methodological variables was eliminated. Lipsey has shown that substantive variables influence the evaluation results. Moreover, he has built an explanatory model of the correctional program effectiveness as a function of study characteristics.

Table 8: Hierarchical Multiple Regression Analysis by Weighted Least Squares for Methodological and Treatment Variables

Step	Variable Cluster	Cumulative Multiple R	Cumulative R-square	R-square change	Change as proportion of total R-square
	Method			.25	.53
1	Samples	.20	.04	.04*	.09
2	Equivalence	.31	.10	.06*	.12
3	Attrition	.36	.13	.03*	.07
4	Control	.40	.16	.03	.06
5	Measures	.44	.20	.04*	.08
6	*ES* Info[a]	.46	.21	.01	.03
7	Interactions	.50	.25	.04*	.09
	Treatment			.22	.47
8	Subjects	.51	.26	.01	.02
9	Dosage	.53	.29	.03*	.07
10	Treatment	.63	.40	.11*	.24
11	Tcontext	.65	.42	.02*	.04
12	Interactions	.68	.47	.05*	.10

* $p < .05$
[a] *ES* Info: Degree of information about effect sizes
(Adapted from Lipsey, 1992, p. 117)

Lipsey's proposed multiple regression explanatory model can be complemented with the ideas recently developed by Rubin (1990, 1992). Rubin proposes to obtain an explanatory model (for example, a multiple regression model) in which the more relevant substantive and methodological variables are combined with predictive purposes. Supposing that we have a regression model in which substantive and methodological variables are included, many questions could be answered such as: what is the effectiveness of the "A" treatment with a duration of "X" months and supposing a maximum design quality, no attrition, and a large sample size? One could try to configure an *effect size surface* capable of predicting future research and, consequently, guiding it adequately. Of course, to accomplish these predictions implies high risks if the explanatory model is misspecified. In such cases, the predictions would be made with extreme caution and always with orientative purposes for future research.

In conclusion, the main aim of this report is to emphasise the importance that meta-analyses on correctional treatment evaluation have to test the potential influence of methodological variables to amend the possible biases in the estimation of the effect size, and the convenience of testing explanatory models that take into account the set of more relevant methodological and substantive variables with predictive purposes. The future of meta-analysis shall go through that displacement from description to explanation.

References

Andrews, D.A., Zinger, I., Hoge, R.D.; Bonta, J., Gendreau, P., & Cullen, F.T. (1990). Does correctional treatment work? A clinically relevant and psychologically informed meta-analysis. *Criminology, 28,* 369-404.

Cook, T.D., & Campbell, D.T. (1979). *Quasi-experimentation: Design and Analysis Issues for Field Settings.* Boston, MA: Houghton Mifflin.

Cook, T.D., Cooper, H.M., Cordray, D.S., Hartmann, H., Hedges, L.V., Light, R.J., Louis, T.A., and Mosteller, F. (Eds.) (1992). *Meta-analysis for Explanation: A Casebook.* New York: Sage.

Cooper, H.M. (1989). *Integrating Research: A Guide for Literature Reviews* (2nd ed.). Newbury Park, CA: Sage.

Cooper, H.M., & Hedges, L.V. (Eds.) (1994). *The Handbook of Research Synthesis.* New York: Sage.

Durlak, J.A., Fuhrman, T., & Lampman, C. (1991). Effectiveness of cognitive-behavior therapy for maladapting children: A meta-analysis. *Psychological Bulletin, 110,* 204-214.

Durlak, J.A., & Lipsey, M.W. (1991). A practitioner's guide to meta-analysis. *American Journal of Community Psychology, 19,* 291-332.

Garrett, C.J. (1985). Effects of residential treatment on adjudicated delinquents: A meta-analysis. *Journal of Research in Crime and Delinquency, 22,* 287-308.

Gensheimer, L.K., Mayer, J.P., Gottschalk, R., & Davidson, W.S. II (1986). Diverting youth from the juvenile justice system: A meta-analysis of intervention efficacy. In S.J. Apter and A.P. Goldstein (Eds.), *Youth Violence* (pp. 39-57). New York: Pergamon Press.

Glass, G.V. (1976). Primary, secondary, and meta-analysis of research. *Educational Researcher, 5,* 3-8.

Glass, G.V., McGaw, B., & Smith, M.L. (1981). *Meta-analysis in Social Research.* Newbury Park, CA: Sage.

Gottschalk, R., Davidson, W.S. II, Gensheimer, L.K., & Mayer, J.P. (1987a). Community-based interventions. In H.C. Quay (Ed.), *Handbook of Juvenile Delinquency* (pp. 266-289). New York: Wiley.

Gottschalk, R., Davidson, W.S. II, Gensheimer, L.K., & Mayer, J.P. (1987b). Behavioral approaches with juveniles offenders: A meta-analysis of long-term treatment efficacy. In E.K. Morris & C.J. Braukman (Eds.), *Behavioral Approaches to Crime and Delinquency: A Handbook of Application, Research, and Concepts* (pp. 399-422). New York: Plenum Press.

Hedges, L.V. (1994). Fixed effects models. En H.M. Cooper & L.V. Hedges (Eds.), *The Handbook of Research Synthesis* (pp. 285-300). New York: Sage.

Hedges, L.V., & Olkin, I. (1985). *Statistical Methods for Meta-analysis*. San Diego, CA: Academic Press.

Hedges, L.V., Shymansky, J.A., & Woodworth, G. (1989). *A Practical Guide to Modern Methods of Meta-analysis*. Washington, DC: National Science Teachers Association.

Hunter, J.E., & Schmidt, F.L. (1990). *Methods of Meta-analysis: Correcting Error and Bias in Research Findings*. Newbury Park, CA: Sage.

Kaufman, P. (1985). *Meta-analysis of juvenile delinquency prevention programs*. Unpublished manuscript, Claremont Graduate School.

Light, R.J., & Pillemer, D.B. (1984). *Summing up: The Science of Reviewing Research*. Cambridge, MA: Harvard University Press.

Lipsey, M.W. (1988). Practice and malpractice in evaluation research. *Evaluation Practice, 9*, 5-24.

Lipsey, M.W. (1992a). Juvenile delinquency treatment: A meta-analytic inquiry into the variability of effects. In T.D. Cook, H.M. Cooper et al., (Eds.), *Meta-analysis for Explanation: A Casebook* (pp. 83-127). New York: Sage.

Lipsey, M.W. (1992b). Meta-analysis in evaluation research: Moving from description to explanation. In H.T. Chen & P.H. Rossi (Eds.), *Using Theory to Improve Program and Policy Evaluations*. New York: Greenwood Press.

Lipsey, M.W. (1992c). The effect of treatment on juvenile delinquents: Results from meta-analysis. In F. Lösel, D. Bender, & T. Blisener (Eds.), *Psychology and Law: International Perspectives* (pp. 131-143). Berlin: Walter de Gruyter.

Lipsey, M.W. (1994). Identifying potentially interesting variables and analysis opportunities. In H.M. Cooper & L.V. Hedges (Eds.), *The Handbook of Research Synthesis* (pp. 111-123). New York: Sage.

Lipsey, M.W., Crosse, S., Dunkle, J., Pollard, J., & Stobart, G. (1985). Evaluation: The state of the art and the sorry state of the science. *New Directions for Program Evaluation, 27*, 7-28.

Lipsey, M.W., & Wilson, D.B. (1993). The efficacy of psychological, educational, and behavioral treatment: Confirmation from meta-analysis. *American Psychologist, 48*, 1181-1209.

Lösel, F. (in press). What recent meta-evaluations tell us about the effectiveness of correctional treatment? In G. Davies, S. LLoyd-Bostock, M. McMurran, & C. Wilson (Eds.), *Psychology and Law: Recent Advances in Research*. Berlin: De Gruyter.

Lösel, F., & Köferl, P. (1989). Evaluation research on correctional treatment in West Germany: A meta-analysis. In H. Wegener, F. Lösel, & J. Haisch (Eds.), *Criminal Behavior and the Justice System: Psychological Perspectives* (pp. 334-355). New York: Springer.

Mayer, J.P., Gensheimer, L.K., Davidson, W.S. II, & Gottschalk, R. (1986). Social learning treatment within juvenile justice: A meta-analysis of impact in the natural environment. In S.J. Apter & A.P. Goldstein (Eds.), *Youth Violence* (pp. 24-39). New York: Pergamon Press.

Rosenthal, R. (1991). *Meta-analytic Procedures for Social Research* (Rev. ed.). Newbury Park, CA: Sage.

Rubin, D.B. (1990). A new perspective. In K.W. Wachter & M.L. Straf (Eds.), *The Future of Meta-analysis* (pp. 155-165). New York: Sage.

Rubin, D.B. (1992). Meta-analysis: Literature synthesis or effect-size surface estimation? *Journal of Educational Statistics, 17*, 363-374.

Sánchez-Meca, J., & Ato, M. (1989). Meta-análisis: Una alternativa metodológica a las revisiones tradicionales de la investigación. In J. Arnau & H. Carpintero (Coord.), *Tratado de Psicología General. 1: Historia, Teoría y Método* (pp. 617-670). Madrid: Alhambra.

Wachter, K.W., & Straff, M.L. (Eds.) (1990). *The Future of Meta-analysis*. New York: Sage.

Whitehead, J.T., & Lab, S.P. (1989). A meta-analysis of juvenile correctional treatment. *Journal of Research in Crime and Delinquency, 26*, 276-295.

Wolf, F.M. (1986). *Meta-analysis: Quantitative Methods for Research Synthesis*. Beverly Hills, CA: Sage.

Wortman, P.M. (1992). Lessons from the meta-analysis of quasi-experiments. In F.B. Bryant et al., (Eds.), *Methodological Issues in Applied Social Psychology* (pp. 65-81). New York: Plenum Press.

Wortman, P.M. (1994). Judging research quality. In H.M. Cooper & L.V. Hedges (Eds.), *The Handbook of Research Synthesis* (pp. 97-109). New York: Sage.

What Works in Correctional Rehabilitation in Europe: A Meta-Analytical Review

Santiago Redondo, Vicente Garrido and Julio Sánchez-Meca

Introduction

During the last decade important research initiatives have been undertaken to evaluate the functionality and profit of different models and techniques applied to delinquents and offenders. Prior to that period, in the seventies and at the beginning of the eighties, a few researchers analysed, in qualitative terms, collections of programmes of offender treatment to evaluate their contingent efficacy. These first inspections obtained, as a rule, negative results and transmitted a generalised pessimism about the possibilities of treating delinquency and crime effectively. The most widely disseminated conclusion of this period was delivered by Martinson, who in 1974 pronounced a kind of epitaph on this topic: in matters of rehabilitative efforts, "nothing works" (Martinson, 1974). This phrase became since then a customary notion of correctional literature (Pearson et al., 1995) and still many authors take issue with this at present.

However, the limits of these first qualitative reviews were great. On the one hand, these inspections were incapable of encompassing and relating the different factors implicated in the treatment programmes, such as the applied techniques' heterogeneity and the diversity of treated subjects, of application contexts, of methodology and of output measures. Furthermore, due to the limited precision of these first reviews, they also showed an evident inability to assess the contingent effects, be they small or partial, of some of the applied programmes. Certainly, when large volumes of information are reviewed in a qualitative manner, only general considerations can be obtained, similar to those where each researcher, according to his or her particular judgement, arrives to conclusions which are excessively generic and inaccurate. Of this manner, if we were to analyse programmes' effectiveness with delinquents and offenders, it would be very naïve to expect the programmes to eradicate the criminal behaviour of most of the treated subjects; therefore, the conclusion could not be other (and quite possible to advance before any efficacy review) than that the programmes failed absolutely. However, research questions so extreme and global, that only will admit global and extreme answers, do not appear to be raised from a scientific perspective, and more yet for a phenomenon so complex and multifactorial as crime.

Some of these problems are also evident in the last example of this narrative review. Palmer (1994), using both direct and indirect evidence, considered many studies of the effectiveness of different treatments for young offenders. He showed that for the majority of the studies, on the whole, experimental programmes showed success of rehabilitation for treatment vs. control groups. Palmer suggests that the results from independent studies, each of which show some improvement, may be classified and taken together, so that the evidence from several small independent samples, each showing low levels of significance, may be more fully assessed. As Wilkins (1996) points out, although this is a plausible analysis, and the findings of many of the studies may seem reasonable, the quality of the research varies widely, and the rigour of any attempts to sum the evidence is doubtful.

Recently, some researchers in the field of rehabilitation assessment have been more modest in their pretensions and, at the same time, methodologically more accurate than the first reviewers. This has been possible thanks to meta-analysis, a relatively recent statistical technique that permits the integration of studies related to a certain topic in order to compare and summarise the current knowledge on the analysed issue (Cooper, 1989; Glass, 1977; Gómez, 1987; Sánchez-Meca & Ato, 1989). More concretely, in the area of delinquency and crime treatment, meta-analysis offers a tool to answer important questions such as the following: Which are the more effective models and psychological techniques in the treatment of offenders? Which are the subjects that benefit more efficaciously? In which places or contexts are the various techniques more useful? And, above all, to what extent are treated subjects favoured above those which are not treated? To answer these questions the reviewers of crime treatment programmes carry out research processes of second order, where they collect a series of programmes that have been applied - and evaluated - during a given temporal period; they then systematically codify the various factors that could be related to the results - features of the treatment, of the subjects, of the context of application and of the methodology used - and they analyse the possible existing relations between these factors and the output measures that were taken for results (for example, psychological adjustment or recidivism). In such a way, through a laborious and systematic process, general conclusions can be obtained about the effectiveness of the treatment of offending behaviour.

According to the usual structure of meta-analysis, a research design was established that connected the various analysed variables in the form that is illustrated in Figure 1. As can be observed, meta-analysis enabled us to investigate the contingent existing relations between treatment factors, subjects, context and methodology, considered here as antecedent or independent variables, and the various output measures (treatment implementation level, institutional adjustment, psychological adjustment, educational adjustment, vocational adjustment, interaction skills adjustment and recidivism) as dependent variables.

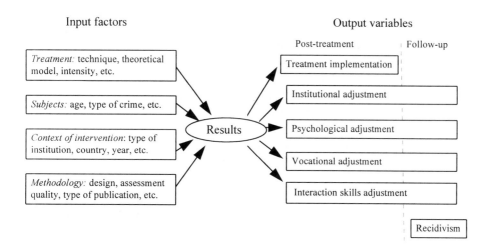

Figure 1: Research design

Up until now seven meta-analytical reviews of treatment programmes of delinquency and crime have been carried out in the world: six in America and one in Europe. The earliest meta-analysis on delinquency was carried out by an American researcher, Anne Garrett, who in 1985 assessed 111 treatment programmes applied to institutionalised juvenile delinquents and obtained an average *effect size* of $r = .18$ (Garrett, 1985). This means that the programmes studied by Garrett achieved, on average, an improvement of 18% in the measures obtained by the treated subjects above those of the not treated (Lösel, 1996; Redondo, 1994). In 1986 and 1987, a group of American researchers conducted two meta-analyses with 35 and 90 *diversion* programmes for delinquents, respectively (Gensheimer et al., 1986; Gottschalk et al., 1987), obtaining an identical *effect size* for both investigations of $r = .10$, that is, an improvement of 10%. In 1989, Whitehead and Lab (1989) analysed 50 programmes applied to juvenile delinquents, and detected an average efficacy of $r = .12$, although their own conclusions were pessimistic. A year afterwards, Andrews et al. (1990) published a review study including 154 treatment programmes of juveniles as well as adults offenders and informed of an average *effect size* of $r = .10$. Lipsey published in 1992 the results of the most ambitious review study carried out to that date. He included in his analysis 397 treatment programmes of juvenile delinquents, applied between 1945 and 1990 - encompassing almost five decades - in those which not less than forty thousand juveniles were evaluated. Lipsey obtained an average effectiveness that was somewhat more limited, between $.05$ and $.08$, that represents a percentage of improvement between 5 to 8%. This less than average efficacy is explained by Lipsey (1992a; 1992b) and additional authors (for example, Lösel, 1996; McGuire, 1992) in terms of the reduction caused by the inclusion in the study of many ineffective programmes existing in so numerous a sample as was analysed in this case. In Europe there has been one meta-analytical review. This was conducted by a German research team (Lösel et al., 1987; Lösel & Köferl, 1989) that studied the effectiveness of the treatment applied in 18 *sociotherapeutic prisons*, obtaining an *effect size* of $r = .11$, which means an efficacy of 11%.

Recently Lösel has updated his 1987 meta-analysis (Lösel, 1995a) with the addition of two more outcome evaluations. The new findings scarcely change the previously obtained results: the revised total effect estimation again revealed a mean correlation coefficient of .11.

To date, however, no research has integrated in its analysis programmes applied in various European countries, contrary to what has happened in the Anglo-American context. This is precisely the novelty of our investigation: we will present in this chapter the main results of a meta-analytical review carried out on a set of programmes applied to delinquents and offenders in different European countries.

Our Research on European Programmes

Method

Literature search As we have discussed more extensively in a previous work (Redondo et al., 1996a), three different channels were used to search for studies that would be analysed. First, a computerised search was undertaken in three data bases, the *Dialogue Information Service* (that accesses the *Criminal Justice Periodical Index*), *Pascal* (a French data base) and *PsycLit*. Second, a direct review was done of journals, books, and monographs on criminology, psychology, education, social work, law, etc. And, finally, a letter was sent to a wide number of European experts and correctional institutions requesting them to forward studies of crime treatment programmes, published or unpublished. This research period covered 1980 to 1993, and the admitted languages were: English, Spanish, Catalan, French, Italian and Portuguese.

The set of 250 references initially located were screened and selected according to the following criteria:

1. Programmes applied to subjects under the control of the criminal justice system (in other words, delinquents or offenders).
2. The use of a strategy directed towards rehabilitation.
3. Incorporation of a scientific evaluation design that would permit the comparability between groups of treatment/control or between pre/post measures.
4. Inclusion of sufficient data for calculating effect size.

After considering these criteria, 49 studies from six countries were included in our meta-analysis. The studies produced 57 independent effect sizes (see Appendix).

Coding variables For the coding process, three instruments were used (see also Redondo et al., 1996a): a coding sheet, a coding book that established the operational definitions of selected variables and computing data bases. In this process information was collected and structured into more than two hundred items referring to document identification, programme philosophy, features of subjects and groups, sampling, setting of application, design and follow-up period, treatment activities, outcome variables and conclusions of the authors.

Two factors were especially important for our analysis according to our research design: treatment and outcome variables.

Eight categories of theoretical treatment models were established:

1. Non-behavioural therapy, such as individual or group psychotherapy (a category where nine studies were classified).
2. Educational-informational treatment, such as school treatment or delivery of educational material (six studies).
3. Behavioural therapy, exclusively founded on classical or operand conditioning models as in the case of token economies, or environmental outlines based on contingencies (eleven studies).
4. Cognitive-behavioural therapy, such as social skills training or psycho-social competence programmes (nineteen studies).
5. Classical penal theory based on retribution, such as models of "shock incarceration" or increasing levels of institutional control (one study).
6. Therapeutic community where inmate-staff relationships were conceived as similar to patient-nurse relationships, or the decreasing levels of institutional control (five studies).
7. Diversion programmes or community treatment (five studies).
8. Others, for instance psychiatric institutions (one study).

Outcome variables were also coded in eight categories with a double possibility of measurement period, post-treatment and/or follow-up measures:

1. Measures of treatment implementation level.
2. Institutional adjustment (behaviour in prison, violence, social climate of institutions).
3. Psychological adjustment of personality and attitudes.
4. Educational-cultural adjustment (school participation, reading books, ...).
5. Vocational adjustment.
6. Interaction skills adjustment (cognitive capacities and emotional factors connected to it - self-control/impulsiveness, cognitive style, etc. -, actual development of interaction behaviour, hygiene and health skills, and general adjustment).
7. Recidivism (new crimes, new police contacts, arrests, return to prison).
8. Other measures.

Due to the great laboriousness and inherent difficulties in the codification process in a study such as this, a series of controls were established to guarantee its reliability. An initial mechanism to adjust the selection and definition of the included variables was the triple coding by independent coders of a sample of twenty studies. After that the observed discrepancies were solved by consensus and the necessary rectifications in the coding instruments were effected. Then, concerning the outcome variables, a test of within-coder reliability was conducted at two different moments, which obtained an agreement index of 94%. Finally, the strictest judgement consisted of finding the reliability among three independent coders, where we found an agreement index of 86.2% for the codification of treatment categories and of 78.5% for the outcome variables categories. Furthermore, a reliability control of the statistical calculations of the effect size was also undertaken. For this, in twenty studies selected at random the calculations of the effect sizes were obtained by two independent coders, with a Pearson correlation coefficient of .83.

Calculating effect size The effectiveness of each programme included in the meta-analysis was calculated through the Effect Size (ES), which is the standardised mean difference, d (Glass, McGaw & Smith, 1981). This index was defined in two ways, depending on the type of study being analysed: (a) For the studies comparing two groups (experimental-control), d was the difference between the means of the two groups divided by the within-group standard deviation; for the one group and pre-test/post-test studies d was defined as the difference between the means of the pre-test and post-test divided by the within-group standard deviation. A positive value was assigned to d when the programme was effective, and a negative value in the contrary case. We express the ESs in terms of Pearson's correlation coefficient (r)[1] (Rosenthal, 1991). When a study presented the results of various programmes applied to different samples, an ES was calculated for each programme and these were considered independent studies. In this way, the 49 selected studies resulted in a total of 57 ES's. Also for each dependent variable its average ES was calculated, distinguishing between the two temporal moments of each register (post-test and the longest follow-up); a global ES in the post-test and in the last follow-up was also obtained. Each ES was weighted by the inverse-variance and the analysis of the moderator variables was made with the variance and regression analysis proposed by Hedges & Olkin (1985). The statistical analyses were made with the programmes DSTAT (Johnson, 1989) and SYSTAT (Wilkinson, 1992).

Results

Descriptive characteristics

Before presenting results on programme effectiveness (certainly the most important), we consider it necessary to offer to our readers some brief information

---

[1] The relation between d and r is about $d = 2r$ (Glass et al., 1981; Rosenthal, 1991).

on the main characteristics of the evaluated programmes. Tables 1 and 2 present the basic data of more relevant codified variables. The first important aspect concerns the *intervention magnitude*, conceptualised as the total number of treatment hours by subject (see Table 2). In other words, this information refers to the question: what was the programme potential? The programme potential constitutes a critical feature of offender treatment, since the magnitude could obviously influence effectiveness. For the set of analysed European programmes we obtained a median of 22.5 hours of intervention by subject (we preferred the median instead the mean because of the asymmetric character of distribution). According to this information it can be affirmed that, on average, the programmes analysed are of low intensity.

Linked closely to this programme issue is the duration and intensity of the programme; the programmes show a median duration of 2.5 months and 3.75 treatment hours per week. The theoretical treatment models more employed were the behavioural and the behavioural-cognitive (see Table 1).

Other relevant descriptive features concern the *total sample size* of participants in the programmes. A total number of 7,728 were evaluated in the analysed programmes, of which 4,284 were included in treatment groups and 3,444 in control groups. This means that our results on effectiveness - and this is one of the most powerful features that a meta-analytic integration offers - refer not to a sole programme or to a small number of offenders, but to a large number of subjects that were treated in many programmes. Consequently, the possibilities of generalisation of our results raise considerably.

The main characteristics of the subjects were: (1) the median age was 19 years old (see Table 2), although there were some missing data; (2) property offences were the most frequent (Table 1), and (3) the vast majority of the subjects were male (median: 100%).

The most frequent settings where the programmes were carried out were juvenile prisons, adult prisons and the community. The programmes were also implemented in custody regimes, most of the times. The countries that contributed more studies were Great Britain and Spain (Table 1).

Another relevant feature is the *follow-up period* used to evaluate some of employed outcome variables, due to the fact that its duration bears a close relationship to the generalisation of programme effectiveness. In average, the follow-up period for those programmes that included follow-up measures (for instance, social skills or recidivism) had a median value of 12 months, while the mean was 19.7 months. Even though the average duration of the follow-up was not as long as would be necessary for evaluating long-time variables as recidivism, this duration was, however, important if we consider that in variables such as recidivism the most critical recidivism rates occur during the first follow-up year (see for example, Redondo et al., 1996b; Sánchez-Meca et al., 1995; Tournier & Barre, 1990).

With respect to the methodological variables, it is noteworthy to say that the quasi-experimental design type was the most employed; the attrition rate in the treated groups had a median of 20%, and also the between groups designs were more frequent than the one-group within-subject designs. Finally, although the majority are data from published studies, about a quarter are from non-published studies; that fact permits us to analyse if the publication bias influences our results.

Treatment effectiveness

The main question in our research can be formulated in the following terms: Are offender rehabilitation programmes effective? In a first analysis, we can see that from the 57 studies analysed, 50 (87%) obtained positive ES's, i.e., favouring treatment groups or the post-test measures in the case of pre-test/post-test designs, while 6 programmes showed negative ES's and in one case the ES was zero ($z = 5.83, p < .001$). Consequently, in the greater part of cases, it can be affirmed that

Table 1: Qualitative variables coded in the meta-analysis (N = 57)

Variables	Freq.	%	Variables	Freq.	%
Theoretical model:			*Regime:*		
- Non behavioural	9	15.8	- Closed	34	59.6
- Educational	6	10.6	- Semi-open	2	3.5
- Behavioural	11	19.3	- Open	11	19.3
- Cognit.-behavioural	19	33.3	- Other	7	12.3
- Classic penal theory	1	1.7	- NA*	3	5.3
- Therapeutic comm.	5	8.8			
- Diversion	5	8.8			
- Other	1	1.7			
Subject age:			*Country:*		
Adolescents (<16)	9	15.8	- Great Britain	26	45.6
Juveniles (16-21)	18	31.5	- Spain	13	22.8
Adults (>21)	25	43.9	- Germany	4	7.0
Mixed	5	8.8	- Netherlands	9	15.8
			- Sweden	4	7.0
			- Israel	1	1.8
Offence type:			*Design:*		
- Property	18	31.6	- Pre-experimental	12	21.0
- People	2	3.5	- Quasi-experimental	25	43.9
- Sexual	4	7.0	- Experimental	15	26.3
- Drugs traffic	2	3.5	- Behavioural	3	5.3
- Alcohol	7	12.3	- Institution comparison	2	3.5
- Mixed	16	28.1			
- NA*	8	14.0			
Programme setting:			*Between vs. within design:*		
- Juvenile reform center	3	5.3	- Between	39	68.4
- Juvenile prison	16	28.1	- Within	18	31.6
- Adult prison	17	29.8	*Publication source*		
- Community	14	24.5	- Published	42	73.7
- Other	4	7.0	- Unpublished	15	26.3
- NA*	3	5.3			

NA : Not available*

any programme was more effective than no programme. A more significant approach consists in calculating the global ES for all the treatment, all the measures and for all the evaluation periods (post-test and follow-ups). The Pearson correlation coefficient was $r = .15$, that corresponds to a standardised mean difference of $d = 0.3039$, statistically significant for $p < .0000$ (95% confidence interval for d: 0.26; 0.35). The Pearson correlation coefficient can be interpreted directly, multiplied by one hundred, in terms of percentage of improvement. This means that treated groups surpassed controls in the set of evaluated variables by 15 points (Rosenthal & Rubin, 1982).

Table 2: Quantitative variables coded in the meta-analysis

Variables	k	Min.	Max.	Mean	S.D.	Median
Programme duration (in months)	46	0.067	41	5.67	7.63	2.5
Programme intensity (in hours week)	46	0.75	56	17.04	23.52	3.75
Programme magnitude (in hours/subject)	45	1.5	9840	687.6	1691	22.5
Sample age (in years)	39	12.5	39.3	21.7	6.9	19
Sample sex (% of men)	52	0	100	93.51	20.86	100
Sample size	57	6	1212	112.5	213.2	36
Attrition (in treated group)	41	0	82.1	23.7	22.3	20
Follow-up (in months)	43	0.5	120	19.7	23.2	12

k: Number of studies. Min.: minimum score. Max: Maximum score. S.D.: Standard Deviation

The average effectiveness is evident. However, the ES distribution of integrated studies is very heterogeneous [$Q(56) = 171.270$, $p < .0000$]. In meta-analysis this verification leads us inexorably to the analysis of the contingent existing relations between outcome and the various factors theoretically associated with it, following our design: factors of subjects, settings, methodology, and treatment.

Table 3: Effect size as a function of crime typology

Class	k	d_+	95% C.I.	r_+	Q_w	DF	p
Property	18	0.261	0.199:0.322	.129	101.85	17	.000
People	2	0.923	0.321:1.525	.419	0.02	1	.991
Sexual	4	0.172	-0.162:0.505	.085	14.99	3	.005
Drug traffic	2	0.241	0.111:0.371	.120	0.85	1	.653
Mixed	16	0.434	0.320:0.548	.212	19.06	15	.265
Alcohol	7	0.337	0.224:0.450	.166	6.32	6	.503
Overall	49	0.300	0.255:0.345	.148	$Q_w = 143.09$	43	.000
					$Q_B = 21.42$	5	.001

k: Number of studies. d_+: average standardised mean difference. 95% C.I.: 95% Confidence Interval. r_+: average correlation coefficient. Q_w: Within-class statistic. DF: Degrees of Freedom. p: probability. Q_B: Between-class statistic

Tables 3 and 4 present the results obtained in analysing the influence of two subject variables, the type of offence and the age, on the ES. The greatest effectiveness was obtained for offences against persons (r = .419), even though this ES corresponds to a very limited number of studies of k = 2, which hinders its generalisation, and in second place in mixed groups integrated by different typologies of offenders (r = .212, k = 16). The least effectiveness was produced with sexual offenders (r = .085, k = 4). This relationship was statistically significant [$Q_B(5)$ = 21.42, p = .001]. With respect to the classification of the subjects by age groups, although significant results were not obtained [Q_B (3) = 5.715 p = .126], it is possible to say that the younger the subjects, the more effective the programme.

Table 4: Effect size as a function of subject's age

Class	k	d$_+$	95% C.I.	r$_+$	Q$_w$		DF	p
Adolescents	9	0.449	0.271:0.626	.219	10.39		8	.319
Juveniles	18	0.405	0.262:0.548	.198	41.18		17	.001
Mixed	5	0.312	0.212:0.411	.154	2.47		4	.781
Adults	25	0.273	0.219:0.328	.135	111.51		24	.000
Overall	57	0.304	0.260:0.348	.150	Q$_w$ =	165.55	53	.000
					Q$_B$ =	5.715	3	.126

Partially related to the subjects' age variable are the programme settings. As can be seen in Table 5, the greatest effectiveness was achieved in juvenile centres (r = .257, k = 3) and in juvenile prisons (r = .193, k = 16), while the least effectiveness was obtained in adult prisons (r = .119, k = 17). This result is consistent with one of the more reiterated conclusions of correctional literature: youths would be more influenced by treatment than adults, whose criminal careers are much more established.

Table 5: Effect size as a function of setting of intervention

Class	k	d$_+$	95% C.I.	r$_+$	Q$_w$		DF	p
Juvenile center	3	0.532	0.114:0.949	.257	0.59		2	.898
Juvenile prison	16	0.394	0.242:0.547	.193	40.91		15	.000
Adult prison	17	0.240	0.183:0.298	.119	78.32		16	.000
Community	14	0.339	0.245:0.434	.167	32.75		13	.003
Other	4	0.475	0.301:0.649	.231	0.55		3	.968
Overall	54	0.295	0.250:0.340	.146	Q$_w$ =	153.12	49	.000
					Q$_B$ =	11.26	4	.023

Table 6 presents the effectiveness of the programmes meta-analysed according to country. The reader should known that this is a weak analysis. It is true that - setting aside the Israeli study ($r = .320$) -, Spain ($r = .239$, $k = 13$) and Germany ($r = .205$, $k = 4$), get the best results; however, on the one hand, the Great Britain results are diminished by one particular study, without which the average ES is similar to other countries ($r = .15$, $k = 25$) and, on the other hand, Great Britain is the country with the highest number of studies.

Table 6: Effect size as a function of country

Class	k	d_+	95% C.I.	r_+	Q_w	DF	p
Great Britain	26	0.173	0.105:0.240	.086	88.34	25	.000
Spain	13	0.493	0.353:0.634	.239	34.19	12	.001
Germany	4	0.419	0.310:0.528	.205	4.58	3	.333
Netherlands	9	0.400	0.285:0.516	.196	9.00	8	.437
Sweden	4	0.318	0.211:0.426	.157	5.27	3	.260
Israel	1	0.674	0.063:1.286	.319	-	-	-
Overall	57	0.304	0.260:0.348	.150	$Q_w = 141.38$	52	.000
					$Q_B = 29.89$	5	.000

In the framework of methodological variables a greater programme effectiveness was observed for behavioural designs, for instance reversion or baseline designs ($r = .395$, $k = 3$), that obviously are connected to behavioural and cognitive-behavioural programmes, that were also the most effective. Contrarily, the least effectiveness was obtained in experimental designs with random assignment of subjects ($r = .067$, $k = 15$).

Table 7: Effect size as a function of design type

Class	k	d_+	95% C.I.	r_+	Q_w	DF	p
Pre-experimental	12	0.361	0.233:0.488	.177	40.90	11	.000
Quasi-experimental	25	0.377	0.317:0.438	.185	61.74	24	.000
Experimental	15	0.134	0.052:0.215	.067	20.79	14	.144
Behavioural	3	0.861	0.451:1.271	.395	12.40	2	.006
Institution compar.	2	0.254	0.060:0.448	.126	4.91	1	.086
Overall	57	0.304	0.260:0.348	.150	$Q_w = 140.74$	52	.000
					$Q_B = 30.52$	4	.000

In order to see if the publication bias could influence the validity of the meta-analysis results, a published versus non-published comparison was made. There were no significant differences between the two sources of publication [Q_w (1) = 2.66, p = .103]. In fact, the non-published studies presented an even higher mean effectiveness than the non-published ones. Consequently, we reject the publication bias as a threat to the validity of our results.

Table 8: Effect size as a function of publication source

Class	k	d_+	95% C.I.	r_+	Q_w	DF	p
Published	42	0.286	0.237:0.335	.142	140.58	41	.000
Unpublished	15	0.379	0.279:0.479	.186	28.03	14	.021
Overall	57	0.304	0.260:0.348	.150	Q_w = 168.61	55	.000
					Q_B = 2.66	1	.103

But, without doubt, the main outcome of our analysis concerns the effectiveness of the different types of treatment applied to offenders. Table 9 shows the ES's obtained by the different treatment models. The greatest effectiveness was observed for programmes founded on behavioural (r = .279, k = 11) and cognitive-behavioural models (r = .273, k = 19). Contrarily, the least effectiveness was achieved in a prison programme based on the classical penal theory or retribution (r = .039). In an intermediate level are the non-behavioural (r = .194, k = 9), educational (r = .175, k = 6) and diversion models (r = .195, k = 5).

Table 9: Effect size as a function of treatment theoretical model

Class	k	d_+	95% C.I.	r_+	Q_w	DF	p
Non behavioural therapy	9	0.395	0.308:0.483	.194	29.32	8	.000
Educational/informational	6	0.355	0.236:0.475	.175	12.13	5	.059
Behavioural therapy	11	0.581	0.407:0.754	.279	19.26	10	.057
Cognit.-behav. therapy	19	0.568	0.403:0.732	.273	38.68	18	.005
Classic penal theory	1	0.078	-0.010:0.166	.039	-	-	-
Therapeutic Community	5	0.251	0.137:0.365	.124	12.90	4	.024
Diversion	5	0.399	0.206:0.591	.195	3.44	4	.631
Other	1	0.036	-0.237:0.310	.018	-	-	-
Overall	57	0.304	0.260:0.349	.150	Q_w = 115.73	49	.000
					Q_B = 55.54	7	.000

In relation to the programme characteristic variables, we included the following: duration, intensity and treatment magnitude. These quantitative variables were analysed through weighted simple regression analysis, with no clear relationship with the ES. Only the intensity of the programme (defined as the number of weekly treatment hours) explained 10.6% of the ES variance; thus, the most intense programmes were the most effective.

As other studies have shown (Lipsey & Wilson, 1993; Sánchez-Meca, 1996), in examining the relationship between the follow-up period and the ES^2, the least effectiveness was associated with the longest follow-up periods, although this was a weak correlation (adjusted squared correlation coefficient: .037).

Finally, we tested programme effectiveness on the various analysed dependent variables, taking the longest follow-up period of each study (see Table 10). A greater effectiveness was found for measures related to institutional ($r = .41$, $k = 7$), psychological ($r = .32$, $k = 3$), work ($r = .28$, $k = 7$) and school ($r = .27$, $k = 3$) adjustments.

The worst results for the test were obtained for the recidivism measures, as we will comment on further. Nevertheless, these results are for guidance only, since the number of studies is quite limited.

Table 10: Average effect sizes on several outcome measures in the last follow-up period

Class	k	d_+	95% C.I.	r_+	Q	DF	p
Overall	45	0.263	0.22:0.31	.13	153.23	44	.000
Recidivism	32	0.243	0.20:0.29	.12	123.48	31	.000
Institutional adjustment	7	0.901	0.53:1.27	.41	9.37	6	.154
Psychological adjustment	3	0.670	0.07:1.27	.32	0.81	2	.665
Social skills	13	0.402	0.29:0.52	.20	32.33	12	.001
School adjustment	3	0.571	0.27:0.87	.27	31.28	2	.000
Work adjustment	7	0.591	0.39:0.79	.28	4.60	6	.595

Recidivism outcomes

It is clear that when speaking of the rehabilitation of the offender, the fundamental outcome variable is recidivism, even though other issues such as social situation, psychological adjustment and so on, are also important improvements. We defined recidivism in a broad sense, including new contacts with the police, new offences, return to prison, revocation of parole, etc. (Sánchez-Meca et al., 1995). From the total of meta-analysed studies, 32 presented data about recidivism, involving 6,012 subjects (3,509 treated and 2,503 non-treated). The mean ES was positive ($r = .12$) and significant ($p < ,001$); that shows the global effectiveness in the treatment of offenders. However, the great heterogeneity found in the ES's means that this general trend is contingent on several moderator variables [$Q(31) = 123.479$, $p = .000$].

---

[2] In order to analyse the relation between the follow-up period and the ES, we employed the weighted regression technique developed by Hedges and Olkin (1985), which gives more weight to the studies with the larger sample sizes. However, we decided to fix as 100 the largest possible sample size to avoid that the few studies with a sample size greater than 100 would have excessive influence in the analysis. In this way, the ratio between the highest and the lowest sample size was $100/4 = 25$.

First, note the strong relation between ES and the treatment model (Table 11). As mentioned in the overall results section, the treatments that were most effective in the reduction of recidivism were the behavioural-cognitive ($r = .265$, $k = 3$) and behavioural ($r = .232$, $k = 6$) therapies, followed by the non-behavioural therapies ($r = .192$, $k = 8$) and diversion ($r = .188$, $k=4$); the only study that applied classic penal theory did not obtain any effectiveness ($r = -.006$).

Analysing the types of crimes (Table 12) we see that the best result pertains to a study that included crimes against the person ($r = .338$); it is based on only one study, and thus must be interpreted with precaution. The second most successful category mixed several types ($r = .193$, $k = 8$), with the sexual crimes obtaining the worst results ($r = .068$, $k = 3$).

Table 11: Effect size on recidivism as a function of treatment theoretical model

Class	k	d_+	95% C.I.	r_+	Q_w	DF	p
Non behavioural therapy	8	0.392	0.304:0.479	.192	28.41	7	.000
Educational/informational	5	0.161	0.037:0.285	.080	6.27	4	.280
Behavioural therapy	6	0.477	0.328:0.626	.232	2.29	5	.891
Cognit.-behav. therapy	3	0.550	0.285:0.814	.265	9.68	2	.021
Classic penal theory	1	-0.012	-0.100:0.076	-.006	-	-	-
Therapeutic Community	5	0.255	0.141:0.369	.127	12.16	4	.033
Diversion	4	0.328	0.179:0.586	.188	3.02	3	.554
Overall	32	0.243	0.198:0.288	.121	$Q_w =$ 61.83	25	.000
					$Q_B =$ 61.64	6	.000

Table 12: Effect size on recidivism as a function of crime typology

Class	k	d_+	95% C.I.	r_+	Q_w	DF	p
Property	6	0.210	0.147:0.272	.104	62.39	5	.000
People	1	0.718	-0.107:1.544	.338	-	-	-
Sexual	3	0.136	-0.217:0.489	.068	14.62	2	.002
Drug traffic	2	0.246	0.116:0.375	.122	0.47	1	.790
Mixed	8	0.392	0.263:0.522	.193	10.34	7	.242
Alcohol	7	0.218	0.105:0.331	.108	12.28	6	.092
Overall	27	0.240	0.193:0.286	.119	$Q_w =$ 100.10	21	.000
					$Q_B =$ 8.01	5	.156

Similar to the overall results displayed in Table 4, recidivism data confirms the superior effectiveness of treatment of adolescents ($r = .205$, $k =7$) and youths ($r = .188$, $k = 6$), in comparison to adults ($r = .101$, $k = 15$; see Table 13).

Table 13: Effect size on recidivism as a function of subject's age

Class	k	d₊	95% C.I.	r₊	Qw		DF	p
Adolescents	7	0.419	0.229:0.608	.205	10.88		6	.144
Juveniles	6	0.384	0.249:0.518	.188	8.86		5	.181
Mixed	4	0.241	0.139:0.343	.120	9.17		3	.057
Adults	15	0.202	0.145:0.259	.101	85.09		14	.000
Overall	32	0.243	0.260:0.348	.121	$Q_w =$	114.0	28	.000
					$Q_B =$	9.48	3	.023

Finally, we must mention the relationship between ES and the design type used in the studies. As Table 14 shows, the pre-experimental studies (pre-test/post-test designs) have the worst results (r = .069, k = 10). This result contradicts prior research that indicated that the pre-test/post-test designs generally show higher ES's than the experimental ones (e.g., Lipsey & Wilson, 1993). The reason for this apparent contradiction is that in the category of pre-experimental studies we included only Thornton's (1987) contribution, which with 1,000 subjects is the only study in our meta-analysis that employed classical penal theory, with negative outcomes (r = -0.006). With this exception, the two experimental studies that obtained recidivism measures (McMurran & Boyle, 1990; Slot, 1983) are the least effective (r = .098), with no statistical significance. However, this result should be interpreted with caution, because of the small sample size (26 subjects each).

Table 14: Effect size on recidivism as a function of design type

Class	k	d₊	95% C.I.	r₊	Qw		DF	p
Pre-experimental	10	0.139	0.075:0.203	.069	48.68		9	.000
Quasi-experimental	19	0.321	0.251:0.391	.159	49.94		18	.000
Experimental	2	0.197	-0.362:0.757	.098	0.54		1	.764
Institution compar.	1	0.504	0.338:0.670	.244	-		-	-
Overall	32	0.243	0.198:0.288	.121	$Q_w =$	99.16	28	.000
					$Q_B =$	24.32	3	.000

Discussion and Conclusions

In his review of meta-analysis studies with offenders, Lösel (1995a) discusses three topics in detail: types of treatment, methodological characteristics and settings. The same author in another paper (Lösel, 1995b), as well as McGuire and Priestley (1995), review the "guidelines for more effective programmes", some of which we present now with the objective of analysing our results.

Type of treatment In Lipsey's meta-analysis (1992a; 1992b) treatment modality was the most important single cluster of moderators. Within the juvenile justice system, the highest effect sizes were found for employment ($r = .18$), multimodal (.12), behavioural (.12), and skill-oriented (.12) programmes. Studies of programmes based on deterrence (-.12) and on vocational training (.-09) even showed negative effects. In programmes *outside* of the juvenile justice system, skill oriented (.16), multimodal (.10), and behavioural (.10) treatments performed best, and where employment/vocational measures were the worst (-.01). With the exception of the modalities of employment/vocational interventions, the other findings were consistent: multimodal (i.e., they recognised the variety of offenders' problems), behavioural, and skill-training measures were more successful than other treatments in programmes inside and outside of the juvenile justice system (such as family counselling, group therapy, etc.). The last finding means that their contents and the methods they employed were designed to teach clients problem-solving, social interaction and other types of coping skills. These are intervention strategies drawn from behavioural, cognitive or cognitive-behavioural sources.

If we look at the meta-analytical review regarding the prevention of antisocial behaviour, this trend finds new support. Durlak et al. (1993) conducted a meta-analysis evaluating controlled outcome studies of primary prevention that had appeared up until the end of 1991. In general, all types of programmes had significant positive impacts on participants, with the mean ES's (divide by 2 to obtain the "r" ES) ranging from 0.25 to 0.50, being the most effective programmes of cognitive-behavioural nature. In a more recent study, Durlak and Wells (1994) conducted a new meta-analytic review of the impact of secondary prevention by evaluating the results of 130 published and unpublished controlled studies appearing until the end of 1991. Again, behavioural and cognitive-behavioural treatments were the most successful strategies, being both of them equally effective in producing moderately strong effects (mean ES of 0.51 and 0.53, respectively), which were almost twice as high as those emanating from non behavioural interventions (mean ES = 0.27).

Our research confirms this overall finding. Also in Europe the cognitive and behavioural treatment modalities are the most effective in the treatment of offenders, with an ES of $r = .27$ in the global meta-analysis, and .26 (cognitive) and .23 (behavioural) with the criteria of recidivism. At the opposite end of the spectrum, the only study that used retribution/deterrence as its theoretical framework did not show any improvement ($r = .039$ and -.006, respectively).

Setting of intervention This matter needs further clarification because it is possible to argue that the most important feature of an intervention programme is "what we are going to do", instead of "where we are going to do that" (see Garrido & Redondo, 1993). However, it seems that programmes located in the community on balance yield more effective outcomes, perhaps due to their possibilities of increasing the generalisation process.

A recent study (Bondeson, 1994) adds new evidence on that question. Bondeson's latest book explores and evaluates the use and effects of three forms of probation sanctions in Sweden (conditional sentence, "pure" probation and probation with institutional treatment). After carefully controlling for a host of influences, Bondeson's quasi-experimental methods lead her to conclude that the greater the intervention, the more disadvantaged people become in terms of survival without further offending. In raw terms, 12 per cent of the conditionally sentenced, 30 per cent of straight probationers and 61 per cent of those placed on probation after institutional treatment recidivated at least once over a two-year period. When these groups were broken down into comparable risk categories, she found the same results. Furthermore all the individuals studied showed less recidivism when their sentences were conditional.

The author, in attempting to reveal the reality of probation supervision and the treatment institutions in Sweden, finds support for what she calls the theory of negative individual prevention. In particular, the special institutions were designed to address issues of unemployment, housing and drug/alcohol misuse. As Rutherford (1996) comments, her findings provide a sombre warning to persons intent on discovering a penal institutional panacea: "despite the aims and fundamental structure of the institutions studied, their negative effects were more prominent than their positive effects and the majority of probationers underwent some form of so-called prisonisation" (Bondeson, 1994, p.186).

However, we think that this research shows exactly the fact we pointed out earlier: *the nature of the intervention programme is the "key variable",* instead of its location. From Bondeson's work we can not conclude that the "pure" probation or the institution plus the probation involved effective programmes at all. It is completely logical that institutions designed to address issues of "unemployment, housing and drug/alcohol misuse" obtain the worst results *without specific programmes directed to improve these problems.* So, our research does not confirm the trend derived from Bondeson's research and some meta-analytical studies: the 14 studies which employed the community as the intervention setting obtained an ES of r = .16, the lowest compared with the categories of juvenile centre (.25) or juvenile prison (.19), among others.

Methodological characteristics Although the results of meta-analyses are not uniform, the major trend is a negative correlation between effect size and design quality: the stronger or more rigorous designs (involving randomisation or experimental validity) obtain lower results than weaker or less rigorous designs. The European meta-analysis confirms this fact. In our research the experimental designs with random assignment show the lowest effectiveness (r = .067), while the pre-experimental and quasi-experimental have similar ES (.17 and .18, respectively). On the other hand, as Garrett (1985) and Gottschalk et al. (1987) have found, among others, our data also present a lower effect size for the measure of recidivism as a criteria of success (r = .12, 32 studies), compared with other non-offending measures   such as institutional adjustment (.41, with only 7 studies) or psychological adjustment (.32, 3 studies). The fact that the number of studies is not too large is balanced for the fact that recidivism is the lowest effect size (see Table 10). This criteria, then, presents the greatest difficulty for any programme that tries to obtain positive effects.

Integrity of the programmes Another characteristic of successful programmes is the way an intervention is put into practice, including events such as training and support of staff, sharing of a plan for programme monitoring and evaluation, and a reasonable connection between stated objectives and methods being used (see Hollin, 1995). Although our meta-analysis did not study this concept exactly, it is possible to assume that the programmes that employed more rigorous treatment theoretical models more strictly supervised the integrity of the implementation and the other circumstances mentioned before. Of the different models that appear in our research, two are defined by the care that was taken in the control and monitoring of implementation: the cognitive-behavioural model and the behavioural therapy model. As we have showed earlier, both of them obtain the best effect size: $r = .273$ and .279, respectively.

Other features associated in the literature with successful programmes such as risk classification, impact on criminogenic needs or the principle of "responsivity" (Andrews, 1995; Lösel, 1995a, 1995b; McGuire & Priestley, 1995) were not able to be studied in our meta-analysis.

Our investigation has some merits and also certain limitations. The main merit resides in having carried out a systematic review of European treatment programmes of delinquency and crime, analysing strategies used, features of treated subjects,   application settings and methodology of evaluation, in connection with effectiveness. Also, we consider a plus that our research has been conceived as an ongoing research project, which supposes that the assessment instruments will permit the integration of future programmes and more extensive analysis on this topic.

But our research also has some limitations that will have to be addressed in future studies. The first concerns the inherent difficulties of the programme location process, by reason of the numerous European languages: probably there are other treatment programmes written in German, Swedish, Danish and also in other languages of east European countries. Some of these reports probably have not been located for their inclusion in our analysis. A second difficulty is related to the low methodological criterion adopted for the acceptance of programmes. With the objective of disposing of the greatest possible information, some studies that used weak assessment designs were accepted. Our results can be obviously influenced by this methodological tolerance. Perhaps in future research, when we could incorporate a greater number of reports on European programmes, this minimalistic methodological criterion will be revised. A third deficiency is related to the exclusive use up until now of univariate analysis, in those which efficacy is analysed in connection with different factors, taken one at a time. The availability of a greater number of studies in the future probably permit the accomplishment of more sophisticated multivariate analysis.

In the foreword to Palmer's (1994) book, Michael Gottfredson says that for some people "the very possibility of rehabilitation is an essential value of our society, and thus the dimmest glimmer of empirical hope is all that is required to maintain rehabilitation as a justification" (in dealing with offenders). Yes, this is true, but probably it is not enough. We must be able to show that we are effective in treating offenders. As the meta-analytical literature indicates, our research provides convincing evidence that in the rehabilitation of offenders, something works. It challenges the "nothing can be done" policy in corrections, showing that criminal behaviour can be reduced by programmes designed to modify the skills, attitudes, or behaviour of offenders. This is not a light objective. Recently the media have turned the spotlight on juveniles and adult violent offenders, and bombarded the public with stories of senseless and random violence, *psychokillers*, gangs, guns, and drug use and trafficking. Howell et al. (1995, p.vii) have reflected on this issue in America in the case of juvenile offenders: "The idea of 'getting tough' on youth, even for a minor first offence, has led to calls for treatming juvenile offenders as if they were adults. This means setting aside rehabilitative goals and dismissing the proven ability of the juvenile justice system to turn most young offenders around. The original basis for establishing the juvenile justice system - to provide an alternative to a harsh, ineffective criminal justice system for children - is in danger of being forgotten".

Perhaps the situation is not so serious in Europe, but we should not be too certain about that, especially if we remember how often European policies follow the ones born in America. Very recently, Robert Ross et al. (1995, pp. 3-4) said that "a substantial body of research has demonstrated that some programmes, conducted by some practitioners, with some offenders, in some settings have been effective. There are no panaceas. No programme will be effective with all offenders or in all settings". This is also true in Europe. We do not need panaceas, but realities. And these support the ideal of rehabilitation.

Appendix

Study	Country	Treatment	n_E	n_C	d_G [a]	d_R [a]
Bayón (1985)	Spain	Nonbehav. ther.	7	7	0.923	-
Bayón & Compadre (1991)	Spain	Cog-behav. ther.	8	_ [b]	0.639	-
Belfrage (1991)	Sweden	Nonbehav. ther.	188	132	0.454	0.454
Beljaars & Berger (1987)	Netherlands	Cog-behav. ther.	32	45	0.439	-
Berggren & Svärd (1990)	Sweden	Therap. comm.	280	_ [c]	0.259	0.259
Bishop et al. (1987)	Sweden	Therap. comm.	42	38	0.035	0.099
Bovens (1987)	Netherlands	Educat./Inform.	91	62	0.263	0.263
Brown (1985)	Great Britain	Behav. ther.	8	8	-0.200	-0.200
Collins & Tate (1988)	Great Britain	Diversion	29	19	0.811	0.811

Study		Country	Treatment	n_E	n_C	$d_G{}^a$	$d_R{}^a$
Cook et al. (1991)	Study 1	Great Britain	Nonbehav. ther.	33	11	-0.207	-0.207
	Study 2	Great Britain	Nonbehav. ther.	11	11[d]	-1.260	-1.260
Cooke (1989)		Great Britain	Therap. comm.	12	-[b]	0.946	0.718
Cooke (1991)		Great Britain	Nonbehav. ther.	120	-[c]	0.603	0.603
Cullen (1987)	Study 1	Great Britain	Cog-behav. ther.	5	9	0.533	-
	Study 2	Great Britain	Cog-behav. ther.	5	9	-0.658	-
	Study 3	Great Britain	Cog-behav. ther.	11	15	1.667	-
	Study 4	Great Britain	Cog-behav. ther.	11	-[b]	3.385	-
Day (1988)		Great Britain	Behav. ther.	20	-[b]	0.311	0.311
Dünkel (1982)		Germany	Nonbehav. ther.	323	889	0.480	0.480
Fisher (1991)		Great Britain	Cog-behav. ther.	6	5	0.848	-
Garrido et al. (1989)		Spain	Cog-behav. ther.	33	28	0.413	-
Garrido & Sanchis (1990)		Spain	Cog-behav. ther.	7	16	0.842	-
Hollin & Courtney (1983)	Study 1	Great Britain	Cog-behav. ther.	4	8	0.632	-
	Study 2	Great Britain	Cog-behav. ther.	4	8[d]	0.965	-
Hollin et al. (1986)	Study 1	Great Britain	Cog-behav. ther.	5	10	0.560	-
	Study 2	Great Britain	Cog-behav. ther.	5	10[d]	0.592	-
Hopkins (1991)		Great Britain	Cog-behav. ther.	8	7	0.472	-
Kravetz et al. (1990)		Israel	Behav. ther.	33	16	0.674	-
Kruissink (1990)		Netherlands	Diversion	124	68	0.421	0.421
Kury (1989)	Study 1	Germany	Cog-behav. ther.	32	106	0.144	0.144
	Study 2	Germany	Nonbehav. ther.	32	106[d]	0.144	0.144
Legaz et al. (1990)		Spain	Diversion	15	6	0.233	0.281
López et al. (1992)		Spain	Diversion	22	-[b]	0.577	-
Martín (1989)		Spain	Behav. ther.	26	25	0.836	-
McDougall et al. (1987)		Great Britain	Cog-behav. ther.	18	18	0.478	-
McMurran & Boyle (1990)	Study 1	Great Britain	Educat./Inform.	13	13	0.000	0.000
	Study 2	Great Britain	Educat./Inform.	15	13[d]	-0.247	-0.247
Members of Demonst. Unit (1986)		Great Britain	Nonbehav. ther.	109	-[b]	0.039	0.039
Moreno & Battestini (1989)		Spain	Educat./Inform.	44	-[b]	0.995	-
Petterson et al. (1986)		Sweden	Therap. comm.	70	61	0.551	0.658
Redondo (1983)		Spain	Behav. ther.	25	-[b]	0.229	-
Redondo (1984)		Spain	Behav. ther.	8	-[b]	1.077	-
Redondo et al. (1991)		Spain	Behav. ther.	288	-[b]	0.475	0.504
Robertson & Gunn (1987)		Great Britain	Therap. comm.	61	61	-0.168	-0.168
Rosner (1988)		Germany	Nonbehav. ther.	420	47	0.405	0.405
Sánchez & Polo (1990)		Spain	Other	103	-[b]	0.036	-
Sastriques (1993)		Spain	Behav. ther.	20	-[b]	1.886	-
Scholte & Smit (1987)		Netherlands	Diversion	71	71	0.216	0.217
Shepherd (1991)		Great Britain	Cog-behav. ther.	15	20	0.211	-
Singer (1991)		Great Britain	Educat./Inform..	152	-[b]	0.282	-0.031
Slot (1983)		Netherlands	Behav. ther.	9	17	0.549	0.419
Slot (1984)		Netherlands	Behav. ther.	6	-[b]	1.011	0.492
Slot & Bartels (1983)		Netherlands	Cog-behav. ther.	29	29	1.066	1.219
Slot & Heiner (1986)		Netherlands	Behav. ther.	22	-[b]	0.559	0.559
Thornton (1987)		Great Britain	Clasic penal th.	1,000	-[b]	0.078	-0.012
Van Dalen (1989)		Netherlands	Educat./Inform.	250	250	0.379	0.281
Weaver & Fox (1984)		Great Britain	Cog-behav. ther.	38	-[b]	0.647	0.647

n_E: Sample Size of treated group; n_C: Sample size of control group; d_G: Global standardised mean difference; d_R: Recidivism standardised mean difference; [a]: d_G and d_R are unbiased standardised mean differences (Hedges & Olkin, 1985); [b]: One group design; [c]: Not available; [d]: Same control group than Study 1; [e]: Control group proceeds from another paper.

References

(Studies preceded by an asterisk (*) were included in the meta-analysis.)

Andrews, D. (1995). The psychology of criminal conduct and effective treatment. In J. McGuire (Eds.), *What works: Reducing reoffending* (pp. 35-62). Chichester: Wiley.

Andrews, D., Zinger, I., Hoge, R., Bonta, J., Gendreau, P., & Cullen, F. (1990). Does correctional treatment work? A clinically relevant and psychologically informed meta-analysis. *Criminology, 28* (3), 369-404.

* Bayón, F. (1985). Psicoterapia de grupos y tratamiento penitenciario: análisis de un estudio práctico. In J.Alarcón et al.: *Tratamiento penitenciario: su práctica* (pp. 49-68). Madrid: Ministerio de Justicia.

* Bayón, F., & Compadre, A. (1991). Efectos del entrenamiento en habilidades sociales en el estilo personal de atribución y en la conducta personal. *Revista de Estudios Penitenciarios, 244,* 127-140.

* Belfrage, H. (1991). The crime preventive effect of psychiatric treatment on mentally disordered offenders in Sweden. *International Journal of Law and Psychiatry, 14*, 237-243.

* Beljaars, I.C.M., & Berger, M.A. (1987). *The Coaching Project: behavioural training by non-professionals for youths with poor community living skills.* Amsterdam: Paedologisch Instituut, Prins Hendriklaan 23, 1075 AZ .

* Berggren, O., & Svärd, H. (1990). The Österaker Project. A further follow-up of the drug misuser treatment programme at Österaker prison. *Kriminalvarden. Forskningsgruppen, 1*, Swedish Prison and Probation Administration (19 pp.).

* Bishop, N., Sundin-Osborne, A., & Pettersson, T. N. (1987). The drug free programme at the Hinseberg prison for women. *National Prison and Probation Administration* (Report 1987:4) (27 pp.).

Bondeson (1994). *Alternatives to imprisonment: Intentions and realities* . Boulder, CO: Westview Press.

* Bovens, R. (1987). The alcohol program: an educational program for drunken drivers in prison. In M. Brand-Koolen: *Juvenile Delinquency in the Netherlands* (pp. 151-157). Kugler publications bv.

* Brown, B. (1985). An application of social learning methods in a residential programme for young offenders. *Journal of Adolescence, 8,* 321-331.

* Collins, S.A., & Tate D.H. (1988). Alcohol related offenders and a voluntary organisation in a Scottish community. *The Howard Journal, 27* (1), 44-57.

* Cook, D.A., Fox, C. A., Weaver, C.M., & Rooth F.G. (1991). The Berkeley group: ten years' experience of a group for non-violent sex offenders. *British Journal of Psychiatry, 158* (1), 238-243.

* Cooke, D.J. (1989). Containing violent prisoners. An analysis of the Barlinnie Special Unit. *British Journal of Criminology, 29* (2), 129-143.

* Cooke, D.J. (1991). Psychological treatment as an alternative to prosecution: a form of primary diversion. *The Howard Journal, 30* (1), 53-65.

Cooper, H.M. (1989). *Integrating research: A guide for literature reviews* (Second Edition). Newbury Park, California: Sage Publications.

* Cullen, E. (1987). Group based treatment for serious institutional offending. In B.J. McGurk, D.Thornton & M. Williams: *Applying Psychology to Imprisonment* (pp. 316-327). London: HMSO.

* Day, K. (1988). A hospital-based treatment programme for male mentally handicapped offenders. *British Journal of Psychiatry, 153*, 635-644.

* Dünkel, F. (1982). Selection and recidivism after different modes of imprisonment in West-Berlin. In: *Research in Criminal Justice. Stock-Taking of Criminological Research at the Max-Planck-*

Institute for Foreign and International Penal Law after a Decade (pp. 452-471). Freiburg: Max-Planck-Institute

Durlak, J. A., & Wells, A. M. (1994, October). *An evaluation of secondary prevention mental health programmes for children and adolescents.* Paper presented at the First Annual Kansas Conference on Child Clinical Psychology. Lawrence, Kansas.

Durlak, J. A., Lampman, C., Wells, A., & Cotten, J. (1993, June). A review of primary prevention programmes for children and adolescents. In J. A. D. (Chair) , *Evaluation of primary prevention: Programmes, outcomes and issues.* Symposium conducted at the fourth biennial conference on community research and action. Williamsburg, VA.

* Fisher, M. (1991). Groupwork with rule 43 inmates at HM prison Wakefield. In: *Psychology Conference of Prison Service* (pp. 227-233). Her Majesty Prison Service, Home Office.

Garrett, C.J. (1985). Effects of residential treatment on adjudicated delinquents: A meta-analysis. *Journal of Research in Crime and Delinquency, 22* (4), 287-308.

Garrido, V., & Redondo, S. (1993). The institutionalisation of young offenders. *Criminal Behaviour & Mental Health,* 3(4), 336-348.

* Garrido, V., Redondo, S., & Pérez, E. (1989). El tratamiento de delincuentes institucionalizados: El programa de competencia psicosocial en la prisión de jóvenes "la Trinidad" de Barcelona. *Delincuencia/Delinquency, 1* (1), pp. 37-57.

* Garrido, V., & Sanchis, J.R. (1990). *La intervención educativa en menores delincuentes: el programa de competencia psicosocial.* In "II Congreso del Colegio Oficial de Psicólogos", Área 6 (pp. 30-38).

Gensheimer, L.K, Mayer, J.P., Gottschalk, R., & Davidson II, W.S. (1986). Diverting youth from the juvenile justice system: A meta-analysis of intervention efficacy. In S. Apter and A. Goldstein (eds.): *Youth violence: Programme and prospects.* New York: Pergamon Press.

Glass, G.V. (1977). Integrating findings: The meta-analysis of research. *Review of Research in Education, 5,* 351-371.

Glass, G.V., McGaw, B., & Smith, M.L. (1981). *Meta-analysis in social research.* Beverly Hills, CA: Sage.

Gómez, J. (1987). *Meta-análisis.* Barcelona: Promociones y Publicaciones Universitarias.

Gottschalk, R. Davidson II, W.S., Gensheimer, L.K., & Mayer, J.P. (1987). Community-based interventions. In H.C. Quay (Ed.): *Handbook of juvenile delinquency* (pp. 266-289). New York: John Wiley and Sons.

Hedges, L.V., & Olkin, Y. (1985). *Statistical methods for meta-analysis.* Orlando, FL: Academic Press.

Hollin, C. (1995). The meaning and implications of "programme integrity". In J. McGuire (Eds.), *What works: Reducing reoffending* (pp. 195-208). Chichester: Wiley.

* Hollin, C.R., & Courtney, S.A. (1983). A skills training approach to the reduction of institutional offending. *Personality and Individual Differences, 4,* 257-264.

* Hollin, C.R., Huff, G.J., Clarkson, F., & Edmondson, A.C. (1986). Social skills training with young offenders in a Borstal: an evaluative study. *Journal of Community Psychology, 14,* 289-299.

* Hopkins, R. (1991). An evaluation of communication and social skills groups for sex offenders at HMP Frankland. In: *Psychology Conference of Prison Service* (pp. 77-91). Her Majesty Prison Service, Home Office.

Howell, J. C., Krisberg, B., Hawkins, D., & Wilson, J. (1995). *Sourcebook on serious, violent and chronic juvenile offenders.* Thousand Oaks, CA.: Sage.

Johnson, B.T. (1989). DSTAT: *Software for the meta-analytic review of research literatures.* Hillsdale, N. J.: Erlbaum.

* Kravetz, S., Florian, V., & Nofer, E. (1990). The differential effects of feedback of trait ratings on worker traits in vocational rehabilitation workshops in a correctional institution. *Vocational Evaluation and Work Adjustment Bulletin, Summer,* 47-54.

* Kruissink, M. (1990). The Halt program: diversion of juvenile vandals. *Dutch penal law and policy. Notes on criminological research from the Research and Documentation Centre, 1*, 1-8.
* Kury, H. (1989). Treatment of young remand prisoners: problems and results of a research project. In H. Wegener, F. Lösel & J. Haisch (eds.): *Criminal Behavior and the Justice System. Psychological Perspectives* (pp. 356-381). New York: Springer-Verlag .
* Legaz, F., López Pina, J.A., Sánchez-Meca, J., & Velandrino, A.P. (1990). *Evaluación del programa experimental de intervención en medio abierto.* Murcia: Instituto de Servicios Sociales de la Región de Murcia, ISSORM.
Lipsey, M. W. (1992a). Juvenile delinquency treatment: A meta-analytic inquiry into variability of effects. In T.D. Cook, H. Cooper, D.S. Cordray, H. Hartmann, L.V. Hedges, R.L. Light, T.A. Louis and F. Mosteller (Eds.), *Meta-analysis for explanation: A casebook* (pp. 83-127). New York: Rusell Sage Foundation .
Lipsey, M. W. (1992b). The effect of treatment on juvenile delinquents: Results from meta-analysis. In F. Lösel, D. Bender and T. Bliesener (Eds.), *Psychology and law. International perspectives* (pp. 131-143). Berlin, New York: de Gruyter.
Lipsey, M.W., & Willson, D.B. (1993). The efficacy of psychological, educational, and behavioral treatment: Confirmation from meta-analysis. *American Psychologist, 48*, 1181-1209.
* López, J.A., Sánchez-Meca, J., & Velandrino, A.P. (1992). *Evaluación del programa experimental de intervención en medio abierto.* Murcia: Fundación Universidad-Empresa.
Lösel, F. (1995a). Increasing consensus in the evaluation of offender rehabilitation? Lessons from recent research syntheses. *Psychology, Crime & Law, 2*, 19-40.
Lösel, F. (1995b). The efficacy of correctional treatment: A review and synthesis of meta-evaluations. In J. McGuire (Eds.), *What works: Reducing reoffending* (pp. 79-114). Chichester: Wiley.
Lösel, F. (1996). What recent meta-evaluations tell us about the effectiveness of correctional treatment. In G. Davies, S. Lloyd-Bostock, M. McMurran, and C. Wilson: *Psychology, law and criminal justice* (pp. 537-554). Berlin: de Gruyter.
Lösel, F., & Köferl, P. (1989). Evaluation research on correctional treatment in West Germany: A meta-analysis. In H. Wegener, F. Lösel and J. Haisch (Ed.): *Criminal behavior and the justice system: Psychological perspectives* (pp. 334-355). New York: Springer-Verlag.
Lösel, F., Köferl, P., & Weber, F. (1987). *Meta-evaluation der sozialtherapie.* Stuttgart: Enke.
* Martín, M. (1989). *Aplicación de una economía de fichas en el centro penitenciario de Tarragona.* Unpublished. Centre Penitenciari de Tarragona.
Martinson, R. (1974): What works? - questions and answers about prison reform. *Public Interest, 10*, 22-54
* McDougall, C., Barnett, R.M., Ashurst B., & Willis, B. (1987). Cognitive control of anger. In B.J. McGurk, D.Thornton & M. Willians: *Applying Psychology to Imprisonment* (pp. 304-313). London: HMSO.
McGuire, J. (1992). Enfocaments psicològics per a la reducció de la conducta delictuosa: investigació recent i implicacions pràctiques. [Psychological strategies for reduction of offending behaviour: recent investigation and practical implications]. *Papers d'Estudis i Formació, 10*, 67-77.
McGuire, J., & Priestley, P. (1995). Reviewing "What Works": Past, present and future. In J. McGuire (Ed.), *What works: Reducing reoffending* (pp. 3-34). Chichester: Wiley.
* McMurran, M, & Boyle, M. (1990). Evaluation of a self-help manual for young offenders who drink: A pilot study. *British Journal of Clinical Psychology, 29*, 117-119.
* Members of the Demonstration Unit, 1981-84 (1986). Increasing the use of probation. *Probation Journal*, March, 87-90.
* Moreno, F.X., & Battestini, R. (1989). L'educació sanitària en una presó de dones. Experiència pilot. *Salut Catalunya, 3* (2), 59-62.

Palmer, T. (1994). *A profile of correctional effectiveness and new directions for research.* Albany: State University of New York Press.

Pearson, F.S., Lipton, D.S., Cleland, Ch.M., & O'Kane, J.B. (1995). Meta-analysis on the effectiveness of correctional treatment: Another approach and extension of the time frame to 1994 - A Progress Report. Presentation at the Annual Meeting of the American Society of Criminology, Boston, Massachusetts, November 15.

* Petterson, T., Sundin-Osborne, A., & Bishop, N. (1986). Results of the drug misuser treatment programme at the Österaker prison. In: *National Prison and Probation Administration* (Report 1986:2) (13 pp.).

* Redondo, S. (1983). Una aplicación de la economía de fichas en la prisión de Madrid. *Revista Española de Terapia del Comportamiento, 1* (3), 303-326.

* Redondo, S. (1984). Empleo de un procedimiento de economía de fichas en un curso de alfabetización de adultos internos en una prisión. *Informes de Psicología,* 145-151.

Redondo, S. (1994). *El tratamiento de la delincuencia en Europa: un estudio meta-analítico.* [Offending treatment in Europe: A meta-analysis]. Doctoral thesis, unpublished. Faculty of Psychology, University of de Barcelona.

Redondo, S., Garrido, V., Anguera, M.T., & Luque, E. (1996a). Correctional programmes in Europe: A pilot study for a meta-evaluation. In G. Davies, S. Lloyd-Bostock, M. McMurran and C. Wilson (Eds.): *Psychology, law and criminal justice* (pp. 510-519). Berlin: de Gruyter.

Redondo, S., Luque, E., & Funes, J. (1996b). Social beliefs about recidivism in crime. In G. Davies, S. Lloyd-Bostock, M. McMurran and C. Wilson (Eds.): *Psychology, law and criminal justice* (pp. 394-400). Berlin: de Gruyter.

* Redondo, S., Roca, M., Pérez, E., Sánchez, A., & Deumal, E. (1991). Environmental outline of a youth prison in Catalonia. Five years evaluation. In J. Junger-Tas, L. Boendermaker & P.H. van der Laan (eds.): *The future of the juvenile justice system* (pp. 411-428). Leuven (Belgium): Acco.

* Robertson, G., & Gunn, J. (1987). A ten-year follow-up of men discharged from Grendon prison. *British Journal of Psychiatry, 151,* 674-678.

Rosenthal, R. (1991). *Meta-analytic procedures for social research* (2nd de.). Beverly Hills, CA: Sage.

Rosenthal, R., & Rubin, D.B. (1982). A simple general purpose display of magnitude of experimental effect. *Journal of Educational Psychology,* 74, 166-169.

Ross, R., Antonowicz, D., & Dhaliwal, G. (Eds.) (1995). *Going straight. Effective delinquency prevention and offender rehabilitation.* Ottawa: Air Training & Publications.

* Rosner, A. (1988). Evaluation of a drinking-driver rehabilitation program for first offenders. In G. Kaiser & I. Geissler (eds.): *Crime and Criminal Justice. Criminological Research in the 2nd Decade at the Max Planck Institute in Freiburg* (pp. 319-336). Freiburg: Max-Planck-Institut.

Rutherford, A. (1996). Review to Bondeson's book: "Alternatives to imprisonment: Intentions and realities". *British Journal of Criminology,* 36, 157-158.

* Sánchez, M.A., & Polo, A. (1990). Modelo de intervención con toxicómanos en el centro penitenciario de preventivos Madrid-1. Programa de rehabilitación en régimen de centro de día. *Revista de Estudios Penitenciarios, 243,* 77-99.

Sánchez-Meca, J. (1996). Methodological issues in the meta-evaluation of correctional treatment. In S. Redondo, V. Garrido, J. Pérez, & R. Barberet (Eds*.), Advances in psychology and law: International contributions.* Berlin: de Gruyter.

Sánchez-Meca, J., & Ato, M. (1989). Meta-análisis: una alternativa metodológica a las revisiones tradicionales de la investigación. [Meta-analysis: A methodological alternative to traditional reviews of research]. In J. Mayor and J.L. Pinillos: *Tratado de Psicología General* (617-669). Madrid: Alhambra.

Sánchez-Meca, J., Marín, F., & Redondo, S. (1995). Evaluación internacional de la reincidencia y de la eficacia penal. [International assessment of recidivism and penal efficacy]. Unpublished research. Centre d'Estudis Jurídics i Formació Especialitzada (Barcelona).

* Sastriques, M. (1993). *Aplicació d'una economia de fitxes a l'aula Pau Casals del centre penitenciari de Tarragona.* Unpublished research. Autonomous University of Barcelona.

* Scholte, E.M., & Smit, M. (1987). Early social assistance for juveniles at risk. *International Journal of Offender Therapy and Comparative Criminology,* 209-218.

* Shepherd, S. (1991). A brief intervention for anxiety and depression. In: *Psychology Conference of Prison Service* (pp. 209-218). Her Majesty Prison Service, Home Office.

* Singer, L.R. (1991). A non-punitive paradigm of probation practice: some sobering thoughts. *British Journal of Social Work, 21,* 611-621.

* Slot, N.W. (1983). The implementation and evaluation of a residential social skills training programme for youth in trouble. In W. Everaerd, C.B. Hindley, A. Bot, & J.J. van der Werf (Eds.), *Development in adolescence: Psychological, social, and biological aspects* (pp. 176-205). Amsterdam: Martinus Nijhoff Pub.

* Slot, N.W. (1984). *The teaching family model in the Netherlands: first results of a community based program for problem youths.* Paper presented at the 14th Conference of the European association for behavior therapy. Brussels, Belgium.

* Slot, N.W., & Bartels, A.A.J. (1983). Outpatient social skills training for youth in trouble theoretical background, practice and outcome. In W. Everaerd, C.B. Hindley, A. Bot & J.J. van der Werf ten Bosch: *Development in adolescence. Psychological, Social and Biological Aspects* (pp. 176-191). Amsterdam: Martinus Nijhoff Publishers.

* Slot, N.W., & Heiner, J. (1986). *Development of community-based treatment programs for troubled youth in the Netherlands.* Paper presented to the ABA-Conference. Milwaukee, USA.

* Thornton, D.M. (1987). Correctional evaluation of custodial regimes. In B.J. McGurk, D.M. Thornton, & M. Williams (Eds.), *Applying psychology to imprisonment* (pp. 467-481). London: Her Majesty's Stationery Office.

Tournier, P., & Barre, M.D. (1990). Enquête sur les systèmes pénitentiaires dans les Etats membres du Conseil de l'Europe: démographie carcérale comparée. *Bulletin d'information pénitentiaire, 15,* September, 4-44.

* Van Dalen, W.E. (1989). Education: a successful instrument for reducing drunken driving in the Netherlands. *Prevention and control/Realities and aspirations, IV,* 717-722.

* Weaver, C., & Fox, C. (1984). The Berkeley sex offenders group: a seven year evaluation. *Probation Journal, 31* (4), 143-146.

Whitehead, J.T., & Lab, S.P. (1989). A meta-analysis of juvenile correctional treatment. *Journal of Research in Crime and Delinquency, 26,* (3), 276-295.

Wilkins, L. (1996). Review to Palmer's book "A Profile of correctional effectiveness and new directions for research". *British Journal of Criminology, 36,* 153-155.

Wilkinson, L. (1992). *SYSTAT: The system for statistics* (6.0). Evanston, IL: SYSTAT Inc.

Epilogue

Psychology, Law and Europe: Current Developments and Problems

Friedrich Lösel

This article is a modified and updated version of a speech that I gave at the banquet of the Fifth European Conference of Psychology and Law in 1994 at Barcelona. I have shortened the more situation-specific, witty parts of the talk and extended the more systematic, scientific ones. However, the overall structure and, in part, the style has been retained in order to give an adequate impression of the conference.

When Santiago Redondo asked me on behalf of the Organizing Committee whether I - as the current president of the European Association of Psychology and Law (EAPL) - could give a lecture at the banquet, I asked him in return what I should talk about. The answer was that I could talk about whatever I liked, for example, about my current research. I accepted, but when I started to prepare my speech I felt doubts. Although worries about the content of a presidential address did not seem to be unusual (e.g., Roesch, 1995), my specific problems had to do with characteristics of the EAPL and the situation at a banquet. For example, my research on protective factors against delinquency (e.g., Lösel & Bliesener, 1994) or on the evaluation of offender treatment (e.g., Lösel, 1995a) probably would be of interest to the big "criminological" subgroup of our association. But would these topics be equally interesting for the subgroups of "forensic" and "legal" psychologists? Would they also fulfill the expectations of our more practice - versus more research-oriented subgroups? Would they not bore those colleagues who are mainly interested in witness problems? Would some people not be dissatisfied with our findings; for example, those who believe in large intervention effects or those who think that nothing works? Would some EAPL members (though certainly only a few) perhaps get so involved in methodological or statistical details and bore their neighbors, or (if their neighbors are particularly interested in methods) even make them forget their dinner?

Therefore, the question was whether I should evoke boredom or disappointment before our dinner. This could ruin some people's appetites (in a country like Spain, which is famous for its cuisine!). No, I decided: I would not report on such research topics. I decided to talk about something that probably interests all participants, something that is simultaneously so complex that it will be easy to phrase in words that may suit a banquet as an appetizer. Therefore, I selected the topic, "Psychology, Law, and *Europe*" I specifically did not choose "Psychology and Law *in* Europe," because this is not a systematic overview on various countries (see, for example, Kury, this volume).

However, I also started to have doubts about whether choosing such a topic was not a particularly serious mistake. Far more than any empirical research, it could well ruin the appetites of many listeners. Perhaps this would be the case for the 49% of the Danes who voted against the Maastricht Treaty. This seemed to be a relatively slight problem, as the EAPL has only very few members from Denmark. However, what about our large group of British colleagues? Although I have read in the German press that John Major has been surprisingly quick in giving a green light to the compromise on the new veto rights in the Council of Ministers, this earned him a red card from the British press with calls for his resignation. Margaret Thatcher's anti-European attitude may be losing its power, but a traditional skepticism based on splendid isolation can still be seen in the spoken language. Our British colleagues "go to Europe" when they come and visit us on the continent. And even among the Germans, who sometimes have viewed themselves as the most enthusiastic supporters of European integration, there is a degree of skepticism about European unification. For example, one state minister gained a lot of publicity against monetary union by raising fears about the "Esperanto money" of the European Union compared to the hard German Mark. It is an irony of fate or perhaps greetings from Sigmund Freud, that the Minister has since had to resign due to a scandal in which he was suspected of using his position to get more hard German Marks for himself.

I overcame my doubts with the tried and tested method of reducing dissonance: my listeners represented by definition a selection of pro-Europeans, at least in the domain of psychology and law. The goal of increasing European cooperation is already expressly written down in the articles of the EAPL. The increasing number of contributions to the European Conferences confirms this positive view. The number of participants has also grown from about 80 at the first conference at Maastricht in 1988 to approximately 220 at Nuremberg, circa 250 at Oxford, and more than 350 at Barcelona. Therefore, we can say that researchers and practitioners in the area of psychology and law say "yes" to Europe.

A politician, and perhaps also the president in me could let the matter rest with such a constructive statement. But a scientist needs problems just like a fish needs water. Therefore, I am afraid I must disappoint those of you who thought we could now turn to the hors d'oeuvres. I shall briefly deal with some problems and developments in the current situation of psychology and law in Europe. These are:

1. The heterogeneity of the different European countries;
2. Problems of political transformation processes;
3. The language problem and the relation to the scientific community in the United States of America;
4. The relationship between psychological research and the practice of law.

Differences between Countries

Is there something like a common supranational field of "European Psychology and Law" or can it be anticipated in the near future? An answer to this question is difficult but rarely a clear "yes." This view is reinforced by analyses in related areas. For example, a recent conference at the Max-Planck-Institute for Foreign and Penal Law at Freiburg addressed the question "Criminology in Europe - European Criminology?" (Albrecht & Kürzinger, 1994). The speakers, who came from different countries, tackled a wide variety of aspects. As an empirical scientist with a weakness for hard data, I began to count the number of times words like "Europe," "European," "European Community," and so forth were used at this conference. By far the most frequent user of this family of words was the Belgian speaker. Perhaps, Euro-skeptics would interpret this fact rather simply: "No wonder, it's Brussels where the money goes." More seriously, there are various good reasons for em- phasizing the Europeanization of criminology and crime control (Fijnaut, 1994). However, most papers at the Freiburg conference revealed that integration is still rather limited in terms of content, theory, or methods in European criminology (e.g., Kerner, 1994).

Eser (1992) has analyzed the possibilities for a transnational criminal justice in Europe. His conclusion is skeptical about the chances of (1) balancing out competing national systems of penal law, or (2) expanding supranational penal law. According to his analysis, the currently most promising and also necessary path is (3) the extension of cooperation on an international level in, for example, the field of mutual assistance in law enforcement. Similarly, den Boer (1995) concludes that pragmatic, low-level cooperation seems to result into more convergence between police systems than the structured, centrally coordinated cooperation envisaged by the Third Pillar (Justice and Home Affairs) of the Treaty on European Union.

Probably, these judgments in the field of criminology, penal law, and policing can be generalized to the area of psychology and law. However, as in biological evolution, signs of heterogeneity should not primarily be seen as negative. Stronger European cooperation and increased exchange about differences will not only contribute to convergence but also to a widening of horizons. It will make local procedures and self-evident truths more relative and open to adaptation in a changing world. Comparative and cross-cultural research could even take advantage of the differences in national conditions and use them as natural experiments. Typical examples are the international victim surveys (van Dijk, Mayhew, & Killias, 1990) or comparative research on crime statistics (Farrington & Langan, 1992). Furthermore, transnational analyses of treatment and prison regimes can contribute to a benchmarking system that is useful for local decisions (e.g., McDougall & Powls, 1994). International perspectives also are important for the development of more effective ways of working with and processing mentally disordered offenders (e.g., Roesch, Ogloff, & Eaves, 1995). Detailed knowledge about various justice procedures and expert witness practices may help to improve the situation of victims in child abuse cases (e.g., Spencer et al., 1990). As Michon (1995) recently has shown, international differences even may be useful for detecting consistent sentencing policies that seem to fit a mathematically formulated law of proportional restraint.

Although psychology and law can cope constructively with national heterogeneity, this problem should not be minimized. Law and its interface to the humanities is more related to cultural differences and traditions than many other areas in psychology. Consequently, jurisprudence is much less anglophone than the natural sciences (Skudlik, 1990). Alignments between different countries are obvious in material law, as can be observed in similar definitions of many offenses. However, even when one tries to assess just incidence or prevalence in longitudinal research, this may depend heavily on details of national crime statistics, age-related definitions of status offenses, the practice of the police, and so forth (e.g., Weitekamp & Kerner, 1994). The importance of national differences is also clear in research on criminal proceedings or in adjudication. It is difficult to attain alignments in those basic principles that belong to the self evident truths of each legal system. An example of this is the determination of criminal responsibility. For example, in Germany, this refers to the extent of the facts, illegality, and guilt; in England, to *actus reus* and *mens rea*; and in France, to the *éléments légal, matérial, et moral*. A systematic international comparison of the normative-dogmatic structure and the criminal procedure is extremely difficult (e.g., Perron, 1996).

National differences are probably less difficult to deal with in topics that are closer to the natural science branch of psychology. This also may hold for cognitive research on the perception and memory of eyewitnesses (e.g., Wells & Loftus, 1984) or on judges' information processing and decision-making (e.g., Wagenaar, van Koppen, & Crombag, 1993). In principle, however, the external and transnational validity is particularly troublesome. I shall recall only the sometimes very uncritical transfer of American laboratory findings on procedural law to discussions on the practice in other countries, even with nonadversary systems (e.g., Haisch, 1989; King, 1986). Alongside different legal traditions, different theoretical and methodological traditions in psychology are also important for the field of psychology and law. French psychology, for example, is more often oriented toward sociological and psychoanalytical approaches than is the case in Germany. There is a less experimental orientation than in, for example, the United Kingdom. These scientific differences are joined by completely heterogeneous financial preconditions, rapidly changing systems, as for example, in the East European countries, and, last but not least, the language problem.

Political Transformation Processes

The fall of the Iron Curtain and the open borders within the European Union have led to dramatic political transformations, particularly in East and Central Europe.

These have also created difficult tasks for crime policy and practice in the justice system. Processes of transformation anomie and related crime in East Europe as well as international organized crime or migration-related offending in other countries are typical phenomena. In Germany, for example, crime rates increased strongly in the former communist states as well as for the groups of asylum seekers and emigrants (e.g., Pfeiffer, 1995). Problems of xenophobia and violence against foreigners also rose (e.g., Willems et al., 1993). The various transformations do not just contain challenges for the police and the justice system. They also confront psychology in the field of law with new tasks of research and practice. For example, basic research has to ask how traditional explanations from learning or socialization theory can be generalized to these phenomena (e.g., Lösel, 1995b). Another question is, how far the results of "classical" longitudinal studies of cohorts from the 1950s (e.g., Farrington, 1995) can be extrapolated to new populations of offenders in a changing world. Questions like these lead to the problem of a theoretically sound multilevel analysis. Reiss (1994) has recently discussed this topic with respect to the societal background of longitudinal studies. He mentions the old example of Young (1932), who showed that proven relationships between delinquency and family disorganization no longer held for boys from Russian immigrant families in Los Angeles. In contrast to other subpopulations, these second- and third-generation delinquents came from intact families in the traditional sense of the term. Global migration as well as the internationalization of business and leisure time make it necessary to pay more attention to different legal cultures and modes of moral reasoning. Concepts like guilt-oriented and shame-oriented cultures are preliminary approaches to this problem (e.g., Bierbrauer, 1992).

Similar problems arise for the practice within the justice system. Various former communist countries are confronted with major problems of coordination, allocation, and distribution in their economies (e.g., Srubar, 1994). These are related to a system of "dual morality" in social networks and inconsistent loyalty to the state institutions. As in other institutions, the necessary changes in the justice system depend not only on the influence of the moral elites in the sense of Max Weber (e.g., former dissidents) but also on functional elites who have professional experience (Srubar, 1994). Furthermore, resistance to new programs, procedures, and institutions may come not only from "conservative" supporters of the former system but also from its low-status clients. For example, democratic changes in criminal justice and the prison system of Romania may even be refused by criminal offenders. During Ceausescu's dictatorship, they had a chance of early release through one of the political amnesties. After the move from dictatorship to democracy there were unrealistic hopes for liberty which led to several prison riots (Gheorghe, 1995). The Council of Europe and other institutions assist in the legal reform process and also in staff training in many East European countries (e.g., Harrimoes, 1995). However, reforms according to European norms are made difficult because of the lack of material and personnel resources (Tari, 1995).

East European political transformations and worldwide migration also have augmented the problems of psychology and law in other countries. In Germany, for example, the number of foreign prisoners has increased strongly since 1990. Figure 1 shows data from the state of Bavaria.

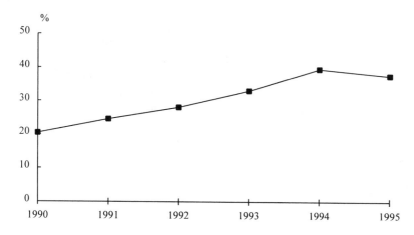

Figure 1: Proportion of Foreign Prisoners in Bavaria

Particularly in remand prisons and in prisons for juveniles, foreigners are no longer a minority; indeed, at times, they already form the majority. More than 100 languages are spoken in Bavarian prisons. One should not only focus on negative aspects of this development. The growth of "minorities" may at least enhance the position of their members in prisons. Hürlimann (1993), for example, surprisingly found that foreign prisoners were overrepresented among leaders in the inmate subculture. On the whole, however, the prison administration has to cope flexibly with many problems of cultural heterogeneity of inmates. For example, they use interpreters from outside and inside, develop information leaflets in various languages, occasionally hire foreign-born officers, serve different food for cultural and religious subgroups, and so forth. Despite various efforts it is scarcely possible to be fair and effective to all individual minority groups. This probably applies less to the protection of rights and formal procedures than to psychosocial care and everyday life in prisons. In particular, rehabilitation programs are hard to apply under these circumstances. Language differences are only part of the problem. Cultural differences in interaction, role behavior, religion, and so forth also lead to difficulties between staff and prisoners as well as within the inmate group. Subcultural rivalry and violence easily arise. For various reasons, transfer to the home countries is frequently difficult. Therefore, it will become increasingly necessary to implement *international* problem solutions in the area of psychology and law. One possibility would be prisons in the country of origin of foreign offenders that are managed according to international legal standards and co-financed by those countries from which offenders are transferred.

Another example of problems due to political transformation and globalization is the field of interrogation and witnesses' statements. Here as well, worldwide migration places new demands on psychology. Traditional statement reality analysis is complicated and probably invalidated by language and cultural differences. Problems of interpretation, verbal and nonverbal communication styles, different roles of men and women, and so forth must always be taken into account. Many psychological tests are not applicable or cannot be used without reservation because norms may be misleading (Haney & Hurtado, 1994; Toker, 1995). Similar problems arise in expert assessments of mental health, of criminal nonresponsibility, in divorce procedures, or in other fields of law. Until now, there has been little systematic research that can be used to solve these problems of internationalization and globalization in psychology and law. However, as we have experienced in work on a training scheme for the Federal Office for the Recognition of Refugees, cautious applications of psychological knowledge can be helpful in such difficult fields of legal practice.

Language Problems and the Relation to the Scientific Community in the United States

One subaspect of national differences is the language problem. It is particularly pleasing to see so many Spanish colleagues at Barcelona. Only a few years ago, not only the Iron Curtain but also the Alps and the Rhine seemed to be true barriers at European conferences. They were dominated by participants from Great Britain, the Netherlands, Scandinavia, and Germany. As the Spanish symposia at Barcelona show, the language problem will also be solved only successively through exchange and cooperation. The national preconditions are extraordinarily heterogeneous (see Table 1).

Table 1: Percentage of Adults Who Speak Various Foreign Languages in European Countries (Taken from: Spiegel Documentation Europe, 1993)

	B	DK	F	D	GR	IRL	I	NL	P	E	GB	EC
English	34	61	31	44	28	100	16	72	25	12	100	44
French	71	9	97	16	8	9	16	31	30	10	21	33
German	19	45	9	100	5	2	4	67	3	1	9	28
Italian	5	1	6	3	2	-	100	2	3	1	2	20
Spanish	3	2	14	4	1	3	2	5	14	99	4	16
2 languages and more	58	71	45	49	38	36	30	88	38	30	33	42

Table 1: Continuation

	A	SF	N	S	CH	EC +
English	42	48	58	73	40	45
French	11	5	2	9	63	31
German	100	14	17	35	88	31
Italian	5	1	-	1	24	19
Spanish	1	2	2	5	7	15
2 languages and more	45	57	63	78	67	44

Simultaneous translations are a very helpful but no general solution, because they are expensive and often too formal. In addition, during the important informal conversations in small groups, the various cultural and language groups often stick to themselves. One may well regret the declining international importance of French or German in scientific communication. However, at least one universal language, which English has become, is very helpful. Perhaps, the Romanic countries may console themselves with the fact that Latin was the dominant language of science for hundreds of years. We cannot and should not, try to turn back the wheel of history in the field of psychology and law. As mentioned above, jurisprudence belongs to the national-language oriented disciplines, while psychology in general is more anglophone (Skudlik, 1990). To a greater extent than the natural-science part of psychology, work in the field of law has to cope with differences in culture and language. However, experience of these differences and learning from them is also dependent on relatively easy forms of international communication. Pragmatic development and the use of one common language does not mean giving up national or cultural identity. English and American native speakers should at least understand that foreign colleagues may be less precise in talking than in thinking, that it is harder for them to engage in spontaneous discussions, and that they do not always have enough time for careful translations. In the scientific community of the EAPL, I have clearly experienced a high level of empathy and support in tackling the language problem.

However, it seems to be easier to overcome the language problem on the personal level than on the publication level. Here, it is also confounded with international differences in quantity and quality of research. Just as in the social sciences in general, North America dominates the field of psychology and law. Papers from other and particularly non-English-speaking countries are rarely read and cited by colleagues in the United States (e.g., Wells, 1994). Things are different in the other direction. Naturally, the work of a few outstanding researchers from Europe is well-known all over the world. The main problem of one-sided "exchange" is on the level of ordinary, mainstream research. However, one-sided selectivity may even bypass great research traditions in other areas of the world. For example, when Tapp

(1976) titled her important paper "Psychology and Law: An Overture," she obviously focused on the United States and not the European developments in forensic psychology since the beginning of the 20th century.

How should "Europe" or other parts of the world react to this situation? Promoting contacts, identity, and the publication market *within* Europe can be one way of coping. However, the development of a separate European psychology and law, as a sort of counterbalance, would also be problematic. It would go against the fundamental internationality of science, and in view of the cultural and language heterogeneity in Europe, it does not promise much success. The relative ignorance concerning European research in the United States is also not intentional and often not even perceived as such there. Thus, increasing the visibility and impact of European research in the United States is an important goal of the EAPL. There are various ways to reach this goal. Again, increased contact is a basic condition to reduce the dominant one-sidedness. Numerous North American colleagues have already participated at our European conferences (see Lösel et al., 1992; Davies et al., 1996), and a number of leading members of the American Psychology and Law Society (APLS) are also members of the EAPL. International exchange of scientists and students, summer schools, NATO Advanced Study Institutes, and other meetings are already creating an ongoing increase in contacts. A joint conference of the EAPL and the APLS might take place in the future.

Another path consists of attractive English-language journals with European or international focus. Insofar, recently founded journals such as "Criminal Behaviour and Mental Health," "Criminological and Legal Psychology," "Expert Evidence," "Forensic Psychiatry," and "Psychology, Crime, and Law" are highly welcome. Here, our colleagues from Britain have an important mediation function. The imbalance in the relationship to Anglo-American psychology and law is, however, not just a language problem. British journals of psychology also have only a limited impact like German journals, and are much less cited than comparable periodicals of the American Association of Psychology (Montada et al., 1995). Perhaps, even British authors submit their most attractive papers to American journals because these have highest rankings according to various criteria (e.g., Feingold, 1989). However, it also seems to be important that researchers in the United States limit themselves to their immediate scientific community much more than Europeans do. Due to the world-wide dominance of the US-community, this does not appear to be local but international. From the perspective of sociology of science, this process may be reinforced by career promotion, support networks, research funding, and, last but not least, the fact that the North-American publication market is large enough.

For these reasons, establishing a European network through the development of the EAPL and other European Associations on various topics of psychology is very important. The recently launched journal "European Psychologist" is a promising attempt to integrate and profile psychology in Europe (see Pawlik, 1996). Perhaps, one day it will have as many subscribers as its big American counterpart. However, for reasons of internationality and quality, European researchers should not restrict themselves to increased English-language publications in their own journals and books. They should also publish in the United States and make Europe-based organs so attractive to American colleagues that they will seek contact and European publication opportunities by themselves. Here, for example, special issues on internationally attractive topics can stimulate exchange. Examples for this are the issues on "institutions" (1993) or "crime and physical health" (1995) published in Criminal Behaviour and Mental Health.

Doubtless, these paths to internationalization seem to be still rather one-sided. Colleagues from France or other countries that strive to protect their own language and culture from "Americanization" may ask why US-Americans should be reinforced in not reading foreign publications. Was not the work of out standing psychologists like Binet, Freud, or Piaget already known in North America before it was translated? Similarly, was not the research of physicists like Einstein, Heisenberg, and Planck originally published and read throughout the world in German? As mentioned above, the international situation in many fields of science has changed since then. However, these examples show that the content and novelty of research should not be overseen in the discussion. It is important that European psychology and law itself preserves or moves toward a profile that does not just imitate North American research but makes its own contribution. I only shall mention two examples: (1) While Anglo-American research on witness credibility is mainly based on experiments from general psychology, European researchers like Arntzen, Scewczyk, Trankell, and Undeutsch have developed their own case-oriented approach that later became widely adopted in child abuse cases (e.g., Steller & Köhnken, 1989; Undeutsch, 1992). (2) Whereas North-American research and practice of offender treatment has focused predominantly on juveniles (e.g., Andrews et al., 1990; Lipsey, 1992), Europe has a specific tradition and relatively more research in the rehabilitation of adult criminals (e.g., Lösel et al., 1987; Redondo, 1994). In combination with more effective prevention strategies, this may help to develop crime policies that are an alternative to the current growth rate in pure incarceration in America (Skolnick, 1995).

Relationship between Psychology and Law in Practice

Traditionally, research in forensic psychology has been concerned mostly with how legal goals could be attained more effectively with psychological means. This "psychology *in* law" (Haney, 1980) or psychotechnical orientation of legal psychology (Loh, 1980) has clearly expanded toward an increasing autonomy of psychology in the last decade. Research relates, for example, more toward the discrepancy between legal schemes and psychological findings or between psychological principles and the effects of law. Both developments are contrasted rather fuzzily as "psychology *and* law" and "psychology *of* law" with "psychology *in* law" (Haney, 1980; Lösel, 1988). The concern is not only to optimize legal procedures but also to develop a more general understanding of law and to promote change in the legal system (e.g., Haney, 1993; Lösel, 1988; van Koppen & Hessing, 1988).

Naturally, after the rapid changes in Eastern Europe, the main research interests and needs lie in the pragmatic area of improving the restructured justice systems. However, other European countries also differ with respect to the relationship of psychological research to legal practice. In various countries, the respective ministries and state institutions have developed impressive research departments (for an overview see Jehle, 1990). In countries like Great Britain or the Netherlands, such pragmatic research *in* the law seems to be more common and accepted within the academic community than elsewhere. In Germany, for example, there is, on the one hand, a long tradition in cooperation between psychology and law (e.g., Kaiser, 1992; Undeutsch, 1992). On the other hand, however, university researchers hesitate to do studies on politically sensitive themes like offender profiling or similar topics of the police (e.g., Lösel & Mai, 1988). In criminology, there was a strong debate on the danger of uncritical, pragmatic research by the institutions of "state criminology" (Brusten, 1986). Although the problem of system-conformity in the selection and financing of research topics should be taken seriously, it should also not be over-exaggerated. Theories, designs, and results from projects at the British Home Office Research Unit, the Research and Documentation Centre of the Ministry of Justice of the Netherlands, the Netherlands Institute for the Study of Criminality and Law Enforcement, the Swedish National Council of Crime Prevention, the Criminological Research Institute of Lower Saxony, the Central Institute of Criminology in Germany or other institutions of "state research" seem not to be systematically different from the work of "independent researchers". Although there is a different focus with respect to the goals and topics of research (e.g., Störzer, 1991), it cannot be seen that they are less "critical." A growing interchange and transfer of personnel between universities and practice-oriented state research institutions can help to further reduce mutual prejudices.

Focusing too much on the needs of practice and policy at the expense of basic research, however, may strengthen the disproportionate emphasis that the justice system places on individual deficit models and individual interventions (Roesch, 1995). A community psychology perspective, for example, can help widening the perspective. In general, the different types of relationship between psychology and law practice are not exclusive but can be combined in concrete projects. Research *on* law does not mean that there is no practical usefulness. However, research that is actually acknowledged by justice can better be engaged in for a longer period of time if it is also useful *in* law (Lloyd-Bostock, 1988). On the other hand, autonomous theoretical approaches can have a strong impact on the practice of law. One example is the influence of the labeling approach for decriminalization, decarceration, and diversion programs (e.g., Scull, 1977). Basic research can also be transformed into technologies, for example, psychological measures of crime prevention based on findings in developmental psychopathology (e.g., Tremblay & Craig, 1995). Furthermore, practice-oriented research *in* law can even be used for testing theories in basic research. One example is the work on offender profiling that is relevant for more general questions of behavioral consistency and for ecological psychology (e.g., Canter, 1994).

Instead of metaphors like "psychology *in, and,* or *of* law," I have proposed a three-dimensional concept for the application of psychology in the field of law (Lösel, 1992). According to this, applied psychology is problem-oriented research that can involve (1) explanatory, (2) predictive, or (3) intervention problems. These three types of problems are often integrated to so-called complex application problems. They refer to three main fields: (1) the psychological assumptions and conditions that underlie the norms of law; (2) the behavior of the citizens toward legal norms; and (3) the application of the norms within the framework of the justice system. The same problem structure can be used for different domains of law, for example, in criminal law, family law, traffic law, and so forth (the third dimension).

Psychologists have strengthened not only their research on legal topics but also their knowledge and understanding of the law and its procedures. Vice versa, in many countries, law scientists and practitioners now seem to be showing a relatively open attitude toward psychology. However, "natural" conflicts remain. For example: (a) psychological versus legal terminology; (b) empirical versus normative thinking; (c) pluralism in psychology versus the goal of uniformity in law; (d) probabilistic psychological findings versus legal demands for certainty; (e) actuality in psychological research versus long-term establishment in law; (f) principles of experimentation versus principles of equal treatment and fixed jurisdiction (Lösel, 1992). As the EAPL aims to bring together psychologists *and* lawyers from research *and* practice, it hopefully will contribute to reducing the dysfunctional consequences of these disparities.

However, there may even be more deep-rooted, unconscious conflicts in the relationship between psychology and law in different European countries. Let us only look at the various logos or symbols used by the different organizers of European Conferences on Law and Psychology:

1. 1988, the First Conference at Maastricht, The Netherlands: No symbol, words only: business as usual? (some psychologists already hold professorships in law faculties); temperate Dutch mind? Some letters and the cover of the program in light green color: hope for further expansion of psychology and law in the Netherlands and more European conferences?

2. 1990, the Second Conference at Nuremberg, Germany: Psychology (Psi) like an old-fashioned candlestick (Wundt founded the first psychological laboratory in Germany!); giving the paragraph (it is the law that really enlightens us!) a solid standing? Law in black and on the right (the conservative side?). Deep green as basic color: Already now a consolidated hope for psychology and law in Europe?

3. 1992, the Third Conference at Oxford, United Kingdom: A light skyblue: symbol of the rational mind and calm temperament of British people? (Scottish, Irish, and

Welsh colleagues might restrict this to the English); the scales of justice in true balance; far away and on the right side: psychology (Rodin's thinker), sitting in contemplation (*on* law?); no action, like Izaak Walton's silent angler at Winchester: an unconscious desire of pragmatic English psychologists?

4. 1994, the Fourth Conference at Barcelona, Spain: Blue color again, but also yellow: southern temperament, stronger feelings, envy between psychology and law? Again, well-balanced scales of justice; but in front now a very dynamic psychology (Psi), attacking law with a three-ponged lance like a torero?

I know my interpretations are wrong from the beginning: Even the colors can have different meanings in different parts of Europe. So only psychoanalysis or perhaps some glasses of Spanish wine may help us to detect the real unconscious meaning of our symbols and relationships between psychology and law.

References

Albrecht, H.-J., & Kürzinger, J. (Eds.)(1994). *Kriminologie in Europa-Europäische Kriminologie? Criminology in Europe-European Criminology?* Freiburg i.Br.: Max-Planck-Institut für ausländisches und internationales Strafrecht.

Andrews, D.A., Zinger, I., Hoge, R., Bonta. D.J., Gendreau, P., & Cullen, F.T. (1990). Does correctional treatment work? A clinically relevant and psychologically informed meta-analysis. *Criminology, 28*, 369-404.

Bierbrauer, G. (1992). Reactions to violation of normative standards: A cross-cultural analysis of shame and guilt. *International Journal of Psychology, 27*, 181-193.

Boer, M. den (1995). *Policing Europe: The police systems of continental Europe.* Leiden: Netherlands Institute for the Study of Criminality and Law Enforcement.

Brusten, M. (1986). Kriminologische Forschung unter staatlicher Regie? Probleme und Konsequenzen des Einflusses staatlicher Behörden auf die Struktur und Entwicklung der Kriminologie. [Criminological research under state control?] In M. Brusten, H.M. Häußling, & P. Malinowski (Eds.), *Kriminologie im Spannungsfeld von Kriminalpolitik und Kriminalpraxis* (pp. 25-38). Stuttgart: Enke.

Canter, D. (1994). *Criminal shadows.* London: Harper Collins.

Davies, G., Lloyd-Bostock, S., McMurran, M., & Wilson, C. (Eds.) (1996). *Psychology, law, and criminal justice: International developments in research and practice.* Berlin: De Gruyter.

Dijk van, J.J.M., Mayhew, P., & Killias, M. (1990). *Experiences of crime across the world. Key findings from the 1989 international crime survey.* Deventer: Kluwer.

Eser, A. (1992). Wege und Hürden transnationaler Strafrechtspflege in Europa. [Ways and obstacles to a transnational practice of criminal law in Europe]. In Bundeskriminalamt (Ed.), *Verbrechensbekämpfung in europäischer Dimension* (pp. 21-54). Wiesbaden: BKA.

Farrington, D.P. (1995). The development of offending and antisocial behaviour from childhood: Key findings from the Cambridge Study in Delinquent Development. *Journal of Child Psychology and Psychiatry, 36*, 929-964.

Farrington, D.P., & Langan, P.A. (1992). Changes in crime and punishment in England and America in the 1980s. *Justice Quartlerly, 9*, 5-46.

Feingold, A. (1989). Assessment of journals in social science psychology. *American Psychologist, 44*, 961-964.

Fijnaut, C. (1994). Kriminologie in Europa. [Criminology in Europe]. In H.-J. Albrecht & J. Kürzinger (Eds.), *Kriminologie in Europa-Europäische Kriminologie?* Freiburg i. Br.: Max-Planck-Institut für ausländisches und internationales Strafrecht.

Georghe, F. (1995). *The prisoners' riots in the Romanian penitentiaries after the revolution of December 1989.* Paper presented at the German-East European Symposium of Psychology and Law, September 1995, Pillisszentkereszt, Hungary.

Haisch, J. (1989). Introduction to part II: Legal thought, attribution and sentencing. In H. Wegener, F. Lösel, & J. Haisch (Eds.), *Criminal behavior and the justice system: Psychological perspectives* (pp. 129-135). New York: Springer.

Haney, C. (1980). Psychology and legal change: On the limits of factual jurisprudence. *Law and Human Behavior, 4,* 147-199.

Haney, C. (1993). Psychology and legal change: The impact of a decade. *Law and Human Behavior, 17,* 371-398.

Haney, C., & Hurtado, A. (1994). The jurisprudence of race and meritocracy: Standardized testing and "race-neutral" racism in the workplace. *Law and Human Behavior, 18,* 223-248.

Harrimoes, E. (1995). The Council of Europe and Eastern Europe. In J. Boros (Ed.), *Structural and legal requirements of prisoners' rehabilitation* (pp. 9-13). Budapest: Ministry of Justice National Prison Administration.

Hürlimann, M. (1993). *Führer und Einflußfaktoren in der Subkultur des Strafvollzugs.* [Leaders and other influences on the subculture in prisons]. Pfaffenweiler: Centaurus.

Jehle, J.M. (Ed.) (1990). *Criminological research and planning in state and supranational institutions.* Wiesbaden: Kriminologische Zentralstelle.

Kaiser, G. (1992). Psychological contributions to criminology: Perspectives of a law scientist. In F. Lösel, D. Bender, & T. Bliesener (Eds.), *Psychology and law: International perspectives* (pp. 22-34). Berlin: De Gruyter.

Kerner, H.-J. (1994). Kriminologie in Europa-Europäische Kriminologie? [Criminology in Europe-European Criminology?]. In H.-J. Albrecht & J. Kürzinger (Eds.), *Kriminologie in Europa-Europäische Kriminologie?* (pp. 75-85). Freiburg i. Br.: Max-Planck-Institut für ausländisches und internationales Strafrecht.

King, M. (1986). *Psychology in and out of court. A critical examination of legal psychology.* Oxford: Pergamon.

Koppen van, P.J., & Hessing, D.J. (1988). Legal psychology or law and psychology? In P.J. van Koppen, D.J. Hessing, & G. van den Heuvel (Eds.), *Lawyers on psychology and psychologists on law* (pp. 1-8). Lisse: Swets & Zeitlinger.

Lipsey, M.W. (1992a). Juvenile delinquency treatment: A meta-analytic inquiry into variability of effects. In T.D. Cook, H. Cooper, D.S. Cordray, H. Hartmann, L.V. Hedges, R.L. Light, T.A. Louis, & M. Mosteller (Eds.). *Meta-analysis for explanation* (pp. 83-127). New York: Russell Sage Foundation.

Loh, W.D. (1980). Perspectives on psychology and law. *Journal of Applied Social Psychology, 11,* 314-355.

Lloyd-Bostock, S. (1988). *Law in practice.* London: The British Psychological Society and Routledge.

Lösel, F. (1988). Rechtspsychologie. [Psychology and law]. In R. Asanger & G. Wenninger (Eds.), *Handwörterbuch der Psychologie,* 4th ed. (pp. 644-653). München: Psychologie Verlags Union.

Lösel, F. (1992). Psychology and law: Overtures, crescendos, and reprises. In F. Lösel, D. Bender, & T. Bliesener (Eds.), *Psychology and law: International perscpectives* (pp. 3-21). Berlin: De Gruyter.

Lösel, F. (1995a). Increasing consensus in the evaluation of offender rehabilitation? Lessons from recent research syntheses. *Psychology, Crime & Law, 2,* 19-39.

Lösel, F. (1995b). Entwicklung und Ursachen der Gewalt in unserer Gesellschaft. [Development and origins of violence in our society]. *Gruppendynamik, 26*, 5-22.

Lösel, F., Bender, D., & Bliesener, T. (Eds.)(1992). *Psychology and law: International perspectives.* Berlin: De Gruyter.

Lösel, F., & Bliesener, T. (1994). Some high-risk adolescents do not develop conduct problems: A study on protective factors. *International Journal of Behavioral Development, 17,* 753-777.

Lösel, F., Köferl, P., & Weber, F. (1987). *Meta-Evaluation der Sozialtherapie* [Meta-evaluation of social therapy]. Stuttgart: Enke.

Lösel, F., & Mai, K. (1988). Polizei. [Police]. In D. Frey, C. Graf Hoyos, & D. Stahlberg (Eds.), *Angewandte Psychologie* (pp. 363-385). München: Psychologie Verlags Union.

McDougall, C., & Powls, J. (1994). International benchmarking. *Newsletter of the European Association of Psychology and Law, 1,* 15-18.

Michon, J. (1995). *The long and the short of prison sentences: On the consistency in sentencing.* Report NSCR TR 95-04. Leiden: Netherlands Institute for the Study of Criminality and Law Enforcement.

Montada, L., Becker, J.H., Schoepflin, U., & Baltes, P.B. (1995). Die internationale Rezeption der deutschsprachigen Psychologie. [The international impact of German-speaking psychology]. *Psychologische Rundschau, 46,* 186-199.

Pawlik, K. (1996). A new voice for psychology in Europe. *European Psychologist, 1,* 1.

Perron, W. (1996). Strafrechtlicher Strukturvergleich. [International comparison of structures of criminal law]. In *Tätigkeitsbericht 1994/1995* (pp. 15-19). Freiburg i. Br.: Max-Planck-Institut für ausländisches und internationales Strafrecht.

Pfeiffer, C. (1995). *Kriminalität junger Menschen im vereinigten Deutschland.* [The criminality of young people in unified Germany]. Hannover: Kriminologisches Forschungsinstitut.

Redondo, S. (1994). *El tratamiento de la delinquencia en Europa: Un estudio meta-analitico.* [Delinquency treatment in Europe: A meta-analysis]. Barcelona: Universidad de Barcelona.

Reiss, A.J.Jr. (1994). Towards comparative societal longitudinal studies. In E.G.M. Weitekamp & H.-J. Kerner (Eds.), *Cross-national longitudinal research on human development and criminal behavior* (pp. 423-437). Dordrecht: Kluwer.

Roesch, R. (1995) Creating change in the legal system. Contributions from community psychology. *Law and Human Behavior, 19,* 325-343.

Roesch, R., Ogloff, J.R.P., & Eaves, D. (1995). Mental health research in the criminal justice system: The need for common approaches and international perspectives. *International Journal of Law and Psychiatry, 18,* 1-14.

Scull, A.T. (1977). *Decarceration: Community treatment and the deviant.* Englewood Cliffs, NJ: Prentice-Hall.

Skolnick, J.H. (1995). What not do do about crime. The American Society of Criminology 1994 presidential address. *Criminology, 33,* 1-15.

Skudlik, S. (1990). *Sprachen in den Wissenschaften: Deutsch und Englisch in der internationalen Kommunikation.* [Languages in the sciences: German and English in international communication.] Tübingen: Narr.

Spencer, J., Nicholson, G., Flin, R., & Bull, R. (Eds.) (1990). *Children's evidence in legal proceedings.* Cambridge: Law Faculty of the University of Cambridge.

Spiegel Documentation (1993). *Europe: Data, facts, trends.* Hamburg: Spiegel-Verlag.

Srubar, I. (1994). Variants of the transformation process in Central Europe. *Zeitschrift für Soziologie, 23,* 198-221.

Steller, M., & Köhnken, G. (1989). Criteria-based statement analysis. In D. Raskin (Ed.), *Psychological methods in criminal investigation and evidence* (pp. 217-245). New York: Springer.

Störzer, H.U. (1991). State criminology: An old phenomenon-A new Problem. In E. Kube & H.U. Störzer (Eds.), *Police research in the Federal Republic of Germany* (pp. 29-45). Berlin: Springer.

Tapp, J. (1976). Psychology and law: An overture. *Annual Review of Psychology, 27*, 359-404.

Tari, F. (1995). Prisoner rehabilitation. In J. Boros (Ed.), *Structural and legal requirements of prisoners' rehabilitation* (pp. 59-62). Budapest: Ministry of Justice National Prison Administration.

Toker, M. (1995). *Forensische Begutachtung von Migranten: Vorgaben und Grenzen.* [Forensic assessment of immigrants: Tasks and limits]. Beitrag zur 6. Arbeitstagung der Fachgruppe Rechtspsychologie in der Deutschen Gesellschaft für Psychologie in Bremen.

Tremblay, R.E., & Craig, W. (1995). Developmental crime prevention. In M. Tonry & D.P. Farrington (Eds.), *Building a safer society: Strategic approaches to crime prevention* (pp. 151-236). Chicago: University of Chicago Press.

Undeutsch, U. (1992). Highlights of the history of forensic psychology in Germany. In F. Lösel, D. Bender, & T. Bliesener (Eds.), *Psychology and law: International perspectives* (pp. 509-518). Berlin: De Gruyter.

Wagenaar W.A., Koppen P.J. van, & Crombag, H.F.M. (1993). *Anchored narratives.* The psychology of criminal evidence. Hemel Hempstead: Harvester Wheatsheaf.

Weitekamp, E.G.M., & Kerner, H.-J. (1994). Epilogue: Workshop and planetary discussions, and future directions. In E.G.M. Weitekamp & H.-J. Kerner (Eds.), *Cross-national longitudinal research on human development and criminal behavior* (pp. 439-449). Dordrecht: Kluwer.

Wells, G.L. (1994). Psychology and law: A jam session. Review of F. Lösel, D. Bender, & T. Bliesener (Eds.), Psychology and law: International perspectives. *Contemporary Psychology, 39*, 490-491.

Wells, G.L., & Loftus, E.F. (Eds.) (1984). *Eyewitness testimony: Psychological perspectives.* New York: Cambridge University Press.

Willems, H., Eckert, R., Würtz, S., & Steinmetz, L. (1993). *Fremdenfeindliche Gewalt: Einstellungen, Täter, Konflikteskalationen.* [Xenophobic violence: Attitudes, offenders, and conflict escalations]. Opladen: Leske & Budrich.

Young, P.V. (1932). *The pilgrims of Russian town.* Chicago: University of Chicago Press.

Subject Index